Breaking New Ground

Breaking New Ground

The Transgressive Poetics
of Claudio Rodríguez

W. Michael Mudrovic

Lehigh
University
Press

Bethlehem: Lehigh University Press
London: Associated University Presses

Associated University Presses
440 Forsgate Drive
Cranbury, N.J. 08512

Associated University Presses
16 Barter Street
London WC1A 2AH, England

Associated University Presses
P.O. Box 338, Port Credit
Mississauga, Ontario
Canada L5G 4L8

The paper used in this publication meets the requirements
of the American National Standard for Permanence of Paper
for Printed Library Materials Z39.48–1984.

Library of Congress Cataloging-in-Publication Data

Mudrovic, W. Michael.
    Breaking new ground : the transgressive poetics of Claudio
Rodríguez / W. Michael Mudrovic.
        p.   cm.
    Includes bibliographical references and index.
    ISBN 0-934223-52-1 (alk. paper)
    1. Rodríguez, Claudio—Criticism and interpretation. 2. Self in
literature. I. Title.
PQ6633.O34Z785   1999
861'.64—dc21   98-39218
                                                                        CIP

PRINTED IN THE UNITED STATES OF AMERICA

For my grandparents
"Papa" and Della

in memoriam

Contents

Acknowledgments

For nearly twenty-five years I have been reading, studying, and most of all living the poetry of Claudio Rodríguez. This book marks a milestone in that process but not its end. When I went to Spain in the summer of 1972, thanks to a travel stipend from the Graduate School of the University of Kansas, my express purpose was to familiarize myself with the then-current trends in Spanish poetry and to decide upon a dissertation topic. My doctoral adviser, the eminent teacher and scholar Andrew P. Debicki, had provided me with a list of authors to investigate. Of all the poetry I read that summer, much has stayed in my memory. Nothing, however, made such a profound impression on me as Rodríguez's *Poesía 1953–1965,* for his work affected me on a personal level more than as a student of literature. I knew immediately that I would study his poetry. Writing my dissertation was the highlight of an exceptional educational experience at the University of Kansas. My most profound thanks to my professors and fellow students, especially Prof. Debicki.

It has been my great fortune—because of a variety of circumstances that I could not have foreseen—to have the opportunity, after many years, to meet the author and his wife Clara, who have befriended me and encouraged me to continue my study. I am grateful for their friendship and generosity.

Many people have contributed in one way or another to the production of this study. Much of this book was completed thanks to the generosity of Washington University in St. Louis: for a new faculty development grant that allowed me to do research in Spain, for a semester leave, and for the many conferences that I was able to attend and at which I read papers on Rodríguez's poetry.

I wish especially to acknowledge my colleagues in the Department of Romance Languages and Literatures at Washington University who have provided a stimulating environment and many opportunities to advance my professional development. At the risk of forgetting valuable contributions from everyone, let me express specific gratitude to Randolph Pope, who read several large sections of the manuscript and who gave me the opportunity to work closely with him on the *Revista de Estudios Hispánicos;* to my mentor, Joseph Schraibman; to my fellow poetry reader, John Garganigo; to the three chairs of the department who placed so much trust in my abilities—Jimmie Jones, Norris Lacy, and Nina Davis; to Charles Oriel, Elzbieta

9

Sklodowska, María Inés Lagos, Akiko Tsuchiya, Eloísa Palafox, Gail Swick, my officemate of ten years Nancy Schnurr, and all the graduate and undergraduate students who have contributed to my growth as a scholar and teacher. My colleagues in the French and Italian sections have been as unequivocally supportive, and I am grateful for the time we have spent together professionally and socially.

I wish to thank the National Endowment for the Humanities, which enabled me to participate in a Summer Seminar under the direction of A. Walton Litz at Princeton University and a Summer Institute at the University of Kentucky held by John E. Keller and Aníbal Biglieri. My fellow participants added significantly to my research and writing skills.

Finally, I would like to thank my friends and family for their unstinting encouragement and confidence in my abilities. To name them all would be impossible, so I will trust that they know who they are and how much their friendship, love, and respect have uplifted and sustained me over the years.

Portions of the text were published in an earlier form in a number of professional journals. I am grateful to the editors for permission to include the following articles in this book:

"Dialogic Perspective, Linguistic Skepticism and the Cultural Code in Claudio Rodríguez's *Conjuros.*" *Letras Peninsulares* 1 (1988): 151–67.

"Dreams, Frames, Impromptu Stages: Spectacle in Poems by Claudio Rodríguez." *Revista Hispánica Moderna* 46 (1993): 313–21.

"Edenic Language in Claudio Rodríguez's *Don de la ebriedad.*" *Anales de la Literatura Española Contemporánea* 18 (1993): 137–56.

"Medieval Models: Claudio Rodríguez and Early Spanish Poetry." In *Estudios alfonsinos y otros escritos,* edited by Nicolás Toscano, 172–82. New York: National Endowment for the Humanities, National Hispanic Foundation for the Humanities, 1991.

"The Title as Pun in Claudio Rodríguez's 'El canto de linos.'" *Hispanófila* 106 (1992): 31–40.

Special thanks to Claudio Rodríguez for permission to include his poems.

Breaking New Ground

Introduction

Born 30 January 1934 in the provincial capital of Zamora in northwestern Spain, Claudio Rodríguez has become one of the most acclaimed poets in contemporary Spain. During the 1980s and 1990s, for example, he received the Premio Nacional de Literatura, the Premio de Castilla y León, the Reina Sofía, and the Príncipe de Asturias (all prestigious awards), and in 1992, he was admitted into the Real Academia de la Lengua.[1] Many readers and critics affirm that he is a poet of Nobel Prize quality. Curiously, Rodríguez has achieved this preeminent status after having published a mere five books of poetry over a span of nearly forty-five years; few readers outside of critical and literary circles are familiar with his poetry. This lack of notoriety may be due to the current marginal status of poetry as art (in comparison with the more lucrative writing of fiction), to Spain's peripheral relationship to the rest of Europe, or perhaps to Rodríguez's approach to writing, particularly his pursuit of authenticity (both personal and poetic), which he readily recognizes may alienate his audience. Yet, when he writes, he touches chords that resonate deeply not only within his compatriots but also within those readers concerned with the issue of genuine, purposeful, meaningful existence, with the issue of what it means *to be*. Let there be no mistaking my position from the beginning of this study: Claudio Rodríguez is one of the greatest Western poets of the twentieth century.

What little we know of Rodríguez's early life derives from Dionisio Cañas's book and from the few comments Rodríguez has made in interviews.[2] These sources nonetheless provide key insights into his development. Rodríguez was barely six years old when the Spanish civil war ended, a detail that not only helps to situate him historically, but also to recognize that he belongs to the first generation of Spanish children to receive their educational formation during the most stringent years of the Franco regime. Much of his attitude toward language and life could be seen as a result of the educational, social, political, and literary atmosphere of that era, especially because of the regime's censorship and writers' needs to employ language ironically.

Perhaps the most significant personal event of these years was the death of his father when the poet was twelve years old. In addition to the loss experienced, two notable consequences followed. First, Rodríguez's father left behind a remarkable library for the time and place. Although it reportedly did not include the poetry of the

Generation of 1927 (the immediate prewar group of poets led by Jorge Guillén, Pedro Salinas, Rafael Alberti, Federico García Lorca, and others), it did contain the classics of Spanish literature and the poetry of Rimbaud and Baudelaire—unusual for a private collection in a provincial city. The readings Rodríguez did, especially in literature and philosophy, led to a precocious intellectual curiosity in these areas that has continued throughout his life. The second consequence of his father's death was the exacerbation of a conflictive relationship with his mother. As a result, the rebellious Rodríguez spent many months away from Zamora, walking the extent of Castile from Sanabria (the westernmost province) to La Rioja. Not only did he come into contact with his cultural and linguistic heritage, so evident in his earlier works; these travels also provided him with central images for his poetry. Not the least of these is walking, synonymous with writing verse, which has led to a lifetime journey, a profound investigation of self, world, and the language that instantiates and mediates them.

IN RETROSPECT

Rodríguez belongs to the group of poets who emerged in the mid-1950s and which literary historians have labeled the "second generation of the post-war era."[3] Unfortunately, this label is misleading. The "second generation" implies that these poets follow the tendencies established by their predecessors. Admittedly, a thematic and rhetorical shift characterizes much of the poetry written in the forties and fifties in Spain, ensuing upon the atrocities and destruction of the Spanish civil war and the triumph of the Nationalists. These authors reject the prewar aesthetic of "art-for-art's-sake" (the "poesía pura" [pure poetry] and "surrealist" poetry written for an esoteric minority, infelicitously labeled "dehumanized" poetry by José Ortega y Gasset) and the erasure of biographical, anecdotal, social, historical, and political specificities in the poetry of Guillén, Salinas, Lorca, and others. The postwar change is led by Dámaso Alonso's *Hijos de la ira*, Vicente Aleixandre's *Sombra del paraíso* (both from 1944), and the work of José Hierro, Blas de Otero, Gabriel Celaya, and others.

But as Jorge Luna Borge has cogently argued, the "break" with the modernist tradition should not be attributed to the "novísimos" who began publishing in the late sixties and early seventies. Their self-publicity and radical style has tended to identify them as the first "postmodernists" in Spain (see Debicki, *Twentieth-Century Spanish Poetry*, e.g.). Luna Borge affirms that the real change occurs in the fifties, with the "second generation."

> Son Claudio Rodríguez, Jaime Gil de Biedma, F. Brines, Angel González, Valente
> . . . quienes más claramente marcan una diferencia y un nuevo rumbo respecto a lo anterior y quienes anticipan por vez primera, lo que años más tarde se adjudicarán los novísimos—ello no quiere decir que no existan diferencias entre ambas generaciones; las hay, pero éstas no son tan poéticamente esenciales como algunos de la del 70 proponen.
> . . . La obra de estos poetas [Eladio Cabañero, A. González, C. Rodríguez, C.

Sahagún y José A. Valente] es una clara muestra de que el compromiso ideológico ya no es importante en poesía. En sus declaraciones al antólogo [Francisco Ribes] los poetas conciben el ejercicio poético como instrumento de conocimiento (ejercicio de autoconocimiento interior) y de comunicación. Se combate el formalismo temático de la poesía social. El poeta más que comprometido con una determinada ideología ha de ser auténtico consigo mismo y su planteamiento vital; esa afirmación de sí mismo y esa indagación en las propias entrañas le permitirá conocer la realidad desde otras perspectivas. . . . Aquí podemos ver ruptura con lo anterior y apertura de horizontes en la poesía española, aspectos éstos muy olvidados a la hora de valorar los presupuestos rupturistas de la estética novísima. El camino, como vemos, estaba bastante andado.[4]

Another way of envisioning this reorientation involves the shift from what Carlos Bousoño describes as a poetics of communication in his landmark study *Teoría de la expresión poética* (2d ed., 1952), to what Debicki has called the poetry of discovery, based on the aesthetic statements of the poets who begin writing during the fifties.[5] To simplify the description of this shift, we might say that modernist poets are highly sensitive filters. They perceive experience, reduce it to its "essence" (free of most if not all extraneous detail), and avail themselves of language as the medium through which to re-create and "communicate" that experience in all its richness, focalized through the filtering perspective of the poet. The poet as indispensable filter, as an artist in control of his/her abilities, presents his/her vision or insight to the reader via language, but by the time s/he finishes stylizing it through form and diction, that experience has become a *product*.

The poets of Rodríguez's era adopt a different stance. Although they rely on lived experience, everyday life serves as the catalyst for another type of experience: that of the act of writing. Rather than communicate to the reader an already digested and transformed experience (an "artifact," a product to be "consumed"), the poets of the fifties engage in the *process* of discovery. In the very act of writing, the poet is affected—psychologically, phenomenologically, intellectually, emotively—by the language employed. To use an analogy with sculpture, if experience is the raw, un-shaped block of stone and language the "tool," the emphasis falls not on the finished product created by the artist's deft handling of his tools, but on the wielding of the tools themselves, the contact between the mallet, chisels, gouges, and buffers, and the stone itself, its fineness, compression, faults, textures, and imperfections that act on the sculptor as he acts on the stone. Self-consciousness about this process defines a shift from the modern to the postmodern.[6] Therefore, in accord with Luna Borge, I would maintain that the most radical shift in paradigms occurs in the mid-1950s, and I would add that Claudio Rodríguez's *Don de la ebriedad* marks a new direction for Spanish poetry.

Self-consciousness and the instability of the process—the "act"-ualization of the *text* as opposed to the "re"-alization of the experience in the *work*—by participation in the act of writing characterizes Rodríguez's poetry in a number of ways and epito-mizes what I call his transgressive poetics. From the beginning of his career, Rodríguez views language as the means of inquiring into his identity, yet he is self-consciously cognizant of its equivocality and instability. His poetics consists of the exploration of the problematic nature of language regardless of the consequences of such an intense engagement in the poetic act. For by surrendering himself to the unexpected outcomes of writing, Rodríguez confronts the elusiveness, equivocality, and instability of his medium and so of his identity, his being.

One of the seminal characteristics of Rodríguez's poetry illustrative of this dynamic is his careful structuring of each volume.[7] Although he writes individual lyric poems (like any other poet), he arranges them sequentially in each work, so that we must read the individual poems not only paradigmatically as discrete moments of lyric expression in relation to the tradition, but also syntagmatically in relation to the other poems preceding and following in the individual work. The sequential structuring of the book, marked in each case by a two-poem section, adds a diachronic aspect that emphasizes the process of writing and reading this poetry. The combination of the paradigmatic and syntagmatic, the interplay of stability and instability, the deconstruction of product and process, work and text, are distinctive aspects of Rodríguez's transgressive poetics. These dualities raise two related issues that need to be addressed in this introduction: (1) the concept/question of the "author" and identity; and (2) transgression.

THE CONCEPT/QUESTION OF IDENTITY

Much has been made of the "death of the author" in poststructuralist, deconstructionist theory, beginning with Roland Barthes's eponymous essay.[8] This de-emphasis of the author's organizing role in the aesthetic process forms part of the larger postmodern questioning and subverting of the grand narratives inherited from the Romantic and Modernist periods.[9] As Kenneth Gergen avers in *The Saturated Self: Dilemmas of Identity in Contemporary Life*, "much of our contemporary vocabulary of the person, along with associated ways of life, finds its origins in the romantic period. It is a vocabulary of passion, purpose, depth, and personal significance: a vocabulary that generates awe of heroes, of genius, and of inspired work."[10] He further notes that

> the vocabulary of moral feeling, loyalty, and inner joy is largely derived from a *romanticist* conception of the self. Although it reached its zenith in the nineteenth century, this view remains very much alive in the present world. It is a perspective that lays central stress on unseen, even sacred forces that dwell deep within the person, forces that give life and relationships their significance. Yet this conception of the person has fallen into disrepair in the present century, largely replaced by a *modernist* view of personality, in which reason and observation are the central ingredient of human functioning. This latter view pervades the sciences, government, and business, and has made many inroads into the sphere of informal relations. Both the romanticist and modernist traditions deserve closest attention, for not only are they among the most important of our lived vocabularies, but they form an important backdrop against which postmodernism must be evaluated.[11]

On the basis of these traditions, we conceive a sense of coherent identity or self-sameness and that a person's words should be an exterior expression of that "core self" or "deeper self."[12] The postmodern view tends to be highly skeptical of the validity of these assertions. A summary rejection of the concept of the author, however, raises several questions. First and foremost, we encounter the much-commented ambivalent relationship between the postmodern and the modern: Is there a rupture between them, or is the postmodern an extension and development of the traditions rooted in romanticism and modernism? James Newcomb has also noted that, "With the reshaping of canons to remedy exclusions based on gender or ethnicity, it would seem that the author and the conditions of the author's existence would have risen to a new prominence."[13] Second, if we completely reject the biographical and therefore historical dimensions of the author, do we run the risk of recurring to a New Critical "tunnel-vision" focused exclusively on the text?[14] And finally (at least for the purposes of this discussion), we hypocritically privilege the figure of the critic at the expense of the author. Drawing principally upon the counteropinions expressed by William Gass, in *The Death and Return of the Author* Seán Burke convincingly argues that theorists such as Barthes, Foucault, and Derrida aggrandize their own "author"-ity at the same time that they proclaim the death of the author; they tyrannize the reader at the same time that they decry the tyranny of the author.[15] Ironically,

> They *created* oeuvres of great resonance, scope and variety. They became more than critics: a vast body of secondary literature has grown up around their work, one which generally has sought not to contest or deconstruct what they say, but rather has re-enacted precisely the predominance of source over supplement, master over disciple, primary over secondary. They have been accorded all the privileges traditionally bestowed upon the great author. No contemporary author can lay claim to anything approaching the authority that their texts have enjoyed over the critical establishment in the last twenty years or so. Indeed, were we in search of the most flagrant abuses of critical *auteurism* in recent times then we need look no further than the secondary literature on Barthes, Foucault and Derrida, which is for the most part given over to scrupulously faithful and almost timorous reconstitutions of their thought.[16]

Although for some time antiauthorial arguments have been interpreted in the extreme, we can specify at least two ways in which these ideas have enlightened our critical thinking and allow a fuller understanding of the act of writing/reading. First, by demystifying the persona of the author, his supposed "death" has given the reader greater latitude to interpret the text. No longer obliged to decipher a univocal "meaning" posited in the author's intent or his biography, the reader now is free to engage in a more symbiotic relationship with the author in the actualization of the multiple possibilities of a text. A greater flexibility, porosity, and malleability of the text enriches our understanding and experience as well as recognizing and enhancing the linguistic capabilities of the writer. The author has not irrevocably died, but the relationship between author and reader has undeniably changed.

Correlatively, the relationship between author/reader and language parallels the distinction between work and text. Rather than a means of communicating, that is, reflecting the mind of the speaker, rather than being created by an "author"-ity, language determines and creates the self. This Lacanian concept of language and the self is in accord with the poetics of discovery. For writer and reader, participation in the act of writing/reading is a means of verifying existence, although both come at this self-affirmation from different directions, and because of the equivocal, unstable, duplicitous nature of language there will always exist a discrepancy between what they find within the (im)precise limits of the text. In that case the reader has a greater latitude, which has resulted in reader-response theories and placing the reader on a par with the writer, what Barthes calls the "birth of the reader."[17] The reader becomes the writer of the text (and the self through the text), reversing the process of the writer and demonstrating their symbiotic exchange at the site of the text, in the arena of shared language.

Let me now consider the application of these theories to the specific case under consideration, the poetry of Claudio Rodríguez. Throughout *Breaking New Ground,* I contend that Rodríguez personally, as well as socially, conceives of himself as a Romantic hero, a Prometheus, and his poetry is the means he has chosen as a lifelong project, a way of gaining status as an individual, a "self."[18] In this sense, Rodríguez continues a modernist tradition posited contradictorily by Paul Valéry. Eugen Simion explains:

> Valéry . . . states that an artist's major work is the artist. The artist writes in order to develop his or her own being into shape. . . . Such is Valéry's idea that by writing his work the artist becomes *somebody else*. . . . The creator is molded by the work, but it is no use trying to find the creator inside the work, because the attempt will lead our curiosity to the discovery of a mask. Created by the work, the creator loses identity.[19]

In effect, for Rodríguez "One work is one section made in its author's inner evolution, a fragment set free in the *act* of writing. . . . The author expects the work to create the self to understand and gain in depth and precision."[20] We also find the *etymon* in his work, "the silver thread which both unites a writer's work, and sets it off against that of others."[21] If we keep in mind Emile Benveniste's dicta that "It is in and through language that man constitutes himself as a *subject*, because language alone establishes the concept of 'ego' in reality, in *its* reality which is that of the being. The 'subjectivity' we are discussing here is the capacity of the speaker to posit himself as 'subject'" and "so it is literally true that the basis of subjectivity is in the exercise of language," we are able to substantiate that whereas to efface the author is antihuman, Rodríguez's poetics of discovery, his engagement with language in the poetic act is an assertion of the human being in time, of human finitude.[22] According to Newcomb, "To efface the author altogether strikes Simion as antihuman. . . . In a very important sense, Simion feels the need to assert the presence of the human in the literary product, for without human presence, for Simion, literature as valued product is barely defensible."[23] The same can be said of Rodríguez, therefore, as for Simion: "the moral *commitment* of the creator of masterpieces matters unspeakably much."[24]

Rodríguez has consistently emphasized the *moral* dimension of his writing, and in his most recent work has highlighted (as does Sartre in *What Is Literature?*) that "the act of writing is a kind of freedom that generates another kind of freedom (the act of reading)."[25]

Nonetheless, Rodríguez recognizes that "In the postmodern world there is no individual essence to which one remains true or committed. One's identity is continuously emergent, re-formed and redirected as one moves through a sea of relationships [i.e., experiences]."[26] In Gergen's words, "[I]ndividuals harbor a sense of coherent identity or self-sameness, only to find themselves propelled by alternative impulses. . . . Such experiences with variation and self-contradiction may be viewed as preliminary effects of social saturation. They may signal a *populating of the self*, the acquisition of multiple and disparate potentials for being."[27] But, "as new and disparate voices are added to one's being, committed identity becomes an increasingly arduous achievement . . . , as social saturation adds incrementally to the population of self, each impulse toward well-formed identity is cast into increasing doubt."[28] Rodríguez epitomizes these concepts, often questioning the efficacy, purpose, and worth of his poetic enterprise. Gergen has provided a succinct description of the double bind of the poet in contemporary life, a theme taken up explicitly and centrally in Rodríguez's most recent work *Casi una leyenda*.

> [T]he technologies of social saturation weaken the capacity of leadership, personality, and community to sustain or rejuvenate the culture's tradition. . . . Any successful attempt at cultural retrenchment must be suffused with a sense of sincerity. . . . Yet to the extent that we ask ourselves what we gain and lose by our actions, what their functional value is, sincerity is in jeopardy. . . . Similarly, as one asks about the personal gains and losses of religious, political, or ethical participation, such commitments are redefined. . . . One may wish to locate modes of sincere commitment, purposes and patterns that are deeply expressive of self. Once the process of saturation goes into high gear, however, such modes are discouraged. The process that generates the longing impedes its fulfillment.[29]

Rodríguez's poetry exemplifies the genitive ambivalence of the phrase "the subject of representation," showing that "The concept of the author is by no means static or immutable."[30] If we consider the text as both self and other, we confront the ambivalent issue of identity. Paul Ricoeur has revealed that the word "identity" is in and of itself ambivalent: It can refer to sameness *(idem)* and difference *(ipse)*.[31] We also recognize that there are some constants along with some traits that continuously evolve within the personality of each individual. We are all alike, yet all different; we have certain idiosyncratic characteristics that define us, yet we are constantly in flux, constantly evolving as our world changes without and our psychology changes within. Constant interaction between interior (genetic, innate, ingrained attributes of self) and exterior (adventitious experience, opportunities or deprivations, historical occurrences, others' [re]actions) can either confirm or destabilize who we are. In short, stasis and change unceasingly interact. Identity is consistent and fluid, integral and integrated. As a subject in process,

Such writers [as Mallarmé, Lautréamont, Joyce, and Artaud—and we can add Rodríguez] take up the position of the "subject in process," a subject unstable within the order of discourse but consequently free to change, to insert itself within textuality without acquiring the transcendental solitude of the epic author. For Kristeva, as for Bakhtin, this carnivalesque subject acquires revolutionary potentialities within discourse precisely because of its motility, its ability to take up new and transgressive subject positions.[32]

To assert, then, that Claudio Rodríguez explores and defines his identity through the act of writing is to evoke a series of paradoxical, oxymoronic dualities and ambivalencies that epitomize the postmodern subject. But Rodríguez is able to define his identity precisely because of and by means of the medium he has chosen: language and the poetic tradition. To write therefore is to posit limits and to transgress them; "to invent language it is necessary to refute it."[33] According to Burke, in "What Is an Author?" Michel Foucault "claims that in fabricating a text an individual can do no more and no less than create a space into which the writing subject continually disappears."[34] As we will see, Rodríguez early discovers a gap in language which I submit is comparable to this "space into which the writing subject continually disappears." But at the same time that he acknowledges this gap, Rodríguez founds his identity upon the exploration of it.[35] Therefore, identity in Rodríguez's poetry is synonymous with *transgression*.

TRANSGRESSION

Given that Rodríguez is self-consciously aware of the equivocality and instability of language and that language is his means of exploring and defining his identity, each of his works is similar yet different from the others. The common denominator, that which makes Rodríguez an exceptional poet, is his willingness—nay, the indispensability, the inexorability—of pushing beyond language through language, of recognizing on a personal level the difficulties and uncertainties involved in the poetic act and yet surrendering himself to them, making as it were a leap of faith. "To transgress," literally and etymologically, means "to step over or across," but it can also mean "to go beyond (a limit, boundary, etc.)."[36] Martin Heidegger, whose philosophy I will discuss in the next section of this introduction because of its influence on Rodríguez, has stated that

> What the word for space, *Raum, Rum*, designates is said by its ancient meaning. *Raum* means a place cleared or freed for settlement and lodging. A space is something that has been made room for, something that is cleared and free, namely within a boundary, Greek *peras*. A boundary is not that at which something stops but, as the Greeks recognized, the boundary is that from which something *begins its presencing*.[37]

In a literary context Tzvetan Todorov remarks,

The fact that a work "disobeys" its genre does not make the latter nonexistent; it is tempting to say that quite the contrary is true. And for a two fold reason. First, because *transgression, in order to exist as such, requires a law that will, of course, be transgressed.* One could go further: the norm becomes visible—lives—only by its transgressions. . . .

But there is more. Not only does the work, for all its being an exception, necessarily presuppose a rule; but this work also, as soon as it is recognized in its exceptional status, becomes in its turn, thanks to successful sales and critical attention, a rule.[38]

Rodríguez's transgressive poetics consists of the awareness and exploration of the problematic nature of language regardless of the consequences of such an intense engagement with the limits and boundaries of signification. Through his poetry, through his act of writing and his surrender to the unknown effects of engaging in the poetic act, Rodríguez seeks to testify to his existence and to define his identity, fully cognizant of the elusiveness, equivocality, and instability of his medium. Often identifying himself with Adam, Prometheus, and Christ, Rodríguez is a prototypical poet, fitting himself within the tradition by altering it, elevating the lyrical to another level of expectations and challenging poet and reader to achieve new insights by going beyond, that is, transgressing, the boundaries of time, space, language, and one's own expectations of self. His willingness to do so makes him not only an exceptional but a superior, an "heroic" or "epic" poet while at the same time exposing and asserting his humanness, his frailties, his failures, and the (im)possibility of achieving his goal.

Rodríguez's transgressive poetics is a paradoxical, oxymoronic fusion of work and text, the paradigmatic and the syntagmatic, product and process. So his "identity" consists of stable, definitive, fixed characteristics and of the elusive, ever-changing, and indefinable. The best evidence of this unity in diversity can be found in Rodríguez's structuring of each of his books, which I mentioned above. Beginning with *Don de la ebriedad* and continuing throughout his career, Rodríguez arranges each of his works around a two-poem section. The positioning of this section determines and reflects the equivocal identity of each work and of the author.

In *Don de la ebriedad* (The gift of inebriation) (1953), Rodríguez's first collection of poems, the poet conceives of himself as Adam discovering the potential brilliance but also the pitfalls and equivocalities of the sign.[39] Although certain images such as light, darkness, dawn, the tree of life, rain, and others are archetypally stable because of their inherent qualities, the poet finds that he can (and must) add his own nuances and individual facets to them, destabilizing and expanding them to the breaking point, but also making them more alive and vital ("tensive").[40] For example, light as a traditional symbol of insight and inspiration becomes so bright that it blinds, disorients, and obfuscates the worldview of the novice poet. Light as blindness becomes conflated with darkness or lack of inspiration, so that night is transformed into insight and illumination. Light and darkness as differential opposites are indistinguishable. The poet deconstructs these stable archetypal symbols to give them new meaning that includes both simultaneously.

This process continues in the second section where Rodríguez imbricates the concepts of metaphor and metonymy. Through the images of awakening and walking Rodríguez deconstructs time and space to show that metaphor (the vertical axis of language) cannot function without metonymy (the horizontal axis) and vice versa. The paradigmatic and syntagmatic aspects that Ferdinand de Saussure discusses and Roman Jakobson's distinction between substitution and displacement no longer hold, producing chaos: The wor(l)d is destabilized as the Adamic poet transgresses the logical limits of language.

As recent studies in chaos theory and fractal geometry have illustrated, chaos is but another form of order. Even though the poet sees himself as not inventing a new language but as piecing together in new ways the fragments of language that have already been used (by himself and others), he discovers a new order through various levels of repetition ranging from phonic alliteration to larger patterns (words, phrases, sentences, structures). This process reveals a gap in language between two totally incompatible meanings that coexist in the same language. This gap will be the focus of the poet's investigation of language and the poetic act in each of his succeeding works. Because of its structure and its focus on the word as the basic unit (or building block) of the poet's expression, *Don* is both an open and a closed text. It demonstrates that we can read Rodríguez's poetry syntagmatically as well as paradigmatically, and it marks the shift from work to text, from a modern to a postmodern aesthetic, defining a new concept of order in chaos, of unity in diversity. By identifying himself as Adam, Rodríguez initiates his transgressive approach to poetry, crossing the gap or boundary between signifier and signified. This crossing takes place in the center section, containing only two poems, which functions as fulcrum and as transition, as center and as gap.

In *Conjuros* (Magic spells) (1958), the two axes of language assume a different configuration. Confronting the issue of originality versus the tradition, Rodríguez here finds himself in a dilemma. On the one hand, his identity as a poet and as a human being depends on the cultural context in which he has been formed. In contrast, he must separate himself from that background to become an individual, unique poetic voice. How can he simultaneously maintain his cultural (social) identity and yet define his individuality, his (personal) identity? This contrast between sameness *(idem)* and difference *(ipse)* determines one axis of the problematic of *Conjuros*, where the cultural context foregrounds this interchange.

The second axis revolves around the concept of irony. The poet realizes that language can cast a magic spell that creates falsehood and/or truth, authenticity and/ or inauthenticity. If he employs irony, the poet risks alienating readers; but irony allows him to explore the gap in language, which leads him to greater insights, greater individuality, and greater intimacy with the readers who can recognize and share his irony. To eschew irony may guarantee him a wider audience and more commercial success, but it denies him the profound experience that will assure his poetic immortality, the perdurance of his voice (his identity) over time. To use irony is to lie, but to lie is to achieve greater truthfulness, just as to alienate himself from his cultural heritage is to negate his identity, but to negate that identity is to assure his individuality and to secure a place for himself in that tradition.

The irony of this situation is that by casting a magic spell with language, the poet himself (the subject) becomes the target (object) of the magic of language. His alienation individuates and exalts him, but it also isolates him and causes him pain. Rodríguez here discovers that his gain via writing exacts its toll. When he writes, when he explores the potential of language to create magical experiences, when he delves into the gap between truth and lie, reality and fantasy, sameness and difference, he individuates himself, but he does so at the expense of his own comfort and tranquility. Writing becomes a painful process that reveals the unknown to the poet. The confrontation with the unknown is what will distinguish Rodríguez's voice even though it does not always lead to the most pleasant discoveries. In comparison with *Don*, *Conjuros* consists of four sections, the third of which is composed of two poems. Beginning with the ambivalence with which he ends *Don*, each section inverts the relationship between irony and truth until the two are indistinguishable. The two-poem section serves as a turning point in this process, though the end result—the poet's discomfort with his discoveries—is the same.

Alianza y condena (Alliance and condemnation) (1965) marks Rodríguez's coming of age as a strong poet. It is a culmination of his previous work and a turning point in his career. Carefully structured in a pattern of center (gap) and excess (overspill), the first three sections of *Alianza* each posit a limiting frame and then spill over and expunge that frame. This fractal-like repetition of ebb and (over)flow in which the speaker comes face to face with his own shortcomings, his own negative and limiting attitudes, culminates in the two magnificent odes that form the final section. The transgressive aspect of this text is its dependence on otherness to determine the independent self, an ironic inversion evocative of Jacques Lacan's psychoanalytic theory of identity, beginning with the Imaginary stage and the formulation of imagoes, passing through the mirror stage and the definition of similarity and difference, and entering the Symbolic, the acquisition of identity by accepting the Law of the Name-of-the-Father. Rodríguez's willingness to accept otherness and loss, the insufficiency and absence embodied in the sign, and the gap in language determine his individuality as a poet in this pivotal work in his career.

The reluctant acceptance of absence to assure presence is borne out in *El vuelo de la celebración* (The flight of celebration) (1976), a consummate elegiac text.[41] The masterstroke of transgression in this work is that the two-poem section is both present and absent; the body of the text (like the sign) is both bridge and barrier. Through the work of mourning, Rodríguez converts the acceptance of death and loss into his quest for identity. The deconstruction of presence and absence, loss and gain, elegy and quest continues Rodríguez's transgressive project in a highly traditional genre, yet Rodríguez gives his own spin to this genre. The troping of elegy and quest sutures the wound of loss, absence, gap, at the same time that the poet continues to explore it, keeping it fresh, open, sore. In this work, repetition—a prototypical elegiac device—and images of light and textuality (weaving, rope, cloth, thread) predominate, exposing the differential gap/suture of the sign. Repetition and the reworking of conventional elegiac imagery belies Rodríguez's artistry, for by repeating (literally and generically), he opens the differential gap in language that defines his individuality and originality.

In his most recent work to date, *Casi una leyenda* (Almost a legend) (1991), Rodríguez revives the figure of the poet as Promethean thief. Using language as constative and performative, the poet as thief is a transgressive figure who steals sacred light and achieves sublime insight for the benefit of others. Ironically, his punishment is his reward. It seems that Rodríguez has deliberately effaced his language in these poems, but this "grotesqueness" only heightens their sublimity. As Rodríguez seeks the most personal, heartfelt, and even painful encounters with himself in the act of writing, in his act of discovery through language, he ironically finds his public image of himself aggrandized and distorted. The grotesque exterior is in discord with the sublime interior, yet the poet's deconstruction of these opposites again defines his transgressive poetics: Ugliness becomes beauty, beauty ugliness; interior and exterior are distinctly separate and inextricably reversible.

Structurally one of Rodríguez's most complex works, *Casi una leyenda* uses the two-poem section as a doorway or threshold, both obstacle and access, to the sublime and as a counterweight of misdirection that urges us to reread the opening poem "Calle sin nombre" at the end of the work. This "closure" reinitiates the reading of *Casi,* but foregoing that closure, leaving the work grotesquely unbalanced, even inviting us to rewrite the final poem, lends dynamism and vitality to the work, leaving it open and flexible, as we anticipate the next step in Rodríguez's oeuvre.

Many critics and commentators have fretted over Rodríguez's "sparse" production and the ever-greater hiatus between the publication of his works. In light of the careful structuring of each work and the precise contribution of each individual poem to the constellation, it is not surprising that Rodríguez should wait until each work comes together of its own accord. In *Twentieth-Century Spanish Poetry: Modernity and Beyond,* Andrew Debicki implies that Rodríguez reworked and polished *Casi* all during the decade of the eighties.[42] For me, such a statement is inaccurate. Although he was collecting material and had composed a few poems, the poetry itself determined its completion; Rodríguez merely waited until the book came together, gelled, on its own. Once he saw clearly the direction he wanted to take, he composed the book within a matter of months, revising significantly "La mañana del búho," which he had published previously.[43] Certainly, the "grotesque," rough, or matte surface of the language, rarely flashing Rodríguez's metaphoric brilliance, attests to its quite unpolished, not overworked character. Making an analogy with the works of Michelangelo, the poems of *Casi una leyenda* are comparable to the sculptor's late works of slaves and half-figures emerging from brute rock, again transgressing and challenging our concept of what "art" is.

In sum, Rodríguez's unique structuring of each work and his evolution as a poet and a human being has required that I avail myself of a different theoretical approach to each work while still maintaining consistency and unity of approach. I have attempted to fit the theory and methodology to the poetry, rather than the other way around. Organizing the exposition around the figure of the poet as Adam in chapter 1, I have used an essay by Umberto Eco, "On the Possibility of Generating Aesthetic Messages in an Edenic Language," the tropes of metaphor and metonymy as delineated by Roman Jakobson, and chaos and repetition theory to explicate the three sections of *Don de la ebriedad*. These approaches show the poet as Adam transgressing the supposed limits of the sign and consequently defining a new pathway for himself in his use of language.

In chapter 2 on *Conjuros*, a thorough investigation of the cultural and intertextual undergirding of the imagery combines with the stance of the poet as *alazon* (ironic boaster) to destabilize language and further to individualize the latecomer poet. The process of establishing the poet's individual voice culminates in *Alianza y condena*, where I have chosen a psychoanalytical approach to portray the poet's coming-of-age. The transition from the imaginary to the symbolic register, passing through the mirror stage to acceptance of the Law of the Name-of-the-Father, structures this portrayal. But fractal geometry, first evident in the chaos-structure of *Don,* is again in evidence in the positing and expunging (or overflowing) of frames in this pivotal work.

Repetition again comes to the fore in *El vuelo de la celebración*, a consummate elegiac work that Rodríguez tropes into his quest for identity. His appropriation of elegiac conventions and transformation of the traditional genre again demonstrates his transgressive poetics. Finally, chapter 5 studies the poet as a Promethean and a Christlike figure by examining the manifestation of the sublime in the context of everyday life. The poet must confront the issues of authenticity of being by acknowledging his finitude. In an attempt to conclude the unending, I present the reading of three of Rodríguez's uncollected poems in the conclusion. Each of these poems represents the figure of the poet, and I have emphasized the Heideggerian subtext as a sort of coda to the following. For to draw together the various theories and approaches I have employed to analyze Rodríguez's poetry, I suggest that we consider the philosophy of Martin Heidegger.

Heideggerian Underpinnings

I do not wish to imply that Rodríguez expounds Heidegger's philosophy in his work or that he is a "disciple" of the author of the monumental and influential *Being and Time*. In fact, I doubt that Rodríguez had read Heidegger prior to the publication of *Don* and prior to beginning his university studies in Madrid. But the mesh between poetry and philosophy (exalted by Heidegger in his postwar writings) is highly propitious for the young poet's development, so that Heidegger's work, especially *Being and Time*, provides philosophical underpinnings with which Rodríguez engages in dialogue.[44] We might even say that Rodríguez embodies the ideal combination of philosophy and poetry that Heidegger envisioned. As an assiduous reader of Heidegger and other philosophical works, Rodríguez often echoes yet transforms Heideggerian concepts; and like Heidegger, he searches for meaning in and through the equivocal, unstable, yet essential medium of language. The poet meditates upon many of Heidegger's precepts but makes them his own, developing them to his own conclusions.

The most fundamental concept of *Being and Time,* which forms the point of departure for all of Rodríguez's opus, is what Heidegger calls *Dasein.* Various commentators have explained that this word, coined by Heidegger, is a compound of the deictic "da-" (meaning "here") and the infinitive of the verb "to be."[45] They point out that, even though the translation of the latter into English is the gerundive "being," the infinitive form must be kept in mind. In fact, the infinitive is descriptive of both a present condition and a future aspiration, in accord with Heidegger's definition of *Dasein* as "possibilities." Before elaborating upon the many nuances and ramifications of *Dasein,* however, we should formulate a basic definition of this term.

Because Western philosophers since Plato have believed that "the unexamined life, the vague and unanalyzed life, is not worth living," Heidegger's project in *Being and Time* is what he calls the *Seinsfrage*: to question what it means to be.[46] According to Heidegger,

> Dasein is an entity which does not just occur among other entities. Rather it is ontically distinguished by the fact that, in its very Being, that Being is an *issue* for it. But in that case, this is a constitutive state of Dasein's Being, and this implies that Dasein, in its Being, has a relationship towards that Being—a relationship which itself is one of Being. And this means further that there is some way in which Dasein understands itself in its Being, and that to some degree it does so explicitly. It is peculiar to this entity that with and through its Being, this Being is disclosed to it. *Understanding of Being is itself a definite characteristic of Dasein's Being.* Dasein is ontically distinctive in that it *is* ontological.[47]

Michael Gelven expounds on this definition:

> What Heidegger means by the term *Dasein* is that entity which is capable of inquiring into its own Being, and indeed, such an inquiry into its Being is what makes Dasein what it is. . . .
> The whole point about Dasein is that it itself can wonder about itself as existing. . . . [T]he *meaning* of existence can be significant only to one who asks about his existence. For this reason, the question of Being itself is possible only because Dasein can reflect upon its existence.[48]

Stephen Mulhall adds:

> [O]nly Dasein exists in the sense that the continued living of its life, as well as the form that its life will take, is something with which it must concern itself. . . . It is therefore determinative of human Being, of Dasein, that its Being is an issue for it.
> . . . for Dasein, living just *is* taking a stand on who one is and on what is essential about one's being, and being defined by that stand. . . . Dasein's essence must lie in this capacity for self-definition or self-interpretation.[49]

These definitions of *Dasein* encapsulate the fundamental thrust of Rodríguez's poetry, for Rodríguez avails himself of language and the poetic act to reflect on his identity, his Being. Throughout his works Rodríguez identifies himself as a poet and, having taken that stand, defines, struggles with, and defends what that entails for him. In truth, to be *Dasein* is a vocation, a career, that *Dasein* chooses because s/he can do only that—examine what it means to be: ". . . Dasein's Being is an issue for it. The continuance of its life, and the form that life takes, confront it as questions to which it must find answers that it then lives out—or fails to."[50]

The choice of a poetic vocation is particularly congruent with Heidegger's philosophy because of the emphasis he places on language: "For Heidegger, to be is 'to speak being' or, more often, to question it."[51] Each of Rodríguez's works responds to the questions "What is the *self*? Who am 'I'?" and his structuring of each work attempts to give form and meaning to his life, his Being, during a certain period of time.[52] But Gelven also warns us that "'Self' . . . is not an entity. It is a characteristic of Being, which is also not an entity. Dasein alone is the entity. One must never ask, then, What *is* a self? but rather, What does it mean to be who one is?"[53] Moreover, Mulhall asserts,

> fully comprehending the specificity of that moment would involve placing it in a context wider than the immediate past and future. It would mean seeing it as the point to which one's life has led, and from which the remainder of one's life will acquire a specific orientation and momentum. Such a contextualization does not require that one's life as a whole should have a single, overarching plot—with everything in it subordinate to a single goal; narrative unity need not be monomaniacal. But it would require avoiding the complete fragmentation implicit in the Kierkegaardian portrait of the aesthetic life; it would require continually striving to understand the twists and turns of one's life as episodes in a single story.[54]

If a fundamental premise of Western philosophy is that there can be no conclusions that do not raise further questions, so "it is never the goal which counts, but only the journey, and even the first small step on the journey."[55] This thinking is evident in Rodríguez's earliest work, *Don*, where the titles "Canto del despertar" and "Canto del caminar," the two central poems, attest to his awakening to his path in life. The imagery of the path and of walking and seeking is, as I have already suggested, a mainstay of Rodríguez's writing.

The affirmation of being and the simultaneous questioning of it is a keynote of Rodríguez's poetry that has its roots in Heidegger's thinking. One could say that Rodríguez accepts Heidegger's challenge to speak being through language and to question being and language in his poetry. Whereas in his later writings Heidegger focuses specifically on the role of the poet and the poet's use of language, his early work includes a profound delving into the roots and recondite nuances of words.[56] Having been a student of philology at Madrid and currently a member of the Real Academia Española, Rodríguez too has always been concerned with the etymological roots and the subtle, often contradictory nuances of words. Writing poetry is one way of investigating these attributes of language and thought because "knowing is a possible mode of Dasein's Being, this is Being-in-the-world."[57]

In addition to the sense of astonishment and illumination that accompanies

Dasein's acquiescence to his/her vocation, *Dasein* encounters its dilemmas, pitfalls, enigmas, and costs.[58] The first of these Rodríguez stumbles upon arises from the play of darkness and light, and leads to the discovery of a disquieting but energizing gap in language. Heidegger addresses this rift expressly in his late essays, included in *Poetry, Language, Thought*. For Heidegger, one of *Dasein*'s primary tasks is to establish truth, to bring truth into the open of a clearing. This *aletheia* ("uncovering" or "unconcealing") is best accomplished in art, as he states in "The Origin of the Work of Art."

> The establishing of truth in the work is the bringing forth of a being such as never was before and will never come to be again. This bringing forth places this being in the Open in such a way that what is to be brought forth first clears the openness of the Open into which it comes forth. Where this bringing forth expressly brings the openness of beings, or truth, that which is brought forth is a work. Creation is such a bringing forth. . . .
> Truth establishes itself in the work. Truth is present only as the conflict between lighting and concealing in the opposition of world and earth. . . .
> But as a world opens itself the earth comes to rise up. . . . The conflict is not a rift *(Riss)* as a mere cleft that is ripped open; rather, it is the intimacy with which opponents belong to each other. This rift carries the opponents into the source of their unity by virtue of their common ground. . . . This rift does not let the opponents break apart; it brings the opposition of measure and boundary into their common outline.
> Truth establishes itself as a strife within a being that is to be brought forth only in such a way that the conflict opens up in this being, that is, this being is itself brought into the rift-design. The rift-design is the drawing together, into unity, of sketch and basic design, breach and outline. Truth establishes itself in a being in such a way, indeed, that this being itself occupies the Open of truth. This occupying, however, can happen only if what is to be brought forth, the rift, entrusts itself to the self-secluding factor that juts up in the Open.[59]

Deconstruction of the archetypal images of light and darkness, the problematic of originality versus repetition, and even the image of the clearing are paramount features of Rodríguez's earliest poems. Even if he had not read Heidegger at that point, the questions that concern him are the same. But perhaps the most astounding event of *Don* is the revelation of the gap in language. In "Language" Heidegger ponders this gap and the ambivalence it posits.[60]

> Does this abyss consist only in the fact that reason resides in language, or is language itself the abyss? We speak of an abyss where the ground falls away and a ground is lacking to us, where we seek the ground and set out to arrive at a ground, to get to the bottom of something. . . . The sentence, "Language is language," leaves us to hover over an abyss as long as we endure what it says.
> . . . If we let ourselves fall into the abyss denoted by this sentence, we do not go tumbling into emptiness. We fall upward, to a height. Its loftiness opens up a depth. The two span a realm in which we would like to become at home, so as to find a residence, a dwelling place for the life of man.
> To reflect on language means—to reach the speaking of language in such a way that this speaking takes place as that which grants an abode for the being of mortals.[61]

It is the poet who is best prepared and must venture into this experience because, as Heidegger says of Rilke, "it is necessary that there be those who reach into the abyss."[62] How does the poet venture into this gap? More specifically, how does Rodríguez engage in this process? Another facet of the meaning of the term *"Dasein"* is "to-be-in-the-world" and especially "to-be-in-time." Heidegger calls this condition of all human beings "thrownness." "To-be-thrown" is to find oneself in the midst of a particular place, time, culture, people, historical circumstance. As Mulhall explains,

> As thrown, Dasein is delivered over to a particular society and culture at a particular stage in its development, in which certain existentiell possibilities are open to it and certain others not. . . . Dasein is also thrown into its own life at a particular stage in its development, which further constrains the range of available choices. . . . In other words, the facts of social, cultural and personal history that make up an individual's present situation constitute an inheritance which she must grasp if she is to project a future for herself; and part of that inheritance is a matrix of possible ways of living, the menu of existentiell possibilities from which she must choose.[63]

Like Heidegger, Rodríguez recognizes that *Dasein* as "Being-in-the-world" is immersed in a particular context along with other human beings. Certainly, the pervasive atmosphere of the cultural code, which Rodríguez employs in *Conjuros,* represents examination of his "thrownness." This inquiry includes both spatial and temporal dimensions, again having its roots in Heidegger's understanding of Being as "average everydayness" or "the realm of the ordinary." Heidegger's concept of "thrownness" may be the source of and is definitely linked with Vicente Aleixandre's statement upon his introduction into the Real Academia:

> Yo diría que el tema esencial de la poesía de nuestros días, con proyección mucho más directa que en épocas anteriores, es el cántico inmediato de la vida humana en su dimensión histórica; el cántico del hombre en cuanto *situado*, es decir, en cuanto *localizado*; localizado en un tiempo, en un tiempo que pasa y es irreversible, y localizado en un espacio, en una sociedad determinada, con unos determinados problemas que le son propios y que, por tanto, la definen.[64]

The many cultural allusions, concrete descriptions of typical Castilian scenes, intertextualities, and concern with the passage of time that characterize *Conjuros* obviously stem from Heidegger and Aleixandre.[65] In addition, the ironic peripateia advance the issue of authenticity and inauthenticity as the poet struggles with his historical context, the poetic tradition, and his attempt to attain knowledge.

> Properly understood, knowing . . . is an activity carried out in a particular context, for reasons that derive from (and with results that are, however, indirectly, of significance for) other human activities in other practical contexts. In short, knowing is simply one specific mode of worldly human activity and so one node in the complex web of such activities that make up a culture and a society.[66]

Rodríguez clearly addresses these issues in *Conjuros* where he calls upon his cultural heritage but also must separate himself from an engulfment that would preclude meaningful existence. This relationship between the individual and society parallels the poet's stance with regard to the poetic tradition, both of which raise the Heideggerian problematic of authenticity. As an act of knowing, poetry represents Rodríguez's way of striving to attain personal and poetic authenticity, individuality, being. The irony in *Conjuros* raises the issue of authenticity and inauthenticity.

Inauthenticity, or what Heidegger calls "fallenness" *(Verfallen),* derives from *Dasein*'s thrownness and immersion in the everyday and is manifest in "idle talk, ambiguity, and curiosity."[67] But this state-of-being is a necessary point of departure for *Dasein*'s wrenching itself away from inauthenticity to authenticity. According to Heidegger's thinking, "one quite frequently loses one's awareness of oneself by one's absorption in the inauthenticity of the anonymous 'they.' . . . In its simplest form, *fallenness is the nonawareness of what it means to be.*"[68] Such inauthenticity is necessary if *Dasein* is to attain authenticity; *Dasein* must recognize and attempt to separate itself from the "they-self." In *Conjuros*, especially in the overt statements of separation in the first section and in the irony, Rodríguez understands that

> To search so deeply in himself he ha[s] to turn a deaf ear to the pleas of his pleasure-loving comrades, who accus[e] him of overseriousness and even morbidity. He realize[s], however, that there [is] an almost natural tendency in himself to avoid such investigations, to yield to the comfortable persuasion of the chatter of the they-self. (That is, he becomes aware of his *fallenness*.)[69]

Continuing this process in *Alianza* requires that the poet accept his role of *Dasein* as "Being-with-others." For that reason, his relations with otherness occupies his attention, in the way Mulhall describes it:

> [I]f Dasein's Being is Being-with, an essential facet of that which is an issue for Dasein is its relations to Others; . . . Dasein establishes and maintains its relation to itself in and through its relations with Others, and *vice versa. . . .* Dasein's capacity to lose or find itself as an individual always determines, and is determined by, the way in which Dasein understands and conducts its relations with Others. And the average everyday form of that understanding focuses upon one's differences (in appearance, behaviour, life style and opinion) from those with whom one shares the world, and regards them as the main determinant of one's own sense of self.[70]

Even in *Don,* Rodríguez is aware of the need to surrender himself ("entregarse") to the poetic act, but it is in *Alianza* that he assumes his social responsibility, which he does by individuating himself. Mulhall's summary of this point is relevant:

> Inauthentic Dasein's selfhood is lost in the they-self; ontologically speaking, there is no self-other differentiation in the "they", and so no internal self-differentiation in its members. . . . [A]n encounter with a genuine other disrupts Dasein's lostness by awakening otherness in Dasein itself; Dasein's relation to that other instantiates a mode of its possible self-relation (a relation to itself as other, as not self-identical).[71]

In the process of determining his individuality in relation to otherness in *Alianza* because of his love for his wife Clara (the "genuine other"), Rodríguez enacts further aspects of Heidegger's thought. The odes that culminate his masterpiece deal largely with the issue of what Rodríguez calls "servidumbre" [servitude]: "[W]hen material is put to use, we encounter its producer or supplier as one who 'serves' well or badly."[72] The poet's role as Rodríguez formulates it is to serve others in the very act of speaking/questioning his own Being. Another key word in the odes is "fundación," referring to the poet/*Dasein*'s founding of Being in the House of Language. Heidegger comments emphatically that

> The nature of art is poetry. The nature of poetry, in turn, is the founding of truth. We understand founding here in a triple sense: founding as bestowing, founding as grounding, and founding as beginning. Founding, however, is actual only in preserving. Thus to each mode of founding there corresponds a mode of preserving. . . . Founding is an overflow, an endowing, a bestowal.[73]

The odes as overflow culminate Rodríguez's lyric coming of age and his acceptance of his role as *Dasein*. But his journey is still incomplete. One of the cardinal definitions of *Dasein* is "Being-in-time"—a concept already touched upon in the recognition of thrownness of *Conjuros*—and hence "Being-toward-death." The death of others can precipitate *Dasein*'s awareness of human finitude, as is the case when Rodríguez's sister and mother die, leading to the elegiac outpouring of *El vuelo de la celebración*. But these deaths impel *Dasein* into a full engagement with the passage of time, what impending death can mean to one in the fullness of one's life, and *Dasein*'s own finitude. This confrontation with "Being-toward-death" also reveals *Dasein*'s obligation to rescue—save, redeem—the transient nature of existence, to show that *Dasein* cares, through *Dasein*'s own Being.

Rodríguez addresses these issues directly in the tripartite central sections of *El vuelo* that correspond to past, present, and future time frames, the three ecstases of time. For, as Gelven explains, "The term comes from the Greek ἔκστασις, which literally means 'standing out.' To focus upon the present, the past, or the future is to 'stand out from' the general flow of time and existence."[74] By accepting its own finitude, *Dasein* enables himself, others, and their world to transcend time. The troping from death to transcendence that Rodríguez accomplishes in the center section of *El vuelo* depends upon the process that he calls "la contemplación viva" [vivid/lived contemplation]. Although Rodríguez has written of this concept in the context of Diego de Velázquez's painting, he may also have had in mind a Kantian definition of union with the object.

> What is of great importance in Kant's analysis is that the knowing situation is possible only through a *union* of the activities of the subject with the data presented or given by the object through sensibility. This means, then, that knowledge is always, to some extent influenced and characterized by the knower. *But if the subject's ontological-metaphysical status is a part of the knowing process, then an examination of that status will reveal something about the so-called objective knowledge situation.* . . . Heidegger is going to argue that Dasein's relation to the world is one of care *(Sorge);* and that the various ways of Being-in-the-world are different ways of caring.[75]

Steiner has identified this concept as *Ent-sprechen*, "'a response to,' a 'corre-spondence with,' a dynamic reciprocity and matching" or "in the liturgical sense . . . participatory engagement."[76] Rodríguez's definition of "la contemplación viva" is remarkably similar to the duty of *Dasein* to connect with the world around it, espe-cially in light of the world's and the poet's transience. The poet's engagement with reality not only demonstrates his "care" but also human relationship with the external world, a world that is constantly slipping away.

> For Heidegger, a human being confronting an object is not like one physical object positioned alongside another. A table might touch a wall, in the sense that there may be zero space between the two entities, but it cannot encounter the wall as a wall—the wall is not in time in the table's world. Only Dasein, the being to whom an un-derstanding of Being belongs, can touch a wall in the sense that it can grasp it as such. . . . That is the way in which Dasein encounters them when it looks after something or makes use of it, accomplishes something or leaves something undone, renounces something or takes a rest. Dasein not only comprehends the objects in its world, but concerns itself with them (or fails to) . . . .[77]

However, Rodríguez discovers that, if he is to attain his goal, authenticity of Being, as *Dasein* he must sacrifice himself, underscoring the poet as *Dasein*'s vulner-ability and messianic self-sacrifice, for the self is grounded in care. The pain exacted of *Dasein* reveals the truth, making the poet's act of "salvación" both a distinction and a burden.[78] But as Rodríguez declares in one of his more quotable lines, "Miser-able el momento si no es canto" [Miserable the moment if it is not song]. For Heidegger, "To sing means to praise and to guard the object of praise in song."[79]

> To sing, truly to say worldly existence, to say out of the haleness of the whole pure draft and to say only this, means: to belong to the precinct of beings themselves. This precinct, as the very nature of language, is Being itself. To sing the song means to be present in what is present itself. It means: *Dasein*, existence.[80]

This understanding is also manifest in *Dasein*'s overcoming the obstacles that would prevent it from experiencing authentic Being, especially the pain involved in the coming to terms with death. In his most recent work to date, *Casi una leyenda*, Rodríguez continues his pursuit of identity and individuality, truth, meaning, and au-thenticity, by defining the role of the poet in contemporary society by accepting "Be-ing-toward-death."

> Heidegger . . . claims that the position from which [beings] must begin necessarily involves a self-interpretation from which they must break away if they are to achieve authentic existence. . . . Authenticity is a matter of the way in which one relates to one's roles, not a rejection of any and all roles.[81]

Rodríguez's debunking of his own public image allows him to shirk off inauthenticity so that he can find authenticity in a confrontation with the inevitability of death. Hence the importance of the word "leyenda." Véronique M. Fóti elaborates upon the concept of *legein* in Heidegger's thinking:

[A] rethinking of *logos* and *legein* (as *die Lese* and *lesen*) is closely linked to the question of what it means to read . . . so as simply to learn, not primarily to read poems, but to read.

In its originary sense, Heidegger indicates, *legein*, like the German *lesen*, means a gathering together that selects and elects, with a view to laying out and laying up *(hinterlegen, bergen, keisthai)* what is thus gathered, to letting it announce itself as *hypokeimenon*. In this laying out, however, *legein* is not concerned to bring that which lies before into its lay, that is to constrain it in conformity with any project. . . . It is concerned, rather, to safeguard, in its lucid articulation, the unconstrained spontaneity of presencing and the differential character of manifestation. The crucial point, then, . . . is that *logos*, as this gathering and gathered letting-lie-before (as language and saying), does not create or impose the configurations of presencing but rather responds to the . . . spontaneity of unconcealment.[82]

In assuming the identity of Prometheus, the poet as *Dasein* participates in a discovery, the unconcealing *(aletheia)* of truth. "Heidegger points out that the very etymology of the Greek *aletheia* shows that truth is a kind of violation or robbery of what is normally the case. Truth is snatched from the usual mode of untruth in the they-self."[83] To reach this truth, to realize its possibilities, *Dasein* must overcome the obstacles of thrownness and fallenness, its resistance to exposing itself to its dread of death, its "Being-toward-death."

[W]e realize that death is something that is not *chosen* by us, but is forced upon us— or, to put it in more existential terms, we are thrown into it. The thrownness of Dasein reveals itself in the awareness that we are going to die. The mood that reveals this to us, however, is *not* the mood of terror or fear or even agonized frustration, but *dread*. . . .

Remaining true to the structure of disclosure, the final characteristic of the meaning of death must be its *fallenness*. According to Heidegger, Dasein tries to avoid the confrontation of the meaning of death. . . .

The inauthentic mood that discloses death is *fear*; whereas the authentic mood focuses not fearfully on an *actual event* but on a possibility in the mood of *dread*. . . . This is why the *inauthentic* way to relate to death is to "fear" death. To *dread*, however, is to be uncannily aware of one's *own possible* dying.[84]

In spite of its avoidance of feeling dread, *Dasein* also understands that its Being is a "Being-alongside" others.[85] Self-sacrifice thereby becomes not only his acting out of one's role as *Dasein* but also his modeling of behavior for those alongside him. For Heidegger stresses that *Dasein* never ventures into the abyss, into danger, for personal reasons: "The more venturesome ones do not venture themselves out of selfishness, for their own personal sake. They seek neither to gain an advantage nor to indulge their self-interest. Nor, even though they are more venturesome, can they boast of any outstanding accomplishments."[86] This duality is seen in the simultaneously performative and constative language of *Casi una leyenda*. This poetry thus fulfills the same purpose that has been said of Heidegger's philosophy:

. . . *Being and Time* is not presented to his fellow-philosophers purely to confirm his own authenticity (although it inevitably attests to precisely that). It is also designed to disrupt the inauthentic self-understandings capable of authenticity, and thereby to serve as a fulcrum upon which they might shift their own lives from lostness to re-orientation, from constancy to the not-self of the "they" to constancy to themselves and to a life that is genuinely their own.[87]

Unfortunately, *Dasein*'s role exposes it to misunderstanding, as Steiner has noted: "Patient in the forest-clearing of Being . . . , dwelling in a house of which he is, at his rare best, a custodian, but never architect or proprietor, the thinker must be prepared to speak seldom, to speak fragmentarily when he speaks at all, and to suffer constant misunderstanding and contradiction."[88] The rejection of his own "legendary" status, the search for authenticity—his "self-effacement"—and the acquiescence of the poet to the pain and sacrifice that his vocation requires of him if his Being is to be authentic is a major theme for Rodríguez in *Casi una leyenda*. If we assert, as Heidegger would say, "authenticity is always an achievement," we comprehend that Rodríguez's striving for identity through his poetry is an attempt to give meaning to life.[89]

In summary, Rodríguez and Heidegger share many attitudes concerning language and poetry. Truly, language is the house of Being:

A house is what gives location and significance to all the other items essential for dwelling (the furniture), but it also shelters and establishes a foundation of human meaning. If language is the house of Being, then all the different ways of Being, all the multifarious ways of existence, are made intelligible and even recognizable only under the curious roof of language. . . . The image of the "house of Being" suggests more than this. It also suggests that language as the very protective enclosure that gives a place for existence and Being to occur cannot be isolated as merely another event or as an entity alongside other entities.[90]

And poetry lets us dwell:

The way in which you are and I am, the manner in which we humans *are* on the earth, is *Baun*, dwelling. To be a human being means to be on the earth as a mortal. It means to dwell. The old word *bauen*, which says that man *is* insofar as he *dwells*, this word *bauen* however *also* means at the same time to cherish and protect, to preserve and care for, specifically to till the soil, to cultivate the vine.[91]

In short, the word itself is the giver of Being, and "To think, to write a poem, is to give thanks for whatever measure of homecoming to Being is open to mortal man."[92] One could adduce many other aspects of Heidegger's philosophy to verify its relationship with Rodríguez's poetry, including his "irrational" use of language and his "dialogic" thought processes that include contradiction.[93] One important moot point of difference would be the moral dimensions of writing. Rodríguez has repeatedly insisted on the moral commitment entailed in his poetry, perhaps to distance himself clearly from Heidegger, who has been roundly criticized for his complete silence concerning the appropriation of his ideas by the National Socialists in Germany and the subsequent atrocities of the Holocaust and the Second World War. But this is not the time or place to rehearse a more thorough and profound introduction to Heidegger or to discuss Heidegger's moral commitment. Suffice it to say that many elements of his philosophy undergird Rodríguez's poetry, but I repeat that Rodríguez does not merely rehash or blindly accept them. Instead, he truly engages Heidegger's thought through his participation in the poetic act, dialoguing, questioning, and enacting his own understanding of Being. The German philosopher provides one point of departure from which Rodríguez continues his own search for knowledge of self and world, of what it means "to be."

BREAKING NEW GROUND

This consideration brings me full circle to a self-conscious appraisal of my own methodology and my approach to writing this book. Having been brought up under the aegis of the New Criticism, I own certain critical prejudices I am reluctant to relinquish. One of these is that I privilege the text over theory, or at least seek to maintain a balance between theory and text. Theory is a tool I can deploy with pleasure to help me explain what it is I find in the text, but I am not a theorist per se. The text and the nuances of language hold more interest for me than the nuances of the intellect played out in theoretical texts. In that regard, I consider myself more of a "practical" or pragmatic reader of the poetic text. Hence, also, my preference for close readings.

Another characteristic I would attribute to my New Critical training is an appreciation for the unity of the text. If I cannot explain a contradiction, an aporia, a discordant tone, it is because I do not possess at this time the critical insight that allows me to do so or because the focus that I have chosen does not at this time address that facet of the text. I do, however, consider the work of art a unity, regardless of how eclectic and at times awkward that unity may appear.

These critical prejudices have not interfered with but rather enriched my embracing of several poststructuralist and deconstructionist principles. Primary among these is the concept of intertextuality and the expansion of the limits of the text to include biographical data, other works by the author, and dialogue with the poetic tradition and cultural heritage. Another fundamental concept that has allowed me to hone my ability to read is the deconstruction of binary oppositions. Rodríguez's poetry, based as it is in the philosophy of Parmenides, Heraclitus, Longinus, Plotinus, Heidegger, and others, is replete with this play of difference that both frustrates and delights poet and reader. One of the most useful and enlightening pieces of critical discussion that has led me to understand this concept has been J. Hillis Miller's discussion of Shakespeare's *Troilus and Cressida*.[94] What Miller calls the dialogic principle—related to but distinct from Bahktin's use of the same term—and his comments concerning deconstructive reading at the end of that article have left a profound impression on my critical insight.

The incorporation of chaos and repetition theory have greatly augmented my critical tools and helped me to understand this poetry. Moreover, an awareness of feminist perspectives has definitely altered and tempered my reading of the representation of female figures in Rodríguez's poetry. I have tried to be sensitive to this aspect and to keep it in mind even though we are dealing with a heterosexual male poet from a highly masculinist society. (We should remember that Rodríguez was educated and formed during the height of the Franco regime, during which time the role of woman in society was a political issue strictly defined by the Fascist regime.)[95]

In short, my critical approach has been eclectic and "practical" in that I have taken advantage of theory to elucidate the text rather than using the text to privilege any particular theory. The unity in this diversity derives from the poetry itself and the author/person/character/nature of the entity we call Claudio Rodríguez.

It is also readily apparent to me that I am obsessive about combing out certain threads of my reading. I can only hope that my reader will accept it as a true critical and linguistic engagement, appreciation, and enjoyment of the text. A related issue concerns the number of poems I have chosen to discuss. On the one hand, I wish to dialogue with those other critics who have written so astutely about Rodríguez's poetry and to add my voice to the polyphony. In addition, my approach and insights have revealed to me a number of gems that have not been included in the Rodríguez canon—poems such as "Amarras" and "Cantata del miedo" from *El vuelo*, for example—that have received scant critical attention but provide rich and moving reading. Again I attribute my dwelling on certain themes to the pleasure and enthusiasm of reading Rodríguez's poetry. My sole purpose has been to share my insights with others and to stimulate even more dialogue on this poetry with my current and future colleagues.

1

Defining the Self through Language:
The Poet as Adam in
Don de la ebriedad (1953)

In the beginning was the Word . . .

Because Rodríguez started writing the poems of *Don de la ebriedad* when he was only seventeen years old—it was published two years later in 1953—critics have tended to slight this work as a precocious anomaly. As a result, even though Pere Gimferrer has lauded it as "sin duda uno de los grandes libros de la poesía española de posguerra," and in spite of winning the Premio Adonais, *Don* has attracted sparse critical attention.[1] The most valuable study to date, one that defines the metapoetic dimension of these poems and lays bare the dialogic tension informing Rodríguez's view of language, is Martha Miller's article "Elementos metapoéticos."[2] But once again this study stops short because it deals with only two poems, both from the first section of the work. Given the complexity and dynamics of the work's language and structure, it is risky to extrapolate a reading of the entire book based on only a few poems.

Throughout this study of *Don,* my approach will be to provide thorough textual analyses of representative poems. This methodology has specific aims: (1) to define the techniques Rodríguez employs and the aesthetic theory these techniques illuminate; (2) to expand the Rodríguez canon through the reading of lesser-known poems so as to challenge and dispel some of the overgeneralizations and misconceptions that have arisen about this work; and (3) to adduce detailed proof to support my readings. Other essential aspects of my discussion entail a sequential reading of the text and a consideration of its structure. These signature features of Rodríguez's poetry provide the continuity that undergirds the poet's entire opus, the consistency woven into the texture of each work upon which difference and variation play. I begin by defining the structure and central theme of *Don*, after which I will examine the sequential exposition of this work, the cornerstone of Rodríguez's opus, which has until now been largely neglected by the critics.

37

Rodríguez has divided *Don* into three sections, which he designates simply as "Libro primero," "Libro segundo," and "Libro tercero." The first and third sections are the longer, containing nine and eight poems respectively, whereas the middle section contains only two poems. These poems, however, are two of the longest in the collection, the only ones with titles (the others are designated sequentially with Roman numerals within each section), and each bears an epigraph. This structure suggests the configuration of a balance on a fulcrum. The two longer sections thus represent opposite extremes of the experience and the instability and volatility resulting from their peripheral juxtaposition. In contrast, the second section as fulcrum centers and stabilizes the work.

This arrangement coincides with Jonathan Mayhew's insightful reading of the duality of the topos of drunkenness in the book's title. He has noted that drunkenness

> can connote unconsciousness, but also heightened consciousness. . . . On the one hand drunkenness involves the breaking down of the boundary between self and other. . . . At the same time, alcohol can be profoundly alienating, creating a barrier between the self and the outside world. The drunk is both gregarious and suspicious, open to the world and closed within himself.[3]

Further reinforcing this duality, a play on words in the title describes the poet's remarkable gift (cf. the Spanish expression "don de la palabra" [lit., the gift of the word]) and his searching for and questioning of poetic inspiration ("¿Dónde la ebriedad?" [Where is the drunkenness?]).[4] We shall see that "Libro segundo" plays a dual role as both center and transition, so that a dichotomy between center and periphery, stability and flux, and any number of other binary oppositions at all levels of the text is deconstructed. *Don* thus describes the poet's first unstable but exciting attempt to define his identity through the act of writing, an attempt that reveals identity as both essence and change. Following the lead of Umberto Eco, then, let us conceive of the poet as a modern-day Adam in the world of language. By observing Adam's progress from a prelapsarian to a postlapsarian state with relation to language, we shall recognize *Don* as the basis for all of Rodríguez's poetry.

EDENIC LANGUAGE: THE POET AS PRELAPSARIAN ADAM IN "LIBRO PRIMERO"[5]

As Rodríguez's inaugural work, *Don* depicts the poet's discovery of the duplicity of language. In this regard, he resembles the Adam portrayed by Eco in his chapter "On the Possibility of Generating Aesthetic Messages in an Edenic Language," which posits "a small-scale working model of aesthetic language . . . to demonstrate a language's own capacity for generating self-contradiction."[6] In their Edenic world, "Adam and Eve have managed to devise a restricted series of semantic units which give preferential status to their emotional responses to flora and fauna, rather than naming and exact classification of each of them" (pp. 91–92). They designate things as either "red" (good, beautiful, edible) or "blue" (bad, ugly, inedible). God upsets this system by calling the apple of the tree of knowledge "blue" even though it looks "red" to Adam and Eve. This contradiction unbalances their pristine system and provokes Adam to experiment with language.

Like Eco's Adam, the poet-speaker of *Don* begins with a simplistic view of language but quickly realizes that language is equivocal. The speaker's discovery of the duplicity of language reveals a dialogic tension and sets up a pattern of oscillation between his optimistic confidence in language and his skepticism and uncertainty. This oscillation extends to all the poems of "Libro primero." As we read these nine poems in sequence, we realize that they grow out of one another, each interacting with the poems that precede it, repeating and extending the dialogue established in the opening poem. It is also apparent that these poems are paired, one repeating another but reversing the argument of the previous poem. In this process, the paired poems grow more and more distinct from one another. The thrust of this oscillation reaches its fullest realization in poem VIII, which presents the greatest contrast with its pair and serves as the climactic moment of "Libro primero." This pairing and divergence of the paired poems replicates on the "stanzaic" level the oscillation found on the semantic and syntactic levels of the poems. The final poem (IX) is significantly unpaired, leaving the oscillation unbalanced, pending resolution in the remaining sections of *Don*. As we shall see as we make our way through *Don*, this pendulum-like swing prefigures the configuration of a balance rocking on a fulcrum, transforming the apparently static structure of the work into a dynamic text.[7]

To deal with the nine poems of "Libro primero," it is necessary to look closely at the first poem again in light of Miller's reading. Thereafter, I will treat the remaining poems in different ways. Some of these poems exemplify more clearly than others the model of development that Eco delineates. These I shall examine closely while summarizing and extracting specific examples from others to support my argument. This procedure will allow me to specify crucial moments in Rodríguez's exploration of language and to arrive at more general conclusions regarding the fundamental characteristics of "Libro primero" as a dynamic unit that unfolds sequentially.

Martha Miller has astutely called attention to the importance of the opening verses of the first poem. These verses encapsulate the experience of "Libro primero" and set in motion the conflicting forces at work throughout *Don*.

> Siempre la claridad viene del cielo;
> es un don: no se halla entre las cosas,
> sino muy por encima, y las ocupa
> haciendo de ello vida y labor propias.
> 5   Así amanece el día; así la noche
> cierra el gran aposento de sus sombras.
> Y esto es un don. . . .
>
> (p. 33)[8]

The pristine view of reality presented in the opening verses relies on the traditional notion that light from above is synonymous with inspiration. Like Eco's Adam,

Rodríguez's poet-speaker begins with a view of language in which the form and substance of the aesthetic message are harmonious, univocal, and unambiguous.[9] The
parallel phrases "Así amanece el día; así la noche / cierra el gran aposento de sus
sombras" would at first glance seem to reinforce this system. But Miller's perceptive
reading demonstrates that the second part of this parallelism creates ambiguity because night's act of closing the chamber of its shadows can describe either dawn or
dusk.[10] We can picture night closing in the shadows at dawn or closing out the light at
dusk. This dual possibility splits the original view of language into a dialogic conflict
by violating "the normative cycle set up by the semiosis."[11]

In Eco's terms, the phrase "Así amanece el día" constitutes a semiotic judgment,
"a judgment inside the normative cycle set up by the semiosis" (p. 94). It coincides
with the semiotic system set forth in the first verse and maintains the consistency of
"our conceptual vision of the universe . . . based on the possibility of extrapolating
from metonymic chains" (p. 91). If we consider this image as representing dawn, it
constitutes another metaphoric variation of the code of light as inspiration. But if it
can also represent dusk, it disrupts that system because night and day cannot name the
same thing without entailing "a subversion in the presumed natural order of things"
(p. 95); that is, "it posits a new type of connotative pairing between semantic units
which had previously been coupled together differently" (p. 95). The personification
of night and the metaphor of the sky as "aposento" disrupts the logic and harmony of
the semiotic system by asserting that the two forms of expression are synonymous,
when in effect the image of the night entails a contradiction. This situation is comparable to Adam and Eve's predicament when faced with God's factual judgment that
the apple is "blue," causing them to invent the word "redblue" to refer to the apple.[12]

The ambiguity of the image of night urges a reversal of a conventional, "Edenic"
concept of language and a substitution of "an anomaly, by which a denoting term
establishes a straight contrast with those connotations which it inevitably produces."[13]
By equating dawn with dusk, day with night, Rodríguez has bifurcated the monologic
perspective with which the poem begins, producing a dialogic tension, so that from
now on we will read "claridad" as "claridad/noche." This new semiosis has an immediate effect on our reading of the subsequent verses.

> . . . ¿Quién hace menos creados
> cada vez a los seres? ¿Qué alta bóveda
> los contiene en su amor? ¡Si ya nos llega,
> 10   y es pronto aún, ya llega a la redonda
> a la manera de los vuelos tuyos,
> y se cierne, y se aleja, y aún remota,
> nada hay tan claro como sus impulsos![14]

Miller states that the questions of vv. 7–9 are rhetorical and that one can answer
them with "la claridad."[15] We could also read them literally as expressing the doubt
and uncertainty of the speaker rather than his absolute confidence. It even makes
more sense to answer these questions with "la noche" because night (darkness) does
make things "menos creados": It changes our perception of reality by making con-

tours less precise and compels us to use a different set of receptors to experience them. The exclamatory sentence of vv. 9–14 extends the ambiguity. Is the subject of this sentence dawn or dusk, "la claridad" or "la noche"? Does it arrive ("llega") or depart ("se aleja")? In short, we do not know if the speaker feels distress or joy. The remainder of the poem reflects this dialogic tension and the oscillation between "claridad" and "noche."

> ¡Oh, claridad sedienta de una forma,
> 15 de una materia para deslumbrarla,
> quemándose a sí mismo al cumplir su obra!
> Como yo, como todo lo que espera.
> Si tú la luz te la has llevado toda,
> ¿cómo voy a esperar nada del alba?
> 20 Y, sin embargo—esto es un don—mi boca
> espera, y mi alma espera, y tú me esperas,
> ebria persecución, claridad sola
> mortal como el abrazo de las hoces,
> pero abrazo hasta el fin que nunca afloja.[16]

An oscillation in the language pulls us in two different directions simultaneously. The iteration of "claridad" in v. 14 swings us back to the beginning of the poem and the pristine system of correspondences there but also causes us to look at the process that has taken place since that first verse and to recognize the changes that have occurred in our perception of its meaning. The phrase "para deslumbrarla" advances this oscillation. "Deslumbrar" forms part of the code of light and illumination ("brillar" is a synonym), but the light is excessive, too brilliant, so that it dazzles and obfuscates the observer, producing an adverse reaction.[17] The subject of this verb and the antecedent of its object are both ambiguous; either could be "claridad" or "forma." The same bifurcation and oscillation found in the image of night, emerges again as "deslumbrarla" looks back to the original semiosis while at the same time it reaffirms the duality "claridad/noche."[18]

A similar duality surfaces in the verb "esperar," which appears five times in the span of five verses (17-21). This verb can mean "to wait" for something, confident of its realization, or "to hope" for something, indicating a greater degree of doubt that it will occur. The duplicity of this verb is especially striking in the question of v. 19 ("¿cómo voy a esperar nada del alba?") where the poet refrains from using the "double negative," the more frequent construction in Spanish. This question suggests that the speaker is confident of the return of inspiration, while he also fears that he has exhausted it. These ambiguities keep the language oscillating between the two aspects of the dialogic tension. We may wish to privilege the speaker's certainty and confidence, but an undercurrent of doubt persistently subverts that tendency.

The final verses culminate the oscillating pattern of the poem. The prepositional phrase "sin embargo" may be read literally ("without restraint," "without qualification," "without doubt") or idiomatically ("in spite of doubt," "nonetheless"). The reappearance of the motif "es un don" again remands us to the opening lines while, compounded by a reversal from "*mi* boca" and "*mi* alma" to "*tú*," the insistent repetition of "esperar" intensifies the oscillation. The image of the harvest reinforces the circadian cycle by means of an intertextual allusion to the gospel according to John (12:24).[19] This intertext supplements the final verses because it suggests sowing as opposed to reaping, but with the same result: unending life instead of/because of death. Poem I thus initiates and prefigures the development of "Libro primero" by defining the dialogic tension and intensifying the interaction between its two aspects.

In the second poem, the poet-speaker continues to explore his new perception of language, making "la noche" the subject of this poem in contrast with "la claridad" in poem I. If "la claridad" represents the moments of poetic illumination and inspiration that produce poems, "la noche" refers to those periods of time when the poet is not writing. If in poem I "la claridad" becomes "claridad/noche," in poem II "la noche" becomes "noche/alba." The opening verses of the poem establish the connection between the closing of night and the coming of dawn and describe a paradoxical situation.

> Yo me pregunto a veces si la noche
> se cierra al mundo para abrirse o si algo
> la abre tan de repente que nosotros
> no llegamos a su alba, al alba al raso
>
> . . . .
>
> y [mi tristeza] no revela que en la noche hay campos
> de intensa amanecida apresurada
> no en germen, en luz plena, en albos pájaros.
>
> (p. 34)[20]

The speaker discovers that the periods between acts of writing are not sterile or empty but actually as enriching and fruitful as the moments of poetic production.[21] He is aware of the great activity of these periods, but it is only after the event that he has proof that inspiration is at work, not just potentially ("no en germen") but fully and intensely ("[sino] en luz plena, en albos pájaros"). The poem as product substantiates the slow, evolutionary process of germination. The speaker nonetheless retains his doubt concerning the return of the impulse that results in a poem. His awareness of the duplicity of the "noche/alba" is discernible in the middle of the poem where the indeterminacy of the future tense (both literal future and future of probability in each instance) and a question (both rhetorical and literal) express the tension between inevitability and skepticism.

> Algún vuelo estará quemando el aire,
> no por ardiente sino por lejano.
> 15 Alguna limpidez de estrella bruñe
> los pinos, bruñirá mi cuerpo al cabo.
> ¿Qué puedo hacer sino seguir poniendo
> la vida a mil lanzadas del espacio?[22]

The speaker concludes by asserting the unity of night and dawn as a poem emerges directly from the night itself.

25   Así yo estoy sintiendo que las sombras
      abren su luz, la abren, la abren tanto,
      que la mañana surge sin principio
      ni fin, eterna ya desde el ocaso.[23]

It is ironic that the poem ends with "ocaso." The very act of bringing the poem to fruition plunges the poet into another hiatus, another "noche/alba," causing another subversion of the primordial code: A rupture of the circadian rhythm coincides with its replenishment and revitalization; partum becomes fertilization; the seed harvested (the poem) renews the process of germination. Poem II maintains many of characteristics of poem I (ambivalent semantics and syntax, circadian cycles, and the imbrication of two semiotically incompatible concepts), but it does so as a mirror image.

In accord with the development delineated by Eco, "The following stage in Adam's experiment confers special status on the *substance of expression*" (p. 97; original emphasis). Adam finds a rock and writes "red" on it, but he uses the juice of blue berries to do so; then he writes "blue" on it but with red juice (pp. 97–98). Poems III and IV of "Libro primero" represent an equivalent stage in Rodríguez's poetic evolution. Because it is an evergreen, conserving its green color throughout the year, the holm oak (also called an evergreen oak) described in poem III would appear to represent the transcendence inherent in a work of art. The dialogic perspective reveals that, in spite of its external appearance, the holm oak actually belongs to the transient world: Its substance contradicts and subverts its form. Serving as emblem for the poem, the holm oak embodies the ambivalent nature of all art. This ambivalence includes the poet, causing him to examine not only the validity of participation in the poetic act but his own existence as well. The poet establishes the holm oak as an emblem for the poem and his existential dilemma in the opening verses.

      La encina, que conserva más un rayo
      de sol que todo un mes de primavera,
      no siente lo espontáneo de su sombra,
      la sencillez del crecimiento; apenas
5   si conoce el terreno en que ha brotado.
      Con ese viento que en sus ramas deja
      lo que no tiene música, imagina
      para sus sueños una gran meseta.
      Y con qué rapidez se identifica
10   con el paisaje, con el alma entera
      de su frondosidad y de mí mismo.

                                       (p. 35)[24]

Mention of the sunlight and spring in vv. 1–2 along with the perennial greenness of this tree recall the primordial perspective at the beginning of poem I. This characterization would lead us to discern the Edenic, transcendent nature of the holm oak if not for the negation and doubt expressed in the phrases "no siente" and "apenas / si." These phrases split our perception of the tree. The speaker may admire the tree for its innocence, spontaneity, and transcendent appeal or disdain it for its ignorance and

lack of awareness. The tree's act of imagining the "meseta" could be either an inge-
nious, generative process or only an illusion. Because the poet-speaker re-creates this
tree from his anecdotal world and creates it in the poem, he recognizes its limitations,
undercutting its existence and reality in the very act of creating it. That subversion
extends to the scene around it and includes the participant, that is, the poet in the act
of writing and the reader in the act of reading. The creation of the poem (through
writing or reading) makes the participant aware of his/her nature as a sentient human
being. But recognizing the imperfections and failures of that act also reflect on the
participant, causing an existential crisis. The poet's identification with the tree and
the ambivalence he has discovered in it stand out in sharper relief in vv. 18–28.

> Así estoy yo. Qué encina, de madera
> más oscura quizá que la del roble,
> 20 levanta mi alegría, tan intensa
> unos momentos antes del crepúsculo
> y tan doblada ahora. Como avena
> que se siembra a voleo y que no importa
> que caiga aquí o allí si cae en tierra,
> 25 va el contenido ardor del pensamiento
> filtrándose en las cosas, entreabriéndolas,
> para dejar su resplandor y luego
> darle una nueva claridad en ellas.[25]

The sentence beginning with "Qué encina" is ambivalent because of its neutral
punctuation. Is it an exclamation or a question? Does it express exaltation, doubt, or
mild sarcasm? The adjectives "intensa" and "doblada" could refer to "encina" or to
"alegría." Even more important is the indefiniteness of the last word of the sentence,
the deictic "ahora." Does it refer to night, just following "el crepúsculo," or to dawn,
the absent supplement of dusk? Is the speaker exhausted but elated because of the
intensity of his participation or dispirited and disappointed because of a lack of fulfillment? Even the intertextual reference to the New Testament parable of the sower
(Matt. 13:1–9) in vv. 22–24, along with the semantic ambivalence of the phrases "el
contenido ardor," "filtrándose," and "*entre*abriéndolas," casts doubt upon the success
of the sowing. The preposition "para" indicates the purpose of the sowing, but does
not assure the realization of the crop, in accord with Christ's rationale for using parables
(Matt. 13:10–17). The questions that close the poem sustain this duality and confirm
the association between the tree/poem and the poet.

> Y es cierto, pues la encina ¿qué sabría
> 30 de la muerte sin mí? ¿Y acaso es cierta
> su intimidad, su instinto, lo espontáneo
> de su sombra más fiel que nadie? ¿Es cierta
> mi vida así, en sus persistentes hojas
> a medio descifrar la primavera?[26]

These interrogatives can be both literal and rhetorical. The speaker asserts his
ability to create as he gives form to this tree (this poem), but concomitant with the act

of creation he destroys it, belying his creation with the questions and doubts latent in the equivocality of language. The final question stresses this ambivalent attitude toward the act of representation. While other trees are budding and putting forth new growth, the "persistentes hojas" of the holm oak do not change. This tree does not participate in the dynamic renewal taking place in the spring. In comparison with other visible changes in nature, the holm oak is static. What appeared to be its transcendent aspect—its perennial greenness—becomes an indication of its stasis. Although the outward form of the holm oak is consistent with the concept of transcendence, its actual substance—the lack of change and renewal—belies our original, Edenic view. The last word of the poem, "la primavera," reasserts the natural rhythm of the seasons but places the holm oak outside that cycle. In the image of the evergreen but static holm oak, Rodríguez has confirmed that the poem is both product and process. He has discovered that he can create with language, but that the equivocality of language subverts and destroys in the very act of creation. Because of his identification with the tree, he sees the ambivalence of participation in the creative act and of his own existence.

In the same way that poem II mirrors poem I, poem IV plays off of poem III. Based on the Adamic concept of writing "blue" with red ink (the reverse of poem III), the fourth poem sustains the oscillating pattern of "Libro primero" but aggravates it by widening the distance between itself and its pair through reversals and ambiguities. This poem revives the image of light in its description of dawn, which the poet equates with the desire to write. The choice of this image connects the poem with a long tradition of poems about the dawn. But here it seems that Rodríguez is parodying a traditional view of dawn as a fleeting moment that cannot be captured or reduplicated. In contrast with that view, Rodríguez defines dawn as a never-ending desire only exacerbated by the production of a poem. Reversals and ambivalencies subvert a traditional view of dawn from the first verse.

> Así el deseo. Como el alba, clara
> desde la cima y cuando se detiene
> tocando con sus luces lo concreto
> recién oscura, aunque instantáneamente.

(p. 36)[27]

The poem begins as if in medias res, in an almost formally logical style which quickly degenerates into nebulous grammar. This ambiguity diverts attention away from mimetic reality or symbolic meaning and draws it to the language itself. By placing the abstraction "deseo" before the image of the dawn, the speaker alerts the reader to the text's subversive nature. The verb from which "deseo" derives has an ambivalent meaning related to the act of breathing (synonymous with inspiration). The more positive of these, "aspirar," means "to draw breath," hence to receive poetic inspiration; the converse is true of its counterpart, "anhelar," "to breathe with difficulty." Although the poet returns to the image of light as poetic inspiration and connects with the poetic tradition of poems about the dawn, reversals and ambivalencies signal that his experimentation with language has taken a new turn.

In the subsequent image of the doves, the speaker's tone is ambivalent. These verses could indicate that the speaker rejoices because inspiration has finally arrived or that with the arrival of day the exciting and productive moment of creativity has passed too quickly and been lost.

> Después abre ruidosos palomares
> y ya es un día más. ¡Oh, las rehenes
> palomas de la noche conteniendo
> sus impulsos altísimos! . . .[28]

The final verses sustain the indeterminacy found in the language of poem IV: "hasta que llegue / por fin a ser mi sangre y mi tarea / corpóreo como el sol cuando amanece." The subjunctive mood belies a sense of closure in the final verse, signaling that the process is still incomplete. Instead of temporarily consuming and destroying desire, the completed poem affirms the continuous nature of this desire as a process that only reasserts itself more emphatically when the poem materializes. The search for fulfillment in the creative act continues unabated and intensified in spite of/because of the poem, leaving the poet dissatisfied, notwithstanding his accomplishment. As the holm oak in poem III appeared to represent transcendent reality only to be subverted and made into a symbol of stasis, in poem IV the transience of dawn is converted into an unending search for satisfaction in the poetic act.

Rodríguez's exploration of language evolves further in poems V and VI where he becomes more self-conscious about the act of writing and continues to foreground language in and of itself. First the poet-speaker discovers a new perspective on language by distancing himself from it, but then he realizes that language has slipped out of his grasp and become autonomous. In poem V, the speaker hopes for a new idiom that will allow him to transcend the limitations of language. The neutral punctuation of the opening verses makes the tone uncertain: "Cuándo hablaré de ti sin voz de hombre / para no acabar nunca . . ." (p. 36). The speaker may be quietly questioning the nature of language or anxiously declaiming his frustration with its inadequacies. This duality points to his dilemma: He wants to accomplish what other poets have achieved, but he must do so in his own way. He realizes that he must draw on the poetic tradition but also separate himself from it. Ironically, by separating himself from the tradition, he continues it. For that after all is what distinguishes great poets: They understand and make use of poetic traditions and modes of expression, but they use (and often misuse and even abuse) those traditions in fresh and exciting ways. That is what the speaker aspires to do also. The crucial moment occurs later in the poem when he repeats the opening verse and then isolates the word "Cuándo" in the next verse: "Cuándo hablaré de ti sin voz de hombre. / Cuándo. Mi boca sólo llega al signo, / sólo interpreta muy confusamente" (p. 37). Focusing on "cuándo" allows the speaker to recognize that language itself embodies the concept of time. This recognition allows him to step outside of language (he now refers to his mouth instead of his voice). We can still read this epiphanous moment dialogically as either his lament about the limitations of language or his surprise as he overcomes a barrier that had been frustrating him. In either case, this discovery leads the speaker to experiment with language to understand it better.

Though still ambivalent, the final verses of poem V evince a first attempt to use a new idiom. The speaker wishes to "sobrepasar el tiempo y convertirlo / en seca fuente de llanura . . ." (p. 37). Michael Riffaterre would call the phrase "seca fuente de llanura" an ungrammaticality because a fountain by its very definition cannot be dry.[29] Normally we think of a "dry spring" as one that has stopped putting forth water because of drought or exhaustion. Here the conversion of time into a dry spring has the opposite meaning. This dry spring is equated with the plains where wheat is grown. The plains are most productive if the end of summer—the season of maturation—is dry so that the sun can ripen the grain. The speaker's factual judgment "seca fuente" succeeds in communicating compactly the contradictions he has discovered. The more he doubts and wavers, the more he invents and subverts with regard to language, the more individual and unique his poetry becomes.

In poem VI, the speaker discovers that *"nomina sint numina,"* that words may be gods with minds of their own.[30] That "las imágenes" function autonomously and that he has lost control of language both upsets and fascinates the speaker.[31] The autonomy of language threatens the poet with lack of identity but also gives him greater latitude to establish his individuality in the language that emerges from his participation in the creative act. Throughout this poem the speaker grasps at words. The result is a collage of different types of discourse that represent both his search for a personal means of expression and the fragmentation of his identity. Within the same sentence, he may juxtapose the discourse of mysticism with agricultural and scientific discourse, the symbolic with the colloquial, the logico-philosophical and metaphysical with images of the hunt. He even goes so far as to use a surrealistic image: "el alcohol eléctrico del rayo" (p. 38). Because "rayo" can be either a destructive, impermanent bolt of lightning or a piercing, exhilarating ray of sunlight (both belonging to the code of light), the ambivalence of the poet's experience with language stays in the foreground. The shuffling of different types of discourse reflects the range of the speaker's experimentation as well as his lack of control.

The equivocal search for a new direction which begins in poem IV attains its fullest expression in poems VII and VIII. One of the most enigmatic and problematic poems of "Libro primero," poem VII relies on "calculated redundancy" to demonstrate the "incantatory power of language"; but the incantation is ambivalent from beginning to end.[32] Abrupt stops and starts, chaotic shifts from one image to the next, along with indeterminacy, contribute to the foregrounding of language. The opening verses (which also conclude the poem) set forth the poet's call for poetic inspiration: "¡Sólo por una vez que todo vuelva / a dar como si nunca diera tanto!" (p. 38). The subjunctive mood makes this incantation ambivalent, capable of being read as both a plea and a command. We can see the poet as doubting and pleading for the return of inspiration or in full control of his materials and like a magician commanding them to appear. The enjambment ("vuelva / a dar") creates ambiguity: Should everything "return *in order to* give" or "give *anew*"? Does the speaker invoke a unique event or one that is habitual and repeated? As a result of these ambiguities, nothing is certain except the incantatory aspect of the statement.

Several verses and images are repeated in the poem, often with some modification. The figure of the "ritual arador . . . en pleno crucifijo de los campos" (p. 38) is a metaphor for the poet, whose act of writing is equivalent to sowing and reaping. Given this metapoetic dimension, we can see the speaker as looking at another poet from the outside, wishing that he too could form part of the poetic tradition, or delighting in the fact that he has become a plowman/poet producing his own "pan caliente / de citas" (poems inviting the reader to partake), having labored over them "surco a surco y grano a grano" (line by line and word by word; vv. 21–22).[33] In another repeated phrase—"Pero siempre es lo mismo" (v. 9), "Pero ya es lo mismo" (v. 19)—it would seem at first that the change from "siempre" to "ya" marks a difference. On close examination, however, both phrases are ambivalent because both express amazement and disillusionment. The iteration only compounds their indeterminacy in both instances.

Interspersed amid these ambivalent redundancies are moments of intense originality. The exclamation in the center of the poem, "¡Arboles de ribera lavapájaros!" (p. 38), exemplifies the poet's ability to create with language. This verse is so disconnected from the context that it nearly becomes pure sound and rhythm. The main problem is the word "lavapájaros," a neologism that could modify either "árboles" or "ribera." The indeterminacy of this verse demonstrates the magician-poet's ability to create totally new realities. Its rhythm and phonologic pattern also call attention to the language itself rather than its meaning. On the other hand, the reader has little or no idea how to interpret it, nearly causing communication to break down. We could say of the poet-speaker what Eco says of Adam: "[W]hen he sings out his dilemma, he is fascinated by its rhythm, for language is beginning to crumble to pieces in his mouth; he has found the way to give it a totally free rein" (p. 101).

When the poet repeats verbatim the incantation that opens and closes the poem (in all senses of those verbs), we wonder whether a change has occurred. Do we read these verses differently than at the beginning? Has there been a development, opening the poem like a spiral, or has the poem turned upon itself, closing like a circle? Has the speaker invoked the inspiration he sought? Has he summoned his abilities and created something new? Or is he still trying to find his voice and write the poem that will separate him from poetic tradition and thereby allow him to continue it? Although the poet has used redundancy and incantation, although he has given free rein to his language and invented words and expressions in novel and original ways, a question remains as to the success of his endeavor. The ambivalence of the poet's incantation—his simultaneous originality and loss of control—reinforces the oscillating pattern of "Libro primero" and further involves the reader in the actualization of the text. This poem also prefigures and contrasts with the use of repetition in "Libro tercero."

Poems VI and VII represent the poet's most extreme use of language in "Libro primero." It is only by stretching the possibilities of language and destroying communication with the reader that he is able to understand the true nature of language and the poetic act. "Adam has arrived at a comprehension of the system at the very moment in which he is calling the system into question and therefore destroying it" (see Eco, "The Possibility of Generating," pp. 101–2). In contrast with the frenetic disquiet of poem VII, the next poem is remarkable for its muted, reflective tone. Because he has taken language to an extreme, the speaker has developed a new view of the poetic act. Although he continues to use redundancy, he now combines that device with a traditional image—rain—giving his poem (and the entire "Libro") focus and coherence. We must recognize, however, that the image of the rain is another factual judgment: "because . . . rainwater falls from heaven . . . it is also cognate with light."[34]

In poem VIII, the poet would seem to have reached the goal he defined in poem V ("Cuándo hablaré de ti sin voz de hombre"). But the rain arrives in the midst of the poem, not at the beginning or the end. In this way, he indicates that it is the process of writing that leads to the discovery of meaning, suggesting a reciprocal relationship between language (form) and knowledge (substance). Through language we achieve an ontological understanding, but that knowledge affects our epistemological view of language, regenerating it, "haciendo de ello vida y labor propias," "convirtiéndolo en seca fuente de llanura." It is only by way of language that the poet is able to go beyond language. The final word of the poem, "lava," confirms this view, for this cleansing "signifies not only purification . . . but, more fundamentally, regeneration through the effect of the transitional powers (implying change, destruction and recreation)."[35]

Just as the poet equates day and night in poem I, in poem VIII he makes rain synonymous with light. Rather than setting up an incompatible situation ("claridad/ noche"), he brings about a metamorphosis, a transformation in which substance becomes form and form substance, without either surrendering its original quality. If we think of this phenomenon in terms of the sign, Rodríguez's poet-speaker has discovered that the sign both unites and separates signifier and signified.[36] The traditional image of the rain receives fresh treatment because it represents language itself. Language has taken on a tangible, sensorial form, a reality of its own that has a perceptible impact on speaker and reader. Poem VIII takes us back to the image of light in poem I but gives fresh impetus to the oscillating pattern of *Don*. Yet the very tranquility and simplicity of expression in this poem heightens our awareness of the power of language to create experience. The measured, contemplative tone of poem VIII does not exclude the dialogic tension which had built to the chaotic effect of poem VII, but it does modify it.[37]

If in poem VII the magician-poet attempts to create new realities with language through its incantatory power, in poem VIII he realizes/discovers his humility because he has realized/brought about a reciprocal relationship between being and language. Poem IX then expresses the poet-speaker's desire to surrender himself, to extinguish his individuality and through the poem to become part of the poetic tradition. Because of the dialogic perspective, the question of his success at this self-sacrifice hangs fire.

> Como si nunca hubiera sido mía,
> dad al aire mi voz y que en el aire
> sea de todos y la sepan todos
> como una mañana o una tarde.

5   Ni a la rama tan sólo abril acude,
     ni el agua espera sólo el estiaje.

(p. 40)[38]

The poem begins with a contrary-to-fact statement and hinges on a number of imperatives which could indicate the speaker's joyful relinquishment of self as well as his anguished plea that he might surrender himself. The syntax of vv. 5–6 is extremely equivocal, again demonstrating the ambivalence of the speaker's situation. Even the image of the flower in the middle of the poem is equivocal because it is uncertain whether the speaker identifies with the flower or feels his distance and difference from it.

¡Que todo acabe aquí, que todo acabe
de una vez para siempre! La flor vive
tan bella porque vive poco tiempo
15   y, sin embargo, cómo se da, unánime,
dejando de ser flor y convirtiéndose
en ímpetu de entrega. . . .[39]

This image evokes a passage from the epistle of James (1:9–11) and defines the conclusion the speaker reached in poem VIII: the reciprocal nature of form and substance.[40] James quotes Isaiah (40:6–8), a passage that reinforces the reciprocity seen in the relation between the isolated poem as "fragment" and all of poetry, the individual poet and the poetic tradition.[41]

The final image of the poet's voice as a stream carving its channel is as ambivalent as the image of the flower. The voice becomes a river—in itself an ambivalent symbol—but the body is more problematic: "Sobre la voz que va excavando un cauce / qué sacrilegio este del cuerpo, este / de no poder ser hostia para darse" (vv. 25–27).[42] The voice as stream and the body as host seem to represent the ambivalence of signs. On the one hand, a sign can flow freely from signifier to signified and constantly changes as it makes its own course; on the other hand, it can frustrate and cancel that movement, designating an abyss between signifier and signified as indicated by a difference between the poet's act of giving and Christ's. The speaker's attitude is also ambivalent. Does he minimize the importance of the body because the voice has achieved transcendence? Or does he lament his inability to surrender himself completely in his recognition of the limits and inconsistencies of language? Poem IX, the unpaired poem, truly leaves us suspended in ecstatic doubt, awaiting a resolution in the remaining poems of *Don*.

WARP AND WOOF: THE INTERPLAY OF METAPHOR AND METONYMY IN THE "CANTOS" OF "LIBRO SEGUNDO"

The tripartite structure of *Don* with its two longer sections flanking the center section suggests the configuration of a balance resting on a fulcrum. Because "Canto del despertar" and "Canto del caminar" are the only two poems with titles and bear the additional weight of an epigram preceding each, "Libro segundo" has a centripetal effect that informs its centrality, stability, and dominance in the structure of the collection. Yet, as the center section, "Libro segundo" is not only the stable fulcrum on which the two longer sections balance and rock but also the second of three sections in sequence. "Libro segundo" serves as the arena of contention between the opposing axes of verticality and horizontality, center and periphery, fixity and flux, the paradigmatic and the syntagmatic. These opposing forces take the form of two different types of language at odds in the "Cantos." We could adduce any number of binary terms to describe this dichotomy, but we can best appreciate this tension if we address the tropes of metaphor and metonymy.[43]

Although metaphor dominates "Canto del despertar," the insistent encroachment of metonymy plays against it. Where metaphor posits the synchronic, paradigmatic, vertical axis of language, arresting progress and creating stability and centrality, metonymy undercuts this effect with a horizontal, diachronic, or syntagmatic thrust. Ironically, this countermovement intensifies the effect of metaphor. After the opening verse, which establishes tension between the two tropes and forms a frame for the section with the last verse of "Canto del caminar," the poet tries to separate the tropes—as much as that is possible.[44] Then he gradually intermingles them so that by the end of the poem only the slightest shift in focus reveals that both coexist in the same language. In that regard we might use the analogy of a Moebius strip to describe the way language functions in "Canto del despertar."[45] The gradual imbrication of the vertical and horizontal forces of metaphor and metonymy not only heightens the intensity of the metaphoric but also leads to the destabilization of language. This process mirrors and amplifies the oscillating pattern of "Libro primero."

The pendulum swings in the opposite direction in "Canto del caminar" where metonymy is prevalent. Because this poem is considerably longer than any other in the collection, "Canto del caminar" defines an even longer swing than "Canto del despertar" and prepares us for a final sweep through the poems of "Libro tercero." In general, this second poem lacks the archetypal resonance manifest in "Canto del despertar" (and most of the poems of "Libro primero"). We recognize many of the same devices of "Canto del despertar," but the context has altered, so that we must approach the combination of metaphor and metonymy from a different angle. Given the blurring of the tropes brought about in "Canto del despertar," we realize that a radical shift in paradigms has occurred. Instead of seeing language as the double-sided Moebius strip, we must now change our analogy to the Venn diagram, a trompe l'oeil that oscillates between two different perceptions of three-dimensional space.[46] In "Canto del caminar," we must read metonymy as if it were metaphor and vice versa. The interaction between metaphor and metonymy in the "Cantos" of "Libro segundo" contrasts centrality and stability with periphery and flux, and intensifies Rodríguez's transgressive handling of language.

"Canto del despertar" opens with a conflation of the tropes, forming a frame for the "Libro." When the speaker states, "El primer surco de hoy será mi cuerpo" [The first furrow of the day will be my body] (p. 45), the linking verb "ser" defines a metaphoric equivalence between a furrow and his body. Having read poem VII of "Libro primero," we know that "surco" is a metaphor for a line of poetry. This verse associates the agricultural code with the metaphoric axis, so that whenever we encounter this code, we will recognize it as metaphor. Yet the future tense defers the metaphoric comparison, creating a metonymic dimension based on linear time. When we envision a furrow, we see a horizontal line corresponding to the written verse and to the poet's drawing upon previous poems and his anticipation of future ones. Here intertextuality underscores the linear development from one poem to the next and from one "Libro" to the next, characterizing it as metonymic.[47]

This opening verse is emblematic of the forces in contention throughout "Canto del despertar": It discloses tension between the vertical thrust of metaphor and the horizontal progress of metonymy, the synchronic and diachronic axes of language. At the same time, it posits a central theme of *Don:* The poet "awakens" through writing, making writing a means of constituting the self. But the concept of self is ambivalent because the traits of the self are both specifically defined and constantly evolving, paradigmatic and syntagmatic, synchronic and diachronic, essence and process. As a description of the poet's awakening to his vocation, *Don* is a contradictory experience. It is an open and a closed text, capturing the ambivalent shift in paradigms from a structuralist to a poststructuralist (postmodern) attitude.[48] The interplay of metaphor and metonymy in the "Cantos" embodies this contradiction.

After exposing the tension between metaphor and metonymy, the poet provides the clearest distinction of the tropes and renders the characteristics of each in verses 2–8. In spite of his attempt to distinguish them, traces of metonymy can be found in metaphor and vice versa.

> Cuando la luz impulsa desde arriba
> despierta los oráculos del sueño
> y me camina, y antes que al paisaje
> 5   va dándome figura. Así otra nueva
> mañana. Así otra vez y antes que nadie,
> aun que la brisa menos decidera,
> sintiéndome vivir, solo, a luz limpia.
>
> (p. 45)[49]

Verses 2–5 have a decidedly metaphoric quality. If the furrow represents a line of poetry, the "oráculos del sueño" in v. 3 are the seeds in the furrow—the words in the poet's verses. This image lends itself to various interpretations because oracles (like poets) are divinely inspired messengers whose words must be interpreted; the preposition "de" could mean "from" or "of," and "sueño" can mean "sleep" or "dream." Do these oracles awaken from sleep, or do they induce us to dream when they awaken? The personification of the light (traditionally, poetic inspiration) as a farmer walking his fields and promoting the seeds' germination also signals the metaphoric aspect. The various levels of meaning in these verses reflect the overdetermination of metaphor. In contrast with these metaphoric qualities, the anaphora of the phrases "Así otra" and "antes que" in vv. 5–6 mark the metonymic axis because of the causal and temporal connections they make. The phrase "sintiéndome vivir, solo, a luz limpia" echoes "va dándome figura" in v. 5, and both restate the opening theme. Throughout the poem, the reworking of ideas in different contexts produces a progressive development through metonymy even though the phrases are metaphoric. Here we see the anticipation of being ("El primer surco de hoy *será* mi cuerpo"), its taking shape ("va dándome figura"), and its realization ("sintiéndome vivir"), a metonymic process that pertains to the topos of awakening.[50]

In spite of the seemingly obvious contrast between the metaphoric and the metonymic, an undercurrent is manifest. Intertextual allusions to poem I of "Libro primero" in the phrase "Cuando la luz impulsa desde arriba" and the parallelism "Así . . . Así" decenter the poem and stress horizontality. On the other hand, in the metonymic verses, the abrupt run-on line "Así otra nueva / mañana" calls attention to morning as metaphor belonging to the topos of awakening. The personification of the breeze as "menos decidera" also evokes metaphor. Although the poet seems to privilege one trope over the other, traces of metonymy can be found in metaphor and vice versa. The intermingling of the tropes expands in the next lines, where the act of writing has ambivalent consequences. These ambivalencies prefigure the tension that greater interpenetration of metaphor and metonymy will produce.

> Pero algún gesto hago, alguna vara
> 10   mágica tengo porque, ved, de pronto
> los seres amanecen, me señalan.
> Soy inocente. ¡Cómo se une todo
> y en simples movimientos hasta el límite,
> oh, para mi castigo: la soltura
> 15   del álamo a cualquier mirada! Puertas
> con vellones de niebla por dinteles
> se abren allí, pasando aquella cima.[51]

Although at first metonymy prevails in the anaphora of the indefinite adjectives ("algún" and "alguna") and the parallel syntax, these metonymic devices give way to metaphor. As one metaphor succeeds another, we discover that though metaphors, they function metonymically. The poet's gesture—the act of writing—becomes a magic one: His pen is a "vara mágica."[52] But the fabrication of this new world has ambivalent results. The world he creates points him out, perhaps because he has a special talent it recognizes and wishes to acclaim. But it may also be accusing him, alienating him from his own words. This duality is germane to the idea that metaphor is a special ability of only the most original poets but also a form of lying, a trope that destroys the usual perceptions of reality by creating a new one.[53] Writing is also an act of theft (plagiarism) because the poet makes use of others' words. The response "Soy inocente" could be interpreted as an exaltation of the poet's heightened consciousness as he creates with language or his defense against these accusations.

The poet underscores this ambivalence as he strings one metaphor after another. The phrase "los seres amanecen" presents the same ambivalence of the first verses of the poem. On the one hand, the verb pertains to the topos of awakening and supports the metaphoric aspect. But this phrase also echoes v. 3 ("despierta los oráculos del sueño"). This restatement of the same idea in different terms is metonymic because it repeats the earlier idea but modifies it. Further ambivalence arises in "castigo." Rodríguez is punning on its archaic but positively marked "learning" in contrast with the modern but negatively marked "punishment."[54] Using archaic meanings evokes the history and evolution of language, another sign of metonymic diachrony, while maintaining metaphoric verticality.

The poet then embodies this ambivalence in the "álamo" (vv. 14–15). The word "soltura" can refer literally to the blitheness of this tree and figuratively to the facility and lucidity of one's diction. In offering this image, the poet is caught up in his ecstatic vision but also guilty of impropriety: He delights in this beautiful scene, there for anyone to appreciate, but he feels shame for having exhibited its intimacy to anyone ("a cualquier mirada"). The metaphor of the "puertas / con vellones de niebla por dinteles" (a possible intertextual allusion to the Book of Exodus and the Passover) could refer to the eyes of the poet or reader awakening, becoming more penetrating when the poet creates new realities with words; or it could refer to words themselves and what they are capable of revealing. But there is also a sense of taboo that the poet transgresses as he quests for higher levels of knowledge.

Although metaphors seem to regain their prominence here, their ambivalence increases because they are used metonymically, one following the other to modify, develop, and restate the preceding concept as the poet strives to capture his perceptions. Dialogic tension in these verses gives further evidence of their overdetermination, whereas intertextual allusions recall various moments of "Libro primero." For example, the figure of the magician appears in poem VII, and the verses "¡Cómo se une todo / y en simples movimientos hasta el límite . . . !" remind us of poem IX.[55] The word "cima" could refer to poem IV, another poem describing dawn, but an ambivalent, enigmatic one that contrasts with the evocation of dawn in verses 2–3 of poem I. These allusions reinforce a diachronic reading and confer a horizontal, metonymical quality on the poem. That axis conflicts with metaphoric overdetermination and the constant reinforcement of various topoi on the metaphoric axis. In contrast with the predominantly metaphoric aspect, anaphora returns in vv. 18–24 to produce metonymic chaining. But here again each link in the chain relies on metaphor, indicated by the agricultural code.

> ¿Qué más sencillo que ese cabeceo
> de los sembrados? ¿Qué más persuasivo
> 20   que el heno al germinar? No toco nada.
> No me lavo en la tierra como el pájaro.
> Oh, para mi castigo, el día nace
> y hay que apartar su misma recaída
> de las demás. . . .[56]

When the poet repeats metaphoric threads from the previous verses here, the interaction between the two tropes intensifies. This is especially evident in the repetition of "Oh, para mi castigo" and in the transformation in "el día nace." This phrase varies the earlier "los seres amanecen," which in its turn had echoed "despierta los oráculos del sueño." Here the poet is grappling with the issue of derivativeness, the inscribing and transforming of traditional imagery so that it becomes fresh and new, preventing that one poem seem like all the rest ("hay que apartar su misma recaída / de las demás"). To write original poems, the poet must draw on poetic tradition, metaphorically and synchronically repeating images and themes that have always concerned poetry; but he must rework them to make them fresh. When he does so, he breaks with tradition at the same time that he contributes to it by adding to the metonymic chain. The poet's contribution to the tradition is synchronic and diachronic, static and dynamic, paradigmatic and syntagmatic. This problem is a variation of the tension between the tropes that we have observed in the reworking of his own images.[57]

From this point onward, the intertwining of metaphor and metonymy grows exceedingly intricate. Verses 24–26 mark a nodal point in the text: "Aquí sí es peligroso. / Ahora, en la llanada hecha de espacio, / voy a servir de blanco a lo creado."[58] The deictics "aquí" and "ahora" are indicators of space and time, respectively, which express a contrast between stasis and movement. "Aquí" pinpoints a specific locus of perception, indicating centrality and stasis; in contrast, "ahora" evokes the continuous passage of time as "now" slides constantly forward. Curiously, though, we could reverse the order of these two adverbs, and the meaning of these verses would not change significantly. They might even make more sense in light of the spatial dimensions of "aquí" and "en la llanada hecha de espacio." As indicators of time and space, these apparently innocuous deictics signal that metaphor and metonymy are interchangeable and synonymous (cf. the Moebius strip).

The speaker then sets up another metaphoric equivalence when he says "Voy a servir de blanco a lo creado," but as in the first verse of the poem, spatial movement and temporal futurity inherent in the verbal construction "ir a" defers that event, negating the "here" and the "now." The poet has become acutely conscious of the poetic tradition and sees himself merging with it, but he does not know if that is good or bad. Does he stand out as an original poet, joining the tradition? Or does he lose his identity like one furrow among many, one day just like any other? If the poet is a stationary target, all of reality ("lo creado") provides the arrows or projectiles that can cause ecstasy and pain, such as those in the following verses.

> Tibia respiración de pan reciente
> me llega, y así el campo eleva formas
> de una aridez sublime, y un momento
> 30   después, el que se pierde entre el misterio
> de un camino y el de otro menos ancho,
> somos obra de lo que resucita.
> Lejos estoy, qué lejos. ¿Todavía,
> agrio como el moral silvestre, el ritmo
> 35   de las cosas me daña? Alma de ave,
> yacerás bajo cúpula de árbol.[59]

Metaphor and metonymy are so densely interwoven in these lines that any attempt to disentangle them results in only a partial reading. I will therefore abbreviate

my discussion and point out only a few of the metaphoric and metonymic entangle-
ments that comprise them. The images of v. 27 show how imperceptibly we move
from one side of the Moebius strip to the other. The phrase "tibia respiración" foregrounds the metaphoric aspect by describing the aroma of freshly baked bread. As
breath (inspiration), the aroma brings the poet to life. But this inspiration reaches him
either because of his spatial contiguity with the world around him or because of his
reading of others' poetry—indications of metonymy. Also, the image of the life-giving breath is another metonymic variation on the topos of awakening. In contrast,
"pan reciente" at first appears to be a literal (metonymic) part of the poet's anecdotal
world. But if we recall poem VII of "Libro primero," we know that bread forms part
of the agricultural code and is a metaphor for the poem.

The phrase "y así" (v. 28) extends the confusion of the tropes. Does it link the
next image metonymically with the image of bread by suggesting cause and effect, or
does it present a metaphoric equivalence? A temporal confusion arises in the abrupt
run-on line in vv. 29–30. The phrase "un momento" stops time, elevates the moment
above the temporal flow by singling it out, similar to the effect of metaphor; but the
addition of "después" in the following line reinforces the sequence of moments (metonymy).[60] These verses conflate the tropes to such an extent that it is nearly impossible to differentiate them.

At the end of this long, complicated sentence, the poet posits another metaphorical association: "somos obra de lo que resucita." Is this metaphor a restatement of the
phrase that generated this sentence ("voy a servir de blanco a lo creado"), or does it
confirm a metonymic process? Now, instead of serving as the target for "lo creado,"
the poet states that we (all who participate in the poetic experience) are the "obra," the
product of an ongoing process, writing/reading as the constitution of identity. The
verb "resucita" varies the topos of awakening generated by the title of the poem, but
ambivalence arises when we ponder whether the verb is transitive or intransitive. Is
this a cause-and-effect relationship (we as targets are created by that which gives us
life), in which case metonymy obtains? Or is it a parallel one (we attain being because
we are capable of reviving something—words, poems—from the past, the routine
and the commonplace of daily life), indicating metaphor? Because both readings are
feasible, process and product are indistinguishable; the horizontal impulse of metonymy and the vertical force of metaphor have become superimposed, reminding us
of the Moebius strip.

The neutral punctuation of the phrase "Lejos estoy, qué lejos" leaves the tone
undecided. The speaker could be expressing his exaltation because he has escaped
time through metaphor and because his ability to transform the world through metaphor excites him. Or he could be despairing because he is still caught in the flow of
time, unable to transcend it along with all the other things subject to its ravages. The
question "¿Todavía . . . el ritmo / de las cosas me daña?" continues this ambivalence,
interrupted and reinforced by the adjectival phrase "agrio como el moral silvestre."
Does "agrio" modify "el ritmo"? If so, it underscores the speaker's despair. If on the
other hand the speaker (present in the phrase "me daña") compares himself with the
"moral silvestre," he stands out as a distinct genus that produces a unique fruit. This

question expresses the speaker's despair because of his inclusion in "el ritmo / de las cosas" and his disdain for that transience because through his poetry, he has been able to individuate and rise above the temporal flow.

These verses are among the most enigmatic in the poem, arising from the intense interaction between metaphor and metonymy that has been building to a crescendo. Rodríguez is exploring the limits of language, trying to determine just how much stress words can bear. He delights in observing how one phrase interacts with others, how meaning can alter as he combines words, how minor changes can produce radical shifts in meaning. Because they push language to the limit, these verses approach incomprehensibility and frustrate exegesis. Information theorists would say that these lines entail a great deal of "noise," a concept that echoes the latter poems of "Libro primero" (esp. IV–VII) and foreshadows the chaotics of language in "Canto del caminar" and "Libro tercero."[61]

This tension reaches its maximum expression in vv. 37–38, the climactic moment of "Canto del despertar": "¡Noche de intimidad lasciva, noche / de preñez sobre el mundo, noche inmensa!" Here the interplay between the tropes is extremely complicated. The image of night, "expressive of fertility, potentiality, and germination," is an archetypal symbol that forms part of the topos of awakening permeating this poem and pertaining to the metaphoric axis.[62] But in addition to these properties Rodríguez anaphorically repeats the word "noche" and links it with the image of night-as-dawn in poem II of "Libro primero." By synchronically invoking the mystic poets, he diachronically connects the image with San Juan de la Cruz (whose verses form the epigraph of this poem), presenting another intricate conflation of metaphor and metonymy.[63] Each repetition of the image introduces a metaphor with erotic overtones. These variations on the agricultural code describe copulation ("intimidad lasciva"), conception ("preñez"), and imminent birth ("noche inmensa"). Taken in sequence, they delineate a process of writing, a cause-and-effect relationship indicative of metonymy that repeats but modifies the process described in the opening verses of the "Canto." Metaphor and metonymy are so thoroughly interwoven in these verses as to make them indistinguishable. Often only a slight adjustment in focus reveals that the two tropes coexist in the same words.

The final verses reveal a change in attitude as a result of the speaker's experimentation with and transgression of the limits of language. Although the horizontal thrust of metonymy has intensified the vertical tension of metaphor, their interplay has also destabilized language. In these verses, the speaker struggles with the indeterminacy of language.

> Ah, nada está seguro bajo el cielo.
> 40   Nada resiste ya. Sucede cuando
> mi dolor me levanta y me hace cumbre
> que empiezan a ocultarse las imágenes
> y a dar la mies en cada poro el acto
> de su ligero crecimiento. Entonces
> 45   hay que avanzar la vida de tan limpio
> como es el aire, el aire retador.[64]

The neutral punctuation of vv. 39–40 maintains the dialogic tension between despair and ecstasy, and the syntax of vv. 40–44 creates more indeterminacy given the curious placement of the adverbial clause beginning with "cuando." At first it seems that the situation arises at the same time that "mi dolor me levanta y me hace cumbre," phrases that emphasize the verticality of metaphor and the simultaneity of events. But the relative pronoun "que" suggests a different reading. If we set the adverbial clause off with commas or consider it preceding "sucede," a situation of cause and effect results—the horizontal, linear progression of events in time, also apparent in the verb "empiezan" and repetition of the preposition "a." The syntax in vv. 43–44 is also ambiguous: The subject could be either "la mies" or "el acto."

The final image of the poem leaves us struggling with the ambiguity and indeterminacy of language embodied in metaphor and metonymy. Like many of the deictics of this poem, the adverb "entonces" is ambivalent. On the one hand, it can refer to a metaphoric moment located outside of time ("cuando mi dolor me levanta y me hace cumbre"); on the other hand, it may refer metonymically to a cause-and-effect relation amid a series of moments. The phrase "hay que avanzar la vida" urges a continuation in time but also suggests that the poet is mired in inertia and stasis.

In the final verse, repetition of "el aire" (with its possible intertextual allusion to Lorca's "Romance de la luna, luna") indicates metonymy. But the adjectives "limpio" and "retador" personify the air and suggest ambivalent characteristics. The former can be either a pristine state, an inherent quality of purity and innocence that uplifts the poet, or a process of purification that he experiences over time as he strives to attain the same purity. The latter adjective connotes resistance and defiance—something that opposes and thwarts the poet—as well as a challenge and a stimulus that keeps him moving forward. In these ambivalent possibilities, we see the contrasting characteristics of metaphor and metonymy. Awakening can represent a single moment (the moment of awareness that a process has taken place) or a process that does not admit noticeable differences between one moment and the next, only imperceptible shadings of light and darkness, nuances of change. Just as the poem is both product and process, so becoming and being describe the same phenomenon, as the last lines of the poem suggest in their ambivalent closure.

"Canto del despertar" depicts a gradual development from beginning to end. Although it starts with an emphasis on metaphor, metonymy stealthily encroaches until the two are inextricably intertwined, heightening the tension between them to the breaking point (near incomprehensibility because of "noise" in the message). Metonymy heightens the effect of metaphor and destabilizes language. "Canto del despertar" recapitulates the process that takes place in "Libro primero," halting the progress of the work and establishing the centrality, stability, and verticality of "Libro segundo" as the fulcrum. But by generating its own development, this poem propels the book forward toward the next poem and the next section where destabilization becomes the territory of exploration. This impetus contrasts with the characterization of "Libro segundo" as stable fulcrum because of its movement and flux.

Just as "Canto del despertar" scribes an arc from beginning to end, amplifying the oscillating pattern initiated in "Libro primero," so "Canto del caminar"—the longest poem in *Don de la ebriedad*—makes a longer swing in a contrary direction, reversing the tendencies in the former poem and preparing us for the final sweep through the poems of "Libro tercero." In fact, the poet now explicitly contradicts many of the stances he took in "Canto del despertar." To continue with the overarching analogy that we have used to describe the experience of "Libro primero," in "Canto del caminar" the poet is a postlapsarian Adam. While still in the Garden of Eden, Adam partici-pated in the pleasure and excitement of discovery, to which the exclamations and exuberance of "Libro primero" attest. Because of his experimentation with language in "Libro primero" and "Canto del despertar," the poet as Adam transgresses the lim-its of language, and his world changes in ways he had not foreseen.

This new world of exile disconcerts him as it expands to include less pleasing experiences. He continues to explore, but now his world is much more extensive, more hostile, less familiar. It is topsy-turvy, fragmented, chaotic: Things look differ-ent; words no longer have the same meaning. Before, even when his experiments with language got out of hand, he delighted in the play and in the dizzying discovery of the capacity of language. Now he is aware that inspiration is not always forthcom-ing and that language often betrays the poet. New emotions such as frustration, con-fusion, disorientation, and fear require different modes of expression. This new con-text entails even more profound discoveries as the poet constitutes his self through writing.

If in "Canto del despertar" metaphor predominates with metonymic devices un-dercutting and heightening metaphor's effect, in "Canto del caminar" metonymy—the "other" trope, more characteristic of narrative than of poetry—usurps the lime-light.[65] If, in the former poem, Rodríguez pushes language to the limit, inflating and burdening the signifier with contradictory signifieds, testing just how much weight words can bear, in this poem he seems to pare language down to the bone, as if he were asking how little archetypal resonance, how few semantic dimensions words can have and still communicate poetically.[66] When metaphors do appear, they allude to metonymic processes and often follow one another in desultory succession, pro-ducing turbulence and fragmentation.[67] In effect, although we observe the same tech-niques employed in "Canto del despertar" (the agricultural code, personification, anaphora, intertextuality, etc.), this new context alters their effect. Because of the conflation of the tropes in "Canto del despertar," we must make a radical shift in our reading: *We must now read metonymy as if it were metaphor and vice versa.*

The basic pattern of this poem repeats that of "Canto del despertar": First the poet tries to distinguish the tropes as much as possible, then he combines them in various ways. But if from the beginning we read metonymy as metaphor, the dynamic of their interaction leads into a labyrinth.[68] In this labyrinth, the poet confronts certain bifurcation points at which he halts his progress to assess where he has been, where he is, and which direction he will take next.[69] Progress through the labyrinth consists of movement and stasis. But instead of aligning metaphor with stasis (verticality, stability, centrality—the fulcrum) and metonymy with movement (horizontality, in-stability, periphery, transition), the context now acquires a third dimension—a gap. Now the interaction of metaphor and metonymy represents activity, movement, dynamic though turbulent flow. In contrast, the poet sporadically inserts small "islands" of stasis, bifurcation points that cause him to stop, to question, to assess.[70] The continual shifting of the tropes via supplemental play—the system of difference that is language—leads the poet to the discovery of a disquieting gap in the sign: its simultaneous plenitude and insufficiency, the presence of an absence that makes presence problematic.[71] If we now add the notion of chaos to our discussion of metaphor and metonymy, we can formulate an understanding of Rodríguez's incursion into hitherto uncharted territories of language.[72] The opening verses of "Canto del caminar" provide a distinct contrast with those of "Canto del despertar."

> Nunca había sabido que mi paso
> era distinto sobre tierra roja,
> que sonaba más puramente seco
> lo mismo que si no llevase un hombre,
> 5   de pie, en su dimensión. Por ese ruido
> quizá algunos linderos me recuerden.
> Por otra cosa no. . . .
>
> (p. 49)[73]

At first glance, these verses offer very little information. About all we know is that the speaker has gone for a walk in the countryside and has discovered a difference in the sound of his footsteps when he treads "tierra roja." This image should ring a bell with us because it pertains to the agricultural code. But it is so underdetermined, so anecdotal, so lacking in archetypal resonance, that it seems meaningless. Only an avid horticulturalist would know that red soil contains too much ferrous oxide (too much acid) to sustain an abundant crop (like wheat). The red soil suggests aesthetic dryness, a lack of inspiration also evident in the hollow sound of the speaker's footsteps.

Walking constitutes another feature of these verses that at first is so underdetermined that we might overlook its significance. Walking is a metonymic activity, a rhythmic, linear movement through time and space, similar to language. This activity contrasts with the opening verse of "Canto del despertar." Instead of describing a metaphorical situation (stasis), it connotes movement; but where the furrow defines a horizontal line undercutting and intensifying the metaphoric, here the poet's body must be in a vertical position ("de pie") to move forward. The text itself thus indicates that we must read the metonymic activity of walking as a metaphor for writing/reading.[74] "Canto del caminar" is a metonymic variation of "Canto del despertar." But walking (like awakening) functions metaphorically as it describes the coming into being, a search for knowledge (of self, of the world, of language) and fulfillment, through writing.

Once we have identified these contrasts, others appear, illuminating the change in the poet's understanding of language. This poem begins with an emphatic "nunca," which contrasts with the first word of the first poem of "Libro primero" ("*Siempre* la claridad viene del cielo"), marking a turning point. This comparison leads to still other contrasts: "tierra" as opposed to "cielo" and sound ("sonaban," "ruido") in contrast with light ("claridad"). Just as the red soil connotes aesthetic dryness and a lack of inspiration, so "ruido," associated with the poet's footsteps, comments upon the poet's self-consciousness about language and the act of writing (as opposed to the heightened consciousness experienced in "Libro primero" and "Canto del despertar").[75] Intertextuality in this context sets up a metaphorical comparison between a former state of being and a new state of becoming. The past tenses "había sabido," "era," and "sonaba" look back to a more innocent time and point to a change that has taken place because of the poet's experience with the duplicity and instability of language. Use of the subjunctive in both the contrary-to-fact "llevase" and the speculative "recuerden" point to his disorientation and insecurity, a questioning of his existence also evident in the phrase "en su dimensión." The mention of the poet's transgression of borders ("linderos") confirms that he has entered unexplored territory, a liminal space where language signifies in unexpected and disorienting ways.

These opening verses rely primarily on metonymic devices (anecdotal reality, anaphora, intertextuality) as opposed to the metaphors that dominate the beginning of "Canto del despertar." But now we read these metonyms as if they were metaphors, proving once again, albeit in a different way, that metaphor and metonymy are indistinguishable. We turn to the metaphoric face of the coin in the next verses where a series of images succeed one another in a turbulent flow, emblematizing in both their form and their content what N. Katherine Hayles calls "the postmodern turn toward fragmentation, rupture, and discontinuity."[76]

> . . . Cambian las nubes
> de forma y se adelantan a su cambio
> deslumbrándose en él, como el arroyo
> 10   dentro de su fluir; los manantiales
> contienen hacia fuera su silencio.[77]

These metaphors of turbulence and noise emphasize movement and metonymic change through time and space ("Cambian . . . de forma," "se adelantan," "fluir"), showing that clouds and streams are subject to the external forces of wind and gravity.[78] Like them, the poet has no control over inspiration. He captures his dilemma in the contradictory semantics with which he describes the fountains (vv. 10–11): The verb "contienen" seems to conflict with "hacia fuera."[79] If we read this expression figuratively and colloquially, we understand that the silence paradoxically emerges from noise/language, just as the whiteness/blankness of the page stands out because of the words on it.[80] Here the babble of the fountains represents an outpouring of words with little or no substance, recalling the proverbial expression "Shallow brooks run noisy."

We encounter the first bifurcation point (or island of stasis) in v. 12: "¿Dónde estabas sin mí, bebida mía?" The switch from a self-conscious meditation on the sound of his footsteps and the change in his outlook to the direct address of the "bebida" brings us up short. Whom does the speaker address? Is it the clear, sobering water of "los manantiales" (meditation) or the inebriating wine (inspiration)?[81] Does he assert the power derived from the drink? Or does he lament his abandonment and the loss of the drink's effect? The imperfect tense of the verb reprises the past tense of vv. 1–7, as the speaker pauses to evaluate his current circumstances. But this verse poses an enigma. At first, we may assume that it belongs to the chaotic string of images beginning with the clouds. We may not recognize it for what it is: an island of stasis in the midst of turbulent movement, a breach in the text that points to a gap in the sign. Only after this pattern repeats and instances of the direct address accrete will we discern the significance of these static moments and know that whenever the poet recurs to the second-person singular, he signals one of these bifurcation points.[82] The recognition of this gap leads poet and reader to more information about language and to a first experience of the gap in the subsequent lines.[83]

> Hasta la hoz pregunta más que siega.
> Hasta el grajo maldice más que chilla.
> 15   Un concierto de espiga contra espiga
> viene con el levante del sol. ¡Cuánto
> hueco para morir! ¡Cuánto azul vívido,
> cuánto amarillo de era para el roce!
> Ni aun hallando sabré: me han trasladado
> 20   la visión, piedra a piedra, como a un templo.[84]

In these verses, we see the juxtaposition of anaphoric repetition and parallel syntax with metaphors. But similar to the conflation of the tropes in "Canto del despertar," the anaphoras introduce metaphors while these evoke metonymic processes. Anecdotal details from the poet's surroundings are converted into metaphors through personification. The sickle no longer reaps, but merely presents a visible question mark, an indication of the silence inherent in language and the superficiality the poet now experiences as he searches for meaning. Instead of inspiring him (a synonym of "chillar" is "cantar"), the grackle curses. By comparing the sound of a wheat field in the wind with a concert, does he mean that noise becomes music or that music (and so his song, his poetry) is noise? This ambiguity, grounded in the conflation of the tropes, breaks down binary opposition by privileging the marginal or secondary.[85] The decentering of the metaphoric throws several other issues into doubt, especially the poet's identity, and contributes to the discovery and subsequent exploration of the gap.

Although these verses seem turbulent and fragmented because of the rapid movement from one image to another, metaphor and metonymy weave them together. In fact, an underlying connection between images suggests the presence of a pervasive semiotic web.[86] For example, "ruido" (v. 5) connects with "silencio" (v. 11), "chilla" (v. 14), "concierto" (v. 15), and "roce" (v. 18); walking finds echoes in the clouds, the stream, and the fountains, and the verbs "viene" (v. 16) and "me han trasladado" (v. 19).

Verses 16–20 point more directly to the gap and the speaker's disorientation in the wilderness that is language. The oddly run-on exclamation "¡Cuánto / hueco para morir!" emphasizes the gap and anticipates future references to death that are connected with the islands of stasis later in this poem.[87] Again the tone is ambiguous: so much open space seems to mock the repletion implied in the field of grain. Is he talking about hollowness, emptiness, lack of production, or an overabundance that leads to anonymity and a lack of individuality and uniqueness? In the colors blue and yellow representing the sky and the wheat field respectively, do we find a harmonious natural blend, a world full of vibrant colors and significant symbolism (blue sky = transcendence; abundant crop = poetic production) or a clash, a rift between transience and transcendence, a vast expanse of empty space? Do the exclamations express ecstasy or despair? Once again, the commingling of the tropes produces dialogic tension, turbulent flow, and ambivalence.

The word "roce" forms a nodal point in the text, bringing together different meanings and providing further confirmation of a semiotic web undergirding the superficial fragmentation. Derived from the verb "rozar," this word pertains in part to the agricultural code. On that level, "rozar" means "Limpiar las tierras de las matas y hierbas inútiles antes de labrarlas, bien para que retoñen o bien para otros fines."[88] Metapoetically, the poet as postlapsarian Adam is involved in an act of renewing poetic space (words), of exploring new linguistic territory, of clearing away the accumulated, hackneyed meanings and usages of words and "resowing" them.[89] Other meanings of "rozar" are associated with the act of writing and allude to the poet's lack of inspiration or his disorientation with regard to language because "rozar" can also mean "Entonar el cantante con inseguridad o con voz poco clara una nota determinada" and "Embarazarse en las palabras, pronunciándolas mal o con dificultad." With regard to the image of the concert, "rozar" can mean "Pasar una cosa tocando y oprimiendo levemente la superficie de otra o acercándose mucho a ella," recalling the way some instruments (e.g., violins) are played. But this act can also produce a strident, unpleasant, or noisome sound (cf. the ambivalence of the concert). Curiously enough, "rozar" derives etymologically from the Latin *ruptiare* from *ruptus* meaning "broken." Along with "hueco," it describes the gap the poet has discovered, though this new information is still too fresh for poet (or reader) to realize its full impact. The word "roce" forms a nodal point that irradiates a variety of meanings, reinforcing the perception of the semiotic web or labyrinth underlying this poem.

The image in vv. 19–20 defines the poet's changing understanding of language. The temple that has been moved "piedra a piedra" defines a hyper-real situation because the poet has lost sight of his original view of things. Language has become for him (and for us too by now) a simulacrum.[90] Through his experimentation with language and his use of imagery taken from his rural Castilian surroundings, Rodríguez has destabilized his view of reality. Does language allow him to understand himself and his reality, or does the world around him enable him to define his experience and his identity with language?[91] Which is metaphor and which metonymy? Which is the original, which the copy? The poet uses the image of the temple to describe his "mirada"—literally his sight, but figuratively his worldview. He feels disoriented, confused, and unstable, for "Once we have entered into this space, the distinction between the copy and the original ceases to have meaning. At this point we live within the hyper-real, and ourselves have become it."[92] Because of the poet's experimentation, the context of language has changed and along with it the sense of self; the poet as Adam now finds himself "a stranger in a strange land." The next perception of the

gap occurs after a series of oblique images anchored in the poet's anecdotal surroundings. Slippage from one image to the next—the constant erosion of context—continues the sense of the hyper-real.

> ¡Qué hora: lanzar el cuerpo hacia lo alto!
> Riego activo por dentro y por encima
> transparente quietud, en bloques, hecha
> con delgadez de música distante
> 25   muy en alma subida y sola al raso.
> Ya este vuelo del ver es amor tuyo.[93]

To what does this act, "lanzar el cuerpo hacia lo alto," refer? It may form part of
the agricultural code, describing the growth of a plant (the act of becoming) or the
dissemination of seed (writing). Or it may refer to the fountain. Both the spike of
grain and the fountain have the visual form of a "lanza." Next we slide to an image of
irrigation, inspiration beneath a deceptive surface and therefore unperceived or un-
recognizable. Or perhaps, in contrast with the earlier image of the "arroyo," we see
that "Still waters run deep" as the poet discerns more clearly the reason for his disorientation.[94] But this image slips into music (the sound of running water) and then into
the image of a bird. When we finally discover that these images all describe the poet's
sight—"la visión" which has become a simulacrum, has shifted context, finds itself
disoriented and unable to focus on one image long enough to constitute identity—the
gap reappears, cloaked in the image of a bird that like music can soar in the air and
skim along the ground. The flight of the bird reworks the contrast between sky and
earth in vv. 17–18 as well as the distinction between the tropes, inspiration and its
lack, and provides the second instance of the direct address. Paradoxically, the turbulent juxtaposition of images pushes us to the edge of the gap, while at the same time
we sense a separation and distance between dynamic flow and vacuity.

As mentioned above, another important feature of "Canto del caminar" is the
contradiction of stances taken in "Canto del despertar." This intertextual play functions both metaphorically and metonymically, as in vv. 38–39 and 41.

> Desde siempre me oyes cuando, libre
> con el creciente día, me retiro
> 35   al oscuro henchimiento, a mi faena,
> como el cardal ante la lluvia al áspero
> zumo viscoso de su flor; y es porque
> tiene que ser así: yo soy un surco
> más, no un camino que desabre el tiempo.
> 40   Quiere que sea así quien me aró.—¡Reja
> profunda!—Soy culpable. Me lo gritan.[95]

The affirmation that he is a furrow (v. 38) brings to fruition the promise made in
the first verse of "Canto del despertar": "El primer surco de hoy será mi cuerpo." Yet
the abrupt run-on line and the negation in vv. 38–39 cast these verses into a turbulent
ambiguity, a network of swirls and eddies of meaning. Does the poet delight in his

individuality, having joined other poets through his writing, thus constituting his identity? Or does he feel he has lost his individuality, become just another anonymous furrow in an endless succession? The problematic negation of the comparison with the road plays against that of the furrow. A furrow is neither as long nor as wide as a road, so perhaps the poet feels he is just one of the common many, not an outstanding poet. Likewise, the "cardo" is a common weed, but a plant that blooms even in the most severe droughts. The poet has achieved an identity, but perhaps not the superlative one he had envisioned.

Then, however, the syntactic and semantic ambiguity of the phrase "que desabre el tiempo" advances the process. Rodríguez is punning with the verb "desabrir," which literally means "to embitter." At first, it seems to describe an un-opening ("des-abrir"), a reversal of the act of opening (but not exactly the same as a "closing"). Etymologically, "desabrir" means to take away the flavor (figuratively, the joy) of something and hence to vex, irritate, or bother.[96] But we do not know if "un camino" or "el tiempo" is the subject of the verb or if "el tiempo" is "time" or "weather." In any case, the verb alludes to a destabilization, certainly a characteristic of the language in these verses.[97] The destabilization of language marks a continuation of the process of constituting identity, lending a sense of hopeful striving toward a goal. While the poet compares his former view with his present state (metaphor), he also continues the process (metonymy) through intertextuality.

This roiling of the metaphoric and the metonymic is also manifest in the development found in the similar phrases "y es porque / tiene que ser así" (vv. 37–38) and "Quiere que sea así quien me aró" (v. 40). Both expressions explain the speaker's situation through cause and effect. Verse 40 modifies that impression by personifying the causal force as a farmer (recalling the opening verses of "Canto del despertar"). When the speaker interjects "—¡Reja / profunda!—" we wonder if he is serious, delighting in his identity as a poet (even if he is no more than a noxious thistle), or if he is sarcastic, seeing himself as an unproductive weed rather than a fruit-bearing plant. Does he rejoice because he has inherited outstanding abilities, or does he resign himself to his inherent defects and limitations? Also, does "reja" refer to a plowshare, or is it a visual image of the furrows as the bars covering the windows of Spanish houses? If the plowshare, is it a metonymic extension of the farmer or a metaphoric comparison? If the bars, that which normally stands vertically here lies horizontal.

When he states "Soy culpable," he directly contradicts his earlier "Soy inocente." If the earlier statement is ambivalent, so is this confession. The speaker may be decrying his shortcomings, or he may be defiantly proud of himself even if he is like a thistle. If before he exalted in and defended his innocence, here he humbles himself after searching within and recognizing his sin of pride, the sin of being a poet, the chosen one who, like Adam, is responsible for all sins, all emotions. But he is also like Christ, and the shouts accusing him remind us of the ambivalence of Christ's condemnation.[98] "Quien me aró" thus adopts divine proportions. Does the poet repent or ironically exonerate himself?[99]

Throughout this passage, intertextual play combines with metaphoric and metonymic devices, puns, and syntactical ambiguity to roil the linguistic flow. These sundry techniques create a dynamic turbulence as Rodríguez causes us constantly to shift our ground, to see new connections, to compare different viewpoints; in short, he disrupts our normal patterns of reading. His transgression of the limits of language has hit "warp speed" in this poem, producing a turbulent, dynamic flow, which continues in the following verses:

> Como un heñir de pan sus voces pasan
> al latido, a la sangre, a mi locura
> de recordar, de aumentar miedos, a esta
> 45   locura de llevar mi canto a cuestas,
> gavilla más, gavilla de qué parva.[100]

If metaphoric language holds sway in vv. 33–41, in these lines metonymy gains ascendence, noticeable in the anaphoric chaining and references to processes. In spite of the simile, the kneading of bread with which this passage begins refers to a process because the dough must be kneaded and let stand several times so that the yeast can ferment and the bread rise. Linguistic redundancy in the subsequent series of anaphora replicates the repetitive processes involved in such acts as baking bread or harvesting grain. At the same time that there is backtracking through repetitive cycles, progress is made.[101] The sheaf of grain ("gavilla") that the poet harvests (his poem, his "canto") has ambivalent meaning. Echoing vv. 38–39 ("yo soy un surco / más"), the poet may see his poem as just another sheaf added to the heap; or he could see it as just another sheaf, but one belonging to an outstanding harvest. The neutral punctuation of the phrase "de qué parva" allows us to gloss it as a questioning of his role (his vocation as poet); as an exclamation of his pride in his unique ability, his special talent; or even as sarcasm. We veer back toward the metaphoric in the next verses, although the metaphors are juxtaposed metonymically.

> Que os salven, no. Mirad: la lavandera
> de río, que no lava la mañana
> por no secarla entre sus manos, porque
> 50   la secaría como a ropa blanca,
> se salva a su manera. Y los otoños
> también. Y cada ser. Y el mar que rige
> sobre el páramo. Oh, no sólo el viento
> del Norte es como un mar, sino que el chopo
> 55   tiembla como las jarcias de un navío.
> Ni el redil fabuloso de las tardes
> me invade así. . . .[102]

In the image of the "lavandera," we again discover that a metaphor defines a metonymic process. The washerwoman does not try to do the impossible—wash the morning; she does what she knows best. If she tried to wash the morning, she would bleach all the color (beauty) and stains (unpredictability) out of it, as white clothes are spread in the sun to whiten them. By doing what is true to herself (washing clothes instead of the morning), the washerwoman defines her role. In comparison, the poet must write about that which he knows best, use images from his world and express himself in his own way. He is involved in the process of defining his identity and must accept who he is to "salvarse a su manera." The washerwoman, part of the poet's anecdotal surroundings, metaphorically parallels the process in which the poet is involved.

The swirling of metaphor and metonymy continues in vv. 51–57. The image of the sea is a colloquial expression for a storm, an intensification of the turbulence of the search for identity.[103] The speaker sees himself as the "chopo," buffeted by the storm while standing in the midst of a "páramo," a dry, bleak plateau or waste land (cf. "tierra roja"). He prefers this turmoil to the tranquility of some afternoons— which also affect him deeply but not as much as the storm. Through writing, the poet begins to sense his identity; the images he chooses from his surroundings, the way he moves from one to the next, his transgression of the parameters of metaphor and metonymy, turbulence and confusion, give him insight into who he is.

The dynamism and turbulence of these verses, their strong visual impact, and the beauty of the images build to a climax. To return to our own visual image, it is as if we were looking at a Venn diagram and our eyes kept shifting dizzily from one side of the figure to the other. For that reason, it is even more of a shock when we feel the bottom drop out from under us, that is, when we reach another island of stasis that deepens our perception of a gap in the sign. The hint of tranquility in the image "el redil fabuloso de las tardes" pushes the poet over the edge and again causes him to confront the gap.

> . . . Tu amor, a tu amor temo,
> nave central de mi dolor, y campo.
> Pero ahora estoy lejos, tan lejano
> 60 que nadie lloraría si muriese.
> Comienzo a comprobar que nuestro reino
> tampoco es de este mundo. . . .[104]

Repetition in the phrase "Tu amor, a tu amor temo" not only stresses the unknown identity of the interlocutor, it confuses subject with object and love with fear. The images of v. 58 reflect a duality of inside/outside, the "nave" suggesting an enclosed interior space and the "campo" a vast exterior space. How can the "tú" be both subject and object, love and fear, inside and outside simultaneously? As we shall see, the other is an estranged self (the postlapsarian versus the prelapsarian Adam) that corresponds to the simultaneous presence and absence, plenitude and insufficiency, of the sign.

These reversals coincide with a pronounced shift in the tone. In the previous verses, the interaction between metaphor and metonymy increases in intensity until it is undercut by this gap. The poet then laments his distance from his goal, echoing words he pronounced in v. 33 of "Canto del despertar": "estoy lejos, tan lejano." Where before that distance offered him a challenge or represented progress, it now causes him despair to contrast the hope, striving, and exaltation of that earlier state of being with his present confusion, disorientation, and frustration. He ponders what he has accomplished and sees that so far he has not left a significant mark ("nadie lloraría si muriese"). His words seem hollow and meaningless; he is still searching for his identity as a poet. The biblical intertext in vv. 61–62 alludes to the Beatitude "Bienaventurados los pobres en espíritu, porque de ellos es el reino de los cielos" (Matt. 5:3). The poet is obviously parodying those words: He considers himself one of the poor in spirit, yet he is not only exiled from the Garden but even a stranger on earth.

He returns to a self-conscious contemplation of his act of walking in vv. 72–79, evident in the anaphoric but unhurried repetition of the verb "seguir." His starting and stopping, the uncertainty of his search, leads to the reappearance of the gap, now more pronounced and more enabling because it represents the acquisition of more insight even as it befuddles and disorients because of the instability and hollowness it produces.

> Sigo. Pasan los días, luminosos
> a ras de tierra, y sobre las colinas
> ciegos de altura insoportable, y bellos
> 75 igual que un estertor de alondra nueva.
> Sigo. Seguir es mi única esperanza.
> Seguir oyendo el ruido de mis pasos
> con la fruición de un pobre lazarillo.
> Pero ahora eres tú y estás en todo.[105]

Halting progress with a period after the verb "sigo" in both vv. 72 and 76 is a contradiction: How can the speaker go forward if he is always stopping? It seems as though he is courting the gap, trying to confront it because that is what will bring him more information, more insight into language, and greater knowledge of self. As he moves forward and as time advances ("Pasan los días"), he observes the light (his inspiration) and compares it with the death of a baby lark—a songbird whose death metaphorically represents a threat to the poet's young voice and the uncertainty of his existence through song. He also revives the auditory image of his footsteps and in their hollowness tries to find satisfaction. Some critics have glossed the image of the "pobre lazarillo" as the poet's blindness, his inability to find inspiration. The "pícaro" is not blind, however, but poor, innocent, and abused. After excessive deprivation, he delights in even the humblest of pleasures.[106] These images of the lark and the "lazarillo," metaphors that describe the speaker's halting attempts to find his identity and become a poet, again result in the perception of the gap.

Now we can see that all the turbulence between metaphor and metonymy in effect has led to the perception of the gap. In the accumulation of these moments that we perceived as stasis, we see a much more profound and dynamic process taking place. Let me recapitulate the major moments of this process as we have observed it until now. The first instance appeared as an interrogative ("¿Dónde estabas sin mí, bebida mía?"). We wondered at that time if the poet was addressing the sobering water or the inebriating wine and why he used the second person. The second instance (v. 26) compared the image of a bird to music which is the sound of running water, and to sight, the poet's hyper-real vision. These images compose the other's love, which the poet fears (v. 57). As he contemplates that fear and the discomfort it causes him, he picks up that thread again.

Pero ahora eres tú y estás en todo.
80 Si yo muriese harías de mí un surco,
un surco inalterable: ni pedrisca,
ni ese luto del ángel, nieve, ni ese
cierzo con tantos fuegos clandestinos
cambiarían su línea, que interpreta
85 la estación claramente. . . .[107]

The appearance of this "tú" has the effect of an illumination, of inspiration itself: The other exists and is present in everything the poet sees. He realizes that if he were to die now, his poetry would be "un surco inalterable." For better or for worse, his reputation as a poet and therefore his identity at least would not deteriorate. Because he has written poetry, his identity—even if mediocre—would not be affected by external factors. The images of coldness in "pedrisca," "nieve," and "cierzo" may suggest the immutability of death, but by describing these natural elements with metaphors, a reversal takes place. Instead of deteriorating his reputation, death would enhance it. The snow is called "ese luto del ángel," changing the traditional black of mourning into a pure, angelic whiteness; the north wind is so cold that it burns "con tantos fuegos clandestinos." Death would not decay his identity as poet but affirm it; death would not destroy but solidify it.

This radical reversal in the poet's outlook has come about because of his perception of the gap. Stasis and doubt have led to change and understanding. Each time the poet has encountered this gap he has increased his understanding of language and of himself. Ironically, walking leads to confusion (turbulence), but stopping allows him to discover, to understand. If writing is a means of obtaining knowledge, as Rodríguez and other members of his generation have so frequently stated, Rodríguez avers that writing consists not only of language but of the silence implicit in language—those moments when the poet stops writing and ponders what he has learned through his writing and what more needs exploring. Silence is the pause between words, when the poet must determine which word will follow, which direction his thinking will take. Language as a differential system is a labyrinth of starts and stops, movement and stasis, flow and repose, experience and meditation. Indeed, how can we distinguish writing from not writing, language from silence, metaphor from metonymy? The following verses explore this enigma and lead to another encounter with the gap.

85   . . . ¿Y qué lugares
más sobrios que estos para ir esperando?
¡Es Castilla, sufridlo! En otros tiempos,
cuando se me nombraba como a hijo,
no podía pensar que la de ella
90 fuera la única voz que me quedase,
la única intimidad bien sosegada
que dejara en mis ojos fe de cepa.
De cepa madre. Y tú, corazón, uva
roja, la más ebria, la que menos
95 vendimiaron los hombres, ¿cómo ibas
a saber que no estabas en racimo,
que no te sostenía tallo alguno?[108]

Verse 93 illuminates the identity of the other, the "tú" the poet has addressed sporadically throughout the poem. This other is the poet himself, because he equates the "tú" with his heart, a rare grape, seldom harvested. When he metonymically addresses his heart as the "other" outside him but contiguous with him and then converts the heart metaphorically into a grape (connected metonymically with the topos of drunkenness and the act of writing), he also addresses his inspiration. The direct address used at key moments throughout the poem relates the concept of self and other with the sign. Just as metaphor and metonymy are intertwined and indistinguishable (as the two sides of the Moebius strip blend into one another), so it is impossible to separate self from other, identity from language, being from becoming.[109]

By describing the grape as unsustained by a vine, the poet comments upon the arbitrariness of the sign, the unbridgeable gap between signifier and signified, the word and its referent, and also upon a gap he perceives in his identity, the constant shifting and uncertain play between being and becoming. Writing is a two-edged sword: It is the means of achieving identity, of constituting the self, but it is also that which places the self in question, subverts, and destabilizes it. The imperfect tenses reflect the speaker's disillusionment with his former self and his former outlook on the world of language. This disillusionment is nonetheless an illumination that defines his identity at the same time that it tells him what he is not. At this point, he dramatically calls attention to this absence by making a complete stanzaic break—a visible gap in the text, an empty space, a silence.

The final section of "Canto del caminar" functions as a coda, summarizing the major features of the poem, but also launching us into the next "Libro." When the poet resumes after the gap, he returns to a "pared-down" language and a subtle use of metaphor. The crepuscular light described in the following verses pertains to the code that pervades *Don*. This blend of day and night, light and darkness, symbolizes the poet's newly-acquired attitude.

> —He hablado así tempranamente, ¿y debo
> prevenirme del sol del entusiasmo?
> 100   Una luz que en el aire es aire apenas
> viene desde el crepúsculo y separa
> la intensa sombra de los arces blancos
> antes de separar dos claridades:
> la del día total y la nublada
> 105   de luna, confundidas un instante
> dentro de un rayo último difuso.[110]

The first two verses after the stanzaic break show the poet backing off from the despair that characterizes his discovery of the gap, but they also show him questioning if he should avoid the exuberance he feels when his inspiration illuminates innovative metaphors. The intensity of metaphor ("el sol del entusiasmo") tends to exhaust inspiration. Yet the loss of inspiration has led the poet to an even keener insight into language, the world, and himself. Certainly, that insight has revealed a disquieting gap. But the poet must ask if the presence of this absence precludes the enthusiastic language of metaphor. The image of light in these lines speaks of the gap. It is a crepuscular light, barely perceptible since it is "Una luz que en el aire es aire apenas." This intermediate stage in the circadian cycle contrasts with the dawn, which the poet has equated with the arrival of inspiration. It brings a different type of light, but light (insight, inspiration) nonetheless. Night follows with its stars, other forms of light that produce even more acute insights. The poem ends by splicing metaphor and metonymy in a turbulent flow that will conclude this "Libro" by closing the frame, but also carry us forward into "Libro tercero."

> Qué importa marzo coronando almendros.
> Y la noche qué importa si aún estamos
> buscando un resplandor definitivo.
> 110 Oh, la noche que lanza sus estrellas
> desde almenas celestes. Ya no hay nada:
> cielo y tierra sin más. ¡Seguro blanco,
> seguro blanco ofrece el pecho mío!
> Oh, la estrella de oculta amanecida
> 115 traspasándome al fin, ya más cercana.
> Que cuando caiga muera o no, qué importa.
> Qué importa si ahora estoy en el camino.[111]

These verses display the two types of language battling for supremacy in the text: The metaphoric tendency toward verticality, centrality, and stability tries to restrain the horizontal impulse of anaphoric repetitions and intertextual allusions. The phrase "marzo coronando almendros" looks forward to poems of "Libro tercero" (and later poems by Rodríguez), whereas the reference to night refers not only to "Canto del despertar" but through it to the poems of "Libro primero." By evoking the mystic poets—San Juan in the "almenas celestes" and Santa Teresa's ecstasies in "la estrella de oculta amanecida / traspasándome"—the poet looks back toward the poetic (metaphorical) tradition, but also anticipates poems in "Libro tercero" (most notably poem I). This anticipation suggests that in the interplay between the metonymic and the metaphoric, between the two sides of the Venn diagram, lies the gap.[112]

In addition, the mention of the target in vv. 112–13 repeats the image in v. 26 of "Canto del despertar." We must ask if that target—centering on the speaker's heart— is not a blank space, the gap itself, the speaker's questioning of his identity as a result of/by means of writing. The penultimate verse may allude to Icarus, the mythical figure who transgresses the limits of his wings in an attempt to reach greater heights. This mythical figure plays off the figure of Adam by suggesting similarities and differences between them. But is it metaphor or metonymy? Is there a comparison or a further development?

In symmetry with the opening verse of "Canto del despertar," the last verse acts as a framing device. Because both contain metonymic elements intermingled with the metaphoric, they dissipate the frame at the same time that they mark it. The repetition of "Qué importa" causes us to question the poet's tone, and the deictic phrase "ahora estoy en el camino" does not tell us if he is standing still to confirm where he is (emphasizing the horizontal) or if he is walking forward on this road (describing the vertical). The image of the road captures this ambivalence: A traditional archetypal symbol for one's path or vocation in life, it also indicates an active search and a horizontal line stretching forward indefinitely. The metaphoric dimensions of this archetype close the frame and end the section, while the metonymic aspects propel us forward into the next section and a continuation of the quest for identity.

Before drawing some general conclusions about "Libro segundo," let me return to the epigraphs that introduce these poems and of my subtitle for this section. The quote from San Juan de la Cruz is from stanza 17 of the "Cántico espiritual," which allegorically describes the soul's search for Christ: ". . . y cuando salía / por toda aquesta vega / ya cosa no sabía. . . ." In placing this passage at the beginning of "Libro segundo," Rodríguez suggests a metaphoric comparison between the soul and the poet-speaker of *Don de la ebriedad*. Because of the poet's inspiration, the new light that has been shed on his world, he may see everything as new and different. He has left behind a former self, an old way of viewing the world, and arrived at a new perspective because of his experience with language and the poetic act. On the other hand, the light has dazzled and blinded him, disorienting him and making his world strange and alien. Does this quote summarize the blissful, enthusiastic experience of "Libro primero" or anticipate the change in the poet's outlook that occurs through his discovery of the gap in language and in himself? Does it describe the result of a process or the moment of transition itself?

The fragment from Rimbaud's "Comédie de la soif" (thirst being Rimbaud's equivalent for "tierra seca") sets up a contrast between two traditional types of art, the Northern or Germanic style and the Southern or Italian style, a distinction that has existed since the Renaissance. Rodríguez has quoted only the second half of the sentence, but it is useful to have the entire sentence to see this contrast: "Choisirai-je le Nord / Ou le Pays des Vignes?"[113] These two styles of art reflect the two different types of language at odds in the "Cantos." Even the language Rimbaud uses points to this duality. On the one hand, he "flatly" says "le Nord," while on the other he uses a metaphor for the south: "le Pays des Vignes." This metaphor connects metonymically with the topos of drunkenness because the vineyard produces the vines that produce the grapes used to make wine, which causes drunkenness. Rodríguez is also punning with the French as he puns with the title of *Don de la ebriedad*. In its oral form, "ou le Pays des Vignes?" can also be a question (only the accent mark is missing in the written form as Rodríguez has fragmented it in the epigraph). This question, like the title, asks, "¿Dónde la ebriedad?"

Just as these epigraphs are ambivalent, having both metaphoric and metonymic aspects, so I have chosen the terms "warp" and "woof" for the subtitle of this section. The allusion to weaving comments upon the text, especially the intermingling of metaphor and metonymy. "Warp" and "woof" are the horizontal and vertical threads that must be woven together to make the "textile." But perhaps only skilled weavers are able to keep these two terms straight as to which is horizontal and which vertical. In choosing these terms, I wish to highlight the confusion of metaphor and metonymy that takes place in the "Cantos," resulting in both the weaving and the simultaneous unraveling/deconstruction of the text in the presence of the gap and the destabilization of language.

In his experiments with language in "Libro primero" and "Canto del despertar," Rodríguez has laden the signifier with an immense richness of meaning. His combination of the metaphoric and the metonymic places a tremendous strain on language. Although this combination enables him to weave the fabric of the text, it also tears it asunder. Viewed as the connective tissue of the text, that which gives form and structure to the stuff of metaphor, metonymy is in effect an empty substance. Linguists assert that connectives have no meaning in and of themselves; they merely establish the relationships (temporal, spatial, causal) between the more substantive nouns and verbs. Likewise, pronouns and deictics are "floaters" or "shifters" because their referents change constantly.[114]

By interweaving metaphor and metonymy in the same language of the text, Rodríguez stumbles upon a lack, a gap in the plenitude of metaphoric discourse. Without that lack metaphoric language has no structure or direction and is incapable of achieving plenitude. Without silence, words lose their impact. Without lapses in the poet's inspiration, poetry itself would cease to exist. But the addition of that supplement problematizes the concept of plenitude because if it inscribes a lack, plenitude can never obtain. When Adam transgresses and eats of the fruit of the tree of knowledge, he suddenly finds himself in exile in a world where everything is unfamiliar. When the poet adds this supplement of absence to the plenitude of metaphor, it is as if he bursts the signified, creating a vacuum and leaving behind a jumble of imagery. The codes and topoi with which he had lived and which he had taken for granted become fragmented and dispersed. As a result, when he now encounters a signifier, he discovers a vast emptiness within it. His transgression leaves him no other choice than to explore that void, even though it affords him uncertainty, fear, disorientation, and frustration.

The supplement of emptiness—the poet's lack of inspiration—thus becomes the center, destabilizing the fulcrum and privileging the peripheral, the fluid, the liminal, the chaotic. In "Libro tercero," the poet will continue his exploration of the void as a postlapsarian Adam seeking his identity and fulfillment in the poetic act. The next step in our investigation of *Don de la ebriedad* will consist of a long walk through the rarefied space of the poems of "Libro tercero." There we should expect to find in true metonymic fashion a repetition and amplification of the characteristics of "Canto del caminar."

ADAM IN EXILE: REPETITION AND THE RENEWAL OF LANGUAGE IN "LIBRO TERCERO"

Throughout this study of *Don*, my approach has been to provide thorough textual analyses of representative poems. The continuation of this approach with the poems of "Libro tercero" will lead to an even greater appreciation of Rodríguez's first book. Many of these poems represent virtually unexplored territory because their opaque imagery, hermetic frame of reference, and abrupt shifts from one idea to another fragment the poems, disrupt communication, and tend to alienate the reader. The opacity and fragmentary nature of these poems counterbalance the exuberance of the first section but also lead to a more profound delving into language and the self. Let us then set the stage, first by defining the speaker's stance and next by specifying the techniques that underlie the apparently chaotic poems of "Libro tercero."

In comparison with his stance in the first section of *Don*, the poet-speaker is now a postlapsarian Adam exiled from the innocent exhilaration of his first encounter with language. The innocent Adam pressed his experimentation to the limit, transgressing the boundaries of the sign to such an extent that he has thrown his world into chaos. He now finds himself at an impasse and must begin his exploration anew. This new beginning appropriately takes place in the spring, a transitional season of unstable weather and turbulent winds comparable to the poet's uncertain awakening to the potential of language and the discovery of his identity. In "Libro tercero," the poet meanders through a wilderness of language probing the gap he discovered in "Canto del caminar." This gap—his lack of inspiration and originality—in contrast with the heightened consciousness produced by "la claridad" in "Libro primero" here results in a heightened *self*-consciousness concerning language.

Structurally, "Libro tercero" broadens and extends the oscillating sweep of "Canto del caminar," making one long (though convoluted) swing of the pendulum through the eight poems of this section. This continuation of the trend seen in the previous sections is confirmed by the subtitles preceding the first two poems. Not only do these subtitles in themselves indicate sequence ("Con marzo" [With March] is followed by "Sigue marzo" [March continues]), they are also parenthetical echoes of the full titles of "Libro segundo," suggesting a continuation of the same tendencies exposited there. Also, poem I is the longest poem in the peripheral sections, further linking it with the "Cantos" and leading us into the succeeding poems.[115]

Given its turbulent, chaotic nature, "Libro tercero" also continues the stylistic features that emerged in the use of metonymic devices in "Canto del caminar." For that reason, we might again avail ourselves of chaos theory to describe this section as a fractal, and I will refer frequently to different aspects of chaos to describe these poems. I feel, however, that it will be advantageous to investigate these poems using another critical concept: the principle of repetition.[116] Beginning with Gilles Deleuze's distinction, Hillis Miller provides an enlightening discussion of two alternative theories of repetition.[117] On the one hand, Platonic repetition entails the existence of a "solid archetypal model which is untouched by the effects of repetition. All the other examples are copies of this model."[118] When copies of the model are produced, they are identical to the original, which remains intact, unmodified by the reproductions. The second or Nietzschean mode of repetition assumes that each thing is uniquely different from every other thing. In lieu of copies, there exist what Deleuze calls "simulacra" or "phantasms," "ungrounded doublings which arise from differential interrelations among elements which are all on the same plane. This lack of ground in some paradigm or archetype means that there is something ghostly about the effects of this second kind of repetition."[119]

Miller then expands the relation between these two theories by discussing a passage from Walter Benjamin's "The Image of Proust." There Benjamin makes a "distinction between the rational, willed, intentional remembering of the daytime, and that kind of involuntary memory which Benjamin calls forgetting."[120] The first of these, coinciding with the Platonic form of repetition, "works logically, by way of similarities which are seen as identities, one thing repeating another and grounded in a concept on the basis of which their likeness may be understood."[121] The Nietzschean form of memory is not grounded but arises out of the interplay of the "'opaquely similar' . . . in which one thing is experienced as repeating something which is quite different from it and which it strangely resembles."[122] Miller's summary leads to a consideration of the main issue of "Libro tercero": the exploration of the gap, "the empty space which the opaque similarity crosses."[123]

For the poet as postlapsarian Adam or the latecomer ephebe (to use Harold Bloom's term), the two types of repetition and the gap they produce represent a linguistic Scylla and Charybdis. On the one hand, a "mimetic" imitation of other poems threatens to result in sterility and lack of originality, in effect, the drowning of the poet's emerging voice in a monotone or in a flood of stronger voices. On the other hand, as already experienced in the latter poems of "Libro primero," too much individuality, too much free play in the signifier, threatens a breakup of communication on the barrier of language.[124] The focus of this investigation of "Libro tercero" will be the "middle ground" where Rodríguez attempts to steer a course between a sterile, mechanical repetition of what has already been said and a mode of expression that is too idiosyncratic and hermetic.[125] We might call this middle ground "repetition with a difference."[126] Now let us look at particular poems—some in detail and others as representative of certain concepts and techniques—to examine the different levels on which repetition functions in these poems and the changes that occur as we move through the poems of "Libro tercero."

Rodríguez spells out many of the problems he now encounters with writing in the opening poem, which serves as a thesis statement for the entire section. Yet at the same time that he recognizes problems, he discovers the potential for original expression through repetition. Because of his instability and disorientation, the speaker has difficulty defining his dilemma with sustained archetypal metaphors such as those he uses at the beginning of "Libro primero" ("la claridad," "la noche," "la encina," "el alba"). His attempt to negotiate this difficult pass relies on repetition and exemplification, but the repetition entails variation, and the exemplification is ambiguous, based on a shifting sense of ground.[127]

> Lo que antes era exacto ahora no encuentra
> su sitio. No lo encuentra y es de día,
> y va volado como desde lejos
> el manantial, que suena a luz perdida.
> 5   Volado yo también a fuerza de hambres
> cálidas, de mañanas inauditas,
> he visto en el incienso de las cumbres
> y en mi escritura blanca una alegría

> dispersa de vigor. ¿Y aún no se yergue
> 10   todo para besar? ¿No se ilimitan
>   las estrellas para algo más hermoso
>   que un recaer oculto? . . .

(p. 55)[128]

The excessive length of the first declaration is a clear indication of the poet's awkwardness as he tries to fit an alexandrine verse (fourteen syllables with caesura—a gap) into his established hendecasyllabic pattern. The phrase "no lo encuentra" repeats the previous "no encuentra su sitio" with the substitution of a pronoun. This variation augments the indeterminacy because it is unclear what the antecedent of "lo que" is in the first place. Already the lack of ground is manifest. The poet then exemplifies what he means with the image of the "manantial." The adjective "volado" could mean that the force of the fountain is either uplifted or dispersed by the wind. Syntactical ambiguity in vv. 3–4 exacerbates the confusion, for we cannot be sure what the subject of the verb phrase "va volado" is: It could be "manantial" or "lo que." Which is the ground, which the figure? This metonymic exemplification becomes even more ambiguous because of the synesthesia of the modifying phrase "que suena a luz perdida." When the poet repeats "volado" in v. 5, he makes a comparison with a comparison, another confusion of figure and ground. In addition, the expression "estar volado" can mean "to be worried, feel anxious, be ill-at-ease." This slight variation—a slippage of the signifier—is due to ellipsis, a device Rodríguez uses throughout "Libro tercero" for a variety of effects.

In both repetition and exemplification, we see the poet attempting to define his dilemma, but each time "The defined enters once more into the definition, disqualifying that definition," so that "The example will then only present again the original opacity."[129] Where we begin on uncertain ground (the indeterminacy of the referent of "lo que"), we feel it shift again and again.[130] Grammatical, syntactical, and semantic ambiguity embody the poet-speaker's disorientation and his uncertain ground.

By beginning with the imperfect tense and comparing "antes" with "ahora," Rodríguez establishes a nostalgic tone for the ecstasy of his poetic experiences, recognizing that his experiments with language have led him to an impasse. The images in vv. 5–8 point to a dichotomy of nostalgia and gaiety.[131] Are the "hambres / cálidas" fasts the poet has imposed on himself to heighten his ecstasy, or are they an adventitious lack of inspiration? Are the "mañanas inauditas" unusual moments of illumination, unprecedented touches of originality, or events that have never materialized? Does he speak of the past or the present ("antes" or "ahora")? The metaphor "el incienso de las cumbres"—an image that he will repeat with variation throughout the poem—describes clouds on the mountain peaks, but the speaker's relation to that image is undefined.[132] Does it refer to an uplifting, quasi-mystical poetic experience or to the inability to see those peaks? When he says that his writing is "blanca," does he mean that it is pure and transcendent like the clouds, or that the page is blank, impeding his poetic vision? The abrupt enjambment in vv. 8–9 emphasizes the ambivalence and the rapid turns the poet's inspiration (like the unstable weather of

March) can take. The questions of vv. 9–12 express hope and desperation, gaiety and nostalgia.

The motif of nostalgia for a lost or unattainable "jouissance" in language has its model in the opening declaration.[133] It then repeats—always with a difference, however slight or marked—on many different levels of the text (semantic, syntactic, metaphoric, metric, phonetic, structural, etc.).[134] More evidence of repetition with a difference can be found in the if-clause and its resultant negation in vv. 12–19.

> ... Si la vida
> me convocase en medio de mi cuerpo
> como el claro entre pinos a la fría
> 15 respiración de luna, porque ahora
> puedo, y ahora está allí... Pero no: brisas
> de montaraz silencio, aligeradas
> aves que se detienen y otra vez
> su vuelo en equilibrio se anticipa.
>
> (p. 55)[135]

The simile of the clearing in the pines compared with the poet's heart "en el medio de mi cuerpo" again functions exemplarily. If we consider a pine forest as a sacred place, the clearing would be the very center of this precinct, while the shadows and density of the pines contrast with the light of the moon in the clearing.[136] But the poet metaphorically transforms the light of the moon into its "fría / respiración." While breath is synonymous with light as inspiration, does the clearing illuminate and inspire, or does it chill and take the breath away? The ambivalence of this image repeats that of "el incienso de las cumbres," both of which echo but negate the dialogic tension that delighted the speaker in "Libro primero" because of the lack of ground, producing a ghostly effect (moonlight as opposed to sunlight—"la claridad").

In another pirouette of the unstable winds of March, the bottom quickly falls out of whatever exuberance this image generates when the speaker leaves the if-clause unfulfilled, creating more gaps. Instead of "la fría / respiración de la luna," the poet receives "brisas / de montaraz silencio." These breezes should bring him inspiration because they too pertain to the code of air, but they bring him only a silence that is "montaraz," that is, "salvaje, grosero," as if the poet had been isolated and lost his ability to communicate.[137] The image of the birds again exemplifies with a variation on the model. While they alight momentarily, they are already preparing to take off again, emblematic of the poet's words and his inspiration, both of which are unstable and fleeting. But we also recognize an ambivalence in these images and in the simile of the clearing. Do they "demonstrate the nostalgia with which the text asserts its gaiety or the gaiety with which it exposes its nostalgia"?[138]

Between vv. 19 and 20 there is a stanzaic break, a visible gap in the text (cf. "Canto del caminar") that repeats a rupture in the formal rhyme scheme between vv. 17 and 18 (where the rhyme is absent) and the other gaps we have noted (caesura, abrupt enjambment, suspensive periods, the clearing, etc.). After the stanzaic break the poet begins the poem anew by repeating the opening phrase.

20   Lo que antes era exacto, lo que antes
        era sencillo: un grano que germina,
        de pronto. Cómo nos avanza el solo
        mes desde fuera. Huele a ti, te imita
        la belleza, la noche a tus palabras
25   —tú sobre el friso de la amanecida.
        ¡Y que no pueda ver mi ciudad virgen
        ni mi piedra molar sin golondrinas
        oblicuas despertando la muralla
        para saber que nada, nadie emigra!

                                                    (pp. 55–56)[139]

Verse 20 repeats the beginning of v. 1 and then redoubles upon itself, substituting "sencillo" for "exacto." These repetitions inscribe difference as an absence, but absence itself then forges a new vision of language. Whereas v. 1 overflowed into v. 2 because of an excess of syllables, unless we break one of the synalephas of v. 20 to *create* a gap where one would not normally be, we count only ten syllables. These aberrations in the formal properties of the poem replicate the gaps we find on other levels. Because we must create a gap in this repetitive sequence, this verse represents a turning point in the poet's attitude.[140]

This stanzaic segment repeats the interplay between figure and ground, destabilizing the origin and creating a constant shifting of ground between "original" and "copy." First of all, we do not know whom the speaker addresses with the second-person pronouns in vv. 23–25. Moreover, confusion of figure and ground arises between nature and art, a relationship that resembles that of original and copy, speech and writing.[141] The confusion is particularly evident in the phrase "tú sobre el friso de la amanecida." "Friso" is an architectural term that describes the dawn, but the dawn is another metaphor for inspiration. "From oneness to twoness, from figure to literal ground, the relation is continuously reversible. Each state of the object is both the literal ground of the other and the figure of it."[142] The personified figure of the poet's muse materializes in the gap between the frieze and the dawn. The image of the city wall and the swallows provides another exemplification of this confusion arising from the matrix of the poet's inspiration.[143]

After this image in v. 29, another stanzaic gap interrupts the poem. Has the poet run out of things to say? Or does this silence speak eloquently of what he is discovering about language? Does the gap now mark a revelation?[144] When the poem resumes, it begins with an ambivalent image: "Oh, plumas timoneras." The speaker compares himself with a fledgling that perhaps cannot fly because it lacks important feathers. But this could also be an exclamation of joy as he discovers the possibilities of his new wings. The image expresses nostalgia and gaiety.[145]

Although the beauty and richness of the final stanza of this poem warrant a continuation of this detailed analysis, I would prefer at this point to turn to other poems that testify to the variety of ways in which Rodríguez deploys repetition to achieve stunning effects and to probe still further the limits of language. Before doing so, one more level of repetition in the last part of this poem merits examination. In vv. 43–46 and in the final verse of the poem, Rodríguez makes use of intertextual allusions. The verses "Es la mirada, / es el agua que espera ser bebida. / El agua. Se entristece al contemplarse / desnuda y ya con marzo encinta" allude not only to Baudelaire's "I Love the Memory" but also to Jorge Guillén's "El manantial," the image used in the first exemplification in this poem; and the final phrase "confundiendo el dolor aunque es de día" (v. 58) obviously plays off San Juan's "Cantar de la alma que se huelga de conoscer a Dios por fe."[146] How does intertextuality function here? Do previous poems inspire the poet to produce new imagery by combining ideas and placing them in a new context? Or is he merely mouthing another's words, resulting in empty repetition?[147] And what is the relationship between these intertextualities, the poet's allusions to other poems in *Don*, and the repetition of phrases within this poem? Do the allusions to other poems in *Don* constitute a middle ground between inter- and intratextuality?[148]

In summary, this initial poem links "Libro tercero" with the tendencies set forth in "Canto del caminar" and initiates a horizontal progression through the final section. Poem I serves as a thesis statement of the problems that will preoccupy the poet in this section, but it also illuminates the various possibilities that repetition offers the poet. The principle of repetition functions on every level of the text, so that what might appear to be fragmentary and chaotic results in a new order, new revelations about the capacity of language to signify.[149] In accord with the image of Scylla and Charybdis as the two forms of repetition, the remainder of the poems will show the poet-speaker steering his way between gaiety and nostalgia, between mimicry and originality, as he attempts to negotiate this turbulent gap and to define himself as a poet.[150]

Poem II continues this trend, as the subtitle indicates. We could divide this poem into two parts predicated on the repetition of the words "Todo es nuevo quizá" in vv. 1 and 14. The first 13 lines can be seen as the poet's attempt to recapture the lost enthusiasm and innocence of "Libro primero" by adopting a new viewpoint that spring metaphorically motivates. But his enthusiasm is constantly undercut by doubt, his assertions undermined by equivocation in language. In the second half of the poem he thereupon decides to consider a "worst-case scenario" that leads to surprising discoveries. For although he may begin with a pessimistic anticipation of disaster by recognizing that nothing he can say has not always already been said, he stumbles upon an echo chamber of resonances that, far from being a dull repetition, illuminates the exciting potential of language in a myriad of ways. Instead of finding himself straightjacketed within the limitations of the already said, he discovers a whole new realm where language sends him bouncing in a giddy, frenzied delirium among multiple resonances.[151] Stumbling upon this alternate view of language opens the poem to more varied effects and allows Rodríguez to continue his transgressive exploration of language. Although poem II begins with a sententious declaration, the adverb "quizá" alters the rhythm—keeping poet and reader off-balance—and undercuts the surety with which the poet makes this declaration.

> Todo es nuevo quizá para nosotros.
> El sol claroluciente, el sol de puesta,

> muere; el que sale es más brillante y alto
> cada vez, es distinto, es otra nueva
> 5   forma de luz, de creación sentida.
> Así cada mañana es la primera.
> Para que la vivamos tú y yo solos,
> nada es igual ni se repite. Aquella
> curva, de almendros florecidos suave,
> 10 ¿tenía flor ayer? El ave aquella,
> ¿no vuela acaso en más abiertos círculos?
> Después de haber nevado el cielo encuentra
> resplandores que antes eran nubes.
> Todo es nuevo quizá. . . .
>
>   (p. 57)[152]

Both spring and love (alluded to indirectly in the dedication—"Para Clara Miranda") are emblematic of the poet's instability and lack of confidence with regard to his inconstant gift.[153] The seasonal renewal of spring and the phenomenon of a first love encourage him to believe that even though he may repeat what others have already said, he will do it somewhat differently and thus give it new meaning because he as an individual is going through these rituals for the first time, just as lovers awaken to the beauty of spring and feel that no other spring has been exactly like it.[154]

But he constantly undercuts this hopefulness with doubt. If the phrase "El sol claroluciente" makes us think of a sunrise or a bright part of the day (morning or midday), our perception takes an immediate turn in the opposite direction in the very next phrase, emphasized by the somber fact that the light is dying. What we might have viewed as a hopeful situation takes a quick turn toward the pessimistic thanks to the abrupt run-on line, the verb "muere," and the revelation that this is not dawn but dusk. However, since it is spring, the days are getting longer. Just as each day in spring is longer and brighter, so the poet desires his inspiration and confidence to grow. But we question how this objective correlative functions. Does it describe what is happening within the speaker, or is it something external, something the speaker sees but does not experience for himself?[155] The placement of the subordinate clause beginning with "Para que" in v. 7 produces a similar ambivalence. Does it express the assurance of a logical result, or does it express what is necessary for this situation to obtain?

The main clause "nada es igual ni se repite" both is and is not a contradiction. These two phrases are redundant; both mean the same thing, and they repeat what the poet has already said several times: "todo es nuevo"; "es distinto"; "es otra nueva"; "es la primera." Yet each time the poet repeats the same idea, his form of expression varies. This clause adds a new twist to the iteration because the poet now uses a negation to affirm. His statement is both true and not true; it repeats, but with a difference.[156] Ironically, the more the poet insists that everything is new, the more he repeats himself—with a difference.

To exemplify what he means, he next embarks on a series of metaphors taken from the spring around him. At first these scenes appear to be random examples adduced haphazardly from his circumstances. But upon examining them closely, we find common denominators among them: They are "opaquely similar"; they too repeat differently. The third image in this series (vv. 12–13) is one of the most beautiful in Rodríguez's poetry, but it too activates certain contradictions. Most obviously, it speaks of a spring snowfall, epitomizing the instability of March weather. Second, it sets up a contrast between "después" and "antes" that reverses the temporal exposition of the image (first clouds, then snow) and the duality of cause and effect. The most outstanding feature of the image is predicated by the personification of the sky. The dispersal of the clouds allows the sun to come out, whose light reveals that the dull gray clouds have metamorphosed into "resplandores." Darkness has become light even as spring has reverted to winter. Snow is synonymous with both water and light because it comes from the sky (cf. Cirlot on rain) and thus emblematic of the poet's inspiration; but it is also cold and numbing, the antithesis of spring.

After this glorious image, which culminates the first part of the poem, the poet repeats the first line but stops after "quizá"—another repetition with a difference.[157] We could interpret this repetition and stopping on the word "quizá" as a moment of illumination when the poet says, trying to convince himself that everything is new, that perhaps we should consider the opposite side of the coin: What if things aren't new? What if everything he says has already been said? This possibility seems to lead in a pessimistic direction. Just when the poet had captured a stunning image that might allow him to recuperate the enthusiasm of "Libro primero," he starts to despair. But this hypothesis allows him to examine what he anticipates as a negative situation and to discover even more brilliant "resplandores" in what appeared to be gray clouds. After truncating the first line in this repetition, he launches into a long sentence that sends language bouncing in different directions.

> Todo es nuevo quizá. Si no lo fuera,
> 15 si en medio de esta hora las imágenes
> cobraran vida en otras, y con ellas
> los recuerdos de un día ya pasado
> volvieran ocultando el de hoy, volvieran
> aclarándolo, sí, pero ocultando
> 20 su claridad naciente, ¿qué sorpresa
> le daría a mi ser, qué devaneo,
> qué nueva luz o qué labores nuevas?
>
> (p. 57)[158]

The poet achieves a ludic "jostling" of language by anaphorically stringing phrases together and playing one word off another in sundry ways. For example, the phrase "las imágenes" placed at the end of v. 15 recalls the beginning of poem VI of "Libro primero": "Las imágenes, una que las centra / en planetaria rotación . . ." [The images, one that centers them / in planetary rotation] (p. 37). The recuperation of these lines activates an exchange between the two texts, juxtaposing the jubilant experimentation of "Libro primero" with the difficulties of the present moment. This comparison evokes the larger phenomenon of the past encroaching upon the originality of the present, a past emphasized in the overdetermination of v. 17 ("los recuerdos de un día ya pasado") and the metonymic iteration of the verb "volvieran" at the beginning and end of v. 18. The solar-system-like spinning described in poem VI of "Libro primero"—reminding us of the change of seasons—is superimposed upon the circadian rhythm in vv. 2–3 of this poem. When the poet begins to play with the conceit "ocultando-aclarando" reminiscent of Golden Age literature, he imbricates two types of movement—revolution and rotation—and thus weaves together past and present, light and dark, bouncing language from one dimension to the other. Examples of this almost ludic play can be found in "aclarando" and "naciente" which echo the earlier "el sol claroluciente," the interjection "sí" which repeats the already repeated "si" of the if-clause, and "claridad"—an obvious allusion to the first line of *Don* and the permutations of that verse we have seen throughout *Don* as well as the light/darkness conceit in this poem. The interweaving of these resonances, often with paradoxical effects, sends language bouncing from one dimension to another.

The metonymic string of questions that concludes this hypothesis sounds more like a series of exclamations. We might even wonder how Rodríguez can say "¿qué sorpresa / le daría a mi ser, qué devaneo . . .?" with a straight face because if we are paying attention to the language, we have been surprised, we do feel delirious, frenzied, giddy, because of the way language has bounced us around. What appeared to be a preoccupation, a troubled consideration of the loss of metaphoric originality—a possible disaster for the poet (according to Aristotle)—has led to the discovery of other ways to make language signify in spite of repetition, imitation, and the encroachment of previous poetic experience. What appeared to be a loss of inspiration and a breakdown into chaos has become an entirely new way of looking at language.[159]

A gap in the rhyme scheme in vv. 22–23 alerts us to a subtle change in tone. The final verses form a coda and open the possibilities of interpretation to the point of indeterminacy.

> Agua de río, agua de mar; estrella
> fija o errante, estrella en el reposo
> 25 nocturno. Qué verdad, qué limpia escena
> la del amor, que nunca ve en las cosas
> la triste realidad de su apariencia.
>
>   (p. 57)[160]

The binary images in vv. 23–25 might suggest an unresolved dialectic between movement and stasis, transience and transcendence, or other binary values. But these images are ambivalent because they could be equivalencies as well as oppositions; both terms can represent the same thing as well as an either/or situation. The phrase "estrella / fija o errante" provides the clearest definition of this ambivalence. We could read this as an ellipsis for "estrella fija o [estrella] errante," a contrast between the permanent and the transient. But we could just as easily deny ellipsis, in which case both adjectives modify the same star, making it paradoxical and equivocal. Finally, although the poet admits the hackneyed idea "Love is blind," he underscores that that is precisely the essence of love. Lovers may be deceived because they do not see reality clearly, but perhaps they see beyond the surface and discover what others caught up in mundane, superficial appearances cannot see.

Because of Rodríguez's ludic approach to language and his synchronic and diachronic exploration of the middle ground, repetition does not limit but rather expands the possibility of expression. Just as in "Libro primero" light becomes synonymous with darkness, day with night, just as in "Libro segundo" metaphor and metonymy become indistinguishable, so here in "Libro tercero" originality and repetition cease to be antinomies and present the poet with more ways to transgress the limits of language.

Poems I and II introduce the potential of language through repetition and an exploration of the gap. If these poems tend toward Scylla, the next four poems show him moving toward Charybdis, the more idiosyncratic and hermetic side of the gap. To accelerate the discussion, I will highlight certain aspects of repetition and other techniques in the next poems that illustrate Rodríguez's poetics in this section. Then we will look more closely at the final poem.

Though not easy to discern because the poet establishes no explicit frame of reference, again destabilizing figure and ground, the anecdotal level of poem III consists of the speaker's leaving his city at dusk. This action represents the ephebe poet's desire to free himself from the oppressive shadow of the familiar and the already said that haunts his search for originality. The voice he hears and addresses with "tú" could be either his mother's or his muse's, neither of which accords him the independence he seeks. Repetition functions subtly in this poem, adopting two basic manifestations: first, echoes of the first four poems of "Libro primero"; and second, the repetition of words often with slight variations. These two manifestations give rise to contradictory forces, for whereas intertextuality holds the speaker back, the anaphoric repetitions move him forward as he attempts to create distance between himself and the past.[161]

The speaker's inability to escape from the past is evident in the opening verses that echo the first verse of *Don*: "Siempre me vienen sombras de algún canto" [Always there come to me the shadows of some song]. His tone of complaint, of almost infantile anger, is perceptible in the rhetorical questions and the repetition of the accented "cuándo" in the verses that follow: "¿Y he de hacer yo que sea verdad? ¿Podría / señalar cuándo hay savia o cuándo mosto, / cuándo los trillos cambian el paisaje / nuevamente y en la hora del retorno?" (vv. 3–5).[162] Several more repetitions show him walking away, trying to distance himself from his confinement, leading him to cross a bridge and look back at his city: "El contagio de ti, de mí, de todo / lo que se puede ver a la salida / de un puente, entre el espacio de sus ojos" (vv. 8–10).[163] A bridge archetypically symbolizes a transition from one stage to another, but here the bridge both separates and links, just as the speaker is ambivalent about what he sees when he looks back through the "eyes" of the bridge's arches, a hackneyed metaphor. Does he see what he leaves behind through a fresh perspective, or is his vision still circumscribed by the old and familiar? Further repetitions, most notably of the word "llegar," move him forward, farther out into the countryside. But the shifting of figure

and ground that pervades this poem calls into question whether the speaker is pursuing or being pursued, whether he is talking to himself or to another: "A la subida.
Acosadoramente / cerca, hasta con el miedo del acoso, / llegas sobrepasando la llegada,
/ abriéndote al llegar como el otoño" (vv. 11–14).[164]

The coming of sunset should bring relief from the heat of the day: "el gran peligro
de las luces / en la meseta se nivela en fondo / cárdeno" (vv. 15–17).[165] Comparing
that external event with the leaving behind of his past ("así mi tiempo ya vivido"; v.
17), the poet wonders whether this sunset presages—like the flight of a bird—"alto o
bajo, la tormenta / o la calma" [high or low, storm / or calm] (vv. 19–20). The prospect
of spending the night in the countryside leads him to the recognition that he is not yet
mature enough to abandon all support. His footsteps, a metaphor for writing, may
betray him and bring destruction as well as mark his assurance and define his presence. The parallelism of the syntax and the slippage of the word "noche" (from night
to death) mark the speaker's arrival at a moment of illumination.

> Porque una cosa es creerme solo
> y otra hacer ruido para andar más firme;
> una cosa la noche, otra lo próximo
> de aquella noche que pervive en esta
> 25   y la desmanda.—¡Calla, álamo, sobrio
> hachón ardido de la espera! . . .
>
>   (p. 58)[166]

The dash before the exclamation and the image of the "álamo" signals the groundlessness of the gap and the insight that produces the image of a dead tree as a "sobrio
/ hachón ardido de la espera." This tree recalls the "álamo" in "Canto del despertar,"
contrasting the litheness (eloquence) of that tree with this dead, burned-out tree (lack).
Also, this third poem of "Libro tercero" parallels the poem about the "encina" from
"Libro primero," producing another contrast of eternal life versus death but also the
cyclical and dynamic versus the static and lifeless, here reversed again. "Sobrio"
counters the drunken ebullience of "Libro primero," and the word "espera" recalls
verses near the end of poem I of "Libro primero": "mi boca / espera, y mi alma
espera, y tú me esperas / ebria persecución" (p. 33). Repetition and intertextuality
inform our reading of the final verses also.

>   . . . Y calla,
> y mueve lindes de su voz en coro
> de intimidad igual que si moviera
> 30   voces del aire mientras yo te oigo
> —te estoy oyendo aunque no escuche nada—,
> sombra de un canto ya casi corpóreo.
>
>   (p. 58)[167]

In addition to the slippage from the imperative to the declarative ("calla"), from
"voz" to "voces," from "coro" to "intimidad," and the conceit "yo te oigo / —te estoy
oyendo aunque no escuche nada—" with its repeated gaps, the final verse evokes the

ending of poem IV of "Libro primero": "corpóreo como el sol cuando amanece" (p. 36). We would assume that the poet anticipates the arrival of dawn, that having confronted fear, aimlessness, and lack of shelter, he will now be more independent and find the originality he has sought. But because poem IV of "Libro primero" is ambivalent, the intertextual allusion undermines that optimism. This ambivalence is borne out when the speaker discovers in the next poem that he has come back to his city. Does he return with a new perspective, or has he returned to find that nothing has changed? Has he gone in circles, or has the circle traced something new?[168]

Poem IV is a meditation on risk-taking and concludes with the poet's commitment to continue exploring the gap. At first, because he has gone in circles and returned to his starting point, he feels discouraged: "La aventura / ha servido de poco" [The adventure / has provided little] (vv. 4–5). But through the recuperation of the archaic meaning of the word "actor," he discerns that the wall of Zamora ("la bien cercada" [the well-surrounded by walls]) and the Duero limit but also extend, protect but also explore and inspire. The poet continues to turn the negative into a positive without repudiating the negative.

> 5   ... Sin mí el cerco,
> el río, actor de la más vieja música.
> Aún y aunque sonden sigilosas huellas,
> amplísimas de rectas y de curvas,
> el valle, el oferente valle, acaso
> 10   valle con señaleras criaturas.
> ¡Tanto nos va en un riesgo! ...
>
>   (p. 59)[169]

Rodríguez here puns on the archaic meaning of "actor," playing it against the more obvious modern meaning. According to the modern meaning, a poet is an impostor, a skilled artisan who repeats the notes/words that someone else has composed, ironically similar to the medieval concept of the artist. But a musician—any artist— also interprets the music and thus puts his/her own stamp on it, in effect rewriting it, as poet and reader do with a poem. This interpretation derives from the archaic root "auctor," the author who draws from other sources but adds his/her own personality and point of view to the material, making it fresh and new. The placement of the adjectival phrase "más vieja" before the noun suggests the origin of music, the uncontaminated view of art without the self-consciousness of the intervening years of repetition. But we can also read in this same phrase that music (and so poetry) has grown stale because of repetition. The river thus becomes a doubly ambivalent symbol.[170]

Phonic play then translates into semantic and syntactic play as the language, steadily more equivocal, caroms between different possibilities. The verb "sondar" can be read in at least two ways. On one hand, it means "to cause to sound" or "to put into words" and "to make known," but it can also mean "to examine, explore, try, fathom." The auditory property of this verb contrasts with the adjective "sigilosas." Is the silent and secret revealed, put into words, made known? Or is it merely explored, examined, but not understood or verbalized? It is even unclear whether "huellas" is the subject or object of the verb until we reach "el valle," at which point the interchange between the anecdotal and the metapoetic (figure and ground) is intense. "Huellas" can refer on one level to the poet's footsteps (writing) or on another to the linguistic sign, the trace, so that "el valle" becomes the gap to be explored by the poet. The phrase "amplísimas de rectas y curvas" recalls both the speaker's literal wandering and chaos theory, turbulence, and the apparent disorder of the nonlinear; but these images also point to the discovery of a new order within the apparent disorder and confusion of gaiety and nostalgia, as we discover in the ambivalence of the exclamation in v. 11. The speaker may be lamenting his lack of gain, focusing on what he has lost in spite of his effort. By participating in this process, by taking this risk, he has lost his inspiration, his originality, and his unself-consciousness. But he may also recognize that his efforts have not been in vain. Whatever he has lost is worth the new things he is discovering.[171] When in "Libro primero" language slipped out of the poet's control, he delighted in the giddy feeling. A similar experience in the new context of "Libro tercero" reverses and tempers the relationship between exhilaration and despair, nostalgia and gaiety.

The images in vv. 11–14, although ambivalent, suggest a moment of illumination and affirms the poet's desire to explore further in spite of the risk and dangers involved: "La mañana, / en la mitad del tronco verdeoscura / y en la copa de un fuerte gris hojoso, / siente mil aletazos que la alumbran" (p. 59).[172] Morning typically represents a fresh beginning and a new outlook. Here morning is embodied in a tree, whose trunk is rooted in the earth but whose branches reach into the sky. Yet other ambivalencies characterize this image. The trunk of the tree is "verdeoscura." Is the green a rich color indicative of vibrant life or a dark shade with negative connotations? Is it emblematic of the intensity of life, or is it ominous, difficult to see, and hard to distinguish? Morning is also evident in the leaves of the treetop; these leaves are "de un fuerte gris," a color that could be silvery, shiny, and brilliant or ominous, cloudy, and sombre. The "aletazos," which give light (inspiration), refer metonymically to birds and flight. Again associating metonymically, the spring, trees, and birds suggest nests and fledglings that—much like the poet—are testing their wings and learning how to fly. This image dominates the final verses of the poem, for the poet must decide if he will wait or if he will continue to take risks, as he says: "Y entre senderos / del espacio, ¿quién vuela? O ahora o nunca" [And amid pathways / of space, who flies? Either now or never] (vv. 19–20).

From this point until the final words that make his decision known, the poet indeed takes a risk by contemplating—ironically, even sarcastically—avoiding risk: "Bien se conoce . . . / que puede más la huida que la busca" [One well knows . . . / that fleeing can do more than searching] (vv. 21–22). Is Rodríguez really going to step back from the edge, to wait until later to test his poetic wings rather than risk flight now? That option might allow him to survive longer and achieve a modicum of success: "no quizá por durar igual que todo / lo que muere y al fin da por segura su elevación" [not perhaps for lasting the same as everything / that dies and at last knows for sure its lifting] (vv. 23–25). But that would be a losing exchange, "Mañana a costa de alas y de túnicas" [Morning at the cost of wings and of tunics] (v. 26). He contemplates choosing the first path that he comes upon, a path with little inspiration, only the inspiration of his own cowardice: "(la primera / senda sin otro viento que mi fuga)" [(the first / path without another wind than my flight)] (vv. 27–28); and he sees himself following the sun like a common plant, "el tropismo solar del agavanzo" [the solar tropism of the wild rose] (v. 29), instead of distinguishing himself.

His final words—an emphatic repetition—do not respond literally to the choice "O ahora o nunca" but conversely. It is not a question of deciding whether to fly—to explore the gap, to take chances, to push language to the limit despite the danger of failing—but *never* to let himself hold back. His emphatic repetition of the word "nunca" at the end of the poem is not a negation but an affirmation of his commitment to a poetic exploration of language and of himself. What an ironic and transgressive poetics! By negating, Rodríguez affirms. By recognizing the gap in language, its equivocality and arbitrariness, the absence within the presence, he makes language signify in new ways. By confronting and exploring the lack of inspiration, he makes poetry.

Corresponding to the latter poems of "Libro primero," poems V and VI of "Libro tercero" are among the more opaque and enigmatic in the collection. Difficulty arises from the indeterminacy of ground, ambiguous antecedents, the apparently random juxtaposition of exemplary images in a free association of ideas, and a pervasive contrast between two different tones—doubt and assurance, frustration and elation, perplexity and clairvoyance. These characteristics show the poet tending toward the hermetic, individualistic side of the Scylla and Charybdis of repetition. Moreover, the indeterminate positioning of the speaker with regard to an image indicates a lack of ground which creates uncertainty. When he states in poem V that "Las estrellas no queman al pisarlas. / Cuando se miran desde abajo, queman" [The stars do not burn when we step on them. / When we see them from below, they burn] (vv. 13–14), we cannot determine his position. Is he ecstatically above the stars, stepping on them, or is he far below, looking up at them? In addition, the verb "quemar" is ambivalent; fire can stimulate, encourage, and regenerate as well as destroy. Is the poet lacking a stimulus because he cannot see or feel the inspiration the stars provide, or is he excited and determined because they inspire him?

Poem V also has erotic overtones that deal with the loss of virginity. This situation is ambivalent because the speaker feels eager and enthusiastic, confident in his desire and his ability, but also frustrated and yearning for fulfillment. Does the "ella" in the following verses refer to Aphrodite or to Erato: "Ella exige muchas / vidas y vive tantas que hace eterna / la del amante, la hace de un tempero / de amor, insoportablemente cierta" (vv. 7–10).[173] The ambivalence of the speaker's position is further evident in his observation, "El fruto muestra su sazón. La rama / ya avisa, tiemblo a tiemblo, su impotencia" [The fruit shows its ripeness. The branch / now warns, tremble by tremble, of its impotence] (vv. 11–12). Is the branch impotent because it is unable to bear fruit or because it is so laden with fruit that it cannot sustain such weight? The final verses of the poem are fragmentary and enigmatic.

> Sencillamente amar una vez sola.
> Arcaduz de los meses, vieja y nueva
> 25   ignorancia de la metamorfosis
> que va de junio a junio. Ve: no espera
> nada ni nadie en mí. ¿Qué necesitas?
> Nada ni nadie para mi existencia.
>
> (p. 60)[174]

From the sententious and impersonal infinitive phrase in v. 23, through the image of the passage of time that results in a "vieja y nueva ignorancia," to the elliptical monologue/cryptic dialogue that ends the poem, the speaker's search for genuine love parallels the poet's search for inspiration and transcendence in the poetic act. The lack of ground and duplicity of tone create the sensation of rushing through a gap, being out of control and in peril of breaking up.

Poem VI represents another turning point in the poet's exploration of the possibilities of repetition. Here he ponders the concept of "repetition forward," "the potential for reexperiencing the past in a new key—revising its initial meanings so as to signal an individual growth within repetition."[175] This potential arises when the poet incorporates an allusion to the Book of Ecclesiastes.

> No es que se me haya ido: nunca ha estado.
> Pero buscar y no reconocerlo,
> y no alumbrarlo en un futuro vivo . . .
> ¿Cómo dejaré sólo este momento?
> 5   Nadie ve aquí y palpitan las llamadas
> y es necesario que se saque de ello
> la forma, para que otra vez se forme
> como en la lucha con su giro el viento.
> Como en la lucha con su giro. . . .
>
> (p. 61)[176]

The first verses disorient us because the subject of the verbs and antecedent of the pronouns is unknown: The poet allows us to overhear his thoughts but has provided no context, no frame of reference, making us unsure of his meaning. His problem consists in giving form to what he senses at this moment, capturing it in language (copying it "mimetically") so that future readers can reexperience it. But he realizes that language is as unstable as the wind. By recalling this image from Ecclesiastes (1:4–9), the poet repeats a topical situation but recontextualizes it.[177] He retraces the circle, but his retracing produces a change. He has grounded his experience in an archetypal topos, synthesizing the grounded with the ungrounded. This synthesis "recovers new possibilities in repetition and yet avoids the alternative of the utter abandonment of meaning or some clarity of value."[178]

The speaker recognizes this situation in the image of the grapevine: "Ayer latía por sí mismo el campo. / Hoy le hace falta vid de otro misterio, / del pie que ignora la uva aunque ha pisado / fuertemente la cepa. Hoy" (vv. 13–16).[179] The agricultural imagery of the vineyard compares the poet with a vine in need of grafting onto a sturdy rootstock in order to produce a new variety of grape. The poet perceives that his precursors felt things directly without the stigma of "influence" and the onus of originality. Now he realizes his dependence on former poets and their poems to nourish him and to produce through him a new type of fruit. The conclusion of the poem shows the poet accepting this duality because it leads to the renovation of creativity and inspiration.

> Oh, más allá del aire y de la noche
> (¡El cristalero azul, el cristalero
> de la mañana!), entre la muerte misma
> que nos descubre un caminar sereno
> 30   vaya hacia atrás o hacia adelante el rumbo,
> vaya el camino al mar o tierra adentro.
>
> (p. 61)[180]

The poet recognizes a paradoxical situation: By surrendering his individuality, he will assure originality and find poetic fulfillment. In these verses, he rejects the inspiration of air and night (the ungrounded) for that of death, a new perspective that releases him from his enabling origins into the adventure of time precisely because he has gone back to the past to retrieve former possibilities.[181] "Repetition becomes the fulfillment of possibilities only latent in the past, the completion of what only the present can awaken."[182]

The parenthetical exclamation that forms a gap between air and night on one hand and death on the other exemplifies this process. This image personifies night as a glazier, providing a new variation on the venerable image of the "windows of dawn."[183] It also recalls the opening poems of "Libro primero" and the deconstruction of light and darkness, dawn and dusk, day and night, here extending that play to life and death, repetition and originality. The poet realizes that his inspiration will renew and his originality be assured if he retrieves the past, if he "recollects forward."[184] His apprehension (pun intended) of this concept is evident in the final two poems of "Libro tercero."

If poems I and II of this section lead us into the exploration of the chaos in the gap in language, the final two poems broaden the horizon to include a consideration of the entire volume. Poem VII is remarkable chiefly because of the tension it motivates via synchronic and diachronic repetition ("strange loops"). The opening verses refer to the gap the poet has been exploring and are extremely equivocal.

> ¡Qué diferencia de emoción existe
> entre el surco derecho y el izquierdo,
> entre esa rama baja y esa alta!
> La belleza anterior a toda forma
> 5   nos va haciendo a su misma semejanza.
>
> (p. 62)[185]

Although the poem opens with an exclamation, the tone is ambivalent. This phrase can express both the poet's exasperation and frustration with language and his exaltation and excitement about what he has discovered. The sententious declaration in vv.

4–5 is not only paradoxical but even tautological. At first, it would appear to describe the Platonic concept of repetition that posits "La belleza anterior a toda forma." Each copy of the original model is an unchanged mimetic repetition. But the second half of the statement undermines this idea: "nos va haciendo a su *misma semejanza.*" The redundancy of the words I have emphasized points out that "la belleza *anterior* a toda forma" is itself a likeness ("semejanza"), disavowing the originality of the original.[186]

This imbrication of the two types of repetition manifests itself again at the end of the poem, where the poet repeats: "Rama baja y rama alta. / La belleza anterior a toda forma / nos va haciendo a su misma semejanza." Because he repeats the same words that in themselves create a contradiction, we cannot help but recall poem VII of "Libro primero," which repeats verbatim the opening phrase "¡Sólo por una vez que todo vuelva / a dar como si nunca diera tanto!" (pp. 38–39). In my discussion of that poem, I note the ambiguity of the phrase "vuelva / a dar" and its contrast with the adverbial "Sólo por una vez." Rodríguez's iteration of the formal structure (the repetition of the same words at the beginning and end of the poem) in poem VII of both "Libro primero" and "Libro tercero" activates repetition with a difference on yet another level. The synchronic repetition (within the poem) plays against the diachronic repetition (between the two poems). A middle ground of inter- and intratextuality comes into play, making us see the two peripheral sections of *Don* as two aspects of the same experience—repetition with a difference. A constant balancing between the two peripheral sections proves that "Libro segundo" is the fulcrum on which both rest and a gap between them. Center becomes periphery and periphery center—one cannot exist without the other—just as the two types of repetition are each contained within and subvert the other.

The final poem is a masterpiece of repetition with difference. The gap has illuminated a vast, new, previously unsuspected world, but the unknown both attracts and frightens the novice poet. Repetition and ambivalence in the final poem exploits the gap to set the entire structure of *Don* in motion. Again, the neutral punctuation of the first verse posits two incompatible interpretations, a dialogic split that operates upon our reading of this poem and of *Don* in its totality. When the speaker says, "Cómo veo los árboles ahora," we do not know if this is an exclamation or a question. As an exclamation, it pulls us back to "el planteamiento, enérgico, convincente, claro y coherente" of the opening verses of *Don*, expressing the poet's enthusiasm for the change that has taken place because of his experience with language throughout this book.[187] If, on the other hand, we read it as a question, we again confront the doubt, uncertainty, and lack of resolution that has steadily grown since the image of night closing the chamber of its shadows. The reprise of the innocence of "Libro primero" brings the collection full circle, unifying and closing the experience. But if we read this verse as a question, we understand that the poet is still perplexed and uncertain about language and his identity. As we shall see as we work our way through the images and repetitions in this poem, this questioning leaves the process unresolved, looking ahead to future works and lamenting the brevity of life and the unreliability of inspiration, at the same time that it creates closure.

The poet-speaker now finds himself in an equivocal position, circumscribed by and yet beyond language. This site is marked by the binary oppositions he selects from the world around him.

> Cómo veo los árboles ahora.
> No con hojas caedizas, no con ramas
> sujetas a la voz del crecimiento.
> Y hasta a la brisa que los quema a ráfagas
> 5   no la siento como algo de la tierra
> ni del cielo tampoco, sino falta
> de ese dolor de vida con destino.
> Y a los campos, al mar, a las montañas,
> muy por encima de su clara forma
> 10 los veo. ¿Qué me han hecho en la mirada?
> ¿Es que voy a morir? . . .

(p. 63)[188]

Using images that capture the essence of autumn ("hojas caedizas") and spring ("ramas / sujetas a la voz del crecimiento"), the poet undercuts the cycle of the seasons at the same time that he suggests it. Is it that a tree is defined by neither one nor the other (spring nor fall) but both equally, deconstructing the opposition through a continual play of difference? Or is it that the concept of "tree" persists unchanging in spite of/because of the various changes through which it passes? As emblem of the poet's identity, the tree represents a stable concept and something that is constantly evolving; it is both Platonic and Nietzschean. If writing is a way of knowing oneself, has the poet defined himself, or have the changes wrought by the very act through which he endeavors to find himself problematized his identity by constantly deferring the signified?

The image of the breeze in vv. 4–8 deconstructs the opposition "tierra/cielo" with a similar effect. Both a cold wind and a hot one can "burn" plants, and fire can be regenerative as well as destructive, oppositions related to the cycle of spring and fall in vv. 2–3. When the poet claims that the breeze is not "de la tierra / ni del cielo tampoco," he is saying in effect that it is both and neither, another description of the gap where he finds himself. That the breeze is "falta / de ese dolor de vida con destino" makes us wonder if it is without purpose or direction, wandering, lost, incapable of fulfillment, or if its destiny is death and the breeze has transcended its concrete manifestations to become immune to death.[189] By considering the breeze the poet's inconsistent ("a ráfagas") inspiration, we see him questioning what he has attained through his writing. The ambivalence of the language creates a myriad of echoings back and forth between a positive and negative interpretation that unsettles us and makes us giddy because of the constant flux, the intense play of difference that takes place in these verses.

The ambiguous syntax of vv. 8–10 problematizes the speaker's position in relation to the things he observes. Is it he or they who are "muy por encima de su clara forma"? Is the "clara forma" something concrete but variable or abstract and unchangeable? The phrases "muy por encima" and "su clara forma" remind us of poem I of "Libro primero." Does the speaker participate in the same type of ecstatic experience now as then, or is there distance (i.e., difference) between then and now, with the poet nostalgically observing from afar? These verses epitomize the two types of repetition but deconstruct them and problematize the speaker's attitude toward his experience with language and poetry (cf. gaiety versus nostalgia).

The questions of vv. 10–11 form a nodal point that pulls together the poet's ambivalent emotions. His preoccupation with his eyesight alludes to his inspiration. But does he have more insight, or is he blind (cf. "deslumbrar" from poem I of "Libro primero")? Is he exulting or despairing? Does his question "¿Es que voy a morir?" express disdain or fear of death? When in v. 13 he asserts, "Sí, ebrio estoy, sin duda," the same ambivalence obtains; drunkenness can be an ecstatic elation and a distrustful alienation.[190] By recognizing that he is drunk, he is estranged from himself and sees his questioning as foolish. But after all, he is still drunk, so that hyperconsciousness and self-consciousness become one and the same even though they represent two distinct and incompatible perspectives. The images of morning and air in vv. 14–25 further elaborate the deconstruction of binary opposites of time and space, leading the poet to a consideration of the concepts of "remembering forward" and "being by becoming."

> La mañana no es tal, es una amplia
> 15 llanura sin combate, casi eterna,
> casi desconocida porque en cada
> lugar donde antes era sombra el tiempo,
> ahora la luz espera ser creada.
> No sólo el aire deja más su aliento:
> 20 no posee ni cántico ni nada;
> se lo dan, y él empieza a rodearle
> con fugaz esplendor de ritmo de ala
> e intenta hacer un hueco suficiente
> para no seguir fuera. No, no sólo
> 25 seguir fuera, sino a distancia.
> Pues bien: el aire de hoy tiene su cántico.
> ¡Si lo oyeseis! . . .

(p. 63)[191]

By comparing "la mañana" with "una amplia / llanura sin combate," the poet deconstructs the binary opposition of time and space, the fleeting and the constant, the abstract and the concrete. The adjectives "eterna" and "desconocida" are problematic not only because they could refer to either "mañana" or "llanura," but also because they are qualified—and the repetition here is significant—by the adverb "casi"! These images represent the concept of "remembering forward" "porque en cada / lugar donde antes era sombra el tiempo, / ahora la luz espera ser creada." While on the one hand we note the contrasts "lugar/tiempo," "antes/ahora," "sombra/luz," the verb "espera" blurs the distinctions. If "la luz espera ser creada," it is there already waiting to be created, but not yet created, so not yet present. When the poet "remembers forward," he repeats what other poets have said, but he does so with a difference by forgetting what they have said in his repetition.[192]

The highly equivocal image extended in vv. 19–27 conflates the air with a bird that inhabits it, reminding us of Benjamin's emblem of the sock.[193] Just as the air and the bird symbiotically define one another, so being and becoming—both characteristics of the poet's definition of his identity in the creative act—are mutually exclusive and inclusive. The final lines repeat with differences, closing and opening the poem and the entire collection.

> ... Y el sol, el fuego, el agua,
> cómo dan posesión a estos mis ojos.
> ¿Es que voy a vivir? ¿Tan pronto acaba
> 30   la ebriedad? Ay, y cómo veo ahora
> los árboles, qué pocos días faltan ...

$$(p.\ 63)^{194}$$

Sun, fire, and water—all symbols of inspiration (light, regeneration, and irrigation)—perform an equivocal function. The poet's experience with the poetic act makes him ecstatically drunken, out of control, but by alienating him, it provides a greater awareness of self and so a more "sober," profound knowledge of who he is. The repetition of the question "¿Es que voy a vivir?" contains a significant difference but is just as ambivalent as the earlier "¿Es que voy a morir?" The poet may want to die now, so as not to lose the tremendous excitement that his experience with poetry has provided: "¿Tan pronto acaba la ebriedad?" Or he may fear that he will die and that he will not be able to continue his experience with poetry. The parallel questions "¿Es que voy a morir/vivir?" paradoxically are the same question and yet significantly different. The same can be said of the poet's repetition of the opening verse, again a repetition with a difference. In this iteration, the order of the words has changed, and their arrangement on the line is different, emphasizing the word "ahora." Such a subtle change opens the phrase more even though we anticipate closure because of the repetition.[195] The subversion of closure concomitant with the very act is underscored in the final phrase. Echoing the "quadrivalence" of the poet's question "¿Es que voy a morir/vivir?" this phrase can lament the brevity of life and this marvelous aesthetic experience, or it can eagerly anticipate the next encounter with poetry. The suspensive periods further subvert closure and are eloquent with silence.

The enthusiasm in poem VIII takes us back to the beginning of *Don* while the anxiety it expresses pushes us forward into the next book. The contradictory tones move us in two directions simultaneously—backward to the beginning, closing the work, and forward to the next work, keeping the experience open to new discoveries. The entire volume of *Don* rocks like a balance on a fulcrum. What seems to be a static, closed work of art because of its tight structure and hermetic language becomes a dynamic, open work that both captivates and alienates the reader. Only by surrendering to the rigid discipline of the text's sequentiality can we actualize more fully its destabilizing and exhilarating vacillations.

Each of Rodríguez's subsequent works repeats—synchronically and diachronically and always with differences—the process of *Don*. Each strives for a definition of the poet's self through language and the aesthetic act with regard to the moment in which it is composed and the process through which that composition passes. Each shows the poet delving into the unknown (in himself and language), and each transgresses the limits of language by deconstructing binary counterparts. In the chapters that follow, I will show how each work repeats this process, but I will emphasize the variations in focus, structure, language, and tone in this constant search for the self and transcendence through language and the poetic act.

2

Tradition and the Ironic Talent
in *Conjuros* (1958)

> Enter ye in at the strait gate . . .
> Because strait is the gate and narrow is the way,
> which leadeth unto life,
> and few there be that find it.

A major change takes place in Rodríguez's second work, *Conjuros* (1958), manifest in the greater variability of his verse form and the organization of the work as a whole, but most significantly in the process of each poem.[1] In *Don de la ebriedad,* the poet begins with a metapoetic issue and couches his imprecise perceptions in (largely archetypal) images, enabling him to concretize his abstract experiences with language and the poetic act. In contrast, the poems of *Conjuros* are firmly rooted in a tangible, everyday reality, as their titles attest. These vignettes of provincial Castilian life resonate with symbolic proportions, though they never completely lose their properties as concrete realities.[2] The interplay between the representational and the symbolic, a facet that has existential and aesthetic implications for the poet, has intrigued readers of *Conjuros* since its publication.[3]

At first, following the precepts of the New Critical approach, we described a movement from the concrete to the abstract, which tended to separate these two levels.[4] With the shift to poststructuralist critical theories, Andrew Debicki and others have stressed the inextricability of the two levels. This "realismo metafórico" [metaphoric realism] (Bousoño's term is still apt) would appear to bridge the gap between signifier and signified by imbricating the representational and the symbolic, the transient and the transcendent. But just as the title of *Don* is a play on words describing an ambivalent experience, so in *Conjuros* the poet is a magician who wields language to cast poetic spells (on everyday reality, on the reader); but he too comes under the spell of language and is ironically affected by participation in the poetic act.

Embedded in the mimetic scenes that comprise the poems of *Conjuros*, a vast network of allusion enriches and intensifies the interaction between the two levels and foments an ironic duality. This cultural code consists of four general (often overlapping) categories: aspects of medieval life (especially agriculture, religion, war, and the hunt); customs and scenes of daily rural life; intertextual allusions (to the Bible in particular); and idiomatic, colloquial language. This historical, cultural, literary, and linguistic heritage from which the poet draws inspiration and identity points to the theme of time—specifically, the passing of time and those entities which survive its passage. The poems of *Conjuros* stem from a recognition of the transience of human existence and a desire to transcend temporal limitations. Art, especially the poetic act, represents one means of achieving transcendence.

The poet's problem in *Conjuros* is to draw upon his inherited traditions and cultural formation but simultaneously to individuate himself, to make himself stand out from that background and not let his voice become forgotten with the passing of time. Although he realizes that he depends on his heritage to identify him as a person and a poet, he also finds himself enmeshed in a web of predetermined meaning from which it is difficult to extricate himself. To separate himself from his heritage is tantamount to denying his identity. Ironically, the cultural code identifies the poet and destabilizes his identity, unites him with others and requires that he separate himself from them. Thus "realismo metafórico" designates union and separation, imbrication (anonymity and indistinguishability) and rupture (individuality and distinction). I argue, therefore, that both views of this interplay (the prestructuralist and the poststructuralist) coexist dialogically in these poems, reflecting the ambivalent relationship between signifier and signified: the gap and the bridge between them, presence and absence, appearance (representation) and reality (meaning).

Irony is at the heart of this duality. First, alazony (boastfulness) distances us from the speaker, allowing us to observe a change in his outlook as we read through *Conjuros* sequentially. The first two sections establish and complicate the irony through an interplay of the representational and the symbolic, signifier and signified. This leads to a chiasmus (a turning point) in "Libro tercero," which contains only two poems, the structural hallmark of Rodríguez's works.[5] The poems of the final section bear the mark of the chiasmus. The difficulty—and ultimately the delight—in reading *Conjuros* consists in discriminating between appearance and reality, irony and straightforwardness. Those readers who can appreciate and step back from the interplay of the representational and the symbolic by recognizing the irony are those who will attain the greatest intimacy ("solidarity") with the speaker. As we trace the speaker's progress through *Conjuros*, we will examine the ways Rodríguez draws upon his cultural heritage and the shifting degrees of irony and sincerity that define his relation with his heritage, his understanding of the sign, and his search for identity.

THE ALAZONIC MAGICIAN: APPEARANCE VERSUS REALITY IN "LIBRO PRIMERO"

Conjuros begins with a startling incantation that establishes the speaker's alazony in "Libro primero":

¡Dejad de respirar, y que os respire
la tierra, que os incendie en sus pulmones
maravillosos! Mire
quien mire, ¿no verá en las estaciones
5   un rastro como de aire que se alienta?
Sería natural aquí la muerte.
No se tendría en cuenta
como la luz, como el espacio, ¡Muerte
con sólo respirar! . . .

(p. 69)[6]

The opening command—either hypnotic suggestion or overpowering incantation—pronounced by the poet-magician, urges that we surrender ourselves to the aesthetic experience. But his command gives us pause: Does he really want us to "Stop
breathing" and to let ourselves as molecules of air be incinerated in the earth's lungs?!
The idiomatic expression "Mire quien mire," the question, and the almost nonchalant
"Sería natural aquí la muerte" all suggest an overconfidence that makes us suspicious.
When we encounter his second exclamation—"¡Muerte / con sólo respirar!"—it seems
that the speaker contradicts himself: First, he tells us to stop breathing so that we can
live more intensely; then, he says we will die if we merely continue breathing. While
these contradictions are confusing, both statements imply that by dying we will attain
a more intense appreciation of life, echoing Christ's words in Matt. 16:24–26, the
intertext that underlies the poem.[7]

This paradox is anticipated in the title of the poem, "A la respiración en la llanura"
[To breathing on the plains], where we discern a duality latent in the mimetic level
(breathing the pure air of the Castilian countryside). Breathing consists of inspiration
(life) and expiration (death) in the vast cultural network which can both stimulate and
absorb the poet ("la llanura"). Hence we begin *Conjuros* where we left off in *Don:*
Because of the free play of the signifier and the duplicity of language, life and death
are synonymous. But this melding of life and death is excessive. It even sounds as
though Rodríguez is mocking the naive, exuberant view of language in *Don*! We must
conclude that these verses instantiate the speaker's alazony, "which is Greek for
braggartism but in works on irony is shorthand for any form of self-assurance or
naïvety."[8] Although at this point it is extremely difficult to distinguish between appearance and reality, this boastful, self-assured tone—which reappears throughout
"Libro primero"—signals an ironic perspective and distances us from the speaker.

We can verify the irony here by applying Wayne Booth's four steps for determining if a passage is ironic.[9] First, "The reader is required to reject the literal meaning"
(p. 10), not hard to do because we cannot stop breathing and go on living for very
long, nor will we die if we continue breathing. In step two, "Alternative interpretations or explanations are tried out . . ." (p. 11). One might protest that all literature is
in a sense metaphoric and that these verses merely introduce us to the semiosis of
Conjuros. But Booth says that where metaphor encourages us to pull meanings together, irony is "subtractive," causing us to nullify the surface meaning.[10] Another
possibility might be to assert that Rodríguez is acceding to the dominant tendencies

of Spanish poetry in the 1950s—the "rehumanized," "social" poetry of the postwar era.[11] This reading fails to explain the exaggeration and distance it creates. We are obliged to assess the implied author's position (the third step in Booth's process).[12]

I suggest that Rodríguez recognizes the aesthetic limitations of social poetry and that he seeks a more perceptive readership at the same time that he rejects the hermeticism and esoteric attitude of the prewar period ("art for art's sake"). Instead of the strident thematics and rhetoric of social poetry or the elitism of art for art's sake, Rodríguez simultaneously invites and challenges the reader to participate in a profound and often difficult introspection through language. This exploration of self constitutes his transgressive poetics, his desire always to push beyond the envelop of the sign as a way of knowing himself better. The use of irony in *Conjuros* represents the next step in this process of transgressing linguistic boundaries, for as Booth asserts, "Irony obtrudes itself and thus obtrudes its author's claim to skill. It risks disaster more aggressively than any other device. But if it succeeds, it will succeed more strongly than any literal statement can do" (pp. 41–42). If Rodríguez wishes to distinguish himself and to define his individuality through writing and the poetic act, irony provides the perfect vehicle. Moreover, "Irony as the key to the tightest bonds of friendship! Real intimacy impossible without it!" (p. 14) embodies Rodríguez's search for introspective readers, another theme that pervades *Conjuros*, as we shall see shortly in "Día de sol" [Sunny day] and later in "Siempre será mi amigo" [He will always be my friend]. I propose that we read *Conjuros* ironically, reconstructing the reading of these poems (Booth's fourth step) in accord with Rodríguez's transgressive poetics.

The distance produced by the opening verses allows us to stand back from the text (at the same time that we participate in it) and observe a duality in the speaker's outlook. Ambivalent language in the subsequent verses advances the irony.

>   . . . Fuera de día
> 10   ahora y me quedaría sin sentido
>   en estos campos, y respiraría
>   hondo como estos árboles, sin ruido.
>   Por eso la mañana aún es un vuelo
>   creciente y alto sobre
> 15   los montes, y un impulso a ras del suelo
>   que antes de que se efunda y de que cobre
>   forma ya es surco para el nuevo grano.
>   Oh, mi aposento. . . .

(p. 69)[13]

Ellipsis in the phrase "Fuera de día / ahora" iterates the ambivalence of the opening command. Does the speaker demand light ("Let it be day") or posit a hypothetical situation, expressing his yearning ("How I wish it were day")? When he says "me quedaría sin sentido / en estos campos," does he mean that he would fall tranquilly asleep, that he would be overcome with ecstasy, or that he would lose all consciousness? Is there ironic humor in the statement "y respiraría / hondo como estos árboles, *sin ruido*"? By letting himself relax and giving himself over to the breathing of the plains, he would fall asleep deeply and silently like the trees—without snoring![14]

Because of what we already know about Rodríguez's understanding of language from *Don*, it is difficult, if not impossible, to accept the speaker as totally straightforward and sincere.[15] It is prudent to stand at a distance, to appreciate the possibility of poetic ecstasy—the magic of language—but also to question, to listen suspiciously for subtleties, and to keep both possibilities (the straightforward and the ironic) viable simultaneously. The poet seems to do the same when he describes morning as "un vuelo / creciente y alto sobre / los montes, y un impulso a ras del suelo." We must learn to discriminate between the presence and absence of irony. At this point, the duplicity of language and uncertainty about the speaker's stance make us suspicious because we are unsure of the difference between appearance and reality, sincerity and irony. As we proceed through *Conjuros* and learn to discriminate the ironic from the straightforward, this uneasiness and suspicion will become delight.

After morning is described as flight, it is compared with a liquid that ironically attains form by being spilled. This statement contradicts what we know to be true about liquids, which adopt the form of their containers; but we perceive light only because it strikes an object (a form) and reflects into our eye. Then the speaker says that even before the light adopts form in this manner, morning "ya es surco para el nuevo grano." If the young poet is the new seed, the groundwork has already been laid by other poets; the cultural context from which he draws inspiration is already prepared to stimulate his growth. The unpunctuated "Oh, mi aposento" divulges an ambivalent response to this situation. In the semiosis of respiration, "aposento" is metaphor for the chest, specifically the lungs. Does the speaker refer to his own lungs or the "pulmones / maravillosos" of the plains? Has he been uplifted by what his heritage offers, or does he fear being overwhelmed and buried by it? The ambivalence of water as irrigation and purification reinforces the reciprocity between the poet and his cultural heritage in a motif of gain/loss (Matt. 16:26) that will reappear not only in *Conjuros* but in Rodríguez's later works.

> ... Qué riego del alma
> éste con el que doy mi vida y gano
> 20   tantas vidas hermosas. Tened calma
> los que me respiráis, hombres y cosas.
> Soy vuestro. Sois también vosotros míos.
> Cómo aumentan las rosas
> su juventud al entregarse. ¡Abríos
> 25   a todo! El heno estalla en primavera,
> el pino da salud con su olor fuerte.
> ¡Qué hostia la del aliento, qué manera
> de crear, qué taller claro de muerte!
>
> (pp. 69–70)[16]

The speaker sees irony in the image of the roses that confirm their eternal beauty and perfection by blooming and perishing. But is he trying to convince us with a tangible example, or does he acknowledge images of surrender in the world around him (roses, straw, pines) but feel himself distant from them? It is only by surrendering oneself, by dying to self, that one attains transcendence and immortality (Matt. 16:25). If we follow his advice—"¡Abríos a todo!"—like the rose we will perish.

The revival of the images of the roses, the pine, and the host echo the poet's longing to give of himself through his poetry that we saw in poem IX of "Libro primero" of *Don* (p. 40). The host, symbol of Christ's body, his sacrifice, death, and resurrection, is equated with breath, imbricating the tangible and the intangible, inspiration and expiration, transcendence and transience, individuality and anonymity. In the repetition of the motif that structures this poem—"¡ . . . qué taller claro de muerte!"—creation and destruction are synonymous, taking us back to the initial alazony and blurring the distinction between appearance and reality. The final lines of the poem confirm the mixture of enthusiasm and trepidation that accompany the act of surrendering oneself.

> No sé cómo he vivido
> 30 hasta ahora ni en qué cuerpo he sentido
> pero algo me levanta al día puro,
> me comunica un corazón inmenso,
> como el de la meseta, y mi conjuro
> es el del aire, tenso
> 35 por la respiración del campo henchida
> muy cerca de mi alma en el momento
> en que pongo la vida
> al voraz paso de cualquier aliento.
>
> (p. 70)[17]

These verses summarize the speaker's estrangement from himself at the beginning of *Conjuros* and our suspicion because of the alazony in the opening command. The passivity of surrender causes fear and joy. Several images in these verses are ambivalent. The adjective "puro" could refer to either the speaker (as host, as aspirant) or the day. Is he able to rise because he is pure, or does this movement describe a painful purification process? Does his rising parallel the sunrise, or does it contrast the purity of dawn with the darkness (unworthiness) of the speaker? The "corazón inmenso" may be either a positive or negative image; "comunicar" can mean "contagiar, dañar, pervertir" as well as "to place in relation," just as the adjective "henchida" can mean "full" (suggesting plenitude and ecstasy) or "swollen" (sore and painful), reinforcing "tenso" (excited or worried).

When the speaker states "mi conjuro es el del aire," does he mean that he receives life and stimulation from his cultural heritage, or that he is subsumed by it? This situation obtains only at the moment when the speaker places his life "al voraz paso de cualquier aliento," another ambivalent phrase because "voraz" may be positively or negatively marked; "paso" suggests brevity and transience as well as dynamic movement and vitality; and the modifier "*cualquier* aliento" connotes not only complete abandonment but also the uncertainty involved in such a gesture.

In short, irony in the opening statement of "A la respiración en la llanura" distances us from the speaker and enables us to discern ambivalence in the language of the poem. If not for the alazony, we might accept this opening as optimistic, enthusiastic participation in the cultural context and the magical realm of poetry. Such a reading does not take into account the irony and would cause readers to interpret *Conjuros* as poetry in praise of social solidarity. Such a reading overlooks the poet's continuation of an insightful examination of himself through writing and the ironic consequences of that task. By recognizing the alazony, we become aware of the difficulty of self-examination that the acts of writing and reading entail and of the danger of failure implicit in irony. As we observe the speaker in other poems of "Libro primero," our awareness of this irony will help us achieve a more insightful reading of *Conjuros*.

The speaker's separation from the anonymous crowd appears in the well-crafted "Día de sol" [Sunny day], which includes a variety of agricultural images and biblical allusions. Presumably, the speaker desires to separate himself from others—perhaps other poets or the majority of readers—to bring about a change in himself and in that way to attain transcendence and an undying reputation. It is ironic, however, that at the very moment when he renounces his past and announces the desire to move on to other experiences, he relies heavily on the cultural code.

The structure of the poem is based on the repetition and variation of a negative exclamation. The regular spacing of these exclamations highlights the speaker's vacillation between his desire to break away and the difficulty of such an action, opening a seam between appearance and reality. The title "Día de sol" may refer to his awareness of the need for change, but it also connotes the comfort and complacency of the familiar that exerts inertia and makes change difficult. These contrasting forces are perceptible in the first half of the poem.

> Me he puesto tantas veces al sol sin darme cuenta.
> ¡Ni un día más! De pronto, como se abre el mercado
> o el taller de la plaza, qué faena, qué renta
> se me abre el día de hoy. Id a mi lado
> 5   sin más arreos que la simple vida,
> sin más que la humildad por aparejo.
> ¡No espero más! Oh, sed ropa tendida.
> ¡Que nos varee el sol y el fruto viejo
> caiga y sirva de abono
> 10 a la nueva sazón, y la sustente!
> Repón tu apero, corazón, colono
> de este terreno mío. ¡Que sea hoy el aviente,
> que sea hoy el espadar del lino
> y se nos mulla y quede limpio el grano!

                                                                    (p. 73)[18]

The customs and rituals of daily life, such as the opening of the market or a shop on the main square of a town, here serve as objective correlatives for revelation.[19] But as the phrase "qué faena, qué renta / se me abre el día de hoy" implies, this revelation produces pain and joy, loss and gain. Agricultural imagery also defines the speaker's state of mind at this moment. The poles used to knock ripe fruit from the trees, the description of his heart as a sharecropper, the separation of the wheat from the chaff, and the processing of flax fibers all pertain to the speaker's separating himself from his past.

Being from Zamora and having walked throughout León and Castile, Rodríguez was surrounded by agricultural life.[20] It is natural that he include that imagery in his poems. The use of agricultural imagery derives from a tradition of popular sayings and short pieces of verse, giving rise to another source of inspiration for Rodríguez's poetry: the oral tradition. The *Cancionero del campo* compiled by Bonifacio Gil gives evidence of an oral tradition of sayings and verses representing the wisdom of country folk and their involvement in every aspect of agricultural life.[21] Many of these aspects appear in all their detail in Rodríguez's poetry.[22] Because of his ventures through the countryside and his conversations with country folk, Rodríguez undoubtedly came into contact with this tradition. But he may also have found a model for this imagery in the poetry of Gonzalo de Berceo.[23]

Rodríguez also weaves a biblical allusion into these verses. His urging "Id a mi lado / sin más arreos que la simple vida, / sin más que la humildad por aparejo" echoes Christ's calling of his disciples, especially the wealthy young man whom he urges to divest himself of all his possessions (see Matt. 4:19, Mark 10:21, or Luke 18:22). The agricultural images and biblical allusion juxtaposed with the exclamations "¡Ni un día más!" and "¡No espero más!" embody the poet's difficulty in distinguishing himself, in separating himself from a cultural network that pervades his identity. How can he individuate yet not negate the very essence of himself? This conflict and the speaker's vacillation continue in the last half of this artfully structured poem.

> 15   . . . Me voy por mi camino
>   a la solana eterna, donde en vano
>   tomé el sol con vosotros tantas veces
>   sin darme cuenta. Cuántas, cuántas veces
>   esperé a que por dentro de la piel nos curtiera.
> 20   No pasó de ella. Os dejo,
>   ahí os quedáis. Quisiera . . .
>   ¡Pero ni un día más! Os aconsejo
>   que ya que así estáis bien estad siquiera
>   con llaneza y con fe. ¿Por qué ha venido
> 25   esta mañana a darme a mí tal guerra,
>   este sol a encender lo que he perdido?
>   Tapad vuestra semilla. Alzad la tierra.
>   Quizá así maduréis y habréis cumplido.
>
>   (p. 73)[24]

The discord within the speaker and between him and his cronies intensifies in these verses, producing a sense of rending the fabric of society and the text. First, the speaker declares his independence and individuality as he states, "Me voy por mi camino / a la solana eterna," emphasizing that he is taking his own path. The "solana," an open, sunny area where people gather to work and talk, pertains to the code of light and the transformative effects of the poetic experience.[25] But the catachresis produced by "eterna" has a dual effect. It unites the concrete and the abstract, but creates a friction that threatens to rend the text apart.

Several contradictions support this duality. The speaker says that the time spent with his friends in the "solana" was "en vano" and "sin darme cuenta," and that the sun he received there had only a superficial effect on him. His declaration that he will go to the same "solana" by a different path and leave his friends behind is a contradiction. We sense that the speaker is trying to negotiate a delicate distinction between himself and others. If they too are engaged in the poetic act, they have received illumination; but Rodríguez seeks a more profound experience in the "solana," the poetic space. His vacillation ("Quisiera . . .") hints at reluctance: How easy it would be to remain comfortably ensconced as part of the crowd! The friction between the speaker as Christ and a disciple subtly underscores this irony. Like Christ, he doubts: "¿Por qué ha venido / esta mañana a darme a mí tal guerra, / este sol a encender lo que he perdido?" There exists yet another friction here because morning (poetic insight) has brought conflict to the speaker just as Christ brought conflict instead of peace (see Matt. 10:34 or Luke 12:51). Moreover, the verb "encender" can connote destruction and pain as well as stimulation and enthusiasm in this revival of the gain/loss motif.

The speaker's advice to his (former) companions in the final verses again rings ironic. By placing himself in a superior position to his fellows through alazony, the speaker violates his own exhortation in v. 6: "sin más que la humildad por aparejo." This supercilious attitude will lead to a humbling experience precisely because he has chosen the difficult path of a more profound engagement with the poetic act. These tensions in "Día de sol" initiate the opening of a seam between appearance and reality in the alazon's stance. As we move through "Libro primero," this rift will become more pronounced and betray the falseness of the speaker's perspective at the beginning of *Conjuros*.

The conflict escalates in "El canto de linos" [The song of Linus], another poem in which biblical allusions and agricultural imagery intertwine. This poem derives from the "canción de trabajo," firmly based in country life and the custom of workers to sing before, during, and after work. However, a pun in the title reveals the speaker's ambivalence. A title represents the first step in the reading process "since a title is supposed to inform the reader and facilitate access to the text by stating its subject, its genre, or its code."[26] But it is also set apart from the poem, thereby indicating a concomitant disjunction between them. The relation between title and poem is comparable to that of signifier and signified.[27]

Because on the literal level "linos" refers to flax-plants, most readers attribute this word to the agricultural code and the mimetic level of the text. But the mimetic level veils Rodríguez's punning on this word with a minor classical myth. According to one version of the myth, Linos (Λινος) or Linus was the son of Apollo and Psamathe, daughter of Crotopos, king of Argos.[28] Fearing her father's wrath, Psamathe abandoned her son, who was raised by shepherds, only to be torn to pieces by dogs before he was full-grown.[29] According to Edith Hamilton, "This Linus was, like Adonis and Hyacinthus, a type of all lovely young life that dies or is withered before it has born fruit. The Greek word *ailinon!*, meaning 'woe for Linus!' grew to mean no more than the English 'alas!' and was used in any lament."[30]

Other aspects of the myth bring out the metapoetic dimension of the poem. Linus's father, Apollo (whose priests wore linen robes—and linen, of course, is made from flax), was the patron of music.[31] "The very name of Linus," Charles Gayley affirms, "is taken from the refrain *ai-linon* or 'woe is me,' of the lament anciently sung by country people . . . ," while H. J. Rose asserts that αι-Λινον or αι Λινον derives from "a very old traditional song of harvesters and vintagers."[32] Drawing from several sources and proffering the most complete account of the different versions of this myth, Robert Graves says that

> Linus seems to have been the spirit of the flax-plant (*linos*), sown in spring and harvested in summer. . . . Since the flax-harvest was the occasion of plaintive dirges and rhythmic pounding [to macerate the flax-stems], and since at midsummer . . . young people leaped around a bonfire to make the flax grow high, another mystical Linus was presumed: one who attained manhood and became a famous musician, the inventor of rhythm and melody.[33]

While referring to a workers' song, the title of Rodríguez's poem adopts self-referential dimensions because of the prominence of song and rhythm in the myth. In addition to being a hymn of praise and thanks for fertility and abundance (a figurative meaning of "cantar" is "celebrar, alabar"), this song entails a lament, reprising the gain/loss motif in yet another variation. Leaving for the fields also metaphorizes the speaker's separation from others.

The pun in the title widens the gap between appearance and reality. Indeed, the opening verses of "El canto de linos" situate the speaker between two extremes (the alazonic and the humble) and show him wavering between them, a conflict that pervades the poem.

> Por mucho que haga sol no seréis puros
> y ya no hay tiempo. Apenas
> se mueve el aire y con la luz del día,
> aún lejana en los cerros, se abre el campo
> 5   y se levanta a su labor el hombre.
> Y ved: la hora mejor. ¿Y qué ha pasado
> para que hoy en plena sazón sólo
> nos acordemos de la siembra aquella,
> de aquel trillar, de aquellos laboreos?
> 10   ¡Si la cosecha no es más que el principio!
>
> (p. 76)[34]

The sun as symbol of purification recalls Apollo and the scene around the bonfire in Graves's version of the myth, a solar ritual found in many cultures. Associated with fire, the sun can connote life, spiritual energy, fecundity, transformation, and regeneration. But fire is an ambivalent symbol because it destroys to regenerate and produce fecundity, whereas the sun's rising and setting describes a circadian alternation between light and dark.[35] The connotations of the sun and fire reinforce the duality of the pun and the tension between the representational and symbolic, while circadian and seasonal rhythms refer to the poet's ambivalent attitude toward his cultural heritage. The image of the sun embodies the gain/loss motif.

Still more intertextual allusions are at play here. This line echoes the opening of poem VIII from "Libro primero" of *Don:* "No porque llueva seré digno" (p. 39). In combination, these verses recall the passage in Matthew in which Christ urges his followers to turn the other cheek and to love their enemies "para que seáis hijos de vuestro Padre . . . que hace salir su sol sobre malos y buenos, y que hace llover sobre justos e injustos" (5:45). Along with the similarity and difference between light and rain and the distinction between good and bad, just and unjust, the biblical intertext introduces the figure of Christ (often associated with the sun), and this intertextual play—moving from one text to another—reflects the different levels in the poem.[36] The figure of Christ overlays that of Linus just as Linus overlays the agricultural code in the pun on "linos."[37] Just as "linos" joins and separates the mimetic and the mythic, this allusion defines a similarity between Linus and Christ but also differentiates them. Linus becomes an intermediary figure between two extremes—the agricultural imagery on the one hand and Christ on the other, the mimetic and symbolic levels of the poem—opening the gap between appearance and reality. The speaker identifies with Linus and sees himself as superior to his fellow workers but inferior to the ideal represented by Christ. These fellow workers could be other poets (past and present), while his ideal could be a superior poet (one he especially admires) or a goal he has envisioned for himself but not yet attained.[38]

Throughout the poem, the speaker vacillates between these two extremes. In vv. 2–6, he paints a rosy picture of the ideal. Because of the metapoetic dimension, the images of air and light connote inspiration, while the mountain represents aspiration and transcendence.[39] The question in vv. 6–9 undercuts this view. The perfect tense, the act of remembering, and the demonstrative adjectives show the speaker detained by the past rather than striving toward the future; the interrogative and the subjunctive express confusion and doubt. Another contrast is the shift from "vosotros" to "nosotros." The former suggests that the speaker sets himself apart from the others and that he has a superior perspective in comparison with them. Caught between two extremes, however, he includes himself with his fellows when he realizes that he shares a sense of failure with them.

The tenth verse recapitulates the speaker's ambivalence. We can read this exclamation as an expression of despair at not having attained his ideal or of enthusiastic exhortation to strive toward it. The ambivalence between despair and aspiration replicates the duality in the pun and in the pivotal figure of Linus, deepening the gap between appearance and reality. Intertextual allusions in the ensuing verses develop the interaction between the representational and the symbolic embodied in the figure of Linus and alter our reading of even the most mimetic passages.

> ¡Fuera la hoz, sí, fuera
> el corto abrazo del apero aun cuando

toda la tierra sea esperanza! Siempre,
como el buen labrador que cada año
15   ve alto su trigo y cree
que lo granó tan sólo su trabajo,
siempre salimos a esperar el día
con la faena a cuestas, y ponemos
la vida, el pecho al aire y un momento
20   somos al aire puros. Pero sólo
por un momento. . . .

(p. 76)[40]

On one level, the phrase "¡Fuera la hoz . . . !" sounds logical because flax-plants
are pulled out by the roots instead of cut with scythes or sickles when harvested. As a
command, it captures the poet's rejection of the tradition in favor of originality. If, on
the other hand, we read this phrase elliptically, "fuera" as the imperfect subjunctive of
"ser" becomes a plea: The poet wishes to reap the harvest of the past to guarantee his
reputation and garner a place for himself in the tradition. The words "la hoz," "el
corto abrazo," and "siempre" recall the first poem of *Don* whose final verses are
based on another biblical intertext (John 12:24).[41] The speaker again reveals his ambivalence in the intertextual allusion to the sower in Mark 4:26–29, the "Parábola del
crecimiento de la semilla."[42] The description of "el buen labrador" and the use of the
sickle to harvest wheat contrast with the flax-harvesters, whose transcendent experience is briefer and less certain: "y un momento / somos al aire puros. Pero sólo / por
un momento." The speaker's position is ambivalent. He has rejected one perspective
but not yet attained the other. Has he drawn nearer his ideal, or does he acutely sense
his distance from it?

The reappearance of the "vosotros"-form of the verb bolsters that contrast: "Oíd
desde aquí: ¿qué hondo / trajín eterno mueve nuestras manos, / cava con nuestra
azada, / limpia las madres para nuestro riego?" (vv. 21–24) [Listen from here: what
deep / eternal commotion moves our hands, / digs with our hoe, / clears the ditches for
our irrigation?]. The adjectives "hondo" and "eterno" point to the symbolic plane of
meaning, so that even the commonplace activity of hoeing suggests a loosening, stir-
ring, and freeing of what had been compacted, settled, and restricted, whereas clearing the ditches of obstruction and irrigating imply a release of creative energies and
fertilization. Nor should we overlook the erotic overtones of these verses, which augment the sense of fulfillment and transcendence. Once again, however, the interrogative undermines the speaker's enthusiasm. An abundance of intertextual allusions in
the final verses unite the speaker with the tradition, though it is unclear whether this
union is triumph or failure.

25   Todo es sagrado ya y hasta parece
sencillo prosperar en esta tierra,
cargar los carros con el mismo heno
de juventud, llevarlo
por aquel mismo puente. Pero, ¿dónde,
30   en qué inmenso pajar cabrán los pastos

del hombre, aquellas parvas
que puede que estén frescas todavía?
¿Dónde, dónde? . . .

. . . .
¿Dónde el tordo que salía
40   de allí con la humildad del vuelo abierta
como si aún pudiera volver siempre?
No volverá. Bien sé lo que he perdido.

(pp. 76–77)[43]

Intertextualities lend significance to seemingly innocuous words, as in the case
of the interrogative "¿dónde?" Through emphatic repetition, this word evokes the
classical theme of *ubi sunt?* The speaker may be expressing his despair at the loss of
something difficult to attain again (his inspiration or the originality of former poets)
or his continuous enthusiastic search for the ideal. And of course "¿dónde?" reminds
us of the pun in the title of *Don.* Another instance of this interrogative in vv. 39–41
evokes the Old Testament story of Noah, the destruction of the world by the floods,
and its rebirth and regeneration thereafter (cf. the image of fire as destruction and
regeneration). Instead of a dove, the speaker here mentions a thrush, a songbird, sustaining the metapoetic dimension.

We must again wonder if the speaker laments something lost or rejoices in the
new when he asserts, "No volverá. Bien sé lo que he perdido." The first half of this
verse evokes Bécquer's Rima LIII. Bécquer holds a unique place in Spanish literary
history, for while many consider him the culmination of the Romantic period, others
acknowledge him as the first modern poet in Spain, making him a pivotal figure similar to Linus and the speaker of this poem.[44] By repeating this well-known refrain, the
speaker may be signaling its originality and powerful effect; but he also parodies it
and makes his relationship with Bécquer ambivalent. Does he admire Bécquer or
disdain him? Does he place himself in the same category as Bécquer or supplant him?
The phrase "Bien sé lo que he perdido" repeats the duality: Does he blithely dismiss
an unimportant loss, or does he realize the full extent of a serious loss and regret it? Is
this revival of the gain/loss motif alazonic or serious? More intertextuality and the
ambiguous pronoun "tú" culminate this ambivalence in the final verses.

Tú antes,
tú, el elegido por las estaciones,
35   el de la gran labranza, ven conmigo.
Enséñame a sembrar en el sentido
del viento. . . .

. . . .
Pero tú baila, triunfa tú, que puedes.
No lo digamos. No, que nadie sepa
45   lo que ha pasado esta mañana. Vamos
juntos. No digas más que tu cosecha,
aunque esté en tu corral, al pie de casa,
no será tuya nunca.

(p. 77)[45]

The person addressed in vv. 33–37 would seem to be the ideal, but doubt still exists as to the speaker's tone. The imperatives could express his excitement and exaltation because he has reached a certain level of accomplishment or his anguish and pleading as he realizes his distance from the ideal. The identity of the referent changes in the final verses (43–48). This "tú" could be one of the "vosotros" addressed at the beginning of the poem, but we do not know if the speaker praises or chides that person. Has the other attained a privileged perspective on life, or is he still naive? Is the speaker inferior or superior to the other? Is he alazonic or sincere?[46]

Intertextual allusions to the Book of Ecclesiastes in the final verses sustain the ambivalence of the poem. The speaker of "El canto de linos" can identify with the speaker in Ecclesiastes who sees all as "vanity of vanities; all is vanity. What profit hath a man from all the labour which he taketh under the sun?" (1:2–3).[47] Looking at his poem and his attempt to be original, to distinguish himself from the poetic tradition, the speaker could lament, "The thing that hath been, it is that which shall be; and that which is done is that which shall be done; and there is no new thing under the sun" (1:9). But we can just as easily see that the speaker has joined the tradition and will become the source of future poets' inspiration, meaning that he has attained transcendence even though it has been based on previous poems. Indeed, the book of Ecclesiastes entails that very conclusion.[48] Again the speaker—like Linus—wavers between one perspective and the other.

Another possibility is that the "tú" addressed at the end of the poem is a "desdoblamiento" (doubling) of the speaker himself and as such provides another variant of the central duality. The poet may feel despair because upon finishing the poem, it ceases to be his; it becomes part of the poetic tradition and the domain of the reader. In this regard, the final verse echoes another passage in Ecclesiastes: "Yea, I hated all my labor which I had taken under the sun: because I should leave it unto the man that shall be after me. And who knoweth whether he shall be a wise man or a fool?" (2:18-19). On the other hand, because his poem does form part of the tradition, every time a reader reads it, the poet resuscitates. His act of writing repeats and renews itself in the next poet's intertextual resurrection of his poem or in the reader's actualization of it. We can read this final statement as the speaker's embittered, disillusioned defeat because of the misappropriation of his labor, or as his altruistic surrendering of the poem, his words, and therefore himself.

After placing so much emphasis on the title, I would be remiss if I did not address a remark to the poem's subtitle, "Salida a la labranza" [Leaving for work], which in one sense iterates the title's effect, but in another bridges the gap between title and poem. The word "labranza" can refer to farmland (the field where agricultural activity takes place, i.e., the poem) or to the act of tilling (writing or reading).[49] This intermediate position coincides with the figure of Linus, reflects the poet's ambivalent relation to his cultural heritage, and opens a gap in *Conjuros* between the alazonic and the sincere, the representational and the symbolic, the transient and the transcendent. If not for the pun in the title and the cultural code, many of these aspects might remain submerged in the mimesis of the text.

Another pun in "Al ruido del Duero" [To the noise of the Duero] deepens our awareness of the gap. This poem opens with an alazonic rejection of the past and the speaker's attempt to leave it behind. The apt placement of the war imagery in these verses attests to the importance of the cultural code in determining a conflict in the speaker and begins to show us the ironic reversal to which alazony leads by widening the gap between appearance and reality.

> Y como yo veía
> que era tan popular entre las calles
> pasé el puente y, adiós, dejé atrás todo.
> Pero hasta aquí me llega, quitádmelo, estoy siempre
> 5   oyendo el ruido aquel y subo y subo,
> ando de pueblo en pueblo, pongo el oído
> al vuelo del pardal, al sol, al aire,
> yo que sé, al cielo, al pecho de las mozas
> y siempre el mismo son, igual mudanza.
> 10   ¿Qué sitio éste sin tregua? ¿Qué altas lides
> entran a saco en mi alma a todas horas,
> rinden la torre de la enseña blanca,
> abren aquel portillo, el silencioso,
> el nunca falso? Y eres
> 15   tú, música del río, aliento mío hondo,
> llaneza y voz y pulso de mis hombres.

(p. 81)[50]

The first three verses relate the speaker's deliberate withdrawal from his former lifestyle and the beginning of a new but still undefined perspective on life. But what does he mean when he says he left everything behind *because* he was popular? Was he truly popular, or did he see a need for change? His tone is smug, but if the river represents his cultural heritage, he quickly realizes that it is impossible to escape from it. His excitement intensifies in vv. 4–9 because of the repetitions, the implications of the verb "subir," the string of images, the colloquial interjection "yo que sé" [*sic*], and the paradoxical phrase "igual mudanza." But in spite of the distance he has placed between himself and his past, the sound of the river still accompanies him.

The introduction of the war imagery in v. 10 heightens the conflict but has ironic consequences. This imagery calls to mind the many invasions Spain has undergone throughout its history (which have added so much to its culture) and reflects the speaker's realization that the Duero represents an intrinsic part of his being and a pervasive force in his life. He recognizes the lasting values inherent in the river and acknowledges it as a perennial source of fertility, life, and inspiration by comparing it with "música," "aliento," "voz," and "pulso." The war imagery is used paradoxically because it describes an enriching revelation instead of destruction. The elation caused by this realization (reminiscent of a mystical experience) and the spate of positive images tend to carry us on a wave of high spirits to the end of the poem. But upon reaching the last word, we are obliged to recognize that the sound of the river also accosts the speaker and to reevaluate the poem because of an unsettling effect produced by a pun.

Cuánto mejor sería
esperar. Hoy no puedo, hoy estoy duro
de oído tras los años que he pasado
20   con los de mala tierra. Pero he vuelto.
Campo de la verdad, ¿qué traición hubo?
¡Oíd cómo tanto tiempo y tanta empresa
hacen un solo ruido!
¡Oíd cómo hemos tenido día tras día
25   tanta pureza al lado nuestro, en casa,
y hemos seguido sordos!
¡Ya ni esta tarde más! Sé bienvenida,
mañana. Pronto estoy: ¡Sedme testigos
los que aún oís! Oh, río
30   fundador de ciudades,
sonando en todo menos en tu lecho,
haz que tu ruido sea nuestro canto,
nuestro taller en vida. Y si algún día
la soledad, el ver al hombre en venta,
35   el vino, el mal amor o el desaliento
asaltan lo que bien has hecho tuyo,
ponte como hoy en pie de guerra, guarda
todas mis puertas y ventanas como
tú has hecho desde siempre,
40   tú, a quien estoy oyendo igual que entonces,
tú, río de mi tierra, tú, río Duradero.

(pp. 81–82)[51]

    The pun in the word "Duradero" jogs our sensibilities and signals that there are two perspectives at cross-purposes in the symbol of the river. The abrupt run-on line in vv. 17–18 emphasizes a bifurcation created by the war imagery and presents a sharp contrast with the alazony of the first declaration ("pasé el puente y, adiós, dejé atrás todo"). Beginning with v. 17, we realize that nearly every statement the speaker makes is equivocal, capable of rendering two distinct interpretations—one maintaining the elation of the speaker's discovery of the pervasive force of the river and the other regretting it.

    Reprises of the war imagery scattered through the second part of the poem alter the tenor of that imagery and generate the conflicting perspective. Once again, Rodríguez draws upon the history of Spain by alluding to the Duero as the Christians' natural line of defense during the Moorish occupation. First, there is an oblique reference to the betrayal of Spain by Count Julian ("Campo de la verdad, ¿qué traición hubo?"). A few verses below, the speaker lauds the river as a "fundador de ciudades," that is, as a source of civilization and stability in contrast with the invading nomadic hoard. Moreover, the river is personified as a warrior who acts as a defender rather than an aggressor: "ponte como hoy en pie de guerra, guarda / todas mis puertas y ventanas." In short, the speaker now characterizes the river differently because of a subtle change in his outlook. Although he sees the river as an integral, inescapable part of himself, he ironically personifies it and addresses it directly, externalizing it and pushing it away from him.

Because the image of the river is converted into a dual sign, the speaker's alazony and the discrepancy between appearance and reality comes to the fore.[52] Whereas in the first part of the poem the river signifies fertility, the continuation of life, and the transcendent perspective gained through the creative act, in the second part, "it stands for the irreversible passage of time and, in consequence, for a sense of loss and oblivion."[53] This contrast is borne out by the adverbial time phrases of the text. The adverb "siempre" appears twice in the first 16 verses, whereas a plethora of temporal phrases appears thereafter: "hoy," "los años," "tanto tiempo," "día tras día," "esta tarde," "mañana," "pronto," "algún día," "desde siempre," and "entonces." Irony arises because on the one hand the tenor connoting invasion (negatively marked) leads to an enriching discovery; on the other hand, the tenor connoting defense and order (positively marked) causes disillusionment. The river as cultural heritage received from the past defines the poet-speaker and threatens to drown him.

It is important to stress that both readings defined here coexist on an equal footing, with neither dominating or supplanting the other. Hence, this poem defines the bifurcation of the speaker's perspective and widens the gap between appearance and reality by joining two conflicting perspectives in the dual sign of the river. The final pun may be the speaker's attempt to bring these two conflicting viewpoints into harmony or to gloss over the friction caused by the ironic outcome of his percipience; but it has an ambivalent effect. The war imagery, underscored by the pun, intensifies the conflict between these two perspectives and exposes the text's duality. The alazonic tone at the beginning of the poem again separates us from the speaker so that we can appreciate the process that will lead to these ironic discoveries through participation in the creative act.

The bifurcation evident in "Al ruido del Duero" carries over into "A mi ropa tendida" [To my clothes spread out to dry], the last poem of "Libro primero." Here the speaker's alazonic attitude stands out in sharp, uncomfortable relief, revealing the falseness of his stance because of the gap between appearance and reality and setting the speaker—and the reader—up for an ironic reversal in "Libro segundo." Debicki has provided a cogent reading of this text, such that a discussion of the poem in its entirety is not warranted here.[54] Nonetheless, he raises some questions that can be illuminated by taking the cultural code and alazony into account.

"A mi ropa tendida" derives from the rural custom (still observable in many countries) of spreading clothes on the ground, on shrubs, or on tree limbs so that they will dry in the sun.[55] Debicki states that the text "juggles two language patterns or codes [one representational and the other symbolic], forming two simultaneous levels and two perspectives which do not fit very well with each other" (p. 43).[56] Rodríguez accomplishes this "juggling act" by juxtaposing the subtitle "El alma" with the title and by using ambivalent referents (adjectives and pronouns) that allude equally to "alma" as to "ropa," words with two meanings (one literal and the other figurative), and catachrestic contrasts (e.g., the "lejía inmortal" that Debicki finds so amusing), so as to effect a general defamiliarization of a commonplace event.[57] Yet, the images at the end of the first stanza are puzzling because they constitute an ungrammaticality that at first appears to be illogical and "threaten[s] the literary representation of reality, or mimesis."[58]

¡No tendedla en el patio: ahí, en la cima,
ropa pisada por el sol y el gallo,
por el rey siempre!

(p. 83)[59]

In an attempt to come to grips with this ungrammaticality, Debicki asserts that, "To be stepped on by a rooster would not contribute to the literal or the figurative cleanliness of the clothes, and the image can only startle us, and may suggest a self-parody."[60] Although these images may perplex us at first, the ungrammaticality gives a clear indication that the cultural code is working semiotically beneath the mimetic surface of the text. These images "function as buoys marking the positions of sunken meaning" that must be discovered in another context—in this case, the cultural code.[61] First of all, an expansion of the subcode of religion established in the subtitle is evident in the dual signs "el sol," "el gallo," and "el rey," for all three are associated with Christ. J. E. Cirlot explains the significance of the sun and the rooster.

> As the bird of dawn, the cock is a sun-symbol, and an emblem of vigilance and activity. Immolated to Priapus and Aesculapius, it was supposed to cure the sick. During the Middle Ages it became a highly important Christian image, nearly always appearing on the highest weathervane, on cathedral towers and domes, and was regarded as an allegory of vigilance and resurrection. Davy comments that a vigilance in this context must be taken in the sense of "tending towards eternity and taking care to grant first place to the things of the spirit, to be wakeful and to greet the Sun—Christ—even before it rises in the East"—illumination.[62]

In addition to the religious subcode, the idiomatic expressions "limpio como el sol" and "el rey es mi gallo" contribute to the significance of these verses as part of the linguistic subcode. The first expression sustains the theme of purification, whiteness, and cleanliness—also invested with religious connotations—found in the first part of the text. Martín de Riquer defines the latter expression as a "frase con que se daba a entender el favorito de uno en una contienda de gallos o de cualquier género."[63] The verb "pisar" also has dual meaning. Figuratively, "pisar" signifies "to humble," a meaning that dovetails with the secondary meaning of "refregar" (v. 1) and "jabonadura" (v. 9), both connoting reproof. For the speaker to have altered the unsatisfying state of his life has been an ordeal, but he has finally attained a new insight ("illumination") and can make a new beginning. This fresh perspective can be attributed to the creative act and the transcendent values found in art.

Thanks to the interweaving of meanings produced by the cultural code at this nodal point, the ungrammaticality is no longer enigmatic because "there is another text in which the word is grammatical; the moment the other text is identified, the dual sign becomes significant."[64] The cultural code has resolved the incongruity of these verses without destroying the interplay between the representational and symbolic levels, but rather by condensing and concentrating it so as to augment its effectiveness. The cultural code focalizes the speaker's discovery of his new perspective, and as a result, the impact of these verses is intensified.

Despite this metaphoric tour de force, the disparity between the two levels—a technique Rodríguez may have learned from medieval authors—makes their juxtaposition unsettling.[65] The cultural code brings these two levels together but also creates friction between them, in accord with Rodríguez's transgressive poetics. Let us consider, then, that Rodríguez has purposefully exaggerated this comparison ("My soul is like my freshly-laundered clothing") to call attention to the boastful, overconfident speaker. It is as if he were saying, "Look at this! Watch what I can do with language! I am going to mesmerize you, cast a magic spell on you!" The tone is clearly alazonic (Debicki calls it self-parody), again distancing us from the speaker just as his command "¡Dejad de respirar!" did in "A la respiración en la llanura." Even the colloquial "¡No tendedla!" unites the positive and the negative; indeed, all the techniques described (ambivalent adjectives and pronouns, verbs with two meanings, catachresis, the cultural code) have united and created an abrasive catachresis of the two levels, marking a wide gap between appearance and reality.[66] It is our task to reconstruct our reading of the poem in harmony with what we infer about the implied author's position (cf. Booth).

The speaker seems to step back from his alazonic stance at the beginning of the second stanza, but even so he calls attention to himself, forcing us to recognize him as the boastful alazon.

> He dicho así a media alba
> 20 porque de nuevo la hallo,
> de nuevo al aire libre sana y salva.
> Fue en el río, seguro, en aquel río
> donde se lava todo, bajo el puente.
> Huele a la misma agua, a cuerpo mío.
> 25 ¡Y ya sin mancha! ¡Si hay algún valiente,
> que se la ponga! Sé que le ahogaría.
>
> (p. 83)[67]

In addition to the "reto" (challenge) that Debicki so keenly discerns, the ludic play in the string of idiomatic expressions "de nuevo al aire libre sana y salva," the deliberate reference to the river and the bridge recalling the ambivalent experience in "Al ruido del Duero," the shirt smelling of river water and perspiration instead of fresh air, and the pun on "ahogaría" (!) distance us from this boastful, alazonic speaker and compel us to read ironically. This tone continues in the final verses, again abetted by the cultural code.

> Bien sé que al pie del corazón no es blanca
> pero no importa: un día . . .
> ¡Qué un día, hoy, mañana que es la fiesta!
> 30 Mañana todo el pueblo por las calles
> y la conocerán, y dirán, «Esta
> es su camisa, aquella, la que era
> sólo un remiendo y ya no le servía.
> ¿Qué es este amor? ¿Quién es su lavandera?»
>
> (p. 83)[68]

Three words belonging to the cultural code stand out here. The familiar custom of drinking wine from a "bota" (wineskin) comes to mind when the speaker specifically mentions his shirt in connection with the local "fiesta."[69] This indirect reference to staining his shirt with wine links the speaker's former state of being with drunkenness. He suggests that his way of life was a result of intemperance and a surrender to sensual vices, a lifestyle remedied by the change described in the first part of the poem. Intertextual references reinforce the contrast between these two states of being. The allusion to wine recalls *Don* and the ambivalence of drunkenness, which both heightens and dulls consciousness, unites the drinker with his friends and alienates him from others, a concept that emerges in *Conjuros* in the motif of separation (see especially "Con media azumbre de vino," the sixth poem of "Libro primero"). Wine, as well as being a traditional staple of life, also forms part of the religious subcode because of its use in the Catholic Mass. Hence, the oblique reference to wine in the words "fiesta" and "camisa" promotes the interplay between the mundane and the spiritual, the mimetic and the symbolic.

Finally, the "lavandera" is a traditional figure in Spanish literature, one that usually conveys sexual overtones. Chevalier and Gheerbrandt make these observations about washerwomen:

> La lavandera es . . . una mujer de baja casta. El tantrismo ha hecho de la lavandera un símbolo importante, por una parte al asociar la pertenencia a una casta inferior a la deprivación sexual juzgada como necesaria—símbolicamente o no—para la ejecución de ciertos ritos. . . . La unión del sabio y la lavandera, exaltada por los textos, figura así como una *coincidentia oppositorum*, una alianza de los extremos, una verdadera operación alquímica. La paradoja es por tanto más que aparente, si la lavandera se asocia a la sabiduría y si su danza simboliza la ascensión [del sabio].[70]

The image of the "lavandera" sustains the interplay between the mundane and the spiritual, the transient and the transcendent, in this "alianza de los extremos, una verdadera operación alquímica." But in the final analysis, the speaker's alazonic tone belies and ridicules a serious interpretation of these images. We can envision him strutting like a peacock through the streets wearing an old shirt that everybody recognizes and that isn't really clean "al pie del corazón," and yet everyone wants to know who his laundress is![71] In its catachrestic juxtaposition of the soul and freshly washed clothes, "A mi ropa tendida" caps "Libro primero" by again depicting the alazonic speaker and the gap between appearance and reality that has become more pronounced as we have read through these nine poems. The alazony and this gap point to Rodríguez's transgression of the limits of language through irony. The exaggeration of this stance has been necessary to set up the ironic reversals and a more profound exploration of self that still await him and us in the subsequent sections of *Conjuros*. For as Booth remarks, "nothing undercuts the sense of *importance* of the quest, of *honesty* in unmasking error and facing the truth, of *courage* in facing the horror. Though everything else may be ironized, the nobility of the quest is not."[72]

PERIPETEIA: THE COMPLICATION OF THE IRONIC IN "LIBRO SEGUNDO"

Whereas at the beginning of *Conjuros* the poet-speaker feels exceedingly confident in his ability to cast poetic spells, the second stage in his progress presents a humbling experience in sharp contrast with the self-assured boasting of the alazon. In "Libro primero," his supercilious attitude leads to a change in his perspective caused by his desire to separate himself from others, the widening of the gap between appearance and reality. The radical position he reaches in "A mi ropa tendida" is predicated by his resistance to the introspection demanded by the poetic act, a requisite he discovers as he progresses through "Libro primero." At the beginning of "Libro segundo," he pulls back from the alazonic stance, leading him to despair and to conclude that he is unworthy of the task before him. The irony of "Libro primero" is thus compounded by a peripeteia, a reversal and complication of the ironic in "Libro segundo" where his resistance to introspection breaks down his defenses more rapidly. If at the beginning of "Libro primero" the poet declares, "Die so that you can live more intensely," in "Libro segundo" he comprehends that "Darkness is a light that reveals a fault, but that fault is really a strength." If pride comes before the fall, "Libro primero" depicts the erosion of the pride and "Libro segundo" the fall. The eight poems of this section accelerate and intensify the process begun in the first part of *Conjuros*.

"A una viga de mesón" [To the roofbeam of an inn], the first poem of this section, evinces a subtle dialogic tension between enthusiasm and despair. The poet's special vision reveals hidden meaning to him, although that revelation also has a humbling effect. Although the poem obviously centers on a tangible everyday reality, biblical intertextuality and the cultural code again point to an abstract level, as we see in the opening verses.

> ¡Si veo las estrellas, si esta viga
> deja pasar la luz y no sostiene
> ya ni la casa! Viga
> de par en par al resplandor que viene
> 5 y a la dura faena
> del hombre, que ha metido
> tantos sueños bajo ella, tanta buena
> esperanza. Así, así. ¡No haber sentido
> humo de la ciudad ni mano de obra!
> 10 Siempre así. . . .

(p. 87)[73]

At first reading, we might believe that the speaker is ecstatic. His poetic vision allows him to see the stars (an archetypal image of insight) via the solid, sturdy, and architecturally essential beam of the inn where he passes the night. The underlying allusion to Matt. 7:3–5 undercuts this enthusiasm because the beam illuminates a flaw, a limitation.[74] What appeared to sustain and invigorate the speaker has the ironic effect of destabilizing and unsettling him. Instead of sheltering and protecting, the beam makes him vulnerable, causing him to lament "¡. . . no sostiene / ya ni la casa!" Though the speaker "ha metido / tantos sueños bajo ella, tanta buena esperanza," he now despairs to find that his dreams and hopes are in danger of being exposed, vulnerable. The simplicity and natural beauty of the beam, uncontaminated by the city's smog, unadorned by the craftsmanship of an artisan, is that which defines its essence but imposes limitations on it. The repetition of the neutrally punctuated "Así, así . . . Siempre así" indicates the speaker's grateful welcoming and his reluctant admission of this symbol of himself and his cultural heritage. His insight has allowed him to see the beam in his own eye, requiring him to admit his shortcomings. Another biblical allusion later in the poem produces a similarly subversive effect:

> . . . ¡Contrafuerte
> del cielo, alero inmenso, viga que era
> hace sólo un momento un tronco inerte,
> sé tú, sé la techumbre
> para todos los hombres algún día!
>
> (p. 87)[75]

The architectural imagery of the "contrafuerte" and the "alero" is ambivalent. The beam should protect the speaker from the overpowering insights represented by the sky and the stars, but it has had the opposite effect. When the speaker says "¡sé tú, sé la techumbre / para todos los hombres algún día!" protection is ironically transposed into vulnerability. Just as the mustard seed, the smallest of seeds, grows into the largest of trees (see Matt. 13:31–32, Mark 4:31–32, Luke 13:19), so the speaker hopes that this beam, "que era hace sólo un momento un tronco inerte," will provide insight for all readers of poetry, though he recognizes the difficulty involved in the acquisition of that perspective. Far from desiring social solidarity "para todos los hombres," the speaker advocates individuality through intense introspection. People will share that process, but it will make them all the more individual. Hence the speaker accepts the challenge proffered by this beam:

> Comienza a clarear. Como a una cumbre
> la estoy mirando. ¡Oíd: se me caería
> 25   encima, se me caería hasta que fuera
> digno de estar bajo ella y no me iría
> de aquí! . . .
>
> (pp. 87–88)[76]

Though he expresses his determination to persist in his quest, he nonetheless doubts his worthiness to participate in it. Once again his closing question expresses hope embedded in despair, an ironic reversal of the beginning of the poem.

> . . . Pero, ¿alguien puede, alguien espera
> ser digno, alzar su amor en su trabajo,

su cobijo en su suelo,
30   su techo en la carcoma de aquí abajo
en la que tiembla ya un nido del cielo?

(pp. 88)[77]

In these images of shelter, the biblical passage about building one's house on rock or on sand (Matt. 7:24–27) undergoes a ironic reversal.[78] Instead of representing weakness ("la carcoma de aquí abajo"), the recognition of weakness will be a strength, the transient will become the transcendent, just as the nest, a crude, fragile structure (the transient), pertains to the sky (the transcendent). The beam in the speaker's eye does indeed reveal his fault, but he also perceives the discovery of this fault as a potential strength. "A una viga de mesón" displays the ironic reversal of an ironic discovery. This dual irony is manifest in all the poems of this section, and each advances the speaker's progress by intensifying the impact of this ironic reversal.

By addressing the swallows in "A las golondrinas" [To the swallows], the speaker attempts to distance himself from the effect they have on him, that of reminding him of his failure to transcend his mundane surroundings and the passage of time. The speaker loses patience with these birds (a commonplace of Castilian life), for they are capable of flight and yet fly low, close to the earth—an ironic situation. His direct address of the swallows distances them only to have them pierce his sensibilities more acutely as he realizes that he can transcend time only if he acknowledges it. This situation reminds him of his experience in *Don* and enables him to discover something positive in this unpleasant encounter. Even though figuratively he feels distant from them (they can fly, he cannot), literally they are too close for comfort in the opening verses.

¿Y me rozáis la frente,
y entráis por los solares igual que por el cielo
y hacéis el nido aquí ruidosamente,
entre los hombres? Qué sed tendrá el vuelo
5   de tierra. Más, más alto. ¡Que no os sienta
este cuerpo, que no oigan nada puro
estos ruidos! Cuándo os daréis cuenta
del sol, de que ese muro
busca vuestro calor. ¡Acribilladlo
10   ahora, metedle el pecho hasta lo hondo
como al barro del nido; abandonadlo
si no! Oh, más, más alto. . . .

(p. 89)[79]

The speaker's tone is sarcastic, even angry. To him the swallows seem ignorant on two counts: They not only miss an opportunity to soar through the sunlight; they are also ignorant of the threat posed by the wall (symbol of earth and death). He cannot comprehend why they should want to stay so close to the earth and human endeavors. Consequently, he vehemently urges them to fly higher: "Qué sed tendrá el vuelo / de tierra. Más, más alto." The speaker becomes so irritated with the swallows that he wishes to hide and protect himself from them, indicating that they are affecting him more profoundly than is comfortable for him.

> . . . ¿Dónde, dónde me escondo?
> ¿Aquí, en pleno chillido, en plena tarde
> de junio, en mi ciudad? Y cuántas veces
> 15   con este cielo a cuestas que tanto arde
> os vi entrar en lo humilde, cuántas veces
> quise alejarme con vosotras. Ahora
> es bien distinto. ¡Idos! ¿Por qué hoy no hay nada que huya?
> ¿Qué estáis buscando aún si el hombre ignora
> 20   que vivís junto a él y a la obra suya
> dais vuestra azul tarea
> beneficiando su labor, su grano
> y sus cosechas? . . .
>
> (p. 89)[80]

The large number of questions and the changes in mood epitomized in the flare-up of the command "¡Idos!" distance the speaker from the swallows and show that they have touched a sore spot in him. The question of vv. 19–23 provides insight into this problem. Similar to the swallows whose contributions are ignored by the humans among whom they dwell, the speaker feels that his poetic efforts go unappreciated. Yet he also recognizes the beneficial contributions of the swallows. The adjective "azul" suggests their elevated, ideal nature, and by dwelling among humans, they provide imperceptible blessings on "su labor, su grano / y sus cosechas," agricultural images that describe human endeavors to produce. So the poet enriches the lives of others. This realization leads the speaker ironically to reverse his earlier position and let himself be enriched by this encounter. Now he urges the swallows to come down to the earth and to bestow their blessings on him.

> . . . Mas dejad que sea
> siempre así y aunque no haya luz y en vano
> 25   intentéis sostenerla a fuego abierto,
> seguid, bajad sin desaliento. Ya era
> necesario hacer pie. Cómo despierto
> oyéndoos. ¡Bajad más! . . .
>
> (p. 89)[81]

In closing, the poet laments the futility of his attempt to capture his emotions in language, but he also recognizes that the process is more important than the result and that the attempt is worthwhile even if he fails.

> . . . Si pudiera
> deteneros, posaros aquí, haceros
> 30   blanco puro del aire . . . Si pudiera
> decir qué tardes, qué mañanas mías
> se han ganado . . . Gracias, gracias os doy con la mirada

porque me habéis traído aquellos días,
vosotras, que podéis ir y volver sin perder nada.

(p. 89)[82]

Words and emotions are as elusive as the swallows, as the imperfect subjunctive and the unfinished if-clauses indicate. But the swallows have put the speaker in touch with his aspirations and fears: "me habéis traído aquellos días." This phrase may refer to his first incursion into poetry in *Don* (notice the image "blanco puro"), his enthusiasm, his difficulties, and the way he turned defeat into discovery (especially in "Libro tercero"). The last line of the poem again marks the distance and difference between the speaker and the swallows by reprising the motif of loss/gain, but this verse is extremely ironic. On the one hand, the swallows—symbols of spring and so of eternal return and immortality (the transcendence the poet seeks)—can fly, coming and going without losing anything. They seem unaffected by the passage of time and the transience of life. For that reason, the poet may despair at the contrast they present with him.

But he also discovers that his capacity for loss is a positive rather than a negative attribute. Ironically, it is only through loss that the speaker can gain and only through self-examination and a greater recognition of his weaknesses that he gains more insight, more individuality, and more recognition as a poet (cf. 2 Cor. 12:9–10).[83] The speaker benefits inversely from his encounter with the swallows: They reveal his shortcomings so that he can profit from them, converting weakness and loss into strength and gain. Where at first the speaker saw the swallows as reminders of his failure, his lack of transcendence, they reveal a means of reaching transcendence by lowering (humbling) himself. The presence of these birds has the ironic effect of breaking down his resistance and opening him to self-exploration and examination, a humility the alazonic speaker of "Libro primero" resisted or seemed incapable of assuming.

The ironic consequences of the speaker's self-examination intensify as his distance increases. Humor at the beginning of "Dando una vuelta por mi calle" [Taking a walk down my street] leads to a more insightful recognition of his shortcomings and deepens his insights. This recognition ironically strengthens his resolve to achieve distinction in this process of knowing the self through writing.

Basta, pies callejeros,
no estáis pisando mosto, andad, en marcha.
¿Qué hacéis por esta calle,
aquí, en la calle de mis correrías?
5   Más os valiera andar por otros barrios.
Siempre tan mal guiados,
cómo no íbais a caer. Es trampa,
trampa. ¿Qué cepo es éste?
¿Quién lo amañó tan bien que no hace falta
10   pieza y hoy por la tarde
tanto esta acera como aquel balcón me cazan?

Se abrió la veda para siempre, y siempre,
tras de tres vuelos, la perdiz a tierra.

(p. 93)[84]

The humorous, slightly sarcastic way in which the speaker addresses his feet in
the opening verses calls attention to his anecdotal situation. He has returned to his
childhood haunts, leading him to compare his past with his present, his aspirations
with his accomplishments. Because in Rodríguez's metaphorical semiosis walking is
equivalent to writing and discovering the self through the poetic act, we can see that
the speaker is dissatisfied with his progress in life because he is only "pisando mosto"—
treading already squashed grapes in the process of making wine. He is not moving
forward but merely going around in circles. His humor and his distancing of himself
by displacing responsibility to his feet, "Siempre tan mal guiados," is a defense, an
attempt to evade full recognition of his shortcomings. But this attempt backfires, reversing the detached position the speaker tries to assume.

Repetition of the word "trampa" underscored by the abrupt run-on line marks a
shift from exterior to interior, from anecdotal experience to introspective reflection.
The images of the hunt in vv. 7–13 and the shift from the direct address of his feet
using "vosotros" to the third person verbs underscore this change. The juxtaposition
of a direct address with a more meditative reflection on what he has said and what he
remembers from the past (the structural dynamics of this poem) embodies the duality
now evident in the title. "Dar una vuelta" idiomatically means "to take a walk," connoting a casual, superficial attitude; but it can also literally mean "to turn around,"
figuratively pointing to an ironic reversal in the speaker's progress down the path of
life ("calle" is synonymous with "camino"). This juxtaposition of direct address with
interior reflection intensifies the irony as the speaker converts a negative experience
into a means of knowing himself better. He separates himself from the superficial and
familiar to penetrate his defenses and to know himself better. The more painful and
insightful his probe into himself, the more individual and intense his poetry will be;
thus he will achieve transcendence and distinction.

This poem includes several elements of the cultural code that enrich this process
and contribute to the interaction between the representational and symbolic levels of
this experience. In addition to the images of the "palomar," the "tonel sin fondo /
donde fermenta mi niñez," and the "granero de juventud" (note the catachresis), the
"corro" and the idiomatic language used to describe it stand out.

¡Calle mayor de mi esperanza, suenen
15   en ti los pasos de mi vida, abre
tu palomar y salgan,
salgan al aire libre,
juegue con ellos todo el mundo al corro,
canten sin ton ni son, canten y bailen
20   de tejados arriba! Ved, ved cómo
aquel portal es el tonel sin fondo
donde fermenta mi niñez, y el otro,

siempre lleno de niñas, mi granero
de juventud, y el otro, el otro, el otro . . .

(p. 93)[85]

A typical play activity for Spanish children, the "corro" is a repository for rhythmic, rhymed song and fragments of verse, and represents another source of the oral tradition of popular verse we have already pointed out as forming part of the cultural heritage in *Conjuros*.[86] The circle formed by joining hands symbolizes the way this cultural heritage binds everyone in that society together. But the circle also excludes the speaker, emphasizing his need to draw on that tradition but also to separate himself from it, to individuate. The idiomatic language describing the activity of the "corro" exemplifies this duality. When the speaker urges that the children "canten sin ton ni son," he imitates the rhythm and alliteration of their songs, enriching his poetry; but he also suggests that their words (and his) are nonsense empty of meaning if they are repeated by rote.

His urging "canten y bailen / de tejados arriba" is similarly contradictory. On one level, this expression means "with unrestrained enthusiasm and joy," transgressing any limit or restraint; the *Diccionario de la Real Academia Española* says of this "loc. adv. fam. y fig., según orden sobrenatural, contando con la voluntad de Dios."[87] The metapoetic dimensions of this expression concerning Rodríguez's transgressive poetics are patent: The divinely inspired poet both inscribes a limitation (the rooftops) and transgresses it ecstatically. That act is implicit in his modification of the colloquial "de tejas arriba." Rodríguez has drawn on his linguistic heritage but altered it to reflect his poetics.

A return to the semiosis of walking in the next segment, where the speaker addresses the local mayor, evokes the image of a vagabond. Walking refers to the speaker's lack of direction (going in circles) and waste of time, his lameness and his shortcomings.

25 ¡Alcalde óigame, alcalde,
      que no la asfalten nunca, que no dejen
      pisar por ella más que a los de tierra
      de bien sentado pan y vino moro!
      Perdón, que por la calle va quien quiere
30 y yo no debo hablar así. Qué multa
      me pondrían ahora, a mí el primero,
      si me vieran lo cojo,
      lo maleante que ando desde entonces.
      Alto, alto mis pasos.

(p. 93)[88]

Chevalier and Gheerbrant provide seminal information concerning lameness. If we consider their discussion as a description of the poet-speaker, the meaning of these verses could not be clearer.

Cojear es un signo de debilidad. Equivale también a terminar, para volver a comenzar: es la ausencia de reposo, lo inconcluso, el desequilibrio. En los mitos, leyendas y

cuentos, el héroe cojo acaba un ciclo que puede expresarse por el fin de un viaje y el
anuncio de otro nuevo. El cojo evoca el sol declinante, o también el sol del fin y del
comienzo del año. . . . Cojear, desde el punto de vista simbólico, significa un defecto
espiritual. Semejante defecto no es necesariamente de orden moral; puede designar
una herida de orden espiritual.[89]

As examples of lameness, the same authors cite Hephaistos and Jacob, both of
whom wrestle with a supreme deity. Their lameness is a sign that they have seen a
divine secret, the price they have to pay for the special gift they now possess. "La
claudicación simboliza la marca con el hierro candente de aquellos que se han acercado
al poderío y a la gloria de la divinidad suprema."[90] Again, the painful, humiliating
experience of recognizing his failures has ironic consequences for the speaker as he
becomes even more determined to overcome obstacles and to know himself better.
We can see him "dando una vuelta" in the final lines.

40   Entonces estos años
      qué mal cosido ajuar para la casa,
      qué arras sin brillo para la gran boda.
      Cada piedra me sea como un ascua.
      Los que estáis ahí, al sol, echadme, echadme.
45   Ya volveré yo cuando
      se me acompase el corazón con estos
      pasos a los que invoco,
      a los que estoy oyendo hoy por la tarde
      sonar en esta acera,
50   en este callejón que da a la vida.

                                              (p. 94)[91]

The traditional customs of the "hope chest" and the gift of family heirlooms as a
wedding present form part of the cultural semiosis, just as walking over hot coals
(here the paving stones of his street) pertains to a biblical passage (Prov. 6:28).[92] The
speaker admits his spiritual failings, but these serve to spur him on to improve himself. The footsteps he hears walking down the street refer to his ideal or the precursor
master poet.[93] The word "callejón" echoes the duality of the title. Although this word
signifies a small, narrow street, the augmentative suffix suggests that the narrowest
path leads to the greatest reward (cf. Matt. 7:13–14).[94]

In "Alto jornal" [High wages], Rodríguez draws primarily on biblical allusions
to enrich the poem's significance. The tone of this poem is quite similar to many
psalms where an "experience of reorientation" is celebrated.[95] The poem even opens
with a convention reminiscent of many psalms, but irony appears again when the
speaker's presence finally emerges.[96]

Dichoso el que un buen día sale humilde
y se va por la calle, como tantos
días más de su vida, y no lo espera
y, de pronto, ¿qué es esto?, mira a lo alto
5   y ve, pone el oído al mundo y oye,
anda, y siente subirle entre los pasos

el amor de la tierra, y sigue, y abre
su taller verdadero, y en sus manos
brilla limpio su oficio, y nos lo entrega
10 de corazón porque ama, y va al trabajo
temblando como un niño que comulga
mas sin caber en el pellejo, y cuando se
ha dado cuenta al fin de lo sencillo
que ha sido todo, ya el jornal ganado,
15 vuelve a su casa alegre y siente que alguien
empuña su aldabón, y no es en vano.

(p. 97)[97]

In addition to the similarity with the psalms, several verses echo passages from the New Testament. The word "humilde" in conjunction with the opening phrase is reminiscent of the Beatitudes: "Bienaventurados los mansos, porque ellos recibirán la tierra por heredad" and "Bienaventurados los pobres de espíritu, porque de ellos es el reino en los cielos" (Matt. 5:5 and 5:3, respectively). Both of these describe the poem's hero because he receives "el amor de la tierra" and his work transcends his temporal limitations. The special quality of the transformation of the hero's life is revealed in Matt. 13:13-17, in which Christ quotes Isaiah to justify his use of parables and to point out to the Apostles that they are a chosen group. The hero also belongs to an elite group by reason of his "reorientation." The words "brilla limpio su oficio, y nos lo entrega / de corazón" recall another of the Beatitudes: "Bienaventurados los de limpio corazón, porque ellos verán a Dios" (Matt. 5:8).

Rodríguez also uses idiomatic expressions to characterize the hero's reorientation. The simile of the child who trembles upon receiving Communion maintains the religious reverberations at the same time that it conveys the innocence, awe, and excitement of this moment. The second idiomatic expression, while reinforcing these feelings, adds a note of pride that conflicts with the hero's humility—a contrast reinforced by the word "pellejo," which usually denotes an animal's hide but is often used colloquially to refer to a person's being. The network of meaning implicit in these expressions produces a paradoxical view of the hero and makes manifest the interplay between the representational and the symbolic, the transient and the transcendent.

The irony that emerges in the final lines depends on the cultural code to create two conflicting perspectives—that of the reorientation of the hero and the disorientation of his admirer, the speaker. On the one hand, the hero is portrayed as a successful artisan who has achieved prosperity and respect, characteristics evident in the phrase "con el jornal ganado" and in the word "aldabón." The latter recalls the idiomatic phrase "agarrarse de las aldabas" [to rely on greater protection], but the augmentative suffix amplifies the prosperity (both literal and figurative) the hero now enjoys. The anonymous "alguien" may be the traditional figure of death calling for the hero. However, the climactic moment of reorientation has a lasting effect on the hero's life, so that when death or the thought of death intrudes, the hero is certain that his life has been meaningful and fulfilling ("no es en vano").[98] He feels assured of transcending his temporal limitations and has no preoccupation about the transience of life (see 1 Cor. 15:58).[99]

On the other hand, other passages from the New Testament introduce a contrasting perspective: "Y yo os digo: Pedid, y se os dará; buscad, y hallaréis; llamad, y se os abrirá. Porque todo aquel que pide, recibe; y el que busca, halla; y al que llama, se le abrirá" (Luke 11:9–10). Taking this intertextual reference into consideration, the "alguien" could be an objectivization of the speaker himself, a reading that emphasizes the difference in perspectives, the speaker's distance from the hero, and his anonymity in comparison with the hero (in other words, his disorientation as opposed to the hero's reorientation). This contrast reveals the speaker's failure to reach the state of being attained by the hero—the more surprising because the speaker thought he had reoriented himself (see "A mi ropa tendida"), only to discover his shortcoming in comparison with the hero. The speaker imagines himself calling on the hero in the hope that an appeal to him will not be in vain, that the hero can give him guidance, supply a model for him to emulate, and thereby lead him to the same transcendent perspective. His relation to the hero is ambivalent: On the one hand, he despairs at being so far from his ideal, but on the other, the hero offers him a model toward which to aspire.

Intertextual references and idiomatic expressions enable Rodríguez to achieve many effects in "Alto jornal." First, what appears to be an ordinary workday adopts symbolic proportions and a common laborer is converted into a hero-artisan through biblical allusions. Moreover, the moment of reorientation is made more poignant by the idiomatic expressions. Finally, the contrasts between the hero and his admirer and between their experiences of reorientation and disorientation stand out because of the richness of meaning produced by intertextual allusions. As in so many poems of *Conjuros*, the cultural code figures prominently in "Alto jornal" because it mediates between the representational and symbolic levels and exposes the text's irony in spite of the speaker's distance—or more appropriately, because of it.

The final poem of "Libro segundo," "Lluvia de verano" [Summer rain], is an ironic invocation. Because rain is synonymous with light, it descends precisely in order to "illuminate" the speaker, making him aware of his lack of progress in life (his footsteps).

> . . . ¡Haber sentido
> 5   la pureza del mundo para ahora
> contribuir a esta sazón, al ruido
> de estos pies! ¿Por qué siempre llega la hora
> del riego? . . .

(p. 98)[100]

Normally a summer rain would be a welcome refreshment from the heat and aridity of the Castilian summer. Here, however, the downpour is too harsh, producing an ironic effect.

> . . . Aunque sea en el verano
> y aquí, llega tan fuerte
> 10   que no calma, no nubla al sol, da al llano
> otra sequía más alta aún. Qué muerte

por demasía, pasajera
nube que iba a salvar lo que ahora arrasa.

(p. 98)[101]

Rather than blotting out the strong rays of the sun to bring relief from the intense illumination, the rain intensifies the sun's effect. The cloud that brings the rain is "pasajera," indicative of its transient, superficial event, whereas the purification it brings is so intense that it destroys instead of reviving. The phrase "Qué muerte / por demasía" ironically echoes the opening verses of "A la respiración en la llanura," undermining the alazonic speaker's enthusiasm. In spite of the painful outcome of this insight, the speaker surprisingly invokes its continuation.

> Cala, cálanos más. ¡Lo que era
> 15 polvo suba en el agua que se amasa
> con la tierra, que es tierra ya y castigo
> puro de lo alto! Y qué importa que impida
> la trilla o queme el trigo
> si nos hizo creer que era la vida.

(p. 98)[102]

The verb "calar," though a more quotidian expression for "penetrar" or "traspasar," conveys connotations of a mystical ecstasy resulting from suffering. And the word "castigo," modified as "puro" and "de lo alto," evokes its archaic meaning of "learning" as well as its more modern meaning of "punishment." The rain elevates the dust (symbol of transience) to create earth, suggesting a union of opposites that characterizes the poems and the language of *Conjuros* and the speaker's ambivalent experience with the poetic act. But because the combination makes earth, the speaker signifies his humility and his potential for growth as opposed to his lifelessness.

The final statement of the poem is especially ironic. The rain—this illuminating, purifying, yet painful experience—may impede the harvest or even ruin the crop; that is, the speaker may not be able to achieve the distinction and transcendence he seeks as a poet because of his intensely introspective approach to the poetic act. Although he may not reap the harvest of a wide audience and great fame, he will have lived and written true to himself. The past tenses in the final verse emphasize the brevity of the experience; but again this impression is ironic, since the insight received from the experience is profound and lasting in spite of its brevity. This dialectic of appearance and reality prepares us for yet another reversal at the beginning of "Libro tercero."

Defamiliarization, Distance, and Chiasmus: "Libro tercero" as Turning Point

Beginning with yet another complication of the ironic perspective, "Libro segundo"—the two-poem section of *Conjuros*—forms a chiasmus, a turning point in the speaker's outlook. First, the poet-magician displaces his voice in an act of ventriloquism, making the "Cerro de Montamarta" the speaker of the first poem. To my knowledge, this is the only poem in Rodríguez's opus in which the speaker is not ostensibly the poet himself and marks the greatest amount of distance and irony in *Conjuros*.[103] For the "cerro" (not a mountain, but not exactly a hill either) ridicules the poet—the tiny man at its feet—for having the same aspirations as it. If the poet is a minuscule, insignificant figure in comparison with the "cerro" in "El «Cerro de Montamarta» dice," positions again reverse in "A la nube aquella" [To that cloud up there].[104] The poet-speaker of the other poems of *Conjuros* returns to address us in this poem, one of the most poignant in *Conjuros*. But the cloud of which he speaks is far above him in contrast with the "cerro," whose perspective is superficially superior to the human figure in the previous poem but whose message is undercut by irony. The cloud is an ambivalent symbol representing both the poet-speaker's lofty aspirations and the fleetingness of time, life, and fame. It is this ambivalence in the symbol of the cloud that constitutes the ironic aspect of this poem and leads us into the split vision of "Libro cuarto." A closer examination of the two pivotal poems of "Libro tercero" will demonstrate how irony and the cultural code collaborate in this turning point in the speaker's perspective in *Conjuros*.

Two aspects of the title "El «Cerro de Montamarta» dice" [The "Hill of Montmartre" speaks] stand out for their irony. This local landmark outside Zamora is clearly not well-known; it is not a Kilimanjaro, a Matterhorn, an Everest, or a Mt. Washington. We might compare it perhaps to a Pike's Peak, familiar locally, but otherwise not distinguished. Because it is a "cerro," it occupies an intermediary position between a hill ("colina") and a true mountain ("montaña"), reminding us of the figure of Linos in "El canto de linos" in "Libro primero." This little-known landmark, insignificant in a larger frame of reference, forms part of the representational level of the text and also stands for the poet, expressing his same aspirations and limitations. By placing this expression in the mouth of an inanimate object outside of himself, the poet estranges us from this speaker (the "cerro") and defamiliarizes its message.[105] In a sense, this ventriloquism and displacement of the poet's voice echoes the original effect of the irony in "Libro primero" although the ironic effect is compounded now. In fact, we might not at first recognize that the "cerro" is speaking, causing us to confuse its voice for the human speaker's. In the first seven verses, its aspirations sound very much like the poet's.

> Un día habrá en que llegue hasta la nube.
> ¡Levantadme, mañanas, o quemadme! ¿Qué puesta
> de sol traerá la luz que aún no me sube
> ni me impulsa? ¿Qué noche alzará en esta
> 5   ciega llanura mía la tierra hasta los cielos?
> Todo el aire me ama
> y se abre en torno mío, y no reposa.
>
> (p. 101)[106]

The "cerro"'s desire to reach "hasta la nube" is the same as the poet's to achieve transcendence and to attain lasting stature as a poet. Light and air as signs of inspiration, the imperatives and future tense, and the positively marked verbs ("levantar," "quemar"—as regeneration as well as destruction—"impulsar," "alzar," "abrirse," "no reposar") can indicate aspiration, but the exclamations and the questions undercut this enthusiasm with frustration. This ambivalence heightens the irony when the "cerro" ridicules the humans at its feet who wish to do the same as it: "Helos / ahí a los hombres, he aquí su pie que inflama / mi ladera buscando más altura, / más cumbre ya sin tierra, con sólo espacio." The "cerro" feels isolated and unappreciated by the humans, who do not recognize the reciprocal relationship between them. The "cerro" is what inspires the humans living in its vicinity because it forms their horizon, beginning each day for them (light and morning being synonymous with inspiration) and representing the cyclical changing of seasons.

> 10   . . . Tantos
> soles abrí a sus ojos, tantos meses, en pura
> rotación acerqué a sus cuerpos, tantos
> días fui su horizonte. Aún les queda en el alma
> mi labor, como a mí su clara muerte.
>
> (p. 101)[107]

These images are again ironic for being ambivalent. Do they emphasize the passage of time, or do they lift the observer beyond time? Does a horizon enclose and limit, or does it connote greater distance and freedom? These verses speak metapoetically about the poet's role in society. His verses remind us of time and its constraints (writing and poetry are temporal events; poetry measures time in rhythm, like music), but they also allow us to transcend our mundane surroundings, to convert the passage of time and trivial events, places, and emotions into eternal cycles, transcendent patterns that last beyond the affects of time. The duality of the poet's role is nowhere clearer than in the last sentence above. In addition to the reciprocal relation between the "cerro" as poet and the humans at its feet, the phrase "su clara muerte" attributes a positive marker to death. The "cerro" as poet implies that the aspirations and attempts to achieve provide inspiration for it/him to reach greater heights. Failure (death, succumbing to time's limitations) ironically inspires others to greater heights, greater risks, and a greater chance of failure. The second stanza then becomes an incantation, a plea for a reader who is able to appreciate what this "cerro" as poet is capable of producing.

> 15   Y ahora la tarde pierde luz y hay calma
> nocturna. ¡Que despierte
> por última vez todo a la redonda
> venga a mí, y se dé cuenta de la honda
> fuerza de amor de mi árido relieve,
> 20   del ansia que alguien puso en mi ladera!
> Ved que hay montes con nieve,
> con arroyos, con pinos, con flor en primavera.
> Ved que yo estoy desnudo, siendo sólo un inmenso
> volcán hacia los aires. Y es mi altura tan poca.

25   ¡Un arado, un arado tan intenso
      que pueda hacer fructífera mi roca,
      que me remueva mi grano
      y os lo dé, y comprendáis así mi vida!

                                                    (pp. 101–2)[108]

The mention of nightfall stresses the passage of time and makes the exclamation of vv. 16–20 more disruptive and urgent, underscored by the subjunctive. Ironically, the "cerro" wants everything to awaken at night and to realize its virtues in its "árido relieve." Aridity would suggest a lack of productivity and profile a superficiality rather than "la honda / fuerza del amor." This "cerro" lacks the snow (purity), streams (fertility), pines (sacredness), and spring flowers (beauty and renewal of life) that taller mountains possess. In contrast, it is "desnudo" (barren or honest, genuine, vulnerable) and "un inmenso / volcán hacia los aires," suggesting fire as destruction but regeneration, passion, and upward thrust. Whereas the plow is usually a symbol for the pen and the force of the writer, here it represents the reader's participation in the poetic process.[109] It is again an ironic turn of events that this "cerro," who disdains the humans who try to scale it, depends on those very humans to give meaning to its existence, to justify it. But not just every reader can accomplish this feat, only an intense reader "que pueda hacer fructífera mi roca, / que me remueva mi grano." The irony of the "cerro"'s point of view is brought home one more time in the final stanza.

      Porque no estaré aquí sino un momento. En vano
30   soy todas las montañas del mundo. En vano, ida
      la noche volverá otra vez la aurora
      y el color gris, y el cárdeno. Ya cuando
      lo mismo que una ola esté avanzando
      hacia el mar de los cielos, hacia ti, hombre, que ahora
35   me contemplas, no lo sabréis. No habrá ya quien me vea,
      quien pueda recorrerme con los pies encumbrados,
      quien purifique en mí amor y tarea
      como yo purifico el olor de los sembrados.

                                                    (p. 102)[110]

The "cerro"'s recognition of its own transience intensifies through contrast with the transience of all human existence. Its seeming permanence and the unending repetition of dawn, it implies, are vain illusions, taken for granted by humans, who do not recognize greatness when they see it ("greatness" here defined as a willingness to take risks and to fail—through the use of irony—to attain genuine communication). The direct address of this "hombre, que ahora / me contemplas" who is unable to appreciate this insignificant "cerro"'s effort is doubly ironic. Does the "cerro" address the poet, the person looking at the local landmark and projecting his voice onto it? Or does the poet address the reader? (Notice the disjunction between the singular "hombre" and "contemplas" and the plural "sabréis.") Are the final words in this poem a lament because no reader will be found and the "cerro," though it may merit recognition, will remain anonymous? Or are they a statement of pride even in isolation and anonymity? For the poet does contribute to his culture ("yo purifico el olor de los sembrados") even if no one reads and understands what he says. Can anyone ever understand exactly what a poet says? Or does one read in the poet what s/he wishes to read (just as the poet "reads" the mountain through his ventriloquism)? The "cerro" as poet disdains but also challenges the reader. This defamiliarizing speaker pushes us away to heighten our desire to understand more profoundly, just as his irony in "Libro primero" challenges us to read more insightfully. "El «Cerro de Montamarta» dice" recapitulates the "reto" (challenge) of "Libro primero" but intensifies it through a complication of the ironic twists we have come to expect, fear, and enjoy in *Conjuros*.

A change in perspective and in the locus of the lyric voice activates the chiasmus in "Libro tercero." Instead of the "cerro" looking down on the human figure and disdaining it for attempting exactly what it wishes to accomplish, in "A la nube aquella" the speaker stands on the ground, looks up at a passing cloud, and wishes to join it in its fleeting but transcendent passing. In contrast with the defamiliarized and estranged stance required by the ventriloquism and the inanimate speaker in the "cerro," the speaker of "A la nube aquella" adopts a nonironic stance. Nonetheless, the cloud as symbol and the language employed are inherently ironic and equivocal, complicating the speaker's relation to both. If in the first poem the "cerro" feels unappreciated and misunderstood, isolated from those around him (cf. Christ—a prophet not valued in his own land), in the second poem of this two-poem section, the poet seeks separation and individuality to transcend his mundane surroundings even though that would emphasize his transience.

The cloud as symbol is ambivalent: Archetypically, it represents both fleeting beauty and transcendence because it is constantly changing and dispersing, but it moves in an ethereal atmosphere; semiotically, it represents the sign as both tangible signifier and constantly shifting signified that is the poet's means of expression and yet that which prevents him from capturing his meaning (and his identity) because of the constant play of difference. Hence, we can relate the cloud both to the interplay of the representational and the symbolic, and to the poet's definition of the sign and by extension to his search for identity.

For these reasons, "A la nube aquella" is one of the most important poems of *Conjuros* and contributes yet again to the unfolding of ironic peripeteia. It plays off "El «Cerro de Montamarta» dice" by reversing the locus of the speaking voice and forms the chiasmus of "Libro tercero" by defining a simultaneous union and disjunction of signifier and signified. Ironic duality is perceptible from the very opening verses.

> Si llegase a la nube pasajera
> la tensión de mis ojos, ¿cómo iría
> su resplandor dejándome en la tierra?
> ¿Cómo me dejaría oscurecido
> 5   si es clara su labor, y su materia

        es casi luz, está al menos en lo alto?
        ¡Arrancad esa límpida osamenta
        dejando ver un corazón aéreo,
        fuerte con su latido de tormenta!
10   Qué vida y muerte fulminantes. ¡Sea
        también así en mi cuerpo! ¡A puro asalto
        cobrádmelo, haced de él vuestra faena!

                                            (p. 103)[111]

As in so many of Rodríguez's poems, we discern a dialogic conflict between enthusiasm and despair in the perhaps rhetorical, perhaps sincere questions and the binary contrasts of light/dark, sky/earth, high/low, fleeting/static. Moreover, the if-clause expresses both aspiration and the impossibility of fulfilling that aspiration. The speaker may want to project his emotions onto the cloud as he did with the "cerro" in the previous poem, but the cloud is much higher than the "cerro" and passes too quickly. Yet he also questions what effect that would have on him, because his experience with the poetic act has had the ironic effect of illuminating his shortcomings and unworthiness, his isolation and lack of recognition. Does he aspire to reach the cloud and to identify with it? Or would he rather contemplate the possible effects of something he feels impossible to attain at any rate?

The rapid shift from questions to exclamations and the violence implicit in words like "Arrancad," "tormenta," "fulminantes," and "asalto," rather than providing a resolution, only increase the speaker's ambivalence because the exclamations could express enthusiasm for or frustration with his attempt to attain the transcendent. If we remove "esa límpida osamenta" (in itself a contradictory phrase) from the cloud, we are left with nothing but air, imbricating container and contained, cloud and sky, life and death. The neutral punctuation of the phrase "Qué vida y muerte fulminantes" in the midst of these exclamations underscores the speaker's ambivalence. "Fulminar" means "arrojar [cast] rayos," but "rayos" can be rays of the sun or lightning bolts. Both belong to the code of light and inspiration, but they cause both pain and pleasure for the speaker (cf. "respiración" as inspiration and expiration, life and death). The speaker's relationship with the cloud—the sign, the poetic experience—is ambivalent, reminiscent of the mystic experience, a possible intertextual underpinning for this poem. The subsequent exclamations may be interpreted as meaning either "may it be so" (desire, aspiration) or "so be it" (resignation). The switch to "vosotros" in the verb forms and possessive adjective metonymically slips the process from language and the speaker to the speaker's words (the poem) and the reader. But does the speaker relinquish himself gladly, or does he resign himself to an appropriation by the reader? Because of the duplicity of language, the speaker's position is ironically ambivalent. This mystical ambivalence then leads to another ironic reversal: the valorization of the imminent.

        Si se acercase a mí, si me inundara
        la vida con su vida tan intensa.
15   No lo resistiría. Pero, ¿acaso
        alguien es digno de ello? ¿No se esfuerza

la nube por morir en tanto espacio
para incendiarlo de una vez? Entrega,
palabra pura de los cielos, himno:
20 suena como la voz del hombre, suena
y pasa, pasa así, dinos tu viva
verdad en esta clara hora terrena,
en esta oscura vida que huye y pasa
y nunca en ello podrá ver la inmensa,
25 sola alegría de aquí abajo, nube,
alma quizá en que un cuerpo se serena.

(p. 103)[112]

A flood can be both destructive and enriching. But does the speaker welcome such an occurrence or dread it? His assertion "No lo resistiría" connotes both "I wouldn't oppose it" and "I couldn't stand it." His questions are again ambivalent, expressing both puzzlement and rhetorical certainty (negation). Ironically, the cloud contrasts with the mundane existence of the speaker. Seen as "Entrega, palabra pura de los cielos, himno," the cloud provides comfort precisely because it is so fleetingly beautiful. It adds a note of happiness to earthly life that allows the body—tangible reality, but a reality that must pass away—to know that there is transcendent beauty. The cloud lends its beauty to mundane existence and redeems it precisely because it sacrifices itself. Although the cloud passes quickly, we see how beautiful it is and are touched by its fleeting beauty because it is so impermanent. These contradictory emotions—the beauty of the fleeting—enriches our "dark" lives here below and if only for a moment stops time as we contemplate fleeting beauty—clearly an ironic effect.

By characterizing the cloud as "entrega," "palabra pura," and "himno," Rodríguez equates it with a poem (cf. *Don*, "Libro primero," IX) and implies that poetry has the same effect as the cloud. Although made of language, which measures time and exists temporally, the poem stops time by lifting us outside of the temporal flow. These verses affirm the poet's role and justify his existence. Poetry—like the cloud—captures the transient, makes it transcendent, and adds beauty to life even though it deals with the imminent, as words themselves cannot capture presence, only represent it. This play of presence and absence is foregrounded in the second stanza.

¿Y dónde están las nubes de otros días,
en qué cielo inmortal de primavera?
El blanco espacio en que estuvieron, ¿siente
30 aún su compañía y va con ella
creando un nuevo resplandor, lo mismo
que a media noche en la llanura queda
todo el impulso de la amanecida?
Lejos de donde el hombre se ha vendido,
35 aquel granero, ¿para qué cosecha?

(pp. 103–4)[113]

Although these lines recall the classical theme of *ubi sunt?* and all poems that lament the passage of time and death (cf. Jorge Manrique's *Coplas*), the clouds as symbols of other magical poetic moments still exist and are accessible to us, under-cutting the questions, making them rhetorical and converting *ubi sunt?* into *ibi sunt*, absence into presence. The poet actualizes past poetic experience every time he en-counters "el blanco espacio," a metaphor for the sky but also for the blank page, the potential for the appearance of another cloud, another poem. Poetry not only captures the fleeting moment but also recuperates the entire tradition by making the transient permanent and the absent present. Far from being a commodity that can be bought and sold, the harvest reaped from poetry is kept in a special barn—the poem itself and the tradition to which it belongs. Although the poem seems to end with a lament for the lost beauty of the cloud, it also ironically exalts the moment and those capable of appreciating it.

> Oh, nube que huye y cambia a cada instante
> como si un pueblo altísimo de abejas
> fuera allí trabajando a fuego limpio.
> Nube que nace sin dolor, tan cerca.
> 40   ¡Y vivir en el sitio más hermoso
> para esto, para caer a tierra
> o desaparecer! No importa cómo
> pero ahora, la nube aquella, aquella
> que es nuestra y está allí, si no habitarla,
> ya, quién pudiera al menos retenerla.
>
> (p. 104)[114]

By equating the cloud with a swarm of bees, the speaker emphasizes the vitality and productivity of the cloud's changing and transience. Bees symbolically represent creative power, eloquence, immortality, resurrection, and so the transcendent aspect of poetry.[115] Their work "a fuego limpio" connotes both destruction and regeneration, again indicating dynamic process that conflates transience and transcendence. Rodríguez's use of the adjectives "altísimo" and "limpio" embodies this duality. The first literally refers to the cloud being high in the sky but also to a more abstract quality in contrast with the earth. The set phrase "a fuego limpio" is idiomatic and a commonplace of the cultural code, but it also has obviously symbolic proportions, as we have already seen in "A mi ropa tendida." And where we might expect the poet to lament the cloud's passing with the verb "muere," he uses "nace," another indication of its vitality and its evolving, perpetual renewal. So too a poem and the poetic expe-rience cause us to change, to die to an old self and emerge as a new person. In this image, Rodríguez iterates the central theme of *Conjuros* announced in "Respiración en la llanura" through the intertext of Matthew.[116]

The speaker feels the full ironic impact of the cloud in the exclamation of vv. 40–42. On one level, we can read the verses with despair: Even though the cloud moves through the open sky high above mundane reality, it must eventually fall back to earth and disappear. The act of falling, the direction toward earth, and the transience in disappearance might all call up negative connotations. Yet, if we analyze the meaning of these occurrences, we find that they are remarkably, ironically positive. When a cloud falls to earth, it does so as a fertilizing rain (cf. the irony of "Lluvia de verano," the last poem of "Libro segundo"); and when the clouds disappear, the sun comes out. What on the surface appears to be an ironic situation undergoes yet another ironic reversal because of the duplicity of language!

Does the same process obtain in the final sentence? The imperfect subjunctive, the impersonal "quién," and the speaker's concession of a more desirable possibility ("habitarla" as opposed to "retenerla") might lead us to a wistful but ultimately resigned or even anguished admission of the impossibility of holding on to the cloud. The verb "retener" is ambivalent, however, and can mean "guardar en la memoria."[117] In that case, we *can* maintain the presence of the cloud even though it is absent, just as language retains meaning even though the referent is absent. Such an interpretation, then, belies the statement "No importa cómo" especially because "ahora, la nube aquella, aquella / que es nuestra y está allí" is the poem we are reading. Despite being distant, it is present "ahora" because it is *ours*, that is, because we as readers have participated in the poetic experience. We have never seen the cloud Rodríguez has described. It has never been present for us, but we have experienced the language describing that cloud and the poet's relation with it. Rodríguez has retained it in the language of the poem even though it is absent.

Through our attention to the speaker's irony, we have reached a point of infinite negativity, of constant irony. The ground keeps receding, slipping out from under our feet. This cloud, this poem and the theory of transgressive language implicit in it, represents presence and absence, transcendence and transience, the permanent and the fleeting, the poet's identity and the problematizing of it. The final manifestation of this irony and the interplay of the representational and the symbolic abetted by the cultural code unfolds with more ironic consequences in "Libro cuarto."

THE STAMP OF THE CHIASMUS IN "LIBRO CUARTO"

The eight poems of "Libro cuarto" manifest an ironic imbrication of two distinct perspectives, functioning much like a Moebius strip, and show the speaker switching back and forth between sincere and ironic statements. Many of these poems end with an ironic reversal, but even these reversals are ironized by a constantly shifting ground, destabilized and destabilizing. As always, the cultural code and the mimetic level play a key role in this process, which represents not only Rodríguez's transgressive poetics but also his definition of identity in *Conjuros*. Although we can assert that the speaker of *Conjuros* is someone who constantly strives to know himself and his world better by transgressing the limits of language and seeking only those readers who are capable of keeping up with him, the dynamic process motivated by his transgressions—the ironic reversals we have pointed out—articulate an identity constantly in the process of becoming, problematical and destabilized. Because of the risks he takes in his transgressive search, risks that threaten to destroy him but also identify him, it is impossible to formulate a stable representation of the speaker. He fits the pattern described by Booth in his discussion of unstable irony.[118]

"Visión a la hora de la siesta" [Vision at the hour of the siesta] sets the tone for "Libro cuarto" because it imbricates the individual and the social, dream and reality, with an ironic twist in the final verse, in addition to its deft deployment of the cultural code. By questioning the definition of reality and raising existential concerns, the poet again points to the ambivalent nature of the representation. These mimetic scenes are separated from the symbolic, yet inextricably intertwined with it, indeed indistinguishable from it. The poem opens with what appears to be a quite unremarkable domestic scene: a woman sewing in front of a window. But several factors produce a magical effect that converts the scene into spectacle.

> ¡Si esa es mi hermana y cose cuarto adentro
> tan tranquila y, de pronto,
> ¡quitadla!, le da el sol y un simple rayo
> la enhebra, y en él queda bien zurcida,
> 5   puntada blanca de la luz del mundo!
> y, ¡cerrad las ventanas!, ese rayo,
> eterna levadura, se nos echa
> encima, y nos fermenta, y en él cuaja
> nuestro amasado corazón y, como
> 10 la insurrección de un pueblo,
> se extiende, avanza, cubre
> toda la tierra ya, teje y desteje
> la estopa hostil del hombre y allí, a una,
> en el mesón del tiempo, siempre caro,
> 15 allí, a la puerta, en el telar hermoso,
> vamos tejiendo, urdiendo
> la camisa de Dios, el limpio sayo
> de la vida y la muerte. . . .

(p. 107)[119]

First we notice the speaker's surprise as he begins the poem with the interjective "si" and multiple exclamations because this woman reminds him of his sister. The act of sewing produces magical effects in "Visión."[120] As if in a puff of smoke, "¡quitadla!," the woman vanishes: A ray of sunshine as needle embroiders her as a thread in the tapestry of life. The startling effect of this scene initiates a series of transformations—characteristic of dreams—in which commonplace domestic activities adopt symbolic proportions, a poetics comparable to Vermeer's paintings which the focal scene resembles.[121] Next the speaker compares his heart with a mass of dough on which the sunlight (inspiration) functions as yeast, causing his heart to ferment and expand. Another activity involves the weaving of cloth (the text), here converted into "la camisa de Dios, el limpio sayo / de la vida y la muerte" (vv. 17–18), that is, all of creation, the very texture of reality itself.[122]

The poem reaches a climactic moment in a series of rapid metamorphoses as a breath turns into a breeze and then becomes a voice which by singing a hymn unravels the cloth and releases the threads that compose it. We get a sense here of a multitude of lives—in truth all of humanity—affected by the song.

```
                . . . Pero, ¿ahora,
            qué pasa?: cuando estaba
    20      viendo colgar del cielo
            la bandera inmortal, como en los días
            de fiesta en mi ciudad cuelga la enseña
            roja y gualda, oídme, cuando
            veía ese inmenso lienzo en el que cada
    25      ligera trama es una vida entera
            ocupar el espacio,
            he aquí que un aliento, un tenue oreo,
            después una voz clara
            se alza, y con tal temple,
    30      con tal metal esa voz suena ahora
            que hilo a hilo cantando se descose
            una vida, otra, otra,
            de aquel gran sayo, y se oye como un himno,
            escuchad, y de pronto . . .
```

(pp. 107–8)[123]

At this point, the speaker awakens and returns to "ordinary" reality as the dream vanishes and the poem seems to end: "De pronto estoy despierto y es de día" [Suddenly I am awake and it is day]. But this abrupt dissolution of the dream and the return to wakefulness leaves us in doubt as to what happens when the speaker awakens. Does he feel disillusionment because his exciting vision has vanished? Or does he breathe a sigh of relief that this nightmare—the unraveling and dispersal of reality—has ended? When the dream vanishes, does the spectacle vanish too, or does it consist of ordinary reality? Was the speaker dreaming, or was he simply lost in his thoughts? Is there a dividing line between dream and wakefulness?

When we examine the poem retrospectively in the light of these provocative questions, we discover another conflict pervading it. Each time Rodríguez introduces the commonplace activities, he incongruously juxtaposes them with political imagery. The rising of the bread is compared with "la insurrección de un pueblo / [que] se extiende, avanza, cubre / toda la tierra ya . . ." (vv. 10–12); "la camisa de Dios" reminds the speaker of "los días / de fiesta en mi ciudad" where he sees "la enseña roja y gualda" (vv. 21–23), the Spanish national flag. The song that unravels the cloth could be a patriotic anthem.

The symbolic dimensions of the everyday activities of sewing, baking bread, weaving, and singing juxtapose the aesthetic act with politics. What is the relationship between art and politics? To what extent does art reflect society? To what extent can it shape society, politics, our thoughts and actions? Does insurrection liberate, or does it subvert and destroy? Is patriotism heartfelt loyalty and devotion to country or "redneck" conservatism and jingoism? Does art have an expansive, uplifting effect on society, or does it rend and unravel the very fibers that hold society together?[124] By juxtaposing art with politics, Rodríguez confronts the duality of art as spectacle, urging us to go beyond the surface, to look at the purposes and possible effects of the spectacle before us precisely because of the possibility of irony. Perhaps he is describing a universal phenomenon of disillusionment. Spectacle creates an illusion. But, at one time or another, we undergo a disillusionment with life because of the passage of time and an awareness of our limitations, both external and internal. From that point on, we not only recognize a different reality behind the glittering surface but begin to seek it, to eschew childish, egotistical illusions in favor of a deeper and richer appreciation of life, to admire the skill and risk involved in the execution of the spectacular.

The poet's "vision," then, parleys both truth and deception.[125] How are poet and reader to ascertain which is which, which is irony, which earnestness? Can the poet rely on poetry to define his identity and to give him lasting renown? To what extent is the poet confined within the tradition and the society that has formed him? To what extent is the reader implicated in the neg(oti)ation of that identity? What is trivial, what resonant with symbolism and meaning? What is the relationship between the mimetic and the symbolic?

Several critics have remarked that the grackle in "Incidente en los Jerónimos" [Incident in the Jeromians] is a metaphorical (or even allegorical) representation of the poet. But what role does the cultural code—especially the detailed architectural imagery of the temple—play in this poem? And how does irony—the mark of the chiasmus—affect our reading? "Incidente" picks up a thread we have seen in other poems in *Conjuros*: the poet's separation of himself from others and his desire to distinguish himself. The grackle supports this concept because, according to Cirlot, this black bird is a "symbol for creative, demiurgic power and for spiritual strength" and "signifies the isolation of him who lives on a superior plane."[126] Chevalier and Gheerbrandt stress that its symbolism is full of contradictions: "Demiurgo y héroe civilizador, clarividente y profeta, pájaro solar y a la vez tenebroso, anuncia desgracia y muerte y a veces protege."[127] This bird is an apt representation of the poet and captures the irony that stamps the poems of "Libro cuarto." The contradictory qualities of the grackle are foregrounded in the opening verses along with the repudiation of a former way of life because of the poetic act.

> ¡Que ahora va de verdad, que va mi vida
> en ello! Si otros días
> oisteis mi chillo en torno de este templo,
> olvidadlo. ¡Que ahora
> 5   no veréis a este grajo
> picar el huevo ni saquear el nido!
> Ya nunca merendero,
> nunca buscando el hato,
> las albardas del hombre,
> 10 porque nada hubo allí sino ruin salsa.
> Oídme, el soto, el aire,
> malva, cardillo, salvia, mijo, orégano,
> tú, mi pareja en celo,
> todos, oídme: aquello no fue nunca
> 15 mi vida. Mala huelga.

(p. 109)[128]

A major symbol in "Incidente" is the poetic space, the temple into which the grackle flies. Although this place is ostensibly a specific Castilian landmark (it could be any number of chapels or churches in Spain—the exact location and identity of this particular scene is irrelevant), the architectural imagery marks its symbolic function. First the speaker identifies it as a "templo," a sacred place. Then a spate of architectural terms points to symbolic proportions. The grackle enters through a "ventano," a liminal space that represents the crossing of a threshold and the transgression of the sacred area. It is equally significant that a "ventano" is smaller and narrower than a "ventana" in accord with Rodríguez's insistence on the narrow path and the exclusivity of the challenge his poetry presents. More architectural description appears in the next verses, where the speaker compares his early attempts at poetry with the innocent enjoyment of festivals.

> ... Dejadme
> donde ahora estoy, en el crucero hermoso
> 35 de juventud. Y veo
> la crestería en luz de la esperanza
> arriba, arriba siempre.
> Paso el arco fajón, faja de fiesta,
> y el floral capitel. ¡Que siga, siga
> 40 el baile! ¡Más, doncellas, primavera,
> alma del hombre! Y tú, ve de jarana,
> viento de tantos años.
> Deja caer este día como un fruto
> de libertad. Recuerda
> 45 nuestras andanzas de oro,
> tú recuerda, recuerda
> la fugaz alegría
> de los hombres, su fiesta
> tan pobre en días y tan rica en tiempo.

(pp. 109–10)[129]

The "crucero" marks the intersection of the transept with the nave, which corresponds with the heart of a person with arms out-stretched. This symbol of Christ's crucifixion is ambivalent because it also represents resurrection, a metaphor for participation in the poetic act (as we have seen in the use of irony and the definition of the poet's identity in the previous sections of *Conjuros*).[130] The "arco fajón, faja de fiesta, y el floral capitel" designate another liminal space between the dome and the columns supporting it, between heaven and earth, love and sex, as well as the joy and productivity of this period in the poet's life. His statement that their feast is "tan pobre en días y tan rica en tiempo" means that this period in his life was a short but intense celebration. The deft combination and elaboration of these two strains of imagery in "Incidente" leads to an ironic conclusion. The metapoetic dimension stands out as Rodríguez draws upon his knowledge of birds in the following verses.

> ... ¡Que empieza
> 65 ya el sofoco, que el buche

> lo llevo mal cumplido como en tiempo
> de muda, que ya apenas
> si me bulle el plumón! ¿Quién me ha metido
> en el cañón de cada pluma la áspera
> 70 médula gris del desaliento? . . .

(p. 110)[131]

When birds molt, they cease to sing. So the poet, when he undergoes a transition, ceases to write. But does the writing of a poem produce a temporary silence, or does silence produce the poem? Which is the transitional state—writing or silence? When the speaker mentions the fluid flowing though the shaft of the grackle's feathers, he refers to the ink in his pen, metaphor for his words and the emotions they convey—or fail to convey because "el desaliento" could refer to his despair or a lack of inspiration ("des-aliento"). This description is not exempt of a touch of humor, as we see when the poet draws on the traditional comparison of the church with a ship ("nave").

> Qué marejada, qué borrasca inmensa
> 75 bate mi quilla, quiebra mi plumaje
> timonero. Este grajo,
> este navío hace agua. Volver quiero,
> volver quiero a volar con mi pareja.
> Sí, festiva asamblea de las tardes,
> 80 ah, compañeros, ¿dónde,
> dónde estáis que no os oigo?
> No importa. Llegaré. Desde la cúpula
> veré mejor. Y ahora,
> vereda va y vereda viene, ¿en qué aire,
> 85 por qué camino voy? ¡Que ya no puedo
> ni ver siquiera, que zozobro y choco
> contra la piedra, contra
> los muros de este templo, de esta patria!

(p. 111)[132]

By comparing the church with a ship, the poet subtly alludes to this space as his life and his passage through time. The humor emerges when he says, "Este grajo, / este navío hace agua." Passing through these stormy seas can cause the ship to take on water, threatening it with foundering. But the expression "hacer agua" can also mean "to urinate," caused here by the speaker's fear that he may not be recognized as a poet if no one can appreciate his subtle ironies. His desire to fly with his mate, that is, to dance with his partner at the "fiesta," is another metapoetic statement about writing and attaining the dizzying enjoyment of art (dance, poetry).

Recurring to ship imagery, the speaker admits that he is foundering: "¡ . . . que zozobro y choco contra la piedra, contra / los muros de este templo, de esta patria!" This link between the temple and his homeland engenders an ironic conclusion. The speaker breathlessly but determinedly strives to reach the top of the dome, to attain the heights of poetry. But the dome represents both the heights and an enclosure, a limit that does not allow the grackle-poet to escape to higher regions. The speaker even states that he would prefer to be tethered to the ground, taking advantage of the frequent custom that children have of tying a string to a bird's leg so that it can fly but not fly away.

> ¡Niños, venid, atadme,
> 90   prefiero que me atéis los pies con vuestro
>   cordel azul de la pureza! Quieto,
>   quisiera estar en paz por un momento.
>   Llegaré. Llegaré. Ahí está mi vida,
>   ahí está el altar, ahí brilla mi pueblo.
> 95   Un poco más. Ya casi . . .
>   Tú, buen aliento, sigue
>   un poco más, alicas,
>   corazón, sólo un poco . . .
>   Así, así . . . Ya, ya . . . ¡Qué mala suerte!
> 100   ¡Ya por tan poco! Un grajo aquí, ya en tierra.

(p. 111)[133]

In these final verses, it at first seems that the grackle has become fatigued; unable to get out of the dome, it has beat its wings against the stones of the cupola, tired, and fallen to the floor. Like Icarus, the poet has striven to attain new heights but has overreached himself and fallen. But another possibility suggests a more ironic twist on this scene. What if the grackle has reached the top of the dome? The dome itself rests on the pillars that support it and link it to the earth.[134] And if this space represents the speaker's "patria"—Spain—even if the poet attains a preeminent position, even if he is the best poet in Spain, he still may not receive the recognition he deserves as a poet because of Spain's marginal position in European/Occidental letters. He may even be better than poets in other countries, but he is limited from flying in that broader context (the wider sky), limited to and by the Spanish context that the cultural code represents in *Conjuros*. Should he then desist from writing? Will this "incidente," a seemingly minor occurrence, lead to serious consequences? The answer to these questions can be intuited in the following poem, "La contrata de mozos."

On one level, "La contrata de mozos" [The contract of youth] constitutes a "pregón," a merchant's sales pitch typical of Spanish culture. On another level, the biblical parable about workers hired to work in the fields (Matt. 20:1–16) forms the basis for the poem. Set in juxtaposition, these two levels bring into contrast a ludic, comic tone and a serious, tragic one. Hawking grapes, the speaker is promoting his own poetry, seeking "buyers," that is, those who can read his poetry and know that it is of high quality. The uneasy relationship between the two tones, however, results in an ironic conclusion. The representational level consists of the speaker parodying the seller's verbal tricks to induce the buyer to make a purchase. He threatens to fold up his tent and move to another location where the buyers are more savvy and his product will be recognized as worthwhile:

> ¡A cerrar ya! ¡Vámonos pronto a otra
> feria donde haya buen mercado, donde
> 10   regatee la gente, y sise, y coja

con sus manos nuestra uva, y nos la tiente
a ver si es que está pasa! ¿A qué otra cosa
hemos venido aquí sino a vendernos?
Y hoy se fía, venid, que hoy no se cobra.

(p. 112)[135]

The reference to the verbal art of bargaining, the wise buyer's handling of the fruit (the verbs "sisar" and "tentar" especially), and the idiomatic language of the phrase "a ver si es que está pasa" reinforce the representational level in a ludic, parodic, ironic way. His feigned anger, as if to say "Why aren't you buying? Why have we even come here?" and his clearly insincere promise that one will not have to pay add to the ironic tone. This tone changes subtly to a more embittered one, though still employing the mercantile code.

Hemos venido así a esta plaza siempre,
20   con la esperanza del que ofrece su obra,
su juventud al aire. ¿Y sólo el aire
ha de ser nuestro cliente? ¿Sin parroquia
ha de seguir el que es alquiladizo,
el que viene a pagar su renta? Próspera
25   fue en otro tiempo nuestra mercancía,
cuando la tierra nos la compró toda.
Entonces, lejos de esta plaza, entonces,
en el mercado de la luz. Ved ahora
en qué paró aquel género. Contrata,
30   lonja servil, teatro de deshonra.

(p. 112)[136]

The metapoetic aspect stands out again in the word "contrata." If poet and reader enter into a mutual agreement, the speaker believes that poetry had reached a state where the poet was a servile entertainer who betrayed him/herself by pandering to the audience, using language that was blatantly emotional and dominated by thematics (the "social" poetry of the forties and early fifties, the immediate postwar era in Spain). By putting this situation in terms of Golden Age theater and giving it a wry twist ("teatro de deshonra"), the speaker shows the theatricality, conventionalism, falseness, and superficiality to which poetry had been lowered. His poetry, relying as it does on irony and the equivocality of language, requires a fuller commitment of both parties—poet and reader—in the lyric exchange. This disillusionment reflects the dissatisfaction of the workers who were hired early in the morning in the biblical parable. They expect to receive higher wages than those hired in the late afternoon, but are paid the same. Whether we come early or late to faith, the reward is the same. But what if no one hires those looking for work? In a few moments, I will return to this biblical intertext to discuss the outcome of the poem. But first the speaker returns to the mocking, ironic tone in his description of other poets:

Ved aquí al mocerío. A ver, ¿quién compra
este de pocos años, de la tierra

del pan, de buen riñón, de mano sobria
para la siega; este otro, de la tierra
40   del vino, algo coplero, de tan corta
talla y tan fuerte brazo, el que más rinde
en el trajín del acarreo? ¡Cosa
regalada!

(p. 113)[137]

The abrupt run-on line, the "pie quebrado" (truncated verse), and the idiomatic expression meaning that the buy is "dirt cheap" make these verses resonate with sarcasm and irony! The characterization of these two poets—one "de buen riñón" who has a sober hand good for "cutting down" others, the next "algo coplero" whose brute strength is good for lifting and hauling because he is short and "strong-armed"—are less than flattering portrayals. What terrific humor! What biting sarcasm! What irony!

In the second stanza, the speaker wavers between despair and hope. At the same time that he fears that no one will be able to read his poetry, he also generates great enthusiasm as he looks not at the past but at the future.

Y no viene nadie, y pronto
45   el sol de junio irá de puesta. Próspera
fue en otro tiempo nuestra mercancía.
Pero esperad, no recordéis ahora.
¡Nuestra feria está aquí! Si hoy no, mañana;
si no mañana, un día. Lo que importa
50   es que vendrán, vendrán de todas partes,
de mil pueblos del mundo, de remotas
patrias vendrán los grandes compradores,
los del limpio almacén. . . .

. . . .

y así han pasado una mañana y otra
60   pero nuestra uva no se ablanda, siempre,
siempre está en su sazón, nunca está pocha.
Tened calma, los oigo. Ahí, ahí vienen.

(p. 113)[138]

The word "feria," repetition of the verb "venir," and the adverbs "siempre" (also contrasted with "nunca") and "ahí," along with the vehement rhythm of the final verse build excitement and expectation about the arrival of a reader who can appreciate "nuestra uva." This grape—metaphor for the poet's words—is of course special because "no se ablanda," "nunca está pocha." That is to say, the poet has invested enough of himself in his poetry as to have complete confidence in its merit and its ability to endure the passage of time.

The final verses would then appear to undercut that view with an ironic twist: "Y así seguimos mientras cae la tarde, / mientras sobre la plaza caen las sombras" [And thus we continue while the afternoon falls, / while over the plaza the shadows fall]. At the end of the day, the biblical workers thought they had been defrauded, that they would earn more money, but they were quickly disabused of that idea. Does the poet-speaker feel the same sense of disappointment when apparently no reader arrives who can appreciate his efforts? Dusk and shadows covering the plaza underscore the passage of time and a movement in descent. On one hand, then, the speaker may be expressing his disillusionment with his irony and the rose-colored view that encouraged him to expect that others would understand him. But on the other hand, Matthew's account of the parable ends with its own ironic twist: "The first shall be last and the last shall be first." The phrase "Y así seguimos" could be a staunch affirmation of the poet's determination to continue writing in this way, to continue his exploration of his identity through language, and to continue believing in the merit of his work in spite of the apparent lack of success. At least he fulfills his end of the bargain.

The poet defines his ironic vision and his concept of the ideal reader of his work in "Siempre será mi amigo" [He will always be my friend]. The two stanzas of this short, jewel-like poem posit a contrast between two different perspectives.

> Siempre será mi amigo no aquel que en primavera
> sale al campo y se olvida entre el azul festejo
> de los hombres que ama, y no ve el cuero viejo
> tras el pelaje nuevo, sino tú, verdadera
>
> 5   amistad, peatón celeste, tú, que en el invierno
> a las claras del alba dejas tu casa y te echas
> a andar, y en nuestro frío hallas abrigo eterno
> y en nuestra honda sequía la voz de las cosechas.
>
> (p. 114)[139]

The speaker distances himself from the type of person he describes in the first stanza, as we can see in the placement of the negative and the use of the demonstrative adjective "aquel." This person has a superficial view, being what we might call a "fair-weather friend." He goes out into the country only in the springtime to forget his problems. The phrase "el azul festejo" not only refers to the clear skies and fair weather but to the illusion and lighthearted atmosphere "de los hombres que ama." This phrase echoes Jesus's words from Matt. 5:43–48.[140] It is easy to deal with those we love but much more difficult to forgive those who have wronged us. Indeed, this person is unable to see the unpleasant beneath the superficial brilliance ("el cuero viejo tras el nuevo pelaje"), and so the speaker rejects superficial friendship, knowing that it will not be lasting or genuine.

In contrast, he calls the "verdadera / amistad," which the second stanza juxtaposes with the first, a "peatón celeste," a catachresis that defines the confluence of opposites that we have seen on several levels in *Conjuros*. This pedestrian could have his feet very firmly on the ground yet have his mind and eyes on the sky. Or he could be walking on clouds, still walking but in a rather miraculous way. This contrast is underscored by the variation from the distant third-person to the more intimate second-person address. Furthermore, this person does not merely go out into the country (implying that he could return to his house for shelter if the weather becomes inclement) but leaves his house behind. And he does so "en el invierno / a las claras del alba," when the weather is sure to be anything but welcoming. Giving himself more completely to an exploration of the world, he makes marvelously ironic discoveries: "en nuestro frío hallas abrigo eterno / y en nuestra honda sequía la voz de las cosechas."

The contrast between these two figures not only describes a change that has occurred in the speaker's outlook in the preceding sections of *Conjuros,* but also the type of reader Rodríguez seeks for his poetry. He does not seek readers who will see only the superficial beauty of his language, who will miss its equivocality and the irony with which he imbues his poems, but those who are capable of making the same introspection that he makes and of participating in the ironic and unexpected, painful, and simultaneously joyful discoveries to which language leads him. In "Libro primero," the speaker realized a difficult separation of himself from his friends, those readers who see only the superficial. Rodríguez rejects superficial brilliance in favor of a more profound and insightful introspection to acquire knowledge of himself and his world through the act of writing. His use of irony in *Conjuros* reflects the risk that he is taking. It is only by recognizing that risk and participating in his exploration of self that we can appreciate the impact of this short, almost terse poem. The speaker of this poem has an ironic perspective, but he speaks to us sincerely, without irony. If we have not followed his progress from the beginning, if we have not been able to appreciate his irony and the ironic consequences of what he has done, we will read the poem superficially. But if we have followed him in his ironic quest, we will read this poem from the inside, sharing his perspective as we have shared his experiences and his ironic discoveries.

After specifying the type of reader necessary to comprehend his poetry, Rodríguez offers a stiff challenge in the next poem, "Un ramo por el río" [A branch in the river]. At first glance the title of this poem may impress us as being quite flat. After all, it is a commonplace to see a branch being carried downstream by the river, especially during the flooding of spring months. But when we read the poem, we realize that this branch has been thrown into the river as part of an annual ritual. This ceremony may have its roots in Roman or pagan mythology, perhaps Quirinal in origin, serving as a propitiation to river gods to assure the supply of water to fertilize crops and the continuation of life. Already we can see that this symbolic act has metapoetic dimensions referring to the writing of poetry.[141]

There is, however, another level of the text because the branch represents death, and part of the ritual involves children throwing rocks at it to drive it away. Personification of the branch as "la muerte" suggests the biblical texts of the stoning of the adulteress and Mary Magdalene. This female figure is saved by Christ twice, literally and figuratively, and through her anointing of him with spikenard, participates in his death and his resurrection, at both of which she is present. These two levels—the ritual and the biblical—are tightly intertwined in the opening verses. The question we must ask is whether the speaker is sincere or ironic in his enthusiasm for the ritual. Does he incite people to participate in this sacrificial act or does he point out their superstition? Are the exclamations which open the poem pleas or commands?

> ¡Que nadie hable de muerte en este pueblo!
> ¡Fuera del barrio del ciprés hoy día

en que los niños van a echar el ramo,
a echar la muerte al río!
5   ¡Salid de casa: vámonos a verla!
¡Ved que allá va, miradla, ved que es cosa
de niños! Tanto miedo
para esto. Tirad, tiradle piedras
que allá va, que allá va. Sí, lo que importa
10 es que esté lejos. . . .

(p. 115)[142]

   We have already seen that "Fuera" is an ambivalent word, and the "barrio del ciprés" refers metaphorically to a cemetery (the "ciprés" is a tree commonly found in Spanish cemeteries) but also to the society in which he lives. Remaining in one's house may signify a lack of concern for public events and communal interests or a desire to close one's eyes to reality, to the presence of death and the blessings of everyday life. The speaker sounds mocking as he downplays their fear of death/life, calling it a "cosa de niños"—child's play. The feminine pronoun "la" in vv. 5 and 8, while referring to death, vaguely hints at the female figure whom I have suggested is Mary Magdalene. The use of "vosotros" introduces more ambivalence because the speaker addresses the people of his "pueblo" both as a character in the scene (he even sounds like one of the more avid boys instigating his fellows) and as the poet addressing the reader. The exclamations, the commands, the children, and the festive atmosphere all suggest a carnival atmosphere entailing the ambivalent celebration of life and death.[143] The question in vv. 10–14, a complicated concatenation of images, is equally ambivalent:

. . . ¿Recordáis ahora
cómo la flota eterna
de las estrellas sobre el agua
boga todas las noches, alta armada
invencible? . . .

(p. 115)[144]

   The reference to Spain's past power—or perhaps more accurately the illusion of power and the fleetingness of earthly fame and fortune—in the evocation of the Invincible Armada points to self-deception and disillusionment. This historical allusion forms a comparison with the stars reflected in the water of the river. The speaker suggests that even the stars are fleeting, not eternal as we are want to think. They, like the river, become ambivalent symbols of the transient and impermanent as well as the distant, unattainable, transcendent (cf. the cloud in "A la nube aquella"). The speaker's question can be either rhetorical or sincere. Does he want us to remember or to forget the image of invincibility? His exclamations sustain the carnivalesque tone but end enigmatically.

. . . ¡Ese ramo
15 a flor de agua también, a flor de vida!
¡Nadie se quede en casa hoy! ¡Al río,

> que allá va el ramo, allá se va la muerte
> más florida que nunca!
>
> (p. 115)[145]

The description of death as "más florida que nunca" seems like a contradiction.[146] It is here perhaps that we become aware of the ritual. The branch that has been thrown into the river is a flowering branch, reminiscent of Christ as the flowering rod. Also the adjective "florida" can refer to flames and suggests both destruction and regeneration as well as something impervious to or in contrast with the water of the river. Figuratively "florido" can mean "escogido, selecto."[147] The idiomatic expression "más . . . que nunca" uses a negation but is affirmative. As if that were not perplexing enough, the poet has appended three verses to the end of the poem, in which exclamations are totally lacking and the tone changes remarkably.

> . . . Ya no se ve. Dios sabe
> 20 si volverá, pero este año
> será de primavera en nuestro pueblo.
>
> (p. 115)[148]

The abrupt change in tone and rhythm, abating the tense excitement, suggests that the river and the branch have outstripped the boys throwing the rocks, and the ritual has come to an end. But it also shows us the speaker standing on the banks or perhaps from some vantage point, meditating on the significance of the branch. In throwing this flowering branch into the river, in sacrificing, making an ablution, the people have had to destroy life in order to assure its continuation. This act has mythical, archetypal proportions, echoing a tale such as Theseus and the Minotaur or sacrificial acts such as spilling wine as a libation, the burnt offerings of the Old Testament, and of course Christ. To chase away death, we have to sacrifice a part of life to death. Why, then, isn't the speaker as enthusiastic in the final stanza as he was earlier?

Here again we find the stamp of the chiasmus, for the speaker identifies with the branch. As the difficult, introspective, genuine poet, he too must sacrifice himself. Sometime in the future his work, his self-sacrifice may receive recognition. But whether it does or not, he must continue on the narrow path. Just as the river represents both the transient and the timeless, so the poet must sacrifice himself to ensure the continuation of the tradition. A part of life must be sacrificed to death to regenerate life. Rodríguez has chosen that narrow, difficult path, and we must follow him if we are to resurrect him.

In "El baile de águedas" [The dance of Agathas], Rodríguez describes a rural dance to present an ironic, skeptical view of life and art. A most significant aspect of this poem is found in its title, a dual sign that initiates a dialogic conflict.[149] On the one hand, dance universally and symbolically represents

> the corporeal image of a given process, or of becoming, or of the passage of time. . . .
> There is a universal belief that, in so far as it is a rhythmic art-form, it is a symbol of
> the act of creation. This is why the dance is one of the most ancient forms of magic.
> Every dance is a pantomime of metamorphosis . . . which seeks to change the dancer

into a god, a demon or some other chosen form of existence. Its function is, in consequence, cosmogonic. The dance is the incarnation of eternal energy.[150]

This particular dance, however, adds an ironic twist to the symbolic and paradoxical proportions of dance in general because of a reversal of the male/female roles. Gustavo Correa explains that this is a

> baile para celebrar la fiesta de Santa Agueda . . . que tiene lugar el cinco de febrero. . . . En la provincia de Zamora en España, existen las cofradías de mujeres llamadas "águedas" que organizan la fiesta. En el baile del día señalado, las mujeres invitan a bailar a los hombres.[151]

Hence, the ironic perspective governs "El baile de águedas" from the very beginning. The structure of the poem embodies this conflict. In the first part (vv. 1–30), the speaker prepares for the dance with hope and anticipation, whereas in the second part, he attends the dance but is disappointed by his apparent lack of participation. In each case, however, irony aggravates the interplay of the representational and the symbolic, subverting the transcendent aspects of the dance and producing a skeptical outlook.

Although several aspects of the text lead to the perception of a transcendent level of meaning arising in the mimetic scene, many of these transcendent meanings are undercut by ambivalent symbols.[152] The words "raíl" (v. 12) and "febrero" (v. 32), for example, point to both the transient and the transcendent.

> Ya están ahí, ya vienen
> por el raíl con sol de la esperanza
> hombres de todo el mundo.
> . . . .
> . . . Estoy en medio
> de la fiesta y ya casi
> cuaja la noche pronta de febrero.
>
> (p. 119)[153]

"Raíl" refers to the wagon tracks in a country lane, metonymically and metaphorically evoking the wheel that made the rut (wheel = circle = endless time) and the road of life. The month of February appears to be a mere anecdotal detail, but is a symbol of purification, an important theme in *Conjuros* (cf. "A mi ropa tendida").[154] Yet both symbols refer to the passage of time and erode the transcendent aspects of the scene. The description of clothing worn at this dance would also seem to emphasize the symbolic level by associating it with history and tradition.

> Cuánto manteo, cuánta media blanca,
> 20 cuánto refajo de lanilla, cuánto
> corto calzón. ¡Bien a lo vivo, como
> esa moza se pone su pañuelo,
> poned el alma así, bien a lo vivo!
>
> (p. 119)[155]

This traditional attire seems at first to be a woman's, especially because the speaker remarks upon a "moza" putting on her kerchief; but he equates the kerchief with the soul and the girl's flair in wearing it with spiritual qualities. In this way, he creates an uneasy relationship between the superficial and the spiritual.[156] This variant of the matrix along with the reversal of roles indicated in the title induces the reader to take a second look at the other clothing. In the past "manteo," "media," and "refajo" were garments also worn by men (the "corto calzón" was worn exclusively by men), generating a conflict between past and present. We then perceive an ironic undercurrent in the nostalgic tone of the subsequent verses.

> Echo de menos ahora
> 25   aquellos tiempos en los que a sus fiestas
> se unía el hombre como el suero al queso.
> Entonces sí que daban
> su vida al sol, su aliento al aire, entonces
> sí que eran encarnados en la tierra.
>
> (p. 119)[157]

By juxtaposing these verses with the conflict in the description of the clothing, the speaker expresses a tacit criticism of the insincerity and lack of integrity of his contemporaries. He recognizes the need for more transcendent values in life, but the values he seeks cannot be attained by making merely superficial changes. The description of the clothing undermines the nostalgic tone and sustains the text's duality.

The final verses lay bare the ambivalence of the dance and intensify the dialogic interaction. Because the roles are reversed, the speaker cannot choose his partner, but must wait until someone selects him. His desire to participate in the transcendent aspects of the dance is thwarted, and he is unable to stop time from slipping away. He is especially disappointed when he sees a young dancer partaking with another of the transcendent experience of the dance. In contrast, the dancers, oblivious of their transience, appear frivolous when compared with the imponderable issues the speaker has confronted and the incisive insight he has acquired.

> Oyeme tú, que ahora
> pasas al lado mío y un momento,
> 45   sin darte cuenta, miras a lo alto
> y a tu corazón baja
> el baile eterno de Aguedas del mundo,
> óyeme tú, que sabes
> que se acaba la fiesta y no la puedes
> 50   guardar en casa como un limpio apero,
> y se te va, y ya nunca . . .
> tú, que pisas la tierra
> y aprietas tu pareja, y bailas, bailas.
>
> (p. 120)[158]

A dual tension is at play in the roles of the dancer and the speaker. The latter feels that he is on the periphery, able to observe but unable to participate because he has not been chosen. Even so, through his observation and description of the event and his feelings, even in the young woman's rejection of him, he does participate. Ironically, the dancer fails to achieve transcendence because s/he is little more than a transient vehicle by which the dance itself is perpetuated. Therefore, the speaker and the dancer have similar relationships with the dance: both participate and fail to participate in the transcendent experience. By extension, the dance is eternal, but cannot exist without the participation of the individual, timebound, earthbound dancers. Both the dance and the dancers are on a fine edge between transience and transcendence because their relationship is correlative: Each highlights the fundamental nature of the other by virtue of their antithesis, yet neither can achieve fulfillment without the other.

Looking at this text metapoetically, we can see that Rodríguez has made a complex and equivocal discovery. If the "águeda" represents the poetic muse, both poet and reader seek to participate in the sublime atmosphere of the poem (the dance). In doing so, they seek transcendence, a suspension from the transience of everyday reality. The results of this endeavor are ambivalent, however, because it is the dialectic between the poet/reader and the poem, the pedestrian and the sublime, the transient and the transcendent, the representational and the symbolic, that determines the realization of the poetic act, discovery and knowledge.[159] Hence, the speaker has acquired a skeptical outlook on the nature of reality—which includes art—and is now able to acknowledge the ironic aspects of his discovery.

Although "Pinar amanecido" [Dawning pine grove] is the last poem of "Libro cuarto" and *Conjuros*, the ironic chiasmus that marks these final poems disavows closure. As usual, binary contrasts bring about an ironic reversal. In "Pinar" the speaker contrasts the pine-grove—a solitary but sacred place, the locus of poetry—with the city where people live in close proximity to one another but form no intimate bond. This contrast produces two conflicting tones: When the speaker addresses the "viajero" directly, his tone is sincere; but as he describes the city, he slips subtly into irony and even sarcasm. We will see, however, that the sincere address of the other results in an ironic reversal on the speaker. The initial verses validate the sincerity of the speaker and his appreciation of the pine-grove as a sacred precinct that represents the poetic space.

> Viajero, tú nunca
> te olvidarás si pisas estas tierras
> del pino.
> Cuánta salud, cuánto aire
> 5   limpio nos da. ¿No sientes
> junto al pinar la cura,
> el claro respirar del pulmón nuevo,
> el fresco riego de la vida? Eso
> es lo que importa. . . .

(p. 121)[160]

Once one has participated in the poetic experience (as writer or reader) in "estas tierras / del pino," one is inexorably changed by it. The speaker represents this change as a healing, healthful experience. The word "salud" metaphorizes the physical effects of healing into a state of grace and salvation.[161] The speaker understates the curative, revitalizing effects of this experience by omitting exclamation marks in the phrase "Cuánta salud . . . ," by using the rhetorical question "¿No sientes . . .?" and by the simplicity and directness of his statement "Eso / es lo que importa."

This tone changes gradually in the next verses (9–27). First we notice that they consist of a series of four exclamatory sentences, overstating the case. This series begins with the phrase "¡Pino piñonero . . . !"—a change in address whose alliteration and rhythm make us suspicious of the speaker's sincerity; it sounds too childlike.[162] These verses go on to describe "la cercanía hermosa / del hombre" who lives in the city. Even though these people live in close proximity and walk through the streets arm in arm, there are walls between them, separating them, preventing them from forming true intimacy and bonding:

> . . . ¡Todos juntos,
> pared contra pared, todos del brazo
> por las calles
> 15   esperando las bodas
> de corazón!
>
> (p. 121)[163]

The brevity of these lines also points to the lack of inspiration, paucity of emotion, and superficiality of life in the city. The "corro / de los niños" observed in the city (vv. 17–23) ironically reveals that these people are like children, afraid to let go of the others' hands and to stand apart independently. The speaker's terse conclusion "Es solidaridad" in v. 24 criticizes a "dependencia mutua entre los hombres que hace que no puedan ser felices si no lo son los demás" [a mutual dependence among men that means that they cannot be happy if all the others are not also happy].[164] If this irony seems too subtle, the image of the mother dove in vv. 24–27 is more explicitly critical.

> . . . Ah, tú, paloma
> 25   madre: mete el buen pico,
> mete el buen grano hermoso
> hasta el buche a tus crías.
>
> (p. 121)[165]

As children, we have a concept of mutual dependence and of our happiness dependent on others crammed down our craws. Life in the city is mundane, banal, exempt of poetry, of the questioning of oneself and one's attitudes that the poetic act requires. The speaker insistently urges the "viajero" to look ("vea, vea"). The adjective "hermoso"—a trite, banal modifier, not at all expressive and incisive as poetic adjectives should be, as we will see in contrast shortly—points to the weakness of his enthusiasm for life in the city. Having given this ironic and negative portrayal of life in the city, the speaker again addresses the "viajero," marking his return to sincerity. We note irony, however, in the biblical allusion: "Y ahora, viajero, / al cantar por

segunda vez el gallo, / ve al pinar y allí espérame" (vv. 28–30).[166] Certainly, this
intertext entails a disillusionment as the "viajero" must disabuse himself of the superficiality he observes in the city to see the reality of the situation, just as Peter had the
illusion that he would not deny Christ. But this disillusionment has ironic consequences, as we have seen in the speaker's experiences in "Libro segundo." This subtle
shift prepares us for the ironic reversal we will perceive the next time the speaker
addresses the "viajero" and allows us to move more quickly and decisively into the
irony.

> Nunca digamos la verdad en esta
> 40   sagrada hora del día.
> Pobre de aquel que mire
> y vea claro, vea
> entrar a saco en el pinar la inmensa
> justicia de la luz, esté en el sitio
> 45   que a la ciudad ha puesto la audaz horda
> de las estrellas, la implacable hueste
> del espacio.
> Pobre de aquel que vea
> que lo que une es la defensa, el miedo.
>
> (p. 122)[167]

Repetition of the phrase "Pobre de aquel que vea" underscores the clearly ironic
"Nunca digamos la verdad." In effect, the person who is able to see clearly and to
appreciate the insights afforded by the pine-grove (participation in the poetic act) is
not at all poor or woeful. The military imagery of the invading horde of stars and the
open air attests to the intensity of poetic experience, to the painful destruction of the
old self but the light and purity of the new vision of self. The adjectives "inmensa,"
"audaz," and "implacable" express much more than the insipid "hermoso" used in the
description of the specious unity in the city. The speaker again understates his irony
by refusing to use exclamation marks. The poem culminates with an ironic reversal as
the poet again addresses the other.

> Qué sutil añagaza, ruin chanchullo,
> 55   bien adobado cebo
> de la apariencia.
> ¿Dónde el amor, dónde el valor, sí, dónde
> la compañía? Viajero,
> sigue cantando la amistad dichosa
> 60   en el pinar amaneciente. Nunca
> creas esto que he dicho:
> canta y canta. Tú, nunca
> digas por estas tierras
> que hay poco amor y mucho miedo siempre.
>
> (p. 122)[168]

The past participle of the title "Pinar amanecido" has become a gerundive adjective, suggesting that the process continues. The placement of the repeated "nunca,"

echoing the first verse of the poem, points to a change. This "viajero" is someone who is always traveling, synonymous with the poet's continual effort to know himself better. (We have already seen the image of walking as metaphor for writing.) And so, if we have not already realized it, this traveler may be the perceptive reader who shares the poet's outlook, but it could just as likely be a "desdoblamiento" (a doubling or unfolding) of the speaker himself. If the other is the self, then this speaker's criticism of the lack of love, unity, and friendship that he sees in others is a criticism of his own lack. In the very last line of the book, the poet discovers yet another shortcoming in himself, forestalling closure, continuing the poetic process, pushing us onward into *Alianza y condena* and an exploration of the self as other. *Conjuros* has delineated a profound examination of the self promulgated by a series of ironic reversals. Although this stage in the process has come to an end, the process continues.

3

The Gaze, the Other, and the (Re)Constitution of the Self: The Poet's Coming of Age in *Alianza y condena* (1965)

> And this is the condemnation,
> that light is come into the world . . .
> . . . that you should put away the old self
> of your former way of life,
> corrupted through deceitful desires,
> and be renewed in the spirit of your mind,
> and put on the new self . . .

Alianza y condena is considered Rodríguez's masterpiece, for in this book the poet regenerates and reconfigures his previous discoveries about language and the poetic act and solidifies his poetic voice. In comparison with *Don de la ebriedad* and *Conjuros,* the two-poem section of *Alianza* is the last of four "Libros." Given that these two poems are odes—celebrations of childhood and hospitality, respectively—we could say that this section culminates the work and that the preceding sections progressively lead up to these crowning effusions. The dynamics of the work are more complex, however, as the structure is configured by two contradictory vectors.

First, the center of each of the first three "Libros" diminishes from three poems to one poem to a gap between poems, each a turning point in its respective section. Concomitant but in contrast with the diminishment at the center, at the end of each section a spilling over or excess progressively increases. In "Libro primero," this excess consists of "Noche en el barrio," which, along with "Eugenio de Luelmo," forms part of the closing frame, producing a minimal spillover. The pattern of "Libro segundo" demarcates the frame more definitively, with "Espuma" (the first poem) paralleling "Frente al mar" (the penultimate) and "Girasol" in the exact center between them. As a result, the substantial "Ciudad de meseta" falls completely outside the frame, a significant increase in the spillover.

Finally, "Libro tercero" is composed of sixteen poems that can be divided into two groups of eight and then subdivided into four groups of four. Each of these four groups adumbrates a different figure from classical mythology, all representing the speaker as poet and transgressor: Prometheus, Orpheus, Dionysus, and Apollo. Although they delineate a progression from beginning to end, these figures interact with one another in myriad ways, creating a pattern in which the two groups of eight and the four groups of four play against one another in a dynamic interaction of similarity and difference. To account for this tight symmetrical structure, we must conceive of the center as the gap or threshold between the two middle poems ("Adiós" and "Noche abierta") and the entirety of "Libro cuarto" as the spillover or excess, which increases inversely with regard to the diminishment of the center. In addition, the two odes are divided into seven parts in all, the same number of poems that compose "Libro primero." Again we recognize a fractal-like structure and a *mise en abïme* pattern of rejection/acceptance in the design of *Alianza*. This process has ethical and aesthetic implications in the poet's search for meaning and identity in a dialectic of self and other.

The contradictory vectors of the structure reflect the relationship between the two terms of the title—"alianza" and "condena"—which unites but also plays these terms against one another. If the speaker allies himself with the "negative" position (which I shall define more specifically in the discussion of "Brujas a mediodía"), he risks condemning himself to ethical and poetic oblivion. Ironically, this negative position forms part of the speaker's character, requiring that he accept it as a part of himself so that he can then repudiate and move away from it. If he opts instead for the "positive" aspect (condemning the negative), he will ally himself with lasting (sublime and transcendent) values, achieve his ethical goals, and give meaning to his aesthetic endeavor. Both "alianza" and "condena" adopt ambivalent meanings since we can interpret each positively and negatively. A further irony resides in the conjunction "y"—a semantically insignificant or marginal word compared with "alianza" and "condena," yet one located at the center of the title. This conjunction forms a crux, uniting the terms of the duality and at the same time setting them in opposition.

This ironic duality appears in each section of *Alianza*, each time producing a different configuration of the dialectic between self and other, similarity and difference, acceptance and rejection. This trait can also be seen in the poetic process that forms the basis of each section. The poems of "Libro primero" resemble those of *Don:* They stem from a concept that the poet attempts to grasp by embodying it in concrete images (e.g., the witches of "Brujas"). Yet they also delineate the four steps of identifying irony that forms the basis of *Conjuros*. Rodríguez reverses this situation in "Libro segundo," where the speaker encounters specific scenes in which he unveils transcendent meaning, reminiscent of *Conjuros*. These discoveries lead to an ironic consequence: While he recognizes them in the world around him, he realizes his own lack of these values, a play of difference that recalls the experiences of *Don*.[1] The third section of *Alianza* combines the two previous processes—reflecting the play of difference in the title—whereas the two odes that constitute "Libro cuarto" invert the relationship again.

In addition to fleshing out these concepts, this discussion will focus on the inter-action between self and other, particularly the speaker and various male and female figures who are reflections of himself. The changing relationship of self to other throughout *Alianza* resembles Jacques Lacan's definition of the development of sub-jectivity. "Libro primero" represents the premirror stage or what Lacan calls the Imagi-nary order.[2] Here the poet depicts the imagoes that define his character and formulates the direction of his search for individuality by means of the gaze.[3] Frames and mirror images of otherness in "Libro segundo" designate this section as the mirror stage.[4] Recognizing the similarities and differences between himself and the others he ob-serves in the mirror (the world around him) allows the speaker to advance the process of individuation. The mythological figures of "Libro tercero" embody the Law of the Name-of-the-Father.[5] The speaker can identify with each of these masculine figures, an identification (similarity) that enables him to individuate (be different). A psychoanalytical reading of the poems and a consideration of their arrangement in *Alianza* will illuminate the process of (re)constituting the self in which Rodríguez is engaged in this work.

THE PREMIRROR STAGE: THE GAZE AND IMAGOES OF THE SELF

"Libro primero" entails the same aspects that characterize the irony in *Conjuros*, now transposed onto the speaker's relationship with life: (1) a rejection of surface meaning; (2) a consideration of alternatives; (3) a decision about his position; and (4) a reconstruction in harmony with that decision. We can compare this section of *Alianza* with Lacan's premirror stage in which the speaker recognizes his ideal egos and for-mulates the terms of his search: his desire to bring about a shift in his outlook, to emend his attitudes.[6] The ambivalence of alliance and condemnation can be seen in the imagery and in a shift in tone in many of these poems. In the individual poems and in their arrangement in the section, we note a rejection (condemnation) of one posi-tion followed by a striving toward (alliance with) another. This tipping of the scales occurs synchronically (within individual poems) and diachronically (throughout the section).

Using bold brush strokes, we can depict "Libro primero" as a triptych: "Brujas a mediodía" [Witches at noon] and "Gestos" [Gestures] set forth the problem in its most negative light, open the frame, and determine the direction of the speaker's search; "Porque no poseemos" [Because we do not possess], "Cáscaras" [Husks], and "Por tierra de lobos" [Through the land of wolves]—all two-part poems at the center of the section—render the transition; and finally "Eugenio de Luelmo" and "Noche en el barrio" [Night in the neighborhood] counterbalance "Brujas" and "Gestos," bracketing the three center poems. The final two poems substitute the imago of Eugenio for that of the witches, but they invert the perspective: If the speaker must accept the witches as part of himself in order to distance himself from them, he must also admit that he is still distant from the values Eugenio represents to move closer to them. This structure demonstrates the alliance/condemnation (acceptance/rejection) motif underlying "Libro primero."[7]

Accepting and Condemning the Witches' Magic Spell

Given that Rodríguez employs the same poetic process as in *Don*—embodying an abstract concept in a concrete image—it may not be readily apparent that the witches of "Brujas a mediodía" [Witches at noon] constitute an imago within the speaker's psyche. Indeed, the alienation created by their grotesqueness exacerbates his reluctance to accept them as his. Read from a psychoanalytic perspective, the title and the subtitle "Hacia el conocimiento" [Toward knowledge] invoke contradictory plays on words, slips of the tongue, verbal manifestations of ambivalence that turn the tables on the speaker to reveal that these indeed are his attitudes.[8] Normally, midnight is the "witching hour," the opportune time for witches to appear and torment their victims. Yet these witches (the speaker's "nightmares") appear at noon! Through familiarity with Rodríguez's semiotic codes, we might infer that noon is the brightest part of the day, so that at this moment the speaker perceives these witches most clearly and is most aware of the threat they pose to him. But because it is noon—the differential opposite of midnight—the witches are disempowered and have less impact. The awareness of these witches is most acute, yet the very recognition of them allows the speaker to move "Hacia el conocimiento," toward knowing them (and himself) better, toward a different perspective (a condemnation of the witches moves him toward an alliance with their opposite).[9]

As Margaret Persin perceptively demonstrates, "Brujas" begins with a definition of the bewitchment by asserting what it is not.[10] Jonathan Culler points out that "in most cases the logical presuppositions of positive and negative propositions are the same, but rhetorically, pragmatically, literarily, negations are much richer in presuppositions."[11] More importantly, perhaps, Harold Bloom reminds us that "In the Freudian *Verneinung,* a previously repressed thought, feeling or desire enters consciousness only be being disowned."[12] Here negation signals the presence of irony, the rejection of superficial meaning.

> No son cosas de viejas
> ni de agujas sin ojo o alfileres
> sin cabeza. No salta,
> como sal en la lumbre, este sencillo
> 5 sortilegio, este viejo
> maleficio. Ni hisopo
> para rociar ni vela
> de cera virgen necesita. . . .

(p. 127)[13]

The speaker informs us that this witchcraft, though "sencillo" and "viejo" (elementary and well known), is more serious and pernicious than old wives' tales, superstitions, magic tricks, or even the religious rituals of blessings and exorcisms. The speaker's distant (but far from neutral) tone, his insistent negation, the hypnotic rhythm and alliteration ("este sencillo / sortilegio, este viejo / maleficio"), and the odd line breaks suggest that his tone is ironic. Add to this the connection between witch-craft and the title of Rodríguez's previous work, *Conjuros*, in which irony is the pre-dominant mode, and we might deem that the speaker mocks the witches and considers them an external threat from which he wishes to distance himself. The following verses confirm that they reside within him, at the very core of his being:

```
                          . . . Cada
          forma de vida tiene
   10     un punto de cocción, un meteoro
          de burbujas. Allí, donde el sorteo
          de los sentidos busca
          propiedad, allí, donde
          se cuaja el ser, en ese
   15     vivo estambre, se aloja
          la hechicería. . . .
```
                                                    (p. 127)[14]

The witches emblematize the speaker's lack of moral fiber: his superficiality, materialism, lasciviousness, deceit, dishonesty, falsity, and egotism. His grotesque description of them points to his repudiation of these traits as repulsive.

```
                    . . . No es tan sólo el cuerpo,
          con su leyenda de torpeza, lo que
          nos engaña: en la misma
          constitución de la materia, en tanta
   20     claridad que es estafa,
          guiños, mejunjes, trémulo
          carmín, nos trastornaban. Y huele
          a toca negra y aceitosa, a pura
          bruja este mediodía de setiembre;
   25     y en los pliegues del aire,
          en los altares del espacio, hay vicios
          enterrados, lugares
          donde se compra el corazón, siniestras
          recetas para amores. Y en la tensa
   30     maduración del día, no unos labios
          sino secas encías,
          nos chupan de la sangre
          el rezo y la blasfemia,
          el recuerdo, el olvido,
   35     todo aquello que fue sosiego o fiebre.
```
                                                    (pp. 127–28)[15]

The speaker portrays these witches as tawdry, lurid prostitutes with overly painted faces ("trémulo / carmín") and toothless mouths ("secas encías").[16] The witches trick and deceive him with winks behind his back ("guiños"), prepare sinister magic potions ("mejunjes," "siniestras / recetas para amores"), and suck all emotion and life out of him ("nos chupan de la sangre / el rezo y la blasfemia, / el recuerdo, el olvido, / todo aquello que fue sosiego o fiebre").[17] In *Don* clarity blinded, but blindness led to more insight; here insight ("tanta / claridad que es estafa") is a fraudulent but fruitful perspective. "[E]ste mediodía de setiembre" is the moment of greatest deceit and of greatest insight. The hottest, driest month of the year, September is a time of great light but also of dryness and a blistering heat that desiccates life but leads to harvest. The more recent spelling of the month, which omits the "p," could intimate more than idiosyncratic usage or modern convention: perhaps a loss of traditional values or a laziness that produces distortion or deformation connected with the grotesque image of the witches and their toothlessness (a lack or gap), but also a fruitful new perspective rooted in a willingness to accept change and the instability of language.[18]

A third link in this chain of metaphors appears in "la tensa / maduración del día." The enjambment as well as "maduración" (as opposed to "madurez") emphasizes a continuing process in contrast with a definitive conclusion. The preposition "de" is also ambivalent: Is the day coming to maturity at this tense moment, or does the light of day have a maturational effect on the speaker, who is coming into his own? These ambivalencies are borne out in the final verses of the first part of "Brujas."

> Como quien lee en un renglón tachado
> el arrepentimiento de una vida,
> con tesón, con piedad, con fe, aun con odio,
> ahora, a mediodía, cuando hace
> 40   calor y está apagado
> el sabor, contemplamos
> el hondo estrago y el tenaz progreso
> de las cosas, su eterno
> delirio, mientras chillan
> 45   las golondrinas de la huida.
>
> (p. 128)[19]

To read a crossed-out line is to go beyond the superficial (to reject surface meaning), to plumb the palimpsest of the text, to read beyond the explicit meaning of words, indeed to go beyond words and to find meaning ("el arrepentimiento de una vida") in the obliteration of words. At this paradoxical moment of noon, the speaker notices the heat (perhaps discomfort, perhaps passion: "tesón," "piedad," "fe," "odio"), and he seeks something that will assuage him, some explanation of the meaning of his life. Besides its curious blend of the personal and the impersonal, its inclusiveness and its indefiniteness, the meaning of the verb "contemplamos" ("to see, to observe" but also "to step back and to meditate" on what has been observed) sustains the ambivalence. We might also ask whether a contrast arises between "el hondo estrago" and "el tenaz progreso": Is there destruction or progress?[20] Does the phrase "las cosas" function literally (materialism) or abstractly (affairs, life in general)? Is the delirium ecstasy or stupor, and is its eternal quality sublime or painfully transient? Does it lift us to a timeless ecstasy, or do we continually suffer the fate of the material and transient?

The final image captures the ineffable in a commonplace facet of Spanish life.
The swallows could be an objective image of the speaker's repulsion for the witches
or perhaps the witches themselves screaming as they flee chaotically from this expo-
sure at noon. The onomatopoeic repetition of the /i/ has a powerful aural impact,
allowing us to see that the witches can be read not only as the speaker's shallow moral
attitudes but also as language itself, the deception and destruction that placing one's
faith in words (especially as a poet) can engender. All these ambivalencies reflect the
ironic implications of the titles *Alianza y condena* and "Brujas a mediodía (Hacia el
conocimiento)." They also point to the first step in the speaker's progress, the rejection of superficiality. Often the emphasis on marginal aspects of language (slips of the
tongue, puns, alliteration, oral/aural aspects) foregrounds latent (ironic) meaning.

The Baudelairean grotesqueness of the first part of "Brujas" is tempered in the
second part, moving away from the "negative" and toward the "positive" as the speaker
begins to consider alternatives. In this second part (and in the next poem "Gestos,"
opening the frame), the speaker strengthens the nexus between the ethical and the
aesthetic, defining writing as a gesture and including words among the most ambivalent of gestures. The second part of "Brujas" begins with a catalog of metonymic
elements that suggest wider resonances but fall short of the symbolic.

> La flor del monte, la manteca añeja,
> el ombligo de niño, la verbena
> de la mañana de San Juan, el manco
> muñeco, la resina,
> 5   buena para caderas de mujer,
> el azafrán, el cardo bajo la olla
> de Talavera con pimienta y vino,
> todo lo que es cosa de brujas, cosa
> natural, hoy no es nada junto a este aquelarre
> 10   de imágenes que, ahora,
> cuando los seres dejan poca sombra,
> da un reflejo: la vida.
>
> (pp. 128–29)[21]

The items composing this catalog echo the list of superstitious spells and rituals
at the beginning of the first part of "Brujas," but this pedestrian listing reduces them
to "home remedies" or commonplace beliefs and then subordinates them to the bewitching power of words, "este aquelarre / de imágenes." This transition serves as a
springboard into the essential question of *Alianza*, as the interrogatives in the subsequent verses indicate.

> La vida no es reflejo
> 15   pero, ¿cuál es su imagen?
> Un cuerpo encima de otro
> ¿siente resurrección o muerte? ¿Cómo
> envenenar, lavar
> este aire que no es nuestro pulmón?
> 20   ¿Por qué quien ama nunca

busca verdad, sino que busca dicha?
¿Cómo sin la verdad
puede existir la dicha? He aquí todo.

(p. 129)[22]

These issues recall Lacan's view of language as a representation of a representation and the relationship between the real, the Imaginary, and the Symbolic.[23] Words
present a reflection of life, but the reflection should not be mistaken for life itself.
What, then, is reality? What is truth?[24] The remaining questions amplify this cardinal
problem. The sexual act—"Un cuerpo encima de otro"—could represent either ecstasy and transcendence ("resurrección") or loss of self, uncertainty of identity, change,
and transience ("muerte"). Is "dicha" luck or happiness? Are the final questions rhetorical or literal? When the speaker declares "He aquí todo," is he totally perplexed
by the immensity of his questions, or does he hint that he has an answer to them (or at
least some insight)?[25] Regardless of the questioning, he designates where he will seek
identity and meaning: in the suture.

        Pero nosotros nunca
25   tocamos la sutura,
        esa costura (a veces un remiendo,
        a veces un bordado),
        entre nuestros sentidos y las cosas,
        esa fina arenilla
30   que ya no huele dulce sino a sal,
        donde el río y el mar se desembocan,
        un eco en otro eco, los escombros
        de un sueño en la cal viva
        del sueño aquel por el que yo di un mundo
35   y lo seguiré dando.

(p. 129)[26]

This suture is a liminal space, sometimes a remedial darning and sometimes beautiful embroidery, but always the site of rupture (a gap) and overlapping ("un eco en
otro eco"), the representation of a representation ("los escombros / de un sueño en la
cal viva del sueño").[27] Just as words evoke images and emerge from the repression of
a loss, just as one poem engages in dialogue with another, echoes and rewrites it, so
Rodríguez employs words to represent his identity and his understanding of himself
and his world.[28] That is why he can state without contradiction, "yo di un mundo / y lo
seguiré dando," though the preterit would indicate a completed action and the future
progressive one that will continue indefinitely.[29] Rodríguez exemplifies this contradiction in a series of images and in the slippage from one signifier to another.

35   . . . Entre las ruinas
        del sol, tiembla
        un nido con calor nocturno. Entre
        la ignominia de nuestras leyes, se alza
        el retablo con viejo
40   oro y vieja doctrina

de la nueva justicia. ¿En qué mercados
de altas sisas el agua
es vino, el vino sangre, sed la sangre?
¿Por qué aduanas pasa
45   de contrabando harina
como carne, la carne
como polvo y el polvo
como carne futura?

(pp. 129–30)[30]

These transformations attest to the constant slippage *(glissement)* of language because of the gap/suture, the bar between signifier and signified.[31] Appropriately, Rodríguez supplies stanzaic breaks after the phrase "He aquí todo" (introducing his discussion of the suture) and after these images with Christian overtones of bread and wine, death and resurrection. Echoing the catalog at the beginning of both sections of "Brujas," these images suggest that language is quicksand or a sinkhole wherein no solid footing can be reached. Yet it is in this liminal territory that Rodríguez seeks to found his identity, his aesthetics, and his ethics. The final stanza returns to the image of the witches, demystifying them and yet stressing the perplexing ambivalence they hold for the speaker.

Esto es cosa de bobos. Un delito
50   común este de andar entre pellizcos
de brujas. Porque ellas
no estudian sino bailan
y mean, son amigas
de bodegas. Y ahora,
55   a mediodía,
si ellas nos besan desde tantas cosas,
¿dónde estará su noche,
dónde sus labios, dónde nuestra boca
para aceptar tanta mentira y tanto
60   amor?

(p. 130)[32]

The witches are portrayed as banal beings the speaker disparages. Does he capitulate to them, giving in to their temptations—his vices—again? If he rejects the superficial, why does he wish to kiss them and to accept from their mouths "tanta mentira y tanto / *amor*"? It is only by admitting that these witches—ugly and banal as they are—belong to him that he is able to overcome them. Though they seem to exist outside him, they are in truth his deeply ingrained attitudes, his imagoes. Acceptance of them becomes rejection, and this rejection will lead to his greater capacity to love others and himself. These witches form part of the self and personify those attitudes the speaker wishes to emend so that he can find love. His search for love—hinted in the dedication of *Alianza* to his wife Clara—serves as an analogy for Rodríguez's ethical and aesthetic search for meaning and identity in a dialectic of self and other in this work.[33]

"Gestos" reinforces the connection between action (the ethical) and writing (the aesthetic). Because of the spontaneity of the gesture of writing and the exploration of the unknown (the unconscious) it entails, the speaker questions the significance of his actions and contemplates his act of writing as an aleatory process that takes place at the periphery, at the point of suture between the speaker and reality, the poet and the canon, in the territory of language.

> ... Cuando actúa mi mano,
> tan sin entendimiento y sin gobierno
> pero con erradunda resonancia,
> 5   y sondea, buscando
> calor y compañía en este espacio
> en donde tantas otras
> han vibrado, ¿qué quiere
> decir? Cuántos y cuántos gestos como
> 10   un sueño mañanero,
> pasaron. ...
>
> (p. 131)[34]

The hand synecdochically represents the act of writing, an act transformed into a handshake "buscando / calor y compañía." The poet reads others' works and writes to make contact with them and to seek recognition from the reader. But this act is pure chance, similar to the cards one is dealt. Will he receive a winning or a loosing "hand"? All is "sólo azar entrañable." The poet understands that there can be a great disparity between intention and consequence and that he has little control over how his poems are read.

In the second stanza of "Gestos," the speaker rejects a superficial perspective on life in favor of a more insightful evaluation. His reference to the pomp of patriotic parades and flag waving and the superficial repetition in the phrase "de fantasías y de dinastías" is succeeded by his call for a more profound vision and more heartfelt gestures. He does not, however, advocate a return to past values, which would interfere with and halt his writing.

> Nosotros, tan gesteros pero tan poco alegres,
> raza que sólo supo
> tejer banderas, raza de desfiles,
> 30   de fantasías y de dinastías,
> hagamos otras señas.
>
> . . . .
> No, no son tiempos
> de mirar con nostalgia
> esa estela infinita del paso de los hombres.
> 40   Hay mucho que olvidar
> y más aún que esperar.
>
> (pp. 131–32)[35]

Like an owl, the speaker will fly through the night (the unconscious) and trust that when he reaches the end of his quest, he will have produced a singular poetic expression.[36]

```
                    . . . Tan silencioso
             como el vuelo del búho, un gesto claro,
             de sencillo bautizo,
             dirá, en un aire nuevo,
      45     mi nueva significación, su nuevo
             uso. Yo sólo, si es posible,
             pido, cuando me llegue la hora mala,
             la hora de echar de menos tantos gestos queridos,
             tener fuerza, encontrarlos
      50     como quien halla un fósil
             (acaso una quijada aún con el beso trémulo)
             de una raza extinguida.
```

                                                      (p. 132)[37]

Even though his gesture will have been fossilized and eroded by the passing of time, he hopes to discover a jawbone (a fragment of his poem, his self) with a kiss still tremulous, still vital, still capable of expressing emotion. The "raza extinguida" with which he closes this poem could refer to extinct creatures (e.g., dinosaurs) that still fascinate and provoke a profound response in us. If we think of the poems of Manrique, Fray Luis, or Quevedo, for example, we may note that the language is archaic, the conventions and codes outdated, the traditions and customs described no longer in existence; yet these works still speak to us, still await us "con el beso trémulo." In "Gestos," the poet continues his rejection of superficiality, his criticism of a shallow gesture, and his questioning of the arbitrariness of language, but we also see him formulating his direction and his values as he moves away from alliance with the superficial and toward a perspective that will not condemn him to oblivion.

Transition: A Consideration of Alternatives and Reevaluation of the Self

The three poems in the center of "Libro primero" form a modulation in the speaker's progress as he considers alternative perspectives, moving him away from his negative attitudes and toward positive ones. The first of these poems "Porque no poseemos (La mirada)" [Because we do not possess (The gaze)] stands as one of the most important statements of *Alianza*. Here the speaker perceives the impact of the other in a reversal of the direction of the gaze. The concept of "La mirada" deals with the differentiation between looking and seeing, seeing and being seen.[38] In accord with Lacan's notion that desire is the desire *of* the Other (not *for* the Other), the speaker realizes that his identity, his (re)constitution of self, depends upon the Other.[39]

Slips of the tongue, puns, and indeterminacy establish a play of language set in motion by the repetition of the title in the first line. The completion of the sentence "Porque no poseemos, / vemos" [Because we do not possess, we see] causes us to look at the title and to question if the subtitle does not also complete—or extend—the title. By collapsing the two statements, we read the paradoxical "Porque no poseemos (la mirada), vemos" [Because we do not possess (the gaze), we see]. The repetition of the "-emos" morpheme rings ironic, and the conjunction "porque" is problematic.[40] How can we see if we do not possess the gaze? Do we have more (in)sight because we do not "see"? This confusion belies a sententious confidence and alerts us to the unexpected effects that sight and the gaze, seeing and being seen, have for (re)constituting the self. The conflation of sight and the gaze, subject and object, and the slippage of signifier into signified only to become signifier again, evolves further in the next verses.

> . . . La combustión del ojo en esta
> hora del día, cuando la luz, cruel
> de tan veraz, daña
> 5 la mirada, ya no me trae aquella
> sencillez. Ya no sé qué es lo que muere,
> qué lo que resucita. Pero miro,
> cojo fervor, y la mirada se hace
> beso, ya no sé si de amor o traicionero.

(p. 133)[41]

The image of fire (which destroys and regenerates) and the preposition "de" are ambivalent: Does the intensity of the speaker's look set reality ablaze (penetrating the surface, destroying a superficial meaning but creating new insight)? Or does his look reflect into his eye, so that the truth his look reveals affects him ironically: "La luz, cruel / de tan veraz, daña / la mirada"?[42] The poetic act can be a discovery of what is painful to realize. If the word "sencillez" reminds us of the speaker's innocence and delight, repetition of the phrase "ya no" and the parallelism "qué es lo que muere, / qué lo que resucita" mark his awareness of alternative perspectives and a deeper understanding of the nature of reality, the poetic act, and his own identity.

Because of this change in perspective, the meaning of "la mirada" shifts. In v. 5, the look belongs to the speaker; his illumination brings him pain along with greater insight. Verse 8 reverses the direction of the gaze; if the speaker does not know if the gaze as kiss conveys love or betrayal, he does not know what effect his look will have on him when it rebounds from that which he contemplates. When the gaze reverses direction, it no longer belongs to him; it becomes the gaze of the Other.[43] Punctuated by the repetition of the verb "Quiere," the ensuing verses express the purpose of the speaker's look. Yet this gaze/kiss now adopts a third-person volition of its own: The speaker does not say "Quiero," although he is the one who desires.

> 10 Quiere acuñar las cosas,
> detener su hosca prisa
> de adiós, vestir, cubrir
> su feroz desnudez de despedida
> con lo que sea: con esa membrana
> 15 delicada del aire,
> aunque fuera tan sólo
> con la sutil ternura
> del velo que separa las celdillas
> de la granada. Quiere untar su aceite,
> 20 denso de juventud y de fatiga,
> en tantos goznes luminosos que abre

la realidad, entrar
dejando allí, en alcobas tan fecundas,
su poso y su despojo,
25   su nido y su tormenta,
sin poder habitarlas. Qué mirada
oscura viendo cosas
tan claras. . . .

(p. 133)[44]

Repetitions abound in these verses: the infinitives "acuñar" and "detener," "vestir" and "cubrir"; the parallelism "detener su hosca prisa / de adiós" and "cubrir / su feroz desnudez de despedida"; the alliteration in the latter phrase and in "su poso y su despojo"; the metaphoric repetition "con esa membrana / delicada del aire," "con la sutil ternura / del velo que separa las celdillas / de la granada." With these images, the speaker attempts to capture the essence of what he would like to attain: to grasp forever the beauty of the world around him, to penetrate to the core of "las cosas," and to rescue their essence from the destruction of time's passage.

He wishes the same for himself as poet: to reach immortality through an-other's recognition of his poetic abilities. Although his gaze oils the hinges of reality and allows him to enter into a deeper understanding of life through language, he must also rely on an-other's opening of his world, his language, his poem, to ensure his identity. Because he does not possess the gaze, he can only observe, send his gaze out in hope that it will return to him from the Other. His exclamation "Qué mirada / oscura viendo cosas / tan claras" is summarily equivocal, playing with the concepts of sight and the gaze, seeing and being seen, light and darkness, self and other. This equivocality is sustained when he repeats the verb "Mira" in v. 28 and again in v. 34.

. . . Mira, mira:
allí sube humo, empiezan
30   a salir de esa fábrica los hombres,
bajos los ojos, baja la cabeza.
Allí está el Tormes con su cielo alto,
niños por las orillas, entre escombros
donde escarban gallinas. Mira, mira:
35   ve cómo ya, aun con muescas y clavijas,
con ceños y asperezas,
van fluyendo las cosas. . . .

(pp. 133–34)[45]

Whom does he address: himself or the (reader as) Other? Do these metonymic images—smoke rising from chimneys, men leaving a factory, children and chickens on the riverbank—merely present mimetic scenes; or do these scenes transcend mundane reality? Does smoke allude to fire, to a reaching toward the sublime?[46] Do we see the emptiness and the misery of a life that entails only working in a factory, never lifting one's head, one's sight, to higher aspirations? Will the routine of industrial society prevent others from recognizing the poet's skill? Does the scene on the riverbank suggest the transcendent innocence of childhood or its loss?[47] These contradictions culminate in the final verses of part I of "Porque no poseemos."

> . . . Mana, fuente
> de rica vena, mi mirada, mi única
> salvación, sella, graba,
> 40   como en un árbol los enamorados,
> la locura armoniosa de la vida
> en tus veloces aguas pasajeras.

(p. 134)[48]

The poet hopes to do the impossible by engraving the scenes before him on his gaze, which is in one respect like the river whose waters rush past. This image of the gaze as "fuente / de rica vena" reworks an image of *Don* which, as we have seen, is an intertextual echo of a verse from Baudelaire.[49] Registering what the poet has observed, the poem is the representation of a representation of a representation, and thus ephemeral, transient, absent before it is present, like words written on water. But just as intertextuality continues a tradition, water and especially a fountain symbolize an eternal source of life and inspiration, "mi única / salvación" as the speaker says. Writing, then, like the lovers' initials carved in a tree trunk (scars, sutures), becomes a way of preserving—however dimly—"la locura armoniosa de la vida": love, the desire to be desired, the gaze of the Other, the always future perfect achievement of the unfeasible.[50] The description of what he sees—his (in)sight—captures the fleeting moment—that which we can never "possess"—with another fleeting moment (the representation of a representation); yet words contain a trace of the sublime and the potential actualization of that trace in the gaze of the Other.

The tone of part I of "Porque no poseemos" is anxious, imploring, and ironic, belying the sententious, affirmative statement with which it begins. The tone of part II changes notably as the speaker considers alternatives in his rejection of surface meaning and a reevaluation of his stance. In this part of "Porque no poseemos," repetition is less frequent, so that the tone modulates to a more tranquil, contemplative key. This transition suggests a contrast between an ineffective, unproductive activity to a passivity that allows the speaker to arrive at insightful discoveries.[51] Coinciding with this reversal, the direction of the gaze rotates, disclosing its reciprocal nature.

> La misteriosa juventud constante
> de lo que existe, su maravillosa
> eternidad, hoy llaman
> con sus nudillos muy heridos a esta
> 5   pupila prisionera. Hacía tiempo
> (qué bien sé ahora el por qué) me era lo mismo
> ver flor que llaga, cepo que caricia;
> pero esta tarde ha puesto al descubierto
> mi soledad y miro
> 10   con mirada distinta. . . .

(p. 134)[52]

The transcendent, timeless essence of reality is personified as a diminutive creature knocking on the speaker's eyelids, inviting him to open his eyes, to receive illumination and (in)sight from the Other. The knuckles of this personified being are
"muy heridos": On the surface, reality looks shabby, familiar, and so commonplace
that we see only the worn-out, scratched, stained surface beneath which resides "la
misteriosa juventud constante / de lo que existe, su maravillosa / eternidad."[53] The
ordinariness and familiarity of the signifier disguises the potential of the signified, but
the personified signifier comes to the speaker to open his eyes to its new but hidden
meaning.

The speaker indicates—in the parenthetical expression and at the end of the second sentence—that his outlook has undergone modification, for "esta tarde ha puesto
al descubierto / mi soledad." If before he was unable to distinguish between death and
resurrection, love and betrayal, giving and taking, now he has become aware of his
aloneness (loneliness and solitude caused by separation). Rather than taking, he realizes that he must give; rather than aggressively seeking his own satisfaction, he must
risk making himself vulnerable to the Other. This realization describes interpersonal
relationships, but we can also envision this change in attitude as the speaker's understanding of the poetic act, his relationship with the poetic tradition and the world
around him, and his own transience and the need to seek recognition of his identity.
Awareness of the falseness of his former pernicious attitudes recalls the witches through
ocular imagery.

> . . . Compañeros
> falsos y taciturnos,
> cebados de consignas, si tan ricos
> de propaganda, de canción tan pobres;
> yo mismo, que fallé, tantas ciudades
> 15   con ese medallón de barro seco
> de la codicia, tanto pueblo rapaz,
> al que a mi pesar quiero,
> me fueron, a hurtadillas,
> haciendo mal de ojo, y yo seguía
> 20   entre los sucios guiños, esperando
> un momento. Este de hoy. . . .

(p. 134)[54]

The speaker expresses his disdain for his "compañeros" (other poets) in the adjectives "falsos y taciturnos" and "cebados" and in the contrast between "ricos" and
"pobres," "propaganda" and "canción." These latter terms point to a metapoetic level
as well as to an ethical one; the speaker's companions can hypocritically put up a
false front (propaganda), but they lack the true beauty of life (song). The aristocratic
"escudos" on the outside of dwellings disguises the "barro seco de la codicia"—greed
that is unproductive and self-defensive. The speaker himself was under the spell of
the evil eye, but he continued functioning in that milieu, using its same tricks and lies
("sucios guiños").[55] This reference to others and the past emphasizes the contrast with
the speaker's current illumination and the change in his outlook.

> ... Tiembla en el aire
> la última luz. Es la hora
> en que nuestra mirada
> se agracia y se adoncella.
> 25 La hora en que, al fin, con toda
> la vergüenza en la cara, miro y cambio
> mi vida entera por una mirada,
> esa que ahora está lejos,
> la única que me sirve, por la sola
> 30 cosa por la que quiero estos dos ojos:
> esa mirada que no tiene dueño.

(pp. 134–35)[56]

Ironically, it is at sunset (the approach of darkness) that the speaker can see his goal more clearly: the gaze of the Other, "esa mirada que no tiene dueño."[57] His perspective prior to this moment made him the "slave" of others (his contemporaries, his fellow poets) because they were slaves to their greed, falseness, pride, rapacity; each tried to "master" others through lies, curses, and tricks solely for personal gain.[58] Now ashamed of his former attitudes, the speaker seeks to free himself from a perspective that will only condemn him to being one among many. If he allies himself instead with "esa mirada que no tiene dueño," if he seeks honesty and truth with himself and with others, he will gain the recognition he seeks and transcend his temporal limitations. The gaze of the Other will determine the autonomy of the self.

If we reconsider the opening of the poem, we understand that the speaker's condemnation and exorcism of certain traits from his personality (greed, pride, egotism) lead him to see what he truly seeks in life. He recognizes that he must ally himself with a gaze that exists outside of himself to confirm his individuality. He must admit the Other to affirm the self. He must condemn the transient ego to ally himself with transcendent values. Ethically speaking, he must alter his interpersonal relationships (especially those with women) and humble himself to the presence/absence and desire of the Other. Metapoetically, he must write for himself and be true to his own feelings as if his ideal reader does exist somewhere, risking that every reader may misinterpret his writing, misread his intentions, betray him, prevent him from achieving the recognition and poetic immortality he desires.

Like "Porque no poseemos," the next two poems, "Cáscaras" and "Por tierra de lobos," show the speaker condemning the superficiality and emptiness of life that does not allow him to strive for higher values and to dare to individuate himself. Through this criticism of human nature and society the speaker expresses his desire to adopt alternative attitudes. The first part of "Cáscaras" [Husks] contains another catalog, this time of surfaces that prevent him from experiencing the true beauty and richness of life. He specifically mentions "El nombre de las cosas, que es mentira," "el traje / que cubre el cuerpo amado," "las cuatro copas que nos alegran," "la cautela del sobre," and "la inmensa cicatriz que oculta la honda herida."[59] These coverings, surfaces, are deceits ("ese prieto vendaje / de la costumbre, que nos tapa el ojo / para que no ceguemos, / la vana golosina de un día y otro día / templándonos la boca") that are hypocritical and harmful ("son un engaño / venenoso y piadoso").[60] They protect us from insight into reality and into ourselves, insight into a truth that may be difficult to accept.

This consideration leads to the formulation of two important questions in part II of "Cáscaras": "¿dónde / la oportunidad del amor, / de la contemplación libre o, al menos, / de la honda tristeza, del dolor verdadero?" (vv. 13–16) and "la cáscara y la máscara / . . . / ¿han de dar vida a tanta / juventud macerada, tanta fe corrompida?" (vv. 17, 23–24).[61] These questions ask "What is truth?" and "What will stand the test of time?" In reply to the hypocrisy and superficiality of life, the speaker addresses himself as "tú" and affirms the direction he wishes to take: "Pero tú quema, quema / todas las cartas, todos los retratos, / los pajares del tiempo, la avena de la infancia" (vv. 25–27).[62] The second-person "tú" posits the existence of an-other (himself as Other) to whom the speaker gives urgent and wise advice. The attempt to reach this goal, his change in attitude, is fraught with risk; but he is determined to leave his old attitudes behind because "El más seco terreno / es el de la renuncia" [The dryest terrain / is that of renunciation] (vv. 28–29).

Ironically, he must leave them behind without leaving; he must still negotiate "Por tierra de lobos" [Through a land of wolves]. He must separate himself from the world in which he lives and yet continue to live in that world. Parallelism and repetition with difference reveal the irony of the speaker's situation, the simultaneity of alliance and condemnation, acceptance and rejection, and the difficulty of finding such a place for himself. Each part of this poem begins with five verses establishing a parallel contrast, yet each contains a contradiction.

> Arrodillado sobre
> tantos días perdidos,
> contemplo hoy mi trabajo como a esa
> ciudad lejana, a campo
> 5   abierto.
>
> *   *   *
>
> Erguido sobre
> tantos días alegres,
> sigo la marcha. No podré habitarte,
> ciudad cercana. Siempre seré huésped,
> 5   nunca vecino.
>
> (pp. 139, 140)[63]

In part I, the humiliation and submission that cause the speaker to fall to his knees also allow him to distance himself and to evaluate his life and his work, just as he sees the city at a distance. In contrast, even though in part II the speaker stands erect and begins walking toward the city, he realizes that he will still be distant from it even after he has entered it. In spite of parallelism and repetition, there is also difference: The speaker must accept otherness in order to individuate; he must separate himself from others and yet remain among them. We could even say that he must separate himself from others *in order to* remain among them. These lines open each of the poem's two parts. By examining the "pictures" within these framing verses, the change in the speaker's attitude epitomized in this section of *Alianza* comes to the fore.

The speaker's heart, which he addresses as "tú" in part I of "Por tierra de lobos," represents his own self, but the direct address distances him from himself and moves him toward the gaze of the Other (separation and individuation). The speaker complains that his heart blames him for having fallen to his knees. His heart represents that part of himself that would prefer the easy way out: that of not confronting the truth about himself. The speaker rejects such an approach, however.

> Y tú me culpas de ello,
> corazón, duro amo.
> Que recuerde y olvide,
> que aligere y que cante
> 10 para pasar el tiempo,
> para perder el miedo;
> que tantos años vayan de vacío
> por si nos llega algo
> que cobije a los hombres.
> 15 Como siempre, ¿eso quieres?
>
> (p. 139)[64]

The heart, a harsh master ("duro amo"), would like to keep the speaker as its slave by having him follow a superficial, mundane path. But the speaker understands that he will not distinguish himself if he follows that path, and he returns to the gain/loss motif that we have highlighted in earlier poems.

> En manada, no astutos
> sino desconfiados,
> unas veces altivos
> otras menesterosos, por inercia
> 20 e ignorancia, en los brazos
> del rencor, con la honra
> de su ajo crudo y de su vino puro,
> tú recuerda, recuerda
> cuánto en su compañía
> 25 ganamos y perdimos.
> ¿Cómo podrás ahora
> acompasar deber
> con alegría, dicha
> con dinero? Mas sigue.
>
> (p. 139)[65]

In the second stanza, the speaker reexamines an earlier period in his life. His lengthy enumeration of the vices, coldness, and spiritual poverty he encountered includes "la muerte," "la envidia," "cobardes," "pobreza," "arrogancia," "carcoma," "notas / de sociedad, linaje, favor público," "adulación," "avaricia," and "enemigos," "aquellos hombres . . . tan sólo ávidos / de municiones y de víveres."[66] The often-cited examples of Rodríguez's imagery "la adulación color lagarto / junto con la avaricia olor a incienso" [adulation the color of a lizard / along with greed the color of incense] is a criticism of the military (whose olive-green drab reminds the speaker of a lizard, a cold-blooded, scaly reptile who likes to bask in the sun) and the clergy (who cloak their greed in the smoke screen of incense). Although I would not deny Rodríguez's specific criticism of the roles the military and clergy have played in Spanish society, in a broader frame of reference most of us expect soldiers and priests to have higher ethical and moral standards because of the discipline and moral commitment of their respective orders. The speaker comments on the corruption and degradation of values pervading even these sectors of society. He remembers "Aquellas / mañanas con su fuerte / luz de meseta, tan consoladora" (vv. 50–52)—his hope for the future— only to recognize how blind and pacified ("amortiguado") he was by these scenes, concealing the truth even about his feelings for the girls he saw, "Aquellas niñas que iban al colegio" (v. 53).[67] His blindness was a protection that now makes his disillusionment more acute.

In contrast with his more innocent past depicted in the image of "aquellas mañanas" and "aquellas niñas," part II of the poem looks at the more recent past, the dark side, the night, the moral darkness through which the speaker now walks as he approaches the city he can never inhabit though he will enter and reside there. The implication is that the speaker has participated in some sordid sexual scenes, linking these verses with the image of "Aquellas niñas."

> 10 No me importó otras veces
> la alta noche,
> recordadlo. Sé que era lamentable
> el trato aquel, el hueco
> repertorio de gestos
> 15 desvencijados,
> sobre cuerpos de vario
> surtido y con tan poca
> gracia para actuar. . . .
>
> (p. 141)[68]

These adventures result in the disgusted avowal of the hypocrisy of hieratic old men, "hombres / con diminutos ojos triangulares / como los de la abeja, / legitimando oficialmente / el fraude, la perfidia, / y haciendo la vida negociable" (vv. 20–25) and the outrage of prim, proper old women.[69] They are as guilty as he, though for different reasons.

> Como en la vieja historia oí aquellas
> palabras a alta noche, con alcohol,
> 35 o de piel de gamuza
> o bien correosas, córneas, nunca humanas.
> Vi la decrepitud, el mimbre negro.
> Vi que eran dolorosas las campanas
> a las claras del alba.
>
> (p. 141)[70]

Neither the men nor the women have very Christian attitudes: the men because they live vicariously through the speaker (black wicker is a symbol of solemn, sacred protection) and the women because they inflict remorse and punishment rather than pouring out love and joy (they get up at dawn to go to Mass when they could remain in bed).[71] The emphatic repetition of "Vi" distances the speaker from them and enables him to repudiate their hypocrisy.

It is fitting that the title alludes to the Freudian symbol of the wolf (male sexuality). Sexual overtones and the reactions of men and women to sexuality (priests and "beatas" [saintly women]) add another level to this poem and the speaker's quest for a change in his outlook. He recognizes that until now he too has been a hypocrite and a "wolf" ready to pounce on innocent lambs ("aquellas niñas"). To condemn the hypocrisy of others requires that the speaker admit his own shortcomings. This brings us to a consideration of the final three verses in each part, aware that an ironic reversal is hinted in the repetition, parallelism, and mirroring of syllabic patterns.

>   A veces, sin embargo, en esas tierras
> 60   floreció la amistad. Y muchas veces
>   hasta el amor. Doy gracias.
>
>   *   *   *
>
> 40   Es hora muy tardía
>   mas quiero entrar en la ciudad. Y sigo.
>   Va a amanecer. ¿Dónde hallaré vivienda?
>
>   (pp. 140, 141)[72]

After the lengthy catalog of vices and superficialities that he recalls from his childhood, in the midst of this thoroughly repugnant society, the speaker unexpectedly comes upon friendship and love. Even though he is immersed in the negativity of this "tierra de lobos," he still finds something for which to be grateful. The simplicity of his statement "Doy gracias," along with the terseness of the punctuation and the line breaks, lends humility and awe to the miracle of these bright spots in his life (highlighted by the verb "floreció"), and so he kneels.

If we then compare that realization with the speaker's search for lodging at the end of part II, we might expect that he will be as delightfully surprised; but the anecdotal situation is symbolic of wider issues and points to the risk the speaker is taking. He has been walking through the countryside where he has come to grips with his desire to individuate, to stand apart from the crowd. Now as he arrives at (or returns to) the city, he is fully cognizant of what awaits him and how he has responded in the past. Despite the late hour, he is determined to confront that past, so that he can bring about the change he seeks. Does the contrast between "Es hora muy tardía" and "Va a amanecer" mean that he has spent the entire night looking for a place to stay without success? Or does the dawn mean that now he is looking for a legitimate place for himself because he will face the truth (dawn, light, illumination) and establish his place, his individual identity (personal and poetic)? The future tense of "hallaré" leaves the result pending. This "stranger in a strange land" is on a journey to find himself, and the search is risky. Even if he finds himself, he may be left out in the cold. Who will take him in? Who, if anyone, will read his work and recognize its truth, its honesty, its penetrating self-analysis?

Reformulating the Ego Ideal: Eugenio de Luelmo

The final poems of "Libro primero" counterbalance the first two and tip the scales in favor of the speaker's search for a new perspective on life and on himself. Dedicated to and written in homage of a local character, "Eugenio de Luelmo" proposes a male personage in contrast with the witches. Individuated by the specificity of his name, Eugenio is a "duende"-like figure who represents traits of the ego ideal the speaker strives to emulate. The subtitle, "Que vivió y murió junto al Duero" [Who lived and died next to the Duero], seems to provide little more than the most general anecdotal information about this person from the speaker's past. The mention of the Duero even goes so far as to locate the setting of the poem in Zamora, Rodríguez's birthplace, adding a biographical dimension that grounds the poem even more specifically in a tangible reality. But if we consider these references, it becomes apparent that Eugenio lived (in the fullest sense of the word) his entire life next to an ambivalent symbol of the passage of time and eternity. As a eulogy, this poem creates an aura around its central figure that defines his special status for the speaker as his ego ideal.

The first part of this three-part poem places in sharp relief the contrast between two different perspectives on life: Eugenio's in contrast with those around him (including the speaker). Yet because Eugenio has died, we infer that the speaker now rejects other attitudes in favor of the perspective Eugenio embodies. The opening statement expresses the admiration he feels as he recalls Eugenio's character.

> Cuando amanece alguien con gracia, de tan sencillas
> como a su lado son las cosas, casi
> parecen nuevas, casi
> sentimos el castigo, el miedo oscuro
> 5   de poseer. . . .
>
> (p. 142)[73]

The verb "amanece" replicates the speaker's sense of delight as he recalls Eugenio's "gracia," his ability to bring out the essence of simple things and to make them look new and extraordinary. The odd line breaks that isolate the adverb "casi" at the end of vv. 2 and 3 contribute to the atmosphere of suspense and serendipitous revelation, while "sencillas," "las cosas," "el castigo," and "poseer" remind us of the witches and heighten the contrast Eugenio represents. This personage stimulates contradictory emotions in the speaker, underscoring the tension between the two perspectives.

> . . . la eficacia de este hombre
> sin ensayo, el negocio
> del mar que eran sus gestos, ola a ola,

10   flor y fruto a la vez, y muerte, y nacimiento
     al mismo tiempo, y ese gran peligro
     de su ternura, de su modo de ir
     por las calles, nos daban
     la única justicia: la alegría.

                           (p. 142)[74]

Eugenio made an impression on others even though his actions were spontaneous, never studied or rehearsed. Like the sea, he was a constant source of liveliness, motion, change. As flower and fruit, he was transient beauty and lasting fullness (the word "fruto" is more abstract and suggests more permanence than "fruta"); as death and birth, he destroyed but regenerated. For these reasons, the speaker feels the contradictory "gran peligro / de su ternura." His admiration for Eugenio is even more pronounced in the next verses.

15   Como quien fuma al pie
     de un polvorín sin darse cuenta, íbamos con él
     y, como era tan fácil
     de invitar, no veíamos
     que besaba al beber y que al hacerle trampas
20   en el tute, más en el mus, jugaba
     de verdad, con sus cartas
     sin marca. . . .

                           (p. 142)[75]

Looking back at his contact with Eugenio, the speaker can perceive things he had not noticed before. His comparison of himself with "quien fuma al pie / de un polvorín sin darse cuenta" expresses the intense emotions produced by his recollections. While others simply caroused or "killed time" drinking, Eugenio "besaba al beber," indicative of the pleasure and sensuality with which Eugenio did even the simplest things in life. Others cheated at cards, but Eugenio always played honestly, symbolic of his sincere and straightforward approach to life: He was incapable of deceit. It is not difficult to see why the speaker remembers and praises him. The tone changes in the final verses, however.

          . . . Él, cuyo oficio sin horario
      era la compañía, ¿cómo iba
      a saber que su Duero
25   es mal vecino?

                           (p. 142)[76]

Eugenio's purpose in life was to accompany others and to add richness and delight to their lives (cf. the role of the poet). The betrayal of Eugenio's innocence now stings the speaker, and he laments Eugenio's death and his loss. The personification of the Duero as a "mal vecino" suggests that life itself (the passage of time) betrayed Eugenio, embittering the speaker's remembrance because he is aware of lost opportunities. Yet the speaker also discovers and gains something in spite of this loss. Eugenio lived life to the fullest and did not let the passage of time interfere with his pleasure. In fact, he may even have seen it as a stimulus to a greater enjoyment of life. Instead of getting involved in the petty games of master and slave, Eugenio stands out as an individual (we know his name) because he had a different perspective and remained honest and true to that outlook throughout his life in every aspect of life.

We receive a more complete picture of Eugenio as the poet's "genio" in part II.[77] First the speaker describes how Eugenio was able to convert the negative into the positive, the commonplace into the extraordinary. He compares Eugenio to an oven that could intensify life and add meaning to everyday limitations. Ironically, the more specific and visual the details, the more Eugenio is transformed into a "duende." His distinctive gait—"Como alondra / se agachaba al andar, y se le abría un poco / el compás de las piernas" [Like a lark / he squatted as he walked, and the compass of his legs / opened a little]—his deafness, his odors ("a cal, a arena, a vino, a sebo" [of lime, of sand, of wine, of grease]), his activity ("Esa velocidad conquistadora / de su vida" [That vanquishing velocity / of his life]), and even the odd combination of his temperament ("su sangre / de lagartija, de águila, y de perro" [his blood / of a small lizard, of an eagle, and of a dog]), combined with the mention that he was seventy-two years old, provide a rich, multifaceted image that lends uniqueness and distinction to this character. These individualizing specificities have the ironic effect of converting Eugenio into a magical gnome or elf but also an ideal who enriches the life of those around him with his traits: "se nos metían en el cuerpo como / música caminera" [they worked their way into our bodies like / traveling music].

The speaker accentuates Eugenio's ephemeral qualities with the question that closes this part of the poem: "¿cómo vamos ahora / a celebrar lo que es suceso puro, / noticia sin historia, trabajo que es hazaña?" (vv. 31–33).[78] Trying to make an accurate appraisal of Eugenio's effect is like trying to capture a will-o'-the-wisp, especially because the speaker has to rely on his memory of a time when he and others were "Ciegos para el misterio / y, por lo tanto, tuertos / para lo real" (vv. 28–30).[79] These references to sight and the elusiveness of the signified refer to the speaker's longing for the ego ideal Eugenio represents. Because he is still in the premirror stage, the speaker can only formulate imagoes (the witches and the elf) and express his preference for one over the other.

As the speaker defines Eugenio's character in greater detail (though still metaphorically), he moves away from the attitudes embodied in the witches and toward the ideal Eugenio represents. A marked change in address and equivocal language in part III illustrate this shift and the speaker's ambivalent position at this moment in his search. The direct address of Eugenio and the insistence on the first person in the opening verses of this section establish an ambivalence between the speaker's intimacy with Eugenio and yet his distance from and yearning for the attainment of this ideal. This ambivalence foregrounds the play between self and other; the imago of Eugenio forms part of the speaker and yet he feels a distance from his ideal: "No bajo la cabeza, / Eugenio, aunque yo bien sé que ahora / no me conocerían ni aun en casa" (vv. 1–3).[80] His inclination to bow his head could reflect either shame or humility in light of his past actions, his ability to recognize a need for a change in his attitudes, and his resolution to change them. He is in fact proud of his determination, and he needs to keep his sights set on his ideal and not lose heart in the face of this difficult, risky endeavor. The tone shifts in the following verses as the speaker meditates on his ideal and his attempt to achieve it, but again we see the contrast between distance and intimacy, evanescence and coalescence.

> La muerte no es un río, como el Duero,
> 5   ni tampoco es un mar. Como el amor, el mar
> siempre acaba entre cuatro
> paredes. Y tú, Eugenio, por mil cauces
> sin crecida o sequía,
> sin puentes, sin mujeres
> 10 lavando ropa, ¿en qué aguas
> te has metido?
> Pero tú no reflejas, como el agua;
> como tierra, posees.
>
> (p. 144)[81]

This meditation on the passage of time and death (with its intertextual debt to Manrique's *Coplas*) is couched in sententious terms but refers to the loss of someone intimate. The mention of the Duero particularizes the situation and yet universalizes it. Love and death are universal experiences, yet both are private and intimate. Eugenio forms part of this same phenomenon. The "mil cauces" to which the speaker refers coincide with the water imagery of the river and serve as metaphor for the many roads by which Eugenio has made his way into the lives of others.[82] In contrast with the water imagery, the speaker perceives Eugenio as "tierra." While Eugenio has penetrated the lives of all who knew him and so becomes disperse and evanescent, he has coalesced as a tangible presence and unity within the speaker, who has assimilated Eugenio's character as his ego ideal. Because of that act, his perspective on reality has undergone a transformation, to which the following catalog attests.

> Y el hilván de estas calles
> 15 de tu barriada al par del río,
> y las sobadas briscas,
> y el dar la mano sin dar ya verano
> ni realidad, ni vida
> a mansalva, y la lengua
> 20 ya tonta de decir «adiós», «adiós»,
> y el sol ladrón y huido,
> y esas torres de húmeda
> pólvora, de calibre
> perdido, y yo, con este aire de primero de junio
> 25 que hace ruido en mi pecho,
> y los amigos. . . . Mucho,
> en poco tiempo mucho ha terminado.
>
> (p. 144)[83]

The play of "mucho" and "poco" and the verb "terminado" show that the speaker rejects the shallow routine and emptiness of his former attitudes (the endless web of undifferentiated streets, the social formalities of shaking hands and greeting people, the unappreciated acts of being in the sun and breathing). His assessment allows him to see that he has broken with the past but not yet achieved his goal. In the final verses, he returns to the contrast between shame and pride with which he began this section.

> Ya cuesta arriba o cuesta abajo,
> hacia la plaza o hacia tu taller,
> 30   todo nos mira ahora
> de soslayo, nos coge
> fuera de sitio.
> Nos da como vergüenza
> vivir, nos da vergüenza
> 35   respirar, ver lo hermosa
> que cae la tarde. Pero
> por el ojo de todas las cerraduras del mundo
> pasa tu llave, y abre
> familiar, luminosa,
> 40   y así entramos en casa
> como aquel que regresa de una cita cumplida.
>
> (pp. 144–45)[84]

When he states "todo nos mira ahora / de soslayo, nos coge / fuera de sitio," the speaker iterates the ambivalence of the opening verses of part III. On the one hand, he expresses the disconcerting, uncomfortable effect that his new perspective on reality has on him; but on the other, he feels surprise and delight in the simple act of breathing or in seeing "lo hermosa / que cae la tarde." He compares Eugenio to a key that opens "todas las cerraduras del mundo," so that "así entramos en casa / como aquel que regresa de una cita cumplida." These final verses remind us of the idealized protagonist of "Alto jornal," suggesting that a change has occurred in the speaker's pursuit of his ideal. In that poem, the speaker used the third person, creating a contrast between the hero and himself. In this poem, he has switched to the direct address of Eugenio and used "nosotros" to indicate his progress. Nonetheless, he returns to the distance when he refers to "*aquel* que regresa." He has made some progress but still feels distant from his goal; he has incorporated the imago of Eugenio as his ideal but still feels separation and difference; he has rejected his former attitudes, yet must still strive toward a new perspective. "Eugenio de Luelmo" looks backward to mark the speaker's progress and forward to anticipate the road that still lies ahead of him.[85]

The final poem of "Libro primero" stresses this impetus toward the future, tipping the scales away from former unacceptable attitudes and toward the acquisition of a new perspective. The aspect of "Noche en el barrio" that stands out most sharply is its verbs, which are reinforced by the choice of adjectives. Subtle shifts in the modes of these verbs highlight the rejection/acceptance motif and the seesaw movement of "Libro primero," reminding us of *Don* and strengthening the connection between that work and this first section of *Alianza*. Because at first we are unable to determine the mode of the verbs, when we do realize that they are imperatives, they have a greater impact.

> Nunca a tientas, así, como ahora, entra
> por este barrio. Así, así, sin limosna,
> sin tregua, entra, acorrala,
> mete tu cruda forja
> 5 por estas casas. De una vez baja, abre
> y cicatriza esta honda
> miseria. Baja ahora que no hay nadie,
> noche mía, no alejes, no recojas
> tu infinito latir ávido. Acaba
> 10 ya de cernirte, acosa
> de una vez a esta presa a la que nadie
> quiere valer. . . .

(p. 146)[86]

It is not until the fourth line that we are sure that these verbs are not descriptive third-person indicative but prescriptive imperatives. This temporary suspension causes the verbs to impact on us all the more, especially when the poet follows them with incisive adjectives. The string "entra, acorrala, / mete" is followed by "tu *cruda* forja," and "baja, abre / y cicatriza" is reinforced by "esta *honda* / miseria." Moreover, the image of a bird of prey receives additional weight from the verb "acosa" as well as from the emphatic line breaks, the alliterative "ya," and the repetitive "de una vez," all intensifying the effect of the night.

These opening verses subvert the title and recall Rodríguez's understanding of the metaphor of night. We would expect a "noche en el barrio" to be a quiet, tranquil time when activity and energy levels begin to subside. But since the opening poems of *Don*, Rodríguez has viewed night as a time of activity and growth. If illumination leads to darkness and confusion, darkness brings more light, more knowledge, as the subsequent verses of "Noche" relate. A subtle shift in the verbs plays against the imagery, producing an equivocal tone.

> . . . Sólo oiga,
> noche mía, después de tantos años,
> el son voraz de tu horda luminosa
> 15 saqueando hasta el fondo
> tanta orfandad, la agria pobreza bronca
> de este bloque en silencio que está casi
> en el campo y aloja
> viva siembra vibrante. Desmantele
> 20 tu luz nuestra injusticia y nos la ponga
> al aire, y la descarne,
> y la sacuda, y la haga pegajosa
> como esta tierra, y que nos demos cuenta
> de que está aquí, a dos pasos. Protectora
> 25 nunca, sí con audacia.

Acusa. Y que la casta,
la hombría de alta cal, los sueños, la obra,
el armazón desnudo de la vida
se crispen.

(p. 146)[87]

In lieu of the direct commands of the opening verses, the speaker here takes
recourse to the subjunctive, with the relative pronoun "que" omitted through ellipsis.
The verbs now express more of a pleading tone than a forceful command. This shift
signals the speaker's ambivalent positioning in the rejection/acceptance motif, also
visible in the phrase beginning with "Desmantele." Here the injustice he sees so clearly
is compared with the darkness, while night as light will expose and dismantle the
injustice. Where the verbs "desmantele," "descarne," and "sacuda" attest to the violence and force of this phenomenon, the subjunctive softens and defers the action.
The speaker is realizing a change that has already occurred and yet is still pending.[88]
The juxtaposition of "Acusa" (v. 26) with "Y que . . . se crispen" (v. 29) summarizes
that paradox. The verbs in the first stanza of "Noche" reflect the ambivalence of the
rejection/acceptance motif of "Libro primero." Another shift in the verbs in the final
verses forestalls closure: Night is not an end but a beginning.

30   Y estás sola,
        tú, noche, enloquecida de justicia,
        anonadada de misericordia,
        sobre este barrio trémulo al que nadie
        vendrá porque es la historia
35   de todos, pero al que tú siempre, en andas
        y en volandas,
        llevas, y traes, y hieres, y enamoras
        sin que nadie lo sepa,
        sin que nadie oiga el ruido
40   de tus inmensos pulsos, que desbordan.

(pp. 146–47)[89]

To communicate the tranquility of night settling on the city, the poet uses the
present tense and slows down the pace with a "pie quebrado" (truncated line), several
commas, and parallelism. This parallelism then leads to contrasts, first perceptible in
the participles "enloquecida" and "anonadada," and then in the future ("vendrá") versus the past ("historia"). This contrast becomes more dynamic and overt in the interplay between the phrases "al que nadie" and "al que tú." In spite of the appearances of
night's settling in, and in contrast with the "nadie" who will never arrive, night is
extremely active, though deceptively so. The idiomatic expression "en andas y en
volandas" could be glossed as a redundant form of the more compact "en volandas,"
but the contrast between "en andas" ("walking") and "en volandas" ("rapidly, as if
flying") epitomizes the tension between acceptance and rejection, alliance and condemnation. The personification of night and the concatenation of the verbs "llevas, y
traes, y hieres, y enamoras" (an urgency slowed by commas) reduplicate this tension.

If the present indicative of the final verb "desbordan" closes the frame of this section (just as these two poems "Eugenio" and "Noche" counterbalance the first two, "Brujas" and "Gestos"), the signified literally "spills over" that frame. In spite of the speaker's insistent repetition of "nadie," *he* has heard the intense pulse of night, and *he* has become aware of activity in the stasis and light in the darkness.

Like the final poems of the three sections of *Don*, "Noche" closes the frame and yet forestalls closure, in accord with the rejection/acceptance, alliance/condemnation motif of "Libro primero." Similar to the intertwining reversals of a Moebius strip, the speaker's attitudes have shifted. At first, he has to accept the witches as part of himself in spite of his description of them as otherness, so that he can then reject and move away from them. As he does so, he finds himself in flux between the rejection of his former attitudes and the formulation of new ones, culminating in the description of Eugenio de Luelmo as his ego ideal. Even though he wishes to embrace Eugenio and all that he represents, the speaker must acknowledge his distance from that ideal and his determination to strive toward it. "Noche en el barrio" brings "Libro primero" to a close but simultaneously spills over into "Libro segundo," where frames and the imposition and dissipation of them play a major role.

THE MIRROR STAGE: FRAMING THE OTHER, FRAMING THE SELF

The paramount feature of the speaker's attempt to bring about a (re)constitution of himself consists of framing the Other.[90] In "Libro segundo," the speaker encounters several scenes in the world around him. After marking off the boundaries around the desired trait metonymically proximate with him, the speaker would appropriate that trait for himself to bring about the desired change. In keeping with the experience of *Conjuros*, where "realismo metafórico" determines the poetic process through the description of a concrete object or scene, ironic peripeteia cause the speaker's discovery to backfire on him. Although he sees himself reflected in and wishes to unite himself with the Other, the speaker also acknowledges his difference from the Other and his lack of the desired trait. "Libro segundo" represents the aesthetic mirror stage in which the poet individualizes and becomes a "strong poet" through identification and differentiation with the other in the mirror.

If we conceive of these scenes as poems written by others, we see that the poet recognizes himself in them at the same time that he wishes to incorporate a certain characteristic of them in his own poetry.[91] But he discovers that he lacks what they possess. It is the recognition of this *lack* that ironically differentiates and individuates him because he will construct his identity on an exploration of that gap.[92] The poet finds himself in an impossibly paradoxical situation: Although he wishes to unite himself with Otherness (the poetic tradition), recognition of the Other in these scenes always leaves his desire unsatisfied because he always discovers a lack. By finding what he is missing, the poet individuates but continually searches for identity. "Identity" is "sameness" or *idem* (unity with the tradition, with the Other in the Imaginary order) and "difference" or *ipse* (individuation, emergence into the Symbolic, into personal language).[93]

To achieve individuality, the speaker in "Libro segundo" frames (contains) the signifier within a certain network of language (his ethical search for meaning and the poetic tradition, the synchronic and the diachronic) only to find that the signified spills over (transgresses) the frame, nullifying it.[94] The dogged pursuit of that which constantly slips away from him is what gives Rodríguez's poetry its individuality.[95] This transgressiveness identifies and individuates him although it defines him as lack or flux, a signified that always reverts to a signifier, constantly spills over its borders and slips out of his grasp.[96] Transgression is transitive and intransitive, intentional (sin) and accidental (excess, exuberance, jouissance). The poems of "Libro segundo" exemplify this ambivalence in the use of frames.

Because it epitomizes many of the principle features of this section and the speaker's paradoxical experience during the mirror stage, many commentators have addressed "Espuma" as one of the most outstanding poems of *Alianza*.[97] This poem forms part of the paradigm of framing (and its transgression) in "Libro segundo." If "Espuma" opens the frame, the penultimate poem "Frente al mar" closes it because both poems depict seascapes. Such a design appropriately locates "Girasol" as the turning point or trope, but it also places "Ciudad de meseta" outside the frame yet inside "Libro segundo." This pattern of overflow, of exceeding (transgressing) the frame, repeated throughout the second section, receives its initial treatment in the opening verses of "Espuma."

> Miro la espuma, su delicadeza
> que es tan distinta a la de la ceniza.
> Como quien mira una sonrisa, aquella
> por la que da su vida y le es fatiga
> 5   y amparo, miro ahora la modesta
> espuma. . . .
>
> (p. 151)[98]

Calling attention to the act of looking, the opening verb "Miro" stages a scene in which the speaker as spectator and participant sets himself apart from the scene and yet suggests a comparison with it.[99] This contrast is abetted by the image of the "ceniza." Foam and ash are delicate (they share that quality metaphorically). They both evidence dynamic forces and represent transitional states, and yet each is quite distinct: Foam is a product of the water's movement (the trapping of air bubbles), but ash is the residue of fire's destructive force (the release of gasses).[100] This opposition is again manifest in the objectification of the speaker as "Como quien mira una sonrisa"—wherein the first-person speaker becomes an objectified third person and the foam becomes a smile, a fleeting, intangible sign of emotion and of the Other's gaze—and in the contrast between "fatiga" and "amparo."[101] Fatigue is the result of expended effort just as the ash is residue of fire, and "amparo" is produced by an encounter and exchange between people. Yet the poet has ironically inverted the order ("espuma-ceniza," "fatiga-amparo"), confusing frame and excess, observer and observed, self and other.

When the speaker repeats the opening statement, the additions he makes with "ahora" and "modesta" cause the sentence to spill over into the following verse.[102] The enjambment stresses the adjective "modesta," personifying the spume, and produces erotic overtones in the ensuing verses.

> . . . Es el momento bronco y bello
> del uso, el roce, el acto de la entrega
> creándola. El dolor encarcelado
> del mar, se salva en fibra tan ligera;
> 10   bajo la quilla, frente al dique, donde
> existe amor surcado, como en tierra
> la flor, nace la espuma. . . .

(p. 151)[103]

Although the poet situates the speaker in a concrete scene, his imagery adds several layers of meaning to it. Nonetheless, the dialectic between sameness and difference (the two meanings of identity) remains in force, so that each signified becomes a new signifier. This singular incident—"el acto de la entrega" produced by the "roce," the interface, the suturing of sea and land on the liminal territory of the shoreline—is a transient moment both "bronco y bello" and an eternal becoming: "creándola." Just as each wave washing over the rocks on the seashore produces a unique and yet sempiternal event, so making love unites contradictory experiences of time and identity. Like snowflakes, the foam is infinitely different and limitlessly the same. Ironically again, the immense movement and energy of the sea manifests itself in the delicacy and transience of the foam. The sea embodies this antithesis because it can archetypally represent the source and generation of all life and be a symbol of sterility and death. As woman and/or (m)Other, the sea can be benevolent and terrible.[104]

The traditional images of the keel and the dike (which resembles a furrow, a fissure, or a rift) connote erotic overtones and echo the connection between plowing and writing. Comparing the spume with a flower that blossoms from the plowed earth recalls the birth of Venus (Beauty) from the waves. The female figure evoked contributes to the metapoetic layer now superimposed on the erotic one which has evolved out of the anecdotal scene. The pronoun "ella" in the next sentence could refer equally to "espuma," a female figure, and the abstract Beauty of poetry.

> . . . Y es en ella
> donde rompe la muerte, en su madeja
> donde el mar cobra ser, como en la cima
> 15   de su pasión el hombre es hombre, fuera
> de otros negocios: en su leche viva.

(p. 151)[105]

The delicate thread of the foam (similar to the dike, the liminal, mutable interface between sea and land) becomes "the locus of the discourse of the unconscious" and "marks the passage from the imaginary to the symbolic, from demand to desire."[106]

Death, like waves, breaks on this "rompeolas" [breakwater], as the sea achieves being: "cobra ser." The intermingling of different levels of the imagery comes to a nodal
point in the idiomatic expression "en su leche viva."[107] On a visual level, anyone who
has been to the seashore and seen the foam has observed that its whiteness is milky, in
sharp contrast with the rocks and the water. This milkiness has erotic overtones of
sexual fluids, especially semen (reinforced by the simile of the man "en la cima de su
pasión") and a mother's milk. Further, this expression can figuratively connote innocence and essence, purity and sterility, transience and transcendence. Compounding
this multivalency, we do not know to whom "su" refers nor whether "viva" refers to
"leche," forming part of the idiomatic expression, or to some other noun ("ella," "la
muerte," "su madeja," "la cima de su pasión"). In short, this nodal point spills over
the limits of the signifier. Yet, if it were not for the limit, the transgression could not
occur. And so in the very next verse the speaker reinstates the presence of the frame as
he continues to subvert and transgress it.

> A este pretil, brocal de la materia
> que es manantial, no desembocadura,
> me asomo ahora, cuando la marea
> 20 sube, y allí naufrago, allí me ahogo
> muy silenciosamente, con entera
> aceptación, ileso, renovado
> en las espumas imperecederas.
>
> (p. 151)[108]

"Pretil" and "brocal" represent the bar or barrier separating signifier and signified. Lacan has inverted Saussure's original formulation of the relationship of signifier
and signified, giving precedence to the former. Rodríguez gives prominence to the
bar, the interface, the liminal space, a place of lack that is a place of production.[109] If
we conceive of the sea as the unconscious, the interface between the conscious and
the unconscious, the points of contact between the Imaginary and the Symbolic—a
"discontinuous and conflictual" space—is where Rodríguez locates his quest for individuality and identity.[110] For him this space "es manantial, no desembocadura": As
fountain, it supplies an eternal source of inspiration that will characterize his poetic
identity. Language (the poem) is the interface between the poet and reality, interior
and exterior; it represents a place of search for knowledge of the self and the world
rather than a means of communication of an experience.[111]

Although he says that this space is not a "desembocadura" (reminding us again
of Manrique), he loses himself there: "allí naufrago, allí me ahogo."[112] Crashing on
the barrier reef of the sign and drowning in that rift or gap (symbol of feminine sexuality) nonetheless leaves him unharmed ("ileso, renovado") because he drowns "en
las espumas *imperecederas*." The poet imposes a frame (his drowning, his "death")
and yet transgresses it. He submits himself to the limits of language—the bar between
signifier and signified, the Phallus—and yet that limit, that interface, has as its "law"
the multivalency and equivocality of the sign.[113] By subjecting himself to language,
the poet achieves what he knows is a contradiction and an impossibility. In the

neg(oti)ation of meaning, he finds signification; in the denial of self, identity.[114] Subjecting himself to the constraints of the poetic tradition commits the poet to difference, rebellion, transgression. To reach the sublime (the transcendent), the poet must rely on the anecdotal (the transient).[115]

In short, we can paraphrase Weber's description of the relationship between the Imaginary and Symbolic by saying of the speaker and his world that "each . . . sets itself apart *from* the other, but in so doing reveals its dependency upon the other and thereby sets *itself apart*."[116] The switch from the singular "Espuma" of the title to the plural "espumas imperecederas" of the final verse underscores the ambivalence of the frame: The speaker distances himself from the scene and yet includes himself in it.[117] "It is only by means of identifying with another, even if that other is its 'own' mirror-image, that the ego is constituted. . . . [T]he ego can only emerge by binding itself to the other; but for it to fulfill its image of wholeness . . . , it is bound to deny the bond that constitutes it."[118]

In comparison with "Espuma," "Viento de primavera" [Spring wind] is one of the least commented poems in Rodríguez's opus. It is worthwhile to examine this poem briefly, for it describes the splitting of the subject in his passage from the Imaginary to the Symbolic (as we are employing Lacan's terms to define Rodríguez's aesthetic trajectory).[119] By beginning with a third-person objectivity that describes the subject's reaction to the "viento de primavera," the poet could be parodying and rewriting Guillén's "Impaciente vivir," even though the images are clearly Rodríguez's.[120]

> Ni aun el cuerpo resiste
> tanta resurrección, y busca abrigo
> ante este viento que ya templa y trae
> olor, y nueva intimidad. Ya cuanto
> 5   fue hambre ahora es sustento. Y se aligera
> la vida, y un destello generoso
> vibra por nuestras calles. Pero sigue
> turbia nuestra retina, y la saliva
> seca, y los pies van a la desbandada,
> 10   como siempre. . . .

(p. 152)[121]

The speaker evokes an ironic defense against the promise of spring's arrival and the intimacy it symbolizes for him when he seeks "abrigo"—an overcoat on an anecdotal level, protection or defenses on a psychological level. His hunger and thirst (vv. 5 and 9, respectively) give evidence of his lack and his desire, but in both instances, the context undercuts those concepts: The hunger has become sustenance, and his saliva (water, moistness) is dry. This is not to say that he has received food or drink, but merely that a signifier ("hambre," "saliva") now connotes an ironic signified (sustenance, dryness), its differential counterpart. Because of the habitual defenses he has erected (putting on an overcoat when it is cool and windy), the speaker is unable to have a clear vision of himself ("sigue turbia nuestra retina"). He thirsts for change and wanders randomly despite "este viento que ya templa y trae / olor, y nueva

intimidad" and "un destello generoso [que] vibra por las calles" (wind and light).[122]
His clouded eyes prevent him from finding "esa mirada que no tiene dueño." But this
wind takes on corporal presence and has a startling effect on him.

```
10              . . . Y entonces,
          esta presión fogosa que nos trae
          el cuerpo aún frágil de la primavera,
          ronda en torno al invierno
          de nuestro corazón, buscando un sitio
15        por donde entrar en él. Y aquí, a la vuelta
          de la esquina, al acecho,
          en feraz merodeo,
          nos ventea la ropa,
          nos orea el trabajo,
20        barre la casa, engrasa nuestras puertas
          duras de oscura cerrazón, la abre
          a no sé qué hospitalidad hermosa
          y nos desborda y, aunque
          nunca nos demos cuenta
25        de tanta juventud, de lleno en lleno
          nos arrasa. . . .
```

(p. 152)[123]

The diverse levels evident in the image of the wind that "ronda en torno al invierno
/ de nuestro corazón"—a displacement typical of *Conjuros*—creates an interplay between the literal and the metaphoric. Never separating completely, this distinction
demonstrates the trajectory of the subject's splitting and his individuation. The ag-
gressiveness of this new attitude, this new perspective on life, is most apparent in the
active verbs "ronda," "ventea," "orea," "barre," "engrasa," "abre," "desborda," and
"arrasa," as well as in the abrupt enjambment in vv. 15–16 and in the images "al
acecho" and "en feraz merodeo," which suggest an animal of prey or a thief. The
idiomatic "no sé qué" anticipates the emergence of the first-person subject but at this
point is still equivocal. Although it may be an indication of the emerging subject, it is
a common idiomatic expression in which the "I" is not yet a distinct identity. The next
step in the subject's individuation is manifest in the alliteration and the verbs of the
next lines.

```
                . . . Sí, a poco
          del sol salido, un viento ya gustoso,
          sereno de simiente, sopló en torno
          de nuestra sequedad, de la injusticia
30        de nuestros años, alentó para algo
          más hermoso que tanta desconfianza y tanto desaliento,
          más valiente que nuestro
          miedo a su honda rebelión, a su alta
35        resurrección. . . .
```

(pp. 152–53)[124]

Here the alliteration of the (turbulent) fricative /s/ onomatopoeically reproduces the sound of the wind, making it an even more tangible presence. Surprisingly, however, the two main verbs of this passage, "sopló" and "alentó," are in the preterit! The split between the saying and the said (*"énonciation"* and *"énoncé"*) further defines the subject. The preterit distances him, "[f]or that Self consists essentially in an alienation: not from itself but from the other"; and it allows him to overcome "nuestro / miedo a su honda rebelión, a su alta / resurrección."[125] If the speaker uses the inclusive "nuestro" here, it is because all human beings possess this fear. But this particular subject is able to overcome his fear and emerge as a first-person "yo" in the following verses, where the contrast preterit/present again appears.

> . . . Y ahora
> yo, que perdí mi libertad por todo,
> quiero oír cómo el pobre
> ruido de nuestro pulso se va a rastras
> tras el cálido son de esta alianza
> 40   y ambos hacen la música
> arrolladora, sin compás, a sordas,
> por la que sé que llegará algún día,
> quizá en medio de enero, en el que todos
> sepamos el porqué del nombre: «viento
> de primavera».

(p. 153)[126]

The emphatic "yo" employed by the speaker is still equivocal. As Weber explains, "The word 'I' thus entails a double reference: on the one hand, it refers to the speaker designating himself as part of the content of a particular statement [*énoncé*]; on the other hand, and at the same time, it refers to the speaker designating himself as the subject of a more general process of enunciation that is irreducible to any determinate statement."[127] We have already encountered this phenomenon in "Espuma" in the speaker's opening "Miro." "Espuma" thus forms a frame, within which "Viento de primavera" begins the subject's emergence. When he repeats the verb "sé" in v. 42, his profile is much more distinct than in the earlier idiomatic "no sé qué."[128] The future "llegará" and repetition of the poem's title propel us into the next stage in this "narrative," but placing the title (the signifier) within quotation marks suggests that this phrase has a special meaning (signified).[129] The words reveal a contrast between the concrete and the abstract, but as in *Conjuros,* these levels are not and never will be separate. In semiotic terms, the poet shows that the bar between signifier and signified separates and unites; the interface between the unconscious and the conscious is a separation and a passageway.[130] Because he has broken the title in the last two lines of the poem, the poet implies a crack in the frame that opens the glimpse of the unconscious but also distorts the information, a reference to the multivalency of language that we encountered in "Espuma."[131]

The same is true of the next poem, "Gorrión," where the sparrow of the title is an image of the speaker as Other in the mirror. This brief poem recounts the observation of a common, unexceptional bird personified as "este granuja astuto." This astute ragamuffin obstinately refuses to fly away, preferring to continue among people's feet "metiendo en su pechuga / todo el polvo del mundo" [putting on its chest / all the dust of the world]. It even disdains flight ("Ya dio al aire a los muertos" [It already gave its dead to the air]), provoking the perplexed speaker to wonder, "¿Qué busca en nuestro oscuro / vivir? ¿Qué amor encuentra / en nuestro pan tan duro?"[132]

If we consider the sparrow as a mirror-image of the speaker, the following questions arise: What do the sparrow and the speaker have in common, and how are they different? Given that the speaker personifies the sparrow as a "granuja astuto," we infer that the bird possesses "street smarts," everyday wisdom or common sense that perplexes and escapes the speaker. After all, this bird could be soaring through the (sublime, transcendent) stratosphere, but it remains amid the dangers of people's feet, eating stale bread and splashing dust (earth, transience) on its breast. The speaker might like to soar through the pure air of poetry, but he like the sparrow finds himself in the midst of an "oscuro / vivir."

Two enigmatic phrases stand out in the description of the sparrow that illuminate the distinction between it and the speaker. The first is the terse opening line of the poem: "No olvida. No se aleja" [It doesn't forget. It doesn't go away]. Repetition of the negative emphasizes the sparrow's persistence. It accompanies human beings instead of flying away because, like a dog, it depends on humans and feels a sense of loyalty and devotion, qualities the speaker admires. The second phrase, "Ya dio al aire a los muertos," recalls the biblical anecdote in which Jesus invites a potential disciple to "Let the dead bury the dead."[133] The implication is that those who choose not to follow Him but attend to mundane duties are without eternal life.

Taken together with the final verse ("metiendo en su pechuga / todo el polvo del mundo"), these phrases evoke the Imaginary order in which the child identifies with the (m)Other and sees the world around it as an extension of itself. To remain in the Imaginary, to refuse or be incapable of separating and individuating oneself, can have deleterious effects.[134] The obstinate loyalty and dependence of the sparrow illuminates the speaker's own dependency on the poetic tradition (e.g., biblical intertextuality). Instead of "letting the dead bury the dead," the speaker—like the sparrow—has refused to separate himself, to individuate, and so he condemns himself to a miserable existence, to a death in which he already splashes dust on his own dust (to use another biblical intertextuality). The speaker's reaction to the sparrow is ambivalent; he admires and disdains it; he finds it charming, amusing, but perplexing, frustrating. This conflict reflects the oedipal conflict, so that the sparrow encompasses contradictory feelings that the speaker is beginning to admit openly. "This Other of desire is . . . the *locus of the discourse of the unconscious*; it can only be placed as the difference between the 'said' and the 'saying,' between signified and signifying, or more exactly as the movement of signifiers which itself always takes place upon 'another stage.'"[135]

"Lluvia y gracia" [Rain and grace] epitomizes the paradoxical relationship between self and other, similarity and difference, in the striving to achieve individuality by means of a mirror image. In this poem, the speaker can identify with the other male figure in the poem (a reflection of himself), an identification (similarity) that enables him to individuate (be different). A consideration of the representation of the other in this poem will illuminate the process of (re)constituting the self in which Rodríguez is engaged in *Alianza*.

In his book *Poetry of Discovery,* Andrew Debicki has aptly pointed out that "The very specific description in lines 1–4 [of 'Lluvia'] anchor the poem in an immediate reality, making us see the man's running as part of a literal scene."[136] These verses set in motion an intriguing interaction between that specific scene and its symbolic repercussions.

> Desde el autobús, lleno
> de labriegos, de curas y de gallos,
> al llegar a Palencia,
> veo a ese hombre.

(p. 155)[137]

As Debicki states, "If these lines were omitted, the symbolic level would dominate and we would lose the feeling that the wider meaning lies in and emerges from concrete reality."[138] Although I am in complete agreement with this statement, I would like to expand upon it to arrive at a fuller understanding of the interplay between the mimetic and the symbolic and a redefinition of the term "realismo metafórico" by considering the use of the mirror.

At first, following the precepts of the New Critical approach, we described a movement from the concrete to the abstract that suggested a gap between them. With the shift to poststructuralist critical theories, Debicki and others have stressed the inextricability of the two levels. However, in *Spanish Poetry of the Twentieth Century: Modernity and Beyond,* Debicki has stated that "Unlike traditional (say, medieval) allegory, the kind created by Rodríguez never collapses the real and allegorical planes into single meanings. Instead, the planes form parallel and coexistent layers, which are related but also set in conflict with each other."[139]

I would argue that, similar to the two sides of a Moebius strip, at once inside and outside, the two levels are collapsed from the beginning and yet remain separate, "set in conflict with each other," that they are both parallel and yet superimposed and intertwined one with the other.[140] That is to say that in principle "realismo metafórico" would appear to bridge the gap between signifier and signified by imbricating the representational and the symbolic, the transient and the transcendent, at the same time that it accentuates their separation and difference. Just as the word "identity" encompasses similarity and difference and the formation of identity depends on our relationship with an-other, so too Rodríguez's poetics and his exploration and definition of his self entails this paradoxical relationship.

In addition to grounding the scene in a concrete, anecdotal setting, the opening verses posit the presence of the speaker juxtaposed with the image of an-other: "veo a ese hombre." The window of the bus from which the speaker observes the other provides a frame and a glass, a mirror that simultaneously reflects and reverses the image of the speaker in the guise of the other. This barrier separates and distinguishes the speaker from the other, but it also allows him to see the other as if the other were himself. The frame of the mirror allows him to identify with the other—noting the similarities between them *(idem)*—and to differentiate and distinguish himself *(ipse)*, as the glass is both reflective and transparent.

Toward the end of this discussion, I will return to the opening verses, but for now let us examine the scene observed, keeping in abeyance the observer's positioning in front of the mirror. As the other man gets off the bus, it begins to rain in a true downpour. Debicki has pointed out the ambivalent symbolism of the rain which functions both to castigate and to purify, a symbolic ambivalence manifest on the linguistic level.[141]

```
5    Comienza a llover fuerte, casi arrecia
     y no le va a dar tiempo
     a refugiarse en la ciudad. Y corre
     como quien asesina. Y no comprende
     el castigo del agua, su sencilla
10   servidumbre; tan sólo estar a salvo
     es lo que quiere. Por eso no sabe
     que le crece como un renuevo fértil
     en su respiración acelerada,
     que es cebo vivo, amor ya sin remedio,
15   cantera rica. . . .
```
                                                            (p. 155)[142]

The intensification expressed in the verb "arrecia" (v. 5) expands the anecdotal level, an effect to which "refugiarse" contributes. It is as if an armed conflict has broken out, causing the man caught in the rain to seek self-preservation. The comparison with a murderer tinges the scene with ethical overtones and heightens the desire to escape "el castigo del agua." Ironically, the speaker describes this escape as a misunderstanding: The other does not comprehend that "castigo" can signify an opportunity to learn as well as a punishment, nor does he see "su sencilla servidumbre."[143] Whether this phrase refers to the man or the rain (the "su" is ambiguous), the man is reluctant to adopt the humility required of him. He sees only the danger and wishes to protect himself ("estar a salvo"). His act of running is egotistically defensive and protective.

The images in the next sentence (vv. 11–15) continue to function duplicitously and thereby foreground and redouble the life-giving qualities and fertilizing effect of water and air as archetypal images. The rain has caused this man to run and to breathe deeply and rapidly—to "suck air." Such exercise is literally and figuratively refreshing and good for his physical and spiritual well-being. The rain penetrating his body from the outside provides a cleansing and purification, while the rapid exchange of air has the same effect from the inside, a duality again reminiscent of the Moebius strip.

The ambivalent images "que es cebo vivo, amor ya sin remedio, / cantera rica" (vv. 14–15) could modify "un renuevo fértil / en su respiración acelerada," or it could be a parallel continuation of the phrase "Por eso no sabe." The rain and the air are "cebo vivo" in that they present a lure and temptation for the man as fish, offering him sustenance but also concealing a hook (purifying but castigating).[144] Both are "amor ya sin remedio," but this phrase is equally ambivalent. Is it a love that is fatal (without a known cure or remedy) or inevitable (a true love that nothing can prevent from occurring)? The "cantera rica" is perhaps the most enigmatic and multivalent image in this series. Although the quarry renders an endless supply of high-quality stone, the rocks are heavy, formless masses that need shaping, fine detailing, and polishing. As a metapoetic symbol of inspiration, the quarry is the source of the raw material of inspiration, but the poet must recognize its potential fecundity and use language artfully, like a sculptor shapes stone. These natural elements work synergistically to produce a positive effect in spite of the severity of the experience—if only the man were aware of it. But because he does not recognize these beneficial consequences, he continues to flee.

<pre>
15   . . . Y, ante la sorpresa
         de tal fecundidad,
         se atropella y recela;
         siente, muy en lo oscuro, que está limpio
         para siempre, pero él no lo resiste;
20   y mira, y busca, y huye,
         y, al llegar a cubierto,
         entra mojado y libre, y se cobija
         y respira tranquilo en su ignorancia
         al ver cómo su ropa
25   poco a poco se seca.
</pre>

(p. 155)[145]

Because of the interplay between the mimetic and the symbolic, this experience of fecundity reverberates with ambivalent and ironic meaning. A surprise can be good or bad, a delight or a shock, so that the fecundity of the rain overwhelms the man, causing him to stumble and pull back. Even though he feels clean in the darkest, most interior, most intimate part of himself, and that this cleansing is "para siempre," he can resist neither the cause nor the effect. The verb "resistir" could mean that he is powerless to *defend himself from* what is happening (the cause) but also that he continues to flee, unable to *tolerate* it (the effect). Fleeing from the immense power of the rain, the man finally finds shelter and enters "mojado y libre." Does "libre" mean that he has finally freed himself from the violence and the punishment of the storm? Or does it mean that the rain has purified him and cleansed him of his shortcomings? His drenching has produced both discomfort and renewal. Similarly, does the phrase "y respira tranquilo en su ignorancia" express his new pure and innocent state following purification or his relief at having escaped the discomfiting and threatening?

The repetition of words and alliteration of several phonemes produces the same ambivalent effect in the final verses. The anaphoric repetition of the conjunction "y" simulates on the mimetic level the man's shortness of breath because he has been running. But does this shortness of breath suggest ecstasy, intensity, and fullness of emotion, or does it connote a lack of vitality (inspiration), a lack of fitness (morality), and the inability to continue (writing)? Does the alliteration in the final verse (especially of the phoneme /k/) represent a relieved return to comfort, dryness, and warmth (a regeneration), or does it figure the hollowness, shallowness, aridity, and repetiveness of this man's life?

Having appreciated the ambivalence of this experience on the anecdotal and symbolic levels, let us now return to the point of departure, the opening verses. Although we may be in accord with Debicki that these opening verses anchor the poem in a concrete reality, we must grant that they are far from devoid of symbolic resonance. In retrospect, even the most specific anecdotal information adopts symbolic significance, just as the symbolic resonances of the scene play against and yet never quite disengage themselves from the concrete circumstances. The bus as vehicle is a traditional symbol of one's passage through time along the road of life. It is no small matter that the bus is "lleno / de labriegos, de curas y de gallos": The speaker needs to be a hard worker like the "labriegos" if he is to overcome his shortcomings and strive toward the higher ethical and spiritual dimension of life personified by the priests. The roosters not only recall Peter's denial of Jesus, evocative of the man's flight from what is good for him, but also the circadian rhythms of the sun and the theme of resurrection and a new beginning.[146] Even the city of Palencia transcends its specificity. The name of this city derives from the Latin "pala," which refers to the wooden implement washerwomen use to beat the water and soil out of their clothes. Figuratively and metonymically, this implement represents a spanking, a punishment, a means of atonement for having done wrong.[147] We note, then, that the poem reverses the relationship and interaction between the mimetic and the symbolic in the manner of the twists in a Moebius strip. The two sides—inside and out—are collapsed into one and yet distinct and separate from each other.

This chiasmatic relationship is further evident in the title "Lluvia y gracia," which in turn echoes the title *Alianza y condena*. Whereas at first we might construe "lluvia" to refer to the anecdotal level and "gracia" to the symbolic, a return to the title after reading the poem reveals the ambivalence of both words. Because, as Cirlot points out, rain like light descends from above and thus represents poetic inspiration, the symbolic cleansing and purification caused by the rain in this scene also allude to the effect of language and the poet's participation in the aesthetic act, adding a metapoetic level of signification to the rain as castigation and purification.[148] Likewise, "gracia" can refer not only to a special gift that comes to us (ethically and aesthetically speaking) from a higher source, but also to an affective response to this scene. The observer on the bus has disdainfully laughed at the man caught in the downpour, disparaging and ridiculing him for getting wet and not finding shelter. The conjunction "y" unites the two terms of the title but also separates and places a barrier between them. Again, this semantically insignificant term (in comparison with "lluvia" and "gracia") occupies a central position and has symbolic implications in the anaphoric repetition later in the poem.

We can underscore this ambivalent and paradoxical relationship between the two levels if we now return to the concept of the mirror. As I stated above, the window of the bus represents a frame and a glass in which the speaker sees himself reflected as if in a mirror. By framing the other in the mirror and separating himself from him, the speaker points an accusatory finger at the other's lack of awareness and reluctance to submit himself to the castigating purification of the rain. He disdains the other for not being able to acquiesce to ("resistir") the immense fertility and renovation offered by the rain. But what has *he* done during this incident but remained on the bus? Unlike the other, he has not even exposed himself to the castigation, the purification and all of the blessings that can accrue from taking a risk. By framing the other, the speaker has also framed himself (pun intended). He, like the other, has been reluctant to accept the punishment he deserves and has not dared to take the necessary risks. Yet in the act of writing he *has* arrived at a certain awareness and *has* castigated himself by proclaiming his own reticence. The other in the mirror embodies the speaker through similarity and difference, while the frame around the mirror equates and separates self and other.[149]

Otherness, especially in the mirror-stage poems of "Libro segundo," forms an integral and dynamic part of this process. The ambivalence of the term "identity" stands out in "Lluvia y gracia" as the other reflects both similarity and difference. Like the other in the rain, in *Alianza y condena,* Rodríguez recognizes his desire to flee from the intensity of the experience of writing. This simple incident enables the protagonist of *Alianza* to comprehend what he must do if he is to achieve the change he seeks. Only when he breaks down his defenses and looks more scrutinizingly at himself, even at the risk of painfully confronting his shortcomings (his lack), will he be able to find "esa mirada que no tiene dueño." As a human being, that means finding love by learning to be independent and to give of himself. As a poet, it entails freeing himself from the poetic tradition by being true to himself.

The turning point in this process takes place in "Girasol," another of Rodríguez's most well-known poems.[150] Debicki has stated accurately that it is impossible to reduce this poem to a unified experience. He draws that conclusion on the basis of the similarity and difference between the personification of the sunflower as pregnant woman and defeated soldier, the one representing order and the other chaos.[151] Given the psychoanalytic approach I have adopted and the consideration of "Libro segundo" as the mirror stage, I submit that this poem is even more complex and irreducible than we might at first think, because its imagery and its language contain a plethora of contradictions.

First, let us consider the title. Chevalier and Gheerbrandt include "girasol" under the entry "heliotropo."[152] Curiously, these two words designate the same object but reverse the order of the morphemic elements composing them: "Gira-" and "-tropo" mean "to turn," while "-sol" and "helio-" refer to the sun. Literally, "girasol" means "turns the sun." This nomenclature is ambivalent, as Chevalier and Gheerbrandt point out: "El nombre común del heliotropo indica suficientemente su carácter solar, el cual resulta por otra parte, no solamente de un tropismo bien conocido, sino también de la forma radiada de la flor."[153] It is a sun that turns to follow the turning of the sun; it is subject and object, rotation and revolution, stasis and dynamism, center and periphery. The prefix "gira-" and the suffix "-tropo" indicate that this flower is a trope: metaphor and metonymy, product and process, transience and transcendence.[154] If the speaker sees an image of himself in the sunflower, that trope is a contradictory, paradoxical one that cannot be reduced to a simple subject or object, *énonciation* or *énoncé*, similarity or difference.[155]

Similar dualities can be found in the first half of the poem where the speaker compares the sunflower to a pregnant woman. Frequently, we commentators of Rodríguez's work have stressed the literal level as the point of departure toward the symbolic, even though that literal level remains in force through its interplay with the symbolic. In this poem, however, the images "cara" and "regazo" precede the word "flor," and ironically all three are synonymous, "identical": "Esta cara bonita, / este regazo que fue flor . . ." [This pretty face / this lap that was flower . . .]. The sunflower's "face," its distinguishing feature, its identity in terms of difference, is its "regazo," a rounded abdomen indistinguishable from any other such abdomen as the sunflower is a common flower, without much variation.

The speaker then enters in the first person to place himself in juxtaposition with the sunflower: "y yo lo quiero, y ahora / me lo arrimo . . ." [and I love it, and now I draw it near to me . . .]. As in "Miro" at the beginning of "Espuma," the speaker sets himself apart and expresses his unity with the sunflower-(m)Other as he draws it toward him. The subsequent concatenation of images ("y me entra / su luminosa rotación sencilla, / su danza, que es cosecha" [and there enters me / its luminous simple rotation, / its dance, which is harvest]) produces another paradox because it equates process and product, transience and transcendence, movement and stasis. We have already noted that "rotación" can indicate the circularity of the sunflower's shape and the movement of the flower as it follows the sun.[156] The dance is an ambivalent image (already discussed in the analysis of "El baile de águedas" in *Conjuros*), and a harvest can be the act of reaping as well as the grain reaped. Do these images represent transience in the passage of time or transcendence and stasis? Are they metonymic or metaphoric? If the speaker draws the sunflower toward him, what will he see? The result is still ambivalent, as the transition between the image of the pregnant woman and that of the defeated soldier illustrates.

The temporal phrase "esta tarde / de setiembre" on one level underscores the passage of time, the slipping away of the day and the year. But we could also understand them as pointing to cycles of change and renewal through their supplemental opposites: afternoon/morning, autumn/spring. Rodríguez has used the more contemporary spelling of the month, suggesting that perhaps something has been lost, but that language is in a constant state of renewal.[157] The division of "buena / ventura" in the enjambment of vv. 8–9 (the midpoint, the turning point of the poem and the "Libro") reinforces these dualities. Is this good luck the outcome (effect) of a process that has led the speaker to a discovery? Or is it the omen, the presage (cause) of future success or good fortune? Does it signal the product of the past or the promise of the future (cf. "cosecha")? These phrases lead to a change in personification along with a change of address.

. . . de buena
ventura porque ahora tú, valiente

10   girasol, de tan ciega
        mirada, tú me hacías mucha falta
        con tu postura de perdón, tras esa
        campaña soleada
        de altanería, a tierra
15   la cabeza, vencida
        por tanto grano, tan loca empresa.

(p. 156)[158]

The "tú" calls attention to the otherness of the sunflower in contrast with the earlier use of "yo." But as in that earlier instance, otherness is a reflection of self, of sameness and difference. The poem simultaneously juxtaposes the sunflower as pregnant woman and as defeated soldier (metaphorically, synchronically), as well as the sunflower with the speaker (metonymically, diachronically), bringing about an ironic quadrature in accord with this mirror-stage rite of passage.[159]

When the speaker remarks the sunflower's "ciega / mirada," does he admire its self-abnegation and self-sacrifice (as woman and soldier) for a cause larger than its individual self (the continuation of life, the preservation of certain rights and principles)? Or does he complain that the sunflower (as [m]Other) does not return his gaze, does not desire him as he desires it, does not admire him as he admires it? Is the flower altruistic or selfish? If the speaker doubts the sunflower's motives, he also doubts his own because he sees himself in this mirror-image. Does he praise himself as valiant, or does he criticize his hypocrisy and self-interest? Does the sunflower's "postura de perdón" request the speaker to forgive it for its selfishness/egotism, or does the flower offer to forgive the speaker for his "altanería"? Seeing the sunflower as his reflection, does the speaker seek forgiveness? Whereas "vencida" refers to "cabeza," to whom does the head belong? Who feels shame and defeat—the sunflower or the speaker? Whom has the grain defeated? Does the sunflower's dependence on the beloved sun lead to an unwanted pregnancy and sadness because of loss?[160] Or does the flower's abundant fertility and productivity shame the speaker into recognizing his own lack of resolve, his difference from the self-sacrificing woman/soldier? The speaker's final pronouncement, "tan loca empresa," could express his scorn for and desire to distance himself from this "enterprise" which has led to the soldier's defeat and the sunflower's destruction. Or it could express his delight and amazement as he recognizes that he has made a new beginning, undertaken a new approach to life ("empresa" derives from "emprender" meaning "to begin"). His realization that he lacks the resolve of self-sacrifice and self-abnegation that characterize the sunflower is in effect a discovery of what he must acquire so that he will be able to achieve his goal. As with the word(s) "buena / ventura," "Girasol" represents a turning point, a change in direction, a troping: an ambivalent, complex illumination ("sol," "helios") of a lack that is a promise, a loss that is a gain.

Corresponding with "Viento de primavera" in the structure of "Libro segundo," "Mala puesta" is an enigmatic poem following the intense turning point of "Girasol." A pun in the title provides two different ways of looking at the poem that again focuses on similarity and difference. On a literal level, the speaker is watching a sunset and by means of an objective correlative represents his emotions on seeing the loss of light, signifying a loss of inspiration, direction, insight, and hope. If we read the title not as "Mala puesta" but as "Mal apuesta," however, the sunset is personified as a female figure badly dressed. As this figure divests itself of its light and retires for/into the night, it becomes more vulnerable, but also more honest, more sincere, more humble. This mirror-image contrasts with yet suggests similarities with the speaker, the subject as "fader."[161]

The ambivalence in the title is sustained throughout the poem. In the opening verses, the light can represent either the speaker (a male figure) through the objective correlative or a female figure who might be either prostitute or virgin, seductress or morally upright.[162]

> La luz entusiasmada de conquista
> pierde confianza ahora,
> trémula de impotencia, y no se sabe
> si es de tierra o de cielo. Se despoja
> 5   de su íntima ternura
> y se retira lenta. . . .
>
>   (p. 157)[163]

The loss of light (poetic inspiration) leaves the poet lacking confidence in his ability to distinguish right from wrong, good from bad, celestial from mundane.[164] He no longer feels the "intimacy" of his inspiration and sees it slipping away from him. On the other hand, the light as woman, as other which had been "seducing" him, now withdraws. Is she definitely but warily rejecting the male figure, or is she being even more seductive, inviting, and alluring? The questions that follow this description continue to obfuscate the issue.

>   . . . ¿Qué limosna
> sin regocijo? ¿Qué reposo seco
> nos trae la tarde? ¿Qué misericordia
> deja este sol de un grana desvaído?
> 10   ¿Quién nos habló de la honda
> piedad del cielo? . . .
>
>   (p. 157)[165]

One could answer these (rhetorical) questions with the expected response, "None" or "No one." Or we can say that the speaker is (truly) wondering about what is happening to him, why it is happening, what it means, and where it will all lead. As the sun continues to set, the speaker finds himself betwixt and between, not knowing whether he has conquered or been vanquished.

>   . . . Aún quedan
> restos de la audaz forja
> de la luz, pero pocas
> nuevas nos vienen de la vida: un ruido,

15   algún olor mal amasado, esta hosca
       serenidad de puesta, cuando
       lejos están los campos y aún más lejos
       el fuego del hogar, y esta derrota
       nuestra, por cobardía o arrogancia,
20   por inercia o por gloria
       como la de esta luz, ya sin justicia
       ni rebelión, ni aurora.

(p. 157)[166]

The "audaz forja" could refer to the poet's (loss of) inspiration, his former daring self, the passion and heat of his creativity. Just as in a love affair that has cooled, he remembers moments of passion; but the loved one has left, leaving him with little evidence of her presence. He then enumerates bits and pieces of sensation that remind him of her: "un ruido, / algún olor mal amasado, esta hosca / serenidad de puesta." Whereas these images function on a literal, anecdotal level and a metapoetic, symbolic one, the "derrota" is ambivalent. Who is the victor, who the vanquished? Has the speaker been overcome by the discovery he has made in "Girasol," here represented by the love relationship? Or has he triumphed—for whatever reason, "por cobardía o arrogancia / por inercia o por gloria"—over his own blindness and shortcomings and his reluctance to admit the truth to himself? He finds himself betwixt and between the fields where he has been working (his poetry) and the warm, cozy, intimate hearth of home (his reputation). His "derrota" (defeat and triumph) is similar to the sunset: It has left him in the dark, but he also knows that he has laid to rest a period of his life that will never return, for better or for worse. He has been defeated, and he has vanquished; he has lost, but he has also gained. The light is similar to and different from him: It reflects his situation in a mirror-image, but it underscores the difference between them. He has defeated a part of himself, so that he is winner and loser, victor and vanquished.[167] He has decided to divest himself of his false, superficial passion but has not yet found his true self and must accept that he never will.

Because of its financial imagery "Dinero" is one of Rodríguez's most intriguing poems.[168] Like other poems in this section, it consists of contradictory meanings encompassed in the imagery and questions. First of all, money is a tangible medium of exchange but also an abstract system. Semiotically speaking, it is *parole* and *langue*, signifier and signified, that which is exchanged and the rules and values constituting the economic system. The interplay between these levels functions simultaneously on an ethical and an aesthetic level, doubling, reversing, and shuffling meanings from one level to another without ever losing its denotative value as money.

       ¿Venderé mis palabras, hoy que carezco de
       utilidad, de ingresos, hoy que nadie me fía?
       Necesito dinero para el amor, pobreza
       para amar. Y el precio de un recuerdo, la subasta
5   de un vicio, el inventario de un deseo,
       dan valor, no virtud, a mis necesidades,

amplio vocabulario a mis torpezas,
licencia a mi caliza
soledad. . . .

(p. 158)[169]

Forming the cornerstone of the first question (rhetorical and straightforward) and of the entire poem, the verb "venderé" lends itself to multiple interpretations. Literally, to sell is to exchange one's goods or products for money. The poet's goods are his words, and considering the transition through which he is passing at this moment, he may wonder if he will be able to publish his works. He has rejected his former superficial approach in favor of a more honest and soul-searching perspective. But will the public buy it? Will his new approach appeal to a readership? Although he may find a publisher (because of his reputation), will his poetry "sell"? Will he have to "sell himself out" by using false, insincere words only to make money, to survive as a writer? We could also interpret this future tense—expressive of the poet's doubt—as a question about the propriety of selling intimate, heartfelt expressions: Should he sell his poems? Should he look at them as something that he can and will sell? Or should he write strictly for himself, for his own gratification?

Because of his recent encounter with the sunflower, the poet-speaker finds himself in a moral and aesthetic dilemma. He sees himself now lacking in inspiration, which he expresses in economic terms ("utilidad" refers to profit, while "ingresos" is his income). But also on a literal level his lack of inspiration deriving from his new perspective makes him feel useless ("inútil") and without gain (i.e., he has lost something, but does not yet know what he has gained). When he states that "nadie me fía," he can mean that he is not trustworthy, that he has created mistrust in others, and also that no one will give him a loan (he is "alone," isolated, abandoned). And on a metapoetic level, he may believe that he has not earned the reputation he deserves (or does not deserve the reputation he has earned).

The statement after the question only intensifies his quandary. This solipsistic statement plays on the different possible meanings of "dinero" and "pobreza" on the monetary, ethical, and aesthetic levels simultaneously. Money may allow him to participate in the sexual act (for example, with a prostitute or gold digger), but he has a better chance of finding true love if he is poor (his spouse will love him for himself, not for his money). On another level, money will bring him material pleasures and creature comforts, but leave him spiritually bankrupt; in contrast, he may be materially poor but spiritually and vitally fulfilled, excited about the simple pleasures of life (the "alianza/condena" motif). On still another level, he needs to call upon a richness of inspiration and wealth of lexical expression in order to write, but he must also humble himself and seek the most honest and profound emotions if his poetry is not to come off as verbal pyrotechnics—all display and no substance. He needs to be familiar with the rich past (the poetic canon) but to speak with his own voice.

Verses 4–9 set up a series of parallelisms and contrasts. The first parallelism contrasts monetary imagery with human motives and emotions: "el *precio* de un *recuerdo*, la *subasta* / de un *vicio*, el *inventario* de un *deseo*." The second set interacts with the first and creates multiple contrasts: "dan *valor, no virtud*, a mis *necesidades*, / amplio *vocabulario* a mis *torpezas*, / *licencia* a mi caliza / *soledad*." Does "valor" mean its true worth or merely the monetary value we affix to things? Or perhaps even superficial bravado as opposed to virtue? The word "necesidades" could be interpreted in reference to Lacan's distinction between need (physical satisfaction), demand, and desire.[170] "Vocabulario" obviously pertains to the metapoetic level but could also refer to a variety of experiences (some very "cheap," some "bargains," some out of his price range) in which he learns more about himself and the world (note that this phrase parallels "la subasta de un vicio"). Finally, "licencia" could refer to permission or privilege (as in a driver's license or a fishing license), but it can also mean "wantonness" and "licentiousness." One will give purpose and meaning to his life, whereas the other will determine his loneliness because of his inability to make permanent attachments. Poetry allows the poet to explore all the possibilities of life and justifies his existence. The speaker's tone in the next verses is at once snidely sardonic and stoically philosophical.

> ... Porque el dinero, a veces, es el propio
> 10   sueño, es la misma
> vida. Y su triunfo, su monopolio, da fervor,
> cambio, imaginación, quita vejez y abre
> ceños, y multiplica los amigos,
> y alza faldas, y es miel
> 15   cristalizando luz, calor. No plaga, lepra
> como hoy; alegría
> no frivolidad; ley,
> no impunidad. ...

(p. 158)[171]

Again, the word "dinero" adopts contradictory meanings epitomized in "sueño" and "vida" (an obvious allusion to Calderón). Money can be an unbelievable benefice and an illusion; it can lead us to new adventures and opportunities and become an all-absorbing obsession that drains life of meaning and enjoyment. The catalog of what money can do can be read in two completely different ways because "triunfo" can be for or against (uplifting or defeating), and "monopolio" can connote a stingy, greedy obsession or a rare privilege. The phrase "quita vejez" can be read cynically to mean that a person with money will not look so old to someone interested in financial gain, or it can mean that one will feel younger and not notice the passing of time because of an optimistic outlook. The alliterative "alza faldas" is similarly ambivalent: Taken cynically, it states that some people (male and female) will do anything for money, including selling/buying sexual favors; taken metaphorically, it can mean "to remove obstacles to pleasure" (like "desbrozar el camino"). In short, we should not view money as a "plaga, lepra" necessarily, but as something that reveals the truth, a truth that can bring joy and/or pain.

In vv. 18–19, the speaker iterates the initial question with variations: "¿Voy a vender, entonces, / estas palabras?" [Am I going, then, to sell / these words?]. Given what he has discovered about money (literally), human motivation (ethically), and language (metapoetically), the speaker reformulates his initial question. Instead of the future tense, however, he substitutes the idiomatic "ir a." This change reflects the thoughtfulness with which the poet considers this question, asking it rhetorically and literally. He interrupts his question with "entonces" to call attention to his logic and the conclusions to which it is leading him, further highlighted by the change from "*mis* palabras" to "*estas* palabras." What makes these words—the words of this particular poem—meaningful, significant to the dilemma in which the speaker finds himself? Are they superficial, or do they lead the poet (and reader) to consider larger issues, various options, the full ramifications of the act of writing? The final verses of the poem posit the question in financial, ethical, and metapoetic terms.

>   . . . Rico de tanta pérdida,
> 20   sin maniobras, sin bolsa, aun sin tentación
>   y aun sin ruina dorada, ¿a qué la madriguera
>   de estas palabras que si dan aliento
>   no dan dinero? ¿Prometen pan o armas?
>   ¿O bien, como un balance mal urdido,
> 25   intentan ordenar un tiempo de carestía,
>   dar sentido a una vida: propiedad o desahucio?
>
>   (p. 158)[172]

The speaker's paradoxical declaration that he is "rico de tanta pérdida" encapsulates the gain/loss motif and the irony with which the speaker views his situation. Even though he has discovered his shortcomings, he sees that discovery as a positive realization. Admitting his falseness and superficiality enables him to work through it and to bring about a change in his life. Losing a false illusion of himself has been an enriching experience. He then asks what purpose "la madriguera de estas palabras" serves, an odd image when talking about words. Along with its connotations of an animal's den or a criminal's hideout, marking "words" negatively, "madriguera" also connotes a place where life exists and can be nourished (etymologically "madriguera" derives from "madre," the source of life and sustenance).

The final question boils down to a paradox. By attempting to give order and meaning to life and the emptiness that he would feel without poetry, words offer the speaker two choices, like the two sides of a scale and the two terms of the title *Alianza y condena*. But as we have seen, this "balance mal urdido" is equivocal: The option between "propiedad o desahucio" entails gain and loss on each side. "Propiedad" can refer to a strictly material existence for which the poet will "sell himself out" for fame or fortune or whatever; or it can mean distinction, individuality, and an adherence to one's principles in spite of the consequences (pain and suffering through self-accusation or criticism and rejection by others). With regard to "desahucio," one can be evicted, given up for lost, declared past recovery or help, given over to despair; or one can evict and thereby recover something of value.[173] If the poet allows himself to be governed by material desires or refuses to "pay his rent/his dues," he will have a shallow, meaningless existence; his words will be like empty rooms. If in contrast he "evicts" those aspects of his personality, those defenses which prevent him from seeing the truth about himself, he will reclaim the most precious part of existence: himself, his self-respect and his unique identity. Neither option is easy; each involves loss and gain. Money as a mirror-image of the speaker, as a representative of alterity, is that which the speaker desires and fears.

Rodríguez confronts his unwillingness to go beyond the surface and to take the risk that writing poetry involves in "Nieve en la noche" [Snow in the night], another poem that clearly demarcates a frame and depicts a scene that objectifies the similarities and differences between it and the speaker.[174] Here the speaker observes a snowfall at night from his window, discerning the illusions created by the snow, and he characterizes them in theatrical terms. The "doncella / máscara" [young woman's / mask] that hides wrinkles could be makeup or the masks of classical theater, while these "escenas" [scenes] he witnesses present facades and false fronts, "andamiajes, trémulas / escayolas, molduras / de un instante" [scaffoldings, tremulous / plaster pieces, moldings / of an instant]. Although he sees the brilliant snowfall as an entertaining festival, he also declares that it is a "feria / de la mentira" [fair of deceit]. These images of the snowfall entail the illusion of light and beauty contrasting with the tawdry, sordid reality beneath: "el rostro inocente / de cada copo" [the innocent face / of each snowflake] hides a "ruin tiña" [ruinous poverty] and a "feroz epidemia" [ferocious epidemic], and it creates a deceptive sense of time, a superficial illusion: "ahora / es mediodía en plena / noche" [now / it is noon in full / night].

In the second stanza, the speaker is quick to point out that the snow "nos ciega, / no da luz" [blinds us, / it does not give light]. Like a clever thief it seems to give, making its theft even more cruel. Like a horse that seems docile but which reins "nunca se aventuran / a conquistar" [never dare / to conquer], the snow "no riega / sino sofoca, ahoga" [does not water / but suffocates, drowns].[175] The speaker confesses his disorientation when he declares, "Y borró los caminos" [And it erased the roads]. The mesmerizing imagery of this brilliant spectacle blinds the reader as much as the snowfall does the speaker, so that we might overlook the dark space in the poem if not for a dialogue embedded in the second stanza.[176] This dialogue inscribes the dark space of the speaker's anecdotal world and causes us to experience a defamiliarization. It is as if we have been viewing a film in a darkened theater when someone in the audience suddenly begins a disruptive conversation. For just a few moments, the illusion is broken, and we become abruptly aware of our separation from the aesthetic world and of our presence in time and space.[177] The spectacle of the snowfall overpowers our perception of the speaker's anecdotal world, but the embedded dialogue redirects our focus from the exterior to the interior, from the surface to the depth, from the obvious to the hidden.[178]

> Y tú dices: «despierta,
> que amanece». (Y es noche
> muy noche.) Dices: «cierra,
> que entra sol». Y no quiero
> 40   perder de nuevo ante esta

nevada. No, no quiero
mentirte otra vez. Tengo
que alzarle la careta
a este rostro enemigo
45   que me finge a mi puerta
la inocencia que vuelve
y el pie que deja huella.

(p. 160)[179]

With whom does the speaker converse? We can infer that it is someone who is sleepy and does not wish to be disturbed, someone deceived by the snow into thinking that it is morning and that morning has come too early. Because of the images at the beginning of the poem, we might suppose that it is a woman (Clara? someone else?). But it could also be a part of the speaker that resists the desire to see himself without illusions and to confront those aspects of himself that are in need of revision. If we view this poem from a metapoetic slant, we discover a poet who rejects superficial linguistic brilliance in favor of profound personal emotions and probing self-analysis in order to attain a lasting achievement. Footprints in the snow will not endure, and so the speaker turns away from the brilliant, illusory exterior and seeks more lasting values in the dark, intimate spaces within.

The scene presented in "Frente al mar," which closes the frame of "Libro segundo" before spilling over into "Ciudad de meseta," contains two principal aspects: the sea and the land, which represent the proverbial confrontation between an irresistible force and an immovable object. This encounter serves as an objective correlative or mirror that reflects the speaker's interior conflict, but as in "Dinero," it leaves the speaker with an ironic choice. As the note after the title explains, the scene described pertains to Ibiza, one of the Islas Baleares off the coast of Cataluña. The opening description sets the scene and juxtaposes the two forces.

Transparente quietud. Frente a la tierra
rojiza, desecada hasta la entraña,
con aridez que es ya calcinación,
se abre el Mediterráneo. Hay pino bajo,
5   sabinas, pitas, y crece el tomillo
y el fiel romero, tan austeramente
que apenas huelen si no es a salitre.
Quema la tramontana. Cae la tarde.

(p. 161)[180]

Underscored by synesthesia, the first declaration "Transparente quietud" is tersely ambivalent. Because "quietud" can refer to either sound or movement and "transparente" is something seen but not seen (seen through), there but not there, we cannot say for sure if this phrase refers to the sea or the land or both, or even the speaker's emotions at this moment. It does, however, have the effect of stopping time, halting our movement forward (as this framing poem should). This stasis allows the speaker time to contemplate his situation and to assess both sides of the issue in the land and the sea. The contrast is immediately noticeable in the color of the land, its dryness and hardness that suggest a rigidity, inflexibility, and intransigence (the inability or un-willingness to change), and the austerity of the plant life (barely productive even of the strong aromas of thyme and rosemary) because of the salt air and the dry wind. The sea, on the other hand, "se abre," an incisive (and quite succinct) description that suggests horizons, freedom, potential, openness, and motion.

It is curious, however, that the poet specifically mentions the Mediterranean. If Ibiza is an island circumscribed by water, the Mediterranean is a sea bounded and defined by land. This latent similarity runs counter to the contrast of land and sea, subverting a neat binary opposition. It also prefigures or replicates on this specific level the fractal-like *mise en abïme* pattern of *Alianza* in general. For now, let us consider the land and the sea, noting how the description of each subverts a simple binarism and our preestablished disposition to see the land as rigidity, stability, and stasis, and the sea as flexibility, mutability, and movement. Framed by pointed but deceptive references to the sea, the following verses in truth describe the land, espe-cially the coastline, the suture or liminal space between land and sea.

         Verdad de sumisión, de entrega, de
   10   destronamientos, desmoronamientos
         frente al mar azul puro que en la orilla
         se hace verde esmeralda. Vieja y nueva
         erosión. Placas, láminas, cornisas,
         acantilados y escolleras, ágil
   15   bisel, estría, lucidez de roca
         de milenaria permanencia. Aquí
         la verdad de la piedra, nunca muda
         sino en interna reverberación,
         en estremecimiento de cosecha
   20   perenne, dando su seguro oficio,
         su secreta ternura sobria junto
         al mar, que es demasiada criatura,
         demasiada hermosura para el hombre.

                                                              (p. 161)[181]

Whereas at first we might be deceived into thinking that the "Verdad de sumisión, de entrega, de / destronamientos, desmoronamientos" describes the sea's mobility, its waves crashing on the rocky shoreline, it turns out ironically that "la verdad de la piedra" is its "interna reverberación" and its "estremecimiento de cosecha perenne." Emphasis is placed not on the sea's participation in this "Vieja y nueva / erosión" but on the architectural and sculptural beauty of the rock as it undergoes changes and reveals its "lucidez" standing out against the colors of the sea. When we finally reach the descriptive clause of vv. 22–23 ("que es demasiada criatura . . ."), we recognize that this phrase more appropriately modifies the "interna reverberación," "estremecimiento de cosecha," and "secreta ternura sobria" of the land. As a "femi-nine" noun, "la tierra" is personified as a woman participating in love, more subtly alive and responsive because of its "sumisión," its "entrega," that is, its ability to sacrifice itself, to give itself over to the other by removing barriers and defenses (cf. "Girasol"). The sea, on the other hand, characterized as masculine ("*el* mar"), is more restricted and suppressed than its counterpart.

> Antiguo mar latino que hoy no canta,
> 25   dice apenas, susurra, prisionero
> de su implacable poderío, con
> pulsación de sofoco, sin oleaje,
> casi en silencio de clarividencia
> mientras el cielo se oscurece y llega,
> 30   maciza y seca, la última ocasión
> para amar. . . .
>
> (pp. 161–62)[182]

This "Antiguo mar latino" could refer to the poetic tradition and the whole of Western civilization as a sea with a limited and limiting scope. Consequently, the sea only whispers instead of speaking distinctly or "singing," a clear metapoetic reference to the poet's sense of limitations ("prisionero") and the suppression of his emotions ("con pulsación de sofoco"). Today this sea is calm, still, "sin oleaje," lifeless, static. The phrase "casi en silencio de clarividencia" repeats, reverses, and alters the opening "transparente quietud." The synesthetic combination of sight and sound is repeated and reversed, but now the transparent quality is transformed into clairvoyance, an ability to go beyond the surface, not just to look through or ignore it. Clairvoyance, a "quick, intuitive knowledge of things and people," takes the surface into account but sees clearly that which the surface disguises, just as the speaker has discovered the opposite of what we normally suppose when we think of land and sea. It is as if the sea were caught in a clairvoyant trance, accounting for its quietude and immobility.

But another ironic reversal awaits us. The hypnotic trance and stillness of the sea seems to make time stop, yet the speaker reminds us that it is getting darker ("Cae la tarde") and that "la última ocasión / para amar" is arriving. Anecdotally, we might extrapolate that this is the eve of the speaker's departure from the island and that he has only this last chance to appreciate its fleeting beauty. His modification of this occasion as "maciza y seca" reminds us of his description of the land (which is really what we would expect of the water), but it seems to apply to the sky instead! The sky reflects the time of day, the liminal hour between day and night, juxtaposing time with space (land and sea) and representing the interplay of synchronic and diachronic, metaphor and metonymy, self and other. The final verses offer us the same ambivalent conclusion as "Dinero," as the reference to "espumas" snaps the frame shut, only to have this section spill over into one more poem.

> . . . Entre piedras y entre espumas,
> ¿qué es rendición y qué supremacía?
> ¿Qué nos serena, qué nos atormenta:
> el mar terso o la tierra desolada?
>
> (p. 162)[183]

As the duplicitous language of the title indicates, the speaker sees himself set against the scene before him, separating himself from it and at the same time ready to "face the music" about himself and to see clairvoyantly beyond the surface.

"Frente al mar" shows us how far the speaker has come in comparison with "Espuma." Both poems employ the sea as the central image, both convey erotic over-tones, and both deal with liminal spaces. "Frente al mar" reveals that the speaker has discovered the price he must pay, with "Girasol" representing the turning point in this poetic and personal coming of age. But now, as a result of the decision made in "Nieve," the speaker knows what his decision will be: He will always opt for the most honest approach, even though it may be the most painful. For that reason, "Frente al mar" twice mentions his "transparente quietud" and his "silencio de clarividencia." Loss will always accompany gain, but to gain, one must sacrifice—"alianza" requires "condena" and "condena" leads to "alianza."

"Ciudad de meseta" [City on the plain] is effusive in more than one sense. This poem may originally have been meant to be included in *Conjuros*, but Rodríguez omitted it from that work, revised it significantly to be less specific, and then "tagged it on" to "Libro segundo" as a supplemental addition, further linking this section with *Conjuros*.[184] A comparison of the opening verses of the two versions of this poem will provide insight into the alteration in the speaker's perspective in *Alianza*. The original version—ironically published after *Alianza*—bears a different, more specific title, and the speaker directly addresses the city of Avila.

> "Llegada a la estación de Avila"
>
> Avila, como tu aire
> tan sano no lo hay, pero no vengo
> a curarme de nada, aunque una cura
> le iría bien a mi pulmón, tras estos
> 5   años en mala tierra.[185]

The later version, "Ciudad de meseta," eliminates specific mention of location, begins in medias res, makes the language more ambivalent, and sounds like internal monologue rather than direct address.

> Como por estos sitios
> tan sano aire no hay, pero no vengo
> a curarme de nada.
> Vengo a saber qué hazaña
> 5   vibra en la luz, qué rebelión oscura
> nos arrasa hoy la vida.
>
> (p. 163)[186]

The introduction of the clause with "Como" could signify the same as in "Llegada": In no other place is the air as pure as it is in this city. But because of the syntax we could understand that the speaker is disappointed about not finding the clear, health-ful air that he had expected to find in this city high on the "meseta" and out in the

open. In "Llegada," the speaker admits he has reason for needing that clear air to
bring about a healthful change; in "Ciudad," the statement is more succinct and equivocal. The speaker may or may not need to heal himself. Indeed, we have seen that he
finds himself in an ambivalent position after his encounter with the sunflower. Instead
of seeking a definitive cure, he continues his search. The equivocation in the language
shows that the change in himself that he seeks will not be determined by his external
circumstances but by an intuitive, insightful search within himself, wherever he may
happen to be. The clear air of the "alta meseta" may stimulate his purification and his
growth, but even if it is not as clean and clear as he expected, even that will stimulate
him, perhaps all the more so.

At this point the two versions of the poem diverge radically, coinciding again
(with variations) only in the final verses of the poem, creating another frame. The
poems are so radically different that it will behoove us to concentrate on "Ciudad de
meseta" and to leave "Llegada" for further study (a supplement or excess) to this
discussion of *Alianza*. Walking through the streets of this city on the plains, the speaker
notes the passage of time, but from the transience he sees around him, he receives
new stimulus. Notice particularly the word "desbordar" in v. 20, the overflow or excess that arises from this scene.

> Aquí ya no hay banderas,
> ni murallas, ni torres, como si ahora
> pudiera todo resistir el ímpetu
> 10   de la tierra, el saqueo
> del cielo. Y se nos barre
> la vista, es nuestro cuerpo
> mercado franco, nuestra voz vivienda
> y el amor y los años
> 15   puertas para uno y para mil que entrasen.
> Sí, tan sin suelo siempre,
> cuando hoy andamos por las viejas calles
> el talón se nos tiñe
> de la uva nueva, y oímos
> 20   desbordar bien sé qué aguas
> el rumoroso cauce del oído.

(p. 163)[187]

Like the downfall of an ancient stronghold, the speaker sees his body as having
been invaded and sacked. Although he may feel his life has no solid footing ("tan sin
suelo siempre"), he still receives inspiration from his experiences (people still live in
this city). His reference to wine making and to flowing water (whether of a river or a
fountain) are images of spiritual elation and a metapoetic ecstasy that overflows from
within him and goes beyond the external stimulations with which he comes into contact.

In the second stanza (reminiscent of "Pinar amanecido"), the speaker criticizes
what he sees as the artificial, hypocritical unity of the people who live in this exemplary city. This stanza begins and ends with variations of "Es la alianza," forming a

frame within the frame of the opening and closing verses, another manifestation of the *mise en abïme* pattern. Where we might expect to discover a positively-marked definition of the concept of "alianza," this word—like the air of the city on the plains— has been contaminated. By employing an image of "este aire / montaraz" (with its abrupt run-on line) for "alianza," the speaker expresses the ambivalence between purity, clarity, and invigoration (mountain air) and roughness, surliness, and wild- ness. He is aware of the separation and distance that characterizes human relations and describes the city in bellicose, defensive terms, ending with a question about his purpose in life and how to achieve it.

> Y a saber qué distancia
> 25 hay de hombre a hombre, de una vida a otra,
> qué planetaria dimensión separa
> dos latidos, qué inmensa lejanía
> hay entre dos miradas
> o de la boca al beso.
> . . . .
> 35 Jamás casas: barracas,
> jamás calles: trincheras,
> jamás jornal: soldada.
> ¿De qué ha servido tanta
> plaza fuerte, hondo foso, recia almena,
> 40 amurallado cerco?
> El temor, la defensa,
> el interés y la venganza, el odio,
> la soledad: he aquí lo que nos hizo
> vivir en vecindad, no en compañía.
> 45 Tal es la cruel escena
> que nos dejaron por herencia. Entonces,
> ¿cómo fortificar aquí la vida
> si ella es sólo alianza?

(pp. 163–64)[188]

In the final stanza, the speaker stands before the city's walls, reinforcing the comparison between himself and the place. These walls—defenses—represent a liminal space between inside and outside, just as the city is defined as "fronteriza": on the border between "civilización y barbarie" [civilization and barbarity], on the fringe between different and opposing cultures, but also at the forefront, making advances into the unknown, the wilderness, that which threatens as it attracts (the unconscious). It is a place on the edge between past and future, indicating the speaker's position at this moment in his trajectory when he is able to see the positive in the negative.

> Vieja ambición que ahora
> sólo admira el turista o el arqueólogo
> o quien gusta de timbres y blasones.
> 55 Esto no es monumento
> nacional, sino luz de alta planicie,
> aire fresco que riega el pulmón árido

```
            y lo ensancha, y lo hace
            total entrega renovada, patria
    60      a campo abierto. Aquí no hay costas, mares,
            norte ni sur: aquí todo es materia
            de cosecha. . . .
```

(p. 164)[189]

"Llegada a la estación de Avila" closes with a repetition of its opening lines, making its conclusion ambivalent—closing like a circle, opening like a spiral. In revising this poem for *Alianza*, Rodríguez has eschewed that pattern for a different type of framing and repetition because he modifies the final lines of "Llegada." A juxtaposition of these two versions illuminates the similarities and differences. First the verses from "Llegada."

```
    75      Avila, como tu aire
            tan sano no lo hay, y este vinillo
            se nos cuela con él en hondo oreo.
            Recién venidos y un momento juntos,
            ¡fuera de aquí quien nos recuerde ahora
    80      esa voraz caída de la noche
            sobre los altos campos
            de nuestra tierra![190]
```

In the revised version of "Ciudad," the poet does not specifically mention night, concentrating instead on the horizon, the magical power of dew, and the image of harvest.

```
                        . . . Porque todo
            se rinde en derredor y no hay fronteras,
    70      ni distancia, ni historia.
            Sólo el voraz espacio y el relente de octubre
            sobre estos altos campos
            de nuestra tierra.
```

(p. 164)[191]

The clearing away of barriers—physical, emotional, and temporal—leaves the speaker exceedingly conscious of "el voraz espacio." This adjective is ambivalent for it could reflect his eagerness to continue investigating this immense new territory that lies before him (his own life, his very self), but because it devours him, this space causes him fear—he is aware of the risks involved. The "relente de octubre" may give him the shivers because it is cool and damp, but dew is also a symbol of life and renewal, of "bendición celestial" [heavenly blessing], and of fecundity.[192]

By making the setting of this poem less specific—in addition to Avila, we might think of Toledo, Segovia, Salamanca, or Zamora—Rodríguez emphasizes its liminality between earth and sky (place) and past and future (time) rather than its specificity. As the overflow of the poems of *Conjuros* and of "Libro segundo" of *Alianza* (especially of the framing poem "Frente al mar," which also imbricates time and space), "Ciudad de meseta" repeats and expands upon "Noche en el barrio." Both poems close their respective sections and yet impel us into the next section by anticipating certain characteristics and spilling over their respective frames. "Noche" forms part of the frame as it spills over; "Ciudad" lies outside the frame proper. Its double framing (the repetition of "alianza" inside the verses repeated from "Llegada") and its effusion (the third mention of "alianza" and the change in its meaning) lays bare the *mise en abïme* that structures *Alianza*. The remaining two sections of this work repeat this pattern one more time and cause us to focus on the center as these poems spill over at the periphery.

CROSSING THE BAR: MYTHOLOGICAL IDENTITIES AND THE LAW OF THE NAME-OF-THE-FATHER

Rodríguez has arranged the poems of "Libro tercero" in a highly symmetrical pattern. Consisting of sixteen poems, this section can be thought of as two groups of eight and four groups of four. Such an arrangement takes into account the change in tone between "Adiós" and "Noche abierta," the two center poems, making the center of this section a gap. This gap is the extension of the center poems in the previous sections: the three two-part poems of "Libro primero" ("Porque no poseemos," "Cáscaras," and "Por tierra de lobos") and "Girasol," the turning point of "Libro segundo." It also establishes a mirror-image reversal and creates concentricity and harmonious balance between the first eight poems and the last eight.

In addition, each four-poem section balances its counterpart and includes a peripeteia that could be summarized with the paradox "From evil good arises." The first four poems ("Un suceso," "En invierno es mejor un cuento triste," "Cielo," and "Ajeno") address the theme of otherness. The next four poems ("Hacia un recuerdo," "Un momento," "Tiempo mezquino," and "Adiós") deal with time and space, and separation from the Other. Once past the gap in the center, the poems of the next group ("Noche abierta," "Como el son de las hojas del álamo," "Un olor," and "Sin leyes") focus on the senses: sight, sound, smell, and touch, respectively. The final four poems ("Amanecida," "Lo que no es sueño," "Una luz," and "Un bien") describe an awakening to self. These four poems balance the four opening poems, juxtaposing the self with otherness.

In accord with these themes, each group of four delineates a mythical figure: Prometheus, Orpheus, Dionysus, and Apollo. Each portrays the speaker as poet and transgressor, and each to varying degrees embodies a combination of the human and the divine. Yet in each there is a modification in the portrayal of the poet. As a thief who transgresses Olympus to steal sacred fire, Prometheus receives a severe punishment. Likewise the poet derives his inspiration from a higher source and must pay the price for so singular a gift. Orpheus plays the lyre so well that he can transgress the boundary of death by descending to Hades and convincing Pluto to return Eurydice to

life. But he also violates the injunctions imposed upon him by doubting and looking
backward to be sure that his beloved is following him. He, like Prometheus, is punished with loss and later dismemberment. As we shall see, the speaker of "Libro
tercero" refuses to look back, placing his trust and faith in the Other's word. He thus
begins to distinguish himself from these father figures at the same time that he identifies with them through the theme of punishment (the threat of castration).[193] A contrast of night and dawn, darkness and light, stands out in the next two groups of
poems in the figures of Dionysus and Apollo.[194] The first of these is attractive precisely because of his darker side, whereas his characteristic drunkenness has ambivalent repercussions.[195] It may be that Apollo, the god of the sun, is the most divine and
powerful of these figures, but several tales of classical mythology address his human
desires.[196]

These four figures interact in multiple ways, not only creating a progression from
beginning to end of the "Libro" but also positing comparisons and contrasts. First, we
can juxtapose the Prometheus/Orpheus dyad with Dionysus/Apollo. Then, we can
correlate Prometheus with Orpheus and Dionysus with Apollo, and Prometheus with
Dionysus and Orpheus with Apollo. Finally, we can counterpose each figure with the
other three. When we then compare each of them with the speaker as poet and transgressor, we note the affinity between similarity and difference (the theme of identity).
The subtle changes from one poem to the next in each of the four groups replicates the
process of rejection and acceptance, separation and individuation.

The combination of the poetic processes of the two previous "Libros" underscores these motifs. If in "Libro primero" (as in *Don*) the poet begins with abstract
concepts and embodies them in concrete images, and in "Libro segundo" (as in
Conjuros) he uses a specific anecdotal scene or experience as the springboard for
more profound discoveries, in the third section of *Alianza* he imbricates these procedures.[197] This combination has two major effects: The different procedures effect contradictory forces—centripetal and centrifugal—which contend with one another; and
their overlapping results in a suture, a liminal space where both combine. Combining
the procedures reflects the concept of "identity" as sameness and difference, at the
same time that it bears out Lacan's definition of the subject (the individual, the self):
to be a subject is to be subject to the Other.[198]

The symmetrical arrangement of these poems would seem to contradict the pattern of a frame and spillover that we have seen in "Libro primero" and "Libro segundo."
"Libro tercero" appears to be self-contained, balanced, and rigidly structured, yet it is
a combination of the processes of the previous sections (and works), and there is a
gap at its center. We can consider the odes of "Libro cuarto" as the spillover, otherness overflowing "Libro tercero," just as "Noche en el barrio" with its commands
spills over and carries us into the second "Libro" and as "Ciudad de meseta" was
removed from *Conjuros*, revised, and included in *Alianza*. A look at selected poems
from each of the four groups of "Libro tercero" illuminates the changes characterizing the poet's emergence as a distinct individual in this postmirror stage, a coming of
age through acceptance of the Law of the Name-of-the-Father.[199]

Promethean Guilt and Penance

Female figures play a key role in "Libro tercero," reminding us that Rodríguez has dedicated *Alianza* to his wife Clara. This is particularly true of the first two poems, "Un suceso" and "En invierno," as the speaker separates himself from the (m)Other. These female figures—in the first poem a young woman and in the second a mother—represent the "suture" or overlapping of opposing forces (difference) that the speaker must accept if he is to become an individual. In Lacanian terms, the speaker must accept repression and absence if he is to be autonomous and fully independent. He must accept being shut off from the Imaginary if he is to enter the Symbolic, but the Imaginary and the Symbolic will always be in contact, one influencing the other continuously and reciprocally.[200] Metapoetically, this section resolves the poet's relationship with the poetic tradition, although this resolution is tenuous and always in need of readjustment.[201]

The title of the first poem, "Un suceso," and the epigraph taken from François Villon prefigure the suturing (imbrication) of the two procedures discussed above. A "suceso" can be the outcome or result of a series of events, or it can be the stimulus for another series of events which are to follow as a consequence. We can view the encounter described in this poem as the outcome (effect) of the steps taken by the poet-speaker up to this moment and as the stimulus (cause) of the next steps in this process. Even though the two ideas are imbricated to form an indivisible unit, they are also reversed in their logical order (outcome precedes stimulus, the signified precedes the signifier).[202] The epigraph from Villon is equally enigmatic. Villon is recognized as a poet of great originality and lyricism, yet he was also an outlaw whose thefts often landed him in jail and finally forced him into exile after a reprieve from the death sentence (cf. Prometheus). The play of verb tenses in the cited passage "Bien est verté que j'ai amé / et ameroie voulentiers" [It is very true that I have loved / and that I would willingly love again] determine an equivocal play between past, present, and future.[203] The conditional "ameroie" qualifies the future, suggesting that it may or may not be a possibility in spite of the speaker's desire. Rodríguez establishes a parallel between the outlaw-poet talking about love and desire, and the speaker's relationship with the poetic tradition and originality (autonomy, individuality, subjectivity). This ambivalence carries over into the first lines of the poem and the speaker's reaction to his encounter with a young woman.

> Tal vez, valiendo lo que vale un día,
> sea mejor que el de hoy acabe pronto.
> La novedad de este suceso, de esta
> muchacha, casi niña pero de ojos
> 5   bien sazonados ya y de carne a punto
> de miel, de andar menudo, con su moño
> castaño claro, su tobillo hendido
> tan armoniosamente, con su airoso
> pecho que me deslumbra más que nada
> 10   la lengua . . .

(p. 167)[204]

The sententious statement to which the speaker has arrived as the starting point for the poem contains a contradictory use of verbs. The main clause of the sentence is in the subjunctive ("sea" reinforced by "acabe"), whereas the parenthetical clause "valiendo lo que vale un día" is in the indicative, the reverse of the "normal" use of these modes.[205] Also, we wonder if the speaker is elated by this chance meeting and wishes for the day to end because it could not get any better; or if he is so thoroughly discouraged by this experience that he wants this wretched day to be over. It is further unclear if the speaker is standing back now, contemplating what has just occurred, or if he is narrating the sequence of events as they are happening. This confusion mixes poetic contemplation in the present with a reflection on past events, imbricating the two poetic processes we have seen earlier. Is this metaphor or metonymy, poetry or narration, present or (immediate) past?

The poet then metonymically transfers the cause/effect ambivalence of "suceso" onto this "muchacha, casi niña," reinforcing it with "novedad" and the description of the female figure. "Novedad" can refer to the uniqueness of this encounter and this female who is both woman and child, or to the surprise she causes the speaker. She is both cause and effect, the personification of the suture between self and other. The speaker first notes her gaze—"de ojos / bien sazonados ya"—which seems to define her knowledge of sexual relationships, her self-assurance, and her self-acceptance. A perplexing figure, she wears her hair in a "moño castaño claro" and walks with a short gait, implying that she is acting the part of someone older and wiser at the same time that she exudes confidence and savoir faire.[206]

The speaker's description of "su airoso / pecho que me deslumbra más que nada / la lengua" concludes his description of her, yet the suspensive periods leave the description incomplete—presumably because the speaker is dumbfounded.[207] The abrupt run-on line calls attention to "airoso," which connotes contradictory characteristics (elegant, jaunty, graceful, rising and falling with her breathing or her steps); and "deslumbrar," recognizable from the opening poems of *Don*, refers to the dazzling effect this sight has on the speaker. Is he a lecher chasing skirts in the street? Or is he someone who can appreciate beauty, potential, self-assurance, and elegance because he can objectively and morally evaluate his own desires? Just as this female figure encompasses childlike and adult qualities, the speaker's reaction to her is contradictory.[208] He then moves from observation of the other to explore more closely the effect of this figure on him.

10   . . . Y no hay remedio, y le hablo ronco
                  como la gaviota, a flor de labio
                  (de mi boca gastada), y me emociono
                  disimulando ciencia e inocencia
                  como quien no distingue un abalorio
15   de un diamante, y le hablo de detalles
       de mi vida, y la voz se me va, y me oigo
       y me persigo, muy desconfiado
       de mi estudiada habilidad, y pongo
       cuidado en el aliento, en la mirada

20   y en las manos, y casi me perdono
       al sentir tan preciosa libertad
       cerca de mí. . . .

(pp. 167–68)[209]

In another "transference" of ambivalence (first from "suceso" to "muchacha" and now from her to him), the speaker becomes a split, self-conscious subject, looking at himself looking. He notices that his voice is "ronco"—either hoarse or deep (i.e., masculine). His words "a flor de labio" could be superficial nonsense or urbane flowering (cf. "piropos," "flores" [flattery]) on his lips. His "boca gastada" could indicate that he sees himself as old and worn out in comparison with her, or that he is experienced, "broken-in," accustomed to this small talk. If he is "disimulando ciencia e inocencia / como quien no distingue un abalorio / de un diamante," is he deceiving her into thinking that he is unknowledgeable and innocent, or is he making a fool of himself by pretending to be what he's not? Is his deceit so transparent as to be ridiculous, false, superficial? Is he really dumbstruck, head-over-heals in love, or is he deceitfully taking advantage of a younger, more naive person? (Is Prometheus a thief or a benefactor of humankind?)

The split subject is especially apparent in his statements "y la voz se me va, y me oigo / y me persigo, muy desconfiado / de mi estudiada habilidad." The speaker is self-conscious, seeing himself being seen by the Other, looking at himself looking at the Other, but his motivation remains a mystery. The reflexive phrase "casi me perdono" epitomizes the ambiguity. Not only is the action reflexive (in all senses of the word), but the qualification with the adverb "casi" calls into question the speaker's attitude. Is it that he is almost able to pardon himself because of the uplifting effect of this extraordinary experience? Or is it that he understands how tempted he is by this young woman, "al sentir tan preciosa libertad / cerca de mí," that he can rationalize his feelings for her? The final lines sustain the ambivalence of his motives but mark a change in his attitude as he resists and separates himself from her (imaginary) charm and attraction.

      . . . Bien sé que esto no es sólo
      tentación. Cómo renuncio a mi deseo
      ahora. Me lastimo y me sonrojo
25   junto a esta muchacha a la que hoy amo,
      a la que hoy pierdo, a la que muy pronto
      voy a besar muy castamente sin que
      sepa que en ese beso va un sollozo.

(p. 168)[210]

The separation of the subject from the (m)Other and the Imaginary order stands out in the abrupt runover of vv. 23 and 24. The word "tentación" lends itself to multiple interpretations, including sin, enchantment, allurement, and infatuation. When the speaker states that he feels something in addition to this "tentación," he begins to tear himself away from his former attitudes. He now makes a separation, renouncing his former desire (his former way of desiring). He represses (sublimates) imaginary union with the Other and begins his incorporation into the Symbolic, that which will define him as an individual and an outstanding poet. Such a rupture causes pain and embarrassment, but the break is a necessary one if he is to be truly independent and individual. To be a subject, he must subject himself to the Other, so that he kisses this young woman "castamente." If he wishes to emulate the sunflower, he must renounce the gratification of his own egotistical pleasures.

This metonymic narrative is metaphoric of the ethical and aesthetic stance Rodríguez has taken as a human being and a poet. The relationship between his conduct and his writing evinces the same paradoxical imbrication of the poetic processes of "Libro primero" and "Libro segundo," and in the relationship between metaphor and metonymy, centripetal and centrifugal forces, identity as sameness and difference, self and other. Writing is a means toward discovering and creating the self; an ethical stance is the cause and the effect of writing. The written word is a representation of a representation of a representation, ad infinitum, carrying us away from the "true," the "real," the "essence," the "original"—that is, from the subject, the self; and it is a reality—a signifier—in and of itself.[211] The speaker-poet attains his wish by renouncing it and in that way constitutes his subjectivity, his individuality, his unique voice.[212] His final word "sollozo," which is the signified (tenor) transported by the signifier (vehicle) of the "beso," is a sign of sorrow and joy, pain and relief, defeat and victory, loss and gain.

In the tradition of an Augustinian confession, "En invierno es mejor un cuento triste" [In winter a sad story is better] delves more deeply into this enigma by dealing with the mother figure: The speaker humbles himself as a little boy seeking forgiveness.[213] Yet it is only because of the error of his ways that he can arrive at this moment of repentance. By humbling himself, he grows more mature, whereas before he only circumscribed himself more sharply within the Imaginary order because of his immature behavior. In the first stanza, the speaker admits his wrong and repents.

> Conmigo tú no tengas
> remordimiento, madre. Yo te doy lo único
> que puedo darte ahora: si no amor,
> sí reconciliación. Ya sé el fracaso,
> 5 la victoria que cabe
> en un cuerpo. El caer, el arruinarse
> de tantos años contra el pedernal
> del dolor, el huir
> con leyes a mansalva
> 10 que me daban razón, un cruel masaje
> para alejarme de ti; historias
> de dinero y de catres,
> de alquileres sin tasa,
> cuando todas mis horas eran horas de lobo,
> 15 cuando mi vida fue estar al acecho
> de tu caída, de tu
> herida, en la que puse
> si no el diente, tampoco

la lengua,
20   me dan hoy el tamaño
de mi pecado.

(p. 169)[214]

Following upon "Un suceso," noteworthy is the use of the direct address of the mother figure with "tú." This form of address creates intimacy, sincerity, and directness while at the same time dramatizing the scene, separating the speaker from his mother and from himself as he sees himself repeating a scene from the past but altering it now because he admits his wrong.[215] His references to "historias / de dinero y de catres" and to his "horas de lobo" yield sexual overtones and illuminate the causes of his current repentance. The mother figure takes on characteristics of a universal woman to whom the speaker appeals for forgiveness by confessing his faults. The second stanza reinforces the duality of intimacy and separation by means of frames, contradictions, and equivocal language.

Sólo he crecido en esqueleto: mírame.
Asómate como antes
a la ventana. Tú no pienses nunca
25   en esa caña cruda que me irguió
hace dieciséis años. Tú ven, ven,
mira qué clara está la noche ahora,
mira que yo te quiero, que es verdad,
mira cómo donde hubo
30   parcelas hay llanuras,
mira a tu hijo que vuelve
sin camino y sin manta, como entonces,
a tu regazo con remordimiento.

(p. 169)[216]

The commands, especially the repetition of "ven" and "mira," appeal for the coincidence of their perspectives (internal and external, male and female)—as opposed to their conflict—brought about by the gaze as the speaker calls attention to himself and to his former childish behavior.[217] The window imposes a frame separating them, but it is also a "transparency," a means of seeing through an obstacle (a wall, a defense, a deceit).[218] Instead of being punished as he was in the past (the "caña cruda" suggests physical punishment), the speaker urges his mother to look beyond his former behavior and the reputation he has gained: "mira qué clara está la noche ahora."[219] Even though it is night—metaphor for his wrongdoing, his egotism, and his blindness—it is now clear to him what he has done wrong. He wishes that his mother will see that he now admits his failings.[220]

The final verses ("mira a tu hijo que vuelve") recall the biblical parable of the prodigal son who returns seeking forgiveness.[221] In this instance the son returns to his mother rather than his father. Instead of returning to the womb, however, (metaphor for the Imaginary order and perfect unity with the [m]Other), the speaker climbs into her lap. This symbolic gesture seeks intimacy and love but still maintains separation of the subject from the (m)Other. The repetition of "remordimiento" underscores this change, for the concept has been "transferred" from the mother to the speaker, and the meaning has changed from the disappointment, pity, and dissatisfaction the mother feels for her wayward, disobedient son, to the son's deep regret for his maltreatment of and disrespect for her as (a) woman.

The slippage from one meaning to another depending on the point of view exemplifies the speaker's change in attitude, his separation from his former self (the child versus the adult) and his next step toward autonomy. His subjectivity will always be subject to the Other, but he must subject himself to the Other to gain individuality. He will create "the illusion of fullness, of completeness, of the ego as a self-identical subjective instance" only if he as "The signifying structure of the subject assumes value through its position relative to others, within the chain [metonymy] and without [metaphor]."[222] In ethical terms, if he understands and treats others as if they were subjects, he too will be a subject.[223] In metapoetic terms, he will be an outstanding, individual poetic voice only if he defines himself as the same and different from the tradition.

The achievement of that goal on both fronts depends on a paradox: Ethically he must surrender himself, renounce his desires, and negate his ego(t)ism, while aesthetically he must delve into himself, assert his flaws, and proclaim his uniqueness. These two aspects appear to be at cross-purposes with one another. It is the exploration of the suture between them, the "gap," the imbrication of opposites (metaphor and metonymy, centripetal and centrifugal forces, self and other, sameness and difference, Imaginary and Symbolic, conscious and unconscious), that constitutes the delicate balance, the unique voice of Claudio Rodríguez.

Orphic Descent and Loss

Still within the first half of "Libro tercero" the four poems of the second group present an inverse relationship between time and space. As time becomes more pressing, space as emptiness, lack, or gap, becomes more extensive. This space or gap is the place of the Other, so that as the speaker-poet divests himself of the Other, creating a lack, time becomes an overpowering stimulus, the desire that keeps the speaker seeking to fill the gap of the Other with *objets a*.[224] Instead of investing his energy in transient adventures, however, the speaker seeks a lasting experience in the form of love, which is synonymous with genuine poetry.[225] The titles of these four poems, "Hacia un recuerdo," "Un momento," "Tiempo mezquino," and "Adiós," all refer to fleeting time but also to the speaker's attempt through his song to prevent time from slipping away. The poem becomes the space in which the fleeting finds permanence, the transient transcendence. In the otherness of language that is emptiness, lack, gap unless we fill it with experience and emotion, the speaker compensates for the loss of time.[226]

A tension between past and future arises in the title "Hacia un recuerdo" [Toward a memory]. On the surface, it would seem that to go toward a memory would be to return to the past. Whereas this poem describes a region of Zamora that the speaker has apparently visited often, the poem in effect looks forward to the making of good memories for the future.[227] Surprisingly, this temporal conflict is more tacit than explicit in the poem. In fact, the setting of the scene in the opening verses has a timelessness to it precisely because it describes a place, an area, a space.

> Bien sé yo cómo luce
> la flor por la Sanabria,
> cerca de Portugal, en tierras pobres
> de producción y de consumo,
> 5   mas de gran calidad de trigo y trino.
>
> (p. 172)[228]

Sanabria is a mountainous region of northwestern Zamora tucked between León on the north, Galicia on the west, and Portugal on the south, and famous for its pastureland. As the speaker's comments indicate, it is not an industrialized or populated area but a land "de gran calidad de trigo y trino." The alliteration of "trigo y trino" as well as its placement at the end of the sentence points to the metaphorical properties of this space that produces grain and song, both associated in Rodríguez's poetry with writing. In this marginal, distant, peripheral area, the speaker discovers lasting values and wishes to save this experience not as a dead memory but as a vibrant presence in his life (cf. Orpheus).

This poem is structured around a rejection and negation of the superficiality of visiting that land and the search for more lasting and transcendent experiences. Curiously, the former is personified as "tú," perhaps referring to the land itself, but also perhaps another person (a female figure? Eurydice?) or the alter ego of the speaker himself as the other and as the visit to that region. As he speaks about this experience, rejecting the superficial in favor of the profound and transcendent, we realize that the speaker refers to the act of writing. The words "empresa," "aventura," and "imagen" transport us to that level in the next verses.

> No es el recuerdo tuyo. Hoy es tan sólo
> la empresa, la aventura,
> no la memoria lo que busco. Es esa
> tensión de la distancia,
> 10   el fiel kilometraje. No, no quiero
> la duración, la garantía de una
> imagen, hoy holgada y ya mañana
> fruncida. Quiero ver aquel terreno,
> pisar la ruta inolvidable, oír
> 15   el canto de la luz aquella, ver
> cómo el amor, las lluvias
> tempranas hoy han hecho
> estos lodos, vivir
> esa desenvoltura de la brisa
> 20   que allí corre. . . .
>
> (p. 172)[229]

Because of its crucial appearance in "Girasol," "empresa" ties in with "trigo" and poetic production, whereas "aventura" reminds us of the image of the snowflakes as horses and the speaker's desire to unmask his own hypocrisy and superficiality in "Nieve." Here he again rejects an "image" (either a memory or his poetic language) that will fade quickly, for one of more lasting value. The "ruta inolvidable" could refer to the traditional "Camino de Santiago" and the Milky Way as a richness of light and aspirations, and in that way refer to the "sacred" path of poetry as well as Orpheus's decent into the underworld.[230] Even trivial or commonplace events such as rain and wind adopt symbolic significance. Associated with fertility and inspiration that comes from above, the conjoining of rain and love supports the view of the experience as an encounter between the speaker and a female figure, but he seeks a lasting relationship (again we recall the myth of Orpheus and that Rodríguez dedicated *Alianza* to his wife Clara). The speaker hopes to "vivir / esa desenvoltura de la brisa / que allí corre." The wind almost seems like a child who runs freely over the land, making childhood memories of a carefree, unrestrained exuberance some of the most lasting and idealized memories we have. Even when he is not there in person, the speaker hopes to feel the presence of this experience as it forms part of his perspective and allows him to judge his life differently.

> 20   . . . No, hoy no
> lucho ya con tu cuerpo
> sino con el camino que a él me lleva.
> Quiero que mis sentidos,
> sin ti, me sigan siendo de provecho.
> 25   Entre una parada
> y otra, saludar a aquellos hombres
> para ver lo que soy capaz de dar
> y capaz de aceptar,
> para ver qué desecho,
> 30   qué es lo que aún me es útil;
> entrar en las ciudades, respirar
> con aliento natal en ellas, sean
> las que fueren. . . .
>
>   (p. 172)[231]

The gain/loss motif receives fresh treatment in these verses. Although the "body" of the other—its physical presence—has been lost (the speaker no longer struggles with it), he still wishes to remain on the same road that led him to that powerful and unforgettable experience (cf. Orpheus). Even without that presence, he hopes to use what he has learned and gained from that experience "para ver lo que soy capaz de dar / y capaz de aceptar, / para ver qué desecho, / qué es lo que aún me es útil." He will shun a spiritually meager existence, as the next verses attest.

> . . . No busco
> masticar esa seca
> 35   tajada del recuerdo,

> comprar esa quincalla, urdir tan pobre
> chapuza. Busco el sitio, la distancia,
> el hormigón vibrado y tenso, la única
> compañía gentil, la que reúne
> 40   tanta vida dispersa. . . .

(pp. 172–72)[232]

Unlike others, he will not buy cheap souvenirs (produce shoddy work); he wants his poetry to reflect richer experiences than chewing on a dry crust of bread. His memories and experiences will have more substance, more scope, more depth. His feeling when he visited Sanabria and saw its immense natural beauty is the type of emotion that he seeks to recapture in all his poems. This space as empty expanse but full emotion is placed in contraposition with the two directions of time (past and future, loss and gain) announced in the title. The larger implications of that space appear in the final verses.

> 40   . . . No tan sólo
> tu carne, que ahora ya arde como estopa
> y de la que soy llama,
> sino el calibre puro, el área misma
> de tu separación y de la tierra.
> 45   De aquella tierra donde el sol madura
> lo que no dura.

(p. 173)[233]

The poet-speaker seeks not the immediacy of the experience itself or only for itself, for that experience disappears in the very act of appreciating it as it is happening, just as a flame burns up tow (the passing moment, the immediate sensorial experience). What he seeks is more ideal: "El calibre puro" is metaphor for a perfect measurement or evaluation, but it is ironically "el área misma / de tu separación y de la tierra." Just as the land is open, unobstructed, pure space, so the speaker is separated from the Imaginary order. He will always long to reach that ideal, he will always strive along the road that will take him there, but it must always be beyond his reach if he is to continue writing, if he is to achieve individuality and subjectivity.[234]

The singsong rhythm and hollow rhyme of the final two verses combine emptiness and transience with poignant beauty, richness, and fullness. "Aquella tierra" represents the poet-speaker's ideal, an open space full of lasting emotion in the void of words: in short, a great poem. Maturation suggests the vivid aroma, color, and taste of a fruit, while the sun's light again refers to inspiration, insight, warmth, passion, and transformation of the ordinary and transient into unforgettable vitality. In the poetic process of "Hacia un recuerdo," Rodríguez transforms the diachronic aspect of time into the synchronic aspect of space, and thus the void, superficiality, and "representationality" of language continually re-creates the experience, converting the transient (metonymy) into the transcendent (metaphor).[235] The poet-speaker of *Alianza* wishes to attain that ideal by letting go of his former attitudes (metaphorized by his relationships with women) and striving toward something more permanent (true love). These poems continue to detail his emergence from the Imaginary to the Symbolic, from a transient, unindividuated perspective to a transcendent subjectivity.

Time and space come into conflict again with ironic consequences in "Un momento," another ambivalent title. Obviously, a moment is a brief extension of time that slips away quickly, and hence it evokes a sense of the transience of life and the instability of all that which is affected by it. But we might also read this word as an elliptical expression: "Just a moment, please." This expression tries to halt action, to stop someone or something from going by or away. This concept receives ironic treatment in "Un momento" because "ordinary," everyday life seems interminable, boring, and endlessly repetitious, only to be interrupted by a simple but extraordinary moment of illumination that suddenly changes our perspective and makes even the repetitious and ordinary seem exceptional. Repetition itself adopts significance as everything attains transcendence.

The tedious familiarity of everyday life is marked not only in the opening verses ("Acostumbrados a los días, hechos / a su oscuro aposento palmo a palmo" [Accustomed to the days, made / to their dark chamber palm by palm]) but in the repetition of the phrase "Acostumbrados a los días" later in the poem (v. 15). Alliteration ("su oscuro aposento") and the idiomatic "palmo a palmo" manifest the same idea, causing us to look for more repetitions. In the midst of this insistence on repetition and the dull passing of time that does not seem to pass, "este momento"—a fleeting moment—is converted into "esta región inmensa y sin conquista / que es el hombre" [this immense and unconquered region / that is man]. This spatial representation of a brief temporal measurement irradiates the evanescent, transforming it into a vast extension. As the speaker notes, "Algo / luce tan de repente que nos ciega, / pero sentimos que no luce en vano" [Something / shines so suddenly that it blinds us, / but we feel that it does not shine in vain] (vv. 12–14). The play between illumination and blindness parallels the temporal and spatial, so that this event will be a lasting one ("no luce en vano") even though it is very brief ("tan de repente").

Introduced by the repetition of the opening phrase, the same idea is repeated with an auditory image ("suena tan claro / este momento en nuestra sorda vida") and with an alliteration that is an intertextual echoing of San Juan de la Cruz: "[Q]ue, ¿qué hay que hacer, si aún están los labios / sucios para besar, si aún están fríos / nuestros brazos?"[236] Repetition and variation become the guiding principles of the poem and of the speaker's perspective. What he thought was dull tedious consistency and lack of change suddenly transforms the repeated into the new and unexpected. We could read his questions at the end of the first stanza ambivalently, expressing despair and boredom as well as excitement and eagerness; they are both rhetorical and genuine questions in which repetition signifies ambivalently: "¿Dónde, dónde hay que ir? ¿Fuera de casa / o aquí, aquí, techo abajo?" [Where, where shall we go? Out of doors / or here, here, under cover?]. Again, these questions search for the temporal (one of those special, uplifting, eternal moments of illumination) by means of spatial metaphors.

The dialectic between time and space, repetition and difference, transience and transcendence, solidifies in the opening phrase of the second stanza: "Ahora ya o todo o nada" [Now already either all or nothing] (v. 23). Now is already, either/or is both/ and; all is nothing and vice versa. Now we see the manifestation of transgression in *Alianza*. The more Rodríguez delves into himself and defines his individuality, difference, and subjectivity, the more he spills over beyond his own limitations. The more he explores his inner self through language, the more his poetry acquires a lasting, individual, distinct quality of voice. The transgression of *Alianza* is a transgression of the boundaries of the self at the same time that Rodríguez specifies and delimits those boundaries! He is just an ordinary human being, but by pursuing that elusive trace of his essence as a human being, he stands out. And by standing out in that way, he adds his name and his poems to the interminable succession of great poets.[237]

The final verses of "Un momento" condense the paradox of self Rodríguez is creating through his poetry: "[H]ay que sacar la huella / . . . / . . . aunque sea al cabo / por un momento, éste de ahora, y nadie / jamás sea su amo / mientras, luz en la luz, se nos va" (vv. 27, 29–32).[238] No one will ever be able to dominate this elusive moment, yet one has to pursue it. Rodríguez's unending process of trying to define himself will never reach a conclusion because he changes in the very act of trying.[239] His demarcation of the boundaries of the self always spills over, just as the signified always becomes another signifier in a constant play of difference.

The final words of the poem are exceedingly ironic because a return to/of routine is a return to/of something different: "Y vuelve, / vuelve lo acostumbrado" [And there returns, / returns the customary] (vv. 33–34). The repetition of "vuelve" could indicate boredom or everlasting excitement, and the modification of "acostumbrados" to "lo acostumbrado" distorts the concept, just as Rodríguez changes every time he attempts to define himself. That to which we are accustomed, that which repeats, that which never changes, is change itself. In "Un momento," Rodríguez parodies the traditional concept of the transience of the moment, showing that the evanescent transcends the tedious transience of life. All of life partakes of that moment and becomes transcendent. The task of the poet is to be on the lookout for and to capture those special, intense moments of illumination in his use of language.

But what happens if time does not provide those moments for the poet? In "Tiempo mezquino" [Stingy time], Rodríguez investigates the drought of inspiration, the stinginess of time, by again turning inward to the negative in himself as he continues his repentance and his individuation on moral and aesthetic planes. "Tiempo mezquino" parallels "En invierno es mejor un cuento triste" in that it is a confessional poem about repentance. Although the speaker does not specify this event, it seems to have been an insincere love affair. Recalling this incident from the past has a chilling effect on the speaker and leaves a bad taste in his mouth. Repeated mention of his mouth in the first stanza establishes a link between this love affair and the poetic act.

First he states, "Mal andaban por entonces / mis pies y peor mi boca" [Badly did my feet walk at that time / and worse my mouth] (vv. 3–4), reminding us of "Dando una vuelta por mi calle" (*Conjuros*), another poem about recognizing his erring ways and repenting. As in that poem, in "Tiempo mezquino" the speaker makes reference to his lameness: "iba ya muy coja / mi juventud" [my youth / went along already very lame] (vv. 10–11). But as we have seen, lameness is an ambivalent image. It is a sign of moral imperfection and shortcoming, and it symbolizes that the lame person has struggled with the divine. When he says that his youth was already lame, does he refer to his moral actions or to the insight he already possessed because of his struggles? Did he form part of the society "en aquella ciudad de hosco / censo, de miseria y de honra. / Entre la vieja costumbre de rapiña y de lisonja" (vv. 5–8), or was he already aware of his difference and separation from the prevailing attitudes?[240]

The next mention of his mouth has to do with his current shame and repentance: "Me avergüenzo de mi boca / no por aquellas palabras / sino por aquella boca / que besó" (vv. 12–15).[241] He knows he did wrong, but he also recognizes and admits it. Even though this incident (representative of others like it) is inexplicable ("¿Por qué lo hice?" [Why did I do it?], he queries in v. 11 but fails to answer directly) and in spite of his youth and the accusation of others ("¿Qué tiempo hace / de ello? ¿Quién me lo reprocha?" [How long ago was / that? Who reproaches me for it?]; vv. 15–16), these events have left a bad taste in his mouth: "Un sabor a almendra amarga / queda, un sabor a carcoma; / sabor a traición, a cuerpo / vendido, a caricia pocha" (vv. 17–20).[242] This aftertaste is a trace of the past that still lingers in the present, reminding him of his lust and petty demands.[243]

This first stanza of the poem places time and space in juxtaposition as the memory of that event (which took place in a distant city in the past) returns to occupy the present. By writing the poem in the present and recuperating the incident from the past, the speaker draws some startling conclusions in the second stanza as he realizes that he can create poetry out of the recuperation of the moment: "Ojalá el tiempo tan sólo / fuera lo que se ama. Se odia / y es tiempo también. Y es canto" (vv. 21–23).[244] The speaker discovers the therapeutic benefit of talking/writing about the unpleasant past. His admission of guilt and his reliving of the experience has a cathartic, purgative effect. To relive that experience is to purify himself of its negative effects and to make him worthy of something better. His insistent repetition of the second-person pronoun has the effect both of reliving the intimacy and immediacy of the moment and of distancing him from the past.

> Te odié entonces y hoy me importa
> 25 recordarte, verte enfrente
> sin que nadie nos socorra
> y amarte otra vez, y odiarte
> de nuevo. Te beso ahora
> y te traiciono ahora sobre
> 30 tu cuerpo. . . .
>
> (p. 175)[245]

His final words are enigmatic because they can be read as accusation and forgiveness, criticism and acceptance of human nature. Here the impersonal, sententious third-person speaker contrasts notably with the second person in the previous verses, again suggesting distance.

30   . . . ¿Quién no negocia
con lo poco que posee?
Si ayer fue venta, hoy es compra;
mañana, arrepentimiento.
No es la sola hora la aurora.

(p. 175)[246]

The words "venta" and "compra" revive the loss/gain motif, demonstrating that the experience has been an ambivalent one, an incident that causes shame and yet leads to repentance and growth. Given the emphasis on time in this block of poems and in this poem in particular, the temporal progression "ayer," "hoy," "mañana" in conjunction with "venta," "compra," and "arrepentimiento" further complicates the ambivalence of the incident. The economic terms of gain and loss stand for the moral concepts of giving and taking, using and being used, but it is unclear who was using whom and if being used is not synonymous with giving and gain, as using is with taking and loss, a paradoxical, contradictory relationship. This ambiguity is reflected in the poem's title where "mezquino" can mean "poor, penurious" as well as "avaricious, covetous." Who is giving, who taking? Who gains, who loses?

The alliteration, rhythm, and internal rhyme of the final line again ring hollow, trite, and sententious, but because of the negative, we can also infer that the speaker rejects a superficial view of life in general. To feel repentance for a wrongdoing does not negate the wrong. On the contrary, it shows us how good we know we can be. Good can arise from evil.[247] "Tiempo mezquino" continues the speaker's journey, his rite of passage and coming of age.

The speaker's Orphic descent into the (un)known, his coming face to face with the dark (under)world of his past and present, reaches its nadir in "Adiós." According to the myth of Orpheus, "Farewell" was the last word Eurydice said to Orpheus as she slipped back into Hades after he impatiently turned around to make sure she was following him.[248] Here the speaker appropriates that word for his farewell to his negative attitudes (toward women). Rodríguez's reformulation of this moment from the myth is in harmony with his resignation/determination to follow his own path and to seek the most profound encounters with himself even though he may painfully lose another aspect. He is now willing to make that sacrifice for love, his song, his poetry. The first half of this short but intense poem expresses the speaker's despair and self-accusation.

Cualquier cosa valiera por mi vida
esta tarde. Cualquier cosa pequeña
si alguna hay. Martirio me es el ruido
sereno, sin escrúpulos, sin vuelta,
5   de tu zapato bajo. ¿Qué victorias
busca el que ama? ¿Por qué son tan derechas
estas calles? . . .

(p. 176)[249]

The verb "valiera" echoes the opening of "Un suceso" and provides a frame for the first half of "Libro tercero." Appropriately, this verb is in the imperfect subjunctive and corresponds to the phrase "si alguna hay" in v. 3. These features intimate doubt and negativity on the part of the speaker, whereas the parallelism of the phrases "Cualquier cosa" emphasizes the low regard the speaker has for his life or the high regard he has for even the littlest aspect of the transient world that he is willing to sacrifice himself for its sake. He seems to question whether anything can exist for very long, as the image of the shoe exemplifies. This minimal sound, which disappears so quickly and means absolutely nothing, could refer to the speaker's past and his low ethical standards and to a type of poetry based on such experiences.

The "tu" could therefore be addressed to a female figure (Eurydice) and the speaker's former attitudes toward her, his former self. Certainly he feels "martirio," shame, acute despair, for his lack of scruples. The phrase "sin vuelta" suggests the transience of unenduring emotions. We could also interpret the direct address as a "desdoblamiento" (doubling) of the speaker and the hollow, insubstantial sound of his footsteps, emblematic of his poetry. But the pain and death of martyrdom leads to unending spiritual bliss and immortality. Rodríguez's willingness to face his own ethical and aesthetic shortcomings paves the way for his salvation. The adjective "bajo" modifying the shoe could ambivalently connote a moral degradation and the adoption of humility through repentance.

In light of these dualities the questions of vv. 5–7, being rhetorical and interrogative, lend themselves to a number of interpretations. The first, reminiscent of the speaker's questions in part II of "Brujas," reveals the ironic side of the word "victorias." One could say that "el que ama" seeks surrender of self rather than victory over the other ("alianza/condena"), or one could imagine the speaker redefining the meaning of "victoria" as some benefit that accrues when one does surrender to the other for the sake of love. A similar duality is manifest in the word "derechas" in the second question. The speaker may be wondering why it is necessary to be on such a straight and narrow path. Or "derechas" could mean "direct," "ineluctable," "inevitable," so that he both cringes and marvels at the discoveries to which his poetic experiences have led him. The Orphic aspect of these poems arises in the final verses of "Adiós," but Rodríguez gives his own individual spin to the descent.

> . . . Ni miro atrás ni puedo
> perderte ya de vista. Esta es la tierra
> del escarmiento: hasta los amigos
> 10 dan mala información. Mi boca besa
> lo que muere, y lo acepta. Y la piel misma
> del labio es la del viento. Adiós. Es útil,
> norma este suceso, dicen. Queda
> tú con las cosas nuestras, tú, que puedes,
> 15 que yo me iré donde la noche quiera.
>
> (p. 176)[250]

The condition imposed on Orpheus by Pluto was that he should not look back to see if Eurydice was following him. In "Adiós," the speaker explicitly states that he does *not* look back, meaning perhaps that unlike Orpheus he has a stronger faith and keeps his eyes on the future and on the ideal he has posited for himself. But perhaps he means that now he leaves behind his former attitudes. If Eurydice (love, readership) follows him, good and well; but from now on the poet-speaker will be true to himself, and his music will be made following his own path rather than trying to please others. In psychoanalytic terms, the speaker separates himself from the Other (Eurydice), losing a very important part of himself repressed in the shadows of death (the unconscious, the acquisition of language) but gaining independence and immortality by keeping his eyes always on his ideal, his soul, himself.

"Escarmiento" is an ambivalent word, having the same dual meaning as "castigo": The speaker receives punishment but also learns a valuable lesson. He has learned that even his friends can betray him, whether intentionally or not; he cannot trust others' opinions but must rely on his own values. Ethically, he may see himself still wandering "por tierra de lobos" or simply that even the people he trusts sometimes make mistakes. With regard to his poetry, Rodríguez could be saying that he does not trust the readers and critics of his work because they may wish to flatter him, deceive him, or may even misread, misunderstand, and misconstrue his purposes and aims. If he cannot trust others, for whatever reason or on whatever level, he must rely on himself and his own intuitions.

Verses 10–12 are among the most beautiful and memorable Rodríguez has written. The speaker knows that all of life is fleeting, including the very lips with which he kisses (praises) his beloved (the ordinary things around him). His poems, like his kisses, accept and include that transience. When he repeats the title of the poem, usurping Eurydice's farewell to Orpheus, he openly acknowledges transience and thereby overcomes it. By humbling himself and accepting the ineluctable and inevitable, he is able to appreciate it more and to participate in the everlasting jouissance of love. Orpheus doubted that Eurydice was behind him and, too eager not to lose her, let her slip away from him again. His lack of trust led to his loss of love and joy in his life and ultimately to his savage death at the hands of the Maenads. Rodríguez, in contrast, accepts loss, does not look back, but thus never loses sight of the joy to which he aspires. His acceptance of loss is tantamount to recognizing his own transience, and this recognition allows him to be true to himself, to make the most of that which will not last—all of life itself.

Mention of the word "suceso" in v. 13 again snaps the frame of this descent shut as the speaker both snidely disparages the platitude about death forming a natural part of life and however reluctantly resigns himself to loss and possible oblivion if he follows his own course. The final verses of the poem spill over the frame in ironic fashion. Whereas there seems to be a contrast and separation of the speaker from the other ("tú"), almost as if a divorce were taking place and he tells the other to keep the things they had acquired together, the possible "desdoblamiento" of the speaker into both "tú" and "yo" complicates the ramifications of this Orphic farewell. Is the speaker Orpheus or Eurydice? Is it the self or the other who dispenses with the trappings of a shallow, transient existence? Would it not be that one part of him will still appreciate and live in the material world while the other part seeks a more internal, transcendent perspective based on the experiences of the Other? He almost seems to envy that the other *can* live in that world and to regret that his interior must separate itself. But it is necessary if he is to achieve his goal. He must come face to face with loneliness and separation as well as those aspects of himself that require and produce it.

"La noche" suddenly adopts contradictory meanings. In the Orphic myth, night is a traditional symbol of death. Is this Eurydice consoling Orpheus and submitting herself to the will of Dis? Or is it Orpheus the poet renouncing the world after the loss of Eurydice, submitting himself to his failure to keep the imposed condition? Also, knowing Rodríguez's poetry, we can read night as its opposite, illumination. In that case we see the poet-speaker surrendering himself to possible oblivion (he will be unknown to the majority of readers) because he has decided to pursue his own illumination. He faces darkness both without and within (anonymity, transience versus the [un]known and the unpleasant), but his decision to confront that ([un]explored) territory of the self—his own transience and shortcomings—will ultimately lead to his illumination (knowing himself by being true to himself). The future tense of "me iré" and the subjunctive of "quiera" capture the uncertainty and risk involved in such a venture (cf. "empresa"), but also his resolve to plunge into that unknown. At this point, we end the first eight poems of "Libro tercero" and make a transition into the second half of this section, remembering that to be a subject means to subject oneself to the Other.

Dionysiac Celebration of Darkness

What a tremendous privilege and a rare honor it is for us as readers not only to witness but also to participate in a magical moment in literature! We have that opportunity when we accompany Rodríguez from "Adiós" to "Noche abierta" [Open night] in stepping over the threshold between the Imaginary and the Symbolic, crossing the bar between signifier and signified, traversing the gap/suture between mortality and immortality.[251] Because of its nocturnal setting and its emphasis on the sensorial (sight, hearing, smell, and touch), the third group of poems in "Libro tercero" defines the mythical figure of Dionysus, god of wine, inebriation, inspiration, and sensorial experience. According to Joseph Campbell, Dionysus illustrates "that divine 'enthusiasm' that overturns the reason and releases the force of destructive-creative dark."[252] Each of the four poems of this group inverts the initial sensorial perception, converting night into fire, noise into music, smell into aroma, and dawn into disappointment.

The very structure of "Noche abierta" repeats fractal-like the pattern of "Libro tercero." This poem consists of four stanzas of four unrhymed alexandrine lines— just as the section consists of four groups of four poems—and one extra line of spillover that repeats the opening verse. Along with the obvious stanzaic divisions that reflect the differentiations between the mythological identities, the alexandrine lines are marked by a caesura, another gap or suture. The emphasis on this gap/suture signals the step we have just taken across the center of "Libro tercero" and the change in the speaker's attitude. He now gladly accepts the negative—which itself diminishes, narrowing as it becomes more profound—to convert it into a positive, a transition observed since the very title of *Alianza y condena*.

In fact, we might say that the title "Noche abierta" plays against that of "Brujas a mediodía." Whereas night may normally have negative connotations because of its darkness and mystery, in Rodríguez's poetry it has frequently, if not always, led the speaker to new discoveries and inspiration. Night here is the absence of the Other and the presence of the unconscious. The symbolic separation of Orpheus from Eurydice in "Adiós" leads to the creation of the unconscious, from which the poet-speaker draws insight, inspiration, and identity. The ambivalence of the adjective "abierta" confirms this duality. On one hand, it could mean that it is fully night, totally dark; but on the other, the act of opening has a positive connotation. Instead of feeling closed in by the darkness, the speaker has a sense of liberation and expectancy as the night is open to his exploration.[253] This duality is repeated in the first two stanzas, where the speaker contrasts two different attitudes to the coming of night.

> Bienvenida la noche para quien va seguro
> y con los ojos claros mira sereno el campo
> y con la vida limpia mira con paz el cielo,
> su ciudad y su casa, su familia y su obra.
>
> 5   Pero a quien anda a tientas y ve sombra, ve el duro
> ceño del cielo y vive la condena de su tierra
> y la malevolencia de sus seres queridos,
> enemiga es la noche y su piedad acoso.
>
> (p. 177)[254]

The contrast of the framing phrases "Bienvenida la noche" and "enemiga es la noche," and of such phrases as "va seguro" and "anda a tientas," "con los ojos claros mira sereno el campo" and "vive la condena de su tierra," make the duality patent. This comparison between two different perspectives of the same situation echoes "Alto jornal" and "Siempre será mi amigo" from *Conjuros* as well as the third section of "Eugenio de Luelmo" and "Lluvia y gracia" above. "Noche abierta" evokes the experiences in those previous poems and expands upon them with the third and fourth stanza, complicating the rejection/acceptance motif to show that rejection and acceptance, condemnation and alliance, loss and gain, are so intimately imbricated and commingled that it is impossible to separate them. The connection between this duality and Dionysus is particularly evident in the third stanza.

> Y aún más en este páramo de la alta Rioja
> 10   donde se abre con tanta claridad que deslumbra,
> palpita tan cercana que sobrecoge, y muy
> en el alma se entra, y la remueve a fondo.
>
> (p. 177)[255]

The region of "la alta Rioja" is world-renowned for its wine. Having already defined "ebriedad" as heightened consciousness and loss of consciousness (the duality present in the first two stanzas of this poem), the poet as Dionysus metonymically adopts contrasting characteristics. Indeed, the speaker refers to this productive but harsh landscape as a "páramo." Does he refer to its altitude (heightened conscious-ness) or to its desolation (loss of consciousness)? In this region, night "se abre con tanta claridad que deslumbra, / palpita tan cercana que sobrecoge." Does the speaker describe the stars' brilliance that awes him or the night's blackness that reveals other things that he might overlook in the light of day? The verb "sobrecoger" can mean "to amaze," "to startle," or even "to scare." When he says that night "muy / en el alma se entra, y la remueve a fondo," does he refer to an exciting rearrangement and new combination of sensations or to a roiling and clouding of a liquid with the silt or debris that had settled to the bottom? In effect, these actions are one and the same. So, too, Dionysus is an ambivalent figure. The final quatrain confirms this duality by comparing night with fire, which is both destructive and creative.

> Porque la noche siempre, como el fuego, revela,
> refina, pule el tiempo, la oración y el sollozo,
> 15 da tersura al pecado, limpidez al recuerdo,
> castigando y salvando toda una vida entera.
>
> (p. 177)[256]

The slippage from one word to another in this stanza suggests comparison and contrast, imbrication and separation, just as Dionysus represents two sides of the same figure and as we can compare and contrast Dionysus with Prometheus, Orpheus, and Apollo, and find similarities and differences between these mythical identities and the poet-speaker of *Alianza*. Clearly, the comparison of night and fire suggests similarities and differences. But then we can ask if the slippage from "revela" to "refina" and "pule" is a repetition of the same idea or an attempt to distinguish vari-ous effects. Are "la oración y el sollozo" extensions of "el tiempo" or definitions of what "el tiempo" means? The parallelisms "da tersura al pecado, limpidez al recuerdo" and "castigando y salvando" repeat the concept of similarity and difference.

Each of the mythical identities that characterize the poet in this section are simi-lar and different among themselves and similar and different from the speaker. In crossing the bar between signifier and signified and traversing the gap/suture between the Imaginary and Symbolic orders, poet and reader enter a new territory character-ized by contradictory qualities. The final verse of the poem—appended as a supple-mental overspill of emotion—compels us to return to the first verse and ask which of the two perspectives identifies the speaker at this juncture. When he concludes by saying "Bienvenida la noche con su peligro hermoso," does he view the night as "quien va seguro" or "quien anda a tientas"? Just as Rodríguez has combined the processes of "Libro primero" *(Don)* and "Libro segundo" *(Conjuros)* to create a gap/suture whose forces are centrifugal and centripetal, mythical and idiosyncratic, so this spillover counterbalances the gap and represents the synergistic effect of the poet's definition of his identity. Identity is both sameness and difference, precise and impre-cise, settled and always in flux. Rodríguez's identity as a human being and as a poet is located on the exciting but risky edge, the border, the gap, the suture, in "la noche con su peligro hermoso."

The cottonwood tree of "Como el son de las hojas del álamo" [Like the sound of the leaves of the cottonwood tree]—one of Rodríguez's best-known and most beautiful poems—represents more than the traditional image of the tree of life, although that significance does play a major part in its symbolism. According to Chevalier and Gheerbrandt, Hercules made himself a crown of cottonwood leaves when he descended into Hades. The side of the leaves against his head remained light, but the side exposed to the smoky fires of Hades adopted a darker, somber color. "De ahí procede el doble color de sus hojas, y en esta diferencia se funda la simbólica del álamo. *Significa la dualidad de todo ser.* . . . Este árbol también aparece ligado a los infiernos, al *dolor* y al *sacrificio*, así como a las lágrimas."[257]

Because the sense of hearing is paramount in this poem and there is a slippage from noise to music, this tree also represents a natural form of music that harmoniously combines Dionysian Pan's reedy pipes with Apollo's lyre.[258] Comparable to the union of night and fire in "Noche abierta," the paradox of the poet-speaker's "dolor verdadero" is here communicated through the sensorial image of the wind blowing through the leaves of the tree.

> El dolor verdadero no hace ruido:
> deja un susurro como el de las hojas
> del álamo mecidas por el viento,
> un rumor entrañable, de tan honda
> 5   vibración, tan sensible al menor roce,
> que puede hacerse soledad, discordia,
> injusticia o despecho. . . .
>
> (p. 178)[259]

The auditory image of noise has a dual meaning in the first verse. This pain or grief may be either physical or emotional. Moreover, the phrase "no hace ruido" could be understood as meaning that it is absolutely silent or that it is a sound very different from noise. As a signifier, then, "el dolor" slips from "ruido" to "susurro" to "rumor entrañable" to "tan honda vibración," an intensification of perception. In addition to sound, this phenomenon resembles touch ("el menor roce")—perhaps the hand playing an instrument—and "puede hacerse soledad, discordia, / injusticia o despecho." This perception slides from silence to sound to touch to abstract qualities. We must question, however, whether these four nouns refer to four different aspects or if each of them (like the mythical figures) is not similar to the others. If "soledad" can be "solitude" and "loneliness" (positively and negatively marked), cannot the other three be as uplifting and virtuous as they are critical and disdainful? The subsequent verses sustain this dichotomy in a number of ways.

> . . . Estoy oyendo
> su murmurado son, que no alborota
> sino que da armonía, tan buido
> 10   y sutil, tan timbrado de espaciosa
> serenidad, en medio de esta tarde,
> que casi es ya cordura dolorosa,

>   pura resignación. Traición que vino
>   de un ruin consejo de la seca boca
> 15   de la envidia. Es lo mismo. . . .
>
>   (p. 178)[260]

In Spanish, the verb "sentir" can mean "to hear," "to feel," "to sense," or "to perceive," depending on the context. The speaker's declaration "Estoy oyendo" evokes this full range of meanings, while the present progressive stresses his presence and the immediacy of his perception, as well as adding alliteration (phonic repetition) to this expression and the subsequent "su murmurado son." The binomial phrases "que no alborota / sino que da armonía" and "tan buido y sutil" resolve into the dichotomous "timbrado," which connects with the musical word "timbre" at the same time that it means "stamped, sealed," that is, marked, tattooed, scarred (the gap/suture). This word conflicts with the phrase "espaciosa / serenidad" and anticipates the paradoxical "cordura dolorosa" and "pura resignación" in which "pura" can mean "complete" or "uncontaminated." As in the opening verses, the speaker conflates the auditory with the tactile, so that the synesthesia and the combination of opposites reiterates the gap/suture, "la dualidad de todo ser."

An evocation of the imagery of the witches again establishes a situation of comparison and contrast in vv. 13–15. Now, however, that initial experience—which seemed so negative, based as it was on "traición," "ruin consejo," "la seca boca," and "envidia"—is synonymous with the noise/music, "espaciosa / serenidad," "cordura dolorosa."[261] The imbrication of these terms does not resolve the dialectical tension but rather heightens it and yet simultaneously brings the two terms of it together: "no alborota sino que da armonía." The repetition of "Estoy oyendo"—again placed at the end of a verse—leads us to the climax of this sensorial, sensual, and quite symmetrical poem.

> 15   . . . Estoy oyendo
>   lo que me obliga y me enriquece, a costa
>   de heridas que aún supuran. Dolor que oigo
>   muy recogidamente, como a fronda
>   mecida, sin buscar señas, palabras
> 20   o significación. Música sola,
>   sin enigmas, son solo que traspasa
>   mi corazón, dolor que es mi victoria.
>
>   (p. 178)[262]

The repetition of the verb phrase again calls attention to the immediacy of the speaker's perception and the ambivalence of the verb. In keeping with the title of the poem, we can imagine that this scene represents a moment of aesthetic ecstasy. The verbs "obliga" and "enriquece" reprieve the gain/loss motif, but we do not know for certain if these "heridas que aún supuran" are the speaker's. The economy of gain/loss flows back and forth between the speaker and the other, and the wounds may belong to both. The important thing is that the speaker mutually and reciprocally sacrifices himself, gives himself over to this "dolor," which ceases to be "señas, palabras / o significación" to become "Música sola."

The mystical connotations of "que traspasa mi corazón" (cf. Santa Teresa) include pain (physical and emotional) along with the ecstasy of union with the Other. According to Walter Strauss, the Dionysiac figure "spoke to the 'darker,' more 'irrational' side of the Greek religious sensibility," so that "the Dionysiac way designates, essentially, nonseparation, indeed, union with the gods, through the darker and irrational powers of the body and the soul, in close conjunction with the 'chthonic' elements of the earth."[263] The sound of the wind in this tree, whose roots delve into the earth and whose branches extend into the sky, uniting them in "la dualidad de todo ser," finally slips from music to pure sound to "dolor" which is then transformed into "victoria."[264]

Whereas in "Libro segundo" the speaker recognized this ability in "Girasol" but found himself an observer, in "Como el son" he shows that he is learning how to integrate outside and inside, self and other, pain and pleasure, to turn defeat into victory, humility into pride, lasciviousness into love, through the slippage of language, the "*glissement*" of signifiers over signifieds. As Dionysus represents destruction and creation, so by imbricating the processes of embodiment of an abstraction in a concrete image with "realismo metafórico," Rodríguez has created a disemic symbol (this poem about "el son de las hojas del álamo") that describes his ethical and aesthetic transformation into an individual while comparing himself with traditional mythical figures.[265]

The next poem, "Un olor" [An odor], opens with Rodríguez's typically enigmatic rhetorical/sincere questions that refer to the gap/suture through contrasts.

> ¿Qué clara contraseña
> me ha abierto lo escondido? ¿Qué aire viene
> y con delicadeza cautelosa
> deja en el cuerpo su honda carga y toca
> 5 con tino vehemente ese secreto
> quicio de los sentidos donde tiembla
> la nueva acción, la nueva
> alianza? . . .

> (p. 179)[266]

As in the previous two poems, here the image of an "olor" undergoes a series of transformations beginning with "aire." This word can signify the air or breeze, suggestive of inspiration, although one is more static, the other more dynamic, one passive, the other active. The phrase "clara contraseña" is a contradiction referring to an esoteric signal shared by a limited number of people, but also to a mark or brand (tattoo or scar, i.e., gap/suture). Because it is modified as "clara," it could be "clear" in the sense of "transparent" or "invisible," or "obvious," "clearly recognizable," contradicting the purpose of a countersign!

In addition to the ambivalent interrogative, the adjective and noun play off one another, similar to the interaction of static/dynamic in "aire." The "contraseña" parallels "ese secreto / quicio de los sentidos," the gap/suture/threshold that represents "la nueva alianza." But again there is a dual effect: it seems that the speaker calls this "alliance" into question at the same time that he affirms its presence. Is there a new alliance? Is there an alliance at all? Can we trust this "aire" that puts its figurative finger on this pulse/wound/scar? Or will this alliance become "traición" [betrayal]? Another question later in the text again conflates alliance and condemnation in the gain/loss motif.

> ¿Qué materia ha cuajado
> 25 en la ligera ráfaga que ahora
>   trae lo perdido y trae
>   lo ganado, trae tiempo
>   y trae recuerdo, y trae
>   libertad y condena?
>
> (p. 179)[267]

Here the "olor" is a "ligera ráfaga," but this delicate, almost imperceptible sensation is the site of coagulation. The material—again problematized by the ambivalent interrogative—is "lo perdido" and "lo ganado," "tiempo" and "recuerdo," "libertad" and "condena." If at the beginning of the poem "clara contraseña" and "aire" confuse the concept of "alianza," these binary opposites sustain the blurred distinctions: This breeze brings alliance and condemnation simultaneously, but which is which? In psychoanalytic terms, crossing the bar, transgressing the suture between the Imaginary and Symbolic orders, separates one from the Other, but makes one dependent upon the Other.[268] In ethical terms, learning to sacrifice oneself, to reciprocate the other (learning reciprocity), both humbles and exalts. In metapoetic terms, there is a constant slippage in the play of difference that transforms signifier into signified into signifier in an indefinite *mise en abïme*. The final verses of the poem delight in this play.

> Gracias doy a este soplo
> que huele a un cuerpo amado y a una tarde
> y a una ciudad, a este aire
> íntimo de erosión, que cala a fondo
> y me trabaja silenciosamente
> 35 dándome aroma y tufo.
> A este olor que es mi vida.
>
> (p. 179)[269]

The "olor" has become a "ráfaga" and then a "soplo," indicating greater intensity. The more intense this scent, the more concretely the speaker is able to identify it: "que huele a un cuerpo amado y a una tarde / y a una ciudad." By referring to this "aire" as water/rain "que cala a fondo," the poet places the metapoetic dimension in sharp relief.[270] He compares himself to the earth that receives "aroma y tufo" from the rain. Again, these words are synonymous and different. If "aroma" is positively marked as attractive and pleasing, "tufo" can be a "stink, bad smell, bad breath, or body odor." Moist soil, like the smell of another's body, can be pleasant and repulsive, distinct yet indefinable. Through metonymic contiguity, the speaker himself adopts these contrasts. His life is as tangible and pungent, evanescent and indescribable, as the "olor." His identity is distinctly unique and yet indistinguishable from any other (as an afternoon or a city is similar to any other). He is both an individual and a mythological identity; his words are transient and transcendent, signifier and signified.

The final poem of this group "Sin leyes" turns on the Dionysian theme of revelry and ecstasy. Having the bed as its central image, the two most usual activities in this space—sleep and love—adopt ambivalent, contradictory aspects. Sleep ("sueño") can be the loss of consciousness, contact with the outside world (separation) simply to rest the body; and it can lead to dreaming ("sueño"), heightened contact with the unconscious (union with the Other).[271] Superimposed on sleep as a solitary activity, lovemaking requires the participation of two individuals, but it can be an egotistical, purely physical encounter or a spiritually as well as physically satisfying experience of reciprocity, mutual pleasure, and an expression of love. Both activities of sleep and love are related to participation in the aesthetic act and the possibility of attaining truly reciprocal love as opposed to a hypocritical, superficial experience.

Another expression of this ambivalence concerns Rodríguez's choice of the epigraph that precedes the poem. This "cantiga de amigo" is spoken by a female speaker in contrast with the speaker of "Sin leyes": "Ya cantan los gallos / amor mío. Vete: / cata que amanece."[272] While on one level it may entail an expression of hypocrisy and false appearances—the "amiga" tries to awaken her lover so that he can leave before they are discovered together—these verses also urge the poet to an awakening to the call of the roosters, symbol of Christ's resurrection and triumph over death. This anonymous piece of traditional verse has survived over the centuries precisely because it contains an element of lasting truth and emotion: There is true love here, and the speaker wishes to protect her lover by alerting him, awakening him. The speaker of "Sin leyes" sees the danger of being superficial and egotistical, interested only in material gain or fleeting sensorial pleasure. He would like to have his poems last over time like this traditional verse, but to achieve that immortality, he must give himself over to the night, surrender himself to the darkness, to the pleasure of the other.

Emphasis on the body in this poem leads to a dichotomy of interior versus exterior, but the boundary—like a Moebius strip—constantly shifts, making it indefinable. Such a duality is evident in the following verses from the beginning of the poem.

> . . . ¿El cuerpo
> es la pregunta o la respuesta a tanta
> 5 dicha insegura? Tos pequeña y seca,
> pulso que viene fresco ya y apaga
> la vieja ceremonia de la carne
> mientras no quedan gestos ni palabras
> para volver a interpretar la escena
> 10 como noveles. Te amo. . . .

(p. 180)[273]

We are again confronted with a question that could be either genuine or rhetorical, throwing the entire phrase into equivocality. The body can be either one's own or the other's, the sleeper or the lover, repose or excitement. The binary opposition of the words "pregunta" and "respuesta" posits the terms of cause and effect: Does physical pleasure carry one to spiritual fulfillment, or does moral, spiritual integrity enable one to participate fully in the physical act of lovemaking? The duality either/or could also be read as its supplemental opposite both/and, so that the expected answer to the rhetorical question is that the *soul*, not the body, is both the question *and* the answer. The same can be said of the phrase "dicha insegura." Does this phrase mean that we are not sure why we have so much happiness, but who cares? Or does it address the fleetingness and inconstancy of this momentary happiness?

The dualities body/soul, cause/effect, presence/absence (of pleasure) take us to the interior/exterior, alone/accompanied dichotomies in the sentence that follows. Does the cough come from the speaker or from someone else (on the outside)? Is it his pulse he feels or the vitality and presence of someone with him? These physical, sensorial stimuli either awaken him from sleep causing his dream to vanish, in which case he cannot interpret it and grasp its meaning; or they remind him that he has just made love with another presence, but does not know how to respond in this uncomfortable moment of "awakening" from pleasure and revery.

The figure of actors on a stage—the bed as stage of dreams and scene of lovemaking—calls into question the sincerity or "reality" of the event.[274] Was it so spontaneous and natural that each time it will be different and exciting? Or were the participants rehearsing a scene so familiar that it has lost all naturalness? (A dream can be spontaneous, or it can be a controlled fantasy.) Is the phrase "Te amo" a trite, obligatory way of expressing gratitude, or is it a heartfelt expression of truth? Is the speaker the courteous one, or is he the recipient of that courtesy? Whether awakening from sleep or arousing oneself from orgasmic revery, this moment of transition is an ambivalent one. The phrases "Te amo. Es la hora" appear repeatedly with slight variations in the final verses, stressing the ambivalence of the experience.

> 15   . . . Como una guerra sin
> héroes, como una paz sin alianzas,
> ha pasado la noche. Y yo te amo.
> Busco despojos, busco una medalla
> rota, un trofeo vivo de este tiempo
> 20   que nos quieren robar. Estás cansada
> y yo te amo. Es la hora. ¿Nuestra carne
> será la recompensa, la metralla
> que justifique tanta lucha pura
> sin vencedores ni vencidos? Calla,
> 25   que yo te amo. Es la hora. Entra ya un trémulo
> albor. Nunca la luz fue tan temprana.
>
> (p. 180)[275]

Static repetition and dynamic change occur simultaneously with the passage of time, as the night gives way to the first light of dawn. War imagery heightens the sense of conflict and ambivalence that underlies the sleep/love, solitude/company, separation/union dichotomies. Does the repetition of the phrase "Y yo te amo" convince us of the speaker's tenderness and sincerity, or does it have the opposite effect?

Why be so insistent unless he cannot convince himself, much less the other? Does his love keep telling him not to go yet—in contrast with the "cantiga de amigo"? He seems to say that he has to get up now, "Es la hora." Is this love (this other part of himself) similar to the other in "Nieve en la noche" who does not want to face the light of truth latent in the darkness? Or does this last moment of night offer him the final shreds of insight and honesty, so that he regrets the coming of the light: "Nunca la luz fue tan temprana"?

Even the question in the final verses is a reformulation of the opening verses cited above. But several alterations in the reformulation offer new insights to speaker and reader. Instead of the impartial, objective, but indefinite "El cuerpo," the speaker now uses "Nuestra carne," more personal and subjective in one sense, but also cruder and more sensorial because of the word "carne." The binary "la pregunta o la respuesta" could also be an imbrication because the question is now couched in terms of "la recompensa, la metralla." The juxtaposition of recompense with shrapnel (fragments, destructive or scattered forces) suggests that they are equivalents rather than options, but the parallelism belies this conclusion. And of course "tanta lucha pura / sin vencedores ni vencidos" corresponds to "tanta / dicha insegura," promoting a similar ambivalence. Finally, the verb tense has changed from present to future. But the question again asks for a yes/no choice that we can answer with a resounding yes *and* no. As in the poems of *Don,* which repeat the same lines at the beginning and end of the poem, we are left with an unresolvable paradox.

Sleep and love, solitude and company, separation and union obtain simultaneously. In our personal relationships, we must maintain our individuality and separateness at the same time that we love and relate to others. We maintain a firm sense of identity as difference, while we give ourselves to the needs and perspectives of an-other. In the aesthetic context, too, poet and reader must enter the poetic experience and be able to step back, reaffirming the boundary between self and other at the same time that we transgress and obliterate it. Without the ability to distinguish the Imaginary from the Symbolic, the Other from the self, we risk destruction (transience) rather than striving for transcendence. Separation from the other permits union with the other, and vice versa.

The title "Sin leyes" can imply a complete lack of restraint (boundaries) and an amazingly ecstatic experience, as well as no need for external laws because our internal sense of ethics imposes restraint and moderation from within, intensifying our appreciation of the transgression of restraint by means of *objets a.* In this poem, Rodríguez explores the liminal space between Dionysian destruction and creativity, self and other, the conscious and the unconscious. This evocation of the god of wine and inspiration leads to the full light of day in the figure of Apollo.

Apollonian Ascent into the Light

The arrival of "un trémulo albor" at the end of "Sin leyes" makes a smooth transition into the final group of four, where images of awakening and light predominate in comparison with the night and darkness of the third group. The positively marked titles "Amanecida," "Lo que no es sueño," "Una luz," and "Un bien" and images of light, morning, and awakening evoke the benign mythical figure of Apollo, the sun god, benefactor of music (poetry) and medicine (healing). Yet it is still a chiaroscuro, an interaction between dark and light, that heightens the effect of the light.

Although Apollo may be the logical conclusion of the progression from Prometheus to Orpheus and Dionysus, all of these figures evince a play of light and dark; and the speaker is similar to and differs from these mythical identities. Apollo drives the chariot of the sun, implying the circadian cycle of day and night, light and dark. Moreover, Apollo is not exempt from his moments of lust, as evidenced in his episode with Daphne, for example. Likewise, the speaker is in a process of development in which there is a constant need to reevaluate, assess his shortcomings, and make adjustments in his perspective. Therefore, although it is true that the positive images of awakening and illumination dominate these final poems, the speaker still is aware of the darkness; but he sees how that darkness augments the beauty of the light.

The first of these four poems "Amanecida" [Dawn] offers several indications of the speaker's situation. First, we note the use of the future tense in the opening verse: "Dentro de poco saldrá el sol" [In a little while the sun will come out]. This futurity defers the actual appearance of the sun, even though the light may be visible, the darkness less obscure. Also, the breeze—another element of the description of dawn— still retains "su fresca suavidad *nocturna*" [its fresh nocturnal softness] (v. 2). The light will bring heat and activity, but at this point tranquility and restraint reign. The phrase "lava y aclara el sueño y da viveza, / incertidumbre a los sentidos" [washes and brightens sleep and gives liveliness, / uncertainty to the senses] is ambivalent because "sueño" can be sleep or dream and because the speaker feels both "viveza" and "incertidumbre." This moment defines a threshold/suture between day and night, consciousness and the unconscious, signifier and signified. This bar/threshold, this restraint, amplifies the effect of the light just as the clouds on the horizon, "Nubes / de pardo ceniciento, azul turquesa, / por un momento traen quietud, levantan / la vida y engrandecen su pequeña / luz" (vv. 4–8).[276]

In spite of the anticipation, excitement, and promise of this moment, the poet captures his ambivalence in another of his rhetorical/sincere questions: "¿[C]ómo / puedo dudar, no bendecir el alba / si aún en mi cuerpo hay juventud y hay / en mis labios amor?" (vv. 12–15).[277] If we read this question rhetorically, the tone is extremely optimistic and delights in the prospects dawn represents. But if we read it genuinely, it appears that the speaker does doubt the beauty and optimism that the imminent appearance of the sun would portend. Why does he doubt? What is there he still needs to address?

These verses also evoke intertextual echoes of the two principal imagoes of "Libro primero," the witches and Eugenio. The final verses of "Brujas" are also an enigmatic question that includes mention of the lips and love: "¿[D]ónde estará su noche, / dónde sus labios, dónde nuestra boca / para aceptar tanta mentira y tanto / amor?" Because the speaker could see the witches at noon when they are not supposed to appear, he wondered at that time how much worse things could get. At this moment of "Amanecida," he poses a similar question, wondering if he has not overlooked something and if he can truly trust himself to perceive the darkness and not be blinded by the light. Furthermore, the first two sections of "Eugenio" end with questions that keep the speaker doubting his ability to see self-betrayal and to elevate the ordinary to the level of the extraordinary. As he compared himself to his ego ideal Eugenio in "Libro primero," so now he continues to question his relationship to the light, embodied in the figure of Apollo.

Another aspect of this question that stands out is the truncated final verse, a "pie quebrado" that slows down the forward impulse of the poem and suggests an abrupt doubt in the speaker's mind. It almost seems as if Rodríguez were again parodying the traditional concept of dawn as an elusive, fleeting moment that cannot be captured or detained as it slips into day. If this transitional moment from darkness to light, this crossing the bar, traversing the gap, represents the arrival of poetic inspiration and its elusiveness, perhaps Rodríguez questions whether the illumination in the ethical and aesthetic arenas will deprive him of the ability to write. Has he, like Rimbaud, exhausted his source of inspiration and his need for poetry? Does truly great poetry depend upon suffering and unhappiness? If he is happily married and truly in love, will he be able to continue his introspective search for self, or will love make that search unnecessary?

Had Rodríguez ended *Alianza* with this question, we would certainly have to doubt the efficacy and outcome of the journey he has made both in this work and since *Don*. The remaining poems of this section recur to the figure of Apollo and elaborate upon the speaker's final position. Amazingly enough, Rodríguez relies upon repetition and equivocality to affirm the deeper insight he has gained through writing these poems. "Lo que no es sueño" [That which is not dream] illustrates these techniques. Like so many others that we have remarked in Rodríguez's opus, the title of this poem posits the middle ground on which the speaker stands. On the one hand, he suggests that he has rejected illusion and falsity through his willingness to face reality. He no longer sees the world or himself in an illusory way. Could we surmise, then, that he has achieved his goal of emulating Eugenio if he has divested himself of the witches' spells? Where the entire collection of poems has moved him toward that position, to infer that he has reached an ideal would be another way of saying that he has exchanged one illusion for another. Apollo may be better than Prometheus, Dionysus, and Orpheus, but he too has his faults.

The speaker therefore places himself in a liminal space, the gap that has narrowed as the spillover of joy has increased in the course of *Alianza*. Rodríguez places himself in the space of imbrication between deficit and excess, abyss and overspill, the site of moderation, harmony, and balance, because in this intermediate space he can be an individual and still surrender himself to otherness. Repetition and equivocality are the source of the transgression that makes the poet both divine and human, and defines his identity (sameness and difference). These characteristics are apparent in the opening verses of "Lo que no es sueño."

> Déjame que te hable, en esta hora
> de dolor, con alegres

palabras. Ya se sabe
que el escorpión, la sanguijuela, el piojo,
5   curan a veces. . . .

(p. 182)[278]

The speaker will repeat the command/plea "Déjame" twice more in this poem, forming a leitmotif. In addition to being a command and a request, this phrase incorporates self and other ("tú" and "yo"), which can be either another (Clara? the reader?) or the alter ego of the speaker. Rodríguez builds this poem around the ambivalent contrast between "dolor" and "alegría." At first, it is difficult to determine who is in pain, the speaker or the other. Have the speaker and his beloved had a quarrel, a disagreement between two egos, or have they just finished making love, so that the "dolor" is ironically ecstasy reminiscent of the mystic experience? If "dolor" is ambivalent, "alegres" must also connote equivocation similar to the title. His words are "alegres" because they try to uplift and console, but they can also remind the hearer of an ideal toward which he/she/they need to strive, not yet attained.

The three animals, "el escorpión, la sanguijuela, el piojo," repeat the idea of biting, stinging, causing pain or discomfort, yet each is less innocuous. These words suggest repetition with a difference and at the same time a reversal of expectations because these animals "curan a veces." The word "palabras" in v. 3 indicates that the speaker refers to his ethical and aesthetic discoveries and that he wishes to express these ideas to the listener (himself or/as another). Repetition and reversal of expectations point to the circadian cycle and to the figure of Apollo, god of music and medicine. The cycle of day and night repeats endlessly, making one day seem like all the others. But time also moves forward, just as the progression from Prometheus to Apollo suggests similarities and differences. And, of course, for Rodríguez night is a time of growth and intense introspection, whereas the light of day can blind one to the truth. This blindness, however, is a darkness that leads to greater insight and "illumination"! These characteristics continue to manifest themselves in the subsequent verses of "Lo que no es sueño."

5   . . . Pero tú oye, déjame
           decirte que, a pesar
           de tanta vida deplorable, sí,
           a pesar y aun ahora
           que estamos en derrota, nunca en doma,
10   el dolor es la nube,
           la alegría, el espacio;
           el dolor es el huésped,
           la alegría, la casa.
           Que el dolor es la miel,
15   símbolo de la muerte, y la alegría
           es agria, seca, nueva,
           lo único que tiene
           verdadero sentido.

(p. 182)[279]

In conjunction with repetition and difference, parallelism plays a major role in this poem. The phrases "ahora / que estamos en derrota, nunca en doma" underscore repetition and equivocality. To be "en derrota" can refer to complete capitulation, complete surrender or failure, but it is not clear whether there has been a war in which the speaker has been defeated or if he has learned how to give of himself freely and willingly. (Have the lovers had a quarrel or made love?) "En derrota" can also mean "en camino," a phrase that we have identified as ambivalent in our discussion of "Canto del caminar" (in *Don*). Is the speaker standing still after having come a long way, or is he making even more progress toward his goal? Though the phrase "nunca en doma" negates mastery, it is unclear whether the speaker is horse or rider. Has he attained the individuality and freedom he sought in "esa mirada que no tiene dueño," or is he still trying to master his faults, still painfully aware of his shortcomings and his lack of (self-)control?

The parallelism of the phrases referring to the contrast "dolor/alegría" also promotes ambivalence. What is the relationship between the cloud and "espacio"? Does the cloud stand out as something unique and different in this anonymous, undistinguished emptiness, or is the cloud a blot or blemish on the perfection and beauty of a broad panorama or the sun's illuminating rays? Does "huésped" as "guest" relate the happiness of finding a place of shelter and acceptance, or does "huésped" as "host" place more emphasis on the act of welcoming and always having room to take someone in? In short, the "dolor" is distinguishing feature and blemish, beauty and imperfection, landmark and obstacle to unobstructed clarity of vision, container and contained, the extraneous and the intrinsic or essential; "alegría" is emptiness and farsightedness, visitor and inhabitant. By calling "dolor" honey, symbol of death, and "alegría" something bitter ("hiel"? [gall?]) but "lo único que tiene / verdadero sentido," the speaker inverts sweetness and bitterness. The sweetness of honey can be excessive and so "peligrosamente seductora," reminding us of the witches' charms.[280] Gall is known to be bitter and so represents a known evil; it can also signify a powerful negative emotion (such as disgust or anger) that will provoke us to react (against the witches).[281]

Each of these images defines itself in relation to the other. We would have no concept of depth of field without some landmark or point of reference, yet a landmark stands out because of the space around it; one can be a guest only if someone will extend hospitality, but the host can open his home only if there is someone to receive; sweetness is identifiable by contrast with bitterness. The semiotic implication of difference and the psychoanalytic concepts of self and other are implicit in these descriptions. In "Libro tercero," the speaker has separated and individuated himself from the other, traversing the suture between the Imaginary and the Symbolic. Now he defines himself in relation to the mythological figures of Prometheus, Orpheus, Dionysus, and Apollo, finding that as a human being he possesses universal traits characterized by these archetypes and that he is an individual, different from them. He defines himself in relation to them, but they also exist because of their relation with him and all other human beings.

The final verses of the poem gather momentum through repetition and variation until they spill over into the final verse, a single, seven-syllable word that again offers various interpretations. Note also the change in the relationship between the concepts of "dolor" and "alegría."

> Déjame que, con vieja
> 20   sabiduría, diga:
> a pesar, a pesar
> de todos los pesares
> y aunque sea muy dolorosa, y aunque
> sea a veces inmunda, siempre, siempre
> 25   la más honda verdad es la alegría.
> La que de un río turbio
> hace aguas limpias,
> la que hace que te diga
> estas palabras tan indignas ahora,
> 30   la que nos llega como
> llega la noche y llega la mañana,
> como llega a la orilla
> la ola:
> irremediablemente.
>
> (p. 182)[282]

Separated from "alegría" yet linked to it by the intervening "inmunda," "dolorosa" is now an adjective modifying "alegría," exacerbating the play of difference within each word and between them and vice versa. But "alegría" has now been converted into "verdad," reversing the relationship of the words "el dolor verdadero" to be read "la dolorosa verdad"!

The anaphoric exemplifications in vv. 26–33 place a metapoetic description amid two images of water. The first describes a purification process caused by the passage of time in the image of a "río turbio." The second suggests an endless cyclical renewal in the waves of the sea and circadian rhythms. The pivotal reminder that the poet is speaking at this moment allows the poem and these particular words (with their many repetitions and variations) to partake of both aspects. This poem repeats and renews, marks the passage of time and contains something eternal. Just as the poet is both individual and archetypal, so his poem draws from the tradition, repeating and renewing it. The sea as poetic tradition or language (*langue*, metaphor) represents transcendence, eternal renewal, cyclical repetition, in contrast to the river as a flow of words through time (*parole*, metonymy) that purifies, cleanses, and revitalizes language and poetry.

The word "irremediablemente" can refer to the lovers' quarrel or to the speaker's conflicting interests, the two sides of himself that both welcome and resist change. What are the possible meanings of this word? What does it express? One option would be the speaker's resignation: Lovers always have their quarrels, their difficulties, their disagreements; it is "inevitable." Still the relationship continues as they "resolve their differences." Another possibility is that certain conflicts are "irremediable." The difference of opinion can never reach a rapprochement, the wounds never heal completely: the scar marks the place of a deep wound.

Water as symbol of time (fleetingness and eternal renewal, purification and repetition) augments the nuances of this word. A river flows downhill and the waves of the ocean reach the shore because of the natural laws of gravity and tides. It is impossible to alter or to counteract these movements. But they also bring about a purification and transcendence through constant cleansing (oxidating and aerating) and cyclical renewal; they are "unrelenting," "painfully necessary." So, too, are "estas palabras tan indignas." The poet writes because he has to; it is inevitable, irremediable. Because of the tremendous introspection involved, it is often painful for himself and for others. Yet the poet's course is "unalterable," and it leads to purification and transcendence. "La verdad," "la alegría," and "el dolor" are inextricably intertwined in the uplifting but painful process of writing.

The intense light of "Una luz" [A light] has a similarly paradoxical effect, first evident in the contrast between the purposes it serves the speaker. Though it is easy to understand how this light "me saca fuerzas de flaqueza . . . / . . . de vicioso aliento / hace rezo, cariño de lascivia, / y alza de la ceniza llama, y da / a la sal alianza" (vv. 3–7), it ironically helps him most "en tareas de amor y de sosiego" (v. 2).[283] Even the bitterness of salt can enhance the taste of food, but how can light help with love and quietude?

The entire poem revolves around a description of the light with paradoxical images. It is only when the poet repeats the key words of the opening verses at the end of the poem that we come to understand the interplay of opposites. In v. 18, the speaker describes the light as "de tan cárdena, cobre" [so red as to be copper]. Although copper is associated with the rays of the sun and so with Apollo, this element "Representa fundamentalmente el elemento agua, principio vital de todas las cosas; pero también . . . la palabra, también fecundante; el esperma, que se enrosca alrededor de la matriz femenina."[284] If copper is associated with water and the fertilizing effects thereof, this red color evokes its spectral opposite, green, a soothing, quieting color. The copper provokes the speaker to passion and to relief, to fecundity and to alleviation, as fire and water destroy and regenerate. Poetry represents an essential part of the speaker's identity as Apollo, the sun god. It stimulates him to heated passion, and calms and soothes him. It is a cathartic experience in which red and green coexist, one defining and stimulating the other through the play of difference.

Paired with "Un suceso," the first poem of "Libro tercero," "Un bien" [Good] describes the recuperation of a lost opportunity. In the first poem, the speaker recognized an opportunity and in one sense turned it down because of the immoral implications it roused; but in another sense, he took advantage of that moment to examine his motives and to bring about the individuation delineated in this section. "Un bien," in contrast, provides the speaker with a second chance. The return of a lost opportunity—one the speaker may not even have recognized at the time—signals rebirth and a new beginning for his outlook on life.

Although he personifies this "bien" as a tattered vagabond, the speaker now has the acumen to discern the grace and inner music of this being in spite of its deceptive exterior. This otherness—evoking perhaps the figure of Christ at Emmaus—may at first appear to be an external entity, something the speaker recognizes in the simple things around him such as "el temblor de una hoja, el dar la mano / con fe, la levadura de estos ojos / a los que tú haces ver las cosas claras."[285] This final adjective, used repeatedly throughout *Alianza*, may be a reference to the poet's wife Clara and the new perspective that her love has brought him.

But the abrupt shift from a contemplative third-person in vv. 1–10 to the more immediate and dialogic "yo/tú" address in the remainder of the poem blurs the distinction between self and Other, interior and exterior, at the same time that it delimits the boundary between the "tú" and the "yo." At the same time that the contemplative interior monologue is transformed into a dialogue, we are aware that the special outlook personified in the vagabond is that adopted by and now available to the speaker. His gaze is the gaze of the Other, "esa mirada que no tiene dueño." Whereas in the past the speaker may or may not have seen the latent possibility in the scene before him, this autumn, because of the new perspective he has acquired, he hopes to receive "ese oro / que te cae de tus bolsillos" [that gold / which falls from your pockets], to harvest the rich crop of his insight. The final verses express the speaker's joyful anticipation of this boon and his fearful anxiety about loosing it yet again.

> ... Yo quiero que tu huella
> pasajera, tu visitarme hermoso
> no se me vayan más, como otras veces
> que te volví la cara, en un otoño
> 25   cárdeno, como el de hoy, y te dejaba
> morir en tus pañales luminosos.
>
> (p. 184)[286]

The light step of this vagabond's visit might signify the transience of the moment that the poet hopes to capture and make lasting. But it may also mean that the vagabond has made a lasting impression on the speaker's life and his outlook, so that now, as opposed to the past, the speaker will be able to recognize the latent glow. If in the past "te dejaba / morir en tus pañales luminosos" (the imperfect tense could indicate an habitual failure to recognize that something was dying, but the inability to do anything about it), now, this day, this autumn, the speaker is making a new beginning, like a baby in pure white diapers. He will now be able to nurture that incipient life and purity because of the ethical and aesthetic growth he has made in the course of *Alianza*.

CROWNING GLORY: OVERSPILL AS TRANSGRESSION AND JOUISSANCE

The odes that comprise "Libro cuarto," substantial poems that fulfill the celebratory function of classical odes, constitute the overspill, excess, or jouissance of the tightly structured "Libro tercero," compensating for its gaps and acting as supplemental completion of its process. Rodríguez weaves together thematic and metaphoric threads from previous poems, giving these odes a rich, colorful texture. In spite of the re-working of past material, these poems look to the future. In that regard, the odes crown *Alianza*, bringing what we might describe as Rodríguez's initial poetic im-pulse to an exuberant culmination, while at the same time they are full of promise, optimism, and horizons open to the future.

These odes respectively celebrate "la niñez" [childhood]—the speaker's rebirth, the death of his former, more egotistical, selfish attitudes and his awakening to a new outlook through repentance—and "la hospitalidad" [hospitality]—the reciprocity be-tween host and guest representative of his new ethical and aesthetic attitudes. In "Oda a la niñez," the month of March serves as metaphor for transition: The change in the weather is analogous to the speaker's outlook. Along with this overriding milieu, the topos of a worker leaving home in the morning—going to factory, field, or atelier—portrays a new beginning, a fresh start, and the acquisition of the new perspective. As a result, Rodríguez expands the implications of his personal experience to a universal (or "public") sphere, in keeping with the conventions of the ode as a poetic form, converting the personal into the mythical.[287] Rodríguez thus fits his personal aesthetic and ethical experience within the framework of the universal poetic tradition.

"Oda a la hospitalidad," in comparison, depicts the return of a vagabond to a familiar house. This guest ("huésped") received by the house repairs and restores it, becoming the host ("huésped") for others, inviting them to gather around his table to share his bounty. The dichotomy guest/host, servant/master, reflects the reciprocity the speaker has achieved to find love. The beautiful image of "una mañana clara" alludes not only to the poet's wife but also to the topos of a new beginning. Hospital-ity, then, is a reciprocal giving of love that augments the exchange between two indi-viduals. This topos of self and other also describes the circular relationship between the poet and the lyric tradition, between poet and reader, reader and poem, signifier and signified.

The structure of these two poems will significantly influence our reading of Rodríguez's next work, *El vuelo de la celebración*, as well as recapitulating what we have read in *Alianza*. "Oda a la niñez" consists of four parts divided by Roman nu-merals. These parts loosely correspond with the four sections of *Alianza* and reiterate the symmetrical structure of "Libro tercero." Emphasis therefore falls on the gaps between these four sections, marking different stages in the speaker's development. "Oda a la hospitalidad," on the other hand, contains three parts, making the center section the focal point. This section (ful)fills the gap, balancing emptiness with full-ness, loss with gain, lack with excess, sorrow with joy. I say "balancing," not "replac-ing" or "filling" because the theme of reciprocity in this poem requires that each be defined by the other.[288] These two poems complement one another in the same way that "Libro cuarto" supplements "Libro tercero" as overspill, excess, and celebration, again reminding us of the fractal-like structure of *Alianza*.

To disentangle all the levels and nuances that come into play in the odes would be a monumental task. I will therefore limit my discussion to broader perspectives while supporting my generalizations with reference to and discussion of specific passages. If in "Libro tercero" the speaker defines himself in comparison and contrast with "universal" mythological figures, in the odes of "Libro cuarto," his personal development acquires the dimensions of a "universal" or mythical topos. Specific "intratextual" allusions to other portions of Rodríguez's opus play a major role in establishing the personal level. As stated above, each of the four sections of "Oda a la niñez" loosely corresponds to the four "Libros" of *Alianza*. This parallelism does not preclude the rich inclusion of a variety of intra- and intertextual allusions but merely identifies the prevailing tone and theme of each section.

The opening verses of the first ode remind us of a number of poems and images we have seen in Rodríguez's works, but the direct address of March connects this section with *Don* and indirectly with "Libro primero" of *Alianza*: "¿Y esta es tu bienvenida, / marzo, para salir de casa alegres: / con viento húmedo y frío de meseta?" (vv. 1–3).[289] The isolation of the word "marzo" recalls the subtitles of the first two poems of "Libro tercero" of *Don*, especially because the second of these is dedicated to Clara, as is *Alianza*. This reference to the unstable month of March recalls the speaker's insecurity resulting from his discovery of the poetic act and his vocation in life. That was a time of dynamic changes in his life and his awakening to his identity as a poet. That metapoetic level is complemented by the ethical level that forms the core of *Alianza*: the desire to improve oneself to be worthy of true love and transcendent experience. "Libro primero" of *Alianza* initiates the process of rejecting (condemning) the negative and acquiring (allying oneself with) the positive, a dual movement reminiscent of the tipping of the balance in *Don*.

Other allusions remind us of similar moments in Rodríguez's works. "Bienvenida" evokes the transition in "Noche abierta," another poem that reflects a wider structure, again linking it with *Don*. The "viento húmedo y frío de meseta," in turn, recalls "Viento de primavera" from "Libro segundo" of *Alianza* and the abrupt awakening to a new perspective. Also, the general situation of leaving one's comfortable home in the early morning to go to work reminds us of "Ajeno" and "Alto jornal." But the word "marzo" is central and establishes the overall atmosphere.

The question in these verses implies a serious inquiry as well as disappointment with the weather and a ludic sarcasm that belies superficial appearances. Because of the effort he has expended, the speaker expects (perhaps unreasonably but understandably) that everything will be perfect from now on. He is happy, so why shouldn't the rest of the world participate in that happiness also? Does his encounter with the cold, damp wind disillusion him? Have his expectations collapsed like a house of cards with the first contrary situation? Or is the speaker confidently sarcastic, able to face any type of obstacle, certain of his ability to overcome it because of his new perspective? Again, this question posits an uncertain transition in which both perspectives coexist. The parallel "Siempre ahora" and "Siempre así" (in vv. 4 and 12) sustain this dialectic through intratextual play.

> Siempre ahora, en la puerta,
> 5   y aún a pesar nuestro, vuelve, vuelve

este destino de niñez que estalla
por todas partes: en la calle, en esta
voraz respiración del día, en la
sencillez del primer humo sabroso,
10 en la mirada, en cada laboreo
del hombre.
Siempre así, de vencida,
sólo por miedo a tal castigo, a tal
combate, ahora hacemos
15 confuso vocerío por ciudades,
por fábricas, por barrios
de vecindad. . . .

(p. 187)[290]

It is impossible to read the word "Siempre" at the beginning of one of Rodríguez's verses without thinking of the first line of *Don*. But the addition of the words "ahora" and "así" call to mind the invocation to night in "Noche en el barrio" (which begins "Nunca a tientas, así, como ahora, entra / por este barrio"), contrasting "noche" with "claridad" and "Nunca" with "Siempre."[291] That the speaker is standing on the threshold of his house, locating him in a liminal space, supports the idea of a transitional moment.

Because it would be a daunting task to comb out the multiple nuances of the intratextualities in these verses, let me point out a few more of them and elucidate their implications before moving on to other issues. The phrase "y aún a pesar nuestro" echoes the multiple repetitions of "a pesar" in "Lo que no es sueño," metonymically leading us to the final word of that poem, "irremediablemente." The repetition of "vuelve, vuelve" replicates the final lines of "Un momento" and revives the play of repetition and variation in the word "acostumbrado" and other phrases from that poem ("que, ¿qué hay que hacer . . . ?," "¿Dónde, dónde . . . ?," "aquí, aquí," "luz en la luz"). Similar connections can be made and inferences drawn if we take into consideration the phrases "esta / voraz respiración," "sencillez," "primer humo sabroso," "la mirada," "laboreo," "de vencida," "miedo a tal castigo, a tal / combate," and so on. Rather than immersing this discussion in a network of details, I will concentrate on a more "global" reading, pointing out the more significant aspects for the purpose of understanding the odes as a recapitulation and celebration of the poet's experience in his first three works.

One such word in the verses quoted above is "vecindad." The relationship of the individual to society, the poet to the tradition, and the need to define his "identity" in relation to others has been a principal concern of Rodríguez's poetry. The word "vecindad" has dual metaphoric and metonymic connotations of unity and separation, belonging and not belonging, likeness and difference. This word literally stands on the border between the "negative" first half of this section of the poem (vv. 1–16) and the "positive" second half (vv. 17–32). The final verses of part I, beginning with "Mas," mark a turning point in the speaker's outlook.

. . . Mas tras la ropa un tiemblo
nos tañe, y al salir por tantas calles

```
              sin piedad y sin bulla
        20    rompen claras escenas
              de amanecida, y tantos
              sucios ladrillos sin salud se cuecen
              de intimidad de lecho y guiso. Entonces,
              nada hay que nos aleje
        25    de nuestro hondo oficio de inocencia;
              entonces, ya en faena,
              cruzamos esta plaza con pie nuevo
              y, aun entre la ventisca, como si en junio fuera,
              se abre nuestro pulmón trémulo de alba
        30    y, como a mediodía,
              ricos son nuestros ojos
              de oscuro señorío.
```

(pp. 187–88)[292]

It is ironic that at the moment he emerges from his house (his isolation), enters the street, and crosses the plaza, joining himself (however superficially) with the flow of anonymous others on their way to work, the speaker senses his unique calling and his individuality more acutely. The image of dawn, united with the name Clara (i.e., love), the ringing of bells ("un tiemblo / nos tañe"), and the month of March, opens the way for paradoxical discoveries. The mention of the plaza recalls Aleixandre's "En la plaza" from *Historia del corazón* and has metapoetic overtones of the poet immersing himself in the tradition, as Rodríguez did in *Conjuros*. It is only by immersing himself in the otherness of society that the individual can emerge differentially. As a result, the "ventisca" of March seems like the sunny days of June, dawn seems like noon, the speaker's eyes are rich, insightful, even though it is barely light. The first section of "Oda a la niñez" foregrounds the experience of awakening characteristic of *Don* and reflective of the pattern of tilting balances established in "Libro primero" of *Alianza*.

Part II resembles *Conjuros* in its use of *inter*textuality, social customs, imagery, questions, and its sardonic, critical tone. The opening verses comment upon the emptiness of a superficial existence lacking in poetic insight.

```
              Muchos hombres pasaron junto a nosotros, pero
              no eran de nuestro pueblo.
              Arrinconadas vidas dejan por estos barrios,
              ellos, que eran el barrio sin murallas.
         5    Miraron, y no vieron; ni verdad ni mentira
              sino vacía bagatela
              desearon, vivieron. Culpa ha sido
              de todos el que oyesen
              tan sólo el ciego pulso
        10    de la injusticia, la sangrienta marcha
              del casco frío del rencor. La puesta
              del sol, fue sólo puesta
              del corazón. . . .
```

(p. 188)[293]

The phrase "Miraron, y no vieron" alludes to the passage from the Gospel of Matthew that underlies the contrast between the speaker and the artisan-hero of "Alto jornal." The combination of life-giving forces and the abstractions of "injusticia" and "rencor" overlayed with sociopolitical implications in vv. 9–11 typifies the imagery and social dimension of *Conjuros*. The questions of vv. 13–20 invoke the cultural code.

> . . . ¿Qué hacen ahí las palmas
> de esos balcones sin el blanco lazo
> 15 de nuestra honda orfandad? ¿Qué este mercado
> por donde paso ahora;
> los cuarteles, las fábricas, las nubes,
> la vida, el aire, todo,
> sin la borrasca de nuestra niñez
> 20 que alza ola para siempre?

(p. 188)[294]

As part of the ceremonies of Palm Sunday, the beginning of Holy Week, people in Spain tie long branches of palm to their balconies to mark the route of the procession. The palms represent the triumph of Jesus' entry into Jerusalem prior to his passion and resurrection, and the white ribbons symbolize his purity and innocence as sacrificial lamb. Notably, the ribbons are lacking in the ode, in keeping with the sense of "orphandad": The speaker feels abandoned and alone (as Jesus would on the cross), causing him to lose his innocent, exuberant perspective on life—the process of disillusionment depicted in *Conjuros*. He questions the significance of all that surrounds him and forms part of his world—the market (cf. "La contrata de mozos"), the quarters, the factories, the clouds, the air—without the special perspective represented by "nuestra niñez." Like the March weather ("la borrasca"), the poet's insight "makes waves," disrupts our superficial, routine view of reality, and gives life movement, vitality, and transcendent value. The speaker's tone is sardonic as he criticizes a superficial approach to life.

> Siempre al salir pensamos
> en la distancia, nunca
> en la compañía. Y cualquier sitio es bueno
> para hacer amistades.
> 25 Aunque hoy es peligroso. Mucho polvo
> entre los pliegues de la propaganda
> hay. Cuanto antes
> lleguemos al trabajo, mejor. Mala
> bienvenida la tuya, marzo. Y nuestras calles,
> 30 claras como si dieran a los campos,
> ¿adónde dan ahora? ¿Por qué todo es infancia?

(pp. 188–89)[295]

The question at the end of this passage makes a distinction between "niñez" and "infancia." If "niñez" is the exuberant, insightful, joyous discovery of profound mean-

ing through interaction with the world, "infancia" is childishness, selfishness, egotism, insularity, and defensiveness, as described in the opening verses of this section
of the ode. From the midst of this anonymity and uniformity, the speaker as individual, as poet, emerges.

> Mas ya la luz se amasa,
> poco a poco enrojece; el viento templa
> y en sus cosechas vibra
> 35   un grano de alianza, un cabeceo
> de los inmensos pastos del futuro.
>
> (p. 189)[296]

This "grano de alianza" is the poet's voice that little by little takes form and
acquires passion ("se amasa," "enrojece"). As the cold March wind tempers, giving
way to warmer, gentler breezes, so the poet grows to individuality through an appreciation of and a drawing upon his cultural environment, his literary and linguistic
heritage. This second section of the ode, with its emphasis on individuation, standing
out from the anonymity of the cultural backdrop and separating oneself from the
other, recapitulates *Conjuros* and "Libro segundo" of *Alianza*.

If my hypothesis concerning the structure of "Oda a la niñez" is accurate, part III
pulls together all of *Alianza* with emphasis on "Libro tercero." This section of the ode
consists in large part of a catalog framed by a repeated sentence, "Ved que todo es
infancia" (vv. 5 and 24). The first instance is preceded by a sententious but equivocal
statement.

> Una verdad se ha dicho sin herida,
> sin el negocio sucio
> de las lágrimas,
> con la misma ternura con que se da la nieve.
> 5   Ved que todo es infancia.
>
> (p. 189)[297]

The final word of v. 4 alerts us to the possibility of irony through its evocation of
"Nieve en la noche." This allusion causes us to look for the unspoken, the dark connotations hidden behind the deceitful facade. In effect, the truth cannot be spoken
"sin herida," and even though it may be revealed "sin el negocio sucio / de las lágrimas,"
the alliteration warns of some "trick," some "spell" that deceives hypocritically. As a
result, the word "infancia" again adopts overtones of childishness, a lack of maturity
and independence. The opening images of the catalog that follows gradually and subtly reveal that irony is present.

> La fidelidad de la tierra,
> la presencia del cielo insoportable
> que se nos cuela aquí, hasta en la cazalla
> mañanera, los días
> 10   que amanecen con trinos y anochecen

con gárgaras, el ruido
del autobús que por fin llega. . . .

(p. 189)[298]

The modification of the sky as "insoportable" plus the "cazalla / mañanera" make us suspicious of the word "fidelidad." The earthly vision seems to accompany the speaker like a dog, making the more elevated vision as painful as a hangover. "Cazalla" is an "aguardiente fabricado en Cazalla de la Sierra, pueblo de la provincia de Sevilla" ["white lightning" fabricated in Cazalla de la Sierra, a town in the province of Seville].[299] "Aguardiente" (note the combination of fire and water) is a rather strong drink to be taken in the morning. To support this subtle hint of a hangover or an inability to tolerate the bright light of truth, the parallelism "amanecen con trinos y anochecen / con gárgaras" suggests disillusioned hopes that result in mundane routines to avoid unpleasantness. In spite of his previous statement "Siempre al salir pensamos / en la distancia, nunca / en la compañía," the stiffness, boredom, and grungy feeling after a long trip also recall the experience of "Lluvia y gracia." These images lead us to understand that the speaker is making a serious point through ironic, often humorous contrast.

When he repeats the framing sentence, he tags on an idea that contradicts the opening statement: "Ved que todo es infancia: / la verdad que es silencio para siempre" [See that all is infancy: / the truth that is silence forever]. Rather than having been said hypocritically, truth now is described as eternal silence. Ironically, the truth is that people are hypocritical; no one wants to express or admit that idea because it hurts and requires that all human beings work at being more honest and forthright— with ourselves and with others. According to the speaker, "Años de compra y venta / . . . / nos trajeron el miedo a la gran aventura / de nuestra raza, a la niñez."[300] We are afraid of that innocent openness and honesty, metaphorized as "la niñez" in contrast with the selfishness and childishness of "la infancia." The final verses, reminiscent of the speaker's decision in *Alianza*, describe his determination to strive always for that honesty.

30   . . . Ah, quietos,
quietos bajo ese hierro
que nos marca, y nos sana, y nos da amo.
Amo que es servidumbre, bridas que nos hermanan.

(p. 190)[301]

Echoing the final verses of "A las estrellas" from *Conjuros*, the act of branding (scarification, tattooing) marks one irrevocably, irremediably, identifying one as belonging to a certain group. The red-hot iron hurts as it marks, but it also cures (cauterizes), making the situation paradoxical. For the master of the iron that marks the speaker as an honest person is a master who serves. This image relates intertextually with Christ washing the feet of his disciples on Holy Thursday (Luke 13:13–16) and with the passage from Matthew 20 in which he urges his disciples to serve one another as he has served them. He who humbles himself will be exalted (Matt. 18:4).

Such humility will have the effect of uniting him with others in a true brotherhood radically different from the superficial "alliances" into which we enter for mutual protection or gain.

Part IV of "Oda a la niñez" is a song of praise and thanksgiving, culminating this ode as the odes culminate *Alianza*. Because it corresponds with itself in a number of ways, contrast and repetition predominate in a play of mirrors that results in the source of identity, knowledge of self as sameness and difference. This part of the ode opens with a recognition of the fleetingness of time and the transience of human existence.

> Y nos lo quitarán todo
> menos estas
> botas de siete leguas.
> Aquí, aquí, bien calzadas
> 5   en nuestros sosos pies de paso corto.
> Aquí, aquí, estos zapatos
> diarios, los de la ventana
> del seis de enero.
> Y nos lo quitarán todo
> 10 menos el traje sucio
> de comunión, éste, el de siempre, el puesto.
>
> (p. 190)[302]

The image of the shoes functions on many different levels. Literally, one is buried "con las botas puestas" [with one's boots on], ready for a long journey. But it could also be an image of having walked a long distance: "siete leguas" has biblical overtones and also refers to a children's tale in which a giant advances seven leagues with every step he takes with these special boots.[303] These boots are already worn out by the time one dies. Time's passing wears all things out, and "you can't take it with you": We will be buried with our shoes on, but we have to leave everything else behind. The "zapatos / . . . de la ventana / del seis de enero" is a cultural reference to the custom of children leaving their shoes—usually the oldest and most worn-out pair—on the windowsill on the eve of the arrival of the Wise Men during the Christmas season. One can receive gifts or a lump of coal, depending on one's behavior, what one has merited.[304] This emphasis on shoes and "nuestros sosos pies de paso corto" metonymically refer to walking, a metaphor for writing. All that will remain of the poet-speaker, then, are his actions, his words, to define and identify him.

Likewise, "el traje sucio / de comunión" refers to the Catholic custom of receiving first communion when one is young and innocent. These suits and dresses are traditionally white, recalling the speaker's shirt/soul in "A mi ropa tendida." According to traditional Catholic belief, the whiteness of one's soul depends on how often one sins and determines one's entry into Heaven. The ethical implications of this imagery are clear, but it also has metapoetic significance. If whiteness represents the blank page, the "stains" or "soiled spots" are the poet's words. Will those dirty spots completely hide the whiteness of the page (giving the suit a falsely, hypocritically gray or black color), or will they stand out as distinctive lines that give uniqueness and elegance to the cut of the suit? Rodríguez is reflecting on his poetic achievement

and trying to evaluate the sincerity and honesty of his verses (their "whiteness"). The
following lines summarize his conclusion, as he puts all his poetry into perspective.

> Lo de entonces fue sueño. Fue una edad. Lo de ahora
> no es presente o pasado,
> ni siquiera futuro: es el origen.
> 15 Esta es la única hacienda
> del hombre. . . .

(p. 190)[305]

The poet rejects all he has written in the past as a dream ("sueño"), a phase he
was going through to reach maturity ("Fue una edad"). The present moment is neither
past, present, nor future, but the origin, the starting point. From this moment forward,
Rodríguez will draw upon his experiences but will begin his career anew. He is that
which has been and that which is to come. The suture, the liminal space of nothingness and excess, is "la única hacienda / del hombre." The poet accepts the cleansing/
cauterizing/purifying humility and gives thanks for the pain of the struggle and the
grace of the insight/inspiration it proffers him.

> . . . Y cuando estamos
> llegando y ya la lluvia
> zozobra en nubes rápidas y se hunde
> por estos arrabales
> 20 trémula de estertores luminosos. . . .

(p. 190)[306]

The anaphoric repetition of the conjunction "Y" echoes the earlier "Y nos lo
quitarán todo" but reverses the effect. Instead of dwelling on loss and death, the speaker
now receives everlasting grace and inspiration, everlasting life and transcendence
through his poetry. The poet again evokes "Lluvia y gracia" but also the speaker's
arrival at the city in "Por tierra de lobos" and the suffering of the invasion of night in
"Noche en el barrio" and even "Lluvia de verano" from *Conjuros*. The "estertores
luminosos"—images of thunder and lightning, death and resurrection—also remind
us of the contrast of light and dark so central to the experience of *Don*. Moreover, the
triumphal declarations of vv. 25–28 repeat those of part I of this ode.[307] Whereas in
the first section the day was just beginning and the speaker had to struggle against "la
ventisca" and had not yet arrived at his goal, in these verses the tone is more ecstatic,
less conflictive, because he is finally reaching his goal, having risen above time and
space, the temporal and material limitations of human existence. The present tense in
the final verses of the ode contrasts with the preterit of v. 12.

> Es el momento ahora
> 30 en el que, quién lo diría, alto, ciego, renace
> el sol primaveral de la inocencia,
> ya sin ocaso sobre nuestra tierra.

(p. 191)[308]

The rebirth of the sunrise recalls not only the mythological figure of Apollo but also the circadian rhythms of *Don*, suggesting that the poet-speaker is starting anew. The words "alto, ciego" evoke the image of the sunflower "de tan ciega mirada . . . tras esa campaña soleada de altanería." "Oda a la niñez" ends praising the acquisition of a new perspective and the inexplicable forces that made it possible. The speaker exults in his resurrection and transcendence, and is at peace with himself at having determined his personal and poetic identity and destiny.

As if "Oda a la niñez" were insufficient as a recapitulation and exaltation of his poetic progress, Rodríguez appends "Oda a la hospitalidad" to this celebration of his coming of age. Whereas "Oda a la niñez" consists of four sections, "Oda a la hospitalidad" is divided into three. The second section is shorter and more delicate than the two that flank it, reminding us of the structure of *Don*. If in that first work the center section is both fulcrum of stability and pivotal turning point, so the second section of "Oda a la hospitalidad" "papers over the gap" by counterbalancing the empty space in the center of "Libro tercero" and "Oda a la niñez"; and it functions as a pivot between the flanking sections, remitting us to the conjunction in the title *Alianza y condena*. The center section unites and separates two different interpretations of "hospitalidad," as we have seen in the meaning of "huésped." One can be the recipient and the supplier of hospitality, guest and host; one is able to give and to receive hospitality—a synonym for love and the reciprocal relationship between self and other, poet and reader. The beautiful imagery of "Oda a la hospitalidad" supplementally extends the overflow of celebration, praise, and thanksgiving with a second ode.[309]

The vagabond of part I of "Oda a la hospitalidad" serves as an alter ego of the poet in search of his place in the canon and his individual voice. In the reciprocal relationship of hospitality—between container and contained, receiver and received—this vagabond life finds its "salvación."

> En cualquier tiempo y en cualquier terreno
> siempre hay un hombre que
> anda tan vagabundo como el humo,
> bienhechor, malhechor,
> 5   bautizado con la agria
> leche de nuestras leyes. Y él encuentra
> su salvación en
> la hospitalidad.

(p. 192)[310]

The indefinite setting as well as the anonymity of the wanderer, like the smoke subject to the capricious direction of the wind, will at the end of this section have found a specific location and identity because of his arrival at a special house.[311] Similar to the attraction of a moth to clothing and of one person to another, this house "seduces" the vagabond.

> Como la ropa atrae a la polilla,
> 10   como el amor a toda

su parentela de lujuria y gracia,
de temor y de dicha,
así una casa le seduce. Y no
por ser panal o ancla,
15 sino por ese oscuro
divorcio entre el secuestro de sus años,
la honda cautividad del tiempo ido
ahí, entre las paredes,
y su maltrecha libertad de ahora.

(p. 192)[312]

The play on "divorcio" resembles that on "hospitalidad" and dovetails with the imagery of seduction and the acceptance/rejection motif. During his wanderings, the vagabond realizes that the passage of time is as confining as four walls. He must therefore separate himself from that transient existence and attain liberty by reentering this familiar but run-down house. Each of the synecdochic parts of the house—the squeaking door, the closed window, the tiles on the roof, the uncomfortable furniture, the cold floor, and the family room—provide the vagabond with an opportunity to assess the poor condition into which the house has fallen and then to convert the negative into the positive.

The door, for example, "rechina / con cruel desconfianza, con amargo reproche" [squeaks / with cruel distrust, with bitter reproach]. Because he hears a reproach in that disagreeable noise, the speaker can locate and oil the rusty hinge, so that the door will open more easily. Symbol of hospitality in itself, the door admits the speaker to awareness of his own shortcoming, enabling him to repair it, and then opens easily so that he can admit others. Through the closed window the speaker can see the faded blossoms of an almond tree, symbol of his lost innocence given that these blossoms are white. As symbol of the passage of time, the blossoms are clearly visible. But they will become fruit as they mature. Even though the window "le es muro, / y su cristal esclavitud" [is a wall for him, / and its glass slavery], separating him from that irrevocable springtime of bloom, they protect him from the wind that scatters the blossoms. He is able to see decay but also the continuing process of maturation.[313] This series of images exemplifies the vagabond speaker-poet's ability to turn painful, unpleasant experiences to his advantage. The final verses of this part show the change that will take place in his perspective if he will come face to face with the negative.

. . . Esta es la lucha, este
es el tiempo, el terreno
donde él ha de vencer si es que no busca
recuerdos y esperanzas
tan sólo. Si es que busca
45 fundación, servidumbre.

(p. 193)[314]

The specificity of the demonstratives "esta" and "este" contrast with the indefinite "En *cualquier* tiempo y en *cualquier* terreno" of the opening verse. But this house and all its parts offer only the opportunity; the vagabond must seek more than "recuerdos y esperanzas." These words lock him in the passage of time—past and future—making his existence transient. In lieu of this option, he must seek "fundación, servidumbre," as the parallelism of vv. 42–45 suggests. We have already noted at the end of part III of "Oda a la niñez" that "servidumbre" is the paradoxical master-who-serves. It describes a humble, honest attitude which exalts the most lowly. The preceding word "fundación" relates these concepts to the house as the vagabond's refuge and his offering of asylum to others, the reciprocity of hospitality and love. It also suggests stability, permanence, and transcendence in comparison with the vagabond's transience and lack of "roots."[315]

Again we are confronted with the reciprocal play of metaphor and metonymy that we discovered in *Don*. The metonymic passage of time like the synecdochic repair of the house is still an essential characteristic of the linguistic, aesthetic experience: Language is still a diachronic, temporal element. But by using these characteristics to his advantage, the poet-speaker transcends temporal flow, constructing the edifice of his poetry. The poet's determination to come face to face with his shortcomings is a laborious, painful process that separates him from others (making him an individual), but also allows him to form part of the community (the canon). Alliance and condemnation go hand in hand.

The center section of "Oda a la hospitalidad" provides focus and unity by "papering over the gap," while at the same time functioning as a turning point representing flux and peripeteia. This dual purpose is observable in its structure. The first thirteen verses are composed of a single sentence that compares "esta mañana clara" with the cleansing, purifying effect of rain. The remainder (vv. 13–21, approximately the last third) contains two lengthy questions introduced by "Mas." In this shift from celebratory description to doubtful questioning, the speaker conveys the shift to reciprocity in the concept of "hospitalidad."

Although the comparison of rain and light is one that Rodríguez has employed before, the adjective "clara" adds another dimension to this combination. Because this is the name of the poet's wife, it is possible to discern an ephemeral and idealized female figure catachrestically doing her spring cleaning. As the wife and mistress of the house the speaker has rehabilitated, this female contributes her own special touch. On the ethical, personal level, one can sense the love the speaker feels upon observing this figure associated with spring taking an important part in the rearrangement of his life.[316]

> Y hoy, como la lluvia
> lava la hoja, esta mañana clara,
> tan abrileña prematuramente,
> limpia de polvo y de oropeles tanto
> 5   tiempo, y germina, y crea
> casi un milagro de hechos y sucesos,
> y remacha y ajusta
> tanta vida ambulante, tanta fortuna y fraude
> a través de los días,

10 purificando rostros y ciudades,
  dando riqueza a una menesterosa
  juventud, preparando,
  situando el vivir. . . .

(p. 193)[317]

The active verbs "limpia," "germina," "crea," "remacha," and "ajusta," the flow created by the conjunction "y," repetition of parallelisms, and the present participles "purificando," "dando," "preparando," and "situando" contribute to a dynamic renewal when in reality the speaker is observing the beauty of a spring morning. This external bustle represents his internal activity as he changes his perspective thanks to his new insight. On another level, rain and light are associated with poetic inspiration in Rodríguez's works, lending a metapoetic dimension to this housewife-muse. The contrast between the domestic and the aesthetic in and of itself embodies reciprocity, while the atmosphere of spring and the germinative effects of light and rain suggest eternal renewal and both the bestowing and the receiving of spiritual riches and blessings.

The female other allows the speaker to participate in love, renewal, and the miracle of the beauty of each and every day, but she also causes him to separate himself from it and to question his own participation as bestower/receiver. His questions in the final verses show him turning toward a new perspective.

     . . . ¿Mas alguien puede
  hacer de su pasado
15 simple materia de revestimiento:
  cera, laca, barniz, lo que muy pronto
  se marchita, tan pronto
  como la flor del labio?
  ¿O bien ha de esperar a estar con esos
20 verdaderos amigos, los que darán sentido
  a su vida, a su tierra y a su casa?

(p. 193)[318]

As genuine and rhetorical questions, these verses show the speaker interrogating himself, asking if the changes he perceives are only superficial. In accord with the image of the restoration of a house, he realizes that a "simple materia de revestimiento: / cera, laca, barniz" may deceive him and others if it is just another "cáscara" [husk]. Such an improvement would be transient, "lo que muy pronto / se marchita," and he seeks a more lasting approach to life. His house cannot be a showplace or a museum but must be open to "esos / verdaderos amigos" who can appreciate it. Rodríguez affirms his approach to poetry by rejecting a superficial brilliance of expression and seeking more profound emotions that he will share with those who can appreciate and enhance them, "los que darán sentido / a su vida, a su tierra y a su casa." Both poet and reader fulfill the role of guest and host with regard to language and the aesthetic experience. Both must give to and receive from participation in the aesthetic experience. The reciprocity of love and poetry as "hospitalidad" is explicit at the beginning of part III of this ode, the conclusion of *Alianza*.

Es la hospitalidad. Es el origen
de la fiesta y del canto.
Porque el canto es tan sólo
palabra hospitalaria: la que salva
5   aunque deje la herida. Y el amor es tan sólo
herida hospitalaria, aunque no tenga cura;
y la libertad cabe
en una humilde mano hospitalaria,
quizá dolida y trémula
10   mas fundadora y fiel, tendida en servidumbre
y en confianza, no en
sumisión o dominio.

(p. 194)[319]

The poet has discovered that writing—like love—can often be painful and leave a wound, but that it also redeems the transience of existence. Because of the similarity and interrelationship of poetry and love throughout *Alianza*, I wonder if this work is not a declaration of love, a celebration of Rodríguez's union with Clara, an expression of his gratefulness for the blessings he has received through their love, but also an apology for the role poetry plays in his life. Both love and poetry require the same total commitment, "entrega" (in various meanings of that word). The poet's invitation to accompany him on this journey—an invitation extended "en una humilde mano hospitalaria" to Clara and the reader—requires as much of the other as poetry of the poet. One must subject oneself to that sacrifice in order to attain subjectivity, "la libertad" extended to us in the hand in which we put our hand "en servidumbre / y en confianza, no en / sumisión o dominio." The paradoxical situation of humbling oneself (acknowledging the possibility of castration in the oedipal drama) to achieve subjectivity and freedom is borne out in the contrast between two approaches to life juxtaposed in the next verses.

A pesar de que hagamos
de convivencia técnicas
15   de opresión y medidas
de seguridad, y
de la hospitalidad hospicios, siempre
hay un hombre sencillo y una mañana clara,
con la alta transparencia de esta tierra,
20   y una casa, y una hora
próspera. Y este hombre
ve en torno de la mesa
a sus seres queridos. No pregunta
sino invita, no enseña
25   vasos de pesadumbre ni vajilla de plata.
Apenas habla, y menos
de su destierro.
Lo que esperó lo encuentra
y lo celebra, lejos

30   el incienso y la pólvora,
      aquel dinero, aquel resentimiento.

(p. 194)[320]

A traditional gesture of hospitality and sharing involves inviting others to a meal. The "seres queridos" seated around the speaker's table sharing his bounty are those who share his outlook on life and appreciate his poetry. The speaker's table is unpretentious: "no enseña / vasos de pesadumbre ni vajilla de plata." Rodríguez eschews superficial brilliance for the pleasure of the company. Lacking "incienso" and "pólvora," this meal is not routine ritual or bombastic display (evoking again the clergy and the military). The poem as meal is a transient occasion, but one that binds the participants together and redeems them.

       Ahora su patria es esta generosa
       ocasión y, sereno,
       algo medroso ante tal bien, acoge
35   y nombra, uno por uno,
       a sus amigos sin linaje, de
       nacimiento. Ya nunca
       forastero, en familia,
       no con docilidad, con aventura,
40   da las gracias muy a solas,
       como mendigo. Y sabe,
       comprende al fin. . . .

(pp. 194–95)[321]

Although no longer a vagabond, the speaker still has the humility and gratefulness of a beggar, knowing that all these blessings have been bestowed upon him because of his willingness to give them away to others. Those who have nothing appreciate any simple thing they receive, and because they depend on the generosity of others, they realize the importance of sharing unselfishly. Although this vagabond now has confined himself to the house he has refurbished, the very walls are transparent.

              . . . Y mira alegremente,
       con esa intimidad de la llaneza
       que es la única eficacia,
45   los rostros y las cosas,
       la verdad de su vida
       recién ganada aquí, entre las paredes
       de una juventud libre y un hogar sin fronteras.

(p. 195)[322]

The final verse epitomizes the speaker's paradoxical outlook at the end of *Alianza.* Children confined indoors ("entre paredes") would scarcely seem free to run and play, but the speaker implies that the discipline of truth to which he has committed himself has had a liberating, rejuvenating effect on his life and his poetry. Whereas "hogar" connotes intimacy, warmth, and interior space, this hearth to which the speaker invites us—the passion and illumination of his poetry—is open to all. The hearth as symbol of hospitality incorporates both giving and receiving: giving as receiving, hosting and receiving, being guest as giving of oneself. This paradoxical outlook is the cause of Rodríguez's celebration in the odes that crown *Alianza* with an excess of humble joy.

4

Presence and Absence, Wound and Suture, Elegy and Quest: The Crisis of Identity in *El vuelo de la celebración* (1976)

> For in much wisdom is much grief:
> and he that increaseth knowledge increaseth sorrow.

Those familiar with Rodríguez's opus have probably either bristled with irritation or clucked their tongues disapprovingly whenever I have declared that each of the poet's works is structured around a two-poem section. "A useful theory for *most* of his works," they comment, "but none of the five sections of *El vuelo de la celebración* consists of just two poems."[1] Although I must agree wholeheartedly with the raw truth of this affirmation, I steadfastly maintain that the structure of *El vuelo* depends upon the two-poem section, which in Rodríguez's fourth work is both present and absent, there and not there.

Rodríguez culminates *Alianza y condena*, the preceding work, with the two odes of "Libro cuarto." These two poems complement one another as they supplement "Libro tercero" and all of *Alianza;* and we know that "Oda a la niñez" consists of four parts and "Oda a la hospitalidad" of three. Rodríguez has torn these two complementary poems apart, placing one at the beginning of *El vuelo* ("Herida en cuatro tiempos" consists of four parts) and the other at the end ("Elegía desde Simancas" is divided into three parts). The intervening sections, consisting of the symmetrical distribution of eight, nine, and eight poems, respectively, both separate and unite the two poems that frame them, creating a gap and a bridge, loss and gain, wound and suture.

Responding to the unexpected and violent death of his sister and the death of his mother shortly afterward, *El vuelo* functions as a painfully eloquent elegy. The wrenching apart of these two poems, forming a wound ("herida"), and the subsequent breaching of that gap, the suturing of the wound, is perfectly consonant with the genre of elegy and the themes of grief and consolation embodied in these poems.[2] Like many contemporary poets who have adopted this genre, however—as Jahan Ramazani convincingly demonstrates in *Poetry of Mourning*—and consistent with his poetics, Rodríguez converts the elegy into a quest for consolation and identity since the death of his beloved family members places his own identity in peril.[3] This search depends upon the exploration of the wound (gap) caused by loss and grief, deepening the wound and preventing it from healing at the same time that it promotes healing and consolation (suturing).[4] My discussion delineates the elegiac conventions in this work and the ways in which Rodríguez recuperates, reconfigures, and revitalizes these conventions to trope elegy into quest into language and self.

Whereas the first section corresponds with the immediate moment of grief caused by the loss of the loved one, each subsequent section represents a step in the process of suturing that wound. In the first of the three intermediate sections, the poet decides to confront his pain more directly, coming to grips with the loss of the loved one. The center section of *El vuelo* provides a turning point, a troping. Here the elegist must confront his own mortality, recognizing that he can achieve poetic immortality only by surrendering himself to the transience and loss inherent in life. The next step in this process entails overcoming the difficulty and pain of continuing this quest, in such a way as not to deceive himself (which would result in a superficial, nonlasting expression). The final section counters "Herida en cuatro tiempos" with "Elegía desde Simancas." If the severe pain of the wound and the loss of the loved one defines the transience of all reality and life as a moment of pain, the elegy provides consolation because of the poet's determination to pursue his poetic quest in spite of the pain it exacts of him.

There are, then, four definitions of time set forth in *El vuelo*, distributed on two vectors—the synchronic and the diachronic. The three intermediate sections form the diachronic axis and correspond to a tripartite definition of time.[5] This vector is diachronic because it conceives of time as linear and represents the elegist's confrontation with grief—his work of mourning—over time. But these three views of time occur simultaneously in the present. Ironically, it is the passage of time in the present that forms the consistent basis for the constantly advancing synchronic vector, the axis composed of the first and last poems of *El vuelo*. Representing the transient and lasting moments respectively, these two sides of the same coin are joined and separated by the intervening sections. One poem depends on the other for definition and existence; they are synchronically reciprocal and complementary. The crossing point of the two vectors, the moment of decision and troping when elegy becomes quest, when loss becomes gain, when the transient becomes the lasting, occurs in the center poem, "Noviembre" (allowing for nine poems in section III). Each of the work's five sections depicts a specific sequential moment in the work of mourning, yet each to a certain extent repeats the same experience of grief and consolation, gain and loss, wound and suture, elegy and quest.[6]

OPEN WOUND: THE TRANSIENT PRESENT

The opening section of *El vuelo* bears the title "Herida en cuatro tiempos," a title perplexing for two reasons. First, the word "herida"—a centrally important image—could be either a noun or a past participle used as an adjective. Equally ambivalent, it could refer to a wound causing the sharp and profound pain that motivates this elegiac work.[7] But it could also stand for the gap, empty space, or absence Rodríguez has discovered in language and his relentless pursuit, exploration, and immersion in that gap as the site of quest where he seeks his personal and poetic identity. Another enigmatic aspect of this title is the number four. Certainly, we can identify three major aspects of time: past, present, and future. But why does the poet speak of *four* time frames? What is the fourth aspect of time? To resolve these questions, we should consider the structure of "Herida" in relation to the entire work.

Each of the four sections of "Herida"—in themselves indicative of the four temporal moments to which the title alludes—prefigures the remaining four sections of *El vuelo*, the three intervening sections that serve as barrier and bridge, and the final section (the elegy proper) that has as its subtitle "Hacia la Historia." This phrase combines the futurity of the preposition "hacia" with the completed past of the noun "historia." Therefore, as we move through and toward the elegy, we participate in a quest, linking these two genres in the language of the poems and in the process of finding consolation on the one hand and continually deferring it in the interest of the quest on the other. Exploration of the wound/gap intensifies the pain, deepening the wound and preventing it from healing, at the same time that it promotes healing and consolation through the work of mourning. As the opening of the frame/wound/gap, "Herida en cuatro tiempos" posits the moment of greatest shock, grief, and anger, and prefigures the trajectory of the quest for self through consolation/deferral of consolation in terms of the elegiac work of mourning. A consideration of the four sections of "Herida en cuatro tiempos" will define *El vuelo* as elegy and quest.

The title of the first poem in this section, "Aventura de una destrucción," continues the framing effect of the previous titles, *El vuelo de la celebración* and "Herida en cuatro tiempos." An adventure can entail risk and excitement, danger and exaltation, reluctance and commitment, whereas destruction is ambivalent because of its unknown complement. If the poet searches for identity, he may risk destroying himself, his reputation as a poet and his self-esteem; but at the same time, he may find consolation for the grief and pain that threatens to destroy him. Risk is also involved in his not searching, not doing the work of mourning and falling into melancholia, as well as in his quest for consolation by the only means he knows: by delving more deeply into his emotions (particularly his grief and sense of loss and abandonment) and constantly renewing his engagement with the poetic act. As we have seen in *Alianza y condena*, in this penetrating exploration of self the poet risks the loss of his reader, a loss in the future occasioned by the events of the past ("Hacia la Historia"). The wound constitutes a double-edged experience; it is both absence and presence, risk and necessity, failure and triumph, grief and celebration.

The initial poem in this sequence displays many of the themes intrinsic to elegiac mourning. One of the most important of these is the fabrication of a text to mediate between mourner and loss, a presence that substitutes for the absence of the loved one who has died. Rodríguez combines quest and consolation and the image of weaving (textualizing) in the image of the pillow.

Cómo conozco el algodón y el hilo de esta almohada
herida por mis sueños,
sollozada y desierta,
donde crecí durante quince años.
5   En esta almohada desde la que mis ojos
vieron el cielo
y la pureza de la amanecida
y el resplandor nocturno
cuando el sudor, ladrón muy huérfano, y el fruto transparente
10   de mi inocencia, y la germinación del cuerpo
eran ya casi bienaventuranza.

(p. 201)[8]

As is customary in Rodríguez's poetry, the opening "Cómo" may function as an exclamation and an interrogation. As the former, this statement expresses the poet's familiarity with the nuances, the very fibers of language he uses to weave the fabric of the text and his reluctance to repeat the elegiac act because of the aesthetic risk involved. As a question, this sentence expresses his estrangement from language and his skepticism about the efficacy of writing to secure consolation. The pillow is where he rests his head, but it can also be the cause of anxiety and frustration if he cannot reconcile sleep, if he does not believe in the power of language to capture and make present his emotions, his identity, his world.[9] Dreams can be aspirations or that which prevents us from getting rest. Because of tears, the pillow can bring consolation and rest, or it can be raspy and unproductive, irritating to our sensitivity, keeping us awake.

The first usage of "herida" as an adjective not only plays against the noun but thereby suggests the ambivalence of its meaning. The pillow as language can be rent and worn out by the poet's overusage of certain conventions, but it can also be "permeated" (as opposed to "undone") by his visions and emotions. Does familiarity with the pillow (language and the poetic tradition) wear out, unravel, tear apart the fabric of language, or does it permeate the text, so that each thread and the fiber of each word enriches and lends new meaning? Elegy as genre provides the perfect testing ground for this "risk of destruction." Will it allow the poet to dispel his grief? Or will he merely repeat the tradition and undo his own identity as a poet?

We could interpret the time phrase "donde crecí durante quince años" autobiographically to refer to the period between 1951, when Rodríguez began writing the poems of *Don de la ebriedad* to define himself as a poet, and 1965, when he published *Alianza y condena*, the culmination of his attempt to establish himself as a major figure.[10] The preterit of the verb "crecí" suggests a definitive end to that period of development and growth. A repetition of tripartite parallelism in the second sentence lends more credence to an autobiographical reading. The progression "el cielo / y la pureza de la amanecida / y el resplandor nocturno" develops and refines the image of light as poetic inspiration, one of the definitive images of elegy.[11]

This series is followed by another disguised by the length of the lines and the enjambment: "el sudor, ladrón muy huérfano, y el fruto transparente / de mi inocencia, y la germinación del cuerpo." These images may allude to Rodríguez's three previous books of poetry and assess his aesthetic maturity in each. But they also introduce the motif of sexuality, and are associated with the image of the pillow and synecdochi-cally with the bed, site of rest, dreaming, and sexuality, of which I will say more when discussing the following stanzas in which the bed is explicitly mentioned, causing us to question whether Rodríguez is speaking of his marriage to Clara (which took place in 1959—approximately fifteen years earlier).[12]

The phrase "ladrón muy huérfano" can serve as an example of how these images function. Describing the poet during his first aesthetic effort ("sudor"), the thief is one who robs from others, as the poet draws upon his early models to write. Yet this thief is also "huérfano," suggesting a lack of familiarity with the tradition, a limited num-ber of sources upon which to draw. This gain/loss motif also hints at the primary loss of unity with the (m)other in the oedipal process, the entry into the Symbolic and language.[13] While "sudor" refers to the effort involved, it has connotations connected with the intensity of the sexual act and the anxiety associated with the first sexual experience.[14]

The superimposition of sexuality and poetry is further reinforced by the image of the speaker's eyes.[15] Light, sight and insight, darkness and blindness, are images that Rodríguez has used frequently in his poetry. A major motif of the elegiac genre (and of quest) involves castration and the displacement of sexual desire. The shock of loss and the depth of the wound caused by grief—emblematic of castration, separation, and loss—requires the poet to reexperience the oedipal crisis and the primary loss of unity with the (m)other. The elegiac genre allows the poet to participate in the process of reentry into language at the same time that it renews his quest for identity and individuality (which is ironically separation from and unity with the other—the po-etic tradition). The multivalence and ambiguity of the language of this opening poem entails the interweaving of sexuality and textuality, elegy and quest.

The fragmented and deferred development of the image of the bed and the juxta-position of past and present (gain and loss) reflect the shock of unexpected loss caused by the death of a loved one. Because he has not been able to prepare defenses against it, this loss shatters the poet's confidence in language and compels him to reengage with the poetic act. Again, the penetrating self-analysis inherent in Rodríguez's ap-proach to this project risks the alienation and disorientation of the reader—another potential loss that leads to the poet's gain. This tension develops in the next two stanzas, where the bed—symbol of the blank page on which the poet must write—crystallizes more sharply.

> La cama temblorosa
> donde la pesadilla se hizo carne,
> donde fue fértil la respiración,
> 15   audaz como la lluvia
> con su tejido luminoso y sin ceniza alguna.
>
> Y mi cama fue nido
> y ahora es alimaña;
> ya su madera sin barniz, oscura,
> 20   sin amparo.

$$(pp.\ 201-2)^{16}$$

Characterizing the bed as "temblorosa" projects the speaker's fear and excitement ("adventure") as he discovers the delights of love and as he puts his words down on paper. The intertextual reference to the opening of the Gospel of John in the verse "donde la pesadilla se hizo carne" confirms the metapoetic context as well as a sense of impregnation. But the word "pesadilla," playing off the earlier "herida por mis sueños," foments the revelation of the speaker's anger and bitterness, which reappears in the next stanza in the word "alimaña." The full expression of these emotions, resulting from unanticipated and unprotected grief ("pesadilla"), plays a dominant role in the work of mourning.[17] Previously, the poet has been able (or at least attempted) to ward off this sense of loss by means of the veil of words, the "tejido luminoso" of the rain which is in turn the fertile if bold (i.e., ineluctable, uncontrollable) breath of inspiration.[18]

In a radical reversal underscored by parallelism and the contrasting verb tenses of preterit and present, the bed—the act of writing, of putting one's dreams and visions on a blank "sheet" of paper—is transformed from a nest (a place of comfort and solace) into "alimaña," a threat to the promise of life emblematized by the nest. Therefore, the wood, the material of which the bed is made, is "sin barniz, oscura, / sin amparo." The poet feels that he is exposed, blind, vulnerable: The darkness of the wood negates the light just as the destructive animal casts a shadow of death over the nest. Because he has been unable to prepare for the death of the loved one, the speaker feels bare and defenseless. His conflicting emotions of anger and the need for solace are foregrounded in the final stanza where he refuses to accept reality and recognizes that he has no other way to come to terms with his sorrow.

> No volveré a dormir en este daño, en esta
> ruina,
> arropado entre escombros, sin embozo,
> sin amor ni familia,
> 25   entre la escoria viva.
> Y al mismo tiempo quiero calentarme
> en ella, ver
> cómo amanece, cómo
> la luz me da en la cara, aquí, en mi cama.
>
> (p. 202)[19]

The expression "volver a," meaning to repeat, is particularly apt because repetition is at the core of elegiac mourning.[20] The refusal to repeat—specifically to repeat the act of elegy—along with the strong characterization in such words as "daño," "ruina," "escombros," and "escoria viva" points to the speaker's reluctance to participate in the act of writing and to his skepticism about the efficacy of language. More importantly, he vents his anger—the healthy expression of mourning—as he emphatically repeats not only these negative words, but also the phrases "en este daño, en esta / ruina" and "sin embozo, / sin amor ni familia" and the alliteration in "escombros," "embozo," "amor," and "familia."

The words "arropado" and "embozo" attract attention because of their similarity with the shroud of the dead; the speaker not only does not wish to admit the reality of the loved one's death, but of his own death as well. This refusal is linked with the poet's refusal to continue exploring himself, as the word "embozo" suggests. This part of the sheet that folds over the blanket and covers the face puns on the code of the bed, but it also reminds us of a mask or covering used to disguise identity. Rodríguez has decided that he must write without any sort of disguise or veil between himself and his emotions, which will identify him, make of him an individual, unique poetic voice.[21]

If he is to come to terms with the death of the loved one, however, the substitution of the veil of language is a necessary part of the renunciation of lost desire and the deflection, redirection, and recathexis of desire.[22] To write an elegy is to mediate grief with the veil of language and "calentar[se] en ella." The wound of grief requires the suture of language. The elegy as a traditional genre with its repeated conventions will provide the vehicle for the poet simultaneously to weave the mediating veil of language and to quest for identity in the wound. In Rodríguez's typically transgressive style, he will do more than merely incorporate and repeat the conventions of elegy: He will weave and unweave the fabric of the text, he will draw the suture over the wound but continue to explore it, deferring healing. This ambivalence continues in the final verses, which demonstrate a paramount characteristic of *El vuelo:* inconclusive closure.

> 30   La vuestra, padre mío, madre mía,
>   hermanos míos,
>   donde mi salvación fue vuestra muerte.
>
>   (p. 202)[23]

It is elegiacally significant that the final verse contains the words "salvación" and "muerte." That the poet's salvation depends on the loss of his parents and siblings may be indicative of the guilt he feels, but also of his ability to console himself through writing. Lying in his bed, recalling the unexpected death of his father, the oedipal loss of unity with the mother, and the estrangement and death of his siblings, Rodríguez enacts his own death and comes face to face with his own mortality and the possibility of transcending death in his verse.[24] Although he may feel guilty because he uses the loss of others to gain his own salvation, those earlier losses help him cushion the shock caused by the most recent loss.[25]

This combination of guilt and consolation again arises from the code of the bed, sleep, and dreaming as a rehearsal of his death and a quest for identity and immortality. If the death of the loved one has fragmented and shocked the now distraught speaker, putting his self at risk and causing him to lose confidence in the consolation afforded by the text (a psychological castration), it also forces him to place himself at risk by honestly confronting his mortality and the continuation of his life in the face of these losses. Having received a profound wound, the poet must now hand himself over to that pain. His exploration of the wound will increase the pain and perhaps lead to another loss—that of his reader, who may not be prepared to participate in such an

intense, personal experience. "Aventura de una destrucción" initiates the quest for
poetic immortality and consolation by defining the pain of the wound and the risks
the poet will have to take. Finding himself at risk, the poet must not merely surrender
to risk but actively seek it, immerse himself in it, or risk losing himself.

This risky and exciting "adventure" continues in the second poem of "Herida en
cuatro tiempos," "El sueño de una pesadilla." The grammar of this title obviously
echoes *El vuelo de la celebración* and "Aventura de una destrucción." But it also is a
solipsism because a nightmare is a type of dream. If in the code of sleep a dream is a
poem, a nightmare must be an elegy. The meaning of "pesadilla" as difficulty in breathing during sleep is related to the elegiac sense of castration and the inability of the
poet to produce poetry because of the shock he has received. Furthermore, the *mise
en abïme* of a dream within a dream questions reality—the "reality testing" inherent
in elegiac work.[26] This repetition with difference highlights the poet's engagement
with the poetic tradition in the act of mourning. Repetition as a poetic device represents the *fort-da* game of compensation for loss and the attempt to gain control of the
other's absence through language.[27]

Another key element of elegy is manifest in "El sueño de una pesadilla": the
antiphonal voice.[28] Originally derived from funeral laments and then incorporated
into drama as the dialogic chorus, the antiphonal voice estranges the speaker from
himself and allows him to gain a more distanced perspective on his grief—another
instance of the *fort-da* game that increases the possibility of consolation. The antiphonal voice opens "El sueño de una pesadilla" and emphasizes the contrasting
points of view.

> El tiempo está entre tus manos:
> tócalo, tócalo. Ahora anochece y hay
> pus en el olor del cuerpo, hay alta marea
> en el mar del dormir, y el surco abierto
> 5   entre las sábanas,
> la cruz de las pestañas
> a punto de caer, los labios hasta el cielo del techo,
> hasta la melodía de la espiga,
> hasta esta lámpara de un azul ya pálido,
> 10   en este cuarto que se me va alzando
> con la ventana sin piedad,
> maldita y olorosa, traspasada de estrellas.
>
> (p. 203)[29]

Like the child with the spool that Freud observed, the poet possesses language,
especially its temporal dimension. The opening sentence seems to be spoken by a
wiser, encouraging voice that has more experience than the childlike poet. The sententious simplicity and directness of this statement contrasts with the long, involved,
highly metaphoric and irrational imagery of the next sentence, which describes the
poet's mental state as he tries to conciliate sleep.

In this poem, the poet attempts to do what he both feared and desired at the end of

"Aventura de una destrucción": to wrap himself in the consoling "bed" of language to acquire some control over his grief. The word "anochece" expresses the loss of sunlight (a primary elegiac figure). The protagonist suffers from insomnia (a lack of consolation) because of the loss of this light. Even though he is in bed, his body—or perhaps that of the person next to him—is repugnant to him, like a festering, foulsmelling wound that limits his desire for sexuality. The "alta marea / en el mar del dormir" indicates that he is tossing and turning, unable to fall asleep. "El surco abierto / entre las sábanas" could be a figure for his wound, but also for his poetry (cf. the image of the "surco" in *Don de la ebriedad*) and a feeling of emptiness and void that attracts him but also causes fear, anxiety, and impotence. Because of the shock of the loved one's death—a shock for which he was not prepared—the speaker fears reattachment of his desire to another lest he lose that love also, the sleep to which he does not want to surrender for fear of a nightmare.

Little by little, his eyelashes become heavy, like a cross he does not want to bear. The visionary distortion of the room where he lies as an open field with its whispering sound of the wind (inspiration) gently moving dry stalks of wheat (a symbol of sexual potency as well as elegiac pipes) moves him albeit reluctantly toward poetic illumination and consolation. His aversion to this experience is evident in the reflexive construction "se me va alzando," whereas his anger and pain can be felt in the words "la ventana sin piedad, / maldita y olorosa, traspasada de estrellas." The window is both barrier and passageway (threshold) for the entry of illumination, whereas stars are yet another telling figure of elegiac light, in this case bringing a piercing pain that is debilitating and uplifting in its illumination. The speaker finally cedes to sleep at the end of the first stanza.

> Y en mis ojos la estrella, aquí, doliéndome,
> ciñéndome, habitándome astuta
> 15   en la noche de la respiración, en el otoño claro
> de la amapola del párpado,
> en las agujas del pinar del sueño.
>
> (p. 203)[30]

On the one hand, the words "estrella," "respiración," "claro," "amapola," and "pinar" suggest illumination, inspiration, productivity, and sacred space, all entering through the speaker's eyes, his poetic insight. On the other hand, the star causes pain and restriction, and is surrounded by night or darkness, the opposite of sight. The productive poppy is an eyelid that forms the poet's (in)sight but may be a reference to the veil of language modifying his experience of grief and loss. This translucent veil is caused by the deleafing of the trees in autumn (another loss associated with the approach of winter/death), and though the poppy produces abundant seeds, it is usually red, indicative of the pain that this piercing though filtered light brings with it.[31] This pain is further emphasized by the pine needles, which are perennially green but also sharp and painful. The reengagement with love and language is painful and beautiful, repulsive and attractive.

Ironically, the vision captured in the dream is anything but unpleasant, the complete opposite of what we might call a nightmare. This tranquil vision evokes an ideal springtime and a near halting of the passage of time.

> Las calles, los almendros,
> algunos de hoja malva,
> 20   otros de floración tardía frente
> a la soledad del puente
> donde se hila la luz entre los ojos
> tempranos para odiar. Y pasa el agua
> nunca tardía para amar del Duero,
> 25   emocionada y lenta,
> quemando infancia.
>
> (p. 203)[32]

This idealized version of the pathetic fallacy has as its central figure the almond tree.[33] Because it is one of the first trees to flower, the almond tree is a harbinger of the renewal of spring, a principal image of elegiac consolation.[34] But this early flowering makes it susceptible to late winter chills that can damage the buds and the tree's productivity. This contradictory image of perpetual renewal and premature destruction reveals the shadow latent in the idealism of the scene. We can then see the streets as avenues to new experiences and also limitless vanishing points that lead to no specific destination.

The image of the bridge signifying transition and growth (also present in the almond trees) sustains the pathetic fallacy in this scene. The poet's solitude ("la soledad") is positively and negatively marked as search and growth, loss and gain. The images of eyes and light—indispensable elegiac components—as well as the reference to weaving and textuality in the verb "se hila" indicate an ideal period in the poet's life when he believed in the efficacy of language and his ability to know himself and the world through the poetic act.[35] The nostalgic evocation of that innocence (again, the images of spring and the white flowers of the almond tree come into play) is undercut by the word "odiar." Even though the speaker once had an innocent perspective on the world, his present disillusionment makes itself felt.

This ambiguity in the idealized dreamscape is underscored by the image of the river. The specificity of the Duero provides an oblique allusion to Rodríguez's personal life at the same time that it evokes wider themes.[36] The bridge recalls the Roman structure still in use in Zamora today—another indication of history (the passage of time) and the timelessness of the scene, the ability of art to survive the ravages of time. The reversal of the parallelism in the phrases "tempranos para odiar" and "nunca tardía para amar" again shows the ambivalence of the ideal scene with its backdrop of shadow hidden in the light. This latent disillusionment is consonant with the ambivalent image of the river which seems not to move and yet is always "quemando infancia." Just as water is both fertilizing and destructive, and the river is both eternity and the passage of time, change and stasis, so the ironic allusion to fire in the gerund "quemando" includes destruction and regeneration. We have already noted in our discussion of "Oda a la niñez" the difference between "infancia" (childishness, selfishness, egotism) and "niñez" (innocence, delight, and wonder in the world).

The friction between the idealism of the dream scene and the undercurrent of disillusionment in the ambivalent imagery leads to an angry outburst of self-deprecation. This outburst requires the reentry of the antiphonal, consoling voice, indicative of the work of mourning accomplished in this surrender to the mediation of the dream/ text of elegy.

> ¿Qué hago con mi sudor, con estos años
> sin dinero y sin riego,
> sin perfidia siquiera ahora en mi cama?
> 30   ¿Y volveré a soñar
> esta pesadilla? Tú estate quieto, quieto.
> Pon la cabeza alta y pon las manos
> en la nuca. Y sobre todo ve
> que amanece, aún aquí,
> 35   en el rincón del uso de tus sueños,
> junto al delito de la oscuridad,
> junto al almendro. Qué bien sé su sombra.
>
> (203–4)[37]

Questioning, like repetition, forms an integral part of the elegiac process.[38] These questions recall the bed and dream code, suggesting the speaker's return to unhealthy melancholia as opposed to the healthy work of mourning. More importantly, the eruption of anger releases pent-up emotions and forwards the healing process. The speaker questions the worth of his poetry, especially if it is unable to prevent him and his loved ones from dying. His poetic effort ("sudor") has resulted in neither economic gain, fertilizing enrichment, nor even illicit pleasure ("sin dinero y sin riego, / sin perfidia siquiera ahora en mi cama"). Repetition of the phrase meaning "to repeat" ("volveré a") and the play on sleep, dream, and nightmare as images of poetry again express his reluctance and skepticism concerning participation in the poetic act. If the diminutive suffix "-illa" connotes the insignificance of the nightmare and the poet's recognition of the doubtful worth of his poetry, it also conveys his anger and self-deprecation as he belittles his belief in the mediative qualities of language to console his grief.

This eruption of emotion provokes the response of the antiphonal voice, who again attempts to console the speaker with soothing repetitive commands ("tócalo, tócalo" earlier and now "quieto, quieto" and "Pon . . . y pon"). This voice urges the poet to give himself over to dreaming/poetry so that he can see the dawn, that is, the beginning of a new day (resurrection, renewal) and the sun, "the elegy's arch-figure for the continuing source of physical and spiritual energy."[39] If in the dreamscape shadows lay hidden in the idealization of light, in the final lines the return of the sun takes place in the darkest part of the speaker's life.

But the voice then alters the imagery of darkness even more, transforming the pain of loss into the gap in language. The image of "el rincón del uso de tus sueños" hinges on the word "uso," the habitual, repetitious, boring, ineffectual, unoriginal recourse to the platitudes of language, or the transformative, regenerative, original, and creative reworking of the traditional conventions of genres, such as the elegy, that will continue the striving toward identity through his individual poetic voice. This converts the darkness's crime (death) into the flowering and leafing of the almond tree that with its shadow protects the protagonist from the harsh rays of the sun. The tree's foliage becomes a mediating veil of language affording the poet relief and comfort.

The final statement of "El sueño de una pesadilla" dissipates the nightmare and makes it seem only a bad dream. Although the phrase "Qué bien sé su sombra" returns to the first person, a new identity has emerged, one that combines the two voices of the protagonist and the antiphonal voice. Even though the final image is one of shadow, it provides healing comfort reinforced by the gentle rhythm and soothing alliteration of the /s/. Notably, Rodríguez has chosen not the verb "conozco" but "sé."[40] This verb suggests greater knowledge, a profound recognition of the integral part this shadow/gap plays in the quest for individuality. "El sueño de una pesadilla" (corresponding with the center section of *El vuelo*) is a turning point in the speaker's outlook, enacting his reconciliation of the loved one's death with his continued production of poetry, the troping of elegy into quest.

Following immediately upon the sentence "Qué bien sé su sombra," the title of the third poem, "Herida," reiterates the ambivalence of the wound as intense pain and pleasure. Echoing the title "Herida en cuatro tiempos" underscores this ambivalence: the widening of the gap in language—an ecstatic exploration of the possibilities of the Symbolic—stemming from the pain of surrendering to grief. If in "Aventura de una destrucción" these two emotions are counterpoised to create friction, in "Herida" the paradox of pleasure and pain coexist in the same language. Narrowing the gap between the two extremes produces an intensification of the experience of the gap and the contradictory yet inseparable emotions, just as the "sombra herida" conflates light and shadow, presence and absence. Once again Rodríguez demonstrates his ability to transgress the limits of language. As both rhetorical and sincere question, expressing amazement and doubt, and reinforcing the link between repetition, questioning, and elegy, the opening verses of "Herida" unite several images and codes Rodríguez has been developing in extended metaphors throughout "Herida en cuatro tiempos."

> ¿Y está la herida ya sin su hondo pétalo,
> sin tibieza,
> sino fecunda con su mismo polen,
> cosida a mano, casi como un suspiro,
> 5   con el veneno de su melodía,
> con el recogimiento de su fruto,
> consolando, arropando
> mi vida?
>
> (p. 205)[41]

The verb "está" foregrounds the question of presence, initiating a play between the prepositions "sin" and "con." The image of the flower, traditional symbol of feminine sexuality, recalls the ambivalent early flowering of the almond tree and the sorely red "amapola del párpado" as a symbol of the mediating properties of language. The speaker questions and also delights in the fructiferous process of pollination that produces a rich harvest even though the beauty of the flowers' petals is lost.

In stating that this wound has been "cosida a mano," the poet makes reference to the act of writing, of textualizing his loss and grief, as an act of suturing the wound. His remark that this suturing is "casi como un suspiro" not only calls attention to the connection between grief and writing but additionally introduces the images of breath (wind, inspiration) and voice. He picks up this image in the parallel phrases "con el veneno de su melodía, / con el recogimiento de su fruto." While moving toward consolation through writing, breathing, and singing, however, the pain of the wound as well as the allusion to the shroud in the word "arropando" continues to vie with the positive aspects. The image of venom is particularly conspicuous. Derived from Venus and associated with love, venom indicates the close relationship between pleasure and pain, grief and consolation, intense life and death.

The paradoxical contrasts permeating the language and imagery of this initial question establish the acutely bittersweet tone of the poem and the interaction between presence and absence in language, love, and death. Converting the wound into an embrace, the speaker continues his exploration of its paradoxical effect. The persistent negation in the following stanza transforms absence into presence, pain into pleasure.

```
        Ella me abraza. Y basta.
10      Pero no pasa nada.
        No es lo de siempre, no es mi amor en venta,
        la desnudez de mi deseo, ni
        el dolor inocente, sin ventajas,
        ni el sacrificio de lo que se cotiza,
15      ni el despoblado de la luz, ni apenas
        el tallo hueco,
        nudoso, como el de la avena, de
        la injusticia. No,
        no es el color canela
20      de la flaqueza de los maliciosos,
        ni el desencanto de los desdichados,
        ni el esqueleto en flor,
        rumoroso, del odio. Ni siquiera la vieja
        boca del rito
25      de la violencia.
```

(p. 205)[42]

The ambiguity of the pronoun "ella" (which could refer to "mi vida," "la herida," "la sombra," "la cama," or a particular female figure such as the poet's wife) and the pedestrian language play against one another, as do the conflicting, paradoxical emotions of love, loss, and language. All three of these remit to the primary loss of unity with the mother, entry into the Symbolic, and the mediation of language as a means of consolation for loss. In the repetition of negation, the poet recapitulates the *fort-da* game with a series of images that combine the tangible with the abstract (the spool with language). Enfolding himself in his grief and redirecting, recathecting his desire are images of the poet's reentry into the Symbolic and the gap he has discovered in language, the absence that makes the presence of language possible. This displacement and redirection of desire is essential if the poet is to achieve the consolation he seeks.

Grief and love are simultaneously similar to and different from the act of writing, as we see in the series of negations. Substitution for the absent loved one, which the speaker is trying to define through a process of elimination, is the topic of this stanza. The sentence "Pero no pasa nada" undercuts the embrace and expresses the speaker's surprise and disillusionment. In the economy of gain and loss, repetition and difference, nothing has happened, yet everything is different. The fundamental difference underlying this sense of change within repetition and sameness concerns the speaker's motivation. When he states "no es mi amor en venta, / la desnudez de mi deseo ni / el dolor inocente, sin ventajas," we are reminded of his attitude toward love and writing that moved him from a vested interest in the production of poetry to the profoundly personal, self-analytical introspection that took place in *Alianza y condena*. In the gain/loss economy of elegy, the terms of exchange have been altered. He no longer seeks fame or even the pleasure derived from exposing himself to the act of giving. The death of the loved one alters the speaker's motivation for writing and carries him to a new plane of self-discovery through the poetic act. If he thinks that he can place a price on his sacrifice ("el sacrificio de lo que se cotiza"), he has not given up very much. That which he now sacrifices is of inestimable value.

This line of reasoning leads the poet to distinguish himself from other poets, to individuate even more, similar to the rejection of negative values that he accomplished in *Alianza*. He characterizes these other poets by the superficial, worthless emotions that undergird their poetry: "el tallo hueco / . . . de / la injusticia," "la flaqueza de los maliciosos," "el esqueleto en flor, / rumoroso, del odio," "el rito / de la violencia." The image of "el color canela / de la flaqueza de los maliciosos" is particularly apt because cinnamon comes from a tree related to the laurel, suggesting the myth of Apollo and Daphne, the substitution of the laurel wreath for lost love, and the connotations of victory and immortality these leaves connote.[43] Yet cinnamon comes from the second layer of bark, a sign of superficiality. The speaker mentions only the color, perhaps suggesting that of dried blood, which lacks the vividness and vitality of his open-wound approach to poetry.

The insistence on negation and the many ways in which the poet repeats yet varies that negation reaches a culmination in the final lines of this stanza. The phrase "Ni siquiera" expresses his disdain for others, and because these images recall the witches of "Brujas" and the attitudes the poet has already rejected and condemned, the speaker sets himself apart, defining his basis for poetry and for the act of writing by eliminating all that it is not. The emergence of his approach to poetry in the image of the wound as absence and presence, pain and pleasure, grief and love, occurs in the next stanza of "Herida."

Aún no hay sudor, sino desenvoltura;
aún no hay amor, sino las pobres cuentas
del engaño vacío.
Sin rendijas ni vendas
30   vienes tú, herida mía, con tanta noche entera,
muy caminada,
sin poderte abrazar. Y tú me abrazas.

(pp. 205–6)[44]

The parallel syntax and internal rhyme of "sudor" and "amor" evidence the speaker's frustration with his effort to write meaningful poetry. He does not want to repeat routinely what others have said or what he himself has already said. He follows this repetitive phrasing with words that overlay the erotic and the metapoetic. "Desenvoltura" can refer to dishonesty and deceit in an amorous relationship, but it also has to do with glibness, the facile production of words. In saying the rosary, one repeats words by rote, stringing prayers along "las pobres cuentas" and perhaps deceiving oneself into thinking that one is praying. We can compare this situation with the hollow phrases lovers repeat without meaning them or investing them with truth.

In contrast with this sterile use of language devoid of profound sentiment, the wound comes to the speaker "Sin rendijas ni vendas." The grief caused by the loss of the loved one is a clean and open wound; it has no hidden crevices where infection can fester, and it is not hidden behind a clean, white bandage that can serve as a blindfold ("venda" can mean both bandage and blindfold). In other words, the grief caused by this wound forces the poet to reach a new level of expression, given that he penetrates into its depth and refuses to disguise his pain with a veil of sterile words. Even though he cannot embrace the wound because it is an absence, a loss, a gap, he can relinquish himself to that pain and let the wound embrace him. Having been placed at risk, he places himself at risk. Thus, his writing of an elegy to assuage his grief becomes a quest. Writing this elegiac work raises Rodríguez's poetry to a new level because his motivation—grief, pain, loss, absence—leads him to quest for consolation through language—the substitution of language, presence, gain, and pleasure for loss, absence, and pain.

If the second stanza of "Herida" employs negation to define the poet's approach to writing, the final one presents a more affirmative definition. Paradox and the union of light and darkness, sight and blindness, wound and suture, combines the elegiac project with the poet's quest for individuality and a distinct voice in spite of the necessity of following in the elegiac tradition.

Cómo me está dañando la mirada
al entrar tan a oscuras en el día.
35   Cómo el olor del cielo,
la luz hoy cruda, amarga,
de la ciudad, me sanan
la herida que supura con su aliento
y con su podredumbre,
40   asombrada y esbelta,
y sin sus labios ya,

> hablando a solas con sus cicatrices
> muy seguras, sin eco,
> hacia el destino, tan madrugador,
> 45   hasta llegar a la gangrena.

$$(p.\ 206)^{45}$$

The imagery of these verses reconciles the opposites of pain and pleasure, revulsion and attraction, Thanatos and Eros. The ambiguity of "Cómo" as interrogative and exclamative, of the syntax that makes "la mirada" the wounded and the wounder, of the play of light and dark, sight and blindness, of the synesthetic imagery ("el olor del cielo, / la luz hoy cruda, amarga"), and of the image of the city as body, wound, and word reveals the paradoxical relationship between Thanatos and Eros, defeat and triumph, loss and gain, elegy and quest. The wound simultaneously oozes pus and heals. The life-giving breath ("aliento") and the corruption or decay ("podredumbre") could belong to either the wound or the city, yet both are personified as "asombrada y esbelta." Does the shadow at the root of the word "asombrada" give pain or relief? Does it obscure or protect from the light of the sun? Is the surprise disagreeable or uplifting? Does slenderness suggest lack, slightness, insufficiency, or gracefulness, litheness, and elegance?

The wound causes pain but also provides the entryway into the Symbolic. This process not only recapitulates the primary loss of unity (the first past event) but also advances the reacquisition of the Symbolic (language, poetry). By converting elegy into quest, Rodríguez shows that he does not simply regain what was lost. This substitution of language for loss brings about an entirely new linguistic and poetic ability, similar to yet different from previous incursions into the Symbolic.

The sutured and thoroughly healed mouth of the wound ("sus cicatrices / muy seguras") attests to the reacquisition of a healthy narcissism in which the poet converses intimately with himself. "One of the major tasks of the work of mourning and of elegy is to repair the mourner's damaged narcissism."[46] In addition, the poet speaks "sin eco," without Echo, that is, "without allowing that repair to have permanent recourse either to the melancholy form of secondary narcissism or to the fantasies of the primitive narcissism associated with the mirror stage."[47] It is only in light of this repair of the mourner's narcissism that we can reconcile a new beginning with the arrival at the point of gangrene. In the recapitulation of the oedipal resolution through the act of mourning and elegy, the mourner must sterilize, cauterize, exorcise the gangrene with the light of dawn ("tan madrugador"), illumination, penetrating honesty, and open eyes, if he is to attain consolation. This is obviously a painful process, but one that also produces redemption and immortality.

> Pero
> la renovada aparición del viento,
> mudo en su claridad,
> orea la retama de esta herida que nunca
> 50   se cierra a oscuras.
> Herida mía, abrázame. Y descansa.

$$(p.\ 206)^{48}$$

The pivoting of wound into quest is signaled in the isolation of "Pero" on a line by itself, a visual representation of the closing of the (stanzaic) gap. The positively marked words "renovada," "viento," and "claridad" offset the muteness of the ghost-like wind ("aparición") even though it repeats earlier losses and represents absence (light and wind are intangible though perceptible). Frequently used to cover the bodies of the dead in funereal rites, the broom ("retama") not only introduces a stock figure of elegy—the flower as symbol of the regenerative power of the vegetation deity—but also is a symbol of immortality associated with mistletoe and the golden bough that enables Aeneas to descend into the Underworld and return to life.[49] The verb "orea" conveys the gentleness and pleasure of the reemergence of life, language, and inspiration derived from the suturing of the wound not by closing one's eyes or covering the wound ("vendas") but by exposing it to the light ("claridad"). The speaker is not content with merely reporting that the wound embraces him; now he calls for its embrace so that he may heal. First the pain of loss and death came upon him and forced him to accept its embrace; now he overtly requests [*sic*] that embrace, which abates the pain and leads to consolation.

The two longer stanzas of "Herida" counterpoise different approaches to the wound and the word as Rodríguez reformulates his elegiacs as a poetics of quest. The tremendous compression of elegiac elements in the image of the wound, epitomizing the mourner's struggle with loss, characterizes "Herida en cuatro tiempos" as an opening statement and at the same time prefigures the trajectory of *El vuelo*. The final poem of this section, "Un rezo," brings closure to this section but also serves as an "envoi" that dispatches us into the gap/bridge, wound/suture, elegy/quest of the intermediate, mediating, diachronic sections. In Rodríguez's characteristically transgressive and (in)conclusive fashion, "Un rezo" closes this section only to open the healing process (the suturing, the closing of the wound).

As envoi and prayer, "Un rezo" looks to the past and to the future. It concludes what has come before and sends forth into what follows; it commemorates and dedicates. Repetition and questioning—major facets of elegy—stand out in the first stanza, but these elements only enhance the ambivalence of this statement.

> ¿Cómo el dolor, tan limpio y tan templado,
> el dolor inocente, que es el mayor misterio,
> se me está yendo?
> Ha sido poco a poco,
> 5 con la sutura de la soledad
> y el espacio sin trampa, sin rutina
> de tu muerte y la mía.
> Pero suena tu alma, y está el nido
> aquí, en el ataúd,
> 10 con luz muy suave.

> (p. 207)[50]

Rodríguez opens "Un rezo" with the same word that opens this sequence of poems and that reappears at the climactic moment of the second stanza of "Herida." Here he has included specific punctuation, but as usual this question functions literally and rhetorically, and thus expresses disbelief and relief. The speaker uses the interrogative to pose two alternate and simultaneous questions to himself. In true elegiac fashion, he asks how this death and consolation have come about and how it can be possible for him ever to forget what has happened. Tinged with the mourner's guilt and consolation for the death, this question also asks how the speaker can keep from remembering as well as forgetting. How can he forget and yet remember? How can he remember without pain and forget without guilt? How can he let go of the pain and the guilt? How can he reconcile grief and relief?

The ambivalence is reinforced by the "dolor" itself. Reprieving this word from "Como el son de las hojas del álamo" of *Alianza*, Rodríguez reminds us of the contradictory "dolor que es mi victoria." His commitment to face the truth, to seek his poetry in the depth of his being, no matter how painful that may be for him, here acquires a new dimension in a new context: the loss of the loved one, the gap as wound. The adjectives "limpio," "templado," and "inocente" contribute to the ambivalence by suggesting a wound that is at once acute, incisive, and intense, yet pure and open; temperate, moderate, yet tempered; flexible yet strong; unexpected yet sacrificial. Moreover, a mystery can perplex us and defy logical explanation, but thanks to the religious connotations evoked by "rezo," a mystery is also the miraculous that awes and amazes.

In addition to the repetition of "dolor" and the alliteration in "mayor misterio," the second verse syntactically implies a gradual unfolding and layering that separates the mourner from the cause of grief. The speaker continues to express these concepts in the verb phrase (where the "se" is grammatically ambiguous) and in the repetitive "poco a poco" in the next sentence. This response to his own question (though it does not provide an answer) underscores the impersonality of the verb phrases to indicate more distance between the speaker and his grief. The images of the suture and space, whether due to painful loneliness or soothing, healing solitude, along with the alliteration of fricatives, add a softness and relaxation to the healing of a sore, painful hurt. The prepositions "con" and "sin" establish a play of presence and absence, the presence of language (the suture) representing the absence of the loved one. But this absent presence also refers to the speaker's language; he has achieved distance and healing without self-deceit ("sin trampa") and without the superficial, formulaic expressions of grief through the customs of mourning ("sin rutina").

Recurrence to the direct address of the lost loved one comes as a shock. While the pronouns define the distance between them and make the lost one present though absent in language, they also add a note of intense intimacy.[51] The work of mourning is having a beneficent effect, but at the same time the quest poses a challenge because of the honesty and intimacy with which Rodríguez approaches the poetic act. The death of the loved one encourages the poet to relinquish a former self and a former approach to the poetic act and to plumb even deeper into self with renewed motivation.

Even though the loved one is absent, her presence reverberates in the speaker's life and words. Supporting the distance between addressee and speaker, the images of the nest and the coffin contrast yet combine life and death, comfort and pain, consolation and grief, presence and absence. The repetition of the /u/ in "el ataúd, / con luz muy suave" is soft, soothing, and consoling, as well as sad, haunting, and mournful.

As a result, the light—the prototypical elegiac symbol—marks a blending of light and shadow, a light softened by shadow, a shadow soothed by light. In these images, Rodríguez expresses the mixed effects of sadness and tenderness, grief and consolation, elegy and quest.

In the first stanza of "Un rezo," the emphasis falls on the repetition of loss and grieving, on the mediation of loss with language, and on the representation of the absent in the presence of language. In contrast, the emphasis in the second stanza shifts to redemption of the loved one and the rehearsal of the poet's immortality. To achieve that immortality, the speaker must renew his quest and place himself at risk.

> Te has ido. No te vayas. Tú me has dado la mano.
> No te irás. Tú, perdona, vida mía,
> hermana mía,
> que esté sonando el aire
> 15 a ti, que no haya techos
> ni haya ventanas con amor al viento,
> que el soborno del cielo traicionero
> no entre en tu juventud, en tu tan blanca,
> vil muerte.
> 20 Y que tu asesinato
> espere mi venganza, y que nos salve,
> porque tú eres la almendra
> dentro del ataúd. Siempre madura.
>
> (p. 207)[52]

Elaborating on the phrase "se me está yendo" from the previous stanza, the three time frames of past, present, and future in "Te has ido. No te vayas. . . . / No te irás" prefigure the next three sections of *El vuelo* and capture the contradictory emotions of the speaker. He admits that the loved one is gone, he is reluctant to accept that loss at the same time that he recognizes it, and he realizes that she will always be present for him in spite of the reality that she has died. His request for forgiveness is based on his sense of guilt—for having relinquished her and for not having done so, for doubting her presence, and for thinking that he could ever forget her. It also signals the dedicatory function of the envoi because this is the one place in the entire text of *El vuelo* in which he specifically mentions his sister and her premature death.

The three complements of this request further develop the concept of the envoi as a dedication to the future. First, there is a conventional appeal to the addressee to forgive the hollowness and the insufficiency of this lament, a crying out that makes the air reverberate; he apologizes in advance for his awkward expressions of grief.[53] His apology continues in the images of the roof and the windows. Having no limit, his grief may seem inappropriate or out of proportion because it is so sincere, intimate, and exposed to others. But he also recognizes that he must open his heart and ventilate and refresh his emotions, yet he is lacking windows. He is still reluctant to make those forays into the recesses of his wound, windows being his painful but illuminating insight into self. Finally, he would like to offer an ideal, lofty compensation for her death by investing the openness and beauty of the sky in his words, but he knows that this would be a misdemeanor, a crime that would betray the sincerity of his feelings. This envoi expresses a self-humiliation that heightens the pathos and marks the first step in his reaching inside to confront the insufficiency of his words.

The speaker follows these apologies with a healthy outburst of anger when he refers to "tu tan blanca, / vil muerte." Her death has been both sterile and pure, useless and innocent. He regrets that she will not be able to see the beauty of his words as well as recognizing that his words are in reality ineffectual against her death. The violence and anger—evident in "vil"—reemerges in the words "asesinato" and "venganza," but there seems to be a shift in focus to the future with the conjunction "Y." Now the "que" implies a prayer for what the poet hopes to accomplish with his writing. The switch from the possessive adjectives "*tu* asesinato" and "*mi* venganza" to "que *nos* salve" unites them even though they have been separated. His words will redeem and give immortality to both of them because he will come to grips with his pain and grief and confront them in his poetry.

Instead of visualizing the loved one as a vulnerable, precariously blooming almond tree, the poet now metaphorizes her into a seed, a promise of life and immortality in the springtime renewal of life, growth, and flowering.[54] We would expect the almond to be encased in its shell, protected and guarding potential life. The substitution of the word "ataúd" for the shell indicates that the poet's words will encase her and that she will be an eternal source of life, hope, and inspiration to him precisely because he is not afraid to confront his feelings. The expression of his emotions will always be potent within the casing of his mediating words.

Repetition of the /u/ in "ataúd" and "madura" echoes the soothing and mournful alliteration at the end of the first stanza and alerts us to another richly complex resonance. Isolating the phrase "Siempre madura" at the end of the poem, Rodríguez remits us yet again to the opening phrase of *Don de la ebriedad* and recalls the closing intertextuality of the Gospel according to John, "Unless a grain of wheat shall fall and die . . ." The conflation of opening and closing—fulfilling the purpose of the envoi and of the first section of *El vuelo*—with the word "madura" ironically focuses on a death that is (eternally) capable of producing (eternal) life. This seed is always ripe, always pregnant, always about to burst forth in life if the poet will continue his quest.

The final poem of "Herida en cuatro tiempos" serves the double function of closing the most intense, bitter, and angry section of the work of mourning (the "herida") and dedicates the poet to his quest. The next three sections of *El vuelo de la celebración* will form the gap and the bridge that both separate and unite the two poems that frame the text and determine its structure and meaning. Now that we have laid the foundation of the elegiac process, we can move through these poems diachronically to the lasting synchronic moment of "Elegía desde Simancas."

COMING TO TERMS WITH LOSS: PRESENT REMEMBRANCE OF THE PAST

Foreshadowed by "Aventura de una destrucción," the poems of section II contain images that juxtapose past and present. Each of the scenes and objects the speaker encounters in the world around him reminds him of the loss he has experienced at the same time that they substantiate some aspect of the loved one. These scenes substitute the present object for the lost loved one, simultaneously causing pain and consolation by reminding the speaker of his loss and by recuperating that which has been lost.[55] Personification of these objects as female figures obliquely represents the lost loved one, while frequent images of flight suggest loss and incipient joy.[56]

Another frequent image in these poems—as in all of *El vuelo*—is music, closely related to images of weaving and textuality, prominent elegiac conventions. The writing of these poems begins the process of suturing, of drawing a veil of words over the loss that dominates the speaker's vision. Just as music is composed of the temporal development of sounds that quickly fade to be replaced by others, so poetry depends on the temporal, diachronic unfolding of language. As music creates an uplifting, transcendent experience, so poetry converts the tangible, thus transient signifier into the intangible but transcendent signified, a paradoxical relationship between presence and absence evident in the juxtaposition of past and present in these poems.

The apparent simplicity of "Arena," the first poem in this section, belies its profound poignancy. Without giving us all the anecdotal details, in a few bold strokes the poet portrays himself kneeling on the beach, scooping a handful of sand, and letting it slip through his fingers. This contemplative moment evokes the impermanence of felicity and life that reminds the speaker of the lost loved one.

> La arena, tan desnuda y tan desamparada,
> tan acosada,
> nunca embustera, ágil,
> con su sumisa libertad sin luto
> 5   me está lavando ahora.
>
> La vanagloria oscura de la piedra
> hela aquí: entre la yema
> de mis dedos,
> con el susurro de su despedida
> 10   y con su olor a ala tempranera.
>
> (p. 208)[57]

The adjectives of vv. 1–3 readily convert the indistinct, nondescript sand into a female figure. Indeed, because sand conforms to the shape of its container, it is, according to Chevalier and Gheerbrandt, "símbolo de la matriz." Representing "una búsqueda de descanso, de seguridad, de regeneración," the sand as matrix is associated with preoedipal unity with the mother and the primary loss of that unity.[58] If the sand is the matrix, the adjectives "desnuda," "desamparada," and "acosada" not only describe the vulnerable, defenseless condition of the sand in need of protection from the wind and water, but also adopt erotic overtones. A sense of inconstancy, frivolity, seductiveness, and deceitful agility are emphatically denied by "nunca" as unacceptable characteristics. This description idealizes the female figure and reveals the speaker's childlike, painfully protective attitude toward her.

The ambivalence of this figure begins to emerge clearly in the fourth verse, where we again encounter the motif of presence and absence in the prepositions "con" and "sin." Although this female figure subjects its liberty to higher forces and resigns itself to its fate, it nonetheless maintains its independence. Another paradox can be found in the phrase "sin luto." This phrase may mean that the sand/woman has submitted without bitterness, complaint, regret, or sadness ("luto" can mean "duelo, pena, aflicción"), but also that its liberty is unending, timeless, and incapable of being lost. Consequently, there is no need to mourn. The key image in this portrayal appears in the word "lavando." This verb connotes water and cleansing, but here the poet applies it to the sand. As Chevalier and Gheerbrandt point out, sand is "purificadora, líquida como el agua, abrasiva como el fuego" and thus partakes of the qualities of water and fire: It cleanses and purifies, destroys and regenerates, soothes and burns.[59]

The focus shifts from the characterization of the sand to the speaker's reaction to it in the second stanza. Even durable, hard rock is reduced to these tiny particles, this "empty glory" that the speaker can hold with the tips of his fingers. The phrase "hela aquí" expresses wonder and disdain, contemplation and pathetic poignancy as the speaker ponders this phenomenon. Such contemplation may confer solace, given that it forms part of a natural process. But disdain for the insignificance to which the solidity of rock has been reduced is equally evident. Repetition and alliteration— elements that we have already identified with the poetics of mourning—round off this half of the poem with further references to premature loss. But these images of loss (absence) are perceived through the senses of sound and smell (presence). These contradictions reflect the relationship between past and present that will become more pronounced in the final stanza.

> Vuela tú, vuela,
> pequeña arena mía,
> canta en mi cuerpo, en cada poro, entra
> en mi vida, por favor, ahora que necesito
> 15   tu cadencia, ya muy latiendo en luz,
> con el misterio de la melodía
> de tu serenidad,
> de tu honda ternura.
>
>   (p. 208)[60]

A shift to the direct address of the sand accompanies a change in the imagery to a bird and its song, prototypical elegiac imagery.[61] Repetition of the first command calls attention to the ambivalence of the word "vuela." The speaker may be pleading that the sand leave him alone, that it go away and stop reminding him of his loss; but he may also be urging it to soar, to take wing. On the one hand, the poet has lost his ability and his desire to celebrate because of the death of the loved one; but on the other hand, he is painfully, almost futilely invoking his words to help him go beyond grief and to draw a veil between him and loss. The bird's song adopts metapoetic, elegiac dimensions through which the poet hopes to fill the gap in his life.

Further allusions to music continue to articulate this ambivalence. The abrupt enjambment in the phrase "ahora que necesito / tu cadencia" (vv. 14–15) counterpoises the speaker with the other, separating them at the same time that he requests that she permeate his life. "Cadencia" can refer to the temporal distribution of rhythmic accents in music and poetry, a measurement of time that negates time's passage. This word derives from the Latin meaning "to fall" and can indicate a drop in the tone of voice, a modulation or inflection of voice. The speaker needs to hear the voice of the loved one in his own voice, needs her to be present even though she is absent. He needs to be reminded of her by the sand/bird/song—the veil of words—even though it is painful. The gerund "latiendo" describes the throbbing pain of an infection or sore as well as a vital heartbeat. The act of writing has an abreactive, cathartic effect, as we saw above in "lavando."

The reference to melody confirms this reading. The inflection of voice that the speaker wishes to hear in his words is a mystery, incomprehensible and inexplicable yet present, something that is attractive and pleasant as it is painful and frightening. Serenity connotes the silence with which the melody is interwoven and intimately related. The combination "honda ternura" presents the contradiction of depth (pain, penetration, intensity) and superficiality (softness, lightness, gentleness). The conflation of mystery, melody, serenity, and tenderness with the preposition "de" grammatically embodies this paradox. The juxtaposition of these words encapsulates the paradoxical relationship between past and present, the painful loss and the act of describing it, entry into the wound as quest. The brevity and simplicity of "Arena" belies its profound poignancy.

Although *El vuelo* boasts some staples of the Rodríguez canon such as "Ballet del papel" and "Hilando" among others, this work also contains some of the poet's most beautiful and rich texts that critics have not ventured to tackle. One such poem is "Amarras," which, like the other poems of this section, juxtaposes past and present. Each of the scenes and objects the speaker encounters in the world around him reminds him of the loss he has experienced at the same time that they instantiate the absent one. These scenes substitute the lost loved one with the present object (and the poem as text), simultaneously causing pain and consolation by reminding the speaker of his loss but recuperating that which has been lost, a paradoxical relationship between past and present, presence and absence.

Painting a seascape at low tide, a scene that constitutes the pathetic fallacy characteristic of elegy and depicts the wound as gap and loss, the poet focuses on a rope (both umbilical cord and woven thread) mooring a boat to a dock.[62] This scene represents the original loss of union with the mother, a basic topos of elegiac poetry. When read in the context of elegiac mourning, a clearer example of the *fort-da* game might be difficult to find. Like the child Freud observed playing with the spool, repeating absence and presence and using language as a means of gaining control over his emotions caused by the absence of the mother, the mourner here uses repetition and images of textuality to deal with his loss.[63] "Amarras" epitomizes this experience because the poet probes the wound as he begins to suture it, inscribing gaps in the text as he weaves it. This loss, along with images of separation and the mother, underlies the language of the opening stanza.

Cómo se trenza y cómo nos acoge
el nervio, la cintura de la cuerda,
tan íntima de sal,
y con esta firmeza temblando de aventura,
5   bien hilada, en el puerto. Está la fibra
del esparto muy dura y muy templada,
algo oxidada. Hay marea baja.
Bonanza. Y el yodo en cada hebra,
donde el sudor de manos,
10   entre el olor de las escamas, ciñe
el rumbo, y el silencio del salitre,
en cada nudo.

(p. 210)[64]

The repetition of "cómo" in the first verse echoes the ambivalence of this word as interrogative and exclamative at the beginning of "Aventura de una destrucción" and later in "Herida en cuatro tiempos."[65] This ambivalence opens a gap in the language of the text. At the same time, references to weaving abound in the opening verses, each time varying slightly: "[S]e trenza," "hilada," "fibra," "hebra," and "nudo" all suggest textuality as the speaker describes this seascape. Because of these images, we might think of the rope mooring the boat to the dock as an umbilical cord that unites the speaker with the lost (m)other—the sea at low tide—as well as his siblings. Indeed, "el puerto" is a symbol of the matrix of mother and text. The womb of the mother is that which unites the speaker with his sister. Her death has strained the connection between them, just as the ebbing of the tide has made the rope taut; and it reminds the poet of the primary separation from the (m)other. The text as knot, nodal point, and suture helps the poet sustain the connection with the lost loved ones in spite of the grief and pain occasioned by loss.

If we examine the structure of this stanza and the sentences that compose it, we discover images of a gap at the same time that there is a suturing of that gap. The binary parallelism of the first verse provides the first instance of this pattern. The conjunction "y" joins and separates one from the other, a device echoed in v. 6 in the parallel phrases "muy dura y muy templada" and in the phrase "algo oxidada."[66] Another example of this gap-and-suture motif entails a change in the speaker's focus. The terse sentences at the center of this stanza—"Hay marea baja. / Bonanza."— interrupts the focus on the rope and the knot and expands the perspective to the horizon. It is almost as if the intensity of his contemplation of the rope and the strain and grief it represents are too powerful. The speaker must look away and take in the panorama, before being irresistibly drawn back to the rope. This hiatus describing the absence of the tide and the clear sky—the infinite gap of the horizon where sea and sky meet but never meet—interrupts the flow of the speaker's thoughts with its pauses and the emptiness these images portray.

Before this pause, the speaker had set the scene and focused his attention on the rope and what it means to him. Though he momentarily turns away, reluctant to give himself over to those painful emotions of absence, when he returns to the rope, he concentrates on its intricate details. He mentions "el yodo en cada hebra," "el sudor de las manos," "el olor de las escamas," and "el silencio del salitre"—repetitive, parallel phrases that represent different sensorial perceptions and convey his contradictory emotions as he contemplates his grief. The fiber of the rope (as umbilical cord and connection) has acquired a number of nuances that now form part and parcel of its composition. The iodine stings and stains the rope; the sweat of hard work, of hands pulling the rope, connotes personal investment; the fish scales protect, but are stripped away; the salt is bitter and corrosive, yet it is a staple of life. These emotions determine and constitute the knot that binds the boat to the dock, a knot now under severe strain because of the low tide—the loss of the loved one, which repeats the primary loss of the (m)other. The syntax of this sentence, like a knot, takes many twists and turns, again revealing gaps.[67]

Significantly, the stanzaic break—a patent gap in the text—immediately follows the word "nudo." This arrangement represents the pattern of six of the eight poems included in its section, each with a gap between two stanzas.[68] More repetition characterizes the second stanza, linking it with the first.

> Tiembla el cordaje sin zozobra en
> el pretil del muelle,
> 15 cuando mi vida se ata sin rotura,
> ya sin retorno al fin y toca fondo.
> Pero qué importa ya. Y está la fibra
> del esparto muy dura y muy segura,
> sin la palpitación de marejada,
> 20 del oleaje sucio, de la espuma
> del destino.
> Pero qué importa ya. Y está la cuerda
> tensa y herida.
> ¿Y dónde, dónde la oración del mar
> 25 y su blasfemia?
>
> (p. 210)[69]

In the opening sentence of this stanza, "Tiembla" duplicates "temblando" (v. 4), "cordaje" repeats "cuerda" and the other images of weaving, and "se ata" is similar to "se trenza." The odd line break in vv. 13–14 captures the tension of the rope and the strain of the separation between the stanzas and between the speaker and the lost loved one. As the liminal point of demarcation between land and sea, stability and instability, "el pretil del muelle" further defines the site of the wound where the speaker now stands. The repeated preposition in the phrases "sin zozobra" (in itself a repetitive word), "sin rotura," and "sin retorno" (note the alliteration) emphasizes loss and absence.

The objects of the prepositions, in contrast, suggest a certain tranquility and resignation, so that the phrase "toca fondo" adopts ambivalent meanings. On the one hand, it can indicate that the speaker has reached the nadir of his sorrow and despair and feels that he is irrevocably sunken. On the other hand, by relinquishing himself to that loss, by accepting it as a reality and convincing himself that he can do nothing about these events, he has reached a solid footing and will now be able to move forward in the work of mourning. This phrase marks a gap in language—the coexistence of two totally incompatible meanings in the same words—that characterizes Rodríguez's poetry in general and manifests itself in the remainder of "Amarras."

Verbatim repetition of the phrase "Pero qué importa ya" in vv. 17 and 22 compounds the ambivalent lack of punctuation. In one regard, this expression could invoke the speaker's complete hopelessness and despair, his having "touched bottom." But read in another light, he could be saying in resignation, "All right. I've lost someone very dear to me. Now I need to decide what is important in order to continue my life." Both of these sentences are followed by a repetition with variation of the sentence in vv. 5–7 of the first stanza. If in the first stanza he characterizes the fiber as "muy dura y muy templada, / algo oxidada," in the first repetition he changes his affirmation to "muy dura y muy segura." The internal rhyme highlights the change from "templada" to "segura," suggesting that while strained, the connection cannot be broken.

Does the qualification "sin la palpitación de marejada" imply that as long as the tide is out, the cord will not be tested and so will hold? As long as the speaker can keep his emotions at bay, not allow himself to be jostled by the ups and downs, the ebb and flow of life, he will not suffer. This option provides scant consolation, however, because life is not so predictable and unchanging. His statement thus smacks of sarcasm, bitterness, anger, and despair—healthy expressions of mourning. It could also imply that at this moment when his strength is at low ebb and he feels empty and lifeless, he has an opportunity to recuperate, to catch his breath, to assess his situation, and to recognize that in spite of the tremendous strain, the rope has not broken, the knot has held.

The next repetition substitutes "cuerda" for "fibra," omits the mention of "el esparto," and describes the rope as "tensa y herida." In the wake of the ambivalent "Pero qué importa ya," these changes broach two contradictory possibilities. One is that the rope has been weakened and frayed by the stress; the other is that this wounding has led to greater confidence in its strength. Muscles that do work tire and stretch to the breaking point (cf. "el sudor de manos"), but that trial (in this case the "work" of mourning) increases one's strength. Note that "tensa" can mean "taut" in the sense of firm, tight, well disciplined; and "herida," derived from "herir," can connote the striking or pulsing of a musical instrument (another elegiac convention), the causing of an intense sensation, or the moving of the heart or soul to profound emotion. Although the death of the loved one has wounded the poet, it has also fomented his quest for more profound emotion and more lyrical expression in his poetry.

The final question begins with a repetition of the interrogative "dónde," again pointing to its ambivalence. As an expression of the *ubi sunt?* theme, it defines loss: Something that was present in the past is now absent, gone, irrevocable. But as an expression of quest, it shows the speaker looking to the future, seeking the strong *verbal* expressions of, on the one hand, prayer—that is, hope, praise, inspiration—and on the other, blasphemy—the healthy expression of grief and anger at loss, the release of immobilizing tension and distress (the *fort-da* repetition).

Ramazani has cogently argued that the elegiac poet feels a contradiction because he takes advantage of the death of the loved one to advance his/her own poetic career.[70] In Rodríguez's case, the confrontation with pain, with the difficult acceptance of profound emotions, is consonant with his poetics. To define himself as a unique poetic voice and to achieve immortality through his aesthetic production, he has discovered in his previous works that he must relentlessly plumb his psyche. He must confront his innermost feelings in spite of the often unpleasant and painful consequences of such a self-assessment. Elegy becomes a vehicle for continuing his poetic quest for the most truthful albeit painful poetic expression.

By confronting the loss of the loved one and revisiting the original separation of the self from the (m)other, Rodríguez engages in the poetic act as a means of seeking elegiac consolation and of continuing his quest for self. In the weaving of the text, he sutures the wound at the same time that he continues to explore and deepen it. The elegiac conventions that we have noted in "Amarras" allow Rodríguez to inscribe the wound, the gap in language, and to pursue his poetic identity, as he carries out the healthy work of mourning. As a result, he continues the poetic tradition through repetition of the elegiac genre as he recuperates and revitalizes its conventions, paradoxically conflating consolation and quest, presence and absence, loss and gain, wound and suture.

Unlike "Amarras," "Ballet del papel" is a staple of the Rodríguez canon. Debicki's perceptive discussion of this poem and my own analysis of it in another context obviate a thorough analysis here. Some additional comments and insights are nonetheless warranted in light of the elegiac dimensions of *El vuelo*. Sacks designates staging as one of the principle devices of elegy.[71] Whereas Sacks emphasizes the exchange between antiphonal voices as if in dialogue with one another, a variation of staging more consonant with Rodríguez's poetry can be found in "Ballet."[72] Instances of framing, creating a complex relationship between periphery and center, are frequent in Rodríguez's poetry. Here the interplay between the trivial, mundane scene of paper littering the street and the poet's metaphorical impressions foregrounds the street as stage and the paper as dancers.

The metaphors of birds and of a swarm of bees define different levels of the frame as proscenium. But these frames are paradoxical. First, the speaker describes two types of flight, two types of birds. One skims along the ground, suggesting perhaps weakness, insecurity, or dependency, an inability or unwillingness to soar. The powerful image of the falcon, its prowess in hunting, the control it has over its actions ("aleteo / sagaz"), its dexterity and strength, contrasts with the "vuelo bajo" of the other bird and implies the achievement of great height. Next the bees, symbolic of intelligence because of their ability to communicate the direction of flowers by "dancing" in relation to the sun's position, and of immortality because of the honey (ambrosia) they produce, are nevertheless anonymous, lacking individuality and identity.[73]

The poet introduces both of these metaphoric comparisons with a description of the anecdotal scene. This scene contains elements of fleetingness and loss: The wind scatters the paper and comes from the west at sunset, traditional images of death and loss. But, as Debicki points out, the metaphors of birds and bees are complemented by references to music (the elegiac convention). These contradictions help us realize that the poet rejects these images at the same time that he invokes them just before he reaches the essence of the scene. The different types of paper represent stock characters from a ballet, a puppet show, an opera, or classical drama. Thanks to the previous framing images, these stock figures vaguely profile particulars of the poet's life (his mother and his sister's death) and a general "plot" of life and death. The staging of these figures works against the reminders of loss the speaker finds in the mundane scene before him. Simultaneous with the foregrounding of painful emotions, staging the event distances him from his grief (*fort-da*).

A return to the mimetic scene accompanies the speaker's entrance in the first person and shifts the speaker from audience to participant. This significant step in the poet's ability to limit the encroachment of the past in the present and to gain control over his experience of loss leads to an important elegiac declaration at the end of the poem.

> Va anocheciendo. El viento huele a lluvia
> y su compás se altera. Y vivo la armonía,
> ya fugitiva,
> del pulso del papel bajo las nubes
>
> . . . .
> 30   . . . muy cercano
> de mi niñez perdida y ahora recién ganada
> tan delicadamente, gracias a este rocío
> de estos papeles, que se van de puntillas,
> ligeros y descalzos,
> 35   con sonrisa y con mancha.
> Adiós, y buena suerte. Buena suerte.
>
>   (pp. 212–13)[74]

The rain announced by the wind can function as the pathetic fallacy, the intensification of the speaker's grief, his tears. But rain as water that cleanses and fertilizes creates ambivalence. When the speaker says of the wind that "su compás se altera," he signals a change in his perspective. (He will amplify this change in the next poem "Lágrima" where the tear is bitter and forms a veil that alters his perspective on reality.)[75]

The same duality is evident in the phrase "Y vivo la armonía, / ya fugitiva." In addition to situating the speaker center stage, the phrase "armonía fugitiva" can stress the fleetingness of life and the essence of loss; but it also suggests that the pulsing life that imbues the paper's dance revitalizes him by reviving delightful memories of the past and quickening his poetic acumen. The phrase "mi niñez perdida y recién ganada" recalls the loss/gain motif that in *El vuelo* takes the form of elegy/quest. Instead of a downpour of rain, there is a sprinkling of dew—the delicate dance of the paper.[76] The speaker concludes his recuperation of lost innocence with a classical elegiac topos: *ave atque vale*.[77] The staging of loss allows the speaker to distance himself from his grief. Though he is still aware of loss and grief, positive aspects of the loss begin to assert themselves. The speaker is beginning to let go of his grief and to recognize the positive effects memories of the loved one can have on the present.

The touches of humor in "Ballet del papel" arise partly from the juxtaposition of the mimetic and the symbolic, but this humor is wistful and poignant for that very reason.[78] "Perro de poeta" employs humor much more boldly, such that it may seem an inappropriate component for an elegiac work. Originally written as an homage to Vicente Aleixandre and published before the Nobelist's death, "Perro de poeta" is an enigmatic poem that betrays Rodríguez's mischievous, ludic side. To my mind, this poem demonstrates the progress the speaker has made in dealing with his grief at the same time that it is a tender tribute to his sister.[79]

First, we must recognize that Aleixandre, as Rodríguez's mentor, fulfilled the role of a father figure, as Rodríguez has stated on more than one occasion.[80] In the elegiac context, he represents not only the symbolic entry into language but also poetic inheritance. If the speaker of *El vuelo* needs to heal the wound caused by the loss of the loved one, he must identify himself with the father figure.[81] By specifically mentioning the dog's name, "Sirio," the poet also calls forth the mythology of Orion and the constellation of Can Maior. The poet as hunter (quester) adequately describes the speaker of *El vuelo* as well as Aleixandre, so that a parallel situation obtains between Aleixandre and his dog and Rodríguez and the star in the constellation, a point of light in the darkness of grief that now guides the hunter/seeker.

Oddly enough, Orion was a twin (brother of Arion), and Sirius is a binary star composed of two smaller (twin) stars, just as Rodríguez's sister Mari Carmen was a twin.[82] Another oddity is that Sirio was a black dog, whereas a star is a light in the darkness.[83] These biographical and mythical allusions lie beneath the surface of the poem and add to the interplay between the ludic and the serious, the anecdotal and the symbolic, causing us to wonder if this is not a sarcastic, defiant poem mocking death and the Law of the Father (the Symbolic) in addition to being a humorous, ludic, mischievous, and quite tender expression of respect and gratefulness. Keeping these latent levels of meaning in mind, let us briefly examine the language of the poem—especially its humor—to appreciate the irony at work in this modern elegiac poem.

> A ti, que acariciaste
> el destello infinito del traje humano cuando
> dentro de él bulle el poema.
> A ti, de rumboso bautizo,
> 5   que con azul saliva y lengua zalamera
> lamiste frescos pulsos trémulos de altas bridas,
> unas manos creadoras, con mimo de sal siempre,
> ahora que recuerdo
> años de amistad limpia
> 10   te silbo. ¿Me conoces?

(p. 215)[84]

In the elegiac tradition, the direct address of the absent one invokes his/her presence, a symbolic use that substitutes language for loss. This address is far from direct, however, if we consider that the humorous punning on the canine code is a way of disguising the speaker's address of his sister. Indeed, the altisonant language of vv. 2–

7 appears to mock the speaker's sense of his own overblown reputation. This indirect self-mockery (self-effacement) forms an integral part of the elegist's need for humility. The scene of the dog following faithfully upon its master's heals while the mind of the great poet is amid the stars is comic enough, but by using the phrase "el traje humano," the speaker suggests a puffed-up importance that in the final analysis is merely a mortal.

The phrase "de rumboso bautizo" undercuts this pomposity with its oblique allusion to a dog's habit of marking its territory with its urine. On the other hand, the speaker may be referring to the many pet names that this animal had acquired because its master was a poet, that is, one who names and has a rich command of language. The act of licking the hands of the master is related to the opening verb "acariciaste." Both actions indicate that the one addressed amused the poet, brought him back to earth, and made him laugh at himself when his emotions became too overpowering, when the struggle with language required extreme exertion to rein in his thoughts. The hyperbolic language of these images points to the speaker's irony and reveals a serious invocation of the lost loved one in this memory of her effect on him. Even the whistle as a way of calling this person to memory may refer to the shepherd's pipes, recalling the myth of Pan and Echo, a myth of metamorphosis in which the mourner substitutes music (poetry) for the loss of the loved one. The next lines are nostalgic and include two significant questions.

> Fue hace seis años, cuando
> mi cadena era de aire, como la que tu amo
> te puso en el jardín. Os mirabais, pisabais
> tú su región inmensa y sin murallas,
> 15 él tu reino sin huellas.
> ¿Quién era el servidor? ¿Quién era el amo?
> Nadie lo sabrá nunca
> pero el ver las miradas era alegre.
>
> (p. 215)[85]

Because "Perro de poeta" was originally published in 1959, the above verses recall to the speaker's memory what was probably his first visit to the famous poet's house (ca. 1953, six years prior to the poem's composition). This recollection with its double framing of the past not only demonstrates the speaker's willingness to make incursions into the past to revive pleasant memories, but also remarks upon the special relationship between the poet and his dog. Once again, this relationship describes the invisible bond between the speaker and his younger sister, a bond that gave him freedom and inspired him, and yet united them strongly.[86]

The questions further define the reciprocity of their relationship. The dog accompanies the poet through "su región inmensa y sin murallas," and the poet has the imagination to follow the dog's "reino sin huellas." The delight both poets (Aleixandre and Rodríguez) receive from their companions and the service each renders to the other refers obliquely to the inspiration provided to poets through their contact with these sensitive, innocent creatures. The word "huellas" significantly points to a metapoetic level: the trace in the sign that entices the poet to follow.

The subsequent verses describe the death of the beloved one and hint at the causes and reasons for that death. The context of this telling is a children's tale, an intertext that, as well as lending a nostalgic, fanciful aura to the event, begins a process of mythification.

> Un buen día, atizado por todas las golondrinas del
>   mundo
> 20   hasta ponerlo al rojo,
>   callaste para aullar eterno aullido.
>   No ladraste a los niños ni a los pobres
>   sino a los malos poetas, cuyo tufo
>   olías desde lejos, fino rastreador.
> 25   Quizá fueron sus hijos
>   quienes en esa hora de juerga ruin, colgaron
>   de tu rabo,
>   de tu hondo corazón asustadizo
>   la ruidosa hojalata cruel e impresa
> 30   de sus vendidos padres. Fue lo mismo.
>   Callaste. . . .

                                                    (pp. 215–16)[87]

The image of the swallows first evokes a hearth glowing with hot coals, which suggests a brilliant sunset, the passionate dying of the light. But the shape, the flight, and the piercing cries of the swallows allude to the knifelike violence of the event. Just when the speaker might fall into painful melancholy, however, humor again undercuts the scene: Sirio barked only at bad poets whose foul odor he could smell at a distance. This image may refer to an intuitive ability possessed by the speaker's sister to identify insincere, shallow people. Couching the revenge of these individuals in a story of children tying tin cans to the tail of a dog further stylizes the death. The tale converts the victim into an innocent sacrifice as it satirizes the assassins as sadistic children of envious parents interested only in material gain. Using different levels of stylization (the children's tale and the humorous treatment of bad poets) allows the speaker to distance the pain, bitterness, and anger he feels with a series of linguistic veils. Mythification continues the veiling and distancing in the final verses.

>   . . . Pero ahora
>   vuelvo a jugar contigo desde esta sucia niebla
>   con la que el aire limpio de nuestra Guadarrama
>   haría un sol de julio, junto con tus amigos,
> 35   viendo sobre tu lomo la mano leal, curtida,
>   y te silbo, y te hablo, y acaricio
>   tu pura casta, tu ofrecida vida
>   ya para siempre, «Sirio»,
>   buen amigo del hombre
> 40   compañero del poeta, estrella que allá brillas

con encendidas fauces
en las que hoy meto al fin, sin miedo, entera,
esta mano mordida por tu recuerdo hermoso.

(p. 216)[88]

The juxtaposition of the preterit in "Callaste" with the present in the adverb "ahora" is conjoined in the verb phrase "vuelvo a" as repetition of a past event melding with the present in the scene before him. Even though he is wrapped in mist at night in the mountains (perhaps he is at the top of low clouds), the speaker can still see the stars, especially the constellations of Orion and Can Maior. The mist—droplets of moisture—may be the veil of words (the speaker's tears, his mourning); but by raising his eyes upward, he can see the stars clearly. The stars portend the clear light of a summer's day in the pure air of the mountains, symbols of the speaker's quest for new heights in his poetry.

When he recalls the loyal and weathered hand of his mentor on the black back of the dog, he simultaneously calls to Sirius (the star) and its friends (other stars around it) to provide him with the same loyalty of inspiration that the dog provided for its master. This comparison of Orion the hunter and his dog with the poet shows that Rodríguez now relinquishes himself to a higher spiritual quest in his poetry. If Aleixandre's hand caressing his pet provided him with inspiration, Rodríguez now playfully but fearlessly (half humorously) sticks his hand into the burning jaws and sharp teeth of his grief, the memory of his sister, to achieve a similar poetic stature.

The uneasy combination of two different planes—one occasional, trivial, and humorous, the other symbolic and intensely serious—is a technique Rodríguez has employed often, especially in *Conjuros*. His use of humor in this poem as in "Ballet del papel" demonstrates the extent to which he has come to grips with the specific loss of his sister. We noted earlier that this poem is not divided stanzaically, although a single word ("mundo") is isolated in the center of v. 19, approximately at the midpoint of the poem. This unusual distribution of the words on the page indicates that suturing and healing are beginning to take place. By placing a veil of words between himself and his grief, the elegist has reached a degree of consolation. Having accomplished this feat does not, however, bring an end to the work of mourning. As the imperatives of "Un viento" (the final poem of section II) indicate, the speaker must take the next step in this process in the next section, a coming to terms with his own mortality: the fragile and fleeting condition of life and happiness.

COMING TO TERMS WITH MORTALITY: REENTERING THE PRESENT

"Cantata del miedo," a lengthy poem in three parts, defines the central issue of section III: the elegist's coming to terms with his own mortality. Rodríguez converts the fear of death—a conventional elegiac concern—into quest, however. For if fleeting time and the omnipresent threat of death and loss reveal the misery of the human condition and cause existential crises (as has happened here), they also spark the search for those lasting aspects that will endure beyond the death of the individual.[89] This paradox and the definition of the fear announced in the title constitute the opening verses of "Cantata."

> Es el tiempo, es el miedo
> los que más nos enseñan
> nuestra miseria y nuestra riqueza.
> Miedo encima de un cuerpo,
> 5   miedo a perderlo,
> el miedo boca a boca.
> Miedo al ver esta tierra
> vieja y rojiza, como tantas veces,
> metiendo en ella el ritmo de mi vida,
> 10 desandando lo andado,
> desde Logroño a Burgos. . . .

(p. 221)[90]

Because of the importance of repetition in the elegiac process and the work of mourning as well as in Rodríguez's poetry in general, repetition of the word "miedo" in these verses stands out. The parallelism in vv. 1 and 3 equates time and fear, misery and richness (the loss/gain motif). If fear of the passage of time and death arouse anguish and cause us to withdraw from full participation in life, it also compels us to search for that which is valuable and lasting amid the fleetingness of experience. We can read vv. 4–6 in two different ways then: On the one hand, fear of death hangs over our physical being and stares us in the face, paralyzing all enjoyment of life; but on the other, that fear finds expression in the act of love, a moment of supreme intensity and vitality.

Likewise vv. 7–11 are ambivalent. Mention of the soil invokes the image of a burial and the interment of different experiences of life in the sorrow of loss and the past. Retracing one's steps "desde Logroño a Burgos" (from east to west) suggests undoing all that has been done as a waste of time and effort, a lack of progress and despair with the attempt to advance because all effort results in loss. These lines also speak of a journey, of walking across familiar territory, which in Rodríguez's poetry is an image for writing. Because of the ambiguity of the syntax in this sentence, however, we could just as easily see the speaker walking from west to east, indicating that the act of walking/writing leads to renewal. In other words, the repetition of loss and the reexperiencing of the death of others gives the poet a new appreciation of life and fresh insight into the simple pleasures and commonplace scenes he knows so well. The phrase "metiendo en ella el ritmo de mi vida" alludes to the speaker's own partial death each time he buries a loved one. He stresses his attachment to the transient, but also accents the emotions he invests in the ordinary scenes and events of his life, transforming those transient moments into "rhythm," the stuff of poetry, lasting emotions that imbue mere words with vitality. This ambiguity continues in the syntax, the imagery, and the personification of fear in the subsequent lines.

        . . . Para que no huya,
    para que no descanse y no me atreva
    a declarar mi amor palpable, para
    que ahora no huela
15 el estremecimiento, que es casi inocencia,
    del humo de esas
    hogueras de este otoño,
    vienes tú, miedo mío, amigo mío,
    con tu boca cerrada,
20 con tus manos tan acariciadoras,
    con tu modo de andar emocionado,
    enamorado, como si te arrimaras
    en vez de irte.

                                    (pp. 221–22)[91]

Again, repetition of "para que" and of the negation reveals irony. Although they seem to be different, adding up metonymically, because of the repetition, the four activities of fleeing, resting, declaring his love, and smelling the smoke of autumn bonfires are all equivalent to sedating oneself, closing one's eyes to the transience of life and happiness. The speaker's heightened awareness of this reality prevents him from doing these things and increases his sensitivity to and appreciation of the palpability of love and the almost innocent shiver of smoke. The unspoken sensations of touch and smell convert the smoke into incense, the bonfires into destructive but passionate regeneration of life, and autumn into the promise of spring. Though it is painful to face these feelings, the speaker uses the recognition of his fear as a means of commencing his quest. The fleeing becomes a search, the resting an incessant investigation, the shiver of death the innocent ecstasy of love, of life itself.

The figure of fear is highly enigmatic. By addressing it as another and personifying it as his friend, the speaker reveals that this fear is an intimate part of his life, indeed its very essence. Its closed mouth indicates silence, but it provokes the poet to write; its caressing hands seduce, leading to sensual pleasure; and its seductive walk makes time seem more vivid and immediate rather than fleeting and slipping away. The caricature of this figure—reminiscent of "Nieve en la noche" from *Alianza*—is as attractive as it is repulsive, as magical as it is diabolical.

    Quiero verte la cara
25 con tu nariz lasciva,
    y tu frente serena, sin arrugas,
    agua rebelde y fría,
    y tus estrechos ojos muy negros y redondos,
    como los de la gente de estas tierras.

30 Pequeño de estatura, como todos los santos,
    algo caído de hombros y menudo
    de voz, de brazos cortos, infantiles,
    zurdo,
    con traje a rayas, siempre muy de domingo,

35 de milagrosos gestos y de manos
de tamaño voraz.

(p. 222)[92]

This caricature also reminds us of the description of Eugenio de Luelmo and prefigures the gnomelike "Rey del Humo" in the final poem of this section, "Una aparición." All these impish figures, in which the repulsive and grotesque is the attractive and fascinating, represent the poet's alter ego, making them distorted but accurate portrayals of who the poet himself wants to be.[93] Here the lascivious nose, the cold, unworried brow, and the narrow black eyes depict a sly, inscrutable, but perhaps overly curious, prying figure. Thanks to his Sunday-best striped suit, his small stature, stooped shoulders, weak voice, and short, infantile arms, he seems almost risible, like a mischievous little boy uncomfortably dressed up for an unusually special occasion. He looks both defeated and ready to explode.

As a representation of the passage of time and death, this figure can deceive because of its apparent innocence. But his voracious hands keep taking things from us, and his "miraculous" gestures—making things disappear like a magician—cause even more surprise and pain. We expect to hold onto the beautiful and precious things in life, but this innocent-looking figure is a calculating thief, disguising his true intentions. The final lines of this part of "Cantata" condense the ambivalent and paradoxical nature of grief and quest.

Qué importa tu figura
si estás conmigo ahora respirando, temblando
con el viento del Este.
40 Y es que en él hallaríamos el suspiro inocente,
el poderío de las sensaciones,
la cosecha de la alegría junto a la
del desaliento.

(p. 222)[94]

The punctuation of the first sentence expresses both despair and triumph, while variations on the image of breath ("respirando," "viento," "suspiro," and "desaliento") compound the semantic ambivalence. Running counter to the prevailing direction, the wind from the East could signal the immanence of a storm (grief, sadness, mourning); but since it comes from the East (significantly capitalized), the motif of resurrection and redemption is also present. To breathe this wind would foretell the speaker's own mortality as well as his redemption through the act of poetry. He may be trembling from fear or from the excitement and anticipation of the immanent—destruction and resurrection. A sigh can be an expression of despair, longing, and defeat, but it can also be one of relief, contentment, and satisfaction. Therefore, the powerful sensations of pain, grief, and despair the speaker has experienced and will experience again ("desaliento" connotes expiration of air—death) can be turned into a harvest of joy.

Repetition continues to play a paramount role throughout "Cantata del miedo" and represents the suturing, troping process that takes place in this central section of *El vuelo*. The opening verse of part II of "Cantata" parallels that of part I, where the speaker equates the passage of time with fear ("Es el tiempo, es el miedo") but finds that this fear can cause enrichment as well as misery. This paradoxical process continues with a slight variation in part II, but the speaker adds another layer of mediation in the double repetition of the opening verse.

> Es el miedo, es el miedo.
> Ciego guiando a otro ciego,
> miedo que es el origen de la desconfianza,
> de la maldad, pérdida de la fe,
> 5   burla y almena. Sí, la peor cuña:
> la de la misma madera. Mas también es arcilla
> mejorando la tierra.
>
> (p. 222)[95]

The speaker seems to say that "all we have to fear is fear itself," suggesting that the passage of time is no longer the issue. Rather, it is the fear of confronting reality, his emotions, those matters that cause him pain and yet will lead to greater knowledge. If his fear is the primary concern, he has the courage to take the risk and to triumph. The parallelism of the two verses and the shift from time as fear to fear as fear distances the speaker from the pain of loss (suturing the wound) at the same time that he resolves to confront pain and fear (troping grief into quest).

The intertextual reference to Matt. 15:14 reinforces this double repetition.[96] Not only is the word "ciego" repeated, but the intertextuality (another type of repetition) emphasizes the attitude the speaker rejects by confronting it, allowing the healing process to begin. For when he equates fear with blindness, he adopts a deprecating tone, affirming his commitment to knowledge in spite of the pain. He would rather experience the pain which leads to enlightenment and enrichment than to continue blindly through life. As he states, this blindness, this refusal to confront the serious issues of life directly, "es el origen de la desconfianza, / de la maldad, pérdida de fe, / burla y almena." These images involve the separation of one human being from another; if we cannot be honest with ourselves, we cannot be honest with one another or expect others to be honest with us.

The image of the wedge, driven between two things or into a crevice (gap/wound), implies betrayal since it is made of the same material it splits. This image is based on a proverb: "No hay peor cuña que la de la misma madera," meaning "There is no worse enemy than an alienated friend." As a proverbial intertextuality—another form of repetition—the wedge points in two directions simultaneously, repeating the repetition of the first lines, the biblical intertext, and the concept of honesty with oneself and others. By exploring the wound and facing pain, the elegist can find consolation and healing, although it costs him.

The final statement adds another metaphorical repetition to the series that characterizes this stanza. By itself, clay soil contains too much acid to be fruitful and to stimulate growth; but added with and mixed into other soils, it enhances productivity.[97] "Arcilla" and "tierra" are both types of soil (they are the same), yet the acidity of clay enriches the earth because of its difference. Clay is a metaphor for the speaker's pain, the wound of his loss, which will enrich his life and poetry if he accepts it as a necessary part of life, betraying, wounding, and causing pain, but also enriching and stimulating productivity.

The next stanza of part II of "Cantata" continues the use of repetition and variation in a series of exemplifications. A glass of water, the human body, opening and closing a door, walking through the streets at dawn would all seem to be commonplace circumstances. Yet these images of everyday life adopt magical proportions. Each is introduced by a command, lending them an incantational aura: "*Coge* este vaso de agua"; "*Toca* este cuerpo de mujer"; "*Abre* esa puerta, *ciérrala*"; "*Anda* por esas calles."[98] The poet as magician can discover the sublime, the magical, the extraordinary, in ordinary, concrete, transient moments; because of the pain he has suffered, he can appreciate basic pleasures and find their subtlest nuances. If he does not blind himself to possible pain, he can increase his appreciation of pleasurable aspects of even the most quotidian moments.

The details describing these exemplifications attest to the keen sense of perception the speaker has acquired by accepting his pain. The glass of water is "tan sencilla / y temerosa y misteriosa, y nueva, siempre." By making love to another, "se oye la disciplina de las estrellas, / ahí, en el sobaco sudoroso, en los lunares centelleantes junto / al sexo." Here the allusion to Fray Luis (another intertextual repetition) points to a sublime and mystical ecstasy. But the speaker finds these qualities in the intimacy of smell and sight. These erotic connotations increase the sense of the sublime that exists in the most ordinary circumstances (body odors and birthmarks, imperfections, idiosyncratic though intimate features of life). Both the water and the body "da[n] miedo al contemplar[los]" ["cause fear upon contemplating them"] because both represent risk. To enjoy them is to risk losing them, but knowing that we risk losing them also enables us to enjoy them all the more if we accept that risk, if we do not avoid the pain ("miedo") inherent in the pleasure.

The hinges that allow the door to open and close (a duality we have already noted in several poems by Rodríguez) underscore the ambivalence as their movement and duality become the focus: "ahí, en sus goznes, hallarás tu vida" [there, in its hinges, you will find your life]. The binary oppositions of "audacia/cobardía," "hoy/otras veces," "el estéril recuerdo y el olvido tan adulador" iterate the speaker's attention to the liminal space where pleasure and pain coincide. The images of light, wind, and rain used to describe the dawn are ambivalent as well. At this liminal moment "esta luz grisácea" can be a gray, drab, cloudy menace or a pearly opalescence promising relief and a new beginning. If this light is "pobre de miembros," the speaker may feel alone, that there are few who can accompany him on his early morning walk. But his solitude can cause sadness (because the loss of the beloved leaves him isolated) or be an exclusive pleasure shared by only a few special people. Solitude becomes a pleasurable experience that unites those who can enjoy it: "nos sobrecoge / y da profundidad a la respiración."

That solitude which is our fear is also our love, as the question isolated in the following stanza indicates. Note that this question—as is customary in Rodríguez's poetry—connotes both despair and confidence, true doubt and yet no doubt whatsoever.

¿Nunca secará el sol
lo que siempre pusimos
al aire: nuestro miedo,
nuestro pequeño amor?

(p. 223)[99]

These poignant lines convert the fear into a small, unimportant, and yet tender and meaningful love, and prepare us for the conclusion of this part of "Cantata." The final stanza condenses the temporal planes of future, past, and present, showing that "Cantata" repeats in *mise en abïme* fashion the temporal sequencing of the three center sections of *El vuelo*. Whereas "esperanza" looks to the future and "recuerdo" to the past, "miedo" occurs in the present ("tiempo"), which is both "oscuro" and "luminoso."

Tan poderoso como la esperanza
o el recuerdo, es el miedo,
no sé si oscuro o luminoso, pero
nivelando, aplomando, remontando
nuestra vida.

(p. 223)[100]

The gerunds in the penultimate verse generate equivalence through repetition of the morphemic suffix. To raze is to make straight is to rebuild; in other words, to accept the pain as well as the pleasure of life is difficult but ultimately beneficial.

The third part of "Cantata del miedo" is one of the most moving and powerful instances in Rodríguez's opus, and again repetition is cardinal. These repetitions split the meaning of language and create a double-voiced discourse in consonance with the ambivalent attitudes toward grief and consolation, wound and suture, elegy and quest. As a result, we are unsure whether the opening constitutes a plea or a challenge as the speaker not only personifies but now directly addresses (literally and metaphorically) his fear.

Vamos, amigo mío, miedo mío.
Mentiroso como los pecadores,
ten valor, ten valor.
Intenta seducirme
5   con dinero, con gestos,
con tu gracia acuciante en las esquinas
buscando ese sombrío y fervoroso
beso,
ese abrazo sin goce,
10   la cama que separa, como el lino,
la caña de la fibra.

(p. 224)[101]

The parallel phrases of the first line echo the opening lines of each of the first two parts and also v. 18 of part I. But here the poet has reversed the nouns "amigo" and "miedo," indicative of the change in his attitude, his paradoxical perspective on pain and pleasure. Moreover, the second verse plays against v. 30 of part I ("Pequeño de estatura, como todos los santos"), intensifying the ambivalence. Does he satirically disparage this friend, his fear, or does he invite it to go along with him through the rest of his life? By repeating the phrase "ten valor," the poet calls attention to the dual meaning of this idiomatic expression: (1) to be brave, and (2) to be of value (not to deceive the speaker with its "mentira"). When the speaker asks fear to seduce him, we wonder whether he is being defiant and challenging, or if he now sees the benefits that can accrue from these trials. In that case, he will not resist the threats posed by time and a transient reality, but accept the intensity of life to the fullest—painful or pleasurable—and make a choice between the useful and the useless. Confronting that choice, that "hinge," those "esquinas," brings about the intensity of life as opposed to blindness and evasion.

The linking of images with "con" and "ese" augments the intensity of the sentence, leading to the combination of two intratextualities: "la cama que separa, como el lino, / la caña de la fibra." First the image of the bed recalls the opening section of "Herida en cuatro tiempos" and the linking of the wound (caused by death and the loss of the loved one) with poetry (the poet's dreams and insights). But this image also recalls "El canto de linos" from *Conjuros* and the unforgettable verse "Si la cosecha no es más que el principio." To separate the fiber from the stalk of the flax plant refers to the myth of Linus and his father Apollo and defines a sorting out, a choice between that which is useful, essential, valuable, and that which is useless, discarded, and unproductive.[102] These allusions to his own poetic past again evoke writing and "textualizing" as a means of knowing the self and the project in which Rodríguez is involved in his writing. Repetition in the following verses produces a similar effect, recalling v. 24 of pt. I of "Cantata" and also "Nieve en la noche."

> Quiero verte las lágrimas,
> aunque sean de sidra o de vinagre,
> nunca de miel doméstica.
> 15   Quiero verte las lágrimas
> y quiero ver las mías,
> estas de ahora cuando te desprecio
> y te canto,
> cuando te veo con tal claridad
> 20   que siento tu latido que me hiere,
> me acosa, me susurra, y casi me domina,
> y me cura de ti, de ti, de ti.

(p. 224)[103]

The direct address of the other is particularly effective here because the other is the self just as the healing is pain and gain. Tears are always bitter, but sometimes they are more palatable than at others (we drink a cup of cider, but we use vinegar more sparingly). Typical of his ambivalent outlook, the speaker despises and praises those tears, which he examines but also accepts as his own. The word "claridad" remits us to the first poem of *Don*, reminding us that clarity is a painful blinding ("deslumbramiento") that provides more insight. The word "latido" can connote a heartbeat (life, pulse, activity) and a keen though intermittent pain (sometimes caused by an inflammation, infection, or wound). For that reason, the effect of the "latido" expressed in the subsequent verbs adopts ambivalent propensities, intensified by the repetition: "que me hiere, / me acosa, me susurra, y casi me domina, / y me cura. . . ." "Curar," for example, can mean to heal, but also to inure and to make one cautious. The final repetition of "de ti" slows down the rhythm instead of accelerating it and brings consolation in spite of pain. The sharp sound of the accented /i/ is expressive of the speaker's pain, but the slowing of the rhythm with commas and repetition turns pain into tenderness, the wound into healing. The final lines remind us that the speaker is addressing his friend, his fear, the passage of time, and the possibility of loss. Again his ironic tone produces double voicing.

> Perdón, porque tú eres
> amigo mío, compañero mío.
> Tú, viejo y maldito cómplice.
> ¿El menos traicionero?
>
> (p. 224)[104]

The passage of time and the possibility of loss always accompany us. Admittedly, then, this fear is the most treacherous and complicitous aspect of our lives. But if we know that it is always with us, that it always deceives us, always pains us, there can be no deceit because we know what to expect. The speaker discovers that he can convert his pain and grief into quest and that this fear is an advantage, a friend. In this way, he substitutes his text for the loved one, his quest for his pain, and continues the elegiac healing process.

Rodríguez has published an illuminating article on the "corro de niños," which is intrinsically related to the elegiac paradigms in the next poem, "Lo que no se marchita" [That which does not fade].[105] At one time a customary and frequent part of Spanish life, the "corro de niños" is an activity in which children join hands to form a circle.[106] Chanting and moving rhythmically around the circle, they comprise a special community, a "societal code," that lifts them out of everyday reality into a world of magical illusion.[107] Their songs and gestures have no meaning per se, but they do transport the participants to an intensified, percipient vision of reality. "It is this substitutive turn or act of troping that any mourner must perform," "an alteration, moving from nature to artifice," "the founding of a sign . . . to invent a consoling substitute for the absent one."[108] In this way, the elegist draws attention to his own surviving powers through "a reluctant resubmission to the constraints of language" and the received conventions and inherited codes of elegy. For Rodríguez, the "corro" is especially important in defining the "origen de la realización poética." In the first stanza of "Lo que no se marchita," the "corro" is described as a "puerta abierta" and as a "milagro."

> Estos niños que cantan y levantan
> la vida

en los corros del mundo
que no son muro sino puerta abierta
5   donde si una vez se entra verdaderamente
nunca se sale,
porque nunca se sale del milagro.

(p. 225)[109]

The poet will repeat the phrase "Estos niños" two more times as he moves further
into the irrational but magical world of children. He adopts as his intertext one of the
children's songs which personifies (or confabulates) a dream. In his article, Rodríguez
cites the following verses: "Señora de mi ama / yo la vi bailar / con dos ratoncitos / en
la casa real." Compare these verses with those from "Lo que no se marchita":

Estos niños que al cielo llaman cielo
porque es muy alto,
y que al sueño lo han visto
15   azul celeste, con lunares blancos,
bailar con un ratón entre los muebles
generosos y horribles de la infancia,
y misteriosos . . .

(p. 225)[110]

Further allusions to fairy tales, children's stories, and stock characters (such as
the wolf) amplify the poet's re-creation of a child's innocent and intense view of the
world, including the magnified appreciation of table legs and chair backs and the fear
of opening a closet door. These elements permit us to recognize the theatrical properties of the "corro" because of the illusion, the hyperbolic reality, they create.[111] The
"corro," theater, and poetry (the text) magically create a new reality that modifies our
everyday perspective on life, the troping from nature to artifice that the successful
mourner must perform.[112] In this way the elegist can substitute the text for the absent
loved one. In "Lo que no se marchita," this substitution is especially evident in the
little girl the poet singles out because of her lack of grace and his desire that she
participate in the extraordinary perspective proffered by the "corro."

Contemplo ahora a la niña más pequeña:
la que pone su infancia
bajo la leña.
Hay que salvarla. Canta y baila torpemente
50   y hay que salvarla.
Esa delicadeza que hay en su torpeza
hay que salvarla.

(p. 226)[113]

According to Sacks, "The movement from loss to consolation requires a deflection of desire, with the creation of a trope both for the lost object and for the original
character of desire itself."[114] The "corro" represents the original character of desire in
that the poet must be willing to "join in" the rhythmic cadences of writing, to seek

knowledge, and to risk pain, whereas "la niña más pequeña" represents the lost object, the absent loved one. The phrase "Hay que salvarla" acquires the force of an "estribillo," a refrain advancing the incantatory aspect of the poem. Imperatives, repetition, rhythm, and internal rhyme create the propitiatory dimension of the following stanza.[115]

Acércate, no sé, no sé,
pero quiero contarte
60   algo que quizá nadie te ha contado,
un cuento que ahora para mí es lamento.
Ven, ven, y siente
caer la lluvia pura, como tú,
oye su son, y cómo
65   nos da canción a cambio
de dolor, de injusticia. Tú ven, ven,
bendito polen, dame
tu claridad, tu libertad, y ponte
más cruzado tu lazo
70   amarillo limón. Yo quiero, quiero
que se te mueva el pelo más, que alces
la aventura de tu cintura más,
y que tu cuerpo sea sonoro y redentor.

(pp. 226–27)[116]

When he enters in the first person, the speaker is outside the "corro." Until this encounter, he has not recognized the importance of the "corro" in his life. For this "corro" represents language, the text, and the creation of a new reality that can substitute for the lost loved one. For that reason, he recognizes the impact the "corro" has on him. He states that he is unworthy to witness the "corro" and that it accuses him.

Y cuántas veces, sin merecimiento,
35   estoy junto a este corro, junto a esta
cúpula,
junto a los niños que no tienen sombra.
Y lo oigo cantar, sólido y vivo,
y me alegra, y me acusa,
40   tan lleno de ternura y de secreto,
ofrecido e inútil hasta ahora . . .

(p. 226)[117]

After he has observed the little girl, taken her aside, and through his incantation made her more propitiate for participation by giving her insight into the song of the rain, the speaker surrenders himself to the "corro." By resubmitting himself to the constraints of language, which he uses as a means of modifying his reality, he substitutes the poem for the lost loved one and secures "a consoling sign that carries in itself the reminder of the loss on which it has been founded," "a sign not only of his loss but also of his pursuit."[118]

> Y sigue el corro,
> 75   y vivo en él, en pleno mar adentro,
> con estos niños,
> nunca cautivo sino con semillas
> feraces en el alma, mientras la lluvia cae.

(p. 227)[119]

The rain could be a traditional image of the speaker's tears, but it also has symbolic connotations of cleansing and inspiration. Likewise, writing has a cathartic effect and produces a text that can substitute for the lost loved one. The speaker adopts impetratory aspects of the "corro" as his own in the final stanza.

> Sólo pido que pueda,
> 80   cuando pasen los años,
> volver a entrar con el latido de ahora
> en este cuerpo duradero y puro,
> entrar en este corro,
> en esta casa abierta para siempre.

(p. 227)[120]

The tone of entreaty is clear, but repetition and intertextuality invite us to participate in the creation of a wider frame of reference and a new reality. The word "latido" recalls the same word used ambivalently to mean both pulse and throbbing pain at the climactic moment of part III of "Cantata." This encounter with the "corro" has been a painful exploration of the wound and an uplifting participation in textualization, in the "community" of poets, that allows Rodríguez to heal his wound and continue his exploration of self, his quest for consolation and identity. Most especially, the final verses recall the friends gathered around the table in the former vagabond's restored house in "Oda a la hospitalidad." It is via writing, the (elegiac) text, the poetic tradition, that Rodríguez has repaired his life, and it is by the same means that he will overcome his grief: by returning to the "corro." The middle section of *El vuelo* describes the process of suturing the wound of loss by way of a resubmission to language and the text, a substitution of the text ("lo que no se marchita") for the lost loved one, and a troping of the elegy into a quest for (textual/poetic) immortality.

If "la niña Reyes" to whom "Lo que no se marchita" is dedicated represents a substitution for the lost loved one, "La hilandera, de espaldas, del cuadro de Velázquez" is an even more pronounced example of this work of mourning. Because I have dealt at some length with "Hilando" in another context, I will limit my remarks here to those aspects pertinent to the elegiac experience of *El vuelo*.[121] This poem illustrates many of the concepts we have been investigating, especially those of suturing through textualization and the transferral of desire. The predominant images of spinning thread and weaving initiated in the title reinforce the concept of textualization in two ways. First, the description of this female figure substitutes the written text of the poem for the visual text of the painting while still evoking and inscribing it. This exchange then becomes an intertextual telescoping in keeping with the different spacial dimensions of the painting.

The speaker's experience of visiting the Prado and observing the painting reduplicates Velázquez's visiting a tapestry workshop. But the inclusion of allegorical figures and an intertextual reference not only to the myth of Arachne but also to a painting by Titian portraying the rape of Europa produces many different planes of (the textualization of) reality, which I would describe as levels of healing. Each (inter)textual level distances the elegist from his grief and allows healing to take place, even though it simultaneously inscribes the very loss it intends to compensate.[122] If intertextual telescoping leads us back to loss, it also compensates for the loss through the mediation of the text.

The elegist's focus on specific details of the female figure and his reaction to her bears out this interpretation. The first line of the poem, "Tanta serenidad es ya dolor" [So much serenity is now pain], recalls "Como el son de las hojas del álamo" and the speaker-poet's resolution to pursue his identity through the act of writing, even though that act may require a painful confrontation with difficult issues (such as his grief and loss). Therefore, the two main nouns of this verse are reversible: The serenity the speaker observes in the figure in the painting causes him pain but leads to his serenity and consolation. The synesthetic equivalence of the woman's blouse with music furthers this effect since music (an elegiac convention) adds another layer of mediation distancing the speaker from his loss, and also the passage of time since music unfolds temporally (as opposed to the illusion of space in painting).[123]

Though the spinner remains anonymous and yet substitutes for the lost loved one, her very posture exudes vulnerability and eternal beauty. Because she has her back turned and is engrossed in her work, she exposes the nape of her neck, while having her hair coiled on her head emphasizes the beauty of her form and her features, as well as being another instance of weaving/textuality. Even her skirt outlines her form, and its color of the leaves of the acacia represent a tree of great beauty and a traditional symbol of life.[124] The poet's illusion of time and the painter's illusion of space combine to bring this woman to life in the text even though she has been lost to the elegist in life.[125] The final stanza emphasizes the continued presence of the loved one in spite of loss and the transience of life.

> 20   Con la velocidad del cielo ido,
>   con el taller, con
>   el ritmo de las mareas de las calles,
>   está aquí, sin mentira,
>   con su amor tan mudo y con retorno,
> 25   con su celebración y con su servidumbre.
>
>   (p. 230)[126]

This stanza seems to unravel the text.[127] Yet, though pleasure may be fleeting ("la velocidad del cielo ido"), though we may get caught up in our daily routine ("el taller"), and life may seem to ebb and flow monotonously ("el ritmo de las mareas de las calles"), the loved one remains a vital presence in the life of the elegist: "está aquí." The two nouns that form the final statement inscribe loss and consolation. On the one hand, repetition of the possessive pronoun "su" calls attention to the speaker's distance. He cannot participate in a celebration, saddened as he is by the loss of the loved one; and unlike her, he does not feel inclined to sacrifice himself as the creation of the text requires of him. But on the other hand, because she is present, the speaker not only appreciates her celebration and self-sacrifice, he can participate in it, just as the title *El vuelo de la celebración* and the opening verse of "Hilando" include both loss and ecstasy. In the sundry allusions to spinning and weaving, to the painter's skill and the poet's music, and through the many layers of mediating intertextuality, this poem fosters the healing process by making present yet another female figure to substitute for the absent loved one. We will return to his emphasis on the female figure shortly, but first we must examine the troping process described in "Noviembre," the poem in the exact center of *El vuelo*.

Some readers may question, Why "Noviembre"? Why not "Hilando" or "La contemplación viva," much more substantial and memorable poems flanking "Noviembre"? Why "Noviembre"? Nothing happens here! Once again, Rodríguez has led us to a unique and crucial moment. If in *Alianza* we accompanied him in "crossing the bar," stepping over the gap between "Adiós" and "Noche abierta," in *El vuelo* the gap between "Hilando" and "La contemplación viva" is filled with another gap, a moment of stasis (the eye of the storm) that is at the same time a moment of transition, a turning point, a troping. "Noviembre" is both the abyss and the keystone that supports the structure of *El vuelo*.

The third section of *El vuelo*, which we are now considering, consists of nine poems, with four poems on either side of "Noviembre." In turn, this section is the second of three, the other two of which contain eight poems each (cf. "Libro tercero" of *Alianza*). As I stated in the introduction to this chapter, these intervening sections both separate and unite "Herida en cuatro tiempos" and "Elegía desde Simancas," the two-poem section that has been torn asunder to be both present and absent in *El vuelo*. If "Herida en cuatro tiempos" and "Elegía desde Simancas" are the cornerstones of the structure, "Noviembre" is the keystone, the gap/bridge of section III, the three intervening sections, and the cornerstone sections which begin and end *El vuelo*. In reading "Noviembre," it is essential to keep in mind the concepts of presence and absence, as well as the two definitions of the present tense postulated as immanence and immortality. "Noviembre" is both the wound and the suture, the epicenter of the concentric ripples of the structure and the fault line, the bar, the threshold, the site of the troping.

November is the elegiac month par excellence inasmuch as it is the season when we are most aware of the loss of light, warmth, and vegetative growth as we move closer to winter.[128] We might also adduce the Catholic Church's tradition of beginning November with a remembrance of all who have died, and even the symbolism of the number nine that lies at the etymological roots of this word. According to Chevalier and Gheerbrandt, "Por ser el nueve el último de la serie de las cifras, anuncia a la vez un fin y un nuevo comienzo, es decir, una transposición a un nuevo plano."[129] This may be stretching the symbolic implications too far, minimizing the concrete level and the sense of emptiness and loss in this poem. But it does highlight the troping in which Rodríguez definitively turns loss into quest, the crossing of the bar in "Noviembre."

This poem is divided into three distinct stanzas which promote a pattern of exposition, development, and resolution.[130] At first, we might think that the speaker laments the arrival of November and the monotonous, painful cycle of loss. But in this first stanza, he sets forth the direction his troping will take.

> Llega otra vez noviembre, que es el mes que más quiero
> porque sé su secreto, porque me da más vida.
> La calidad de su aire, que es canción,
> casi revelación,
> 5 y sus mañanas tan remediadoras,
> su ternura codiciosa,
> su entrañable soledad.
> Y encontrar una calle en una boca,
> una casa en un cuerpo mientras, tan caducas,
> 10 con esa melodía de la ambición perdida,
> caen las castañas y las telarañas.
>
> (p. 231)[131]

The stately rhythm and subtle alliterations embedded in everyday language of the first two verses (alexandrine in nature, with a caesura, a gap) alert us to the presence of a secret that is the source of more life. The second sentence (vv. 3–7) expands upon the nature of that secret: the cool, crisp quality of the autumn air and the healing light of its mornings. By comparing the air with a "canción, / casi revelación" (echoing the image of the white blouse in "Hilando"), the elegist achieves two contrary aims. At the same time that he mediates and attenuates his grief by means of the veil of language (song, artifice), he "reveals" it, *un*veiling it as the secret source of his lyric insight and integrity ("dolor").[132] As a poet, he bases his expression on the intensity of his emotions felt genuinely, honestly, truthfully. Yet these emotions arise from a loss, an absence. At one and the same time, his words are a veil and a revelation, the suture and the wound, tempering mediation and painful forthrightness. This duality can be appreciated in the modification of "*casi* revelación" and the alternating values of "su ternura codiciosa, / su entrañable soledad."

The uninflected "encontrar" in the final sentence of the stanza problematizes the meaning. Has the speaker found his direction ("una calle") and his relief/shelter ("una casa"), or is he still desperately seeking them? Concomitant with this search/discovery, which is both grief and consolation, the speaker introduces the two images that he will develop in the second stanza: "las castañas y las telarañas." In keeping with the ambivalence of the infinitive, the phrases "tan caducas" and "con esa melodía de la ambición perdida" are equivocal. The adjective "caducas" can mean either worn out and broken down or fleeting and perishable. Have they lasted a long time, or do they change quickly from one state to another? Both nevertheless suggest loss, but a loss counteracted by the verb "encontrar." Likewise, "perdida" could modify "melodía" or "ambición." Has the melody itself been lost, or does the presence of the melody "represent" absence? Rodríguez is clearly talking about his poetic gesture and the ambivalence of his grief/consolation, elegy/quest (alliance/condemnation, gain/loss). His contemplation of the chestnuts and spiderwebs constitutes the development section in the second stanza, where transition is the main theme.

> Estas castañas, de ocre amarillento,
> seguras, entreabiertas, dándome libertad
> junto al temblor en sombra de su cáscara.
> 15 Las telarañas, con su geometría
> tan cautelosa y pegajosa, y
> también con su silencio
> con su palpitación oscura
> como la del coral o la más tierna
> 20 de la esponja, o la de la piña
> abierta,
> o la del corazón cuando late sin tiranía, cuando
> resucita y se limpia.

(p. 231)[133]

To qualify the chestnuts' color as "de ocre amarillento" would seem to be redundant, but in this way, the poet emphasizes the uncertain state of this fruit. Is it unripe or overripe? Has it blended with the soil, or is it still a seed? In similar fashion, the adjectives "seguras, entreabiertas" are ambivalent, just as the sight of the chestnuts stimulates both elation ("libertad") and fear ("temblor"). Do these seeds fall to the ground and rot, or do they still contain the promise of new life? The poet employs this image to represent the dead loved one and the effect of loss on him, and his own words and their effect as language.

The geometric pattern of the spiderwebs, coming on the heels of a poem about Arachne, encourages us to read them as a sign of textuality and suturing, spanning a gap and closing a wound. Geometry underscores the artifice of this natural work of art (is that a contradiction?), whereas the paronomasia "cautelosa y pegajosa" (a repetition as the concentricities of the spiderwebs, replicating the structure of *El vuelo*) foreground the personified attributes of the webs. The speaker projects his own need to be cautious and yet to attach himself, to reestablish contact with life after the traumatic severance from and loss of the loved one. That the webs are silent yet palpitate could refer to their movement in a breeze or to the promise of life these webs hold since in the autumn the spider lays the eggs that will hatch in the spring.

This movement and latent life remind the speaker of coral, sponge, and the intricate networking of a pineapple that has been split open (cf. "La ventana del jugo"). He also compares it to the systole and diastole of a heart that beats "sin tiranía," without constraints or burdens, free from the preoccupation of grief. Does he see these attributes in nature because he feels them and projects them outwardly? Or does he recognize them around him but feel the need still to acquire them because he lacks them? His next words leave that question unanswered.

> Tras tanto tiempo sin amor, esta mañana
> 25 qué salvadora. Qué

luz tan íntima. Me entra y me da música
sin pausas
en el momento mismo en que te amo,
en que me entrego a ti con alegría,
30 trémulamente e impacientemente,
sin mirar a esa puerta donde llama el adiós.

(p. 231)[134]

The conflict of interior and exterior is underscored in the direct address of another, "tú." The speaker has decided to take a risk, he has decided to hand himself
over ("entregarse"), make himself available to life through his emotions. In the indeterminacy of the addressee (is it a woman, his wife Clara, the morning, the light, the
lost loved one?) we discern his blindness, fear, and impulsiveness. The light, music,
and repetitions—all attributes of elegy—seem to produce a sudden impulse in the
speaker, but it is actually a change that has been developing over an extended period
of time. The final phrase sustains the ambivalence. Does he deliberately not look at
"esa puerta donde llama el adiós"? Does he acknowledge its presence, include it in
his poem, but choose not to look at it? What does this door represent? Is it a door
where his grief is exiting, and he does not want to turn around, to see it again?[135] Is it
the same door that he mentions in "Lo que no se marchita"—a door that leads to
lasting values and immortality for the poet? Or a door that leads to death and loss, the
poet's own mortality? Are these one and the same? The final verses complete this
troping, but a clear-cut resolution is still unattained.

Llegó otra vez noviembre. Lejos quedan los días
de los pequeños sueños, de los besos marchitos.
Tú eres el mes que quiero. Que no me deje a oscuras
35 tu codiciosa luz olvidadiza y cárdena
mientras llega el invierno.

(p. 232)[136]

This stanza entails three temporal perspectives (past, present, and future), corresponding with the three interior sections of *El vuelo* and the tripartite structure of this
poem. The repetition of the phrase "Llegó otra vez noviembre" from the first line
repeats the cyclical turning of the seasons. But here the verb is in the preterit tense
followed by a period, halting the repetition and introducing a finality that situates the
cyclic view in the past. Indeed, the speaker distances his former perspective from him
in the next sentence and emphasizes his abandonment of that limited, shallow perspective in the adjectives "pequeños" and "marchitos."

The act of troping, located in the center of this stanza as "Noviembre" is the
keystone of *El vuelo*, occurs in the next sentence: "Tú eres el mes que quiero." Such
a forthright declaration, equating the person with the month of November, performs a
substitution, a transference of desire from the lost loved one to the present moment,
the speaker's engagement with and commitment to life and his poetic quest. The
ambiguity of the addressee, albeit personified and coming as it does between two
poems in which female figures are foregrounded, opens the pronoun to multiple inter-

pretations, all referring to the present moment, even if that moment involves the painful memory of a lost loved one. Consequently, the switch to the preterit tense in "Llegó" signifies loss as both the painful absence of the loved one and the grateful embracing of a new perspective on life. This troping represents an end and a new beginning (cf. the symbolism of the number nine).

Futurity is expressed in the subjunctive mood: "Que no me deje a oscuras." This entreaty, the incantatory and protractive aspects of language, demonstrates the speaker's willingness to maintain his new perspective and to continue his quest, his troping activity, his writing, in spite of the omnipresence of death and his own mortality ("el invierno"), a central theme of this section of *El vuelo* announced in "Cantata del miedo." The final inscription of "llega," devolving to the present tense but looking toward the future, represents the poet's acceptance of his mortality but his refusal to let that cyclic certainty interfere with his quest for self and immortality through writing and the complete, honest engagement that quest requires of him. "Noviembre" inscribes loss (absence) but also forms the keystone of *El vuelo* as it marks a troping, a recathecting of desire, the elegist's healthy work of mourning.

As a result of the speaker's "turning the corner" in "Noviembre," "La contemplación viva" constitutes another major statement of the new perspective he has acquired and to which he commits himself following his acceptance of the loss of the loved one and his own mortality. Rodríguez has provided insight into this formulation of his poetics in a short meditation on another of Velázquez's paintings, "El bufón «Calabacillas», llamado erróneamente «el bobo de Coria»."[137] In describing Velázquez's aesthetics with a quote from San Juan de la Cruz, Rodríguez establishes a connection between his own poetry, Velázquez's complex genius, and mystical experience of union with the other.

Cuando San Juan de la Cruz intenta aclarar los versos y después dice: «Mira que la dolencia de amor no se cura sino con la presencia y la figura», nos acerca a la contemplación, la contemplación viva. Se trata de una transfiguración, por decirlo así. Pero la interpretación no es tan sólo la versión actual del objeto contemplado, sino la vida total del pintor, del creador, del arte en este caso, en contacto con el objeto, es decir, uno se empieza a preguntar para volver a preguntarse si la existencia es imagen, figura. En efecto, pienso yo, el creador intenta perder su personalidad hasta cierto punto. Por ello el respeto que tiene Velázquez hacia sus tomas, sus objetos, sus figuras, sus retratos. Este respeto o esta transformación consiste, naturalmente, en entrañarse. Entrañarse de tal manera en el objeto, en la figura que el propio creador pierde su personalidad o, mejor que perderla, se alimenta, se reconoce, se renueva en la figura, en la contemplación, llega a haber contemplación viva.

La relación entre las múltiples huellas de las cosas y su secreto tiende hacia un momento vigilante en el que se ha de establecer, es decir, ha de adquirir eternidad sin fugacidad. Esto es esencial.[138]

These comments and the phrase "la contemplación viva" posit an ambivalent relationship between subject and object, self and other. To contemplate means to gaze attentively, to observe, literally to mark out space for observation, and is related to the temple and the outward signs of sacrifice. Contemporary usage has interiorized this activity, but still retains something of the meditation on an external event, object, or person (often God). As Rodríguez's statement indicates, the creative mind identifies so completely with that which it observes that the artist lends life to that otherness. In the case of the poet or painter, that surrendering of self (Rodríguez has used the term "entregarse" as early as *Don*) entails the figuration of otherness in words, shapes, or colors. This figuration in turn contains something of the self, the subject who created it. The enriching complementarity and reciprocity between self and other, subject and object, poem and author/reader, is readily apparent in Rodríguez's poem, "La contemplación viva." The opening verses set forth the anecdotal scene but expunge the boundary between self and other.

> Estos ojos seguros,
> ojos nunca traidores,
> esta mirada provechosa que hace
> pura la vida, aquí en febrero
> 5   con misteriosa cercanía. Pasa
> esta mujer, y se me encara, y yo tengo el secreto,
> no el placer, de su vida,
> a través de la más
> arriesgada y entera
> 10 aventura: la contemplación viva.
>
> (p. 233)[139]

To whom does the gaze belong: to the speaker or to the woman? Does the speaker recognize the power that his new perspective lends to his gaze? Or does he as object, as observed, feel the intensity of the woman's gaze? The experience of passing another human being on the street has a cathartic effect on him. The month of February reinforces the experience of purification by dint of its coldness but also its healthfulness (cf. "El baile de Aguedas" and "Ciudad de meseta"). The adjectives "provechosa" and "misteriosa" are equally ambivalent, implying taking advantage and receiving benefit, wariness and attraction, respectively.

The verb phrase "se me encara" is reciprocal because the speaker must be looking at her for her to return his gaze "face to face." If she has revealed her secret to him, he also has handed his over to her. Even the words "secreto" and "placer" begin to resonate with ambivalence: intimacy versus withholding, true happiness versus painful truth, genuine feeling versus superficial delight. When he calls this reciprocal exchange "la más / arriesgada y entera / aventura," the speaker reminds us of his contradictory stance in the first part of "Herida en cuatro tiempos," "Aventura de una destrucción." Exposing oneself in this type of encounter, handing oneself over to that which passes by and is quickly lost, entails risk and pain, but it also contains the possibility of excitement and joy, and of knowing oneself better. But how different the tone of the two poems! The emphasis on seeing, sight, gaze, and blindness in the next verses intensifies the reciprocity and confusion between self and other.

> Y veo su mirada
> que transfigura; y no sé, no sabe ella,

y la ignorancia es nuestro apetito.
Bien veo que es morena,
15   baja, floja de carnes,
pero ahora no da tiempo a fijar el color, la dimensión,
ni siquiera la edad de la mirada,
mas sí la intensidad de este momento.

(p. 233)[140]

Rodríguez's choice of "transfigura" is a master stroke because it combines exterior reshaping and interior exaltation in this exchange of looks. Such an experience can be painful if it reshapes, but also clearly uplifting. Neither of these persons knows what is happening or what it means. But their blindness ("ignorancia") heightens the desire to know the other and the self, the self through the other. Whereas the speaker can remember certain details about this woman ("es morena, / baja, floja de carnes"—probably not physically striking), he can only fix on "la intensidad de este momento." All other details are lost to him: "el color, la dimensión, / . . . la edad de la mirada." In short, this otherness that reflects his gaze as similar and different is a perplexing combination of the transient and the lasting, interior and exterior, self and other. The speaker finds this moment so intense that he wishes to record not only the specifics of the scene but also his emotional reactions to it, to "transfigure" this incident.

Y la fertilidad de lo que huye
y lo que me destruye:
este pasar, este mirar
en esta calle de Avila con luz de mediodía
entre gris y cobriza,
25   hace crecer mi libertad, mi rebeldía,
mi gratitud.

(p. 233)[141]

Avila, the scene of this incident, alludes to Santa Teresa and the mystic experience, so that the speaker finds "fertilidad" in "lo que huye / y lo que me destruye." The painful and the difficult is also uplifting, exalting, refreshing. Again calling upon the elegiac convention of light and especially the light at noon—which for Rodríguez is the moment of greatest insight and inspiration but also of "deslumbramiento," a brilliance too intense to tolerate—the poet describes the light as "entre gris y cobriza." The color gray is a blend of black and white, while the copper color is a mixture of green and red. These ambivalencies play off one another in a double contrast, a chiasmas of the type Rodríguez has just effected in "Noviembre."

Of the three nouns that conclude this part of "La contemplación viva," "rebeldía" stands out from "libertad" or "gratitud" as more negative. This word declares that the speaker's act of engaging with the world, with "lo que huye / y lo que me destruye," is a difficult one and requires a surrendering of the self to the other and an acceptance of his own mortality. But he also rebels against a superficial approach to life and becomes even more determined and committed to his quest. His gratitude therefore also acquires a double edge: He is grateful for the pain because it leads to growth and ultimately to his redemption through the redemption of the fleeting reality with which he engages in the act of "la contemplación viva."

The complementarity between subject and object, observer and observed, posited in part I translates into Rodríguez's transgressive poetics in part II. Even though he draws a veil of language over the wound to attain consolation by the transferral of desire, he reaches beyond that veil to recognize the wound, the intense emotions underlying the (trans)figurative language of the text as suture. Writing—drawing the veil of language over the absence of the loved one, suturing the wound caused by loss, defining the self—ironically consists of an incisive penetration into self, a removal of protective veils, an intensely painful honesty with self and other in search of the self. This ambivalent veiling/unveiling can be seen in the opening verses of part II.

> Hay quien toca el mantel, mas no la mesa;
> el vaso, mas no el agua.
> Quien pisa muchas tierras,
> nunca la suya.
>
> (p. 234)[142]

The "quien" described in these verses could be other poets whose poetics keep them on the surface of things, not allowing them to delve into the real stuff of life. Surely the tablecloth can be a beautiful work of art, woven, embroidered, of fine linen, but Rodríguez would prefer to see the table itself, to savor the simplicity of the water rather than admire the lovely artifact of the container. The poet (and the critic) can employ beautifully eloquent language, but that is only the container. Unless what goes into that container is pure, valuable, and appreciated for what it is, the exquisite container is just another object destined to a transient existence. Rodríguez drives home this point by affirming his surrender of self to the full appreciation of life, symbolized by this moment in Avila.

> 5   Pero ante esta mirada que ha pasado
> y que me ha herido bien con su limpia quietud,
> con tanta sencillez emocionada
> que me deja y me da
> alegría y asombro,
> 10   y, sobre todo, realidad,
> quedo vencido. Y veo, veo, y sé
> lo que se espera, que es lo que se sueña.
>
> (p. 234)[143]

Even though this gaze has wounded him, has passed him by and disappeared, even though he experiences this loss profoundly, he has gained by surrendering himself. His declaration, "quedo vencido," is an acknowledgment of defeat and ecstatic triumph. The repetition "Y veo, veo, y sé" poignantly emphasizes that the other's gaze has conquered but also liberated him. He has learned that one gets out of life what one puts into it. If we dare to dream, our dreams will become our expectations and our realities. Returning to the gaze, the final verses again set forth the contrast between the transient and the lasting.

> Lástima de saber en estos ojos
> tan pasajeros, en vez de en los labios.
> 15 Porque los labios roban
> y los ojos imploran.
>
> Se fue.
>
> Cuando todo se vaya, cuando yo me haya ido
> quedará esta mirada
> 20 que pidió, y dio, sin tiempo.

(p. 234)[144]

The contrast between the lips (the deceptive surface, the veil of language) and the eyes (honest depth) is clear in the contradictory verbs "roban" and "imploran." Ironically, the eyes are "pasajeros." The isolation, brevity, and phonetic alliteration of the phrase "Se fue" marks the site of loss. This woman (the lost loved one) and her gaze (this moment, this incident, the poet's own life) are fleeting, yet the experience has been intense and lasting.

The gain/loss motif in the final verse is reinforced by the ambivalence of the phrase "sin tiempo." The moment has been extremely brief; this incident takes place in a few fleeting seconds in which nothing is said. Yet that silence, that exchange (gain/loss), between the speaker and the other will last eternally. The words of the poem are insignificant, yet the emotion they convey will perdure because the speaker has surrendered himself to this transience. Recognition of transience, an acceptance of his own mortality and the immanence of all of life and of the pain this causes, enriches the speaker and allows him to hope for immortality in his poetry. A drawing of the veil of language is a refusal to allow language to separate the poet from his commitment to life. His elegiac striving for consolation is a quest for poetic immortality; suturing the wound is an exploration and aggravation of it.

"Una aparición," the final poem of this center section of El vuelo, would seem to form an anomalous part of an elegiac work. But the gnomelike figure (reminiscent of Eugenio de Luelmo) who visits the speaker in what seems to be a drunken hallucination is the poet's alter ego.[145] If we recall that "Una aparición" closes the frame of this section, we can conceive of the apparition as the embodiment of the fear described in "Cantata del miedo." An apparition is anything that appears unexpectedly and is usually associated with a ghost. Based on its etymological roots, however, we can also consider an apparition as something extraordinary, even an epiphany. This visit to the poet by his mortality provides just such an ambivalent and unexpected experience.

This poem is structured principally around the repetition of the verb "Llegó" in vv. 1 and 9, and at the beginning of the second stanza (v. 18). By echoing the use of this same word from "Noviembre" (another structural link with "Cantata"), the poet inscribes finality and loss at the same time that he defines presence. The description of this figure—effected by the accumulation of a number of details—reflects this ambivalence. For example, that he has "un aliento muy oscuro" could mean that he has very strong mouth odor that repulses the speaker. But the association of "aliento" with inspiration suggests the subtle effect and the slow development of inspiration that this figure has on the speaker. "Oscuro" in this sense would mean "indistinct," "nebulous," "uncertain," and even "profound."

Moreover, he arrives "en ayunas, / con apetito seco." This could mean that he is too poor to buy food for himself and suffers from hunger, or that he has been fasting and is eager to participate in an ecstatic vision (cf. mysticism). He also possesses a gaze that is at once "audaz y recogida," and "volvió atrás su mirada." Is he fearful and cautious because someone is following him? Or does he look to the past, as the elegist takes one final look at the loss he has suffered and the fear of his own mortality? The focus on his hands and mouth at the end of the stanza subtly foregrounds the metapoetic dimension of the poet's other:

> con la desecación sobria y altiva
> 15   de sus manos tan sucias,
> con sus dientes nublados,
> a oscuras, en el polen de la boca.
>
> (p. 237)[146]

Throughout this stanza and carrying over into the next by virtue of the verb "Llegó," repeated images of darkness and light as well as certain adverbials ("con," "en," "muy," and "bien") provide unity along with the fragmentation caused by the accumulation of so many descriptive details.[147]

When the poet repeats the verb "Llegó" at the beginning of the second stanza, however, he increases the sense of finality (of loss and of arrival) by ending the sentence there. At this supposed moment of drunken stupor, when it is dawning (literally and metaphorically) in the midst of a rowdy tavern scene (a realistic, nontranscendent moment), the speaker and this figure participate in an epiphanic experience.

> Y dijo: «Hay un sonido
> dentro del vaso» . . .
> 25   ¿De qué color?, yo dije. Estás mintiendo.
> Sacó un plato pequeño y dibujó en la entraña
> de la porcelana,
> con sus uñas maduras,
> con su aliento y el humo de un cigarro,
> 30   una casa,
> un camino de piedra estremecida,
> como los niños.
> —¿Ves?
> ¿No oyes el viento de la piedra ahora?
> 35   Sopló sobre el dibujo
> y no hubo nada. «Adiós.
> Yo soy el Rey del Humo».
>
> (pp. 237–38)[148]

At first, the non sequitur and the lack of logic in this exchange suggests the disorientation of drunkenness and the lack of communication. But if we specify the troping process here, we can see that the liquid (wine, for example) turns into sound (the origin of the cosmos, the word), then into color, and then into a vision, an image, a figure. We can almost feel the squeakiness of the gnome's fingernails drawing this picture in the porcelain, along with his harsh breath and the smoke of his cigarette. These vivid sensorial images produce a crude drawing, similar to something children might draw. The house and the road of this figure (the drawing) within a figure (the gnome) within a figure (the poem) within a figure *(El vuelo)*—replicating the concentricity of the center sections—remind us of "Oda a la hospitalidad," the vagabond who has found his home, restored it, learned from it, and invites his friends to partake of a meal. This illusion of wholeness, comfort, peace, and stability would also seem to be ephemeral, suggesting that all efforts to create the illusion of immortality through art are in vain.

But the gnome's final words propose an alternate reading. The question "¿Ves?" slips into the question "¿No oyes . . . ?" and refers to the sound in the glass. That this sound is "el viento de la piedra" not only suggests that even the rock is transient (cf. "Arena": "la vanagloria de la piedra") but also that permanent inspiration resides in the fleeting. The drawing disappears when the gnome blows on it (another image of inspiration, breath), but the drawing never existed—only its figuration in the language of the poem and the speaker's drunken hallucination. Just as the gaze of the woman in "La contemplación viva" passed quickly by and was lost, the image called up by the figure in this poem is a lasting one, an unforgettable experience. The poet is like the gnome: a vagabond, an illusionist, a magician. Though he reigns over that which vanishes, is transient and ephemeral ("el Rey del Humo"), his magic also figures the transient and makes it permanent. The poet himself is transient, ephemeral, mortal, and yet his drunken hallucination, his magic, his words, create an everlasting image.

LOSS AS GAIN: PRESENT ANTICIPATION OF THE FUTURE

Of the five sections that form *El vuelo de la celebración*, one might argue that the fourth is the most "celebratory." This is not to say that doubt, pain, guilt, and grief are totally excluded from these eight poems. Far from it. Indeed, this celebration extols loss, the wound, the gap in language, and the transient nature of life. Ironically, Rodríguez's identity—his immortality—depends on this other that is absence, wound, lack, transience, mutability. It is only through the celebration of loss and absence that he can affirm his self.

It has been said that this fourth section "contiene sobre todo poemas de temática amorosa."[149] Given that on two occasions the speaker declares "la mañana es clara" and "el alba es clara," punning on the name of his wife, we can assume that the female figure in these poems is Clara. The elegist recathects his libido from the lost sister and mother to his wife. That she now subsumes all of these roles transforms her into an archetypal figure representing all of reality, life itself, and most significantly *language*. For both woman and language embody difference—a gap—that determines the poet's identity. In sum, the fourth section of *El vuelo* shows the speaker's process, his acceptance of risk and the challenge involved in living life to the fullest.

The complex and enigmatic "Tan sólo una sonrisa" that opens this section explores the peril and challenge that confronts the elegist at this moment of determining his future investment in life and the poetic act. It also reveals the poet's ironic situation: As elegist, he would heal the wound of loss with the suture of language; but as poet, he has discovered that language contains a gap that he must seek if he is to write truthfully and attain poetic immortality. How can he at one and the same time heal the wound and open the painful gap, exposing himself to loss? That is the dilemma exposited in "Tan sólo una sonrisa."

At first glance, this poem might seem to be nothing more than a repetition of the episode in "La contemplación viva." But enough superficial differences exist to make us question how different their significance is for the speaker. Although each poem describes a passing encounter, the woman in "Tan sólo una sonrisa" seems to be much younger than the one in the previous poem. Whereas the speaker is captivated by the eyes of the first woman, in this poem he is attracted to the woman's smile. If the gaze was a silent signifier that opened upon a vast expanse of communication, the smile is much more enigmatic, causing the speaker to question his own motives as well as those of the other. This encounter raises many more moral, metaphysical, epistemological, and ontological questions for the speaker because it brings out the peril and risk, both internal and external, involved in a commitment to life.

The opening verses encapsulate this conundrum: "Sólo se pierde lo que no se ama. / ¿O lo que se ama?" The affirmative question of the second verse undercuts and problematizes the negative sententious declaration with which the poem begins. Are we as human beings susceptible to losing that which we do not value? Or can we only experience loss if we do value something or someone? Also, the verb "perder" reprises the gain/loss motif that we have noted earlier. That motif now has an additional dimension because of the elegist's loss of the loved one. If the poet has lost something, what has he gained? If he does not lose anything, can he gain?

The abstract quality of this argumentation tends to distance the speaker from the incident. That distance quickly gives way to the specifics of the encounter, yet the smile becomes the receptacle of this questioning. Regret for the lost loved one has brought the speaker to this crucial moment. He has been examining himself closely, scrutinizing his emotions, but he has lost contact with the outside. The smile he sees disrupts his meditation on self and reincites a reciprocal contact with the world. The process of introspection and individuation ("altas tapias por fuera / y ventanas por dentro") separates the speaker from others, just as loss of the mother is the first separation an individual experiences. Seeking the self through writing also requires separation and loss. If the loss of the loved one replicates the loss of the mother, causing pain, the process of individuation through writing also involves pain but ultimately leads to individuality. In fact, the speaker seems disconcerted by his indiscreet and perhaps even lecherous thoughts upon encountering this young woman.

> Aunque no te conozco, niña apenas
> pero con carne prieta de mujer,
> 10 tengo la silenciosa
> llave febril con la que estoy entrando,
> sin claridad y sin fijeza,
> y quizá a deshora,
> en tu boca entornada
> 15 sólo por un momento, como el amor del aire
> o la sorpresa de la soledad.
>
> (p. 241)[150]

In describing this person as "niña apenas / pero con carne prieta de mujer," the speaker's dilemma is apparent. Is she an innocent young girl, or is she a knowing woman? The adjective "prieta" could refer to her dark complexion, but along with "carne," it has a lascivious connotation. Because of her smile, the speaker has insight into her contradictory nature, but he describes his insight as "la *silenciosa* / llave *febril.*" These ambivalent adjectives increase the uncertainty in this situation. Moreover, the speaker says that he enters "sin claridad y sin fijeza, / y quizá a deshora." What are his motivations when he looks at this young woman? What is the source of those feelings—the observer or the observed? Has he sought this insight, or has it simply occurred? How much control does he have over these feelings and his ability to discover them? The phrases "como el amor del aire / o la sorpresa de la soledad" epitomize this ambivalence. Is the air something insubstantial, fleeting, imperceptible, making its love vacuous? Or is it the very breath that sustains life? Does "soledad" mean "solitude" or "loneliness"? Is the surprise delightful or unwelcome? This confusion intensifies in the next stanza.

> Y la columna del aliento,
> tan fugitiva e imperecedera,
> el movimiento oculto de tus labios carnosos,
> 20 con demasiado aplomo y embusteros,
> me hacen vivir en ellos:
> en tus encías, en tus dientes, no
> en tus ojos.
>
> (p. 241)[151]

The reversal of the contrasting terms "columna" and "aliento," "fugitiva" and "imperecedera" replicates the chiasmus of the opening verses. Does the adjective "oculto" mean "hidden" or "bewitching," "alluring"? Does he see the movement, or is he deceived into seeing it? Does he deceive himself into thinking that he has found a message in the signifier? Or is he arbitrarily projecting a message, an attitude, a knowledge, of which the woman is unaware? The abrupt enjambment in vv. 22–23 confuses the speaker's position. Is he aware that he is focusing on the physical aspects of

her mouth (the gums, the teeth) rather than her eyes? Or does he reject the purely
physical attraction for the spiritual? Does he invest his feeling of life in the transient,
or does he discover deeper emotions that will last beyond time? There is no resolution
to this dilemma in the final stanza.

> Adiós, adiós. Recordaré, a la sombra
> de otros labios más claros que los tuyos,
> 30   esta aventura silenciosa.
> No ha sido nada: sólo una sonrisa.

(p. 242)[152]

The repetition of the salutation "adiós," the contrast between "sombra" and
"claros," "otros" and "tuyos," and the future tense of a verb looking at the past
("recordaré") problematize "esta aventura silenciosa." Does "silenciosa" mean that
this encounter has not resulted in a lasting experience for the speaker? Or does it
mean that an unspoken but very real communication (with the other and/or the self)
has taken place? This fleeting smile has been all and nothing, has had a lasting impact, and has sped by and been lost.

To return to the original formulation of this dilemma, the speaker has questioned
whether he should or should not invest in this chance passing. Will it lead somewhere, or is he just deluding himself? If he loves and loses, will it not be painful for
him? Should he then not invest his time, energy, emotion, and self in this experience?
Is the young woman deceiving him, or is he deceiving himself? Because this woman
is not his spouse (evoked in "otros labios más claros"), is this a lesser commitment?
Should he disdain this experience and the possibilities it offers him? If he does that
now, will he fail to take advantage of a more promising situation? How does one
know when one is being deceived, when one is deceiving oneself? How does one
know which experience will be more valuable than another? How much is lost when
one is seeking gain? How much is gained when one loses?

This smile symbolizes the speaker's engagement with reality and life. As a signifier,
it may be empty and meaningless, or it may point to an even more profound perspective (the gaze). The signified to which it refers may be fleeting, subject to decay and
loss, or it may have a lasting impact. Has this poem been successful, has the encounter been a fruitful learning experience? Or does it merely repeat "La contemplación
viva"? There is both peril and promise in the speaker's continued engagement with
life: peril of deceit (deceiving or being deceived), pain, loss; promise of adventure,
mystery, knowledge, growth. This enigmatic smile (a laugh without sound), this ineffable and unfathomable encounter, embodies the speaker's dilemma as he begins the
next phase of his mourning and his quest: the celebration of the fleeting.

The encounter in "Tan sólo una sonrisa" represents an act of reading. The poet
must be willing to surrender himself to the text of reality, to read and interpret it. Even
though that act entails the discovery and exploration of the gap which renews his loss
and reinstates his pain, that surrender is necessary if he is to continue to achieve the
knowledge of self and the growth that writing requires of him. Having dealt with the
loss of the loved one and with his own mortality, the elegist must now confront his

resistance to this pain, which he couches in erotic terms. His ability to "read" is equivalent to his ability to love because both require a surrender of the self. For it is this surrender to pain and loss (the gap) that will enable him to continue writing. His confrontation with the other in section IV of *El vuelo* is a working out of that resistance in which the female other represents all of reality as text and the reciprocal acts of reading and writing, being read and being written, having and being.

This process develops step by step over the next poems, so that we need only summarize the outstanding moments in this process. In "Mientras tú duermes," the speaker contemplates the other as she sleeps. He notes above all the innocence and defenselessness of the person asleep, when all learned gestures of self-protection and circumspection fall away. On the one hand, this observation of the other is voyeuristic and lascivious. But on the other hand, it becomes an invocation of that which the speaker lacks and therefore desires. The ambivalence of this moment (both fleeting and imperishable, innocent and lascivious, contemplative and lascivious) is captured in the final verse: "Te estoy acompañando. Despiértate. Es de día."

Reminiscent of "Visión a la hora de la siesta" *(Conjuros),* "Sin leyes" *(Alianza),* and even poem I of "Libro tercero" of *Don,* "(Con marzo)," the awakening at the end of this poem raises several doubts. Does the vision disappear with the awakening, or does participation in experience begin? Does the coming of day create a disillusionment, a fleeting moment, a "reality check"? Or does it connote inspiration, vitality, and greater involvement? Does the speaker take advantage of this intense moment of life to surrender himself to it, or does he avoid it by reminding the other of his presence, invoking her defenses, to protect himself from this intensity? Which is having and which being? By waking the other, the poet's act of reading comes to an end, as does the act of writing the poem. Is his waking the other a way of halting his painful recathection with reality, or does he urge himself to participate even more fully in it?

The next poem, "Música callada," shows the speaker in the midst of a struggle to overcome his reluctance. The title of this rambling, disjointed poem expresses the same ambivalence seen at the end of "Tan sólo una sonrisa" and "Mientras tú duermes." Is the music very soft but perceptible, or is it silenced? Has the poet lost his inspiration and his ability to fall into the gap in language? Or is that inspiration calling to him albeit faintly? In two instances, the speaker defines this paradox explicitly. In the first stanza, he states, "Y toco el quicio / muy secreto del aire, y va creciendo / la armonía, junto con el dolor" (vv. 15–17), whereas in the penultimate stanza, he ambivalently exclaims/questions, "Qué vena tan querida, / tan generosa y cruel con su latido" (vv. 51–52).

The key moment in this poem can be found at the beginning of the second stanza. These verses might seem incommensurate with the remainder of the poem unless we note that the "tú" addressed can be the music, the lost loved one, the female other, or the poet's inspiration. Hence the erotic overtones and the allusion to an indiscretion, a moment of infidelity.

>   Perdona mi ligera
> 25   traición de hace dos meses, pero te quiero, ven,

ven tú, ven tú,
y oye conmigo cómo crece el fruto,
porque sin ti no sé,
porque sin ti no amo. . . .

(p. 244)[153]

At first, this statement seems to disrupt the poem and to digress from the opening imagery and the central theme: the speaker's footsteps on a wooden floor. His footsteps evoke for him the impermanence and mutability of reality, but as we have seen, walking is synonymous with writing for Rodríguez. The speaker's pacing corresponds with the rambling development of the poem that leads up to this declaration. The female other whom he has betrayed provides a vehicle for the poet to address a myriad of issues—personal and poetic—simultaneously. The sound of his footsteps echoing on the wooden floor leads to a contemplation of "El sonido callado" (v. 41). The poet associates the process of pollination, germination, flowering, and bearing fruit with this sound. But the song of this fruit needs to be protected by its peel or shell, which also isolates it, distinguishes it, individuates it from the rest of the world. When the speaker exclaims, "¡Cómo / suenan la almendra, la manzana, el trigo!" (vv. 39–40), he sees that all are united in the production of "música callada" (because all are fruit), but also that each has a distinct identity. He then embodies the memory of his favorite sounds from childhood in the person of the other.

El sonido callado. Oigo las calles
generosas e injustas de mi pueblo
como en mi infancia,
en esta fiesta de tus labios, de
45   tu carne que es susurro y es cadencia
desde las uñas de los pies, sonando a marejada,
hasta el pelo algo gris, como el rumor del agua
quieta o el de los chopos al atardecer.

(p. 245)[154]

Although images of sound and other sensorial qualities predominate in these verses, the speaker cannot sustain his vision and declares, "No sólo estamos asombrados, mudos, casi ciegos / frente a tanto misterio, sino sordos" (vv. 49–50). These intense moments of insight are so overpowering, awesome, and brilliant that they "mask" the music latent in them. They create a wall, a shell, an exterior (lips, toenails, graying hair), surfaces that conceal the music within, a transient physicality that disguises the lasting beauty of the music behind the facade. In the final verses, the speaker seems frustrated in his attempt to attain that beauty, but the alliteration of the /s/ in the final verse is ambivalent.

¿Qué más? ¿Qué más? ¿Es que oiremos tan sólo,
después de tanto amor y de tanto fracaso,
55   la música de la sombra y el sonido del sueño?

(p. 245)[155]

This questioning of his ability to overcome blockage, the defenses that prevent him from surrendering himself to the gap in language, continues in "Hermana mentira." The poet recognizes that language can deceive, that it can be a lie as well as being truthful and intimate like a sister; and he denounces that falseness: "ahora estoy maldiciendo / su ilusión y su trampa" (vv. 34–35). Nevertheless, he is still struggling and feels that the morning air (clear, cool, inspiring) is accusing him: "Pero, / ¿por qué me está acusando / el aire?" (vv. 7–9); "Pero, ¿por qué me está mirando el aire / con vileza y sin fe?" (vv. 37–38).

In this poem, the speaker questions his willingness to surrender himself to the gap in language and to take the risk of renewing his pain. His denunciation and frank admission of his difficulty is only the first step; he must go beyond that. Significantly, he reprises the gain/loss motif at a critical moment: "¿Qué es lo que pido, qué es lo que he perdido, / qué es lo que gano ahora?" (vv. 10–11). This pivotal questioning assesses what he is accomplishing now and what his goals are for the future, in keeping with the futurity of this section of *El vuelo*.

The turning point comes in "Voz sin pérdida," as its title suggests. By making the central image of this poem "Este viento de marzo" and linking it with the direct address of the other, Rodríguez reminds us of the first two poems of "Libro tercero" of *Don*, the second of which is dedicated to Clara, his wife. The speaker not only is recathecting his emotions onto this female figure (as mother, sister, spouse), he is also recalling the uncertainty of the postlapsarian transition of his first incursion into poetry. If at that moment his world was thrown into chaos because of his illuminating discoveries about language and self, the death of the loved one now has had the same effect and has led him to a similar adjustment in his perspective on life and the poetic act. The association of the March wind with the other's voice provides the transition, which the poet makes at the beginning of the second part of "Voz sin pérdida."

> He oído y he creído en muchas voces
> aunque no en las palabras.
> He creído en los labios
> mas no en el beso.
>
> (p. 249)[156]

These verses posit a parallel but chiasmatic relationship between "voces" and "palabras," "labios" and "beso." By believing in the lips but not the kiss, the speaker has placed his confidence in the transient but concrete reality instead of the emotion conveyed by the lips, an allusion to his superficial approach to life. This situation would seem to be the opposite of the first relationship between "voces" and "palabras." He listened to the sound of the words, the quality of the voice, the intangible but perceptible, rather than placing his faith in the words themselves. This incommensurability between the parallel phrases is the crux of the poem. In this way, the speaker shifts his attention back to the "música callada." He again crosses the threshold and accepts the fall into language, the presence of language that marks an absence. If the body of the other is transient and yet the speaker risks the pain of loss in making love to it, then the kiss (the intangible, the lie, the presence that marks an absence, the signifier that can mislead as well as lead to the signified) is also suspect if not for the mouth. The mouth, the lips of the loved one, give meaning to the kiss as do the identity and character of the loved one. The final verses of the poem are ironic because we as readers have the option of *"reading"* them as ironic.

> Que mientan ellas, las palabras tuyas.
> 15 Yo quiero su sonido: ahí, en él, tengo
> la verdad de tu vida, como el viento,
> ya sereno, de marzo. Oyelo. Habla.
>
> (p. 249)[157]

If the speaker hears the truth in the sound, he will know that the words are ironic. Words can lie, but that lie is a truth because of the sound and the source of the words: "la verdad de tu vida." Notice the use of the verb "tengo": The speaker can possess, but what he possesses is being. The March winds may be calm now, but we know that March is unstable, the winds can change direction from one moment to the next. Likewise, life is uncertain; but if we know that and accept that inconstancy as a constant, we hear the "música callada." As Rodríguez states at the end of "Cantata del miedo," the known evil is "el menos traicionero." Knowing that all of reality is transient and that to celebrate life is to expose oneself to the risk of loss and pain, the poet can hear the "música callada" and give himself freely to the fall into language, the gap, the absence that is presence, and continue to seek his immortality as a poet.

For that reason, the final words of "Voz sin pérdida," like its title, are ambivalent. "Oyelo" can be either a command to the other or to the self to accept that paradoxical situation which constitutes life, or it can be an ecstatic recognition: "I hear it! Listen to it! Isn't it beautiful!" "Habla" could equally be a command to the other or to the self to speak so that the poet can decide if what is said is honest, authentic, or it can be a declaration: "That which the March wind says is the truth; my poem, my words also tell the truth because they accept the lie, the gap, the loss, the absence." This poem marks the elegist's reentrance into language, the reconstitution of his "Voz sin pérdida."

The speaker's joyful though painful acquiescence to crossing the bar, falling into language, surrendering to loss and absence takes place in "Ahí mismo," an extremely erotic poem in which the female genitals represent the gap, the bar separating and uniting signifier and signified. Here the union of self and other, light and dark, experience and innocence, having and being, is the indefinite but very perceptible difference between them, the imprecise boundary separating joy and pain, agony and ecstasy. The other's body is metaphor for the transient and the permanent, the known and the unknown, light and darkness, as evident in the opening statement.

> Te he conocido por la luz de ahora,
> tan silenciosa y limpia,
> al entrar en tu cuerpo, en su secreto,
> en la caverna que es altar y arcilla,
> 5 y erosión.

> Me modela la niebla redentora, el humo ciego
> ahí, donde nada oscurece.

(p. 250)[158]

This act of knowing ("conocimiento") depends on a contrast between opposites. The reciprocity between knowledge of self and/through/of the other is evident in the opening verb phrase "Te he conocido" and in the light that exists in the darkness. The female genitals are described as a cavern, and yet that cavern is full of light. The contrast between "altar y arcilla" juxtaposes the permanence of stone (the altar) with the malleability and mutability of clay. The altar is a place of immolation and surrender, death and resurrection; and clay can enrich the soil or impoverish it, as we have seen in other instances in Rodríguez's poetry. The poet also describes the genitals as "erosión," a destruction by slow disintegration (the passage of time), but also eroticism (Eros), the drive to preserve life, just as in Freudian terms the death drive and the pleasure principal are inextricably intertwined.

When in the next verse the speaker states, "Me modela la niebla redentora, el humo ciego," he ironically receives shape, contour, identity from the amorphous (mist and smoke), and he reverses the relationship between self and other, sculptor and sculpture (another use of clay). His identity, his knowledge of self, depends on his knowing the other; note the contrast between "Te he conocido" and "Me modela." The "secreto" and "misterio"—ambivalent images Rodríguez uses throughout *El vuelo*—of the female body redeem as they blind, another phrase with religious overtones (cf. Paul's conversion), just as mist and smoke are transitional states.

The poet continues to develop these concepts with a series of images in vv. 8–25. The darkness within is described as "transparencia" and "luz de abril," whereas the cavern is transformed into a chalice. Even though this offertory cup is made of stone, it is subject to the erosion of time (cf. "Arena"). Geologic images of stone and different land forms ("grietas," "estratos," "el relieve calcáreo") describe the female genitals visually and tactilely, but also evolve the images of the cavern as "altar y arcilla, / y erosión." The vaginal lips ("los labios crudos") are "tan arrasadores / como el cierzo, que antes era brisa": They incite (the breeze as inspiration, erotic desire) and culminate the sexual act (the north wind—symbol of coldness, death, loss of sexual potency). The cavern is presented in a series of ambivalent but climactic images:

> ahí, en el pulso seco, en la celda del sueño,
> en la hoja trémula
> iluminada y traspasada a fondo
> 20   por la pureza de la amanecida.
> Donde se besa a oscuras,
> a ciegas, como besan los niños,
> bajo la honda ternura de esta bóveda,
> de esta caverna abierta al resplandor
> 25   donde te doy mi vida.
> Ahí mismo: en la oscura
> inocencia.

(p. 250)[159]

The adjective "seco" could refer to a lack of potency and the sterility of this act, but it could also indicate the intensity of the climax, of the moment of release. Not only does "sueño" mean sleep and dream (unconsciousness and heightened consciousness); "celda" can be the prisoner's enclosure and isolation or the locus of the mystic's union with the divine (loneliness versus solitude). And the tremulous leaf (both frightened and thrilled) traversed by the pure morning light contrasts opacity with clarity. To kiss "a oscuras, / a ciegas, como besan los niños" is to kiss either because one has been told to (as one tells a child to kiss and the child obeys because s/he trusts completely), or spontaneously because children love without questioning. The phrase "donde te doy mi vida" reinstantiates the duality of self and other at the same time that it expresses the surrender of one to the other. To give one's life to another is to die to self but also to continue one's life in the life of the other (cf. "la contemplación viva").

The final phrase of the poem repeats the title. Ironically, we know the specifics of that place (the female genitals), and yet these genitals as gap are an indefinite and mutable place, a constantly shifting reference described by deictics. The separation of adjective and noun in the phrase "en la oscura / inocencia" individualizes self from other yet combines the concept of darkness (gap, wound, loss, absence) and innocence (incapable of harming or injuring).[160] The sexual act is a union of opposites that weakens and strengthens the self; in spite of its repetitive nature, it is always different, new, unknown. So, too, is the act of writing/reading, participation in the aesthetic act. We often learn something about ourselves by surrendering ourselves to the other—the text. That which separates some from others—poets, critics, lovers—is the extent to which they fall into the gap, accept the risk of pain and loss, embrace the absence in the presence.

Rodríguez makes the transition to the next poem, "Salvación del peligro," by converting the concatenation of images into a catalog of metonymic items. Providing a sense of plenitude through sheer proliferation, this catalog of the world's simple beauty compensates the speaker for the loss he has sustained. As he says in the first stanza, "Esta iluminación de la materia, / con su costumbre y con su armonía, / . . . / salvan mi deuda" (vv. 1–2, 13). In spite of the familiarity of this commonplace world ("su costumbre") and in spite of its temporal limitations, fleetingness, and mutability, the speaker reaches out eagerly to touch it "sin recelo, / con la alegría del conocimiento" (vv. 7–8). The accumulation of details—which point to subtle qualities latent in the commonplace (the metal is strength, the linen textuality, the creeping thyme on ocher soil a contrast between vitality and sterility)—leads to one of the most often cited passages of *El vuelo*.

> peligrosa la huella, la promesa
> 35   entre el ofrecimiento de las cosas
> y el de la vida.
>
> Miserable el momento si no es canto.
>
> (p. 252)[161]

While summarizing Rodríguez's poetics, this statement is particularly poignant in light of the elegiac purpose of *El vuelo* and the work of mourning that has taken place in these poems. The barely perceptible, almost fragile interface between transience and the enduring meaning of reality ("la huella, la promesa") is dangerous ("peligrosa") precisely because one must accept "el ofrecimiento de las cosas" to attain "el de la vida." A seed remains just a seed unless it falls to the ground and dies, which leads to abundant life.

The title "Salvación del peligro," then, is ambivalent and ironic. The poet must preserve, rescue, redeem fleeting reality, that which is subject to the ravages of time, to preserve, rescue, redeem himself from that same fate. It is only through his celebration of the transient that he can preserve the moment, converting it into song.[162] Through his recognition of absence in the presence of the signifier, he is able to invest "hollow" words with significance and give lasting presence to his absence.

Of all the poems in *El vuelo,* "Sin adiós," the last poem in the penultimate section, is one of the most tranquil and consolatory. The gentle rhythms of the language harmonize with the seascape and the theme of love, elegiac symbols of natural flux and tranquility. The parallel between interior and exterior that makes of this scene an "objective correlative" of the speaker's consolation and peace is established in the first stanza.

> Qué distinto el amor es junto al mar
> que en mi tierra nativa, cautiva, a la que siempre
> cantaré,
> a la orilla del temple de sus ríos,
> 5 con su inocencia y su clarividencia,
> con esa compañía que estremece,
> viendo caer la verdadera lágrima
> del cielo
> cuando la noche es larga
> 10 y el alba es clara.

(p. 253)[163]

The contrast between the open expanse of the ocean and the interior, captive land is reinforced by the phonic play in "el amor . . . junto al mar," the paronomasia of "nativa, cautiva" and "su inocencia y su clarividencia," and the contrasts of innocence and insight, night and dawn. Even though the speaker's grief has been long and his sadness painful (the rain as "la verdadera lágrima"), the cleansing, nourishing properties of water (river and rain) have produced a change that the speaker now recognizes. The future of the verb "cantaré" and the promise of a clear dawn after the rain are indications of the tranquility he has acquired and the optimistic outlook he has gained after working through his loss and his grief. However, just as his mourning has led to consolation and greater insight, just as his concept of self was shattered only to return more strongly, this contrast becomes imbricated complementarily and reciprocally in the next stanza.

Nunca sé por qué siento
compañero a mi cuerpo, que es augurio y refugio.
Y ahora, frente al mar,
qué urdimbre la del trigo,
15   la del oleaje,
qué hilatura, qué plena cosecha
encajan, sueldan, curvan
mi amor.

(p. 253)[164]

Just as "augurio" is both sign and meaning, signifier and signified, symbol and interpretation, just as "refugio" is the place of shelter and the protection sought, so the speaker's body is a "compañero"—someone other and yet an intimate companion who is always there and understands him better than anyone else. This combination of estrangement (difference) and unity ("identity") mirrors the elegist's relationship with the lost loved one: He has assimilated her and made her present in his life even though she is absent, forever lost. So, too, he speaks of his relation with language because the words "urdimbre" and "hilatura" refer to weaving and spinning, creating textuality. The grain of his native land and the waves of the ocean are synonymous, as are the acts of spinning and weaving, growing and reaping. This dialectic characterizes the poet, for these two aspects determine the shape and direction of his life ("encajan, sueldan, curvan / mi amor"). If this duality is true of the poet himself, the presence of the female other only augments this interaction and definition of self ("identity") through similarity and difference.

El movimiento curvo de las olas,
20   por la mañana, tan distinto al nocturno
tan semejante al de los sembrados,
se van entrando en
el rumor misterioso de tu cuerpo,
hoy que hay mareas vivas
25   y el amor está gris perla, casi mate,
como el color del álamo en octubre.

(p. 253)[165]

By attributing the same ambivalent qualities to the other, the speaker establishes a reciprocal, complementary relationship with her, a chiasmatic give-and-take, gain and loss. The poet instantiates this chiasmas in the disposition of the waves and the crops, morning and night, in vv. 19–21. The melding of their bodies results in the color "gris perla, casi mate" as black and white produce a liminal gray and the lusterless finish of a pearl suggests moistness and softness along with the opaline iridescence of this precious gem. The comparison of this color with that of the poplar leaves in October evokes the myth of Orpheus and the leaves he wears on his head when he descends into the underworld in search of Eurydice. But because it is autumn, these leaves will have lost the fresh greenness of spring, making their color even more silvery, perhaps a visual metaphor for the waves of the ocean at dawn "hoy que hay mareas vivas," which might account for "el rumor misterioso." More metaphors for the female body develop this duality in the poem's final stanza.

> El soñar es sencillo, pero no el contemplar.
> Y ahora, al amanecer, cuando conviene
> saber y obrar,
> 30 cómo suena contigo esta desnuda costa.
> Cuando el amor y el mar
> son una sola marejada, sin que el viento nordeste
> pueda romper este recogimiento,
> esta semilla sobrecogedora,
> 35 esta tierra, este agua
> aquí, en el puerto,
> donde ya no hay adiós, sino ancla pura.

(pp. 253–54)[166]

It is easy to dream because all we need do is fall asleep, close our eyes to reality, and let ourselves be carried away. It is much more difficult to be open eyed and to engage life fully, to surrender ourselves willingly to participation, and to make something lasting of that contact. That is precisely the speaker's task (and pleasure) at this liminal moment when he makes love with the other (the sea, all of reality). His comparison of the other with "esta desnuda costa" encompasses the emptiness, barrenness, absence, and loss inherent in reality and language along with the attraction, desire, and allure of the constant mutability of the seashore (another liminal space as we have seen earlier in "Amarras" and "Frente al mar"). All of this is equated with the lost loved one, one of many possible interpretations of the "tú" addressed here.

The possibility of another storm (another loss, another encounter with pain and turmoil of self) exists in "el viento nordeste," but the love of this other—described here as a "puerto," similar to the "caverna" in "Ahí mismo"—is not a point of departure ("ya no hay adiós") but a safe haven, a protective sheltering port where the poet can find stability, "sin que el viento nordeste / pueda romper este recogimiento." The word "recogimiento" reverberates with different connotations: withdrawal ("refugio"); spiritual absorption ("la contemplación viva"); harvest ("cosecha"); and retreat (in the religious sense of the word). Compared with "esta semilla sobrecogedora, / esta tierra, este agua," this "recogimiento" is the future promise of loss (the seed must die or it will remain just a seed) and of a propitious situation for growth and more abundant life.

ELEGIAC SUTURE: THE TRANSCENDENT PRESENT

The final section of *El vuelo*, consisting of the three-part "Elegía desde Simancas," forms the counterpart to "Herida en cuatro tiempos." United and separated by the three intervening sections, these two poems constitute the two-poem section that is both present and absent in *El vuelo*. Given that "Herida en cuatro tiempos" is the painful expression of the overwhelming presence of absence (the wound caused by the loss of the loved one), "Elegía desde Simancas" is the obverse side of this coin, a celebration of presence in spite of absence. It seems ironic or perhaps redundant that Rodríguez should end his elegiac work with a formal elegy, but this strategy pulls together the two extremes of mourning: absence and presence, grief and consolation, wound and suture, loss and quest. This poem encompasses and concentrates in one statement the entire range of emotions that have evolved throughout *El vuelo*. Because it replicates the structure of "Oda a la hospitalidad," it shows that the poet has reached a similar conclusion: He has arrived at the same commitment to distinguish himself through writing by confronting the most difficult aspects of life in spite of the pain this procedure causes him. Despite the structural similarities between the ode and the elegy, however, the difference in tone, language, and imagery attests to the continuing evolution of the self.

Before examining the elegy in detail, a few comments concerning the title and subtitle "Hacia la Historia" are warranted. This poem was presumably written during and/or following the poet's visit to Simancas and its medieval fortress outside of Valladolid, overlooking the Pisuerga River valley. Because Rodríguez mentions history in the subtitle, the historical significance of Simancas may have a bearing on our reading of the poem. Simancas was originally a Roman settlement (a beautiful Roman bridge still crosses the Pisuerga), and according to the *Enciclopedia Sopena*, "es célebre en la Historia por la victoria obtenida en 939 por Ramiro II de León sobre el califa Abderramán III."[167] This struggle between what might be called the forces of "good" and "evil" echoes the elegist's struggle with grief and his eventual triumph over it.

At one time, the fortress served as a "prisión de Estado," but since 1539, it has served as a repository of important historical documents related to Spanish history. "El castillo de Simancas es hoy el Archivo general de la nación, que encierra 33 millones de documentos . . . que vienen a ser como un libro abierto de la historia de España."[168] This collection of documents provides the backdrop for the current document, *El vuelo*, the elegist's response to an event in his personal history. How does his document compare with these others? Will his words last over time as the Roman bridge, the medieval castle, the village, and these (un)remarkable moments in the history of the Spanish nation? These seem to be the questions motivated by the poet's visit to this out-of-the-way village, for the historical setting emphasizes the passage of time, the arbitrary endurance of some events and the oblivion of others.[169] The presence of the Pisuerga subtly underscores this ambivalent view of time as both fleeting and eternal, the old and the ever new.[170]

The subtitle "(Hacia la Historia)" gives greater definition to this ambivalence. On one hand, the poet is gazing upon the past, finding a Roman bridge, a medieval castle, historical documents, and a village that has changed little (at least on the surface) over the centuries. But the preposition "hacia" also suggests futurity, a look forward. The poet's philosophy, as it has evolved in *El vuelo*, is that one must live life to the fullest to overcome the omnipresence of death, the passage of time, and a sense of emptiness ("Miserable es el momento si no es canto") and to make life worthwhile.

This affirmation expresses Rodríguez's poetics of delving honestly and profoundly into himself to identify himself by writing truly exceptional poetry.

If in "Herida en cuatro tiempos" the speaker feels that he is immersed in the nothingness of the present moment (the wound), here in "Elegía desde Simancas," he finds himself in the gap between past and future, but with those terms reversed. The future will be History (with a capital H) if the poet will live life anticipating not his absence but his continued presence in language. Language marks an absence, but it is also present and can make that absence present if the poet engages with his world, explores his emotions, and salvages the passing moment from destruction. The present moment, then, is both a gap (a wound, an emptiness) and the point of contact between the future and the past (in that order).[171] Just as the three middle sections of *El vuelo* separate and unite the two-poem section, the present moment is loss and gain, wound and suture, gap and connection, elegy for what is absent and quest for eternal presence. This paradox is manifest in the contrast of light and darkness, past and present, in the opening verses of the elegy. Note also the predominance of the elegiac conventions of spring, light, resuscitation, and breath.

> Ya bien mediado abril, cuando la luz no acaba
> nunca,
> y menos aún de noche,
> noche tan de alba que nos resucita,
> 5   y nos camina
> desde esta piedra bien pulimentada,
> respiramos la historia, aquí, en Simancas.
>
> (p. 257)[172]

The spring month of April (dedicated to Aphrodite, the goddess of love) along with "alba" and "resucita" suggests a new beginning when the days get progressively longer following the equinox. This renewal of light and life even takes place at night, a possible allusion to the poet's grief (the loss of light) which has led him to greater insight. The unusual verb phrase "nos camina" along with "nos resucita" could mean that the light orients even in moments of darkness and grief, but it also communicates a sense of examining closely and making repairs.[173] Likewise, the preposition "desde" is ambivalent: The light could reflect off the stone (the streets of Simancas, the white stone of the castle, or even the Earth itself). The light as stimulus elicits a response from the speaker. But it could also refer to the speaker's path as he reaches this decisive moment and must decide which direction to take. In this situation, the light determines his future course, differentiating past (reflected light) and future (light as horizon). That this rock is "bien pulimentada" could mean that it is well worn because of the passage of time and the number of feet that have trod upon it, or it could suggest the refinement and shaping of stone to create a work of art (the castle, the poet's life and work).

In either case, past and future converge on this moment when we "respiramos la historia." Considering the many written documents contained in the archives of Simancas, this history represents the poetic tradition (the past) that the poet repeats and renews with his own act of writing, particularly significant when we talk about the elegy.[174] Rodríguez equates this specific place with the passage of time (loss versus constant renewal, the specific moment versus the entire expanse of time). This union of time and space leads to a comparison between the architectural structure of the castle and the documents it houses.

> Y se va iluminando
> la curva de los muebles,
> 10   las fibras de papel ardiendo en la peña madre,
> el ábside de los pergaminos,
> la bóveda de las letras. Y los nombres cantando
> con dolor, con mentira, con perjurio,
> con sus resabios de codicia y de
> 15   pestilencia y amor. . . .
>
>   (p. 257)[175]

The imbrication of architecture and nature combines art and life: The furniture is both artifact and practical equipment; the snow on the mountaintops at dawn resembles pages of fire; parchments are supportive or decorative structures; the dome that protects these documents is the sky.[176] The image of roundness that repeats in "curva," "ábside," and "bóveda" suggest a Guillenian perfection and the height of the "peña madre" aspirations of the sublime, whereas the gerunds "iluminando" and "ardiendo" lend color and warmth to the impersonal: Words are transient objects unless we invest them with insight and activate them.[177] Similarly, the names of authors or the words in this archival material are "cantando"—broadcasting, making public, declaring or singing, celebrating—a whole panoply of human emotions and reasons for making these declarations "con dolor, con mentira, con perjurio, / con sus resabios de codicia y de / pestilencia y amor." For example, we could read "pestilencia" as death, loss, catastrophe, that is, reasons for writing, acts preserving the moment for posterity. Writing transforms the brute event, mediates via language (and emotion) meagre reality, as we see in the following image of a fountain.

> 15   . . . Y se va alzando
> el cristal, donde un nuevo recocido
> limpia sus poros y moldea a fondo
> su trasparencia, junto a las encinas
> en alabanza con su sombra abierta.
>
>   (p. 257)[178]

The cleansing and shaping of the water's transparency and the fountain as symbol of life and fertility is set against a backdrop of "encinas," evergreen trees symbolizing eternal life. The "sombra abierta" of these trees echoes the phrase "noche tan de alba" at the same time that it contrasts the shadowy trees with the clarity of the water. The juxtaposition of light and darkness, the static and the dynamic, reaffirms the reciprocity and complementarity of the two and points to the theme of loss and gain, transient and lasting, elegy and quest.[179] In the next stanza, the simple act of eating bread in the morning—with its eucharistic overtones of sacrifice and resurrection—represents drawing on the past through the act of reading.[180]

> 20 La corteza del pan, que ahora está en manos
>   de la mañana,
>   y la miga que suena
>   a campana
>   nos aclaran, serenan,
> 25 aún ocultando la mirada ocre
>   de la envidia,
>   el hombro de la soberbia, los labios secos de la
>   injusticia,
>   la cal de sosa, el polvo del deseo,
>   con un silencio que estremece y dura
> 30 entre las vértebras de la historia, en la hoja
>   caduca y traspasada en cada vena
>   por la luz que acompaña
>   y ciega, y purifica el tiempo
>   sobre estos campos, con su ciencia íntima,
> 35 bajo este cielo que es sabiduría.

$$(p. 258)^{181}$$

The cover of the book is like the crust of a loaf of bread, whereas the soft white interior calls the faithful to partake in the ritual. The act of reading provides insight and inspiration ("nos aclaran") and comfort ("serenan") because we can still find vivid human emotions in its pages: "la mirada ocre / de la envidia, / el hombro de la soberbia, los labios secos de la injusticia." We can read "la cal de sosa" as caustic invective and "el polvo del deseo" as lasting human love.[182]

Ironically, all this vivid emotion arises from silence—perhaps the past, the books that make no noise on their own, the history of Spain, or even the isolated and rural countryside, because "las vértebras de la historia" could be a mountain chain surrounding the valley or the spine of the books ("vértebras" is synecdochic for "espinazo"). "La hoja / caduca y traspasada en cada vena / por la luz" may refer to the new spring leaves in the sunlight of the rural scene or to the insight and inspiration offered by the lines written on the pages of a book ("hoja," "vena"). The leaves are "caducas," indicating that they have been here indefinitely (spring keeps renewing life across the centuries) and that they are thin, fragile, vulnerable to destruction.[183]

This light "acompaña y ciega": We forget the light outside (we take it for granted) unless sometimes it is so bright that we must narrow our eyes. We can forget that we have a book in our hands and are reading words on a page because we get so absorbed in the characters and the voices accompanying us. To read is to forget completely the passage of time in our world and to enter into another concept of time and space, a time and space that we can reevoke again and again, endlessly. Books are fields that produce great abundance because of their "ciencia íntima," the act of writing and reading, sowing and reaping, the marvelous miracle of life.

In the final verse, the sky recalls the architectural term "bóveda," again combining art and life. The fields beneath the sky and the books beneath the dome of the library represent "sabiduría," knowledge of self through knowledge of the world (of books). We can see here how "conocimiento" and "sabiduría" are reciprocal and complementary, just as the fountain and the holm oaks at the end of the first stanza.[184] Reading, returning to the past via the written word and history, becomes a way of renewing life through loss. As a result, this first section of "Elegía" corresponds to the past-in-the-present experience of loss and gain described in section II of *El vuelo* at the same time that it counterbalances the concept of the present tense and the sense of loss expostulated in "Herida en cuatro tiempos."

Consonant with the tripartite structure of the intervening sections of *El vuelo* (and with "Oda a la hospitalidad"), in part II of "Elegía desde Simancas," the moment of troping obtains. These verses define the turning point, the transformation of elegy and loss into quest and gain. Yet, because of the inextricability of these concepts, the images of part II are extremely ambivalent. This section begins with the description of a sunrise that recalls to some extent "Noche en el barrio" (from *Alianza*).

> Nunca de retirada, y menos aún de noche,
> alta de sienes,
> tan sencilla, amasada
> en la cornisa de la media luz,
> 5   entre rejas del conocimiento,
> en la palpitación del alma
> llega la amanecida.
> Y el resplandor se abre
> dando vuelo a la sombra.
>
> (p. 258)[185]

Several words related to the head—"sienes," "cornisa" (derived from the Greek *korone,* meaning crown or wreath), "conocimiento," and "alma"—make dawn synonymous with inspiration and insight, reinforcing the juxtaposition of "luz" and "sabiduría" at the end of the previous part of the elegy. The personification of dawn as a proud but simple woman, perhaps a kind of caryatid on a cornice, the lover on the other side of the "reja" covering a window, or the palpitation that love causes in the soul, makes this a figure of someone always arriving, even at night (dark moments of grief).

The last line of this statement, however, is ambivalent. Does the light chase away the shadows of night, routing them in an aggressive, bellicose advance? Or does light create shadow, allowing the world to stand out in bolder relief and to elevate, gravitate, "lighten" the shadow? Reminiscent of the memorable lines from *Don,* "Así amanece el día; así la noche / cierra el gran aposento de sus sombras," this image inscribes and excises shadow, and represents the loss/gain motif and the troping from elegy to quest, the turning from grief and loss to consolation, quest, and the promise of eternal presence. As a result of his visit to Simancas (the past), the speaker has a clearer picture of himself, seeing himself in the other writers, the other voices there. He provides several images of that self in the next verses.

10   Como lince de caza en la ladera,
      al acecho, mirando casi con su hocico,
      como el milano real o la corneja
      cenicienta, en el tiempo
      de invernada, así vienen ahora
15   la rapacidad, el beso,
      la imagen de los siglos,
      la de mi misma vida.

                                        (pp. 258–59)[186]

As a lynx or a bird of prey, the speaker is always alert to the possibility of finding sustenance, ensuring his survival. As the "milano" is a diurnal hunter and the "corneja" nocturnal, and because all three must seek sustenance "en el tiempo / de invernada" when food is scarce, these perceptive animals can sustain life even in lean times, similar to the poet's finding inspiration even in moments of grief and loss. This characteristic is for him both "la rapacidad" and "el beso," a taking advantage of the loved one's loss and a tender demonstration of his affection for the beloved.[187] In perusing other documents (the elegiac tradition of poetry), the poet sees that he is not unlike others and that future readers will be able to judge his motivation as he does when he reads others.

                         Hay nidos
            de palomas, y halcones
20   ahí, en las torres, mientras canta el gallo
            en el altar, y pica
            la camisa ofrecida y humilde y en volandas
            en la orilla derecha del Pisuerga.

                                        (p. 259)[188]

Both doves and falcons reside "en las torres," which could be the tall, elegant structures of a fortress or, provincially, a villa, a summer cottage. The rooster who sings on the altar (a symbol of Christ's death and resurrection) contrasts with the humble, commonplace scene of the rooster pecking at clothing spread in the sun to dry. Because this image reminds us clearly of the experiences described in "A mi ropa tendida" and "Lluvia y gracia," there can be little doubt that the poet refers to the motivation for writing. His specification of "la orilla derecha del Pisuerga" concretizes this scene, creating a contrast between the mimetic and the symbolic, but it also suggests a contrast with the left bank, the other side of the issue, the "sinister" side, showing Rodríguez's concern for the moral aspect of writing.

In the midst of these images, the ambivalent question of v. 24 stands out: "¿No ha sucedido nada o todo ha sucedido?" The contrast between negation and affirmation, "nada" and "todo," rhetorical and straightforward questions, posits a chiasmatic turning point. This verse problematizes the distinction between art and life, fantasy and empirical reality, history and representation. In this regard, the speaker follows in the footsteps of Segismundo, Don Quijote, and the art of Velázquez. The verb "suceder" also recalls poems such as "Un suceso" (from *Alianza*), "Una aparición," and "Tan sólo una sonrisa."[189] A large part of the elegiac project involves proving oneself worthy of inheritance from the past, an issue Rodríguez confronts in this moment of troping. The final lines address the air—an indication of the troping—and invoke continued inspiration, insight, and life. Ironically, air is present but invisible; it is "todo" yet "nada."

> 25 Aire que nos acunas
> y que nunca nos dejas
> marchitar porque arropas
> de mil maneras,
> tan seguro y audaz, desde los coros
> 30 del pulmón,
> hasta la comisura de los labios,
> ven tú. Eres todo.
>
> (p. 259)[190]

Air as inspiration—the breath of life and aesthetic insight—is an invisible, "absent" substance that leaves a mark on us by protecting us from dying. The verb "arropar" would suggest something wrapped around (perhaps even a shroud), but the air also works from the interior, giving substance (body) to life. The air does its task "de mil maneras, / . . . desde los coros / del pulmón, / hasta la comisura de los labios." This image compares the many tiers of alveoli with a choir loft as the source of song that modulates and is shaped by the vocal tract all the way to the corners of the mouth.[191] These references to speech and song as well as the anatomical (architectural) structure formed by shaping the air emphasize the reciprocity and complementarity of interior and exterior, all and nothing, presence and absence, gain and loss.[192] By declaring to the air "Eres todo," the speaker tropes the absence of the lost loved one into the very breath of life, so that he transforms his elegy into poetic quest and dedicates himself to celebrating the absence that is present: the air, the lost loved one, the transience of life itself—his inspiration.

The final part of "Elegía desde Simancas," like its counterpart section IV of *El vuelo* and the final part of "Oda a la hospitalidad," looks to the future from the tranquility of the present. The poet knows full well what it takes to achieve an outstanding poetic expression, the effort and pain, but also the great satisfaction and triumph. Picking up a thread from the previous part of the elegy, the speaker contemplates his approach to life and poetry in terms of vocal expressions to begin this final statement.

> La historia no es siquiera
> un suspiro,
> ni una lágrima pura o carcomida
> o engañosa: quizá una carcajada.
>
> (p. 259)[193]

The term "la historia" refers to that which will outlast the ravages of time: the full surrender to life and the expression of that surrender through writing. Saying that life does not even measure up to a sigh ("un suspiro") or a tear—a silent signifier that can be honest and pure, a grave, continuous worry, or deceitful and false—the speaker is defining his poetics and his approach to life through diminishment and negation.[194] Perhaps all of life is nothing more than a sarcastic, ridiculous jest ("una carcajada"). This bitter, discouraged outlook represents the nadir of human existence and a nihilistic vacuity. The speaker posits this low point, this extreme negativity, as the counterpoint to his dedication to poetry, to the salvation of the fleeting through the act of writing as he has defined it. In spite of the transience of life and its apparent meaninglessness, he points to the written word in books.

```
 5   Pero aquí está el sudor
     y el llanto, aquí, al abrigo
     de la lana y el cuero repujado,
     en la seda, el esparto,
     en la humildad del sebo,
10   en la armonía de la harina,
     en la saliva en flor, lamida y escupida
     y pidiendo
     pulpa de dátil o un amor cobarde
     en las ciudades esperando el tráfico.
```

(p. 259)[195]

The effort and grief of life ("el sudor / y el llanto") can be found between the protective covers of a book. Expression can be as smooth as silk or as course as esparto grass; it can be as humble as the suet used in candles, or as harmonious as the flour used for bread; it can be as crude as a lustful appetite ("la saliva en flor") seeking sweetness and delight ("pulpa de dátil"), or too embarrassed to declare love openly. And it can be found in the most mundane, empty, and impersonal places, "en las ciudades esperando el tráfico." But amidst all these books, this wide range of human emotions and situations, the speaker needs to find himself.

```
15   Estoy entre las calles
     vivas de las palabras: muchas se ven escritas,
     finas como el coral,
     color rojizo oscuro,
     en manuscritos; otras
20   batiendo alas en tantas paredes,
     dichas a pleno labio,
     mientras tú estás enfrente, cielo mío,
     y no me das reposo. . . .
```

(pp. 259–60)[196]

Some of the words in manuscripts are floridly written in red ink, beautiful to look at and passionately written; others remind us of the grackle in "Incidente en los Jerónimos" (from *Conjuros*), capable of flight but caught within the walls of their own making, honest words ("dichas a pleno labio") but never soaring. In contrast with these, the poet sees the open sky as an invitation but also a challenge to soar. The sky invigorates and excites him, and makes him uncomfortable, uneasy, never still ("y no me das reposo"). A perfect counterpart to the opening nihilistic verses of this section, the final verses supply a kind of coda to the entire experience of *El vuelo*, and yet this closure looks to the future and the continuing surrender and resurrection that poetry provides for Rodríguez.[197]

> . . . Calla, calla.
> Aquí ya no hay historia ni siquiera leyenda;
> 25   sólo tiempo hecho canto
> y luz que abre los brazos recién crucificada
> bajo este cielo siempre en mediodía.
>
> (p. 260)[198]

The repeated verbs "Calla, calla" can be read as commands, injunctions, pleas, or invocations of the silence out of which the poet's words will arise. These commands may be addressed to the sky—the poet's ideal and the challenge it presents to him— because poetry demands painful concentration from the poet, who here tries to resist the inevitable. They may also, however, be addressed to the poet himself as he urges himself to listen and to make the effort required of him without complaining even though it is painful.[199] These words could also be declarations, descriptions of those moments when the sky is a silent source of inspiration, the privileged moment when true poetry emerges, as the final verses attest. Again, by silencing, by negating, Rodríguez defines his transgressive poetics.

By stating that his poetry is neither history nor legend, the speaker denies that he is merely reporting what has happened and what he has felt, or that he is aggrandizing and exaggerating it. His poetry is "tiempo hecho canto," the transient and the lasting, elegy and quest interacting with one another in the liminal interface between them: the wound, the gap, the silence. It is "luz que abre los brazos recién crucificada," the prototype elegiac image, also a symbol of inspiration, here converted into a Christ figure. But just as Christ was crucified, he rose from the dead. The theme of resurrection following pain and death is an apt image of what Rodríguez hopes to accomplish with his poetry. He hopes that by surrendering himself to the pain of loss (the wound as the gap in language), he will ensure his poetic immortality. For his ideal—the sky above him that both provokes desire and challenges—is to be always honest with himself in his quest to attain immortality, the perfect moment of noon when there is no shadow, "a blinding yet purifying displacement from physical to spiritual vision."[200]

5

Prometheus Double-Bound:
The Role of the Poet in Contemporary Life
in *Casi una leyenda* (1991)

I am the door . . .
The thief cometh not, but for to steal . . .
I am come that they might have life,
and that they might have it more abundantly.

Given that for Claudio Rodríguez the poetic act is akin to crucifixion because of the tremendous effort, sacrifice, and pain it can cause, it may seem astonishing that he should want to write yet another book, to submit himself to that surrender, and to probe deeply into himself, in spite of the rewards, joy, and pleasure that can accrue from such an experience. But that is exactly what he does fifteen years after the publication of *El vuelo de la celebración*, when he releases his most recent work to date, *Casi una leyenda*.[1] Jonathan Mayhew has written a perceptive and insightful article analyzing Rodríguez's use of repetition in this work.[2] Beyond a doubt, repetition theory—as well as chaos theory—provides valuable insights into *Casi*. Nonetheless, I will examine this work in light of various aspects of the sublime, the poet as Promethean thief, and the relationship between writer and reader to see how Rodríguez defines the role of the poet in contemporary society.[3]

Though it may be a critical commonplace to say so, with the publication of *Casi*, Rodríguez shows that each of his works raises the stakes of participation in the poetic act for both writer and reader; each elevates the level of aesthetic, linguistic, and psychological intensity as the poet delves more deeply into himself. An ironic result of the incisive, self-sacrificing activity of writing that characterizes Rodríguez's poetics is that the more the poet personalizes and individuates his thoughts and his utterances, the larger his image becomes in the public eye.[4] The poet then must explore even more incisively into himself in the hope of deflating his image. Yet such a self-effacement, self-humiliation, and demystification only adds to his aggrandizement, resulting in a "double bind."[5] The title *Casi una leyenda* encapsulates this ambivalence.[6] On the one hand, the poet may be reacting sarcastically to the (to his thinking)

333

overblown proportions of his (legendary) image. But on the other hand, he is still striving to attain a certain personal ideal, a vision that still eludes him, for which he yearns and which he is committed to seeking through the poetic act.[7]

In *Casi una leyenda,* Rodríguez portrays the poet as a Promethean and a Christlike figure (the thief and the benefactor, the human and the divine). In his self-sacrifice, the poet conjoins penetrating appraisal of the colloquial, trivial, transient self with his striving for poetic immortality afforded by the poetic act. Both avoided and sought, his necessary confrontation with and acceptance of the inevitability of death are Heideggerian and sublime. These dualities are also visible in the complex structure of the work. The body of *Casi* consists of three sequences of five poems each, which Rodríguez has titled "De noche y por la mañana" [At night and during the morning], "De amor ha sido la falta" [Love has been at fault], and "Nunca vi muerte tan muerta" [I never saw death so dead].[8] Preceding these symmetrical groupings (which we might call the "main acts"), the poet has placed a substantial three-part "overture" ("Calle sin nombre"), while between them he has intercalated two "interludes." The first, "Interludio mayor," consists of the masterful "El robo," whereas the second, "Segundo interludio de enero," is the two-poem section that is the hallmark of Rodríguez's works. This interlude contains "Un brindis por el seis de enero" and "Balada de un treinta de enero," which offset "Calle sin nombre" and "El robo."[9]

The second interlude functions as a counterweight, making the overture and intermediate poems mobile, unfixed, fluid, in comparison with the three more "monolithic" sequences of five poems (although it seems superfluous to comment that Rodríguez deconstructs this binary opposition of fixed/fluid). What makes this structure unique is that the counterweight exhorts us to reread "Calle sin nombre" at the end of the work. By recontextualizing the overture as "coda" or "epilogue," a dynamic progression of the speaker from Promethean to Christ figure, from the oneiric (grotesque, distorted, stumbling) to the sublime (ecstatic, soaring), obtains. Ironically, this closure (making the structure symmetrical, balanced, complete) also has the effect of beginning the cycle of poems anew, so that they repeat indefinitely.[10] But if we finish our reading of *Casi* with "*Secreta*," the last poem of the third sequence, the structure seems lame, deformed, unsymmetrical (grotesque).[11]

By concluding our reading with the rereading and recontextualization of "Calle sin nombre," we "complete" the work and bring it to closure (the sublime). But this closure is illusory because it leads to an interminable repetition, rereading, and rediscovery of the poems. To stabilize the work in that way is to reach the sublime (the ideal, perfect, polished, finished) but also to make the work sterile, repetitive, static, as well as perpetually in flux and renewal. On the other hand, if we end our reading with "*Secreta*," the incompleteness and unsymmetricality liberate the counterweight, making the text dynamic and vibrant even though it seems to be imperfect (incomplete, grotesque), even though it seems to "limp along."

The structure embodies the theme of the work in the figure of the poet as Prometheus and Christ: The role of the poet in contemporary society is to remind us—through his example and his words—that we should imitate Christ (by being Prometheus, a thief) and thereby "complete" the work of redemption always already fulfilled by Christ's crucifixion and resurrection.[12] These figures also define the gain/loss economy of the sublime, which turns on pain and a confrontation with finitude. As Suzanne Guerlac remarks,

> A moment of negation is at work in the series of terms associated with the sublime because of the slippage from positive pain to delight. That the sublime can be said to "turn on pain" is thoroughly ambiguous, since pain is both posited and canceled. The interpolation of delight into the grounding binary opposition superimposes upon that distinction one between presence and absence. . . . While the relation between pleasure and beauty is an immediate one, that between pain and the sublime is mediated by an absence or separation. It is marked by negativity.
>
> If the sublime for Burke involves "the strongest emotion which the mind is capable of feeling," this is so because pain, upon which the sublime is said to turn, is considered to signify death—an absolute in relation to sensation. Death, like the infinite, is "presentable but by language"; yet pain is said to serve as a sign for death. . . . The force of the sublime in the *Enquiry* is thus a function of that play of presence and absence that marks the process of signification in general and that finally refers us to that ultimate absence—death.[13]

One other aspect of this work warrants especial mention as part of this process. At first, the language of *Casi* may seem "flat," "matte," or "opaque" in comparison with Rodríguez's previous works, that is, repetitive and lacking in brilliant metaphors. It is almost as if the poet were intentionally expunging superficial brilliance, forcing the reader to reach beyond the dull signifier to the sublime signified. This denial of "beauty," this "uglifying" of the surface, lends more gravity to the content and heightens the impact of the sublime by denying the artifice of art.[14] If the grotesque is a significant part of the sublime because of the interaction of opposites, Rodríguez compels the reader to "swallow a bitter pill" to heighten the sublime impact of his thought.[15] This experience with language replicates the poet's often painful exploration of self, making the poems of *Casi* descriptive of the poet's experience and prescriptive for the reader's participation in and actualization (the putative completion) of the text.[16]

In both its structure (form) and theme (content), *Casi una leyenda* is the epitome of the supplement in Rodríguez's poetry, as the reader's participation supplements the poet's act of writing. Descriptive and prescriptive, performative and constative, this work completes what is already complete; it adds (im)perfection to (im)perfection; it imbricates and deconstructs the grotesque and the beautiful to reach the Sublime. In short, *Casi una leyenda* is a (re)enactment—a repetition and a renewal—of Rodríguez's transgressive poetics and his (re)definition of self and his vocation as poet in yet another context and at another stage in his life.[17]

OVERTURE AND FIRST ACT: THE SEARCH FOR WISDOM

"Calle sin nombre" [Street without a name] functions as an overture or prelude to all of *Casi una leyenda*, and each of its three parts foreshadows the three major sections that follow. Whereas earlier in his career Rodríguez used the image of the road ("camino") to represent his poetic path, in *Casi* he substitutes the street ("calle"). That this street has no name may refer to the anonymity and ostensible lack of individuality the poet feels, and it can define his sense of disorientation and alienation (perhaps because he has not written for several years or perhaps because the city does not inspire him as much as the countryside).[18] It may also emblematize the poet's inability to give voice to his poetic desire. Denis Donoghue explains that "The myth of Prometheus answers to this pattern of feeling when it is interpreted as testifying to the endlessness and the namelessness of man's desires."[19] Indeed, the first part of the poem creates an oneiric atmosphere; it is as if the poet were lost, unable to find his bearings, because he cannot name (or find the name) of this street.[20] As if in medias res, a long, convoluted sentence and ambivalent imagery introduce this work with a disorienting effect.

> ¿Y no hay peligro, salvación, castigo,
> maleficio de octubre
> tras la honda promesa de la noche,
> junto al acoso de la lluvia que antes
> 5 era secreto muy fecundo y ahora me está lavando
> el recuerdo, sonando sin lealtad,
> enemiga serena en esta calle?
> ¿Y la palpitación oscura del destino,
> aún no maduro hoy?
>
> (p. 11)[21]

Sometimes posed as a question and at others used in a declaration, the beginning of sentences with the conjunction "y" [and] will become a leitmotif repeated not only in "Calle" but throughout *Casi*. As often in Rodríguez's poetry, these opening questions can be straightforward or rhetorical. As genuine questions, the poet's disorientation and his search for wisdom (meaning, knowledge) and/or identity ("nombre") is self-evident; but as rhetorical questions the speaker's sense of incredulity, frustration, and perplexity is also manifest.

The opening sequence of nouns, "peligro, salvación, castigo," epitomizes Rodríguez's poetics and posits the poet as a Promethean figure. As we have come to understand through reading his poetry, the aesthetic act involves a risk or leap of faith that the speaker has called "aventura" in *El vuelo* and here has explicitly called "peligro." Taking that risk leads to "salvación," poetic immortality that redeems the poet and his world, and "castigo," pain, retribution for the risk and the effrontery the poet demonstrates in participating in the poetic act. Just as Prometheus dared to transgress Olympus to steal fire, a redemptive act on behalf of humankind, and received a painful and prolonged punishment for his audacity, so the poet experiences his participation in the act of writing. The "maleficio de octubre" embodies the enchantment and magical attraction of a beautiful, dynamic autumn and the sense of fleeting beauty, loss, and immanent barrenness, a bittersweet combination of agony and ecstasy. "Calle sin nombre" begins, then, with a sense of disenchantment and frustrated expectations.

Rodríguez confuses the issue further through a number of displacements, equivocations, and ambivalencies. First, hypallage (a reorganization of normal word order to distort meaning) displaces the adjective "honda" from "noche" to "promesa," foregrounding the hope engendered *in* the night in contrast with the depth and darkness *of* the night, a period of poetic gestation in Rodríguez's idiolect. Also, the prepositional phrase "junto a" here and in other poems in *Casi* conflates and confuses metaphor and metonymy. Because this phrase literally speaks of contiguity, we could read it as meaning that the "acoso de la lluvia" is adduced *in conjunction with and in addition to* "la honda promesa de la noche" as a reason for high expectations; as such, it functions metonymically. But this phrase as Rodríguez uses it also purports a comparison: The "acoso de la lluvia" is a substitution for "la honda promesa de la noche," a metaphoric amplification of the initial image.

The poet augments this equivocation with the contrast of past and present ("antes ... ahora") and the abrupt enjambment of vv. 5–6. At first, we might think that the rain is cleansing (in keeping with the images of water, rain, and washing that we have seen throughout Rodríguez's opus); but then we learn that it is cleansing his memory.[22] If the first reading is ambivalent (cleansing is purifying but also painful), the second compounds the equivocation. Does having his memory cleansed by the rain distill and purify those scenes from his life, or does it fade them and wash them away, leaving the poet without memories? Does the gerund "sonando" complement "lavando" as part of the progressive tense? Does it describe the rain as betrayer ("sin lealtad, enemiga serena")? Or does it describe "recuerdo"? If memory betrays the speaker, the rain will be an "enemiga *serena*," battling against the tricks of the mind to alter and idealize memories (life itself). In that case, the rain will reveal the truth as opposed to the lie of memory, the betrayal of the mind.[23]

Likewise, the second question could repeat the first one ("¿Y [no hay] la palpitación oscura del destino ... ?"); or it could complete the later sequence ("¿ ... me está lavando / el recuerdo ... [y] la palpitación oscura del destino ... ?"). The speaker is caught in a maze of language, as if he were lost in an unfamiliar city late at night in the rain, lending an oneiric dimension to this scene. This disorientation is sustained in the synesthesia and the ambivalent questioning of the next verses.

> 10   Oigo la claridad nocturna y la astucia del viento
> como sediento y fugitivo siempre.
> Pero ¿dónde está, dónde
> ese nido secreto de alas amanecidas
> de golondrinas?
>
> (p. 11)[24]

The combination "claridad nocturna" is paradoxical in itself, but the speaker states that he *hears* that which should be visible. Does that mean that he can do the impossible, see the unseen? Or does it attest to his continued disorientation? By personifying the wind as astute, he suggests that his poetic insight is both deceptive and knowledgeable. This duality is reinforced by the adjectives "sediento y fugitivo"; his inspiration is seductive but elusive, enticing but deceitful; he desires it, but it is not easy to apprehend. The emphatic repetition of "¿dónde?" certainly voices the speaker's disorientation, but has he lost something that he possessed in the past, or is he trying to find something new? That which he seeks is a natural image in the midst of a city: The wings of morning suggest flight, the soaring of the imagination—even in the swallows' nest, anchored in a hidden place. Tension between the static and the dynamic, dark and light, attraction and disorientation, continues in the final verses of this part.

> 15 Alguien me llama desde
>   estas ventanas esperando el alba,
>   desde estas casas transparentes, solas,
>   con destello y ceniza
>   y con la herencia de sus cicatrices mientras
> 20   esta puerta cerrada se hace música
>   esperando una mano que la abra
>   sin temor y sin polvo. ¿Y dónde los vecinos?
>
> (pp. 11–12)[25]

Although the speaker hears someone calling to him and desires to make contact with that person, several aspects of the scene intensify his confusion and disorientation. The indefinite "alguien" and the deictic "estas" used with "ventanas" and "casas" creates a sense of surreal confusion, while the placement of "desde" and "mientras" at the ends of their respective verses suspends attention, disorienting and shifting expectations. We can imagine the speaker in the middle of a dark city street with several tall buildings and windows around him, seeking a voice that calls to him through the darkness and the rain. The windows (sites of observation or insight) are blank because there is no light, and the houses seem transparent, unreal, because they blend in with the darkness.[26]

The reality surrounding the poet is promising and inviting but also ill-defined, alienating, and disorienting. It presents a spark or gleam of insight and inspiration ("destello") and the lack of warmth and substance, the transience and loss of material reality ("ceniza").[27] The scars borne by these houses represent both wounds and signs of healing, the marks of time (aging) they have acquired either because of their architectural design or because of weathering. Because these scars are termed an inheritance, these images include gain and loss, venerability and decrepitude, identifying characteristics and imperfections.

Nonetheless, the poet has the ability to transform his limitations into advantages, as the image of the door suggests. Though the door is closed, the poet can convert that experience into music, song, poetry. A closed door can operate as a stimulus, calling out to the poet to open it, to find out what is on the other side, just as the speaker hears a voice calling to him; but the door can also prohibit access. Both the door and the hand that opens it (notice here the indefinite article and the use of the subjunctive) must be "sin temor y sin polvo." These phrases could apply equally to either noun. The door may be inviting to be opened, and it is kept in good condition, clean and polished, again presenting an inviting, attractive, welcoming image. But it takes someone with courage to accomplish this task, a hand that will also respect and appreciate the beauty of the door and its purpose, one that will not get it dirty and leave it in bad condition. The hand must be that of a special poet who will not mar the beauty of this means of access that is also a protective barrier, one that will convert the door into music.

The final question combines the previous ones by repeating both the conjunction and the interrogative. Condensing the images of the nest and the house along with the metapoetic dimension of the voice and poetic experience (the Promethean motif), this question encapsulates the speaker's disorientation, alienation, frustration, desperation, and incredulity. Neighbors are those who live in the city with him, those people who share his life and his times, his hopes and his fears. The speaker feels both intimacy with them and estrangement from them; he feels their proximity and their distance.[28]

As we shall see, this first part of "Calle" is related to the first major section of *Casi*, "De noche y por la mañana." But before discussing the five poems of that section, let us examine the remaining two sections of this poem to see how they also reflect important characteristics of the next section and those following. The first verse of part II, "Está ya clareando" [It is now growing lighter] signals not only a temporal advance (also evident in "De noche") but also a thematic shift. If in part I the speaker wanders confusedly through the night seeking wisdom (insight, inspiration, knowledge), in the second part he has received a modicum of illumination.

But this insight reveals his lack of courage, his reluctance to submit himself to the castigation that results from engagement in the poetic act. He offers (to himself and to the reader) several alibis, ostensible reasons for thinking that writing is a sterile and unproductive act in contemporary life, where words (poetry) no longer carry any weight. After exhausting these social and personal criticisms, however, the speaker comes up against the wall of his own resistance and determines to pursue his ideal in spite of the pain. The acquisition of courage prefigures the theme of the second major section of *Casi*, "De amor ha sido la falta."

The shift in tone and theme is manifest in the similarities and differences between the beginning of part I and that of part II. After the terse announcement of the progression of time, the speaker begins a long, convoluted sentence that concatenates a number of images. Even though he again begins this sentence with the conjunction "y," the question is now a declaration.

> Está ya clareando.
> Y cuando las semillas de la lluvia
> fecundan el silencio y el misterio,
> la espuma de la huella
> 5   sonando en inquietud, con estremecimiento,
> como si fuera la primera vez
> entre el aire y la luz y una caricia,
> ya no importan como antes,
> el canto vivo en forja
> 10   del contorno del hierro en los balcones,

las tejas soleadas
ni el azul mate oscuro
del cemento y del cielo.
La calle se está alzando. . . .

(p. 12)[29]

Along with the imminent arrival of dawn the rain is ceasing. The new "face" that the light and rain give to reality has a fecundating effect. The "semillas de la lluvia," then, are the combination of light and raindrops that lends a new brilliance to the world and a new perspective to the speaker, as "el silencio y el misterio" of night begin to yield insight and inspiration. Resisting the change that he perceives, the speaker tries to deny that his poetry, his words, and his insights ("las semillas de la lluvia") have as much importance as they used to: "ya no importan como antes."

The combination of light and water converts the wrought-iron railing of a balcony into "canto vivo en forja," an image of rosy dawn augmented by "las tejas soleadas" and even more by the contrast of coolness suggested by "el azul mate oscuro / del cemento y del cielo." The tension between street and sky, darkness and light, is accentuated at the same time that it is denied and suppressed. These are beautiful visual images, and yet the speaker denies their importance and negates their vitality.[30]

The basic structure of this sentence is interrupted in vv. 4–8 by a digression describing the speaker's self-conscious awareness of his steps, that is, the poet's self-conscious scrutiny of his writing. On a literal level, we can almost see and hear his footsteps as he treads the damp pavement, leaving a foamy trail of footprints. The erotic overtones of this description unite the transient and fleeting with the ecstasy of the moment. Because it is dawn and everything looks clean and fresh, his writing adopts a newness and enthusiasm "como si fuera la primera vez." Yet it is immediately after this evocation of erotic newness that the speaker denies and resists the beauty he perceives. This juxtaposition augments the tension in the more specific images of the balcony, the rooftops, and the opposition between street and sky.

The terse sentence "La calle se está alzando" forms a frame with "Está ya clareando" and reinforces the ambivalence of this moment. The verb "alzarse" could be read as "to rise," meaning that the street, this ordinary scene, is adopting new dimensions because it is the same color as the sky: The poet's insight allows him to convert everyday reality into transcendent experience. But "alzarse" also means "to rebel against," suggesting that the street scene is in opposition to the sky, rebelling against an overidealization of reality that the poet no longer accepts as a valid perspective on life.

While evincing some progress, the speaker falls back into a skeptical attitude regarding himself existentially and the poet metaphorically when he returns to the conjunction "y" and the interrogative mode. This resistance, a reluctance to accept the vision he sees, then leads him to criticize both self and society more severely.

. . . ¿Y quién la pisa?
15   ¿Hay que dejar que el paso, como el agua,
se desnude y se lave

<blockquote>
algunas veces seco, ágil o mal templado;
otras veces, como ahora
tan poco compañero, sin entrega ni audacia,
20   caminando sin rumbo y con desconfianza
entre un pueblo engañado, envilecido,
con vida sin tempero,
con libertad sin canto?

Me está hablando esta acera como un ala
25   esta pared en sombra que me fija y me talla
con la cal sin tomillo y sin vuelo sin suerte
la juventud perdida. Hay que seguir. Más lejos . . .
</blockquote>

(pp. 12–13)[31]

The speaker wonders what is required of him as a poet and why it is required of him when he lives amid an uninspired and disinterested society avid only for material gain. He wonders how he can expose himself, make himself vulnerable, in such a climate because it causes him to write "sin entrega ni audacia, / caminando sin rumbo y con desconfianza." Despite the inclination to soar that poetry and writing stimulate in him, he nevertheless confronts "esta pared en sombra" that defines him more precisely. The whitewash of the wall makes it white, but it is in shadow, and whitewash does not permit the growth of life, the pungent odor and vibrant color of thyme in contrast with the limy whitewash in shadow.[32]

When the speaker mentions "la juventud perdida," one questions whether he is talking about his own disillusionment with life and writing, with his identity as a poet, or whether he is criticizing today's youth who are—he intimates—unable to appreciate his words, his poetry, his effort ("vuelo"), or any experience that requires effort and sacrifice rather than pure chance ("suerte"). These young people seem to be incapable of soaring unless it is produced by the completely aleatory (winning the lottery, attending a concert, or taking drugs, e.g.).[33] But the poet also recognizes his own disenchantment and the limitations he places on himself. For that reason, he urges himself forward: "Hay que seguir. Más lejos . . ." The final verses in this section thus readopt a more positive outlook with a return to the declarative as opposed to the interrogative use of "y."[34]

<blockquote>
Y voy de puerta en puerta
calle arriba y abajo
30   y antes de que me vaya
quiero ver esa cara ahí a media ventana,
transparente y callada
junto al asombro de su intimidad
con la cadencia del cristal sin nido
35   muy bien transfigurada por la luz,
por el reflejo duro de meseta,
con pudor desvalido,
asomada en silencio y aventura.
Quiero ver esa cara. Y verme en ella.
</blockquote>

(p. 13)[35]

Renewing his search for the door that will provide access to the sublime experience he described in part I, the speaker employs the same tone evident in "Nieve en la noche," an earlier moment of determination to avoid superficial brilliance and self-deceit: "quiero ver esa cara." The combination of several factors—the verb "clareando" in v. 1; the (female) other and the window in "Nieve"; the gender of the noun "cara"—suggest that this other is a female figure, the poet's muse. The conception of this other as his poetry emphasizes the clarity and honesty of his vision. The other's face appears in the open part of the window and is illuminated by its transparency and transfigured by the light of the Spanish plateau. The "meseta" even serves as a mirror because the poet identifies openness, light, and air with this image.

On two occasions, he remarks on the silence of this figure: Though transparent and silent, this vision of the other is that which allows the poet to identify himself, to distinguish himself as a poet. This face, "asomada en silencio y aventura," represents tranquility and excitement; it unites self-confidence with the need to take risks. In confronting this otherness which is himself, his alter ego, the poet will alter his ego, his perspective. He will become someone different—a threat to or even denial of his identity—at the same time that he learns to know himself better. His terse, energetic declarations in the final verse evidence his determination and his courage.[36]

In accord with the temporal progression in this poem, part III opens with the assertion "Ha amanecido" and with an affirmation beginning with "y." Corresponding to the third major section, "Nunca vi muerte tan muerta," this part of the poem presages the contradictory pain and pleasure entailed in full surrender to the poetic act. With the dawning of day, the speaker realizes both his suffering and his love that have coincided to bring him to this epiphanic moment.

> Ha amanecido. Y cada esquina canta,
> tiembla recién llovida. Están muy altos
> el cemento y el cielo.
> Me está llamando el aire con rutina,
> 5   sin uso.
> El violeta nuevo de las nubes
> vacila, se acobarda. Y muy abiertas
> vuelan las golondrinas y la ciudad sin quicios,
> el bronce en flor de las campanas. ¿Dónde,
> 10 dónde mis pasos?
>
> (p. 14)[37]

The images of dawn and turning a corner problematize interpretation. If dawn is like a corner, there is a line (the horizon?), angle, or limitation, before which we experience anticipation and after which we may feel satisfaction and plenitude modified and undercut by a certainty that a unique moment has been lost. Each corner is a turning point which, once passed, produces song, but the song is almost a belated aftereffect: Something is lost when representation obtains.[38] Moreover, the corner trembles: from pain and fear, or from excitement and joy? The iteration of the rain (washing as painful cleansing) strengthens this ambivalence. Although "Están muy altos / el cemento y el cielo," it is unclear whether the speaker has risen to the occasion with them (so to speak), or if he views them as far beyond him, too ideal to attain and yet still beckoning, still attracting him. The ambivalence of the parallel but inverted phrases "con rutina, / sin uso" indicates that the poet has experienced these sensations before, and yet something entirely new is happening.

The violet color of the clouds is a particularly evocative image. First of all, clouds often represent, traditionally, that which is changing, transient, fleeting, and unattainable (cf. "A la nube aquella" from *Conjuros*). To this concept, the poet adds the delicate color of violet, which, according to Chevalier and Gheerbrandt, is a "Color de la templanza, hecho de una igual proporción de rojo y de azul, de lucidez y de acción reflexiva, de equilibrio entre tierra y cielo, los sentidos y la mente, la pasión y la inteligencia, el amor y la sabiduría."[39] This perfectly balanced mix of red and blue (cf. "forja" and "tejas soleadas" versus "el azul mate oscuro" from part II), "vacila, se acobarda." As a result, this image evokes a sense of surrender, of submission to crucifixion, both pain and ecstasy, surrender and triumph, death and resurrection, linking this ambivalence with the turning of a corner.

The next three images of the swallows, "la ciudad sin quicios," and the bells explode upon us so quickly that we barely have time to absorb them. Again the leitmotif "y," the flight of the swallows, the lack of barriers (doors, thresholds), and the flowering of the bells quickly pushes the *locus amoenus* into a *carpe diem*. On the heels of this rapid transformation the question "¿Dónde, / dónde mis pasos?" posits the theme of *ubi sunt?* (the past) and the uncertain direction his steps will take (the future). The speaker is clearly excited because he has entered a zone of intense insight, but this "window of opportunity" closes very quickly, giving only a glimpse of what awaits poet and reader in the final section of *Casi*. As eager as he is to participate in this adventure, the speaker is immobilized, overwhelmed, unable to go forward. The final verses are extremely disquieting because a totally different voice (a different part of the speaker's persona?) abruptly brings the overture to a conclusion.[40]

> Tú no andes más. Di adiós.
> Tú deja que esta calle
> siga hablando por ti, aunque nunca vuelvas.[41]

In one respect, these verses teasingly anticipate the final poems of *Casi*, "Nunca vi muerte tan muerta." But the irruption of this alternate voice functions as a barrier and a limitation that brings the overture to a conclusion and reminds us that there are many more poems, many more barriers, that lie between the speaker and his goal. In fact, this alternate voice that bids the poet be silent will reappear in "Manuscrito de una respiración," the final poem of "De noche," as a voice speaking from another text. By drawing attention to that limitation, that "closed door," Rodríguez again posits a tension between metaphor (that which we hope to attain at the end of *Casi*) and metonymy (the next section). To attain the ideal goal, we must submit ourselves to the deferral of satisfaction, to the overcoming of obstacles, to the temporal unfolding of the text that eventually leads to the sublime. At the end of this chapter, I shall reread "Calle sin nombre" as epilogue rather than prelude. This recontextualization will completely subvert the reading I have just elaborated. But such a tour de force will only be possible if we first examine the intermediate sections to establish the new context.

Casi una leyenda has afforded us greater insight into Rodríguez's poetic trajectory and development. As a result of this work, it is easier to comprehend that in each of his books Rodríguez elevates his expression and the reader to a new level of discourse in inverse relation to the profundity with which he delves into himself. One of the major purposes, then, of "Calle sin nombre" and the poems of "De noche y por la mañana" is to instruct the reader how to read this text.[42] If we conceive of the poet as a Promethean figure, we realize that he acquires this insight, knowledge, wisdom, inspiration, not for his own aggrandizement, for he knows in advance that he will be castigated for his transgression. He persists in his task of writing/stealing fire in order to share it with all of humankind and to improve the human lot in the future.[43] The five poems of "De noche," prefigured by "Calle," coerce us into learning how to read, how to share in this wisdom and to profit from it. As Donoghue points out, however, in doing so, the poet makes the reader complicit in the theft; the reader, as the receiver of stolen goods, becomes an accomplice and must bear some of the castigation as well as partake of the benefits.[44] In short, these poems are challenging precisely because the extent of the risk we take and the effort we expend will determine the beauty and clarity of the gift we receive.[45]

Consonant with "Calle," the five poems of the first section delineate a temporal progression from sunset in "Revelación de la sombra" [Revelation of the shadow] to dawn in "Nuevo día" [New day]. The final poem, "Manuscrito de una respiración" [Manuscript of a breath], introduces a new, alternate voice speaking to poet and reader from a supposed other manuscript, similar to the alternate voice that intervenes at the conclusion of "Calle." As the poet contemplates the acquisition of light, wisdom, and inspiration, he implicates the reader in the same process. The title "Revelación de la sombra" initiates this process in the equivocality of the genitive. Is the shadow revealed? Or does the shadow make the revelation? Is a revelation an unveiling and exposing of that which already exists? Or is it a prediction of what will happen (as in the Book of Revelation)? Also, revelation suggests illumination, light, understanding, whereas shadow is darkness, concealment, disorientation, and confusion. To reveal is to expose the hidden, to make the unseen visible; a shadow may be a soothing, cool, comfortable relief from intense light; or it may be a symbol of darkness, coldness, loss, and death.[46] All these contradictory, paradoxical elements come into play as the speaker searches for insight and is reluctant to surrender himself to it. Prometheus knows beforehand that he will be punished, yet he seeks.

"Revelación" is an important statement, but much of the confusion it creates is comparable to what we have already seen in the speaker's nightmarish wanderings in the first part of "Calle." The initial verses rely upon negation, the contrast of light and dark, and an image of flight, all of which are ambivalent.

> Sin vejez y sin muerte la alta sombra
> que no es consuelo y menos pesadumbre,

se ilumina y se cierne
cercada ahora por la luz de puesta
5   y la infancia del cielo. . . .

(p. 17)[47]

The negative markers "sin," "no," and "menos" define this shadow by taking away possible characteristics rather than attributing them to the shadow, veiling as they unveil. The notable exception is the adjective "alta," an adjective that Rodríguez has used symbolically before (in "Alto jornal," for example). But even this word is equivocal because it can mean that the shadow is lofty, elevated, worthy of dignity and respect, or serious, grave, somber, and to be feared. Not only is it neither "consuelo" nor "pesadumbre"; this shadow "se ilumina"! Is the reflexive pronoun literal (it reveals itself) or impersonal (it is revealed)? Is the shadow subject or object? In similar fashion, the verb "cernirse" can mean to soar ("alta") or to hover (imminently). It would seem that the darkness is laying siege to the fading light of sunset, but here the reverse is true: The light of the sunset and the innocence (purity, ideality) of the sky perform this aggressive, militaristic action on the shadow. If night is a period of gestation, a fecund but generative time of inactivity that leads to dawn, the breaking of new light, new insight, we can perhaps deduce that here the light of a previous illumination still has enough force to resist entering the darkness again, because of the threat of another revelation at the next dawn (a dazzling but painful, blinding "deslumbramiento").[48] This ambiguous play of light and darkness continues in the next convoluted sentence, reminiscent of "Calle," which runs from the end of v. 5 through v. 15. The last image in these verses epitomizes this passage:

y la vida que enseña
su oscuridad y su fatiga,
su verdad misteriosa, poro a poro,
con su esperanza y su polilla en torno
15   de la pequeña luz, de la sombra sin sueño.

(p. 17)[49]

An image of the Promethean poet, the moth drawn to the flame represents the fatal attraction of the light.[50] But again "la pequeña luz" is transformed into "la sombra sin sueño," a slippage from light to darkness that conflates attraction and repulsion, desire and fatality.[51] Fast on the heals of this sentence comes the leitmotif "y" and further conflations of light and darkness.

¿Y dónde la caricia de tu arrepentimiento,
fresco en la higuera y en la acacia blanca,
muy tenue en el espino a mediodía,
hondo en la encina, en el acero, tallado casi sin curva,
20   en el níquel y el cuarzo,
tan cercano en los hilos de la miel,
azul templado de ceniza en calles,
con piedad y sin fuga en la mirada,
con ansiedad de entrega?

(pp. 17–18)[52]

The white flower of the fig tree and the acacia stand out against the darkness of the leaves, whereas the shadow remains among the dense branches of the hawthorn even at the hour of greatest illumination ("mediodía") and in the holm oak, a dark evergreen symbolizing eternal life. This play of light and dark is equated with repentance, and repentance is characterized as a caress. Finally, the ambiguity of the word "ansiedad," meaning both eagerness (willingness) and anxiety (reluctance), and the end of this long question are reminiscent of the speaker wandering down the "Calle sin nombre." The final stanza of "Revelación" shows the speaker moving abruptly and frequently from one emotion to another, always ambivalent because of repetition and parallelism.

> 25 Si yo pudiera darte la creencia,
> el poderío limpio, deslumbrado,
> de esta tarde serena . . .
> ¿Por qué la luz maldice y la sombra perdona?
> El viento va perdiendo su tiniebla madura
> 30 y tú te vas yendo
> y me estás acusando,
> me estás iluminando. Quieta, quieta.
> Y no me sigas y no me persigas.
> Ya nunca es tarde. ¿Pero qué te he hecho
> 35 si a ti te debo todo lo que tengo?

(p. 18)[53]

The poet is struggling with his acceptance of inspiration and illumination, questioning why he is the (un)fortunate recipient of these insights, why he is both benefactor and scapegoat, thief and philanthropist. His poetic ability is a castigation and a gift, and he both regrets and exults in having it. Is the "tú" addressed the light or the shadow? The ambivalence of the addressee complicates our reading of the final verses.

> Vete con tu inocencia estremecida
> volando a ciegas, cierta,
> más joven que la luz. Aire en mi aire.

(p. 18)[54]

Is this a rejection of the unwanted or an invocation of the desired, a dispersal of the light or a calling of the shadow, or vice versa? The light creates the shadow, which leads to a greater appreciation of the light and consequently sharper definition of the shadow. Does the speaker invoke the shadow to protect himself from the light, or does he fear the shadow, knowing that a stronger light will appear, and thus he pleads with the light? What is the relationship between shadow and light, signifier and signified? Which is pain, which joy? Which gain, which loss? Which impedes him more, which inspires him more? "Revelación" defines the speaker's predicament as a Promethean figure reluctant to sacrifice himself because he foresees the castigation, but who also knows that he will make that commitment despite the pain.[55]

The title of the next poem, "La mañana del búho" [The morning of the owl] repeats the ambiguities of "Revelación de la sombra" but also expands upon and advances it, further confusing unveiling and veiling.[56] As "sombra" is both shadow and light, here morning functions ambivalently. Is the owl's morning those first hours after sunset when the owl—symbol of the poet, out of phase and synchronization with the rest of society—begins its "day"? Or is it that in the morning, when the sun rises, the owl must seek its roost because its vision does not function? Considering the temporal progression of this sequence of poems, we might lean toward the former. But again the play of light and darkness, attraction and repulsion, underlies the juxtaposition of the two terms.[57] The owl sees in the dark and is blinded, disconcerted, and disoriented by the light; the night represents the owl's day and the day its night. Is it night or day in this poem? Can the owl see or not?[58]

The poem begins with an ominous voice of experience warning us that some days it is better not even to get out of bed. The triteness of this proverbial wisdom is then undercut by leitmotifs: "Hay algunas mañanas / que lo mejor es no salir. ¿Y adónde?" This on the one hand humorous and banal onset of the poem creates distance and makes us wary of the reliability of the speaker, who both is and is not the owl. Is this old coot grumpy because he has to get out of bed? Or is he cautious because he knows he is in danger because he is out of his element? The highly baroque images of the next verses, again ending in a question, continues the teaching/learning process initiated in the irony of the opening verses.

> La semilla desnuda, aquí, en el centro
> de la pupila en plena
> 5   rotación
> hacia tanta blancura repentina
> de esta ola sin ventanas
> cerca de la pared del sueño entre alta mar
> y la baja marea,
> 10   ¿hacia dónde me lleva?
> ¡Si lo que veo es lo invisible, es pura
> iluminación,
> es el origen del presentimiento!
>
>   (p. 19)[59]

The word "pupila" refers to the eye, but because this word is often used colloquially to refer to the iris, "la semilla desnuda" is the true center of the eye and the focus of the poet. Light enters the eye through the pupil, a window that inverts the image on the retina. This aperture is defenseless and exposed ("desnuda") to the overpowering effect of the light ("tanta blancura repentina"). By comparing the light to a wave ("esta ola sin ventanas"), the poet suggests that the light is so intense that the eye begins to tear, blurring vision, clouding the window used for envisioning. This light even causes the lowering of the eyelid, metaphorized as "la pared del sueño." Along with the speaker, the reader might wonder where all this is leading and why Rodríguez is making us work so hard for so little in return.

In addition to being part of the teaching/learning process, this opacity also represents the frustration and difficulty the poet experiences because of his vision, his poetic insight. He may be exclaiming ecstatically and incredulously about what he sees, but he may also be questioning why he should be the one to receive this special insight that blinds him. This vision as "el origen del presentimiento" offers another indication of the figure of Prometheus, whose name means "forethought."[60] His description of the owl in the next verses makes us think that the speaker is looking at himself in the mirror and participating in the specular interplay of self and other, poetic self-consciousness.[61]

> Es este otoño de madera y de ecos
> 15 de olivo y abedul
> con la rapacidad del ala lenta
> ladeando y girando,
> con vuelo viejo avaro de la noche,
> con equilibrio de la pesadilla,
> 20 con el pico sin cera, sin leche y sin aceite,
> y el plumaje sin humo, la espuma que suaviza
> la saliva, la sal, el excremento
> del nido . . .
>
>   (pp. 19–20)[62]

These verses portray the poet as an owl hunting in a forest (his world), taking full advantage of his maturity and skill (autumn). The olive and birch trees are distinctly recognizable and easily identified, and both have a white or silvery characteristic (leaves and trunk, respectively) that would make them reflect light and stand out in the darkness (like the moon). On the hunt, the owl moves deftly and silently through its world. The poet describes its flight as a "viejo avaro," secretly and stealthily moving in the night so that no one will discover his hoard. He is as cautious about revealing himself as he is miserly in hoarding his silver, these moments of illumination in the darkness.

The description of the owl's beak is particularly suggestive because the mouth is metonymically associated with words/poetry. The beak is "sin cera, sin leche y sin aceite": Wax would shine superficially and give the owl away; a milky whiteness would be insipid, bland, even childish; oil would make the beak slippery (urbane) and might let the prey slip away from a less-accomplished hunter. The exclusionary preposition describing the plumage ("sin humo") suggests that the owl's coloring has no gray or white in it, which would give it away in the darkness, or indicate that it is not old and has not lost its skill in detecting and capturing its prey.[63] These feathers form the soft padding that lines the crude interior of the nest, characterized by the digestive process because saliva is indicative of hunger and desire, salt enhances flavor, and excrement (the bird's droppings) represents the fertilizing capacity of the poetic process.[64] The nest is also the intimate interior disguised by a rough exterior. This flattering (preening) observation of the poet as owl highlights his skill, maturity, and undiminished control. The final verses of this stanza summarize the owl's life in comparison with other birds, that is, the poet's poetics in comparison with others'.

```
           . . . Hay un sonido
       de altura, moldeado
25     en figuras, en vaho
       de eucalipto. No veo, no poseo.
       ¿Y esa alondra, ese pámpano
       tan inocentes en la viña ahora,
       y el vencejo de leña y de calambre,
30     y la captura de la liebre, el nácar
       de amanecida y la transparencia
       en pleamar naranja de la contemplación?
```

(p. 20)[65]

The image of the "sonido / de altura" calls attention to the nest as a construction, an artifact woven and redolent of eucalyptus (an evergreen; everlasting life) and to the rhythmic and alliterative language in the preceding verses. If we have not already noticed them, this repetition "del nido . . . Hay un sonido" causes us retrospectively to appreciate such melodic verses as "del ala lenta / ladeando y girando, / con vuelo viejo avaro de la noche" or "con el pico sin cera, sin leche y sin aceite, / y el plumaje sin humo, la espuma que suaviza / la saliva, la sal, el excremento. . . ." The declaration "No veo, no poseo"—in itself rhythmic, repetitive, and alliterative—epitomizes the owl's poetics: If it cannot see, it cannot capture its prey. But because this statement also evokes "Porque no poseemos" from *Alianza* and because the juxtaposition of the two repetitive phrases problematizes their syntactical relationship, we could also gloss this terse statement as an expression of the current moment. The owl at morning cannot see and therefore does not possess (knowledge).

Then the owl compares itself with the lark and the swift. The lark, like the vine shoot, thrives on sunlight and sings early in the day, but it is incapable of perching in trees, staying instead close to the ground (the tendril). Darting through the air, chattering, playing, and flying in circles, the swift's flight is dry and brittle (like firewood), not graceful, skillful, and silent like the owl's. These "poets" write so fast and so stiffly that they get writer's cramps ("calambre"); their inspiration becomes stymied quickly. Unlike the owl, these birds do not hunt the elusive prey because they do not have the skill, speed, and insight; these poets never appreciate "el nácar / de la amanecida y la transparencia / en pleamar naranja de la contemplación," privileged moments of insight and subtle color that the owl as insightful poet is capable of seizing. Equivocation in the individual images is intensified through repetition with difference. Consequently, the next verses express both the speaker's exultation and his perplexity, his capture of the prey and his searching disorientation.

```
       ¿Y todo es invisible? ¡Si está claro
       este momento traspasado de alba!
35     Este momento que no veré nunca.
       Esta mañana que no verá nadie
       porque no está creada,
       esta mañana que me va acercando
       al capitel y al nido.
40     ¿Y este aleteo sin temor ni viento,
```

la epidemia, el mastín y la crisálida
con la luz de meseta?
Cómo cantaba mayo en la noche de enero.

(p. 20)[66]

In addition to recalling the opening verses of "Calle" by repeating the leitmotif, vv. 33–34 repeat and modify vv. 11–12: "¡Si lo que veo es lo invisible, es pura / iluminación. . . ." Where the earlier verses problematize the owl's gaze, these call into question that which the owl observes, both anticipating and placing in doubt an affirmative response. Where before he questions why he instead of others has received this insight, here he wonders whether he has any insight to offer. He is questioning his epistemology and his ontology.

The transformation of this insight into "este momento traspasado de alba" and subsequently into "Este momento que no veré nunca" and "Esta mañana que no verá nadie" employs repetition with difference to instantiate the ever-shifting, ever-fleeting nature of the scene. It passes away so quickly that even the poet is unable to recapture it in language, in which case no one else will be able to appreciate it. And yet this fleeting moment brings the poet closer to the creation of the text, here embodied in the architectural capital—the uppermost part of the column usually decorated with carvings—and the nest, the poet's text. These images conflate the artistic with the natural, the spiritual with the corporal, the religious with the mundane—an imbrication of mimetic and symbolic that epitomizes Rodríguez's poetry.[67]

The slippage from "todo" to "momento" to "mañana," from "nido" to "aleteo" again shifts the emphasis from the ontological to the epistemological. The poet as owl is "sin temor ni viento": He is a mature poet unafraid of flight (unlike the nestling in Don), and the conditions seem to be favorable for flight because there is no wind to buffet the owl, change its course, or require extraordinary efforts. But the wind is also lacking as inspiration, that which will help the owl reach new heights easily. In effect, the range of stimuli or motivations for writing—"la epidemia, el mastín y la crisálida"— is lacking; the poet sees no death or suffering, there is no hound on his trail (time or fame pursuing him), and he is no longer passing through the stages of metamorphosis that motivated him earlier in his career. He has reached such a level of maturity that he wonders what more he could possibly have to say. The Promethean poet is searching for the motivation that will take him to greater heights, insight, and wisdom.

The statement of v. 43 can be read as a perplexed question and as a nostalgic exclamation. In the past, he discovered eternal life and springtime ("mayo") in the darkness and coldness of January. How was he able to do that? Oh, how he wishes he could do that again! The architectural/sculptural imagery persists in the next verses, but it is unclear if the poet compares or contrasts himself with other poets.

Junto al relieve y el cincel, la lima
45   y el buril hay ciudad,
mano de obra y secreto en cada grieta
de la oración y de la redención,
y la temperatura de la piedra
orientada hacia el este

50 con una ciencia de erosión pulida,
   de quietud de ola en vilo, de aventura
   que entra y sale a la vez. Ahí las escenas
   de historia, teología, fauna, mitos
   y la ley del granito, poro a poro,
55 su cicatriz en cada veta ocre,
   el rito de la lágrima
   en riesgo frío y cristalino en lluvia
   y con el girasol que ya se lava
   entre el búho y la virgen.
60 No hay espacio ni tiempo: el sacramento
   de la materia.

                 (pp. 20–21)[68]

The preposition "junto a" could function metonymically, juxtaposing this poet's art with the anonymity and impersonality of a modern cityscape; or it could suggest a comparison between what the sculptor and the poet can do with gross blocks of raw material, the reality of everyday life, by means of their artistry and capacity for fine detail. The similarities and differences between sculptor and laborer-builder, confusing repetition with difference, may be read as a remark concerning the quantity versus the quality of poetic production, the fine detail of the true work of art versus gross proliferation, mundane, utilitarian expansion.

This duality is underscored by the contrast between the religious and sacrilegious in several of the images. Earlier the poet imbued the everyday scene with mystical overtones when he described it as "este momento traspasado de alba" (v. 34). He has also suggested a contrast as well as a comparison between "capitel" (usually adorning the columns of a church or temple, as many of the Romanesque churches of Castile attest) and "nido." The words "oración" and "redención" (v. 47) adopt ambivalent meanings that are both profane and sacred. An "oración" is a statement and a prayer; "redención" can describe an exchange of money in the pawning of material items or deliverance from sin and atonement for guilt.

The redundancy of the words "orientada hacia el este" provokes a pun juxtaposing illumination, resurrection, and greater knowledge with the secular coldness of stone and the lack of passion, warmth, and light. This counterbalancing is sustained in the image of "una ciencia de erosión pulida." Again we note a contrast between a desire for knowledge that is a caress, a polishing, a perfection, and a calculated, pragmatic reasoning that produces superficial brilliance and urbanity. All three phrases describing knowledge as "de erosión pulida, / de quietud de ola en vilo, de aventura / que entra y sale a la vez" repeat the tension between the superficial and the profound, lifeless art and art that captures a tension and vitality, not turning it into static description but keeping it on edge, in motion, deeply felt.[69] The deictic "Ahí," which begins a series of ambivalent images, could be the poet's way of separating himself from a superficial, lifeless drawing upon experience, or his way of pointing directly at that which can enliven, resuscitate, and refresh the conventions of art. But the question remains: Is this a comparison or a contrast? Does the poet set himself apart or include himself?

Again religious overtones problematize this distinction. When the speaker talks of "el rito de la lágrima," does he mean that poetic emotion is nothing more than an empty, mechanical, lifeless ritual, or that it is sacred, heartfelt, and elevating (cf. Eucharist)? "El girasol que ya se lava / entre el búho y la virgen" stylizes the sun rising in the rain between night ("el búho") and morning ("la virgen"). But does this description represent the superficial cleansing by means of insincere tears or a true redemption of Christ (the sunflower) rising between death and eternal life, between the Devil and the Virgin, sin and purity? Is "el sacramento / de la materia" the negation of time and space, life and vitality, because it is concerned only with the material (both tangible reality and material benefit); or is it the transcendence of time and space to achieve life and eternal vitality by dint of the symbolic, metaphoric sacrament, bread and wine converted into the body and blood of Christ?

Through this marvelous description of the dawn in the center of "La mañana," Rodríguez criticizes the superficial brilliance of other poets and rejects that approach by distancing himself from them. He questions his own writing at this time, asking himself if he is a Prometheus with something to say, some wisdom to impart, or a common thief like the others. Like the owl's ambivalent "morning," meaning both dawn and dusk, Rodríguez's criticism is directed both outwardly and inwardly. He questions his own sincerity as sharply and as incisively as he criticizes others' superficial brilliance.

It may seem that Rodríguez is making us work very hard to disentangle and decipher what are in the end unresolvable ambivalencies, that he is exacting an exorbitant amount of energy and giving little in return. We must keep in mind, however, that this difficulty is part of the teaching/learning process that will elevate us to the new level of discourse and intensity of the poetic experience in which Rodríguez is engaged in this text. Though the rewards are not immediate, these difficulties, these linguistic and aesthetic barriers, are leading to even greater heights.

If in the first stanza he looks at his work and describes himself as an owl, mature but not flying, serious, determined, on the basis of what he has already accomplished; and if in the second he evaluates himself and his approach to poetry at this moment, each time comparing himself with other poets and other approaches to poetry; in the third stanza, he looks to the immediate future, presenting a line that he will repeat and modify in each of the next three poems. The opening question asks if it is possible for the poet to attain knowledge if each day is new, if the world keeps renewing itself through change: "¿Qué voy a saber si a lo mejor mañana / es nuevo día?" [What am I going to know if at best tomorrow / is a new day?] (vv. 62–63).[70] But there is also the nonrhetorical aspect: If the world is always changing, there will always be something new to learn! What can I learn now, today? This search for wisdom will carry over into the next poem, "Nocturno de la casa ida" [Nocturne of the house gone], which ends with the declaration "Ya es nuevo día" [Already it is a new day], leading us directly to a poem entitled "Nuevo día." In the final verses of the last poem of this section, "Manuscrito de una respiración," the poet will repeat but modify this question by asking "¿Y qué voy a saber si a lo mejor mañana / es la mañana?" [And what am I going to know if at best tomorrow / is the morning?]. To see how this sequence plays out, let us first examine the series of descriptive and prescriptive images that follows the initial question in this series.

Cuánta presencia que es renacimiento,
65   y es renuncia, y es ancla
del piadoso naufragio
de mi ilusión de libertad, mi vuelo . . .
Adivinanza, casi pensamiento
junto al hondo rocío
70   del polvo de la luz, del misterio que alumbra
este aire seguro,
esta salud de la madera nueva
y llega germinando
hasta el néctar sin prisa, bien tallado
75   en la jara quemada.

(pp. 21–22)[71]

Not only can we interpret "Cuánta" as both exclamative and interrogative, each of these is ambivalent. The exclamatory reading could express either frustration or delight with the ever-changing nature of life and a world that is constantly in flux. Because of these ceaseless permutations, the poet is compelled to change also, to renounce—or at least modify—what he has already learned, what he has taken to be his "knowledge," and to learn all over again. Reality is the "anchor" of a shipwreck, that to which the poor poet as shipwrecked sailor clings to stay adrift in the ever-shifting seas. How much security does he feel if the ground is always shifting and the "anchor" is all that keeps him afloat? This question beginning with "Cuánta presencia" is both a rhetorical expression of the speaker's desperation with the lot of humanity, and his sincere renunciation and search for meaning in a world that seems ephemeral. The act of writing is all he has to hold onto, and as an anchor, that which gives stability and certainty to his life ("mi ilusión de libertad, mi vuelo . . .").

By describing his writing as "Adivinanza, casi pensamiento," the poet evokes the figure of Prometheus, whose name means "forethought." With the ambivalent preposition "junto a" he equates and differentiates his words with "el hondo rocío / del polvo de la luz." Like the dew and the dust of the light, his words are insubstantial and ephemeral, yet they are also fertilizing, refreshing, full of light and insight. His poetic act is an ironic combination of gain and loss, productivity and disintegration. The images of light (insight, wisdom) may be intangible, but light and air promote growth, just as a mystery is something perplexing and unfathomable as well as attractive, enchanting, and stimulating. To germinate is both to lose the capacity for life and to produce new life abundantly (loss/gain).

The final image of a bee pollinating and extracting nectar from the rockrose, a white flower that is wilting ("quemada") because it has absorbed so much light, describes a process that requires time to unfold, blossom, ferment, and intoxicate, a process that requires loss to gain. Although these images challenge and delay both poet and reader, a sense of rising anticipation and of promise as well as frustration continues to emerge.

Es la gracia, es la gracia, la visión,
el color del oráculo del sueño,
la nerviación de la hoja del laurel,
la locura de la contemplación
80   y cuántas veces maldición, niñez,
sonando en cada ala con sorpresa.
¡El manantial temprano y el lucero
de la mañana!

(p. 22)[72]

Repetition of the phrase "Es la gracia" reveals that poetic insight is a special gift from a higher source and a mockery, an illusion, a deception (cf. "Lluvia y gracia" and "Cantata del miedo"). It is a blessing and a curse ("maldición"), a madness ("locura") that like drunkenness is both heightened consciousness and self-consciousness, an oracular insight and an insubstantial dream ("ilusión"), a surprise that delights and shocks.[73] The final exclamation emphasizes this duality by introducing erotic overtones and certifying the complementarity and imbrication of these two aspects. As premature ejaculation or an idealized Venus, poetic insight is exciting and frustrating, gain and loss. The erotic overtones lead back to the image of the poet as owl in the next verses.

Y el placer, la lujuria, el ruin amparo
85   de la desilusión, el roce
de mis alas pesadas, tan acariciadoras,
casi entreabiertas cuando
ya no hay huida ni aún conocimiento
antes de que ahora llegue
90   el arrebol interminable . . . ¡Día
que nunca será mío y que está entrando
en mi subida hacia la oscuridad!

(p. 22)[74]

Gain and loss become indistinguishable in these verses, as the owl's "alas pesadas, tan acariciadoras" can be strong and uplifting as well as a tiring, heavy weight to bear. The poet is caught in a Promethean double bind: He does not know what he seeks, and yet he has a moral obligation to seek all the same, interminably; he has not found wisdom yet, and yet he cannot turn back; and even if he finds wisdom, it will only lead him to pain and greater darkness. The rosy blush of the sunrise ("arrebol") is the promise of eternal life, eternal youth and renewal (Venus) as well as rouge, a hypocritical, false, tawdry illusion.[75] The exclamation echoes the previous verses "No veo, no poseo" and "Este momento que no veré nunca," here substituting having for seeing. On the one hand, the poet knows that if he is true to his poetics, his poetry will continue to be vibrant in the future, though he will never see that happen (Prometheus); but on the other hand, he hopes never to see the day when his poetry might become false and superficial.

The final question of the poem shifts the tone from exclamation to interrogation, chiasmatically inverting the ambivalence: "¿Viviré el movimiento, las imágenes /

nunca en reposo / de esta mañana sin otoño siempre?"[76] The poet as owl wonders if he will live *in order to* attain the images of this morning's insights (if he will survive) and if he will live *via* these images, by means of them, in spite of their elusiveness. Will he ever attain what he seeks? Or will he never be able to rest in spite of the insight he has? Will he finally participate in his endless illumination, "esta mañana sin otoño"? Or will the light constantly torment this owl? The poet is unable to resist this illumination—the darkness of his morning allows him to find sustenance, to fly— and yet he is reluctant to keep flying. If the poetic gift is a blessing and a curse, the final question is both serious and mocking.[77]

As the third poem in this sequence, "Nocturno de la casa ida" [Nocturne of the house gone] represents a turning point in the speaker's progress, establishing a pattern for the succeeding sections. Structured according to the temporal movement from dusk to dawn, this lengthy poem can be understood in three segments in which the speaker tries to break out of the darkness and find wisdom. A meditation on his status as poet, this ebb and flow portrays the need to go beyond his own limitations and to seek a higher level of expression. The three segments in this process are signaled by temporal references: "Es la hora de la puesta" [It is the hour of sunset] (v. 1); "Se está haciendo de noche" [It is becoming night] (v. 40); and "Ven noche mía, ven como antes" [Come my night, come as before] (v. 79). Each of these phrases initiates an attempt at writing, and the poem finally ends with the declaration "Ya es nuevo día" [Now it is a new day], leading directly into the next poem. Given the length of "Nocturno," I will outline the speaker's epistemological and ontological search and point out some of the crucial moments in this trajectory.

The poem opens with a string of images describing the speaker's situation at sunset. Although at first we may get caught up in the anaphoric momentum and the enchanting imagery (silver clouds above a village with smoke coming from the chimneys of the houses), just when it seems that the poet has reached a moment of epiphany, he aborts his sentence and leaves the stanza suspended. This abrupt ending and the terse sentences beginning the next stanza ("Estoy llegando tarde. Es lo de siempre" [I am arriving late. It's the same old thing]) show that the poet rejects the superficial brilliance of the opening statement. These verses are characteristic of Rodríguez's style, and although at first they may seem attractive and uplifting, the poet undercuts and rejects them as false and trite.[78] His self-humiliating rejection of that style and his search for a new form of expression is evident in the following verses.

> Y no hay manera de salvar la vida.
> 20   Y no hay manera de ir donde no hay nadie.
>
> Voy caminando a sed de cita, a falta
> de luz.
> Voy caminando fuera de camino.
> ¿Por qué el error, por qué el amor y dónde
> 25   la huella sin piedad?

(p. 24)[79]

Via anaphora and repetition the momentum builds again, only to fall back in the next segment. Here again the poet limits the length of his utterances at the same time that he modulates his tone through repetition with difference: "Se está haciendo de noche. Y qué más da. / Es lo de siempre pero todo es nuevo" (vv. 40–41).[80] Note the ambivalence of the expression "Y qué más da." On one hand, we can read this idiomatic expression as the speaker's frustration ("Who cares?"). But on the other, it can be a legitimate question, linking this "da" with the end of the truncated, abortive first stanza. The speaker may be questioning what more he can gain from participation in the poetic act (literally and rhetorically).

Rodríguez offsets these short terse sentences and the emphatic monosyllables ("Y qué más da") with the shift in time, the reworking of the leitmotif, a repetition of "Es lo de siempre," and intertextuality with the second poem of "Libro tercero" of *Don* ("Todo es nuevo quizá para nosotros"). In this act of "self-surmounting," the poet recognizes that he is no longer the same person as that Adamic figure first transgressing the limits of language; he cannot rely on the same means of expression or expect to make the same types of discoveries. If he is beginning anew, he may want to adapt the use of repetition, anaphora, and intertextuality, but always keeping in mind the difference between who he was then and who he is now. If in the past his writing was stimulated more by sensorial stimuli, now he is more mature, and his writing is "ya muy lejos / de los sentidos" [now very far / from the senses] (vv. 43–44). Now, "esta noche / de San Juan, la más clara / del año" [this night / of St. John, the clearest / of the year] his inspiration comes from a much higher source. Although this night of the summer solstice is thought to be a night of miracles, when young people build bonfires and leap over them (a fertility rite that would add to the poet's inspiration), the mature poet now looks to the stars—a colder but purer form of fire that distinguishes Prometheus from Linus (cf. "El canto de linos" from *Conjuros*).

> Y las estrellas de blancura fría
> en el espacio curvo
> de la gravitación, y la temperatura,
> 55   las leyendas de las constelaciones,
> la honda palpitación de las constelaciones,
> la honda palpitación del cielo entero
> y su armonía sideral y ciencia,
> están entrando a solas
> con un dominio silencioso y bello,
> 60   vívido en melodía
> en esta casa.
>
> (p. 25)[81]

The stars provide the poet "con un dominio silencioso y bello, / vívido en melodía," more fitting for his maturity. Their entry "en esta casa" refers to the poet's construction, the dwelling place of his being, his poetry. At this point, a conflation of night and dwelling begins, eventually leading to a consideration of the title "Nocturno de la casa ida" in which "casa" is equivalent to "noche." Before he can merge night and poetry in a new form of expression, however, the poet must undergo a second falling back in which he recognizes the deceit inherent in the basic materials of this act of construction.

> Es la desconfianza en la materia.
> Es la materia lejos de los hombres
> que no se hace a sí misma y se está haciendo.
> Es la materia misma la que miente
> 75 como la avena loca del recuerdo,
> como el delirio del cristal nocturno,
> las ventanas del cielo,
> presentimiento de la soledad.
>
> (p. 26)[82]

In the first two segments of "Nocturno" (vv. 1–39 and 40–78), the speaker is engaged in an ontological and epistemological questioning of his poetic identity. If in "La mañana del búho" he speaks ambivalently of "el sacramento / de la materia," here he examines "la desconfianza en la materia," again ambivalently. The combination of the ontological (the world around him) and the epistemological (his poetic insight) destabilizes reality at the same time that it creates a new reality. Language in the poetic act is both destructive and constructive; it participates in the transient nature of empirical reality (language as tangible signifier, as another "object"), and yet it supersedes and re-creates reality (language as signified, as the site of subjectivity, individuality, identity). The catachresis with which he describes the house—"el hormigón traslúcido" [the translucid concrete] (v. 68) and "el hierro dulce" [the sweet iron] (v. 70)—contributes to this impression. As well, the contradictory phrase "que no se hace a sí misma y se está haciendo" plays on the "se" as reflexive and impersonal, and the duality of the final line "el presentimiento de la soledad" is a forewarning of debilitating loneliness and grateful anticipation of enriching solitude.

The final two stanzas, the third segment in this process, constitute roughly half the poem. This segment starts with an invocation and then conflates the images of house and night into a temple: "Y esta casa es un templo como la noche abierta" [And this house is a temple like the open night] (v. 90). Interior and exterior, the ontological and the epistemological, interact in such a way that one calls the other into question and yet each enthralls and affirms the other, as the poet states in the next stanza: "Esta casa, esta noche / que se penetran y se están hiriendo / con no sé qué fecundidad . . ." (vv. 116–18).[83] The interaction between these oppositions not only is expressed in the images taken metonymically from the world around him, examples of which can be seen in such phrases as "la miel sin muerte del romero, el rubio / gallo de pluma fina, / el arco iris de la piel de trucha, / el ámbar de los ojos y el aullido / del lobo de Sanabria" (vv. 95–99); it is also evident in the extremes of birth and death with reference to Christ.[84] The celebration of the birth of Christ ("la cocina y la anguila / de Navidad, la nata / y la harina pequeña"; vv. 100–102) prefigures His death in the loss of innocence and a nostalgia for the past; but complementarily the images of His death ("el sepulcro vacío y el sudario doblado, / la sábana de lino, / la reverberación de la resina, / de la mirra y el áloe"; vv. 108–11) bespeak His resurrection, confusing birth and death, death and eternal life.[85]

The final stanza consists of an invocation marked by musical images and the subjunctive of the verbs "cantar" and "sonar" overlaid upon the dual image of the house/night. The poet sees his role as one who draws on the past to give to the future (cf. Prometheus), who draws on the transient to produce the everlasting, who renews stale language so that his language will then be renewed by others.[86] In these verses, the images pertaining to the house and the night (the ectypal and the archetypal) are metaphors for words.[87]

> ¡Canten por fin las puertas y ventanas
> y las estrellas olvidadas, cante
> la luz del alma que hubiera querido,
> 125   lo volandero que es lo venidero
> como canto de alondra en esta noche
> de la mañana de San Juan y suene
> la flauta nueva de las tejas curvas
> en la casa perdida . . .
>
>   (p. 28)[88]

These exclamations express hope and anguish, joy and pleading, prayer and lament, in accord with the duality of the word "Nocturno" in the title. Since the Romantic period, a nocturne has connoted a dramatic, brooding composition played on the piano, a musical work appropriate to the night. This interpretation is congruent with the metapoetic references to song and music in the above verses and can function as a lament or meditation on darkness. But in a religious context nocturnes are prayers said between midnight and dawn, the darkest part of the circadian cycle and yet the part that leads directly to dawn (light, resurrection). These religious overtones have been occupying a greater scope in the development of this poem (the night of St. John, the birth and death of Christ).

"Nocturno" is, then, both a lament for what is lost, and a renewal, a recontextualizing, a resurrection and carrying forward (of the poetic act, of language, of human experience), so that loss becomes gain as the dark of night leads to dawn. The ontological and epistemological questioning in which the speaker is engaged shows the poet accepting the paradoxical nature of his role. The Promethean poet understands the inexorability of his theft and the punishment and loss entailed as a result. His double bind is that he knows how much pain and pleasure the creative act affords him, and yet he must submit to it, fully aware that he may never know those who will eventually profit from and build upon his sacrifice, for those readers may be in the far future just as he draws upon the past (his own and a more distant past) for his inspiration.[89]

Similar to the other titles in this section, "Nocturno de la casa ida" can lament loss; but if we substitute "noche" for "casa," the loss of night results in the dawning of a new day, which is reason for exultation. This sense of renewal and discovery can be seen in the final verses which conflate "casa" and "noche" and rely on terse sentences reflecting the speaker's determination and insight: "Esta casa, esta noche . . . / Dejadme en paz. Adiós. Ya es nuevo día" [This house, this night . . . / Leave me in peace. Good-bye. Now it is a new day] (vv. 148–49).

Even though in "Nuevo día" the poet secures a moment of illumination and wisdom, it is only a prelude of what is to come. Consequently, a mild undercurrent, a darkness or shadow, tempers this moment. While there is a degree of alleviation in the first two stanzas, the "pies quebrados" (truncated lines) at the end of each stanza create suspense, anticipation.

> Después de tantos días sin camino y sin casa
> y sin dolor siquiera y las campanas solas
> y el viento oscuro como el del recuerdo
> llega el de hoy.
>
> 5 Cuando ayer el aliento era misterio
> y la mirada seca, sin resina,
> buscaba un resplandor definitivo,
> llega tan delicada y tan sencilla,
> tan serena de nueva levadura
> 10 esta mañana . . .
>
> (p. 31)[90]

Rodríguez has often used the image of the vagabond to figure the poet during his times of artistic activity. Though he has wandered aimlessly and without a goal, he has felt a distant calling ("las campanas solas") and an inspiration; but these have been echoes of his past work or imprecise insights, not new inspiration. The contrasts between "tantos días" and "hoy," "ayer" and "esta mañana," posit a turning point—or the culmination of the turning point developed in "Nocturno." The sense of a definitive change is nevertheless attenuated by impending anticipation. The "nueva levadura" suggests that the dough is beginning to rise again, but it is still not a loaf of bread, baked and ready to be eaten. The poet has reached a certain level of illumination, but as the images of the next stanza indicate, his insight is still imprecise.

> Es la sorpresa de la claridad,
> la inocencia de la contemplación,
> el secreto que abre con moldura y asombro
> la primera nevada y la primera lluvia
> 15 lavando el avellano y el olivo
> ya muy cerca del mar.
>
> (p. 31)[91]

How often have we noted the ambivalence of "sorpresa" and "claridad" in Rodríguez's poetry? In the same vein, innocence and contemplation are ambivalent, repeating but advancing the duality. A secret is something hidden, unknown, and something simultaneously revealed, known. It is this secret that opens the first snow-fall (associated in "Nieve en la noche" with a false, superficial brilliance, a deceit) and the first rain which refreshes and cleanses, gives joy and pain. While the hazelnut tree and the olive bear abundant fruit and represent the tree of life, the light trunk of the first (a member of the birch family) and the silvery leaves of the second recall "La mañana del búho" and the ambivalence of morning ("claridad"). The renewing purity of snow and rain are contrasted with the sea, a more static, horizontal image than precipitation falling from above, again suggesting a contrast between metaphor and metonymy, life and death, change and stasis.

This moment of illumination signifies a change in the speaker's outlook, but it is still too premature to reach a moment of plenitude. The ambivalence of the images mutes the light of dawn (the poet's inspiration and insight), signaling just the barest perception of the gap in language that Rodríguez explores in his writing. In the final stanza, we attain a first ambivalent perception of the gap in one of Rodríguez's most memorable verses.

> Invisible quietud. Brisa oreando
> la melodía que ya no esperaba.
> Es la iluminación de la alegría
> 20   con el silencio que no tiene tiempo.
> Grave placer el de la soledad.
>
> (p. 32)[92]

Several paradoxical combinations characterize this statement. First, the phrase "Invisible quietud" echoes the ambivalent moment at the beginning of "Frente al mar" (from *Alianza*): "Transparente quietud." In both cases, the period defining the limits of this phrase captures the tension between the visual and the auditory, the tangible and the intangible, a breeze (movement of air) that is barely perceptible, a melody that is silence. The phrase "Es la iluminación de la alegría" repeats v. 11 ("Es la sorpresa de la claridad") but reverses the terms of the comparison, relativizing the speaker's position with regard to this illumination. Is he contemplating something happening outside of him from which he is separated even though a witness to it? Or is he experiencing this illumination within himself?

Once again, these images problematize the distinction between night and day, interior and exterior, cause and effect, stasis and change. This duality culminates in the masterful statement "Grave placer el de la soledad," in which the contrast between "grave" and "placer" and two meanings of "soledad" (loneliness and solitude) epitomize the tensive relationship between two opposing yet complementary emotions.[93] In the poems of "De noche," the poet is searching for wisdom and insight at the same time that he is teaching the reader to read, seducing the reader to overcome the obstacles to understanding, so that both can participate in the acquisition of knowledge toward which these poems are striving. Once the speaker attains this climactic though ambivalent glimpse of the gap, the poem quickly begins to unravel.

> Y no mires al mar porque todo lo sabe
> cuando llega la hora
> adonde nunca llega el pensamiento

25   pero sí el mar del alma,
       pero sí este momento del aire entre mis manos,
       de esta paz que me espera
       cuando llega la hora
       —dos horas antes de la medianoche—
30   del tercer oleaje, que es el mío.

                                         (p. 32)[94]

The speaker warns the reader and himself not to look ahead at the vast horizon of the sea, but to focus on the immediate, the near-at-hand, the interior "mar del alma," "este momento del aire entre mis manos." The indicative mood in the phrase "cuando llega la hora" belies the futurity, uncertainty, and anticipation the subjunctive "llegue" would express. The speaker urges us not to seek immediate gratification but to delay its attainment. He suggests that the process is more exciting and satisfying than the attainment of the goal, which can only give us the plenitude of its pleasure if we work to overcome the difficulties of the search.[95] The enigmatic interjection placed within dashes in the penultimate line—an interruption and a perplexing enigma—instantiates that type of barrier. Two hours before midnight, ten o'clock in the evening, is the hour of the third wave. This image remits us to the third segment of "Nocturno," the invocation of night that will lead to dawn, the birth that is death that is eternal life, the death of the death of poetry (art without art), and the third "act" of *Casi*, "Nunca vi muerte tan muerta."

Similar to the antiphonal voice that brings "Calle sin nombre" to an abrupt end, the entirety of "Manuscrito de una respiración" [Manuscript of a breath], the final poem in this section, is placed within quotation marks.[96] This voice, ventriloquistically projected by the poet, speaks to him from another text; the other text, the text that the poet is reading, conveys these thoughts, this new text. "Manuscrito" is a palimpsest that reveals the voice and transmits the message if not the exact words of the previous text, filtering the voice of that text through reading in/a "Manuscrito." The palimpsest is a barrier to reading (a translucent but not transparent screen covering the original text) and a window or door that reveals the alternate voice, the voice of the other, in the words of the present text. The self-consciousness of this act of reading and writing problematizes the position of both reader and author, defining a gap between them and yet simultaneously bridging that gap, as the sign unites signifier and signified and calls attention to the abyss between them.[97] The poet speaks for the other, who speaks for the poet. The other voice in the text says what the poet would say/says. The poet is the reader of the text; the poet reads for the reader what the reader reads for her/himself.[98]

As with most of the poems in this section, the title "Manuscrito de una respiración" is ambivalent because of the preposition "de." This preposition suggests that the poem is both *about* inspiration and *belongs* or *pertains to* it. It deals with the nature of inspiration/wisdom (the ontological) and with the means of acquiring it (the episte-mological). It is inspiration *in* the text and *from* the text from the respective points of view of writing and reading. This duality can be seen in the act of breathing, of taking in and expelling breath, of receiving air/life and producing sound (anything from a sigh to a cry) in the act of releasing that air, that life.

The opening verse, which repeats the leitmotif, depicts the breath as a spy, as a traitor and a hero: "Y la respiración que es hondo espía" [And breath that is a deep spy]. A spy discovers and divulges secrets, an agent similar to Prometheus who steals from one and bestows on another. This figure ambivalently encompasses both reading and writing: The Promethean poet must draw insight from the act of reading other poets and then transmit that knowledge through his own act of writing. Each author resuscitates and revitalizes that which has passed away and then surrenders her/himself to the same fate. For that reason the speaker of "Manuscrito" refers to an inscription in stone (reminiscent of an epitaph) and the weaving and sewing of cloth—the making of a text that will last beyond the purely temporal limits of an individual's life.

The question capping the first stanza is therefore equivocal: "¿Es que voy a vivir después de tanta / revelación?" [Is it that I am going to live after so much / revelation?]. This question not only functions rhetorically and literally; it also echoes the final poem of *Don* and the change from "¿Es que voy a morir?" to "¿Es que voy a vivir?" We can see that the speaker—the voice in the text that is and is not the poet and the reader—is enthusiastic about the possibilities generated by a text and overwhelmingly doubtful of them. From the point of view of the spy, the poet wonders if he can escape with this secret, this wisdom, this light, without getting caught and punished; and he wonders if he can accept and tolerate the acquisition of wisdom that is uplifting but dangerous. At the end of *Don,* the Adamic poet questions and exalts in the new perspective he has discovered: "Cómo veo los árboles ahora." The outcome is similar, but emphasis has shifted from ego-consciousness to Self-consciousness.[99]

The ambivalence is further evident in the word "revelación," isolated at the end of the stanza. Who or what is revealed to whom? Rodríguez may be questioning his audience and the possibility that his poetry will be misread.[100] In the second stanza, the image of rest, meditation, and dream refresh the breath of insight and inspiration. The reader takes in the breath of his/her reading and ferments it.

>>La cama me remueve y me depura
con olor muy de marzo,
con mirada de lluvia entre los pliegues
de la sábana y un
20   roce de lana virgen.
La oscuridad del tórax, la cal de uva del labio,
la penumbra del hueso y la penumbra
de la saliva,
la médula espinal mal sostenida
25   por sus alas que duelen
cuando comienza a clarear y llega
un temblor de inocencia.

(pp. 33–34)[101]

The fresh air of March blowing through the sheets hung out to dry and the softness and purity of a blanket of virgin wool permeate the air taken in by the reader while sleeping. Everything from the dark, shadowy depths of the body ("la oscuridad del tórax," "la penumbra del hueso") to the oral cavity ("la penumbra de la saliva") and the lips ("la cal de uva del labio") participates in this exchange, this renovation of inspiration (life) acquired from reading.

These images may also refer to the book itself: the white pages as sheets, the cover of virgin wool. So "la médula espinal" could be the spine of a book and the wings its covers as well as the shoulder blades of a human being or the wings of an angel. Awakening to this inspiration causes aches and pains when the poet begins to process these ideas and to make them his/her own: "duelen / cuando comienza a clarear." These multifaceted images are difficult to comprehend because they are dream-like in nature, reminding us of "Calle sin nombre."

Though we had reached a brief moment of illumination in "Nuevo día," at the end of "De noche" a recession takes place, a backing off from the pain that Rodríguez's poetics exacts of the poet. The speaker of *Casi una leyenda*, the Promethean poet, may have found the inspiration he needs, but the problem of courage, which will be taken up in the next section ("El robo" and "De amor ha sido la falta"), necessitates a backing off, a distancing from the emotions unearthed in the palimpsest and the ventriloquistic voicing (the poem placed in quotation). This "pared medianera" [mediating wall], as the speaker calls it in the third stanza, produces a loss of consciousness and a heightened consciousness, "un desvanecimiento, un nacimiento" [a fainting, a birth] (v. 30). While in "Calle sin nombre" someone calls him and a door becomes music, here the wall separates and increases desire.[102] Here, too, as in "Calle sin nombre," the speaker wants to know who calls to him; the voice on the other side of the wall (the words of the text) is still inconsistent.

> ¿Y quién me llama a través de ella, quién
> me ha escogido, quién
> me está pidiendo algo y no se entrega?
> Y tú te me vas yendo,
> 35   vas y vienes y vas y estás como perdida,
> como huida de nuevo. . . .
>
>   (p. 34)[103]

The image of a bird in flight figures the reader (the poet as owl?) turning the pages of a book "en las riberas de la amanecida" [on the shores of dawn] in the final stanza. The search for inspiration leads the reader away from the text and toward the production of his/her own song: "estás sintiendo ahora / este aire de meseta, el que más sabe, / el de tu salvación que no se oye / porque tú eres su música" (vv. 49–52).[104] The poet as bird takes the air of morning (inspiration from reading) and converts it into song. The duality of reading and writing is apparent when the speaker states "Y me sanas, / y yo te doy las gracias por venir / tan delicada que casi te veo."[105] Is the text, the manuscript, the voice in the text, thanking the reader for revitalizing it? Or is the poet thanking the text for revitalizing him through his reading of it? The ambiguity of the palimpsest includes both possibilities, reinforcing the circular and reciprocal relationship between author and reader, reader and text.

This reciprocity is incorporated in the final lines through repetition and difference: "¿Y qué voy a saber si a lo mejor mañana / es la mañana?" This verse is a repetition from "La mañana del búho" ("¿Y qué voy a saber si a lo mejor mañana / es nuevo día?") which initiated the "nuevo día" motif. But it also links this final statement with "Calle sin nombre" because of the "¿Y?" and with "Revelación de la sombra" because of the parallel syntax of the titles. Earlier the poet wondered how he can know anything if each day is new, if every day his world and his knowledge of it change. Now he looks toward the future in anticipation of knowledge. Ironically, it is the text from the past that is speaking. The reader brings insight and new meaning to the text at the same time that the text inspires and creates meaning, wisdom, a vision of morning. The variation from "nuevo día" to "la mañana" suggests that each future poem will not only confront a new, unexplored reality, but that that reality will be the basis for yet other visions created by new poems and new poets, new readers and new readings. Repetition and recontextualization have expanded the possibilities of language, pointing us toward a rereading of "Calle sin nombre."

The text, like the author (the subject) and language itself, is always in flux, even though the words on the page do not alter significantly once they have been written and the author has died. The first section of *Casi* is a meditation on the ontological and epistemological aspects of the poet's task, a search for wisdom and illumination in that which is always shifting, always already nebulous and ambiguous. In this section, Rodríguez teaches the reader to read by illuminating the ambivalence and slipperiness of language. Without this fundamental basis on which to build, the reader cannot follow the poet to the profound insights that he will strive to attain in the remaining poems of this work. The Promethean poet recognizes the need for wisdom and illumination, and he begins to provide them for the reader. These poems also open a gap in language that will expand in the next section.

THEFT AND SECOND ACT: BUILDING UP COURAGE

The "Interludio mayor" between "De noche y por la mañana" and "De amor ha sido la falta" consists of the three-part poem "El robo" [The theft]. Given its structure, "El robo" parallels and advances the pattern of the overture, "Calle sin nombre," and is comparable to it in that its three parts correspond to the three major sections of *Casi*. But it also represents an advance in the speaker's progress. Whereas the first part of "El robo" looks back at "De noche" and builds upon the rent in language produced in "Nuevo día" and the split speaker of "Manuscrito," the second and third parts of the first interlude anticipate the search for courage in "De amor."

In several interviews granted after the publication of *Casi*, Rodríguez explains that "El robo" is based upon a Zamoran legend ("leyenda") about a thief who tried to steal a pair of golden candlesticks from the Cathedral of Zamora.[106] As the thief was attempting to leave the cathedral, the window through which he was escaping miraculously shrank and captured him. He was found the following morning halfway in and halfway out of the window. Although this tale evokes some of the miraculous events recounted in medieval literature (cf. the *Cantigas* of Alfonso X el Sabio) and represents the oral, popular tradition, the topos is a universal one reminiscent of the Prometheus "syndrome."[107] For this thief must transgress a sacred space (the altar) to steal the golden candlesticks—emblems of light, knowledge, and sacred wisdom. In making his escape through a window—a symbol that we have already discussed in "Calle sin nombre"—the thief is miraculously caught on the threshold. This liminality corresponds to the speaker's stance in "De amor": He has taken the light of inspiration into his hands (his act of writing), but his wavering courage prevents him from attaining full advantage (profit) from his theft.[108]

In addition to the local legend and the Promethean topos undergirding this poem, Rodríguez has preceded "El robo" with an epigraph in Italian: ". . . il fiume, / le zaffiri . . .". These words are taken from Dante's *Paradiso;* but Rodríguez has modified them, altering Dante's original "Il fiume, e il topazii" (Canto XXX). The river (specifically the Duero) remains the ambivalent symbol that has pervaded Rodríguez's poetry. Instead of the yellow topazes, symbols of divine light, Rodríguez has opted for sapphires, brilliant blue stones that reflect the sky, the ideal. Nonetheless, the context of Dante's canto can help situate the speaker of "El robo." In this canto, Beatrice tells Dante that he must drink of the water of the river before he can partake of a higher vision that will satisfy his spiritual thirst. That which the protagonist observes is but a shadow of the truth, but the fault lies not in reality but in the observer.

> Non che da sè sien queste cose acerbe:
> Ma è difetto dalla parte tua,
> Che non hai viste ancor tanto superbe.[109]

To achieve the insights toward which he is striving, the poet must humble himself, must kneel down and drink of this ambivalent symbol of time. Only by surrendering himself to this humbling experience can he satisfy his thirst for greater wisdom. It is precisely this self-abnegation that requires courage.[110] For the poet, this act entails the rejection of superficial linguistic pyrotechnics and comfortable, habitual writing habits. He must be prepared to take risks, to change his style, to experiment, to explore new avenues of expression that arise from a more profound delving into self. "El robo" portrays the poet as a thief who, if he hesitates and wavers in his resolve, will fail to accomplish his task, will disappoint humankind and be a laughing-stock.

Throughout "El robo," the speaker addresses the thief as other ("tú"); but he is obviously addressing himself. This split in the subject between self and other maintains the gap in language opened in "De noche" and allows the poet to explore and widen that gap. The result is a more profound ecstasy and inner peace (freedom) than evident in "Nuevo día," but the poet requires more of himself and of the reader. With these preliminary observations and intertextual topoi as backdrop, we find that the opening verses of the first section of "El robo" create anticipation as the thief (the self as other) is poised on the verge of his transgression.

Ahora es el momento del acoso,
del asedio en silencio,
del rincón de la mano con su curva
y su techumbre de codicia. Ahora
5   es el momento de esta luz tan tenue,
alta en la intimidad del frío seco,
de este marzo tan solo.
Y hay que pagar el precio, la subasta y el fraude
porque tú has prometido y no has vendido,
10   y no has sabido lo que se presiente:
la aventura en secreto, la destreza
de tanta duda.

(p. 39)[111]

Anaphora builds tension in the repetition of "Ahora es el momento" and the prepositional phrases. The aggression implied in "acoso" and "asedio" along with the motivation of "codicia" situate the speaker just as he is about to enter the cathedral to make his theft. The silence, the hiding place in a corner, the distinctive dome of the Cathedral, the darkness and the coolness all theatricalize the scene and increase the tension.[112] Direct address of the other as "tú" intensifies this pregnant moment in which the thief seems to have his hand extended, ready to enter.

But equivocality in the language, especially when the direct address begins, causes us to question who is the aggressor and who must pay the price of this act of robbery. Because Prometheus implicates all of humankind in his theft of the sacred flame in addition to receiving his own punishment, the duality of speaker and reader, self and other, problematizes the scene. Is the speaker warning himself of the dangers involved in this act (writing)? Or is he warning the reader that this act (reading) exacts a price for participation and complicity? In the transaction of the text, writer and reader enter into a contract that must be fulfilled on each side, an economy of pain for gain.[113] Yet at the time when we begin these activities, neither of us is fully aware of the consequences of these actions and the amount of surrender that will be required of us: "y no has sabido lo que se presiente."

The verb "presentirse" is ambivalent and introduces additional equivocation, opening the gap in language. A presentiment can be a foreboding of something about to happen (in this case the theft and consequent punishment). But it can also be the joyful anticipation of a future event (the benefit and pleasure to be derived from the act of writing/reading). "Aventura" is excitement and peril; "secreto," like "misterio," is hidden and relished; and "la destreza / de tanta duda" can mean that doubt is the source and motivation of dexterity or that the dexterity (the skillful use of one's hands, like a pickpocket, a thief, or a writer) is an inherent trait of doubt. In one case, doubt is uncertainty, vacillation, hesitancy that prohibits one from stealing, and in the other, it is the caution, prudence, and circumspection one needs not to be caught. The poet as Promethean thief knows what the punishment will be and has the option of avoiding the transgressive act. But he also knows the benefits that await him if he carries off the theft. Rodríguez follows this declaration with three exemplifications, each in its turn equivocal.

Es el recuerdo ruin y luminoso
y la mano entreabierta con malicia y rapiña
15   y los dedos astutos ya maduros
con el temblor de su sagacidad.
Es cuando el tacto brilla con asombro y con vicio,
la mirada al trasluz,
la encrucijada a oscuras del dinero.
20   Es la orfandad del cuerpo que no sabe
ser aún pobre ladrón, sin beneficio.

(pp. 39–40)[114]

Again availing himself of anaphora ("Es" at the beginning of a sentence is another leitmotif of *Casi*), the poet reduces these exemplifications from four to three to two verses. This condensation heightens the tension of the moment. First, the memory of past experience is "ruin y luminoso." If the thief trembles, it can be for fear or excitement at this crucial moment. Then, contact with the boundary of the sacred produces "asombro" (surprise as good and bad) and "vicio" (a habit that can be "bad" but pleasing, like smoking or drinking, reading or writing). This "encrucijada"—itself an emblem of chiasmus and equivocality—is both motivated and not motivated by pecuniary gain. The value of that which is stolen prompts the theft, but Prometheus obtains no personal gain from his action. Finally, "orfandad del cuerpo" can be cause or effect: The thief steals out of need (humanity needs fire to sustain life), but his theft makes him lose all regard for personal safety and isolates him from the rest of society. This ambivalent situation obtains when the thief (poet or reader) still does not know exactly what the repercussions of the act (of writing or reading) nor what the benefits will be.

The contrast between past and present is accented by the imperatives of the next stanza, which mark this critical moment. Here the symbol of oil facilitates the thief's entry by keeping the hinges from squeaking and giving him away.

El aceite es muy íntimo y rebelde,
tan sospechoso como el pulso. Déjalo, deja que se
resbale y que se esconda,
25   deja que nos ampare y nos anime,
déjalo que me acuse
del delito.
Tú recuerda cómo antes un olor a castaño,
a frambuesa, a cerezo, a caña dulce,
30   a la armonía de la ropa al raso
te alumbró, te dio techo, calle, adivinación
y hasta hoy libertad
entre perfidia y bienaventuranza.
Ahora es el momento de la llave,
35   de la honda cerradura. Acierta o vete.

(p. 40)[115]

Because oil, like the pulse, is "rebelde" and "sospechoso," the speaker cannot trust it. Inconstant and suspect, it may betray him as well as abet the theft by leaving a trace that can be followed. But the speaker advises the other not to worry because that will occur after the fact: He will already have accomplished the deed. The poet then recalls how some of the most delicate but identifiable aromas brought him illumination, comfort, direction, insight, and ecstasy in the past. The oil fulfills the same purpose now, as in a rite of anointing.

Repetition of the phrase "Ahora es el momento" in v. 34 brings this moment to a climax. The images of the key, the lock, and the act of closing ("cerradura" can indicate the object and the action) are particularly overdetermined in a poem about a theft. By modifying the noun "cerradura" with the adjective "honda," Rodríguez points to the symbolic proportions of this act of transgression. The parallelism of the anaphoric phrases "de la llave, / de la honda cerradura" equates key with lock, opening with closing, interior with exterior, self with other. Ambivalently addressing the other and the self, reader and author, the final imperative "Acierta o vete" encapsulates the crucial moment of decision as an urging and a challenge, an invitation and a defiance. The speaker possesses the key (skill, dexterity) to carry out the theft. Does he possess the courage? The final stanza suggests that he has taken a determination and crossed the threshold of commitment.

> Así, al acecho, entre los ladrones,
> la incertidumbre de la soledad,
> tanto delirio en manos
> húmedas de oro,
> 40   con la prudencia de la encina oyendo
> la señal de la liebre,
> el raíl, el alambre
> junto al cauce del río hoy muy templado,
> te doy las piedras blancas del destino.
> 45   Grábalas con tu aliento
> para que sepas que lo que has ganado
> tú lo has perdido.
>
> (pp. 40–41)[116]

"Las piedras blancas del destino" may be the pages of the text that the speaker proffers to the other. As either writer or reader, the other must inscribe them with inspiration: "Grábalas con tu aliento." As writer, one fixes words on the page; as reader, one actualizes the text. The speaker hands over these white stones "al acecho" and "con la prudencia de la encina": Theft makes the other complicit in the crime, yet the holm oak—an ambivalent evergreen standing next to an ambivalent symbol of time ("junto al cauce del río hoy muy templado")—ennobles the act because it is attuned to the slightest sounds, the most innocuous signs of warning. It is not a gift handed over indiscriminately to everyone, but prudently and sagely to a few. It is necessary for the speaker to make this presentation so that both he and the other (writer and reader) can learn from this experience and know "que lo que has ganado / tú lo has perdido." This reworking of the gain/loss motif is equally problematic. Does he recover what he possessed before but had lost? Or does he lose in the very act of gaining? Is it necessary for him to lose so as to gain? Can he regain that which he has already lost? And does he want to do that?

The highly equivocal and duplicitous language of this first part of "El robo" reflects the previous section of *Casi* as the ambivalent address joins and separates self and other, speaker and reader. In contrast, the speaker as Promethean thief urging, challenging, defying himself to steal the sacred fire portrays a more well-defined subject than the lost wanderer in "Calle sin nombre."[117] In the act of *pre*scribing the necessary action and the necessary traits, the speaker *de*scribes his progress. This split between *énoncé* and *énonciation* will continue to develop in the remainder of "El robo" and in "De amor ha sido la falta."

Part II of "El robo" begins with a negation of the previous statement, an about-face that signals a shift from exterior to interior, from inspiration to courage. This center section, like the poems that follow in "De amor," describes the act of crossing the threshold, of transgressing the sacred space. Passing through a series of turning points marked by ellipsis and contradiction, the speaker summons his courage and makes the commitment to transgress the sacred space (the gap in language) even though he knows that it will require a great sacrifice on his part. The opening verses establish a pattern that will repeat itself, with the turning point coming between vv. 6–7. It is as if the thief has cold feet and needs to convince himself to continue.

> No lo has perdido. Espera.
> Cualquiera sabe y menos ahora cuando
> te has olvidado de entregar al aire
> el alma,
> 5   y cuanto más respiras más se te va yendo
> y te llama, y ya nunca . . .
> Pero tu cuerpo y la uva moscatel
> que es quemadura en luz,
> la fiebre y la sorpresa,
> 10   aún te descubren, en alta intemperie
> mientras los dedos suenan, se hacen ágiles
> y hasta familiares con bóveda de humo.
>
> (p. 41)[118]

Whereas he ends the previous part evoking the gain/loss motif, he begins this part denying that anything has been lost. This negation underscores the ambivalence of the previous verses and calls for a reconsideration and a rethinking of the economy of the situation. The conciliatory second verse is almost counteracted by the self-criticism in the portrayal of the nervousness of the thief. He has forgotten to commend his soul to the air, to do what he knows and let the chips fall where they may. He is more self-consciously aware of his labored breathing, yet he still lacks inspiration. It seems as if his resolve, his courage, has deserted him. In contrast with the spirit, the body and the wine he has drunk ("la uva moscatel") cause him to realize where he is; he is now more Self-conscious as opposed to ego-conscious, and this bodily state heightens consciousness.[119] His "fiebre"—like the "quemadura en luz"—can be his false courage created by imbibing wine, or his inherent thirst and desire to do what he knows best. He finds himself cracking his knuckles as his courage grows, and the flexing of his fingers while holding his cigarette shows that his confidence is increasing.

This description creates a humorous, even ludicrous portrait of the thief trying to screw up his courage. The otherness of the thief, seeing and talking to himself from the outside, belies the impression of courage that he wishes—needs—to present even to himself. The split between exterior and interior heightens the irony of this decisive moment. If this thief/poet is truly a professional, why does he need so much prompting? Why does he have "stage fright"? The clichés of the thief cracking his knuckles and calmly smoking a cigarette before a heist undercut the seriousness of the transgression in an attempt to postpone it even longer. The questions, ellipsis, and flat statement that end this stanza ridicule superficial bravado with brutal honesty.

> ¿Y tú qué esperas? ¿Qué temes ahora?
> ¿La claridad de nuevo, el riesgo, la torpeza
> 15   o la audacia serena de tu rebeldía
> junto a la alevosía de la noche
> y la estrategia de la sombra en niebla
> de aquellas lilas que fueron tu ayuda
> con olor a azucena
> 20   donde te refugiaste y poco a poco
> huiste de tu muerte, de aquel crimen,
> mientras vas . . . ?
> Tú bien sabes adónde y lo has sabido siempre.
>
>   (pp. 41–42)[120]

The overblown rhetoric of phrases such as "la audacia serena de tu rebeldía / junto a la alevosía de la noche" and the cliché of a thief tiptoeing in the darkness and hiding behind lilac bushes(!) exaggerate the danger and inflate the heroic image of the thief.[121] The interruption by ellipsis suggests that he is going to jail (or Hell), so please, let's not idealize him, and let's not blow this act out of proportion by looking only at the superficial. This demystification leads to a scrutiny of the barrier itself and the thief's measured assessment of the best means of entry.

> Pero llega el dominio del oficio,
> 25   el del hierro solemne y el acero perverso,
> los goznes decorados, la locura del clavo,
> el ritmo cincelado
> sin notarse la huella de la cruel soldadura,
> y la cabeza del tornillo abriendo
> 30   el giro y el encaje
> de la bisagra;
> la lira de la llave, el astil taladrado y bien pulido,
> iluminado entre los pliegues limpios
> marcado por la luz, por el azufre,
> 35   por el humo de sal y de carbón.
>
>   (p. 42)[122]

Knowledge of his profession ("el dominio del oficio") takes over and enables the thief/poet to evaluate judiciously and coolly the obstacles that stand in his way: the door itself, the decorative and protective devices of the hinges, a multitude of nails that prevent their easy removal, their intricate meshing, and the solidity of the "solemn" iron and the "perverse" steel. The thief may be cursing as he admires the intricacy and strength of this barrier which he is challenged to overcome. His pride as a master thief evokes his wisdom, his skill, his ingenuity. So he takes a key out of his pocket, a key wrapped in clean cloth so that he will not leave any fingerprints, a key that he himself has fashioned and that will allow him to transgress the sacred space. This key is the poet's skill with language, that which allows him to enter forbidden regions; and it is illuminated by a match smelling of sulphur, salt, and carbon—diabolical images which recall the "quemadura en luz" of the wine, "la fiebre," and the "bóveda de humo" in contrast with the innocent Edenic garden of lilacs and lilies. The act of transgression—of turning the key in the lock—occurs in the next verses.

> Nadie ha vencido pero no te han dado
> libertad sino honda
> esclavitud.
> Lo que es desgracia es descubrimiento
> 40   y nacimiento.
> No es el dolor sino es el sacrilegio
> entre el metal y el alma
> mientras la alondra nueva canta en las heridas
> secas y solas de la cerradura.
>
> (p. 42)[123]

The understatement of these verses further reveals the poet's double bind. The possession of this "metaphoric" key has not provided him the freedom to enter but rather has incarcerated him because of the obligation he feels to use his skills. This obligation, this "desgracia," is also "descubrimiento / y nacimiento." Therefore, no one has conquered, neither the thief nor the lock. Both have worked in conjunction to open and to enclose.[124] The transgression of this sacred threshold, accompanied by the singing of the lark in the wounds of the lock (the key turning in the lock), is the falling into the gap in language at the same time that the poet transgresses (steps over) that gap. Like the thief's body, the act of turning the key mediates between the lock and his desire; interior and exterior are imbricated. They contrast and work against one another as they overlap, merge, and work together. So functions the poem between poet and reader. Neither dominates the other; both appreciate the beautiful singing of the lark (the transcendent, the sublime) in the dry and lonely wounds of the lock (empirical reality, the transient, the imminent).[125]

The final verses of this part reemphasize the imbrication of self and other following the crucial moment of falling into/crossing the gap: "¿Y lo que buscas es lo que tú amas? / Tú calla y no recuerdes. ¡Y las llaves al mar!" [And what you seek is what you love? / Hush and don't remember. And the keys to the sea!]. These verses repeat the leitmotif of the conjunction twice, first as a question and then as an exclamation.

This rapid transition defines the gap, the moment of transgression, of falling into/ crossing the gap. The question asks if "lo que buscas" is equivalent to "lo que tú amas," simultaneously equating them as it distinguishes them. Does the thief/poet steal only what he values, that which attracts his attention? As readers, do we find only what we seek in the text, depending upon how much we bring to it? Or does the text itself teach us? Does reality (life, reading) reveal that which is worthwhile, uplifting, illuminating? The declaration establishes a similar relationship between "calla" and "no recuerdes," but now in the imperative mode. That which we as readers bring to the text can interfere with our ability to learn something new from it at the same time that it opens the doors; our knowledge is the key in the lock, opening and enclosing.

The final exclamation is a masterful stroke of poetry, radiant with various levels of meaning contained in this one phrase. By throwing the keys into the sea, poet and reader lock themselves in together and "throw away the keys"—forever. This exclamation articulates the commitment each must make and the isolation (the punishment) such a commitment entails. But we could also read this act as getting rid of the incriminating evidence. It is a subversive act that rebels against society, against the accepted laws (of poetry), against the accepted ways of doing things (writing/reading), and the crimes to which these lead us: We become so enamored of material possessions, of life itself, that we steal, we hoard, we barricade ourselves from the enjoyment of life. The Promethean thief-poet commits a crime, transgressing the laws of humanity and gods; but he does so to free us from the limitations those laws impose upon us, that we impose upon ourselves.

The double bind is an opening that is a commitment, an obligation that is a necessity as well as a duty; a pleasure that causes pain and a punishment that is an exaltation; a debt that is a reward; humility that is self-respect. This second part of "El robo" defines an important turning point in the speaker's trajectory that he will specify more fully in "De amor ha sido la falta." Though the thief finally reaches the altar (the sacred space) and seizes his prize, his inability to escape frustrates his attempt to carry off the theft. Caught by the miraculous window and held on the threshold between inside and out, enclosure and freedom, detention and escape, the thief represents the Promethean poet's double bind. The poet can delve into the inner recesses of self and can hold the sacred truth in his hands, but the more honest, the more daring, the more personal (individual) he is, the greater the risk of his being incarcerated in his own language and his own image.

To become a first-class poet, one must take risks and expose oneself to danger. Rodríguez has done so by constantly pushing himself beyond the limits, through his self-honesty and self-abnegation, in an effort to confront his shortcomings and to improve himself. In that process, he has acquired a reputation, an image, a legendary status as poet, that belies the personal honesty and integrity that he has pursued so diligently. By being more intimate, he has become more legendary, superficial, unreal! The frustration of the thief as Promethean poet continues the pattern of expansion/regression, of attaining heights that lead to greater challenges. The signified continually reverts to a signifier, deferring meaning. At the same time, the poet is aware of his increased understanding (knowledge, wisdom—of self, of his world), and he feels the obligation to continue his search, knowing that it is a quest without conclusion and discouraged by the apparent lack of understanding on the part of his public.

Whereas the second major section, "De amor ha sido la falta," is an advancement over the first and leads to a more profound sense of inner peace and enlightenment, it is also a repetition of the first section, as "El robo" is a three-part repetition of "Calle sin nombre" and yet a very different poem. Part III of "El robo" evinces greater daring, greater risks, and yet the poet/thief is frustrated in his escape to freedom and becomes nothing more than a vague face in bas-relief on the dome of the cathedral, a bas-relief eroded by time, an anonymous, distant face nearly lost in the shadows. This part of the poem opens with a recognition of the inexorability of the thief's endeavor.

> No te laves las manos y no cojas arena
> porque la arena está pidiendo noche,
> la desnudez del sueño,
> grano de mirto.
> 5   Buscaste casa donde no hubo nadie,
> cerca del río,
> pero el destino había ya hecho duro
> resplandor en las alas de la infancia.
> Tú vas por el camino, que es el del sufrimiento,
> 10 de la ilusión, de la ambición, tortura,
> con el trastorno de la lejanía.
> Eres ladrón. Espera.
>
> (p. 43)[126]

The second-person verbs emphasize the dramatic situation and heighten the relationship of similarity and difference between self and other. The speaker's injunction in the first verse recalls the biblical scene of Pontius Pilate washing his hands, a topos that has become part of popular culture. The speaker tells the other (himself) that he cannot renounce his responsibility as a poet/thief. Sand, like water, time, and opportunity, is fleeting, shifting, and inconstant, recalling the biblical passage about building one's house upon the shifting sands or upon a rock (Matt. 7:24–27). To place one's trust in the unstable is to invite darkness and confusion, vulnerability and illusion ("noche, / la desnudez del sueño"). The seed of the myrtle is an extremely ambivalent image. As seed, the "grano" represents the promise of future life (of poetic immortality); and the myrtle is an evergreen and the source of myrrh, the aromatic herb used to embalm the dead and which promises resurrection and immortality. If the poet seeks to build his opus on shifting, uncertain, nonlasting themes, he may gain a lasting reputation, but it will be a lifeless, artificial, grotesque image rather than true life.

The contrast between the house by the river and the vagabond thief's wings reinforces this duality and the inexorability of his chosen path (his "camino"). Instead of settling down next to the always-present river to live out his life alone, this thief wanders a difficult road, "el del sufrimiento, / de la ilusión, de la ambición, tortura," constantly goaded by the horizon to continue his journey, to know more. The definitive statement "Eres ladrón" is an accusation (distancing the speaker from the addressee, self from other) and an expression of pride, as the imperative "Espera" indicates by echoing the beginning of part II: "No lo has perdido. Espera." The imperative arrests the thief, bringing him to a halt, and urges him forward to hope and expect more from the future. This dialogic, double-voiced language exposes the gap between self and other at the same time that it unites two totally incompatible readings in the (con)fusion of self and other. This duality continues in the next verses, where the thief perpetrates his transgression.

> Mira el lirio del valle, los pinares
> entrando en la ciudad cuando hoy apenas
> 15 hay tráfico, alarma
> de policía.
> Cada paso que des es peligroso
> entre escombros y ruinas donde crece la malva
> tan impaciente como
> 20 la media luna delicada en nácar
> de la uña tocada,
> del juego de la yema de los dedos.
> Sigue con calma y llega hasta el altar,
> llega furtivo en danza
> 25 hasta la plata viva, hasta el oro del cáliz,
> hasta el zafiro y hasta la esmeralda;
> llega hasta tu saliva que maldice,
> suave y seca, a tu cuerpo.
>
> (pp. 43–44)[127]

On the one hand, the speaker may be urging the thief to "stop and smell the roses," to see the beauty of the country around him and to avoid the city, another contrast (city versus country) that distinguishes the poet. The city—the anonymity of the poet among others—is a dangerous place for the Promethean thief because it exposes him to the threat of capture by the police (critics?) for his lack of moral principles. On the other hand, the speaker may be warning the thief, becoming his accomplice, his abettor. The city, in contrast with the sacred pine grove and the purity of "el lirio del valle," consists of "escombros y ruinas donde crece la malva." Having been to Zamora, the location of this scene, and walked through the ruins of the medieval fortress on the same promontory as the Cathedral overlooking the Duero, I have been alarmed and saddened at the state of disrepair of this structure and the tall weeds growing on the parapets. This symbol of the transience of human constructions and human glory invaded by an irresistible life force is an ambivalent image because the structure has endured for such a long time in spite of the neglect and lack of maintenance, and it serves still as a proud symbol and identifying feature of the city of Zamora.

The comparison of the mallow with the quick of one's fingernails and the momentary whiteness that appears when one touches the tip of the finger before the blood returns describes the life still latent in the purely material (the horny excrescence of the dead nail, the flesh of the finger through which the blood flows). The poet/thief represents this part of society, the vital, irrepressible flowering of life amid the stones in ruins. With each step he takes, he exposes himself to capture and threatens the stability of the structure of society. The thief's steps (the poet's writing) is dangerous both for him and for society.

The imperatives, "Sigue con calma y llega hasta el altar," are equally equivocal. The thief may be nervous, needing someone to tell him to calm down at this heightened moment of transgression. But he may be completely calm and nonplussed by the situation, in which case the speaker confidently tells him to go on, to reach the sacred light of wisdom, as cool as a cucumber. The thief's furtive steps (again an allusion to writing) are similar to dance, a rhythmic art form (like music and poetry); but the mood created by this dance may be cautious and wary (furtive, surreptitious, secret, sly) or agile, confident, assured, as if rehearsed over and over again.

The chalice on the altar (the sacred space) from which he will imbibe the sacred wine (his poetic inspiration, his immortality) attracts the thief with its "plata viva" (shimmering, glinting); and the gold (representing the sacred, the precious) is encrusted with gems (the sapphire mentioned in the epigraph, the water of the river and the blue of the sky; and the emerald, the rich color of life). The curses of the thief's saliva may surprise and disconcert us at first. Certainly saliva is a symbol of appetite, thirst, desire, a liquid that evokes the thief's thirst for wine (inspiration, poetic ecstasy, "ebriedad"). But this saliva is described as "suave y seca," so that its curse is a gentle one, while the appetite or thirst is a calculated, unemotional desire. This desire curses the body, meaning either that it detests the limitations of the physical world and strives toward an ideal, or that it condemns the body, placing life itself in danger because of overwhelming lust and cupidity. If with each step the thief endangers his own freedom and life at the same time that he is a threat to the rest of society, so here too the altar, the chalice with its jewels, and the saliva (desire) indicate the ideal and the profane, spiritual quest and banal greed, an entering into the sacred space (participation in the sacred) and a transgression, a desacralization of the sacred. The poet recognizes the double bind of his profession, the paradoxical and ironic consequences of this dangerous, subversive act—the act of writing—of regenerating the life of society (language) at the same time that he destroys it (cf. the mallow and the fortress).[128] This act still falls short of the mark, however.

> Y fluye el Duero ilusionadamente . . .
> 30 Estás llegando a tanta claridad
> que ya ni ves que está la primavera
> sobria en los chopos ahí enfrente. Pero
> ¿tú qué te has hecho?
> ¡Si has tenido en tus manos
> 35 la verdad!
> No has podido salir de la marea
> de esta ventana milagrosa y cierta
> que te ahoga y te ahorca.

> (p. 44)[129]

The Heraclitean concept of the river always flowing and renewing itself and yet always the same river is a deceit (an illusion) and an ideal (a dream) toward which to strive. The thief is so intent on capturing his prize that he fails to see eternal life in the trees on the opposite bank of the river. The poet gets so involved in his words, in his writing, in his inner world that he fails to live, to participate in life itself—another double bind: In seeking life, he loses it; in the act of walking/writing, gazing ahead, moving toward the horizon, he cannot see that which is right in front of him. In the very moment of escape, with the precious light in his hands (the light of truth), he gets "hung up" on the threshold. The window—that which provides egress and allows the thief to see his freedom—is also that which limits him and prevents him from reaching his goal—the perfect theft.

For the Promethean poet, language is the means and the obstacle to knowledge; it is both signifier and signified, vehicle and tenor, freedom and restraint, self and other. The verb phrases "te ahoga y te ahorca" graphically define the constraints on the poet's breath (his words, his poetry), yet the window (language and the poetic act) is that which admits light and air (inspiration). Like "ebriedad," "marea" is heightened consciousness and unconsciousness, ecstasy and disorientation; it is a means of self-knowledge and recognition, and of alienation, difference, otherness. It allows the poet to identify and individuate himself, yet it estranges him from himself, making him someone else in the very act of identifying and knowing himself. The visual image of the thief on the ceiling of the Cathedral of Zamora represents that paradox.

> La erosión de la piedra,
> 40   eres tú,
> solo y ocre en el ábside.
> ¡Pero si eres tú mismo, tú, con la agria
> plasticidad de proa de tu rostro
> siglo a siglo, día a día,
> 45   en transfiguración!
> Tú, con tu vida entera
> que despierta y que llama a la ciudad
> mientras está cantando por las calles
> la mañana que roba a la mañana,
> 50   tanto tiempo que roba hasta al amor
> y hasta a mí mismo, sin saber quién eres,
> viejo ladrón sin fuga.
>
>   (pp. 44–45)[130]

The rock as gap, erosion as erotica, apse as open space and enclosure, all capture the image of the self as other, known and unknown, individual and anonymous ("solo"). The poet sees himself in the profile (identity, individuality) of the thief's image in the stone, but that profile is eroding and changing as time passes. The speaker sees his life and his image (his poetry) "en transfiguración!": changing in outward form but illuminated eternally from within. Here the religious connotations of the scene invite a comparison between Prometheus and Christ and emphasize the divine and the human nature of the poet as Christ figure, sacrificed but attaining eternal life through resurrection.

The thief is the object of ridicule; caught in the window, he attracts the attention of all the others in the city as word passes from one person to another. The light of morning enlivens the streets, creating activity, life, vitality, at the same time that it passes and life, vitality, is lost. Time enriches language and makes it fade. We can appreciate great poetry after the passing of time, and yet something is also lost. The poet's identity and reputation are secured, but the poet himself is unknown and unknowable. Language both unveils and veils, preserves and destroys, illuminates and obscures, defines a profile and blurs identity.

The final verse again emphasizes the gap in language which is the substance of language itself: "¡Si estás vivo, estás vivo! Enhorabuena" [But you are alive, you are alive! Congratulations]. The repetition of "estás vivo" underscores the ambivalence of this phrase, whereas the lack of exclamation marks around "Enhorabuena" undercuts and satirizes its meaning and that of the previous phrase. It is as if the speaker were saying, "So you're alive. So what? What's the big deal?," simultaneously recognizing that the legend of the Promethean thief has survived and does have meaning even after all this time has passed. The congratulations can be read as bitterly sarcastic or as confidently self-assured and satisfied with the accomplishment of a difficult task. This gap in the language of the text continues to broaden and deepen as we move through the second major section of *Casi*, "De amor ha sido la falta," and as we make our way toward a recontextualization and rereading of "Calle sin nombre" and the acquisition of profound inner peace and wisdom.

In comparison with "De noche y por la mañana," where the passage of time from sunset to sunrise is a structural motif with variations in each of the five poems, in "De amor ha sido la falta" the motif is love. This motif takes an unexpected turn in the final poems of this section. At the end of the first poem the speaker, using the ambivalent conjunction, states that night lifts him to the sky which is entering "junto a tu amor y el mío" [along with your love and mine]. If this construction defines a separation between other and self, the final line of the next poem brings these distinct loves closer. A contradictory movement is manifest because the speaker finds himself and the other farther away from that love: "muy lejos del recuerdo, el dolor solo, / la verdad del amor que es tuyo y mío" [very far away from memory, the lone pain, / the truth of love that is yours and mine]. This contradictory process, which defines "De amor ha sido la falta" as the dynamic chiasmus or turning point in the speaker's progress, continues to take unexpected turns in the third poem, where the speaker separates himself from a plural otherness: "muy lejos / del amor verdadero, que es el vuestro" [very far away / from true love, which is yours].

When the speaker addresses an ambivalent figure of Basque mythology in "Lamento a Mari," the similarities and differences of self and other crystallize. Here the speaker states directly "Ya no hay amor . . ." [There is no longer any love . . .]. Instead, a cold light at dawn illuminates speaker and other: "y luce el día / . . . / . . . en tu cara y en la mía" [and day shines / . . . / . . . in your face and in mine]. Though he emphasizes otherness in each face, both are united in the enlightenment they receive. The most radical turn in this process results in the final poem, where love and illumination become death: "Con los cinco pinares de tu muerte y la mía" [With the five pine groves of your death and mine]. This process delineates the speaker's individuation as he acquires more courage, but also calls attention to the sharing of experience in spite of separation. Self and other, past and present, Eros and Thanatos depend on and define one another and yet are portrayed as more distinct entities in this section of *Casi*.

Another anomaly characterizes "De amor ha sido la falta." The first poem of this section does not bear a title and consequently does not appear listed in the "Índice." We could assume that the title of this poem (whose first line is "Aquí ya está el milagro" [Here now is the miracle]) is the same as that of this section. But the omission of the title above the poem itself creates an absence or gap, described as a miracle in the first line of the poem. Is this another instance of Rodríguez's sarcasm and irony?[131] How does this gap, this absence of a title, relate to the motif of love as death? These are the parameters that determine our investigation of the center section of Rodríguez's most recent work to date.

The opening poem—to which I will refer by its first verse, "Aquí ya está el milagro," to avoid confusion with the title of this section—consists of only three sentences, the second of which is a question without an independent verb. Erotic overtones pervade this brief introduction, but the ecstasy of the act of love serves as metaphor for the act of writing. Let us assume, then, that these verses refer to the absent title, the ambivalent "De amor ha sido la falta." Love is to blame, but love has been lacking, as the title is both absent and present. If love is equivalent to writing, the lack of love is the lack of writing, a fuller participation in life that leads to fuller participation in the aesthetic act; and love will receive the credit. Love as participation in life is the courage the Promethean poet needs to carry through with his transgressive but beneficial act. Without experiencing love, the poet would never be able to make his sacrifice and to persist in his quest for more knowledge. The Promethean double bind requires the reciprocal participation of self and other, life and language, poet and reader. Absence as presence, presence as absence, is evident in the opening statement.

> Aquí ya está el milagro,
> aquí, a medio camino
> entre la bendición, entre el silencio,
> y la fecundación y la lujuria
> 5   y la luz sin fatiga.
>
> (p. 49)[132]

Although definitive stresses in the opening verse, reinforced by the repetition of "aquí," make an emphatic assertion, the deictic, the reference to an absence that is present (the title), and the equivocal nature of a miracle problematize the assertion. Is the speaker being matter-of-fact about this presence/absence? Or is he marveling at its paradox, the irony of this situation in which the absent is present and the present absent? Does his position "a medio camino" describe the width or the length of the road, the poet's progress in this particular work or his career and life?

Furthermore, repetition of the preposition "entre" equates "bendición" with "silencio" and defers the other extreme, which he then defines as "y la fecundación y la lujuria / y la luz sin fatiga." But we could just as easily equate all of these nouns (bendición = silencio = fecundación = lujuria = luz), adding many contradictory layers to the situation of the speaker. Is he in the center? Or does he stand on the periphery, pointing to the miracle at the center of these equivalent opposites ("bendición" and "silencio," "fecundación" and "lujuria")? The light (the poet's inspiration) may be interminable, but it can be quite fatiguing for the poet to live constantly with that insight.

The question in the center of the poem sustains this ambiguity because we cannot tell if it is a continuation of the previous statement or a distinction the speaker wishes to make: "¿Y la semilla de la profecía, / la levadura del placer que amasa / sexo y canto?"[133] Is he saying, "Here's the miracle, but where is the prophecy?" Or is he saying, "If the miracle is here amid these things, is it also amid the seed of prophecy and the yeast of pleasure?" Is he questioning presence or descrying absence? Because of the syntax and the relationships already established, we must ask whether "la semilla de la profecía" and "la levadura del placer" are the same or different. Are these metaphors, or do they describe a metonymic process? Both seed and yeast promise growth; prophecy as foreplay in an erotic context and as experience, the necessary precondition for writing/reading, are necessary for the achievement of ecstasy. The speaker is exploring and positing the reciprocal interface between experience and language, self and other, erotics and poetics, not privileging one over the other, so that presence is absence, but absence produces pleasure.[134] If we relate this situation to the thief in the first part of "El robo," we recall the ambivalent options "Acierta o vete" and "lo que has ganado / tú lo has perdido." The final verses do nothing to disrupt the reciprocal relationship of gain and loss.

> Esta noche de julio, en quietud y en piedad,
> 10   sereno el viento del oeste y muy
> querido me alza
> hasta tu cuerpo claro,
> hasta el cielo maldito que está entrando
> junto a tu amor y el mío.[135]

If the first sentence in this poem declares "Here is the miracle" and the second questions "Where is the promise for the future?," this final statement shows the speaker surrendering himself to the pain/gain of love and song, the "salvation" or "celebration" of that which slips away.[136] If the beginning of the poem tells where ("aquí, a medio camino"), this sentence declares when ("Esta noche de julio"), how ("en quietud y en piedad"), and what ("me alza") happens to the speaker. Contrasts between darkness and light ("noche," "claro"), stasis and movement ("sereno," "alza"), substance and essence ("cuerpo," "cielo"), self and other ("tu amor y el mío"), maintain the reciprocal interface, as the combination of "cuerpo claro" and "cielo maldito" and the ambivalent "junto a" simultaneously bring them into friction.[137]

The accursed sky—the ideal that is feared, resisted, reluctantly accepted—enters this union of two lovers at the same time that the darkness and the lack of wind lift the speaker to this moment. By conflating metaphor and metonymy in the phrase "junto a," the poet distinguishes and separates self and other while bringing them together. If the poet (and the reader) is to know him/herself, s/he must surrender to otherness. In becoming another, the self is more clearly defined, a double bind that equates love with courage and yet shows that each is cause and effect of the other.

The opening poem of "De amor" situates the speaker at this moment in his progress. That his situation is ambiguous and ambivalent captures the double bind of the Promethean poet who knows that he will be castigated for his transgression (it will be a painful experience), yet it is inexorable that he should take risks. Like love, poetry requires the relinquishing of the self and leads to a greater knowledge of self. Along with love, poetry involves the risk of losing the self, but this risk heightens the pleasure. Love of humanity motivates the Promethean poet to transgress the sacred and to receive an inexorable castigation (it overcomes his lack of courage), but it also increases his intransigence, his commitment, his steadfastness, which allows him to demonstrate his love by means of his courage.

Before moving on to a discussion of the next poem, I am obliged to comment on the length of "Aquí ya está el milagro." This poem consists of fourteen verses containing a tripartite structure. Composed largely of heptasyllabic and hendecasyllabic verses that rhyme irregularly, this poem in no way reminds us of a sonnet in spite of its fourteen lines. But this irregular, erratic, almost intuitive statement prefigures the final poem in this section, also of fourteen lines and a regular prosodic pattern. Though lacking a formal rhyme scheme, the final poem resembles an Elizabethan sonnet and contrasts markedly with "Aquí ya está el milagro." This experimentation, taking risks with poetic conventions, modifies the figure of the Promethean poet, showing that he is both threatened by and threatens expectations, existing conventions (societal and poetic). How does the contemporary poet compare with the Romantic rebel—the poet as pirate, for example? Another anomaly in the title of the next poem leads to a further definition of the individuality of the Promethean poet.

"«The Nest of Lovers»" is the first poem Rodríguez has titled with a phrase in a foreign language. As he modified the epigraph preceding "El robo," it seems that here Rodríguez has modified the title of a poem by Shelley, "The Nest of Love."[138] This alteration is in keeping with the motif of this section and recalls the image of the nest in "La mañana del búho," the second poem of "De noche." But it shifts the emphasis from the abstraction (love) to the participants (the lovers). The parenthetical inclusion of the proper name "Alfriston" after the title informs us that this poem is set in a small town in southern England.[139] This estrangement of place suggests a juxtaposition of two different time frames (Rodríguez's first visit to England in 1958 and this memory written in the 1980s and 1990s) and two different aesthetic attitudes (the Romantic versus the postmodern, the beginning of his career and many years later). By encountering himself at another (foreign) time and in another (foreign) place, the poet can compare himself with the other (Shelley, the poet who died at age twenty-nine, roughly the same age as Rodríguez when he returned to Spain after his "exile" in England as a Lecturer at the Universities of Nottingham and Cambridge) and see the similarities and differences between them.[140]

Reminiscent of "Nocturno de la casa ida," "«The Nest of Lovers»" begins with a long, convoluted sentence (sixteen verses) describing a walk through the English countryside.[141] As in "Nocturno," the speaker breaks off this long sentence in midthought with an ellipsis. Suspensive periods and ellipsis also recall the second section of "El robo," moving us forward in the speaker's trajectory to his second stage. Similarity and difference—self and other (Rodríguez and Shelley), past and present—is the aim of this comparison. The poet's purpose is not to indulge nostalgically in what was and no longer is; in fact, he states clearly in the third stanza that "no hay recuerdo ni remordimiento" [there is neither memory nor remorse]. It is instead to evaluate progress, to define the present self in comparison and contrast with a former self.[142]

Repetition and recontextualization contribute to this play of similarity and difference, especially in the final stanza. This stanza begins with the phrase that follows the ellipsis and stanzaic break after the first stanza (v. 17), also repeated in v. 37: "Y yo te veo porque yo te quiero" [And I see you because I love you] (v. 51). The next verse is another repetition: "Es el amor que no tiene sentido" [It is love that doesn't make sense] (vv. 38 and 52). Constantly undermining the previous phrase, these verses evoke the motif of love but also of loss because we recall the earlier "Porque no poseemos, vemos," previously revived in "La mañana del búho" ("No veo, no poseo"). The speaker sees what he *wants* to see, but this desire, this love, is senseless; love is blind. As the lover sees only the beautiful aspects of the beloved and is blind to the other's faults, so the speaker remembers only what he wants to recall from the past. The phrase "Es el amor que no tiene sentido" can be an accusation (love is responsible, love is to blame; love—of self—prevents us from hurting ourselves with unpleasant memories), but it can also be a definition: Seeing what he wills to see is a type of love because it causes pain, yet it is necessary if he hopes to know more and to share that knowledge with others.

In the third stanza, the speaker urges himself as other to look ahead, at the horizon, at the top of the hill, at a higher goal: "Alza tu cara más porque no es imagen / y no hay recuerdo ni remordimiento / . . . / del enamorado, / el silencio que dura, está durando" (vv. 29-30, 35-36).[143] The poet repeats this command in the final stanza.

> Y yo lo veo porque yo te quiero.
> Es el amor que no tiene sentido.
> Alza tu cara ahora a medio viento
> con transparencia y sin destino en torno
> 55   a la promesa de la primavera,
> los manzanos con júbilo en tu cuerpo
> que es armonía y es felicidad,
> con la tersura de la timidez
> cuando se hace de noche y crece el cielo
> 60   y el mar se va y no vuelve
> cuando ahora vivo la alegría nueva,
> muy lejos del recuerdo, el dolor solo,
> la verdad del amor que es tuyo y mío.

(p. 53)[144]

Several images first mentioned in the opening stanza—the wind, the apple trees, the sea—are now recontextualized as the time frame changes from morning to night, from dawn to dusk. In the first stanza, the scene is "traspasado de alba," in contrast with the final stanza, "cuando se hace de noche." The parallelism of the phrases beginning with "cuando" suggests that this moment of dusk represents not a renewal of former happiness, but the discovery of *new* happiness. When the poet writes, he does not employ language mimetically to reproduce a powerful and memorable experience, but rather discovers a new experience in the act of writing. Language is not a substitute for experience (a suturing of the gap with textualization); the poetic experience does not substitute for the empirical one, which would place a barrier between poet and experience. Rather, language can incorporate and assimilate empirical reality, but to become poetry it must lead to a new experience that fuses past and present, self and other, present and absent. Likewise the reader cannot participate vicariously in the experience of the poem, but must assimilate that experience by making it his/her own. Only through that effort, that pain of surrendering the self to the other, does a lasting aesthetic experience obtain for either poet or reader. The speaker of "«The Nest of Lovers»" presents both a descriptive and a prescriptive example of the aesthetic experience when he distances himself and the reader from present time and place, setting the poem in England and recalling a past experience. Unless we (poet and reader) give ourselves completely to that experience, nothing will last after we die, as Shelley's poem "The Nest of Love" suggests.

The "Momento de renuncia" [Moment of renunciation] described in the third poem constitutes the turning point not just of "De amor" but of *Casi* in its entirety. Located at the center of the five poems of the center section of the work, "Momento de renuncia" is based on an anecdotal incident in which the poet has awakened early and gone for a walk in the city—presumably Salamanca, given that the speaker mentions the river Tormes, seashells, stained-glass windows, and a large, open plaza. Nonetheless, the scene is vague enough to suggest the classic fable of the contest between the sun and the wind, in which each says that he can make the man walking down the road take off his coat. The wind tries first, blowing harder and stronger, but the man holds onto his coat even tighter against the wind. Then the sun shines warmly on the man, forcing him to remove his coat because of the warmth.

Because light and air are metapoetic symbols of inspiration, we might assume that the speaker as poet experiences this contest between two opposing but equally potent aspects of his psyche.[145] One of these (reason) compels him to defend himself even more protectively, pulling his defenses (his coat) around him. This outlook will not permit him to create a lasting achievement. The other—warmth, passion, expansiveness—encourages him to remove his defenses, to be more daring and feel more freedom. The speaker's observation of female figures stimulates his desire.

> Ahora me salen las palabras solas
> y te estoy esperando
> junto al viento envidioso de la luz,
> muy cerca de la plaza. Y estoy viendo

5   los tobillos recién amanecidos
      sonando a horno. Es la primera curva
      querida, vena a vena,
      antes de entrar en el misterio. Cómo
      se me está abriendo el día. Y es por vuestras
10   caderas hondas nunca por los muslos,
      ese olor a sobaco que madura
      con sudor que yo quiero y huele a trigo
      salino, a brea, a fiebre de madera,
      a ilusión de la infancia
15   fácil de despertar como a los hombres
      risueños, pero astutos,
      color de ala de aquella paloma
      que vuela por la plaza
      remontándose en giro de lujuria.

(p. 55)[146]

The speaker's ambivalence is evident in several aspects of these verses. The adjective "solas" in v. 1 could indicate that he has no control over his words and that he responds to what he sees without thinking or reflecting on the consequences. Is he talking to himself, or is he tossing "piropos" to the women he sees on the street? Do his words achieve real communication with those around him (his readers), or is he merely muttering to himself? The verb phrase "te estoy esperando" does not indicate whether the other is expected or if the speaker is waiting in vain for the other to appear. If he is addressing his inspiration, he may feel that he has discovered a special moment and knows that it will result in a poetic experience of knowledge, or that he is looking for inspiration but finds only everyday, commonplace, nontranscendent reality. Will he fail like the wind or be successful like the sun?

The ankles he observes could be part of the mundane world of people (especially women) passing; their footsteps ring out—but is it a hollow sound, or is there some deeper resonance? Is the speaker nothing but a lecherous voyeur, or does his appreciation of these footfalls resonate with rich symbolic meaning? Do these steps turn the corner, attracting the speaker to new illumination and knowledge? Or does he merely fetishize the ankle because it is attached to the leg and provides his imagination with a glimpse of the erotic? The ticking of an oven heating up could suggest true warmth (the sun), or it could emphasize the coldness and emptiness of the moment. We have noted several times the ambivalence of the word "misterio," and we have seen how the word "Cómo" without punctuation can express a question and an exclamation, disorientation and excitement. Does the phrase "se me está abriendo el día" refer literally to the beginning of another day? Or does it describe the acquisition of special insight that delights the poet and increases his desire? The poet is opening a gap in language, but is he excited and eager for that gap to appear, or does he fear it, try to avoid it, wrap his coat (his defenses) tighter around him?

The setting of this scene contributes to the ambivalence. A plaza, though open and airy, is a limited space, suggesting stasis and enclosure. In this regard, a plaza makes us think of verticality and metaphor. But "plaza" is derived from the Greek "plateia" meaning "broad street." Thinking of Rodríguez's use of "calle" and "camino" as a trajectory, a metonymical extension in space, "plaza" also suggests dynamic movement and open possibilities in contrast with stasis and enclosure. This duality manifests itself in the second stanza, where erotic overtones continue to function ambivalently and where Rodríguez begins to engage in some daring imagery.

> 20   En esta plaza de dorado espacio
>   donde la piedra danza con su sombra
>   llega el placer de todos los sentidos,
>   y la visitación de benavides,
>   y la alegría de la carne, el puro
> 25   cuerpo festivo cuando canta el gallo
>   a lo oscuro,
>   y el trino ágil del pezón moreno. . . .
>
>   (p. 56)[147]

In saying that this plaza is "de dorado espacio," the speaker could be suggesting either that it is a gilded, superficial, empty space or that it is sacred, precious, and expansive. The beautiful image of the rock dancing with its shadow sets rock and shadow apart, emphasizing the contrast of light and darkness, heaviness and weight-lessness, static and dynamic; but given that the rock dances, it partakes of the light-ness and airy agility of the shadow. The image encompasses contrast and comparison, similarity and difference.

The phrase "la visitación de benavides" is a perplexing one, but it illustrates Rodríguez's willingness to experiment, to take risks. I assume that this is an allusion to a painting of the Visitation by an artist named Benavides, but the lowercase letters downplay the specificity of the allusion. If we think of the context of the Visitation, we note the similarities and differences between Mary and Elizabeth (especially their pregnancies) and between Jesus and John the Baptist. This context influences our reading of the next images. We can imagine "la alegría de la carne" as the movement of John in Elizabeth's womb as a response to the divine presence of Jesus and the miraculous conception in Mary's womb. But we also think of a more profane and carnal delight in the act of impregnation. The singing of the cock in the darkness could be a rather lewd image for erection and ejaculation, but it can also be a symbol of resurrection and eternal life that Jesus represents. Likewise, "el trino ágil del pezón moreno" could on a literal level describe the movement of a woman's breast as she walks through the plaza (eliciting a lurid response from the speaker); or it could be an image of song, a "trill" of delight experienced by the woman who will nurse a child.

The combination of "trino ágil" with "pezón moreno" illustrates the daring and contradictory nature of Rodríguez's imagery as he makes this renunciation, to which the last verse of this stanza makes reference: "y el resplandor de la renuncia." This image could be a further description of the painting of the Visitation (the holy glow around Mary, who has renounced her own will to do that of God, the divine source of eternal life), but it could also represent the Promethean poet's renunciation of his defenses at the moment of illumination (cf. the fable of the sun and the wind), his commitment to the transgressive act of poetry. The relaxation of his intransigence is a greater resolve, a greater commitment, a more intransigent determination to sacrifice his own safety, his own welfare, for the benefit of humanity, his act of love. He underscores the ambivalence of the gain/loss motif in the next stanza: "Desde esta plaza a cielo descubierto / . . . / estoy perdiendo cada vez más alma / aunque gane en sentido."[148] To lose is to gain; to renounce is to accept and receive.

In the final stanza, this interplay between self and other can be seen in the possessive pronouns. The poet makes his own what is not his to own, just as the readers must surrender themselves to the experience of the text, assimilate it, make it their own if the poet is to achieve his goal of immortality. Poet and reader function reciprocally, as do poet and reality, reader and text.

> Estoy cantando lo que nunca es *mío*.
>
> . . . .
> . . . Basta sólo
> la mañana sin fin que entra y desea
> en *vuestro* cuerpo que es el *mío*. . . .
>
> . . . .
> Y me dejo llevar, me estáis llevando
> hacia la cita seca, sin vivienda,
> hacia la espera sin adiós, muy lejos
> del amor verdadero, que es el *vuestro*.
>
> (p. 57; emphasis added)[149]

Does the speaker address those who pass him in the plaza, or does the poet address the reader? Because of this ambivalence, the relationship between "vuestro" and "mío" is problematical, indicating similarity and difference, self and other, distance and nearness, renunciation (lack, giving up, giving away) and the plenitude of receiving. To fall into the gap in language is to bridge it. To sacrifice oneself is to attain eternal resurrection. "Momento de renuncia" is the crucial turning point in the speaker's progress, where he finds his courage by making himself vulnerable and taking risks. Instead of a battle between two opposing forces, Rodríguez's poetics becomes a cooperative effort in which similarities and differences complement one another. This crossing of the threshold leads to another moment of profound inner peace in "Lamento a Mari," the fourth poem, paralleling "Nuevo día" in "De noche."

As the poet avails himself of the classic fable of the wind and the sun in "Momento de renuncia," in "Lamento a Mari" Rodríguez employs a contradictory figure of Basque mythology. According to Julio Caro Baroja, Mari is a Basque equivalent of Persephone, combining characteristics of the innocent, virginal daughter who inspires Ceres to renew life in the spring, and the spouse of the dark ruler of the Underworld, queen of the dead.[150]

Originariamente, Mari era una joven mortal. Su madre la maldijo por desobediente o la ofreció al diablo con harta imprudencia, y de acuerdo con este hecho se la llevó el enemigo del género humano a sus mansiones subterráneas, desde las que preside las sequías y las lluvias. . . . «Mari» es, pues, a veces, una especia de «Koré» o «Proserpina» vasca. . . . (p. 294)[151]

Although Rodríguez denies that Mari represents his sister who died (the motivation of the elegiac *El vuelo*), it is helpful to make an analogy between these two
female figures, one very real, human, and absent because of death, and the other
mythological who like Persephone is absent but cyclically returns. In accord with the
dual nature of Mari (she is both beautiful and a witch, attractive and repulsive), the
title of this poem is ambivalent. This lament may be addressed *to* Mari, but it may
also be a lament *for* Mari; it is both descriptive and prescriptive, constative and
performative; it may be a love poem or an elegiac statement. This duality splits the
language of the poem, as we observe in the opening verses.

> Casi es mejor que así llegue esta escena
> porque no eres figura sino aliento.
> La primavera vuelve mas no vuelve
> el amor, Mari. Y menos mal que ahora
> 5   todo aparece y desaparece.
> Y menos mal que voy tan de mañana
> que el cuerpo no se entrega, está perdido.
>
> (p. 59)[152]

Besides the equivocation of "casi" and the indefiniteness of "así" and "esta escena,"
it is further unclear whether the expression "es mejor que . . . llegue" expresses the
reluctant acceptance of the inexorable or if it prescribes how the speaker would like
the scene to materialize if he had his choice. Nor can we say for sure that he is addressing Mari or himself when he says "no eres figura sino aliento." We do not know
if we identify with the speaker's point of view, hearing his most intimate thoughts, or
if we are distanced from him as if he were on a stage. Also, the relationship of cause
and effect ("porque") is unclear, along with the images of "figura" and "aliento." The
former would seem more tangible and definite than the latter, but breath is privileged
over the figure. Is the speaker resigning himself to accept what he cannot change, or is
he protesting against a situation that seems unfair or intolerable?

Likewise in the next sentence, he seems to contradict himself. Normally, we
might equate the return of spring with a revitalization of love and life, the cyclical
return of Persephone and Ceres' joy replenishing the vegetative productivity of the
Earth (a renewal of the poet's inspiration). Whereas the seasons may be cyclical and
constant, love is analogical: present or absent, "on" or "off." If we think of the poet's
loss of his sister, we might understand that life goes on in spite of her absence, a fact
to which the speaker resigns himself without much enthusiasm. Once the loved one
has been lost, she cannot like Persephone return from the world of the dead. Yet the
speaker's affection for the lost loved one does not undergo the same ups and downs as
the cyclical seasons. His love is constant and only continues to grow even though the
loved one is no longer present.

Extending this situation to the Promethean poet, we understand that his insight is
constant, but his courage is cyclical. His ability to produce goes through cycles—and
for Rodríguez these cycles have become progressively lengthy—even though their
intensity continues to escalate. This intensification corresponds directly to the ampli-

tude of the cycle. The emotion he feels through participation in the creative act requires that he build up a greater amount of courage, for the intensity—the pain and
delight—takes its toll. In order to receive, the poet must be prepared to sacrifice a
great deal.

This exchange explains the contradictory statements "todo aparece y desaparece"
and "el cuerpo no se entrega, está perdido." Repetition of the phrase "Y menos mal"
reinforces the effect of "casi es mejor." We can read this phrase (meaning "It's just as
well") as relinquishment, resignation, helplessness, and as protest, rejection, and avoidance ("It's a good thing!"). In a world in which nothing is permanent except change,
the speaker welcomes and resists the moment of writing, the poetic act, because it
causes him pleasure and pain. It lets him know who he is but also disrupts and changes
him, calling his knowledge and his self into question. The interrogatives of the next
verses continue to manifest this duality.

> ¿Es lo que fue, lo que es, lo que aún espera
> remordimiento, reconciliación
> 10   o desprecio o piedad? Y ya no hay celos
> que den savia al amor, ni ingenuidad
> que dé más libertad a la belleza.
> ¿Quién nos lo iba a decir? ¿Y quién sabía,
> tras la delicadeza envejecida,
> 15   cuando ya sin dolor no hay ilusión,
> cuando la luz herida se va a ciegas
> en esta plaza nunca fugitiva
> que la pureza era la pureza,
> que la verdad no fue nuestra verdad?[153]

First the poet juxtaposes three time frames (past, present, and future) of remorse
with three possible responses from the offended party: reconciliation, disdain (rejection), and pity. The question contemplates the situation, attempting to understand, to
know, and at the same time expresses doubt about a possible outcome: Which one is
it? Which one will it be? The first expresses vexation, frustration, anger with the
indefiniteness of the situation, whereas the second is openly curious, wondering, eager to see what the result will be. For the poet to write again, must he pass through a
similar ordeal as the loss of the loved one? Does he want to submit himself to that
ordeal yet again? On the one hand, he resists such intensity and pain, whereas on the
other, he knows what the reward can be and can feel himself reaching new heights,
discovering new worlds, attaining a spiritual peace through a mystical experience of
the sublime. The Promethean poet has arrived at such a level of maturity and such
profound insights that his earlier attitudes toward writing are no longer valid. Something has changed in the poet: Is that an advantage or a disadvantage? He is no longer
the same person who began this quest (perhaps because of the loss of his loved one),
so why should he submit himself to this process, knowing full well what awaits him?

The next questions are equally equivocal. Does he marvel at what he has accomplished? (Who could have predicted this would happen?) Or is he complaining bitterly, resisting, reluctant to have another go at it? (Why didn't someone warn him this

would happen?) The speaker is simultaneously embittered, angry, disillusioned, and amazed, awestruck. Alliteration in the phrase "la delicadeza envejecida" and parallelism of the phrases beginning with "quién," "cuando," and "que" suggest similarity and difference, as do the phrases "que la pureza era la pureza, / que la verdad no fue nuestra verdad." The change from affirmation to negation, from the imperfect to the preterite, and from the impersonal to the personal ("*nuestra* verdad") establishes a contrast within the similarity of the parallelism. Purity can lead to the truth, but the truth is not always pure. At this stage in his life, the poet acknowledges what he has gained and what he has lost (failed to attain). He is disillusioned with his lack of progress, reluctant to participate again in a disappointing though honest endeavor that always comes up short; and he is intrigued and amazed by this process that reveals so much, that has taken him so far and yet only increases that which he can know, that which he knows awaits him if he will only participate in this experience again!

The final verses of this amazing poem again juxtapose interior and exterior, self and other, as the speaker both rejects and welcomes another incursion into the poetic act. In these verses, the speaker contrasts his face with the other's (Mari's) which is already ambivalent (beauty and witch), substituting this similarity/difference for "tu amor y el mío," "la verdad del amor que es tuyo y mío," and "el amor verdadero, que es el vuestro."

> ¿Quién buscó duración? ¿Quién despedida?
> Ya no hay amor y no hay desconfianza,
> salvación mentirosa. Es la miseria
> serena, alegre, cuando aún hace frío
> de alto páramo, Mari, y luce el día
> 25 con la ceniza en lluvia, con destello
> de vergüenza en tu cara y en la mía,
> con sombra que maldice la desgracia.
> ¡Qué temprano, qué tarde, cuánto duran
> esta escena, este viento, esta mañana!
>
> (p. 60)[154]

Contrasting self and other, the mythical level (Mari and Prometheus) plays against the personal level (the anecdotal speaker and the poet, the grieving loved one and the rebel). From the questions in v. 20 to the exclamation in vv. 28–29 the tone is simultaneously one of complaint and of wonder, of reluctance and of surrender. Even though it is cold (the wind blows over the high "páramo"), the sun is shining; the rain is equivalent to ashes (fire and water are destructive and regenerative); a "destello" is an indication and recognition of shame and that which motivates to remove the shame ("destello" can be a flash of lightning and a ray of sunshine, connoting destruction and generation, loss and gain); the shadow curses yet condemns misfortune, complaining yet dismissing. The disparity between these contradictory emotions and two incompatible readings we can give this poem exacerbate the gap in the language into which the poet falls and which he explores and bridges.

If we compare "De amor" with the previous section "De noche," we note that the same reciprocal interaction between similarity and difference obtains. Most obviously, both sections contain five poems and are structured around a motif that evolves from one poem to the next. "Nocturno de la casa ida" and "Momento de renuncia" are lengthy, difficult poems that define a turning point in the speaker's progress after he has defined his starting point. Following "Nocturno," "Nuevo día" is like a breath of fresh air, revealing a profound illumination and an inner peace that become even more perceptible in "Lamento a Mari" following "Momento" in the second section. If the speaker distances himself from that intense illumination in the final poem of "De noche," the last poem of "De amor" advances the progress: The speaker does not pull back as radically as he did in "Manuscrito," but partakes of greater risk through greater experimentation.

As I pointed out at the beginning of the discussion of this section, the first poem and the last contain fourteen verses. In comparison with the first poem, however, "Con los cinco pinares" is divided into four quatrains and ends with a couplet, reminiscent of the structure of an Elizabethan sonnet though no rhyme scheme is evident. The appropriation and alteration of the Elizabethan sonnet constitutes a major risk on the poet's part, first because it deviates from the Petrarchan structure (two quatrains and two tercets) more characteristic of the Spanish tradition and also because it repudiates the rhyme scheme. Moreover, the alexandrine verses contain a caesura, which, along with the stanzaic divisions, mark the gap in language; and the rhythm of two strong beats per hemistich approximates this poem to English. These characteristics are consonant with the (lack of a) title of the first poem, the English setting and modification of the title of "«The Nest of Lovers»," and the pattern of complementary and reciprocal similarities and differences, and the riskier experimentation that define the Promethean poet's acquisition of courage in "De amor."

In the previous poems of "De amor," the poet has deconstructed the binary opposites of physical and spiritual love, self and other, renunciation and acceptance, complaint and invocation, attraction and repulsion. In "Con los cinco pinares de tu muerte y la mía" [With the five pine groves of your death and mine], he deconstructs death and life. I submit that the five pine groves, sacred places marking eternal life, represent (among other possibilities) the five books of poetry Rodríguez has written, including *Casi una leyenda*, the work "in progress." These five works "represent" Rodríguez's life: They are a lasting testimony to his existence and his achievement, yet as representation (especially in language) they are and are not an accurate reflection of his life. On one level, Claudio Rodríguez is going to die (as we all will); he will cease to exist. But on another level, he will continue living "legendarily" in the poems he has written. Like the gap between signifier and signified, the "identity" of Rodríguez is created and confirmed, yet denied and negated by these works/words. The Promethean poet's double bind is laid bare: The more honestly and painfully he delves into himself to produce these extraordinarily personal, painful, heartfelt, and individual poems (descriptive of himself), the more legendary, overblown, and false his image becomes. The Promethean poet exists in a no-win, no-lose situation. Another irony of this poem lies in Rodríguez's punning on the name of a relatively unknown town in Sanabria, Los Cinco Pilares [The Five Pillars].[155]

For that very reason, the speaker contradicts himself. If in "Lamento a Mari" he affirmed that "La primavera vuelve mas no vuelve / el amor, Mari," in "Con los cinco pinares" he declares "Es el amor que vuelve." This love is the speaker's courage; his love of life, of poetry, and of humanity is the motivating force behind his willingness to expose himself to risk. Even though in his "anecdotal life" that courage may be cyclical—after all, Rodríguez has published only five books, a modest amount in comparison with some others—in his poetry his courage is constant, otherwise there would be no poetry, no lasting achievement. Reminiscent of Quevedo's "Polvo será, mas polvo enamorado," Rodríguez defines this courage as the life blood flowing through his poetry that engages poet and reader, causing each to continue living even though they—we—die.

> Es el amor que vuelve. ¿Y qué hacemos ahora
> 10   si está la alondra de alba cantando en la resina
> de los cinco pinares de tu muerte y la mía?
>
> (p. 61)[156]

The poem—a collection of arbitrary symbols staining the white page, the hieroglyphic markings etched thinly on the surface of the paper—becomes the interface between poet and reader where there is an exchange of energy, where both participate in the actualization of the language, the experience, the emotion of the text: "¡Si es el amor sin dueño, si es nuestra creación: / el misterio que salva y la vida que vive!"[157] Our transient existence continues to survive in our participation in the text, in the aesthetic experience.

JANUARY AND THIRD ACT: LONG-SUFFERING LOVE

The "Segundo interludio de enero" contains two poems, making this section the focus of the work's structure. Together these two poems, united by the leitmotif of the month of January, are comparable in length with either "Calle sin nombre" or "El robo." As a result, this section is of equal weight with the overture and the first interlude, yet because there are two poems, the second interlude functions as a counterbalance to the other two. Indeed, this is the moment in which the balance tips the scales, propelling the speaker into his final and most intense experience of the gap in language (the sublime) while also irrevocably turning us toward a recontextualization and rereading of "Calle."

Repetition of the month of January and the dates chosen for the titles of these poems overdetermine their meaning. The first month of the year is named for Janus, the god of two faces, who looks to the past and to the future. This split in the gaze leaves a gap in the present, the gap in language into which the poet falls and which he bridges in his act of writing. January is the beginning of the calendar year, but in Spain it is also a cold, dark month, a contradictory combination of a new beginning with coldness, darkness (night), and lifelessness in nature.[158]

The dates Rodríguez has specified are equally ambivalent. The first poem, "Brindis por el seis de enero" [Toast for the sixth of January] takes place on the day of the Adoration of the Magi, when the three wise men arrived in Bethlehem with their gifts for the newborn Jesus. Gold, frankincense, and myrrh (images Rodríguez has used in variations throughout *Casi:* "oro," "olor," and "mirto") imply eternal life and death, the mundane and the celestial, the human and the divine. The sixth of January, traditionally the day when gifts are exchanged in Spain, is a day of giving and receiving, gain and loss. These aspects evoke the poet's ambivalent relationship with the poetic act and his sense of pain and ecstasy deriving from participation in this act of writing/ reading.

The second poem, "Balada por un treinta de enero" [Ballad for a thirtieth of January], refers specifically to Rodríguez's birthday. Given that an early version of this poem appears in Cañas's book and the poet had won the Premio Nacional for his collected works the previous year, I would venture to say that the anecdotal basis for this poem is his fiftieth birthday (30 January 1984). This date at the end of the month contrasts with the other at the beginning and also represents a day of giving and receiving (in more than one sense, as we shall see). The contrast between these dates underscores the conflict between the personal and the public, the thief and the benefactor, past and future, the old and the new, life and death.

It is no coincidence that "Brindis" and "Balada" begin with the bilabial /b/ and that each refers to an utterance, a speech act. Words uttered before drinking a glass of liquor, a toast can commemorate a past achievement or express hope for the future. The mention of alcoholic beverages invokes the duality of "ebriedad" (heightened consciousness and unconsciousness, disorientation); it also echoes rituals such as the propitiation of wine to the gods, the spilling of sacrificial blood, and acts such as signing a document or shaking hands in sign of agreement, trust, and promise. As a symbol of blood, the life force, this imbibing seals an eternal compact through a momentary act, an act accompanied by words.

The ballad serves a similarly dual function. This speech act originated as a means of reporting narrative events and disseminating information to a wide audience by means of rhythm, song, and performance. One of the most traditional and venerable poetic forms, the ballad is also a popular verse form, much less complex than the sonnet, for instance, and stems from a folk origin; it is a form of popular culture. On the one hand, this folk aspect is congruent with Rodríguez's delving into himself to produce his poetry, but on the other, it becomes a public act of performance, stylized representation. The narrative aspect reflects sequential time, linking it with the poet's birthday and such narrative conventions as cause and effect, incident, and plot. "Incremental repetition" is another characteristic of the ballad that we have observed not only in this work but throughout Rodríguez's opus.[159]

Unlike the tone of the ballad, however, the speaker of this poem is quite personal, addressing himself and establishing a dynamic "dialogue" between self and other, or the self as other. Because of the dramatic quality that accrues from this dialogue, the speaker in effect seems to be an actor in the dressing room, preparing for his dramatic entrance, his performance. Featuring the ambivalence of interior and exterior, performance and spontaneity, writing and reading, this ballad relies heavily on the image of the door. In brief, these two poems—the hallmark of Rodríguez's structural design in each of his works—serve as the threshold for the final poetic sequence (the definitive third act) and represent a turning point, a falling into the gap to explore and bridge it.

The speaker of "Un brindis por el seis de enero" seems to become more intoxicated as this short poem unfolds. But is his intoxication disorientation and unconsciousness, or heightened consciousness and greater insight? At first, we might think that he feels the pressure of his ideals and the need to justify his existence (as a poet): "Heme aquí bajo el cielo, / bajo el que tengo que ganar dinero" [Here I am beneath the sky, / beneath which I have to earn money] (vv. 1–2). The emphatic "Heme aquí" and the speaker's positioning with relation to the sky, however, could be an exalting declaration of presence and plenitude, as the speaker is both resigned to the impossibility of his endeavor, the inevitability of his "failure," and defiantly proud of his individuality, his dignity, and his conviction. Playing off the journey of the Magi, following the star and paying adoration to the child Jesus, the next verses develop this ambivalence.

> Viene la claridad que es ilusión,
> temor sereno junto a la alegría
> 5   recién nacida
> de la inocencia de esta noche que entra
> por todas las ventanas sin cristales,
> de mañana en mañana
> y es adivinación y es la visión,
> 10 lo que siempre se espera y ahora llega,
> está llegando mientras alzo el vaso
> y me tiembla la mano, vida a vida,
> con milagro y con cielo
> donde nada oscurece. Y brindo y brindo.
>
> (p. 65)[160]

The sentence that unfolds in these verses, stringing together a number of equivocal and enigmatic images, describes journey and arrival, process and product, writing and reading. As the guiding star and the morning sun—images of light, inspiration, and revelation—"la claridad" represents an ambivalent "ilusión." Rodríguez is punning on this word, on one hand pointing out the deception and disillusionment of a false vision, whereas on the other delighting in a fanciful, magical belief (e.g., the figure of Santa Claus). The uncertainty of the Magi following this star without knowing where it may lead is a "temor sereno" that is equivalent to and different from "la alegría / recién nacida / de la inocencia de esta noche." On one level, the child Jesus is a humble, vulnerable human being, and a prophet and king, just as the Magi are human kings and prophets (seers); but Jesus far surpasses these wise men in the gifts he brings humanity and the ultimate throne he will occupy. On another level, the poet is describing his experience of receiving an uplifting, magical insight (the poetic gift) in the midst of a commonplace event (the traditions of the Christmas season can become repetitive, hollow, and indistinguishable; we are all the "bah-humbug" and the rejuvenated Scrooge).

Furthermore, night contrasts with clarity, so that instead of light streaming in through the windows—that symbolic limen between interior and exterior, surface and depth, self and other—darkness invades the always already darkness. Windows without glass are apertures that facilitate and place barriers between the poet and his insight into self and world. While the glass does not reflect and distort the image, shutters may instead block any attempt at an exchange of interior/exterior. (Shutters—"contraventanas" or "persianas"—are prevalent in European housing, and they can prevent seeing into or out of the house, the loss of warmth and the entry of light.)

Likewise, the phrase "de mañana en mañana" can mean "from one day to the next" in the sense of either a repeated, habitual occurrence or a unique, inimitable, irreversible event. Is the poet defining a singular event or one that is continual, unremarkable, unextraordinary, insignificant? The comparison and contrast of "adivinación" and "visión" and "lo que siempre se espera y ahora llega, / está llegando" bear out the ambivalence. "Está llegando" emphasizes the immediacy of the arrival and yet defers it by never indicating completion.

This abstract imagery is then compared and contrasted with the commonplace yet symbolic gesture of making a toast, lifting one's glass to speak and to imbibe the inebriating liquid. When the speaker notices that his hand is trembling, we cannot be sure whether it is from fear and nervousness, or excitement and joy. Is he merely "bending his elbow," taking drink after drink to become intoxicated, or is he raising the sacred cup in solemn sacrifice and heartfelt offering? His repetition in the phrase "Y brindo y brindo" could signify a repeated action or an extended continuance of his sacred discourse and the gesture of writing.

The aphorism of v. 15 epitomizes Rodríguez's poetics: "Bendito sea lo que fue maldito" [Blessed be that which was cursed]. We recognize the connection with language in the words "bendito" and "maldito" as we also note the contrast between them ("bien" and "mal") and between the verb modes and tenses. We should also see the ambivalence in the subjunctive "sea," indicating futurity and performativity. In the act of making the blessing (the toast), that which is desired is brought about: The transient becomes the permanent and lasting, the pain becomes gain. Even though they are two incompatible, incommensurate opposites ("good" versus "evil"), they are equivalent, identical, and in Rodríguez's case, the basis for individuality and identity in both senses. This toast converts the negative into the positive as it defers and looks forward to that conversion. It is process and product, performative and constative.

The final two verses function as closure and as a negation of closure: "Sigo brindando hasta que se abra el día / por esta noche que es la verdadera" (vv. 16–17).[161] As "está llegando" in v. 11 signals immediacy and deferral, so here the progressive construction, especially via the auxiliary "sigo," is ambivalent, repeating and extending "Y brindo y brindo." The placement and ambiguity of the prepositional phrase in the final verse complicates closure. Does the speaker mean that he continues his toast, addressing it *to* "esta noche" (cf. the poetic tradition of poems titled "To Night" or, similarly, to or for someone or thing)? Or does he continue toasting (drinking) *throughout* the night? Will day arrive *because of* this true night or *at the end of* (following) it? Is there a cause-and-effect relationship, or is it a cycle that will repeat with or without the speaker's consent or desire?[162]

Why does the speaker describe this night as "la verdadera"? Is this a reference to Jesus as the true King and Savior, He who will die to ensure eternal life, He who will receive the gifts of the Magi and give His own life as gift in return? Or is this an extension of the paradoxical "bendito" and "maldito"? The contrast of day and night, of drinking to get drunk and participating in a sacred ritual, of acting (pretending, feigning) and acting (doing, accomplishing) calls attention to the speaker as a character on a stage. Is he a human being getting intoxicated? Or is he a semidivine being participating in a sacred act? The Promethean poet is human and divine, thief and savior, sacrifice and priest; his discursive act—his poetry—is illusion (deceit) and Illusion (magic), an act of stealing and of giving, loss and gain, an act that requires painful honesty and self-abnegation and one that brings ecstasy, exaltation, and knowledge at the same time that it creates a false, legendary figure, so superficial and aggrandized in comparison with the "real" human being.[163]

If "Un brindis" portrays the speaker as an intoxicated (and intoxicating) shaman of the word, "Balada de un treinta de enero" presents him as an actor with stage fright, reluctant to play his part, to step out onto the stage and expose himself to the public, the audience that will judge, crucify, and redeem him (cf. Prometheus as Christ). His dilemma is dramatically set forth in the opening stanza, where the questions function rhetorically and literally, as usual.

> Alguien llama a la puerta y no es la hora.
> Algo está cerca, algo se entreabre.
> ¿Y cómo la creencia se está haciendo
> misteriosa inocencia,
> 5 momento vivo cuando aún los años,
> en rebeldía, enseñan
> soledad o placer? Desde estas piedras
> que se estremecen al juntarse igual
> que cruz o clavo
> 10 de cuatro puntas,
> ¿se oye la señal?
> ¿Se oye cómo el agua
> se está hablando a sí misma para siempre?

(p. 67)[164]

The speaker's reluctance is patent: He thinks it is too early for the guests to arrive for his birthday party, too soon for the knock to announce that he must appear on stage. He is still putting on his makeup, his costume. But the questions are so ambivalent that we can read them as excitement or perplexity, eagerness or fear. The speaker wonders how this is happening to him, yet he throws himself into the fray. His belief ("la creencia") is objective and subjective, and this belief becomes "misteriosa inocencia," ingenuousness and unawareness as "misterio." In like fashion, the years (the passage of time) reveal and teach solitude and/or pleasure; the passage of time can lead to disillusionment with life or more profound knowledge of it (cf. the earlier "Grave *placer* el de la *soledad*"). That these years are "en rebeldía" could suggest that the speaker resists this process or that he learns to accept these things precisely because he struggles with them. How can it be that this is happening? How *does* this happen?

The poet substitutes the image of "piedras" for "años" to develop this idea further. The rocks can be the years he has lived and the words he has written. Placed together, they tremble ("estremecerse" is a variation of "temblar"), and they resemble a cross or a compass with four distinct, cardinal directions. The cross and the nails evoke crucifixion and suffering, but also destiny, direction, purpose, and certainty. Not only does the question "¿se oye?" function rhetorically and literally ("Is it possible to hear it from here?" versus "Do you hear it too? I do!"); repetition again confuses metaphor and metonymy. Is "el agua / . . . hablando a sí misma para siempre" equivalent to "la señal" (metaphor)? Or does it exemplify and re(de)fine (metonymically) this notion? Is the "señal" the sound of running water (the "murmuring brook" as language, discourse, poetry)? Or is there a similarity between them, so that if we can take delight in the sound of running water, we can partake equally in the concatenation of these words, these stones, this series of moments that add up to years, a life, a destiny? The stream talking to itself yet overheard by the speaker (and the reader) is similar to the stream of words written by the poet and read by the reader. But because of the ambivalent interrogative mode, the speaker equates and differentiates these two images, he simultaneously doubts and affirms the power of language and his role as a poet (actor, priest, magician) in contemporary society.

From his dressing room, the speaker as actor can hear the murmur of distant voices that know, as he knows, that life is transient and that we must find some way (such as a play, a celebration, a work of art) to mark and alleviate this constant passing. The next stanza contemplates that paradox in the image of the wheat field from which bread (the body of Christ in the Eucharist) is made.

> Y oigo las aristas de la espiga,
> 15   el coro de los sueños y la luz despiadada,
> preso de tanta lejanía hacia
> el viento del oeste y el polvo del cristal,
> la pobreza en ceniza,
> tanta alegría hacia la claridad,
> 20   tanta honda invernada.
> Y el cuerpo en vilo
> en la alta noche que ahora
> se ve y no se verá
> y no tendrá respiración siquiera.
>
> (pp. 67–68)[165]

The speaker is able to hear distant voices: the wheat field waving in the wind ready to be mowed and made into bread; the crowd of people gathering to witness his appearance, his performance. The words he hears expressing "los sueños y la luz despiadada" are his own words. If the poet uses words, they are words that belong to everyone and express everyone's concerns, especially about the passage of time and death. The "coro" is "preso" just as the "cuerpo" is "en vilo": The wheat and the bread are destroyed in the process of sustaining life. The individual dies in carrying on—

sustaining, eternalizing—the tradition (acting/writing, attending theater/reading). The actor poised on the verge of a performance will adopt another persona; his individual self will disappear, will be seen but not seen, and will die (surrender) to the character he portrays (the illusion of the play). Yet his performance will assure the perpetuity of his name, his identity, his individuality as an actor/poet.

This ontological meditation continues in the next stanza, where the children playing in the snow are literal, metonymic details and metaphor for the human condition. The speaker then compares and contrasts them with the knock on the door.

> 25   Y los niños jugando a nieve y nieve en la plaza del aire,
>   con transparente redención.
>   El tiempo, la traición de óvalo azul,
>   de codicia y envidia,
>   y esta pared con sombra.
> 30   Esta señal certera, esta llamada,
>   este toque con calma ya maduro.
>
>   (p. 68)[166]

Images of death and vitality undergird the details on which the speaker fixes his attention. The children, the plaza as street ("camino"), the sky ("óvalo azul"), and the wall (a construction similar to a poem) all speak to the issue of life and vitality, whereas the snow, the emptiness of air and space, and the shadow contrast "traición" with "redención," evoking overtones of Christ's death and resurrection. The knock on the door adopts ambivalent meaning as a calling to death and to life. The juxtaposition of the speaker's situation (his fiftieth birthday, his reluctance to go out to receive his guests) with the children emphasizes their similarities and differences. Time as eternal, unending cycle of life and meaningless, inevitable passage to death, as dynamic and static in both cases, is like the words on the page (the shadow on the wall): an achievement, a monument, a lifeless work, and a city, a center of life, a text that is in constant flux even though the words on the page do (not) change. So this knock on the door, the poet's call to write, his inspiration, delights and distresses him.

>   ¡Y qué iba yo a saber si estaba ahí
>   llamando puerta a puerta, entre las calles,
>   muy descaradamente,
> 35   con el deslumbramiento de las manos
>   hoy tan huecas y vivas,
>   con escayola! No he tenido tiempo.
>   Es el día, es el día.
>   Y la madera aérea, con granizo
> 40   y las heridas del cristal heladas,
>   el latido de enero y el frío luminoso.[167]

Paradoxically, if the poet goes out into society looking for life, seeking adventure, knocking from door to door, he would never have written his poems. He has not had time to seek life because he has been living it! His hands are empty, yet they are covered with plaster because he has built the wall, written his poems; he has something to show for his life even though his Promethean hands are dirty and empty. If "No he tenido tiempo" means he has not had enough time, it also means that he is timeless, that he will live throughout time because of his accomplishment.

The repetition "Es el día, es el día" points out this ambivalence. Today is his birthday, the day when he "completes" a certain number of years (cf. the Spanish "cumpleaños"), just as January looks to the past; but it is the day when he goes onto the stage to give his performance, to write a new poem, to publish another book. It is also a beginning, a risk, but pleasure, excitement. All his "playing," all his practice, has led him to this moment, the verge of the future. This day is an end and a beginning (cf. January and one's fiftieth birthday).

The drafty windowpanes, the sleet hitting the frost-covered windows, are signs of vitality ("latido" = pulse, "luminoso" = illumination) even in the cold of January. Recalling such poems as "Siempre será mi amigo," "Nieve en la noche," and "En invierno es mejor un cuento triste," we see that this fleeting moment, trivial, personal, and transient as it may be, is the stuff of poetry. The speaker laments the passage of time and celebrates it; like Janus, he looks to the past and to the future, falling into the gap, the transient/eternal present. A repetition of the knocking interrupts and stimulates this meditation, halting it and spurring it forward.

> Alguien llama a la puerta. Doloroso
> es creer. Pero se abren
> de par en par las palmas de las manos;
> 45   los nudillos gastados
> piden, cantan
> en el quicio que es mío este treinta de enero,
> y el dintel sin malicia
> con la fragilidad del sueño arrepentido
> 50   entre las ramas bajas del cerezo.
>
>   (p. 69)[168]

Is this the same person still waiting to be admitted (perhaps the poet's wife impatiently hurrying him along), or is it another friend coming to celebrate/lament with the poet? Earlier in *Casi,* the speaker reflected "Grave placer el de la soledad." Similarly, here he declares/describes and warns, "Doloroso / es creer." *Caveat lector*! Yes, it is a painful experience to participate in the act of writing/reading, but it is also an affirmation of self (paradoxically through the surrender—crucifixion—of self). Just as Jesus trusted completely and surrendered Himself to crucifixion, here the speaker/poet opens his hands to receive the nails, and the knocking—the hammering—of his own bare knuckles on the beam that is cross, threshold, and lintel, that becomes his knocking on the door of immortality, a sound that resembles the barren but promising branches of the cherry tree shaken by the winter wind. This symbol of potency and delicacy, barrenness and fruitfulness, resiliency and fragility, poignantly equates the tree of life with the cross. The final verses of the poem then show the actor prepared to go onto the stage and compares that banal, frivolous, profane performance with Christ's crucifixion.

Ya todo se va alzando. Y estoy viendo
una crucifixión de espaldas. Huelo ahora
a esta resina, a este serrín sin polvo.

Es ahora la hora. Y qué más da.
55   Sea a quien sea sal y abre la puerta.
¿Al mensajero de tu nacimiento?[169]

The verb "alzar" suggests not only the raising of the curtain in a theater, but the raising of Christ on the cross to confront death. Just as an actor sees the play from the reverse side as the audience, so Jesus has a different perspective on the Crucifixion, literally and figuratively. If the speaker (as actor and Christ) smells the resin and the wood, it is because he has become one with them. The resin as sap, as life fluid, and the "serrín" as the act of cutting—the sawdust is "sin polvo"—unite sacrifice and sacrificed, act and result, death and eternal life, living wood and tree.

The alliterative "Es ahora la hora" and the ambivalent "Y qué más da" recall earlier moments in *Casi*, especially "Nocturno de la casa ida" (where the Christ imagery is prevalent and where "donde ya no hay aire" is first mentioned) and "El robo" with its insistent "Ahora es el momento." These echoes suggest the ballad's recurrent repetition and the contrast between past and present. If the knocking came too early before and the speaker was not yet ready, now is the designated time, as we enter the final section of *Casi*, "Nunca vi muerte tan muerta." The commands of the penultimate verses confuse the addressee: Is the speaker talking to himself ("Face the music; get it over with"); or is he addressing the reader (as wife, servant, or stagehand)? Does he urge resignation, or is he peremptory, commanding, in control, in character?

The symbolic action of opening the door—another leitmotif of *Casi*—involves risk and excitement, reluctance and eagerness. The question of the final verse is ironic in a number of ways. Does the speaker refer to the visit of the archangel Gabriel to announce God's choice to Mary? Is this the angel who led the Magi to the birth of Jesus? And, of course, this is the poet's birthday. Was he born at this time? Is that the hour: "¿Es ahora la hora?" This visitor, this guest (the reader?), announces the birth of the poet even though the poet is fifty years old! Rodríguez is playing with the concept of birth as a singular moment and one that keeps repeating and renewing itself each time the reader engages the text. According to this poem, then, the role of the poet in contemporary society is to remind us—through his example as seen in the act of writing as well as through his words, in what he has written—that we should imitate Christ to continue the work of redemption. The Promethean poet is to Christ as reader is to poet.

The title of the third and final section, "Nunca vi muerte tan muerta" [I never saw death so dead], is as ambivalent as that of the two preceding sections of five poems, emphasizing the gap in language. It is unclear whether death is the apotheosis of destruction, loss, and absence, or if death itself is destroyed, resulting in an eternal regeneration of life. This title encompasses the two paradoxical aspects of the sublime, grotesqueness and beauty, pain and ecstasy, transience and transcendence, both united and separated in the act of writing/reading, an act of surrendering one's individuality while defining it. The five poems of this section demonstrate the poet and reader's continuation of the act of redemption through a surrender to death.[170]

"Los almendros de Marialba" [The almond trees of Marialba], the first poem, is based upon a folk song of the region of Zamora, "El tío Babú."[171] This folk song is firmly rooted in a specific colloquial setting that includes the mention of several place-names in Sanabria and reference to a commonplace event: spring rains and a flood. These specific, anecdotal details adopt symbolic proportions, many of which Rodríguez has incorporated into his poem, although he has modified and redefined some of them, as the first verse of this song reveals.

> Cómo llueve por Bardales, tío Babú . . .
> también por Valdelespino.
> Los albillos de Marialba, tío Babú . . .
> se los ha llevado el río.[172]

The name "tío Babú" is a phonetic corruption of "Belcebú" (Beelzebub), a figure similar to the "bogey-man," "an imaginary evil character of supernatural powers, especially a mythical hobgoblin supposed to carry off naughty children."[173] "Tío Babú" is a personification of death, but one that the poet mocks. Moreover, Rodríguez is playing with the similarities and differences between Mari, the figure from Basque mythology that he introduces in the earlier poem "Lamento a Mari," and the name Marialba in this poem.[174] Another paramount similarity is found in the refrain of this song, which evokes biblical passages of the bridesmaids.

> Veinticuatro mozas iban a una boda
> iban veinticinco porque iba la novia;
> porque iba la novia porque iba el padrino,
> veinticuatro mozas iban de camino.[175]

This refrain evokes the passage in Matthew 25, in which the virgins who have brought sufficient oil can accompany the bridegroom when he arrives late, whereas the others miss their opportunity because they did not foresee a long wait. It also reminds us of the scene of the Last Judgment at the end of the same Gospel. Both passages describe an elite group that earns a reward (eternal life and joy) and a group condemned to a dark, cold absence.

The title of "Los almendros de Marialba" immediately calls attention to these intertexts and the ways Rodríguez has recontextualized and modified them. First he has changed "albillos"—a type of grapevine—to "almendros," an ambivalent image associated with death and resurrection (cf. Rodríguez's deployment of it in *El vuelo*). The white flowers of the almond tree promise fruit, the same productivity and fertility connoted by grapes, and represent one of the first signs of spring; yet they are susceptible to late freezes that limit the crop. Rodríguez may be commenting upon his own poetic career which began very early but has produced a limited crop in comparison with other poets who are as fruitful as grapevines. Nonetheless, almonds are rarer and more expensive than grapes, more valuable because of their scarcity; and the almond is a delicious, though bitter fruit.

In addition, the name "Marialba" includes the figure of Mari but appends the image of the dawn. This elaboration evokes the image of Persephone and of the Virgin Mary ("María del Alba") as the mother of Christ, the perpetual renewal of sunrise and resurrection, the bridegroom and the judge at the Last Judgment. The title fuses different levels of meaning (which we could summarize reductively as the transient and the transcendent) through intertextuality, recontextualization, and modification. The opening stanza of the poem is composed of a series of images referring to almond trees and agricultural activity as the late freezes interrupt and forestall milder weather, the putting forth of leaves, and the advancement of spring. The poet then caps this catalog with a question that will become the leitmotif of this poem and a central theme of the final section.

> Las heladas tardías
> entre un febrero poco a poco íntimo
> y un marzo aún muy miedoso,
> la rama noble tras la poda seca,
> 5   la nerviación de la hoja tierna como
> el recuerdo sin quicios ni aleteos,
> la templanza, el cultivo
> con el aceite blanco del invierno,
> ¿todo es resurrección?
>
> (p. 73)[176]

Rodríguez often mentions February as a time of purification and March as an image of the instability of the transition between winter (death) and spring (resurrection). The late freezes that threaten the almond trees' flowers occur at an indefinite point between these images of castigation, purification, and awakening to spring. The economics of pain/gain that characterizes the sublime is repeated in the image of the recently pruned branch ("poda"), in the contrast between the adjectives "noble" and "seca," and in the comparison of the veins of new leaves with memory. This memory is described as "sin quicios ni aleteos," modifiers that refer to an absence of obstacles to the poet's insight and his soaring, his poetry.

The phrase "el cultivo / con el aceite blanco del invierno" could describe the plowing of fields, damp with the melted snow, or the absorption of water and nutrients by the roots of plants. The curious aspect of this image is the use of "white oil" as metaphor for melted snow (water). Oil and water do not mix, yet each is fluid, and each facilitates, enriches, enhances, and sanctifies. Therefore, that which was cold, crystallized, superficial (snow is an image of superficial beauty) undergoes a transformation, a fundamental change in matter (from solid to liquid, from snow to blossom).[177] This alteration describes the work of the poet who draws upon stale, superficial images (the folk song, the myth) to convert them into new growth, blossoming, and productivity (fruitfulness and life).

The interrogative in the last verse is therefore perplexing. Why hasn't Rodríguez used an exclamation or at the very least a declarative statement? This rhetorical and literal use of the interrogative stresses the ambivalence of the sublime experience which entails pain and ecstasy, doubt and certainty, death and eternal life. Although he affirms that all the images cited above are potential signs of the sublime, the speaker also undercuts this affirmation and still doubts, deferring resurrection and ecstasy. The Promethean poet is a thief, castigated, reviled, and guilty of transgression, as well as a protector and benefactor, a bringer of light, warmth, wisdom, insight, and passionate vitality. He reveals suffering as well as ecstasy, the transient as well as the transcendent. Like the almond tree, he announces the arrival of spring, but he also makes himself more vulnerable to the vicissitudes of life. If he causes us to marvel at the example he sets for us, his willingness to abnegate (efface, surrender, sacrifice) himself, he also is an intimidating figure who challenges us, defies us, shames us into recognizing our own weakness and reluctance to follow his example. He questions submitting himself to this endeavor and yet exalts in it (the double bind). A possible reason for the shift from "albillos" to "almendros" in the title is clarified in the next stanza. Here again the last verse stuns us, seeming to contradict what precedes it.

10   No se los ha llevado la crecida del río,
        sin posible remanso, como entonces,
        a estos almendros de Marialba. Ahora
        es el prodigio enfrente, en la ladera
        rojiza. Hay que mirarlos
15   con la mirada alta, sin recodos,
        esperando este viento tan temprano,
        esta noche marchita y compañera,
        este olor claro antes
        de entrar en el tempero de la lluvia,
20   en el tallo muy fino de la muerte.

(pp. 73–74)[178]

In contrast with the vine shoots carried away by the heavy rains and the flooding river, the almond trees are not washed away. This image depicts Rodríguez's desire to produce a lasting achievement with his poetry—not one that has shallow, surface roots, but one that can withstand the vicissitudes of life and the passing of time. Derived from the Latin *prodigium* meaning a prophetic sign, the "prodigio" the speaker observes on the slope in front of him could be the flowering almond trees presaging the arrival of spring, or Christ crucified on Golgotha, a slope stained with blood but also a figure of dawn and resurrection ("rojiza"). As "prodigio," that is, "cosa que parece en contradicción con las leyes de la naturaleza," the almond trees and Christ stand out as different from their surroundings—the landscape, ordinary humanity—and each presages the renewal of life, as does the sublime poet.[179]

The phrase beginning with "Hay que mirarlos" could be addressed to the speaker himself or to the reader, the other who stands next to him and yet stands before him (the poet as Christ, as fellow human being and as savior). The poet is urging the reader (and himself) to look directly at the images he places before us, not sidelong or evasively ("sin recodos"). He then presents us with three successive images that define what we should perceive in the poem: "este viento tan temprano, / esta noche marchita y compañera, / este olor claro. . . ." The wind, the arrival of light at dawn (the fading of night), and the aroma of blossoms are all images of inspiration and illumination expected yet deferred, presaged yet delayed. (The verb "esperar" means both to hope and to expect.)

Insight must be present before entering "en el tempero de la lluvia, / en el tallo muy fino de la muerte." These images of full-blown spring equate the rain with the growth of vegetation, the renewal of life, and the rebirth of productivity. Modification of the stem with the adjective "fino" bifurcates the meaning as both "delicate" and "of high quality" (transient and transcendent). Here again the last verse stuns us, seeming to contradict what precedes it. When we read the word "muerte" where we expect to read "vida," a friction develops between the pain and the joy of the sublime. Given the title of this section, "Nunca vi muerte tan muerta," the omnipresent uncertainty and fragility of life ("la muerte") is the pain that the Promethean poet converts into joy through participation in the poetic act, his surrendering of self that leads to greater definition of self. The "tallo" is a hollow conduit of the vital energy (sap) that produces growth and life. This image echoes the myth of Prometheus who hid the sacred fire in a fennel stalk.[180] The sap as fire, uniting water and flame (destruction and regeneration), is a combination of air, light, and aroma that produces the intensity of the pain/joy of the sublime that is the poet's life blood which he passes on to the readers in his words—hollow forms (like stalks) that convey the meaning and intensity with which he imbues them. This contrast continues in the interrogatives/exclamations of the next stanza and repetition of the leitmotif.

> Cuántas veces estuve junto a esta cuna fría,
> con la luz enemiga,
> con estambres muy dulces de sabor,
> junto a estas ramas sin piedad. Y hoy
> 25   cómo respiro este deslumbramiento,
> esta salud de la madera nueva
> que llega germinando
> con la savia sin prisa de la muerte.
> Sin prisa, modelada
> 30   con el río benigno
> entre el otoño del conocimiento
> y el ataúd de sombra tenue, al lado
> de estos almendros esperando siempre
> las futuras cosechas,
> 35   ¿todo es resurrección?

(p. 74)[181]

Assuming that "esta cuna fría" is the flower of the almond tree, the poet exclaims and questions his appreciation of the opportunity to draw from experience, to take advantage of converting flower into fruit. He may regret lost opportunities, or he may be exalting in the continual opportunities presented to him. The sap that produces new growth and stimulates flowering on such trees is a "deslumbramiento" (a bril-

liant light that both illuminates and blinds) that arrives "sin prisa de la muerte": On
one hand, the flowing sap, like the river metonymically juxtaposed with it, is a symbol of the passing of time and the cycle of blossom, fruit, and harvest; on the other,
the sap is not threatened by the passage of time because it produces an eternal cycle of
life. The phrase "esperando siempre" delays the renewal of life and expresses absolute assurance that such a renewal will occur. Repetition of the leitmotif heightens the
perception of the gap between two incompatible readings of this song *(prodigium)* of
spring, the almond flower as delicate, vulnerable potential and as the cradle of new
life. The poet is simultaneously more reluctant, uncertain, and vulnerable as well as
ecstatic, invulnerable, and assured of inspiration. The final repetition of the leitmotif
caps the penultimate stanza.

> Nunca en reposo, almendros
> de Marialba
> porque la tierra está mullida y limpia,
> porque la almendra está durando apenas
> 40 alta y temblando
> con su fidelidad, su confianza,
> muy a medida de las manos que ahora
> se secan y se abren
> a la yema y al fruto,
> 45 a la fecundación, a la fatiga,
> a la emoción del suelo
> junto a la luz sin nidos.
> ¿Todo es resurrección?
>
> (pp. 74–75)[182]

The almond tree is the essence of change and contradiction. At the same time that
new leaf buds are opening, the tree is dropping its crop from the previous year: Springtime is ironically the time of harvest! Meanwhile, the poet at the foot of the tree opens
his hands—to catch the falling fruit or to receive the wounds of his crucifixion? The
contrast between "la emoción del suelo / junto a la luz sin nidos" juxtaposes and
imbricates earth and sky, transient and transcendent, saturation and emptiness, presence and absence. This time when the leitmotif is repeated, it stands alone, not as an
adjunct to the previous images, not detached from the rest of the stanza and the poem,
but independent of it. Again, as rhetorical questioning and literal appeal for truth, this
question/repetition defines the speaker as dependent upon transience and death, and
yet free of them.[183] This statement unites the speaker (and all of humanity) with Christ
in death and eternal life at the same time that it separates him (and us) from Christ,
requiring that we supplementarily complete the work of redemption. If Christ had
completed the work of redemption, the world would no longer exist as it does, suffering and death would have ended (died) forever. That suffering and death endure in
our world necessitates our participation in the work of redemption (the act of reading), yet if we are believers, we know that suffering and death can have no lasting
effect because Christ has risen. This is the double bind not only of the Promethean
poet but of the human condition as well.

Rodríguez enters the final stanza by repeating a verse verbatim from the earlier "Nocturno de la casa ida," where he alluded to the Night of St. John (the summer solstice).

> Hay un suspiro donde ya no hay aire,
> 50 sólo el secreto de la melodía
> haciéndose más pura y dolorosa
> de estos almendros que crecieron antes
> de que inocencia y sufrimiento fueran
> la flor segura,
> 55 purificada con su soledad
> que no marchita en vano.
>
> (p. 75)[184]

This repetition unites a moment of decision in the earlier poem with this revelation or epiphany. The variation in the next verse—where the poet has changed "hay *un* secreto" in the earlier poem to "sólo *el* secreto de la melodía" here—marks the speaker's progress as well as the similarity and difference of spring and fall, germination and harvest, pain and joy, death and life. The parallelism between "pura y dolorosa" and "inocencia y sufrimiento" exemplifies this ambivalence of the falling flower petals (the melody) and reinforces the distinction and imbrication evident in "secreto," an ambivalent image in Rodríguez's poetry meaning something that is both hidden and revealed. (There can be no such thing as a secret unless someone knows about it.) The ambiguity of the antecedent of "purificada" (is it "melodía" or "flor"?) is followed by a displacement of the withering to "soledad" (loneliness, isolation, abandonment versus solitude, individuality, and glorification). The flower fades, but not in vain: It produces fruit.[185] The final verses return to the image of the river and the intertextual reworking of "El tío Babú."

> Y es todo el año y es la primavera
> de estos almendros que están en tu alma
> y están cantando en ella y yo los oigo,
> 60 oigo la savia de la luz con nidos
> en este cuerpo donde ya no hay nadie
> y se lo lleva, se lo está llevando
> muy lejos y muy lejos,
> allá, en el agua abierta,
> 65 allá, con la hoja malva,
> el río.[186]

The scene that the poet has figured for us in the black and white contrast of the printed page is a springtime brought to life in the reader's mind ("tu alma"). These almond trees are as real and as alive as the ones the speaker has observed. He repeats and alters the earlier verse "junto a la luz *sin* nidos," saying "oigo la savia de la luz *con* nidos." Just as the trees in the reader's mind adopt a life of their own and add life to the almond trees the speaker has observed, so life renews and revitalizes itself through art and art through life.

The sublimity of the final verses, intensified by the stately, rhythmic repetition, is nearly indescribable. The verb phrase "se lo lleva" recalls "El tío Babú" (that obscurely regional and highly personal part of the poet) and emphasizes the sameness and difference of "albillos" and "almendros," Mari and Marialba. The river as passing time destroys and carries away, yet it carries us along (transports us) with "la hoja malva" in "el agua abierta" (note the alliteration of the open vowel /a/). This ambiguity is epitomized in the combination of Mari and "alba" and in the phonetic slippage from Marialba to "malva," a corruption that mirrors that of "Babú-Belcebú" in the intertext.[187] The color "malva," similar to violet, connotes the perfect intermingling of red and blue, warmth and coolness, carnal passion and a Platonic ideal, death and resurrection, the transient and the transcendent.[188]

In "Los almendros de Marialba," the poet identifies with the daring, vulnerable almond tree that announces the arrival of spring but is susceptible to the instability of the weather. He continues to explore the duality of this symbol—the tree of eternal life and the delicate transience and vulnerability of existence—in "Sin epitafio," whose very title expresses an ironic duality. In one sense, a person who dies without an epitaph (a written phrase, a commemorative inscription, a brief composition in commemoration or praise of the deceased person) would have lived an anonymous, uneventful existence, not worthy of commemoration or remembrance. With his death, the person is forgotten, leaving no written statement to attest to his existence. In contrast, if one never dies, there is no need for an epitaph; immortality obviates the purpose and need for an epitaph at the same time that an epitaph serves to preserve memory in perpetuity. Again we see the contradictory imbrication of presence and absence, eternal life and transience, in the context of the written word.

In the opening verses, it is unclear whether the poet is describing an event in the indicative mood or prescribing action with the imperative: "Levanta el vuelo entre los copos ciegos / de cada letra" [Lift flight amid the blind snowflakes of each letter]. Likewise, the reiterated verb "deja" could mean "to leave behind" or "to let alone, to permit, to allow." When "Vete" (v. 7) clarifies the previous verbs as commands, we still do not know if the speaker is addressing himself or another (the reader).

The image of the bird taking flight from the treetops is just as ambivalent. We could gloss these images as the poet's desire to attain poetic ecstasy through a flight starting at the very tops of the trees, which are still earthbound and subject to the passage of time. But we could also read "copos" [treetops] as "snowflakes," an image for the almond tree's white petals. Do these petals fall because they are completing their natural cycle, promising the production of fruit? Or have they been burned by a late frost? Do they stimulate the poet to ecstasy, or do they represent his transience? Because these are the "copos ciegos / de cada letra," the metapoetic implications posited in the title are interwoven more tightly in the imagery. The treetops, flowers, faded petals are aspects of language, of words themselves.

The declaration "La vida se adivina" [Life is perceived] embodies the same duality in its alliteration, the ambivalence of the verb, and the speaker's tone. "Adivinarse" can mean "to anticipate" as well as "to perceive." Is the speaker just now coming to an awareness that still eludes him, that he can barely intuit in these images? Or is he exclaiming about what he knows to be true and urging the reader to strive toward this marvelous discovery? This phrase could also be a pun on the word "divine": Life is in transition from the mundanely human to the divinely ecstatic ("La vida sea divina").

The final verses repeat the opening phrase "Levanta el vuelo" and then play on the words "entre" [amid], "no entres" [don't enter], and "este cuerpo entero" [this whole body]. The isolation of the phrase "donde está amaneciendo" [where it is dawning] in the last line, even though lacking the accent on "donde," could be interpreted as a decisive affirmation and a question. Is the speaker warning (himself and the reader) of the danger hidden in the treetops, the flowers, the fruit that will grow? Or is he urging us toward new heights, away from earthbound dangers, the shifting uncertainty that provokes slippage from "entre" to "no entres" to "entero." What is it, exactly, that he is warning against at the same time that he is urging flight?

If the falling petals of the blossoms (the loss of productivity versus the promise of fruit, the interruption of the cycle versus its fulfillment) is cognate with the dawn (the light, the arrival of inspiration), the speaker urges us both to seek and to avoid that dawn. As the phrase "Levanta el vuelo" can be prescriptive and descriptive, and "donde está amaneciendo" declarative and interrogative, the speaker urges us to avoid the facile and always to strive for higher attainments. Let us never be satisfied with mediocrity, anonymity, the commonplace and transient, but instead make the highest point, the greatest production of fruit, the starting point for even greater achievements. So Rodríguez has done in each of his works; so he will always strive to do; so he urges us to do. As he said in "El canto de linos," "Si la cosecha no es más que el principio" [But the harvest is only the beginning].

The reprisal of the image of "El cristalero azul" [The blue glazier] from *Don* as the title of the next poem and the self-citation of the phrase "El cristalero azul, el cristalero / de la mañana" [The blue glazier, the glazier / of the morning] twice in this poem reevokes the play of inter- and intratextuality, originality and repetition that was a major theme of Rodríguez's first work. Now, thirty-eight years later, he returns to the same image to assess his progress and to define his poetics as similar and different from the novice poet of *Don*. In addition, he draws upon a scene similar to that of "El baile de Aguedas," where dancer and dance, the transient and the transcendent, become inseparable and indistinguishable. By recontextualizing them in *Casi*, Rodríguez adds new facets to these combinations of past and present, self and other, transient and transcendent.

Here the subtitle alerts us that the male figure "el cristalero azul" is transformed into "La muerte." But death is an ambivalent concept in "Nunca vi muerte tan muerta." If death is equivalent to pain, which, in turn, is equivalent to sublime ecstasy, the ironic slippage of language—the merging of the dancer with the dance—imbricates signifier and signified in a constant play of difference and slippage, metaphor and metonymy, the transient and the transcendent. As the poet uses the image of the dance for a symbol of life (its transience and its permanence, that which slips quickly away and that which survives over time), he plays with two basic levels of meaning that are in contrast and in harmony in the text. The speaker's actions and his address of the other bear out this ambivalence in the poem's opening verses.

«¡El cristalero azul, el cristalero
de la mañana!» Y te vas cojeando,
silbando. Entra en el baile
sin funeral, con son de nacimiento
5   hablando con los hombres pasajeros
cuando el camino llega hasta la cima
y lo invisible es transparencia en llama
como el olor a hoguera de noviembre.
Dentro de poco, ¿quién oirá siquiera
10   al girasol que nadie verá nunca?
Todo es oscuro pero tú eres clara.
La vida impura pero tú eres pura.

(p. 79)[189]

Rodríguez has used the image of the limp in other poems. This image, as we have noted, suggests deformity, limitations, imperfections, and handicaps as well as being a sign of contact with the divine, of a struggle in which the human being has held his own with the gods even though he bears this wound, this impediment. The etymological root of the name Claudio also means "one who limps." Not only is he playing with the verb "Y te vas" (meaning "to go along, ahead" and "to go away, leave"), he is also punning on his own name and perhaps his own arthritic condition that causes his leg to stiffen if he is seated too long. This mischievous punning has the humorous and poignant effect of juxtaposing the personal and mundane with the symbolic and divine. The verb "silbando" reinforces this effect. Because the speaker is addressing himself (as he did in "Dando una vuelta," another poem in which the limp and walking figure the act of writing), we can imagine him either whistling in pain because his leg hurts (expelling his breath rapidly as an interjection of pain—an oral gesture) or making music in a colloquial, folkloric fashion.

He then urges himself as other (the glazier, the poet) to enter the dance. This command is ironic if the glazier is "La muerte" taking part in the dance of life. Does he make death a part of eternal life? Or does he see eternal life arising from death, the transcendent from the transient? How can we know the dancer from the dance? The invocation of dawn (inspiration, insight—the glazier) to enter the dance (life) is synonymous with the act of writing: "hablando con los hombres pasajeros." Keeping in mind the cultural context of a "verbena" in which men and women circle the perimeter of a plaza in a promenade that will lead to coupling and dancing, these "pasajeros" are literally "passersby," mortal, transient others whose fate the speaker shares. Yet this is an eternal dance, one without end ("sin funeral").

There is a reference here to the Way of St. James, the stars and the custom of dancing around a bonfire in November (the elegiac month), a pagan-based, Halloween-type celebration of life and death that invokes the return of the sun (light) after the winter solstice. The road also suggests a spiritual and aesthetic journey, as we have seen frequently in Rodríguez's poetry. These ritualistic celebrations—the dance and the bonfire—overlap, as do the images of the bonfire, the stars, and the sun, imbricating the particular with the universal, the colloquial with the symbolic, the transient with the transcendent. Without this combination and the abyss we infer between them, the poet as "girasol," another ironic variation on the image of the sun, will not survive. If all is dark and life impure (vv. 11–12), the "tú" addressed (the glazier, the dawn, the sun, death, pain, ecstasy, the sublime) is clear and pure precisely because it does unite these extreme opposites as well as marking the disparity and distance separating them. The anaphora of the verb "Entra" in the next verses continues to build upon and to build up the momentum of these images and the paradox they represent. Again puns bifurcate the language, juxtaposing life and death in many ways.

> Entra con limpia audacia,
> enterrada en tus alas,
> 15 entra en el baile,
> en cada letra de este nombre, en esta
> lápida que es secreto y sacrificio,
> y fruto y salvación.[190]

The amplification of "entra" into "enterrada" points to the ambivalence of the antecedent ("tú" or "audacia") and the meaning of "enterrada" ("buried, hidden, unseen, protected" versus "pervasive, inherent, characteristic, adorned"). The word "alas" evokes not only the image of a bird, but also an angel, both referring to a cloak or scarf worn by the dancer (death, life; pain, ecstasy). To take part in the dance (in life) is cognate with entering each letter of a name inscribed on a tombstone (cf. the epitaph of the previous poem). These written, engraved words are synonymous with poetry and the aesthetic act (a dance of life and death in signified and signifier). As we have seen in other contexts, the four nouns used to define this stone—the words on it being the words on the page—are all ambivalent, pointing to presence and absence, gain and loss, reaping and sowing, protection from risk and the very act of taking a risk.

Near the end of the poem, the speaker returns to this command and repeats the verses that appear at the beginning of the poem. This technique is similar to the repetition of the same words at the beginning and end of poems VII of "Libro primero" and "Libro tercero" in *Don*.

> . . . Entra en el baile,
> danza con cuerpo vivo,
> con gracia altiva y bella,
> 35 dame la mano y deja
> tu pañuelo en el aire.
> Danza sobre esta lápida.
> «¡El cristalero azul, el cristalero
> de la mañana!»

(p. 80)[191]

The imperatives "Entra," "danza," "dame," "deja," and "Danza" again accelerate the rhythm of the dance literally and figuratively (the dance as image and the language of the poem). But again we are envisioning an act that has yet to take place. The imperatives urge the other to join in the dance, but we imagine the dancing becoming even more vivid, graceful, carefree, and ecstatic. The passage is descriptive as well as prescriptive because of the ironic power of language to represent and to incite to action. Language is simultaneously constative and performative, both and neither.

Repetition of "El cristalero azul" at this juncture suggests that this is the epitaph, the words written on the stone/page. The question is whether the dance of life and death is played out in these words as echoes of the first time Rodríguez employed them (the "originality" of the novice poet in *Don*) or the words and the way the poet has deployed them in this context, in this moment, in this poem ("repetition"). The point is moot because it is both and neither: These words are empty repetitions drained of meaning, hollow, superficial signifiers, and simultaneously incomparably rich, symbolic, multivalent signifieds. Following the trend in *Don* where the same words are repeated at the beginning and end of poems, Rodríguez here extends their impact by adding a coda.

> 40 Antes de que se oiga
>   la melodía inacabada ahí quedas,
>   ahí, muy sola, sola,
>   sola en el baile.[192]

What can we possibly say about the contradictions, ambivalencies, and repetitions in this passage except that they condense the entire impact of the poem? The "tiny dancer" keeps spinning and dancing even though the music ends and everyone leaves the plaza. And this has all happened before the music even began because that is the essence of life: death. The poet, like the dancer, feels alone, isolated, caught in the sublime ecstasy of his own words, which identify and distinguish him; yet everyone who reads the poem (in isolation, of course) participates in a communion with the poet and so with all of humanity, all of the society who attends the dance, whether they can dance as she can or not. The readers' engagement with the language of the poem unites them with the poet and with each other in the dance of language, the presence and absence of the signifier/signified. Such is life, combining the transient and the transcendent, the colloquial and the universal, the personal and the communal, life in death and death in life. What a profound and sublime view of his and our world Claudio Rodríguez offers us in these poems of *Casi una leyenda*!

The motif of death as pain and delight, loss and gain, receives its most poignant and sublime treatment in the fourth poem, "*Solvet seclum*," where the poet avails himself of the grotesque to heighten the sublime. "*Solvet seclum*" is a lengthy poem that deserves greater attention than space allows here. I will forego a detailed analysis and concentrate on only a few of the highlights of this poem to leave room for *my* reader to participate in the work of redemption to which Rodríguez, the Promethean poet, invites all of us. Another indication of Rodríguez's experimentation and risk taking in *Casi*, the title of this poem is in Latin. The phrase derives from the burial of the dead and underscores a more traditional theme, the day of wrath. The first stanza of this traditional requiem is as follows:

> Dies irae, dies illa,
> Solvet saeclum in favilla:
> Teste David cum Sibylla.[193]

The day of wrath is that of the Final Judgment when the dead shall rise, and Christ will decide who shall receive eternal life and who shall be condemned. On a metaliterary level, Rodríguez is attempting to assure that his name, his identity, his "spirit," will survive through his poetry. The phrase *"solvet seclum in favilla"* refers to the destruction of the world in fire and is often associated with cataclysmic, catastrophic, or apocalyptic destruction on a grand scale (such as a war).[194] But the specificity and diminutive of "favilla" adds a note of tenderness and joy to this destruction, making the fire regenerative as well as destructive.[195] Out of the ashes and debris of the old world a new world will arise. Rodríguez sees himself as forming part of and continuing the poetic tradition, as a dancer in the dance. Writing is an exhaustive and a redemptive participation in life. Exhaustion (pain, loss, finitude) is necessary for redemption (joy, gain, immortality) to obtain.

The ironic complexity and complementarity of these two aspects is clearly evident in the opening statement of *"Solvet seclum"*: "No sé por qué he vivido tanto tiempo" [I don't know why I have lived so long].[196] In making this statement, the speaker simultaneously laments and rejoices that he has not already died; he questions and accepts his life. He assumes there must be a reason and purpose to his life, yet he sees it as a waste and an abomination: He feels fortunate and disconsolate. The two possibilities for each cause and effect ("Why am I alive? Why haven't I died?" "It's a blessing. It's a curse.") interact contradictorily, one complementing the other and vice versa, one negating the other and vice versa.

Rodríguez then uses two images to exemplify this situation. The first entails water, which is "la erosión, la sedimentación" (v. 7), "la disolución, la oxidación" (v. 16), "la corrosión en plena / adivinación / y la aniquilación en plena creación, / entre delirio y ciencia" (vv. 21–24).[197] The binarism and parallelism of these phrases foregrounds the chiasmatic relationship between two meanings on one side and two on the other. The second deals with the cyclical changes in nature and life, exemplified in the growth of grapes.

> 25   El campo llano, con vertiente suave,
> valiente en viñas . . .
> Cómo el sol entra en la uva
> y se estremece, se hace luz en ella,
> y se maduran y desamparan,
> 30   se dan belleza y se abren
> a su muerte futura . . .
>
> (p. 82)[198]

The photosynthetic process catalyzes growth and harvest, life and death, as the mature grapes are picked and crushed. But the juice from that grape (the sunlight converted into the fruit) becomes wine, the blood of life, beginning the cycle again and always already deferring destruction: "se abren / a su muerte futura . . ." The linear flow of water as erosion and sedimentation is compared and contrasted with the cyclical transformations of sunlight, juxtaposing and imbricating water and fire, destruction and regeneration, crucifixion and redemption. The speaker summarizes this paradox in the exclamation "¡Si está claro / antes de amanecer!" [But it is clear / before dawning!], which juxtaposes light and darkness, day and night, clarity and obscurity. This exclamation leads into a grotesquely beautiful description of death and decay that heightens the impact of the sublime.

El esqueleto entre la cal y el sílice
35   y la ceniza de la cobardía,
la servidumbre de la carne en voz,
en el ala,
del hueso que está a punto de ser flauta,
y el cerebro de ser panal o mimbre
40   junto a los violines del gusano,
la melodía en flor de la carcoma,
el pétalo roído y cristalino,
el diente de oro en el osario vivo,
y las olas y el viento
45   con el incienso de la marejada
y la salinidad de alta marea,
la liturgia abisal del cuerpo en la hora
de la supremacía de un destello,
de una bóveda en llama sin espacio
50   con la putrefacción que es amor puro,
donde la muerte ya no tiene nombre . . .

(pp. 82–83)[199]

The daring combination of the grotesque with the sublime in these images juxtaposes the dry, hollow bones of a skeleton with the music of a flute, the perforated skull with an ambrosial honeycomb or a beautifully woven basket, the burrowing of the worms with the delicate sound of violins—to give just a few examples, all clearly metatextual—and converts the surrender of life ("putrefacción") into "amor puro." The final verse above connects with "Sin epitafio" but also echoes "Calle sin nombre." In each case, anonymity is counterbalanced and interwoven with the eternal, recalling the title of this section, "Nunca vi muerte tan muerta." As the perfect epitome of death and the negation (the death) of death, the surrender of one's life becomes its redemption and salvation. In aesthetic terms, the Sublime necessitates the juxtaposition of the sublime and the grotesque.

The final stanza begins with another pair of daring exemplifications: "Es el último aire. ¡Ovarios lúcidos!" [It is the last air. Lucid ovaries!]. We must live every moment as if this breath were the last breath we will take. Living is dying, but dying is the source of life (the ovaries). In *Don,* the novice poet used the similar exclamation: "¡Ovarios trémulos!" [Tremulous ovaries!]. If we compare these two statements (recognizing the repetition and difference, sameness and evolution), the tremulous ovaries are excited and uncertain, joyful and fearful, eager and reticent (the novice poet as virgin). In comparison, the lucid ovaries are knowledgeable and innocent, rational and emotional, experienced and always new. The chiasmatic combination of these images results in a series of questions that are literally interrogative and rhetorically exclamative.

> ¿Y se oye al ruiseñor?
> ¿Dónde la cepa nueva,
> 55　dónde el fermento trémulo
> de la meditación,
> lejos del pensamiento en vano, de la vida
> que nunca hay que esperar
> sino estar en sazón
> 60　de recibir, de hijos
> a hijos, en la aurora
> del polen?
>
> (p. 83)[200]

The final poem, "*Secreta*," demonstrates more of Rodríguez's risk taking in this work. This short poem is composed of six stanzas of three hendecasyllabic verses capped by a "pie quebrado" (a truncated verse) of five syllables, with no regular rhyme pattern. This uniformity suggests repetition, yet each of the six stanzas introduces a new image incongruously juxtaposed with the previous image, while the final stanza repeats the opening verse in its third line (v. 23), signaling closure and yet maintaining difference.[201] The title is in Latin (similar to "*Solvet seclum*"), and it is repetitive in spite of its single word because it is taken from the Aristotelian phrase "secreta secretorum," the most esoteric of the esoteric, the most hidden of secrets, the most sublime of the sublime.

Negation in the first two stanzas may disguise the contrast between and reversal of affirmation and negation. The repeated "Tú no sabías" affirms the negative, but negation of the negation in the second stanza results in affirmation.

> Tú no sabías que la muerte es bella
> y que se hizo en tu cuerpo. No sabías
> que la familia, calles generosas,
> eran mentira.
>
> 5　Pero no aquella lluvia de la infancia,
> y no el sabor de la desilusión,
> la sábana sin sombra y la caricia
> desconocida.
>
> (p. 85)[202]

The motif of this section, "La muerte," represents the ambivalent concept of pain (awareness of life's transience) that has caused the poet to rise above death through his poetry (delight in the sublime). For that reason, death is "bella," and this feeling stems from awareness of the transience of the body. Likewise, the family and "calles generosas" represent the opposite of what they might seem. The family would normally be considered a loving support system, the human being's first society, and the streets the lucrative careers or opportunities afforded by the larger society; but here that support, the network of family and society, creates a false sense of security, independence, and personal accomplishment, a false sense that one is immune from the passage of time.

In contrast, the purity and innocence of youth interrupted by grief ("la lluvia") and bitter disillusionment, which the poet paints with the images of a white sheet and an insincere, disappointing love affair respectively, are more crucial contributions to an individual's growth. An additional contrast lies in the ambivalent and enigmatic address: The "tú" is self and other. Addressing the other, the speaker has a superior attitude; the other is less experienced and knowledgeable than he. Speaking with himself, the tone is much more sympathetic and understanding. One voice criticizes and challenges, while the other consoles and encourages; one describes his own experience, while the other warns and advises (prescribes).

The third stanza ellipses the "Tú no sabías," but the same introduction is implied. This pattern of repetition and difference carries over to the fourth stanza.

> Que la luz nunca olvida y no perdona,
> 10   más peligrosa con tu claridad
> tan inocente que lo dice todo:
> revelación.
>
> Y ya no puedo ni vivir tu vida,
> y ya no puedo ni vivir mi vida
> 15   con las manos abiertas esta tarde
> maldita y clara.[203]

The image of light, redoubled by "tu claridad," is the truth that does not allow a person to "forgive" or "forget" the truth. If one possesses the insight that the poet has into reality, s/he will not be able to misrepresent or deny the truth, even when that insight reveals her/his own shortcomings and errors past and present. If the second stanza turns on the conjunction "pero" to reverse the pattern of affirmation and negation, the fourth stanza pivots on repetition and the conjunction "y." Again this repetition hinges on the duality of self and other. The open hands recall the crucified Christ who opens his hands to the nails. Because he has surrendered his life to his destiny as a poet, the speaker can no longer lead life in an ordinary way; his poetic insight will not allow it and has irrevocably changed his life.

Because of his own experience, however, he knows that he cannot make that same decision and commitment for another. Each of us must make that decision individually. The poet can only present himself as a model, honestly calling his life, his insight, "maldita y clara." These two adjectives display the same ambivalence of self and other. "Maldita" can mean cursed, damned, terrible; but its etymology reveals the speaker's humility (his words are ineloquent). Similarly, "clara" puns on the image of light and the name of the poet's wife, suggesting that his love of this other is as ambivalent for him as his poetic insight. She is the all of his life, the center, the joy, but also the greatest challenge, even a bane or a crucifixion. Certainly if he is punning in this way, we wonder if the speaker is not mischievously ironic and comic, and thus tenderly loving.

The final two stanzas of "*Secreta*" further problematize the speaker's attitude as he questions the efficacy not only of his own sacrifice, but of his urging others to make a similar imitation of Christ.

> Ahora se salva lo que se ha perdido
> con sacrificio del amor, incesto
> del cielo, y con dolor, remordimiento,
> 20   gracia serena.
>
> ¿Y si la primavera es verdadera?
> Ya no sé qué decir. Me voy alegre.
> Tú no sabías que la muerte es bella,
> triste doncella.
>
> (p. 86)[204]

The run-on line at the beginning of the fifth stanza bifurcates the deictic "ahora." In one respect, the speaker may be affirming his own act of redemption (salvation) in this reprisal of the gain/loss motif and confidence in the redemptive value of the sacrifice he has made in these poems. In that light, "ahora" means "right now, at this very moment." But in another respect, he could be talking generally about "nowadays, at the height of present circumstances of the contemporary world and my own life," saying that the only way to redeem the perishable, ephemeral value of life is through a "sacrificio de amor." In this sense, the speaker doubts his feeble, ineloquent attempt and questions whether he has attained his lofty ideal.

Moreover, he seems to place the very tenet of his argument in question. The phrase "incesto / del cielo" may refer to a common theological and metaphysical debate about the conception of Christ by the Holy Spirit and the relationship between the humanity and divinity of Jesus as the Son of Man and God himself. On one hand, the poet may be doubting his faith: If one doesn't believe, is this a valid sacrifice? Will it, *can* it, be successful? On the other hand, he affirms that one must take that risk—that leap of faith, an act of faith that is also an "auto de fe" (a painful martyrdom of self for one's beliefs). Whether one is a believer or not, the value of the act is not diminished, as long as the "dolor, remordimiento" are real and one accepts them with "gracia serena."

The poet doubts himself, doubts his own faith in his own words, his own poetic gesture of sacrifice and self-definition; yet he is still willing and committed to making that gesture. He wonders, "¿Y si la primavera es verdadera?" Spring—redemption, resurrection—may or may not occur, but the speaker can be proud of his effort, knowing that he has done his best, that he has demonstrated his courage and made his particular sacrifice.

When he repeats the opening verse in the penultimate and then alters it by adding the person of the other (the addressee), the poet signals closure yet leaves the poem, the work, his work, our work, unfinished and open-ended. The sad maid he addresses at the last moment may represent that other who is less knowledgeable and experienced than the speaker. She (as other) sees only the frivolous, ephemeral side of life and is saddened, even oppressed, by the apparent meaninglessness of life. She may represent the youth of Spain (and of the world) whose hopes are limited by the very nature of the contemporary world. But the speaker's tone is ambivalent: He may be lamenting that she didn't know—but she does now, because the poet has given his example and his words to demonstrate his view that life is painful, but it can also be highly rewarding. This duality is complicated if we remember that the other can be a part of the speaker himself, who chides himself for his reluctance and his lack of courage, but also sympathizes with and understands why he would like to see life as eternal youth, pleasure, and beauty. He has and has not abandoned or *lost* that view, having *gained* new insight into how to attain it and what life really is.

As a final commentary on this poem, I would like to suggest that the truncated lines at the end of each of the six stanzas make a poem in themselves. The *secreta*

> eran mentira
> desconocida
>
> revelación
> maldita y clara
>
> gracia serena
> triste doncella.[205]

Overture as Epilogue: Recontextualization and Rereading

Having examined closely the well-defined structure of *Casi una leyenda*, with its overture preceding the three major sequences separated and joined by the two interludes, the lack of a "coda" proper renders the work asymmetrical, as if incomplete, so that it seems to limp along. If we also take into account the unity and separation of the two-poem section in *El vuelo de la celebración*, separated and united by the three intermediate sections, this lack becomes even more acute. Where is the "Elegía desde Simancas" that will counterbalance and complement the overture of *Casi*, "Calle sin nombre"? Should *Casi* end with "*Secreta*," or is there some "resolution" to the speaker's trajectory that might make us more comfortable with the entirety of *Casi*? Some "closure" even if it negates closure?

As soon as I completed my initial reading of *Casi*, I turned back to "Calle" and discovered a totally different text. I should now like to return to the overture, "Calle sin nombre," and reread it as coda in the new context of the trajectory we have observed in this work. For it seems to me that in the context of the Promethean poet as a Christ figure "Calle sin nombre" is both the Alpha and the Omega, the beginning and the end, the oneiric (unconsciousness) and the ecstatic (heightened consciousness), closure and reopening, highly congruent with the fundamental themes and techniques of *Casi*, and the poet's risks deserve a cognate response from me as reader.[206]

When we first open *Casi*, the street without a name presents us with an oneiric scene. The speaker wanders through an hallucinatory dreamscape in which he cannot find his bearings and his security. The street on which he searches for meaning has no name because the speaker feels disoriented. After reading *Casi* in its entirety, it becomes apparent that the nightmare of that initial reading has been transformed into ecstasy. Though the speaker still feels disoriented and though the language still maintains its double-voicing, the emphasis and the tone have shifted radically. The speaker is now triumphant and delights in the intense vision he encounters. This change does not negate the earlier reading—the pain, the disorientation, the "deslumbramiento"— but it does change the context and place the two readings in a new relation to one another, again defining the sublime.[207]

Reading the opening verses as if looking toward the past rather than the future converts the nightmarish scene into the beginning of a truly sublime, mystical moment of union. The speaker still feels disoriented and dazzled by the anticipation of the light, but his tone is much more accepting as he revels in the anticipation of the arrival of sublime joy.

> ¿Y no hay peligro, salvación, castigo,
> maleficio de octubre
> tras la honda promesa de la noche,
> junto al acoso de la lluvia que antes
> 5   era secreto muy fecundo y ahora me está lavando
> el recuerdo, sonando sin lealtad,
> enemiga serena en esta calle?
> ¿Y la palpitación oscura del destino,
> aún no maduro hoy?
>
> (p. 11)[208]

Instead of ambivalent questions, these interrogatives adopt an exclamatory shading that invites and coaxes rather than creating doubt, fear, puzzlement, and uncertainty. The speaker yearns for but also expects with certainty the arrival of the dawn, his resurrection through the reactualization of his words, his poems, his sacrificial gestures. When he subsequently questions "Pero ¿dónde está, dónde / ese nido secreto de alas amanecidas / de golondrinas?," he does not negate the *ubi sunt?* theme; he dismisses it as unimportant. He does not doubt that he can find this hidden secret anymore; in contrast, he welcomes and embraces the challenge: He has lost something that is gone forever, but he uses that loss to his advantage, to gain. If life is a never-ending process of loss and death, the poet's goal is to live that life to the fullest. Now when he hears the voice calling to him "desde estas casas transparentes," the closed door he encounters is not a barrier or a stimulus to open it, but music itself, the poet's hand (the gesture of writing), opening the transient, insubstantial barrier of empirical reality with his poetic insight and his words.

His final question in the first part of "Calle"—"¿Y dónde los vecinos?"—emphasizes his elation and his optimism through the repetition of the leitmotif. He still questions where his readers are, if he is making contact with others or if he is wandering through a ghost town alone; but now he is optimistic that he will eventually find them and is eager to do so. Because finding those kindred spirits has been one of the purposes of his quest, of laying himself on the line, of submitting himself to pain, suffering, and (self-)humiliation. He wrote these poems—and all his poems—to find those kindred spirits and because he knew he would find them.

On a first reading, the description of the cityscape after the rain, as the light becomes brighter, defining the railing on the balconies, the reddening of the roof tiles, and the bluish color of the buildings and the sky—this description indicates the speaker's first perceptions of his location in the world and orients him in the direction he will take. However, he is still disoriented, wandering, and searching. Upon a second reading, following his trajectory through *Casi*, this greater definition of the world around him adopts magical proportions because of the speaker's and our heightened consciousness. Instead of seeing him stumbling along and then beginning to get his bearings, we see him emerging from the initial darkness (excessive illumination), being drawn into greater delight and consciousness as if emerging from a momentary daze ("deslumbramiento"). The spume of his footsteps on the pavement, "sonando en inquietud, con estremecimiento," points more toward the speaker's excitement, his eagerness, and his delight in this exploration of the unknown. He almost seems to be drawn by a magnetic force; having surrendered himself, he is passively in motion and enjoying a sense of weightlessness and elation: "La calle se está alzando."

If at first we understood his action of stopping at the doors frantically searching for a certain face ("quiero ver esa cara ahí a media ventana"), now the speaker boldly and enthusiastically runs from door to door, rejecting them because they are not true to the image he seeks. He now rejects superficiality not out of dissatisfaction with what he finds but out of assurance and optimism that he can and will find something better—if he keeps trying, if he keeps striving for his ideal.

Whereas at first we might have thought that the desired face was that of a woman—the poet's inspiration, perhaps his wife ("está ya clareando")—now, thinking of the vertical and horizontal framework of muntins holding windowpanes in place, and keeping in mind the speaker's role as poet, we may conceive of him looking for any face, any experience, any illuminating moment in which he will see the face of Christ and see himself, his actions, his identity, reflected in that face, that image. The window allows him both to look through and to see himself reflected, superimposing one image on the other. He will find himself in Christ and Christ in himself.

The final section of "Calle sin nombre," as we saw earlier, is the height of mystic enlightenment after the dark night of the soul: "Ha amanecido." The images of the rain, the altitude, the air, the violet clouds, the soaring swallows, and "el bronce en flor de las campanas" describe his exaltation and his sublime joy in the smallest and subtlest details of the world around him. His question "¿Dónde, / dónde mis pasos?" seems to say, "I want more. Now which way should I turn?," knowing that wherever he turns he will find a lasting ecstasy even though the world around him and he himself are transient (the theme of *ubi sunt?* is *not* negated and lost, only incorporated in a new perspective, a new context).

During our first reading, the final three verses of this poem brought the speaker's budding joy to an abrupt conclusion by introducing a contrasting voice but promising greater ecstasy as we move through *Casi*. Now these words do function as a true coda, bringing all of *Casi* to closure. We might think, reading these verses, that the speaker is sated, that for the moment at least he can absorb no more pleasure, joy, ecstasy, and so he takes his leave. Perhaps for the last time ("aunque nunca vuelvas")? Will he ever be able to recapture this ecstasy? But he could just as well abruptly turn to the reader saying, "You see what I have done? Now, you, stop wandering around. Say good-bye to that superficial, unsatisfying approach to life. Follow my example." This is a "Calle sin nombre" not because it is anonymous and transient but because it must be individual, it must be unique to each individual, it must bear his/her singularity. Each person must determine his/her own course of action to achieve what Rodríguez has demonstrated through his example. Even the poet himself must choose an individual path if he is to achieve his goal. In *Casi una leyenda,* Claudio Rodríguez has given us the example: He has blazed his own trail, he has struck out on his own, he has broken new ground yet again.

Conclusion and Prologue:
The Poet-Artist as *Dasein*

To bring this commentary on Rodríguez's poetry to a specious conclusion—for the poet continues to write and the critical exchange about his poetry has virtually only begun—I would now like to analyze three poems that have not been included in his five published books.[1] Written at three different moments in his career and employing three distinct styles, these poems share a common theme, as each in its own way defines the image of the poet/artist.[2] The first of these poems pays homage to fellow-poet Blas de Otero and includes the figure and workspace of the Zamoran artist (painter, sculptor) Ramón Abrantes. The second depicts the poet as the bullfighter Antoñete, whereas the third forms part of a collection of paired poems and paintings representing the Stations of the Cross. In this third, compact statement, the poet combines his voice with Christ's as he speaks through that "mask." In each of these poems, my focus on the poet/artist is informed by Heidegger's philosophy, especially his concept of *Dasein*, for through participation in the creative act the artist encounters with heightened consciousness what it means to be.[3]

"Blas de Otero en el taller de Ramón Abrantes, en Zamora" [Blas de Otero in the workshop of Ramón Abrantes, in Zamora] commemorates the visit of the well-known, well-established poet to the provincial capital, and more specifically to the studio of the artist Ramón Abrantes. This momentous occasion brings together and juxtaposes the wordsmith and the artist (painter, sculptor) in a space that enfolds both the studio (a place of artistic creation) and the workshop (such as a "taller mecánico" [mechanic's garage] where cars are repaired). These two possible meanings of "taller" encompass both the inspiration and the craft or technical skill needed to produce a work of art. Couched in an everyday setting (similar to many poems of *Conjuros*) and based upon an actual, historical event, this scene—reminiscent perhaps of Velázquez's painting of Vulcan's forge—allows the young poet-witness Rodríguez to define himself as an apprentice.

Two aspects of Heidegger's philosophy stand out in the reading of this title. One is, of course, the setting, underscored in the repetition of the preposition "en" and in the two spaces delimited, the workshop and Zamora. This specific, historical, autobiographical context epitomizes *Dasein*'s thrownness, as he finds himself in the midst of his world, his culture, his everydayness. Yet it is also into this mundane context that the renowned poet has stepped, as if a god, to inspire the work of the smith. (Recall also that Vulcan was lame, a trait Rodríguez frequently attributes to himself and his poetry.) Blas de Otero functions as a part of that context (he is a Spanish poet who addresses his artistic utterances "a la inmensa mayoría" [to the immense majority]) and yet transcends it because of his artistic production, characterized by his protest against the anguish of being.

The second Heideggerian aspect concerns the tools we would expect to find in this workshop. Heidegger's discussion of tools in "The Origin of the Work of Art" stresses the interrelatedness of the everyday and thrownness with *Dasein*'s understanding of what it means to be. For Heidegger, the poet's "ready-at-hand" "tools" are words, so that we encounter a direct link between Rodríguez's concept of poetry as "conocimiento" and *Dasein*'s being-in-the-world. The gerunds used to describe the working of the tools in the poem's opening statement not only describe the poet's (Blas's and Rodríguez's) work with language, but also allude to *Dasein*'s witnessing and testimony of insight into being.

> Por ver cómo corre el Duero
> y cómo la escayola y el cemento,
> cómo el pan, la herramienta
> cantando y acusando entre las manos
> 5   de Ramón y de Julio, y de Marcelo,
> de Tomás y de Antonio,
> sobre todo de Eugenio,
> estabas.[4]

Although the speaker of this poem ostensibly addresses the other poet in apostrophe, he could also very well be addressing himself. In witnessing the visit of the other to this humble context, he realizes his own role as *Dasein*. This purposiveness stands out in the opening prepositional phrase "por ver" and in the accentuated anaphora of "cómo." Typical of the ambivalence of these interrogatives/exclamatives in Rodríguez's poetry, these "cómo" introduce a series of images that are equated because of the parallel structure. The flowing of the Duero enters into the process of making plaster and mortar (used in sculpture or ceramics), as it also is part of the bread-making process, implying that the creation of art is as basic and necessary for existence as bread. This flowing parallels the musical sounds of the tools in the hands of the artists and apprentices. That these tools are "cantando y acusando" lends a metapoetic dimension to the scene since both singing and accusing are verbal acts. They also combine the beautiful with the harsh, the aesthetic with the political or ideological (in the broadest and most philosophical senses of those words).

We might dismiss the list of names of the laborers as merely anecdotal ersatz, given that only one of them has a last name—Ramón Abrantes, the distinguished artist—and the others are unknown. However, we might read "Julio" and "Marcelo" as noble Romans, and "Tomás" and "Antonio" as saints, whereas "Eugenio" is an allusion to Eugenio de Luelmo, the central figure of the eponymous poem from *Alianza y condena*. By beginning and ending his list with Ramón and Eugenio, Rodríguez raises the issue of identity and displays the gamut of possibilities for attaining individuality.

At the end of this catalog and as a result of the hyperbaton, Rodríguez isolates the verb "estabas" to focus attention on presence and "being-there." But as noted, he confuses the addressee in absentia: It could be Blas or himself. In other words, he questions his own identity. Does he stand out as a distinguished artist like Blas de Otero and Ramón Abrantes in this collection of human beings, or is he merely one of the observers of (and perhaps minor players in) a constellation on the edge of and touched by the propinquity of greatness? The imperfect tense of the verb augments the descriptive level of the scene and the sense of presence, but it also marks the absence of the other (and the speaker as other). We could therefore read this sentence as a nostalgic yearning for something that has been lost, that has slipped away with the passing of time (note the Duero), or as a contemplative reflection out of which symbolic meaning resonates and becomes present for the speaker-poet. The question for the apprentice poet is whether he has learned from that moment so that he too will become a major figure, or if that chance has eluded him, consigning him to anonymity. This ambivalence is confirmed in the next sentence, which launches him into further consideration of the scene he has witnessed.

> Sí, entre el barro
> 10   y el alma,
> cuando la luz se hacía melodía
> y manantial y el cielo
> «muy luminosamente rojo», como dices,
> entonces, a dos pasos,
> 15   se abría el puente y abrazaba el agua,
> tan íntima y fecunda,
> y la tejía entre sus ojos limpios,
> y la amasaba libre,
> con el molde sudado y respirado
> 20   junto con los amigos.[5]

In addition to the duality of "el barro / y el alma" ("mud and soul"), the preposition "entre" can be read as either "between" or "amid." Is the apprentice poet caught between two possibilities in a sort of uncertain no-man's land? Or does he find himself immersed in a world that offers him confirmation of his ability on every front? On the one hand, the mud can refer to the materials with which art is made, but on the other, the soul—inspiration, emotion—is also necessary to produce the work of art. The series of metonymic/metaphoric images that follows only intensifies the tension in the apprentice's position. In an inverse relationship with the mud and the soul, the speaker's detailed elaborations of the sky and the land continue to deconstruct these oppositions, reminiscent of the ironic peripeteia of *Conjuros*. Instead of the river, the light becomes "melodía / y manantial": The visual becomes audible and tactile whereas before the fluid became tools "cantando y acusando"; that which slipped away became lasting artistic objects. The elliptical parallelism shows the effect of the light on the sky, but here Rodríguez intertextually cites one of Blas's poems, "Aceñas" [Water mills]. Blas's poem describes the same event but emphasizes the passage of time and loss in his use of the preterit.

> El Duero. Las aceñas de Zamora.
> El cielo luminosamente rojo.
> Compañeros. Escribo de memoria
> lo que tuve delante de los ojos.[6]

Although Rodríguez intertextually concedes primacy (precedence and superiority) to Blas's poem, his (mis)quotation dis-figures or re-figures the original with the adverb "muy," adding alliteration and rhythmic fluidity to the verse. He could be expressing either his admiration of the master poet's representation of the beauty of the moment or his improvement upon the originary utterance because he found it lacking. In this way, he asserts his superiority over the other, at the same time that he concedes his indebtedness. What is the relationship between the apprentice and the master? Does he learn from and depend upon him, or does he supersede him? As the presence of the Duero indicates, Rodríguez is questioning his relationship to the poetic tradition and his identity as a poet.

The speaker then turns his attention to the bridge and the river. The deictics "entonces, a dos pasos" are ambivalent because "entonces" could indicate a sequence of moments or the immediacy of that very moment, while "a dos pasos" defines an ambiguous distance and proximity. Likewise, the bridge both opens itself and embraces the water, contradictory movements, just as the lateral immobility of the bridge contrasts with the countering, perpendicular flow of the river. These dualities repeat in the images of weaving (warp and woof, metaphor and metonymy) and kneading bread: in short, textuality.

Then he returns to the workshop, making a comparison between the bridge as a mold for the baking of bread and the artist's mold that produces an art object. The adjectives "sudado" and "respirado" refer to both, but also function ambivalently. Describing condensation and evaporation, "sudado" can allude to heat, effort, and sweat as well as passion, intensity, and the fertility of work (water); and "respirado" can indicate fatigued, labored breathing as well as inspiration. The final phrase "junto con los amigos" repeats the ambivalence of "entre" and returns our attention to the specific men gathered in Abrantes's workshop at the same time that these friends suggest a collaborative effort in the search for artistic truth and a communion that extends into the future as the poet advances the tradition. The imbrication of the particular with the general, the anecdotal with the symbolic, the transient with the transcendent, again recalls *Dasein*'s "being-in-the-world" as an opening onto the perception of Being.

With the ambivalent image of the Duero as a pervasive backdrop and catalyst for the artists' work, the final two stanzas of "Blas de Otero" show the apprentice poet asserting his individuality. Although the layering of artist, master poet, and apprentice continues, the apprentice distinguishes himself by calling attention to his own craft. If in the first stanza he cites the master poet, in the second he imitates not only his style but also his intensity and purpose.

> Ahí, en el taller tuyo estás tallando
> (copio tu estilo)
> no tan sólo palabras verdaderas
> sino también la salvación, la busca
> 25   y la protesta. Pasa
> el agua, ahí, a dos pasos,
> del Duero.[7]

Although the apprentice readily admits that he is imitating the other's style, the parenthetical statement brackets the speaker off and calls attention to what he has done. Yes, he imitates the other, but in doing so, his alliteration creates the sounds of the artist's workshop and converts the verb "tallar" into a metaphor for writing. He has also changed from the earlier past tense "estabas" to the present "estás." Like the master poet, he draws on past experience but goes beyond the superficial, striving to attain "la salvación, la busca / y la protesta." Faced with the constant passage of time and the transience of the human condition, the poet like the sculptor seeks to create a lasting achievement, one that finds its salvation through its protest, its plaint, its search for authenticity. *Dasein*'s purpose in life, based on his care for the world around him, is to save, to redeem that which slips away in the flow of time, the continuous "being-toward-death." The choppy rhythm and fragmented syntax of the final mention of the Duero reveals the ambivalence of the river as both passing time and enduring identity.

How does the apprentice distinguish himself to attain a lasting expression? The answer to this question is found in the surprising imagery of the final stanza.

> Y el taller, y el latido
> del ritmo de la obra y de la mano,
> 30   están ahí, contigo,
> junto a los muslos de las lavanderas
> sin que el río se muera en nuestros brazos
> porque el agua del Duero es ya cal viva.[8]

The confusion of address in the apostrophe of these stanzas shows that the apprentice individuates by identifying with the master poet. The process of identification and individuation (similar to what we see in *Alianza y condena*) suddenly emerges from the background of the workshop in the image "junto a los muslos de las lavanderas." The insertion of this new element, given its metaphoric dimensions, demonstrates the apprentice's breakthrough to originality. The erotic dimensions of the washerwomen (cf. "A mi ropa tendida"), specifically the mention of their thighs, and the purification process of washing clothes in the river of time evoke a whiteness repeated in the image of the river as "cal viva."[9] Whereas quicklime is used as a corrosive in cemeteries to hasten the decay of the interred body, associating it with death, it is also used as a cohesive in mortar, plaster, and ceramics, making it a symbol of building and creating. Even though the river seems eternal and unchanging, it is as vulnerable and fragile as a babe in arms. But because of the catalyst, the quicklime that produces change and creativity, the apprentice's fertility (erotically signified in the washerwomen's thighs) will ensure that the poetic tradition continues to flow. In Heideggerian terms, *Dasein*'s "being-in-time" and the confrontation with the inevitability of death (the river as passing time, the quicklime of the cemeteries) are the catalysts that push the apprentice to authenticity and lasting expression through heightened awareness of what it means to be.

The next poem I wish to examine, "Toreando" [Bullfighting], bears a resemblance to "Hilando" [Spinning] in *El vuelo* in its imagery as well as its gerundive title. It is easy to see the bullfighter's confrontation with death in the bullring as the poet's own encounter with the death of his loved ones, elegized in *El vuelo*, and the similarity with Lorca's famous elegy "Llanto por Ignacio Sánchez Mejías" [Lament for Ignacio Sánchez Mejías], in addition to the risk *Dasein* takes in confronting Being. The gerund indicates that life itself is an act of constantly but barely evading the onslaught of pain, grief, and death. Knowledge of the specific bullfighter to whom this poem is dedicated, "Antoñete," may be pertinent to the reading of the poem. What we can say for certain, though, is that the name "Antoñete" gives us some insight into the figure of the poet as bullfighter.

First, we note that "Antoñete" is derived from "Antonio," the patron saint of lost items. If this poem is elegiac in nature or at least if the bull represents the pain and grief of loss (perhaps the Law of the Name-of-the-Father), the invocation of St. Anthony's name is apropos. Moreover, "Antoñete" employs a diminutive suffix expressive of admiration for the bullfighter's grace, agility, and rhythm. The phonetic change to the "ñ" and the presence of the tilde adds flair and style to this image, reminiscent of the "duende" that can inspire artists as well as bullfighters (cf. "Cantata del miedo" and "El rey del humo" in "Una aparición," both from *El vuelo*).

As a poem, "Toreando" unfolds gradually, in imitation perhaps of rhythms of a bullfight. At first, there is great expectation; but as the contest continues, tension builds. This process metapoetically parallels not only the advent of inspiration and the confrontation with the unknown experienced in the poet's handling of language but also the involvement of the reader-spectator during the spectacle. Rodríguez is employing repetition and staging techniques that form part of *El vuelo*, and we should expect to encounter a troping, a turning point that pushes us over the edge, over the bar between signifier and signified. What begins as a confrontation with the imminence of danger, pain, grief, and death becomes a search for authenticity, in spite of *Dasein*'s reluctance. The speaker's staging of the bullfight and repetition, especially of the expression "he aquí" (which also appears in "Hilando"), draws us into this perilous, unpredictable, and gripping experience.

> Es esta sinfonía
> del capote que suena
> ¿a qué? He aquí el misterio.

Todo, la tela, el aire
5   de la distancia, toda la embestida
agresiva y solemne,
y cuando el temple llega ya es canto.
He aquí un torero que, aunque tenga nombre,
se lo va dando más, y quiere, y salva.
10   Esa manera de andar por la plaza,
el movimiento interno, el del tanteo,
se maciza,
y se hace tacto y aire al mismo tiempo
cuando llega el embroque.[10]

The truncation of the opening statement in the question "¿a qué?" in v. 3 and the ambivalence of the statement "He aquí el misterio" immediately posit expectation. We may understand that we are about to hear a symphony of movement orchestrated (as it were) by the bullfighter, and specifically by his "capote" (the violet and golden "verónica" used in the first passes of the bull). If the image "sinfonía" stages the scene, the expectation is bifurcated with the word "misterio." As we have seen before, this word has a dual meaning in Rodríguez's poetry similar to "secreto" or even "aventura." It promises something thrilling, exciting, attractive, alluring, that we want to discover, but also something unknown, foreboding, and risky that makes us wary and cautious. In Heideggerian terms, this moment of danger awakens awareness of being and becomes that which saves.[11]

The punctuation and phrasing of the next sentence (vv. 4–7) gathers momentum in accord with the images it presents. "Tela" in particular reminds us of "Hilando" and the images of music and textuality. The run-on line "el aire / de la distancia" halts but promotes the advance of the rhythm as it replicates the still necessary distance between the bull and the *torero*, between the audience and the event. Yet the air also hints at inspiration as the slight suspension of one's breath as the bull charges. The presence of the bull can be felt in the word "embestida," suggesting a beast ("bestia"), whereas "toda" connotes fullness that is both fearsome and ecstatic. This duality is repeated in the adjectives "agresiva y solemne," which characterize the bull's power and color, symbolic of the growing imminence of death, keen awareness of "being-toward-death." Ironically, although the rhythm of these phrases replicates a sense of dynamic movement, no verb appears until "llega" in v. 7, which tells us exactly that: By the time the mood, spirit, or mettle ("temple") arrives, it is already "canto." That is, this "temple" emerges so skillfully, so stealthily from the bullfighter's/poet's handling of his medium, that it simply catches us up in its artistry. "Temple" is a particularly apt word because it refers not only to the bullfighter's/poet's energy, courage, and boldness but also in a musical context to harmony and resolution.

When Rodríguez repeats the phrase "He aquí," it is evident that he is comparing himself as poet to the bullfighter. For even though he has an established reputation, he continues to extend himself, to give more of himself, because of his desire to redeem the transience of his own life and of all life. This statement alludes to *Dasein*'s purpose: to experience authentically what it means to be and to lead others to the same experience because *Dasein* recognizes the meaninglessness of inauthenticity and the "thing-ness" or "fallenness" of inauthentic existence. This awareness is of paramount importance when *Dasein* confronts a critical moment of the possibility of death. By again remarking the staging of the scene in the bullfighter's gait, underscored by a stately iambic rhythm, the ambivalence of "tanteo" as both uncertainty and careful consideration, and the isolation of "se maciza" in v. 12, the speaker prepares us for the critical moment of engagement: "el embroque" (v. 14).

At first, it might be surprising to learn that "embroque" does not appear in the *Diccionario de la Real Academia Española*. The verb "embrocar," however, does. In tauromachy "embrocar" means "coger el toro al lidiador entre las astas": The bull catches the bullfighter "between" its horns. We have seen in many instances that the preposition "entre" is ambivalent in Rodríguez's poetry. Does this word "embroque" mean that the bull *gores* the bullfighter? Or does it mean that the bull *catches* the bullfighter *between* its horns without seriously harming him, only tossing or butting him? Or does it mean that the fight now has become a solemn engagement? This indeterminacy plus the poet's invention of the noun form (or the use of a colloquial expression), demonstrating his skill, marks a troping or turning point in the poem as the confrontation with death becomes a search for such an encounter that will intensify the sensation of life. Notice how the line-breaks and the rhythm change in the second half of the poem.

> 15   Aparición sin tiempo.
> ¿Frontal o circular? ¿Es movimiento
> o es reposo?
> La lejanía, la proximidad,
> helas aquí. Él bien sabe
> la religiosidad del humo y de la sangre:
> lo más vivo. Y le llega
> una revelación oscura, por la izquierda
> o bien por la derecha, y está el cuerpo
> ofrecido, total, aquí en su pecho, en poderío y mármol,
> entre la magia y la sabiduría.[12]

In addition to evoking "Una aparición" from *El vuelo* and the ambivalence of that inebriated encounter with "El rey del humo," the entire phrase in v. 15 is dialogic. An apparition can be either a phantom or a revelation of the hidden. The phrase "sin tiempo" can refer to a specific, transient moment in a sequence—the moment of troping, of apparition—or it can connote a total escape from time, a transcendence of any awareness whatsoever of the passage of time. The bullfighter/poet (along with the audience) suddenly finds himself engaged in an activity that both accentuates the passage of time and halts it, as evident in the questions that follow in vv. 16–17. When the poet repeats the phrase "helas aquí" in reference to both distance and proximity, he equates this conflation with the previous "misterio" and with the "milagro" mentioned in "Hilando." Although it seems that the scene creates a heightened sense of time and space, self and other, in effect those concepts have been imbricated. The relation between audience, bullfighter/poet, and bull/language has vicariously telescoped in both directions of distance and proximity, identification and individuation, the acceleration and suspension of time's passing. Again the ambivalent deictic "aquí" marks an absence and a presence as the poet describes the bullfight and the text.

Because the text of "Toreando" contains a written accent over the "e" of "Él," a practice usually disregarded in the printed form, we can read this phrase as "He well knows," expressive of the bullfighter/poet's control over what is happening. He may have a certain degree of skill that he employs deftly, masterfully; but that does not eliminate chance, spontaneity, the unexpected. *Dasein* lives life on the edge, aware and unaware, trusting in fate yet determining his own fate, in control and totally at the mercy of the unknown and unexpected. Is his "religiosidad" a superficial ritual or a heartfelt devotion? And his religion consists of smoke and blood, incense and wine, fire and water, black and red, death and passionate life, in this unique offering or sacrifice that is ineluctable, in this choice which is a necessity and an obligation, in this risk of death which is intense life: "lo más vivo." The poet reinforces this ambivalence with the phrases "una revelación oscura" and the duality "por la izquierda / o bien por la derecha," deconstructing light and darkness, left and right, good and bad. Heidegger, who was profoundly moved by Hölderlin's verse "Where there is danger there also grows strength, the agency of salvation," would say that the pain opened by language becomes a celebration, sacrifice becomes a gift, as happens in *El vuelo* and in *Casi una leyenda*, respectively.[13]

Because of the religious overtones of this scene, we might read the final verses as a depiction of the crucifixion, although that reading is not as obvious here as in other poems. The chest of the body offered completely emblematizes the vulnerability and innocence of the victim as well as his courage and fearlessness. The curious images of "poderío y mármol" inversely imply a vital, living fragility and an impenetrable, indestructible durability. This play continues in the final verse where "entre" again signals ambivalence, leading to an deconstructive appraisal of both the magic (inspiration) and the wisdom (skill) involved in the production of a work of art, be that the performance of the bullfighter or the poem. Which is spontaneous, unexpected? On which can the artist in his confrontation with the unknown depend more? In the final result, we might question what has happened to Antoñete: Has he given an inspired, truly magnificent performance in which he has killed the bull and so momentarily conquered his fear of death? Or has the bull seriously gored him? Is this poem an homage or an elegy? Is it not both?[14]

In 1991, the Cofradía de Jesús del Vía Crucis of Zamora, with the financial assistance of several community resources, published a book commemorating the fiftieth year of their founding. This book, the *Vía Crucis del arte zamorano*, consists of fourteen poems paired with fourteen color plates by Zamoran artists portraying the Stations of the Cross, the major moments of Christ suffering as He carries the cross, His crucifixion, and His being placed in the sepulchre. Rodríguez has contributed a poem that forms part of this collection. It is, in fact, the first poem in the series, describing the First Station of the Cross when Jesus is condemned to death, and it is paired with a painting by Alfonso Bartolomé.[15]

This painting is a frontal depiction of Christ wearing the crown of thorns. His head is surrounded by a large stylized halo representing the arms of the cross; He is wearing an orangish cloak, and before Him, at chest-height, a skull rests on the pages of an open book. Christ's expression is anything but agonizing. As He looks directly at the viewer, He also seems to gaze hopefully into the future. Even at this first station, a definitive moment that initiates the sequence, Christ seems to be looking beyond suffering to resurrection and glorification.

Rodríguez's accompanying poem is a meditation on this moment when Christ's fate is sealed, but it also comments upon the poet and his purpose in life. The skull resting on the open book in the painting resonates with Rodríguez's view of the sacrifice required of him when he writes, especially the recognition of the possibility of death confronted by *Dasein*. The poem comments not only on this First Station of the Cross, but also on his own ambivalent poetics and the tremendous price he must pay but also the hope of future redemption through the reader's participation in reading. With the simplicity, directness, intensity, and profundity of a passage from St. Paul's epistles, Rodríguez the poet speaks through the mask of Christ in this brief but powerful poem.

> Esta es mi libertad y mi condena.
> Es mi condena y vuestra salvación.
> Y la injusticia será vida a vida,
> rebeldía y amor y sacrificio.
> Así lo quiero. Así. Vedme ofrecido.
> Y mi cruz será cántico, y mi muerte
> vuestra resurrección.[16]

The simplicity of the syntax and the imagery belies the paradoxical depth of the poem, similar to the "matte" surface and the brilliant sublimity of *Casi una leyenda*, published in the same year. The demonstrative pronoun in the first verse, for example, is bewilderingly multivalent. One might assume that it pronominalizes the First Station and the death to which the speaker is condemned, both of which appear in the straightforward title. But then we might wonder what a station is. Certainly, we could think of the analogous but mundane railway or bus station, a temporary stopping point on a journey. These images suggest the journey through life itself and all the vicissitudes involved in the process of living out one's life, one's vocation as *Dasein*. "Station" also derives from the Latin "stare" meaning "to stand." In addition to the stopping/standing still, this vertical posture contrasts with the horizontality of the road, and its tranquility contrasts with the dynamic progress of the journey. These images remind us of the final verse of "Canto del caminar" from *Don de la ebriedad* and evoke the comparison of walking with writing—the path Rodríguez has chosen for his life—and the tension between metaphor and metonymy. Ironically, this station is the starting point that will conclude with Christ's death but that also promises His resurrection: The end is in the beginning. This deconstruction of death and life is overlaid upon the act of writing as a process that taxes the poet but also leads to his redemption and eternal life.

It is not surprising, then, that Rodríguez chooses to place the nouns "mi libertad y mi condena" in what seems to be reverse order when he equates them with this "sentence" of death. This reversal heightens and undercuts the contrast between liberty and condemnation, and also places emphasis on their ironic deconstruction by recalling Rodríguez's *Alianza y condena*. A death sentence does not set him free in a mundane legal or worldly sense, but it does assure his spiritual freedom because he has chosen to accept death. Therefore, what would seem to be condemnation is converted into a release from the anguish of death and the freedom to experience life to the fullest, according to Heidegger's philosophy, which correlates the acceptance of the possibility of death with freedom.[17] The poet accepts the challenge of facing the unknown in his act of writing, knowing the price he must pay for this confrontation with death and the problematizing of his identity, because that acceptance produces a greater intensity of what it means to be and the assurance that he will continue to live through his poetry.

A similar deconstructive play exists in the second verse between the nouns "condena" and "salvación" and the switch from the possessive pronoun "mi" to "vuestra." The poet's acceptance of his condemnation not only promotes the salvation of his readers (as Christ's death redeems all of humankind), but the readers' act of reading redeems, resuscitates, resurrects the poet. Not only is *Dasein*'s being intersubjective, dependent upon its relation to itself in and through others, but to accept one's *Dasein* is "the dynamic embedding of individual fate in communal destiny"; "to accept actively one's individual finitude and the need to choose among finite options . . . involve[s] the community and the individual's afterlife in the destiny of the group."[18] That also implies, however, that the reader will have to pay the same price that the poet has paid. Thus, "Y la injusticia será vida a vida" (v. 3) describes a mutual exchange from one human being to another. It is an injustice, but a reciprocal one that has a redeeming effect for both parties involved. The clearly unjust death of Christ (the poet, *Dasein*) brings about a new justice—salvation—based on one's sacrifice for another's benefit. The phrase "vida a vida" may also recall the relationship between Adam and Christ (always one of the readings of the Easter Vigil in the Catholic Church; see Rom. 5:15–21), but the future tense of the verb "será" defers that redemptive act for the poet's dependence on the reader, *Dasein*'s possibilities, its two modes of "Being-toward."[19]

The perplexing nouns of v. 4 substitute, each in turn, for "injusticia" at the same time that they create a process of illumination and surrender to the justice of the injustice. The sacrifice that at first is resisted because it appears to be an injustice evolves into an offering made for a higher or more pressing claim: love.[20] Again the sequence of the nouns may seem odd, but after all, love (again see St. Paul; Heidegger calls it *Sorge*, care) is the central turning point that provokes the metamorphosis from condemnation to freedom, from injustice to justice, from reluctance to sacrifice, from loss to gain. The pithy, resolute declarations of v. 5 represent the climax of the poem, the moment when the poet crosses the bar, accepts the challenge, but also makes the challenge to the reader, as the poems of *Casi* are both descriptive and prescriptive, performative and constative. Notice also the bifurcation of the verb "quiero" as both

"I like it that way" (acceptance in the present) and "I want it to be that way" (looking to the future), as well as "ofrecido" meaning "I have made my sacrifice" and "I offer myself for the future." This ambivalence is reinforced by the contrast I-you and the imperative "Vedme" as both "Look at me" and "See me as I am," which echoes the classical "Ecce homo," the words pronounced by Pontius Pilate upon presenting Jesus to His accusers at the moment of His condemnation (John 19:5). In this instance, as in the other, it is the victim who surrenders himself to the condemnation.

The iteration of the future tense in the final verses focalizes the dialogism of the poem. The speaker may be affirming the certainty that his sacrifice will become a hymn, a song of praise to God, to other human beings, to life itself, that is, a poem.[21] But it also casts doubt upon the outcome: It is necessary that the readers participate in this exchange, that they "see" the poet's sacrifice ("Vedme ofrecido") for the redemption to occur, because not only the poet's resurrection depends upon it. The elliptical presence/absence of "será" in the second part of this conclusion reinforces the ambivalence and the contrast of "*mi* muerte" and "*vuestra* resurrección," which the "pie quebrado" [truncated verse] of the final line punctuates.[22] The silence of the unfinished hendecasyllabic verse compels us to add: "If only you will see," concomitantly with the resolute affirmation that death *will* become resurrection (as it does for Christ). The truncated final verse abruptly and definitively ends the poem as it points toward the future resolution still pending.

Which brings us to a similar moment in this book. If my readings of Rodríguez's poetry have served to open these poems for other readers, it is now incumbent on those readers to continue the exchange. The three poems examined in this conclusion/prologue all address the image of the poet as artist, yet each, directly or indirectly, encompasses us, Rodríguez's audience, and comments upon our engagement in the artist's accomplishment. As readers, we are the apprentices of Rodríguez as he makes us aware of the passage of time, shows us the beauty of the ordinary world into which we have been thrown, and instructs us in the meaning of being. As spectators of his struggle, we join him in fending off the vicissitudes of life that assail us, and we assimilate his courage, determination, and individuality. As his fellow human beings, we accompany him along the Via Crucis of life so that we too may die and rise with him as he surrenders himself to his calling as poet.

Claudio Rodríguez has broken new ground for other poets and for his readers, but he also continues to write and will continue to challenge us to transgress the limits we place upon ourselves, so that we may participate in the poetic process and continue to discover ourselves through language. In short, through his intense engagement with language as a means of "conocimiento," Rodríguez encourages his readers to found their identities in participation in the poetic experience and to accept the profound changes and instability that such an engagement brings about, in spite of the risks entailed. Although his meticulous structuring of each work, his unique dialogic bifurcation of language, and his original imagery are constants of his poetry, Rodríguez continues to evolve, to break new ground, not just as a poet, but as a human being acutely aware of what it means *to be*.

Notes

INTRODUCTION

1. Rodríguez delivered his "discurso de entrada" on Miguel Hernández, with whom he shares many metaphoric affinities (see esp. *El rayo que no cesa*). See Claudio Rodríguez García, "Poesía como participación: hacia Miguel Hernández" (Madrid: Real Academia Española, 1992).

2. Cañas, *Claudio Rodríguez* (Madrid: Júcar, 1988). Luis García Jambrina also includes a chronology at the beginning of Claudio Rodríguez *Hacia el canto* (Salamanca: Universidad, 1993), 23–31.

3. During the past several years critics have debated—and generally denigrated—the critical practice of generational categorization in Spanish literature. On the one hand, these designations are still convenient ways of organizing our perspectives and our thinking about the literary changes we see in our century, a valid ontological goal of our profession. On the other hand, this system has tended to be exclusive, has misrepresented literary history, and has isolated or at best distanced Spanish literature from wider European and Western movements.

My comments about the so-called second generation of the postwar era support the latter view, though it is still convenient to use these designations. In effect, the label "second generation" misrepresents several historical and literary events. First, Rodríguez's generation is the *first* to feel the full effects of the Franco regime, though this statement of course would seem to omit the valuable and pertinent contributions of Angel González and Gloria Fuertes. Even so, a case could be made that the youth of these authors precluded most if not all experience of a previous political climate. We should also note that the authors of the "first generation of the postwar" were writing while the larger conflict was still in progress in the rest of Europe, undoubtedly affecting their daily experiences and their literary production. A new climate arises in the 1950s when the "second generation" comes upon the scene. Therefore, I would argue that the "second generation" is in reality the "first" of the postwar era.

4. Luna Borge, *La generación poética del 70* (Sevilla: Qüásyeditorial, 1993), 20–21. [Claudio Rodríguez, Jaime Gil de Biedma, F. Brines, Angel González, Valente . . . are the ones who most clearly mark a difference and a new direction with respect to what comes before and who anticipate for the first time what years later the "novísimos" will adjudicate for themselves—that is not to say that differences between both generations do not exist; there are differences, but these are not so poetically essential as some of the generation of 1970 propose.

. . . The work of these poets (Eladio Cabañero, A. González, C. Rodríguez, C. Sahagún y José A. Valente) is a clear example that an ideological compromise is no longer important in poetry. In their declarations to the anthologist (Francisco Ribes) these poets conceive the poetic exercise as an instrument of knowing (the exercise of internal self-knowledge) and of communication. They combat the thematic formalism of social poetry. The poet rather than compromised by a determined ideology must be authentic to himself and his life's goal; that affirmation of one's self and that probing into one's own entrails will permit one to know reality from other perspectives. . . . Here we can see a rupture with what came before and an opening of horizons in Spanish poetry, aspects very much overlooked at the time of evaluation of the ruptural proposals of the "novísimo" aesthetic. The road, as we see, was well travelled. . . .]

5. In addition to the comments by the poets themselves in Ribes's *Poesía última* (Madrid: Taurus, 1963), Debicki cites Enrique Badosa's article "Primero hablemos de Júpiter (La poesía como medio de conocimiento)," *Papeles de Son Armadans* 10, no. 28 (1958): 32–46 and 10, no. 29 (1958): 135–59. Debicki emphasizes, though, "Badosa sets his essay against Carlos Bousoño's view of poetry as communication, expressed in the various editions of the latter's *Teoría de la expresión poética*. But it is more useful as an attack on cruder visions of poetry as vehicle for social messages than as a denial of Bousoño's fuller view of poetry as conveying complex experiences." See Andrew P. Debicki, *Poetry of Discovery: The Spanish Generation of 1956-71* (Lexington: University Press of Kentucky, 1982), 216 n. 14.

6. The "novísimos" merely take this self-consciousness to an extreme by making it explicit. See Jill Kruger-Robbins's excellent introduction in *Frames of Referents: The Postmodern Poetry of Guillermo Carnero* (Lewisburg, Pa.: Bucknell University Press, 1997).

7. Miguel García-Posada identifies this characteristic as a mainstay of Spanish poetry of the twentieth century. See Volume 10 of the collection *Poesía española: La nueva poesía (1975– 1992)* (Barcelona: Crítica, 1996), 19, where he states, "Frente a la tendencia a la yuxtaposición de poemas dominante entre los poetas novísimos, ahora se prefiere el libro orgánico y estructurado. Tal fue el modelo preferido de la poesía pura en los años veinte, donde la primacía la alcanzó el modelo guilleniano, hecho de simetrías y correspondencias, y a él se remiten los poetas que llamo neopuristas, pero otros autores también se decantan por esta vertebración, que se trasluce en los títulos de las secciones y en la propia organización interna, incluida la narrativa." [In contrast with the tendency to juxtapose poems dominant among the "novísimo" poets, now an organic and structured book is preferred. Such was the model preferred by pure poetry in the '20s, where the Guillenian model reached primacy, and to it remit the poets that I call "neopurists," but other authors also lean in that direction, which is visible in the titles of sections and in internal organization itself, including narrative.]

8. Roland Barthes, "The Death of the Author," in *Image—Music—Text*, trans. Stephen Heath (New York: Noonday Press, 1988), 142–48.

9. Seán Burke summarizes this position: "For Barthes, Foucault and Derrida, the expulsion of the subject from the space of language is thus seen to extend right across the field of the human sciences, and to call into question the idea that man can properly possess any degree of knowledge or consciousness. For should it be that all thought proceeds necessarily by way and by virtue of language, then the absence of the subject from language translates into the absence of the subject or consciousness from knowledge. If knowledge itself, or what we take to be knowledge, is entirely intradiscursive, and is thoroughly displaced and dislodged. Cognition and consciousness arise as intralinguistic effects or metaphors, by-products, as it were, of a linguistic order that has evolved for thousands of years before any subject comes to speak. Man can no longer be conceived as the subject of his works, for to be the subject of a text, or of knowledge, is to assume a post ideally exterior to language. There can thus be no such thing as subjectivity whilst the subject or author—as has classically been the case—is conceived as prior to a language which exists as an entirely transparent vehicle or medium for his uses, his designs. . . . The idea of authorial absence thereby connects with the epistemological upheaval in Western thought which the theorists of the 1960s believed to be underway in the linguistic decomposition of subject-centred philosophies. Where philosophy and the human sciences had registered man, or the subject, as the necessary beginning and end of knowledge, knowledge and the subject are seen to be fictive emanations of a language and a writing which endlessly subvert all attempts by the human agent to assert any degree of mastery or control over their workings." See *The Death and Return of the Author: Criticism and Subjectivity in Barthes, Foucault and Derrida* (Edinburgh: Edinburgh University Press, 1992), 14–15.

10. Kenneth Gergen, *The Saturated Self: Dilemmas of Identity in Contemporary Life* (New York: Basic Books, 1991), 27.

11. Ibid., 19.

12. Gergen has supplied the term "core self" (ibid., 203). I have taken the term "deeper self" from Eugen Simion's discussion of Proust and his polemic with Sainte-Beuve. See *The Return of the Author*, ed. James W. Newcomb, trans. James W. Newcomb and Lidia Vianu (Evanston, Ill.: Northwestern University Press, 1996).

13. Newcomb, ed., *Return of the Author*, 4. Among other issues Newcomb makes reference to the seeming contradiction between the postmodern effacing of subjectivity and the concomitant feminist assertions of woman's subjectivity.

14. See Burke, *The Death and Return of the Author*, 15–16.

15. See William Gass, "The Death of the Author," in *Habitations of the Word* (New York: Simon and Schuster, 1985), 265–88.

16. Burke, *The Death and Return of the Author*, 160.

17. Barthes, "The Death of the Author," 148.

18. "In the romantic period persons often viewed their lives as driven by a mission, possibly directed by inner forces or personal muses deep within. One could speak unflinchingly of personal destiny." Gergen, *The Saturated Self*, 161.

19. Simion, *The Return of the Author*, 56.

20. Ibid., 63–64.

21. Burke, *The Death and Return of the Author*, 36. Burke takes this concept from Barthes's *Writing Degree Zero*.

22. Benveniste's comments are quoted in Kaja Silverman, *The Subject of Semiotics*, 1, 44.

23. Newcomb, *The Return of the Author*, 5.

24. Ibid., 138.

25. Ibid., 86.

26. Gergen, *The Saturated Self*, 139. Below I will address the assertion that Rodríguez is committed to his identity as a poet, but he does question whether one can remain true or committed to that "essence" or that it is an "essence" at all.

27. Ibid., 68–69.

28. Ibid., 73.

29. Ibid., 216–19.

30. Burke, *The Death and Return of the Author*, 42.

31. Paul Ricoeur, *Oneself as Another*, trans. Kathleen Blamey (Chicago: University of Chicago Press, 1992), 16.

32. Gergen, *The Saturated Self*, 2.

33. Ibid., 34.

34. Burke, *The Death and Return of the Author*, 16. Foucault's essay can be found in *The Foucault Reader*, ed. Paul Rabinow (New York: Pantheon Books, 1984), 101–20.

35. I will develop this concept shortly in the discussion of Heidegger's philosophy.

36. *Webster's New World Dictionary*, 3d college ed., s.v. "transgress."

37. Heidegger, "Building Dwelling Thinking," in *Poetry, Language, Thought*, 154; emphasis appropriately in the original.

38. Todorov, "The Origin of Genres," *New Literary History* 8 (1976): 160; my emphasis.

39. To elucidate this phenomenon in the first section of *Don*, I have used an essay by Umberto Eco, "Edenic Language."

40. See William Wheelwright, *Metaphor and Reality*.

41. In this chapter, Todorov's statements concerning transgression and genres are particularly apt. See note 38 above.

42. Andrew P. Debicki, *Spanish Poetry of the Twentieth Century: Modernity and Beyond* (Lexington: University Press of Kentucky, 1994), 192.

43. See "La mañana de la lechuza" in Cañas, *Claudio Rodríguez*, 195–97. See also

Encuentros con el 50: La voz poética de una generación (Oviedo: Fundación Municipal de Cultura, 1990), 105–7.

44. Martin Heidegger, *Being and Time*, trans. John Macquarrie and Edward Robinson (New York: HarperSanFrancisco, 1962); in Spanish, *El ser y el tiempo*, trans. José Gaos, 2a ed., (México: Fondo de Cultura Económica, 1971).

45. See Michael Gelven, *A Commentary on Heidegger's Being and Time*, rev. ed. (DeKalb: Northern Illinois University Press, 1989), 27.

46. Ibid., 22.

47. Heidegger, *Being and Time*, 32; original emphasis.

48. Gelven, *A Commentary*, 28.

49. Stephen Mulhall, *Heidegger and Being and Time* (London and New York: Routledge, 1996), 14–15.

50. Ibid., 36.

51. George Steiner, *Martin Heidegger* (Chicago: University of Chicago Press, 1989), 50.

52. "Kierkegaard's philosophical pseudonym, Johannes Climacus shares the Heideggerian view that human beings continuously confront the question of how they should live, and so must locate some standard or value in relation to which that choice might meaningfully be made. . . .

"Climacus goes on to suggest . . . that we start by aiming at a specific goal or achievement to give our life meaning—the pursuit of power or wealth, the development of a talent. Since such goals have significance only insofar as the person concerned desires them, what is giving meaning to her life is in reality her wants and dispositions; Climacus calls this the aesthetic form of life." Mulhall, *Heidegger and Being and Time*, 122.

53. Gelven, *A Commentary*, 177.

54. Mulhall, *Heidegger and Being and Time*, 139–40.

55. Ibid., 194; Steiner, *Martin Heidegger*, 18. Steiner also refers to pilgrimage, journey on p. 62.

56. See the essays collected in Martin Heidegger *Poetry, Language, Thought*, trans. Albert Hofstadter (New York: Harper and Row, 1971), for Heidegger's thinking on poets and poetic language. Also see Véronique M. Fóti, *Heidegger and the Poets: Poiēsis/Sophia/Technē* (Atlantic Highlands, N.J.: Humanities Press, 1992).

57. Mulhall, *Heidegger and Being and Time*, 96.

58. "Heidegger goes on: 'All being is in Being. To hear such a thing sounds trivial to our ear, if not, indeed, offensive, for no one needs to bother about the fact that being belongs to Being. All the world knows that being is that which is. What else remains for being but to be? And yet, just this fact that being is gathered together in Being, that in the appearance of Being being appears, astonished the Greeks and first astonished them and them alone.' These sentences crystallize Heidegger's doctrine of existence and his methodological stance, which is one of radical astonishment. The fact of existence, of being in Being, astonishes Heidegger immeasurably." Steiner, *Martin Heidegger*, 26–27.

59. Heidegger, "The Origin of the Work of Art," in *Poetry, Language, Thought*, 62–63.

60. Following the introduction to *Poetry, Language, Thought*, the translator Albert Hofstadter informs us that Heidegger presented this lecture in October 1950 and repeated it in February of the following year. It was published in 1959 in *Unterwegs zur Sprache* (Pfullingen: Neske, 1959) (xxv). Obviously, Rodríguez would not have had access to this information. It is therefore even more remarkable that Rodríguez's thought should have been so advanced as to coincide with Heidegger's.

61. Heidegger, "Language," in *Poetry, Language, Thought*, 191–92.

62. Heidegger, "What Are Poets For?" in *Poetry, Language, Thought*, 92.

63. Mulhall, *Heidegger and Being and Time*, 169–70.

64. Vicente Aleixandre, *Algunos caracteres de la nueva poesía española* (Madrid: Imprenta Góngora, 1995), 8. [I would say that the essential theme of the poetry of our day, with a projec-

tion much more direct than in previous eras, is the immediate canticle of human life in its historical dimension; the canticle of man as *situated*, that is to say, as *localized*; localized in time, in time that passes and is irreversible, and localized in space, in a specific society, with specific problems that are its own and that, therefore, define it.]

65. I am unaware if anyone has investigated Aleixandre's reading of Heidegger, but it would behoove critics to investigate this topic in many of the poets of the postwar era. See particularly José Angel Valente's "El cántaro," which is based on an image used by Heidegger in his essay "The Thing" in *Poetry, Language, Thought*, 163–86; see esp. 171–72.

66. Ibid., 44.

67. Gelven, *A Commentary*, 106.

68. Ibid., 106.

69. Ibid., 133–34.

70. Mulhall, *Heidegger and Being and Time*, 67.

71. Ibid., 133.

72. Heidegger, *Being and Time*, 26:153–54.

73. Heidegger, "The Origin of the Work of Art," 75.

74. Gelven, *A Commentary*, 182.

75. Ibid., 66–67.

76. Steiner, *Martin Heidegger*, 29.

77. Ibid., 41.

78. See Steiner, *Martin Heidegger*, 50. See also Heidegger's discussion of pain in "Language in the Poem," in *On the Way to Language*, 181-84.

79. Heidegger, ibid., 187.

80. Heidegger, "What Are Poets For?," 138.

81. Mulhall, *Heidegger and Being and Time*, 74.

82. Fóti, *Heidegger and the Poets*, 8.

83. Gelven, *A Commentary*, 132.

84. Ibid., 148–50.

85. In chapter 5 below, I will remark upon Rodríguez's frequent use of the prepositional phrase "junto a," which precisely refers to the concept of "Being-alongside."

86. Heidegger, "What Are Poets For?," 119.

87. Mulhall, *Heidegger*, 143.

88. Steiner, *Martin Heidegger*, 129.

89. Ibid., 74.

90. Gelven, *A Commentary*, 226.

91. Heidegger, "Building Dwelling Thinking," in *Poetry, Language, Thought*, 147.

92. Steiner, *Martin Heidegger*, 146.

93. Steiner has explicitly stated of Heidegger that "His punning—where 'punning' is too feeble a designation for an uncanny receptivity to the fields of resonance, of consonance, of suppressed echo in phonetic and semantic units—has bred, to the point of parody, the poststructuralism and deconstructionism of today" (*Martin Heidegger*, xiii).

94. J. Hillis Miller, "Ariachne's Broken Woof," *Georgia Review* 31 (1977): 44–60.

95. See Carmen Martín Gaite's discussion of the "formation" of the "ideal" woman during the Franco regime in *Usos amorosos de la posguerra*, 10a ed. (Barcelona: Anagrama, 1992).

CHAPTER 1. DEFINING THE SELF THROUGH LANGUAGE:
THE POET AS ADAM IN *DON DE LA EBRIEDAD* (1953)

1. Pere Gimferrer, "La poesía de Claudio Rodríguez," *Triunfo* (19 junio 1970): [n.p.]. Much of the first section of this study of *Don* is a response to the valuable work of Martha

LaFollette Miller, "Elementos metapoéticos en un poema de Claudio Rodríguez," *Explicación de Textos Literarios* 8 (1979–80): 127–36; Jonathan Mayhew, *Claudio Rodríguez and the Language of Poetic Vision* (Lewisburg, Pa.: Bucknell University Press, 1990); and Alan Bruflat, "Ambivalence and Reader Response in the Poetry of Claudio Rodríguez" (doctoral diss., University of Kansas, 1986).

2. J. Hillis Miller's concept of the dialogic as exposited in "Ariachne's Broken Woof," *Georgia Review* 31 (1977): 44–60, is based on Bahktin's but is somewhat different. Martha Miller uses "Ariachne's Broken Woof" as the basis for her reading of the first poem of *Don*. Her article "Elementos metapoéticos" has generated several aspects of my reading not only of *Don* but of Rodríguez's entire opus. Throughout this book, when I use the term "dialogic," I refer to Hillis Miller's discussion, following the lead of Martha Miller.

3. Mayhew, *Claudio Rodríguez*, 26.

4. Luis García Jambrina has also noted this ambivalence in Rodríguez's title; see his articles "De *Don de la ebriedad* a «¿dónde la ebriedad?»" (parts I and II) which appeared in *El Correo de Zamora* (29 marzo and 5 abril 1992). García Jambrina and I arrived at this discovery independently.

5. I am indebted to the National Endowment for the Humanities for a fellowship which enabled me to participate in a Summer Seminar in 1989. I wish to express my thanks to Professor A. Walton Litz of Princeton University as well as the other participants in the seminar for their help with the preparation of these analyses.

6. Umberto Eco, *The Role of the Reader: Explorations in the Semiotics of Texts* (Bloomington: Indiana University Press, 1979), 91. All subsequent references will appear parenthetically in the text.

7. In *Claudio Rodríguez,* Mayhew proffers a provocative and radically different reading of the structure of *Don*. He believes that "the organization of the poems as a sequence is not self-evident" and that "These 'fragments' invite the reader to organize them into a larger whole. . . . In order to make sense of *Don* the reader must create a new order out of the fragments, although the disjunctiveness of the work means that no one definitive order can exist" (28–29). He, therefore, "hopscotches" from one poem to another following what he believes is the thematic unity of *Don*.

I take issue with the use of the word "fragments" to describe the poems of *Don*. Although Rodríguez himself has more recently stated that *Don* forms "un solo poema, dividido arbitrariamente en fragmentos" (*Desde mis poemas* [Madrid: Cátedra, 1983], 16), and both Irene Hodgson ("The Poetic Works of Claudio Rodríguez," [doctoral diss., Purdue University, 1986], 77) and Mayhew (*Claudio Rodríguez*, 144 n. 3), having spoken with the author, report that the poems are not presented in the order in which they were written, for me these poems are well able to stand on their own as independent lyric expressions. At the same time, Rodríguez has obviously arranged them in a pattern, in that way emphasizing their interdependence on one another. This apparent contradiction goes hand in glove with the oscillating pattern of the text which I describe and its simultaneously open and closed nature. Also, if these poems are only "fragments," why did Rodríguez divide them into three distinct sections labeled "Libro primero," "Libro segundo," and "Libro tercero"? Why did he use Roman numerals (as opposed to some more innocuous means) to designate the individual "fragments"? I submit that both the ordinal numbers (significantly following the noun) and the Roman numerals indicate sequence. By examining the individual poems in relation to the larger sequential pattern of the collection, we will gain greater insight into the disjunctions Mayhew perceives so keenly in *Don*.

8. Throughout this study, I have used the Cátedra edition (1983) of Rodríguez's works when citing the poems of *Don de la ebriedad*, *Conjuros*, *Alianza y condena*, and *El vuelo de la celebración*, although I have also referred to the Plaza y Janés edition (*Poesía (1953–1966)* [1971]) for the first three and the Visor edition (1976) for the fourth. For readers unfamiliar with Spanish, I will include translations of the longer passages in the footnotes. Shorter passages will appear in square brackets in the text. All translations are mine unless otherwise noted

and are intended to give as close and literal a translation as possible. However, my discussion may often problematize and subvert these translations. The verses cited here are translated thus: "Clarity always comes from the sky; / it is a gift: it is not found among things, / but very much above them, and it occupies them / making of all that life and labor of its own. / Thus day dawns; thus night / closes the great chamber of its shadows. / And this is a gift."

9. A biblical allusion to the epistle of James (1:17) supports the primordial linguistic system in this poem: "[A]ll good giving and every perfect gift is from above, coming down from the Father of lights, with whom there is no alteration of shadow caused by change." Intertextual allusions throughout *Don* are indicative of Rodríguez's poetics at this point in his development. As N. Katherine Hayles has said about Thomas Pynchon's *Gravity's Rainbow*, we can say that in "Libro primero" and "Canto del despertar" "first language is seen as a process of recovery, an attempt to return to the underlying deeper pattern. Then, language is an instrument not of recovery but of creation, actually bringing the patterns into existence. The next step is to recognize that the distinction between 'reality' and 'created pattern' is meaningless" (*Cosmic Web: Scientific Field Models and Literary Strategies in the 20th Century* [Ithaca and London: Cornell University Press, 1984], 187). We can also see that Rodríguez's frequent inclusion of biblical intertextualities suggests an "origin" that in "Libro tercero" will prove false, even though they support the Adamic vision in this first section.

It is possible to read Rodríguez's poetry from a religious (or quasi-religious) viewpoint, in which case *Don* depicts the speaker's discovery of religious faith (or his discovery of "the Word") with the doubts and ecstasies that accompany such an experience. Although critics have rarely addressed this religious or spiritual aspect, Rodríguez himself has commented (Juan Carlos Suñén, "Entrevista a Claudio Rodríguez," *El Urogallo* 62–63 [julio–agosto 1991]: 12, 13) that "la mía es una poesía que tiene mucho de religioso. . . . Yo tengo mis creencias. Y un sentido religioso de la vida, si no absolutamente católico (no soy practicante, realmente), sí cristiano, un sentido trascendental" [mine is a poetry that tends very much toward the religious. . . . I have my beliefs. And a religious sense of life, if not absolutely Catholic (I am not practicing, really), yes, Christian, a sense of the transcendent].

10. Martha Miller, "Elementos metapoéticos," 129–30.

11. Eco, *The Role of the Reader*, 94.

12. As Eco explains, "This releases them from the logical contradiction and also opens up the possibility of an intuitive and ambiguous grasp of the concept (by way of a fairly ambiguous use of the code). . . . This new term expresses a contradictory fact without obliging the speaker to formulate it in accordance with the habitual logical rules, which would in fact exclude it. . . . The message . . . is obviously ambiguous from the viewpoint of the form of content, but the form of its expression is also ambiguous. It thus becomes embryonically self-focusing" (ibid., 96–97).

13. Ibid., 96.

14. ". . . Who makes beings / consistently less created? What high dome / contains them in its love? But it already comes to us in a roundabout way / and it is still early, it already comes / in the manner of your flights / and hovers, and goes away and, still remote, / there is nothing as clear as its impulses!"

15. Miller, "Elementos metapoéticos," 130.

16. "Oh, clarity thirsting for a form, / for a substance to dazzle it / consuming itself upon completing its work. / Like me, like all that waits. / If you have carried off all the light, / how am I to expect nothing of the dawn? / And, nonetheless, —this is a gift—, my mouth / waits, and my soul waits, and you wait for me, / drunken persecution, clarity alone / mortal as the embrace of the sickles, / but an embrace until the end that never loosens."

17. Philip Wheelwright notes that light symbolizes "certain mental and spiritual qualities. . . . First and most evidently, light produces visibility, it shows forth clear outlines which in darkness vanish. By a natural and easy metaphoric step we can pass from this observable action of light in the physical world clarifying spatial boundaries and shapes to the action of the mind

bringing the boundaries and shapes of ideas into intellectual configuration. Consequently light readily becomes a sign of mental configuration—which is to say, of mind in its most distinctive form" (116–17). However, he adds, "One further quality of light that has acquired symbolic importance is the tendency for excessive light to produce a blinding effect, especially on weak eyes, and thus to become associated with darkness. . . . Light, for those incapable of beholding it, is darkness" (*Metaphor and Reality*, 120–21). Cf. Paul's conversion in Acts 22:6–11 (which Wheelwright also mentions).

18. Miller ("Elementos metapoéticos," 130) lucidly points out other ambivalencies in the latter verses of this poem.

19. "Amen, amen, I say to you, unless a grain of wheat falls to the ground and dies, it remains just a grain of wheat; but if it dies, it produces much fruit."

20. "I sometimes wonder if night / closes upon the world in order to open itself or if something / opens it so suddenly that we / do not reach its dawn, dawn out in the open / . . . / and does not reveal that at night there are fields / of intensely hurried dawn / not in germination, in full light, in white birds."

21. In *Infame turba* (Barcelona: Lumen, 1971), Federico Campbell has asked Rodríguez about these periods of dryness:

> —Entre las publicaciones de tus libros median muchos años. ¿Entras en períodos de aridez?
> —Si se trata de aridez respecto al acto físico de escribir, sí. El poeta muchas veces se está alimentando de cosas de las que no se da cuenta. (236)

> [—Between the publication of your books there mediate many years. Do you enter periods of dryness? —If it has to do with dryness with respect to the physical act of writing, yes. A poet often is feeding upon things which he doesn't notice.]

In a later interview with Blanca Berasátegui, "Claudio Rodríguez: El alma es una colmena vibrante," *ABC,* 20 marzo 1977, he answers more thoughtfully:

> —¿A qué se debe esta intermitencia en el proceso creador de Claudio Rodríguez?
> —Soy de una gran lentitud. Pienso que el cambio vital y espiritual—la poesía es siempre espíritu—se tiene que reflejar en la palabra, en el estilo, y no se puede cambiar de estilo, ni mucho menos de alma, con rapidez. Se necesita, pienso, cierta transición. (36)

> [—To what do you attribute this intermittence in the creative process of Claudio Rodríguez? —I am of a great slowness. I think that vital, spiritual changes—poetry is always of the spirit—has to be reflected in the word, in one's style, and one cannot change style, much less spirit, rapidly. One needs, I think, a certain transition.]

22. "Some flight will be burning the air, / not because it is ardent but because it is distant. / Some stellar limpidity makes / the pine trees shine, it will make my body shine in the end. / What can I do except continue placing / my life at a thousand lances of space?"

23. "So I am feeling that the shadows / open their light, they open it, open it so much, / that morning surges forth without beginning / or end, already eternal since sunset."

24. "The holm-oak, which conserves a ray / of sun more than an entire month of spring, / does not feel the spontaneity of its shadow, / the simplicity of its growth; barely / does it recognize the terrain in which it has sprung. / With that wind that in its branches leaves behind / that which has no music, it imagines / for its dreams a great plateau. / And with what rapidity it identifies / with the countryside, with the whole soul / of its luxuriance and of itself."

25. "Thus am I. What holm-oak, of wood / darker perhaps than that of the oak tree, / lifts my happiness, so intense / a few moments before the dusk / and so wilted now. Like oats / that are sewn haphazardly and which doesn't matter / if it fall here or there if it falls to earth, / the contained ardor of thought is / filtering itself through things, half-opening them, / to leave its splendor and then to give it a new clarity in them."

26. "And it is certain, for the holm-oak, what would it know / of death without me? And perhaps its intimacy / is certain, its intimacy, the spontaneity / of its shadow more faithful than anyone? Is my life / more certain thus, in its persistent leaves / with spring half deciphered?"

27. "Thus desire. Like dawn, clear / from the peak and when it stops, / touching with its lights that which is concrete, / recently obscure, although instantaneously."

28. "Afterwards it opens noisy dovecotes / and then it is just another day. Oh, the hostage / doves of night containing / its highest impulses! . . ."

29. Michael Riffaterre, *Semiotics of Poetry* (Bloomington: Indiana University Press, 1978), 2.

30. Eco, *The Role of the Reader*, 99.

31. Ibid., 101.

32. Ibid., 99.

33. My understanding of this poem improved greatly thanks to a conversation with Jorge Alcázar, a fellow participant in the NEH Summer Seminar.

34. J. E. Cirlot, *A Dictionary of Symbols*, trans. Jack Sage, 2d ed. (New York: Philosophical Library, 1971), 272.

35. Ibid., 22.

36. Mikel Dufrenne has stated the following about this relationship:

It is language which introduces the requisite distance between the signifying and the signified. It is by the mediation of language that the interval is created where thought can come into play. Nevertheless . . . the mediation is one that separates and unites at the same time. If language digs a trench between the world and me, it throws a bridge across it. (Quoted in Gerald Bruns, *Modern Poetry and the Idea of Language* [New Haven and London: Yale University Press, 1974], 261.)

37. "Clearly, neither language nor the world is so harmonious or single-voiced as both were during the period of situation (1) [the pristine state described at the beginning of poem I], but at least he [Adam/the poet] is no longer afraid of the contradictions concealed inside his language system; this is because from one side the contradictions force him to reenvisage the form which he assigns to the world, while from the other they induce him to exploit them for their potential poetic effects" (Eco, *The Role of the Reader*, 103).

38. "As if it had never been mine, / give my voice to the air and in the air / may it belong to everyone and may all know it / like a morning or an afternoon. / Neither does April come only to the branch, / nor does water await only the drought."

39. "Let everything end here, and let everything end / once and for all! A flower lives / so beautifully because it lives so briefly / and, nonetheless, how it gives of itself, unanimously, / ceasing to be a flower and becoming / the impetus of giving . . ."

40. "The brother in lowly circumstances should take pride in his high standing and the rich one in his lowliness, for he will pass away 'like the flower of the field.' For the sun comes up with its scorching heat and dries up the grass, its flower droops, and the beauty of its appearance vanishes. So will the rich person fade away in the midst of his pursuits" (James 1:9–11).

41. "A voice says, 'Cry out!' / I answer, 'What shall I cry out?' / 'All mankind is grass, / and all their glory like the flower of the field. / The grass withers, the flower wilts, / when the breath of the Lord blows upon it. / [So then, the people is the grass.] / Though the grass withers and the flower wilts, / the word of our God stands forever'" (Isa. 40:6–8).

42. For the ambivalence of the river as a symbol, see Cirlot, *A Dictionary of Symbols*, 274.

43. I have chosen the terms metaphor and metonymy for the sake of convenience and to keep the parameters of my definitions flexible. My generic use of these tropes is based upon Roman Jakobson's discussion of aphasia and his definition of the two axes of language. I have chosen Jakobson's definitions because I do not wish to limit my categories as stringently as some theoreticians might (see, for example, Michel LeGuern, *Metáfora y metonimia*), for in Rodríguez's "Cantos" these two tropes become inextricably intertwined and indistinguishable

from each other (see Kenneth Burke, "Four Master Tropes," in *A Grammar of Motives* [Berkeley: University of California Press, 1969], 503–17).

Jakobson's classic study "Two Aspects of Language and Two Types of Aphasic Disturbances" posits that language functions on two axes—selection and combination—which he equates with the terms metaphor and metonymy (Roman Jakobson and Morris Halle, *Fundamentals of Language*, 2d rev. ed. [The Hague and Paris: Mouton, 1975], 67–96; see esp. pp. 74–75). In tracing the development of these concepts, Elmar Holenstein notes the following:

> The combination of sections of discourse is obviously a process that takes place through time. Selection, however, gives the impression of an instantaneous decision. . . . Therefore, the two axes were also coordinated with Saussure's paired concepts synchrony/diachrony and static/dynamic. . . . The syntagmatic axis appears in a static perspective, the paradigmatic axis in a dynamic one. (141–42)

David Lodge's elaboration on Jakobson's theory has been a valuable source for my thinking throughout this chapter. See Part Two of *The Modes of Modern Writing: Metaphor, Metonymy, and the Typology of Modern Literature* (Ithaca: Cornell University Press, 1977). See also chapter 3 of Eco, *Semiotics and the Philosophy of Language* (Bloomington: Indiana University Press, 1984) for another discussion of metaphor and metonymy.

44. In the "Four Master Tropes" (metaphor, metonymy, synecdoche and irony), Kenneth Burke asserts, "It is an evanescent moment that we shall deal with—for not only does the dividing line between the figurative and literal usages shift, but also the four tropes shade into one another. Give a man but one of them, tell him to exploit its possibilities, and if he is thorough in doing so, he will come upon the other three" (503).

45. Floyd Merrell (*Semiotic Foundations: Steps toward an Epistemology of Written Texts* [Bloomington: Indiana University Press, 1982]) describes the Moebius strip and its "warp" in this way:

> Construct a Möbius strip by taking a strip of paper and connecting the top corner of one end with the bottom corner of the other end. . . .
>
> The strip encloses a space, a boundaried but "warped" space. Traveling along one surface (boundary) of the strip (enclosed space), you can go continuously from "inside" to "outside" without removing your finger from the surface (boundary) of the strip (enclosing a space). Recall that the name and the boundaried space named ordinarily combine to form a sign that is like two inseparable wholes. However, along the continuous Möbius strip such a discontinuity between space and name is "transcended" since one side of the surface can suddenly become the other side, and vice versa.
>
> What is the meaning of this? The "warp" in the strip is "like" names that are fused and (con)fused with the boundaried spaces they name. The name may be mistaken for the boundaried space, or the boundaried space may be mistaken for the content of the name when in fact a different boundaried space was intended to be the representation of the name. And so on. To consciously create a metaphor also entails such a "warp" or (con)fusion. Conversely, at nonconscious levels, to interpret a metaphorical name literally or a literal name metaphorically is to (con)fuse name and boundaried space without knowing it. In essence what occurs is that, like running your finger along the surface (boundary) of the Möbius strip, a discontinuous "switch" is (consciously or nonconsciously) perceived in what would otherwise be a continuum.
>
> The Möbius strip is a two-dimensional plane "warped" through three-dimensional space. . . . (26–27)

Merrell further equates this image to the "warping" (we might say the "troping") of metaphor (46).

46. See ibid., 20–21, for a description of a Venn diagram and discussion of the incommensurability of two perspectives in such a figure.

47. I call this intertextuality against the designation of my colleague Stamos Metzidakis (*Repetition and Semiotics* [Birmingham, Ala.: Summa Publications, 1986], see esp. pp. 21–23).

He affirms that "Whenever we are confronted with an intertextual repetition . . ., it automatically means that two *different* texts are involved; one present, the other absent" (43). If, as Metzidakis contends, intertextual repetition "would cover those parts of a text which represent various things from outside its own margins" (21), we will see that inter- and intratextuality become problematic in "Libro tercero" because we have difficulty (1) deciding where the margins of the text begin and end (what are "two *different* texts"?) and (2) making a distinction between "present" and "absent."

48. Similar to N. Katherine Hayles's placement of Stanislaw Lem, we could say of Rodríguez in *Don* that "He is on the cusp of the transition from the old to the new paradigms but not actually within either, for he resists the synthesis the new paradigms offer at the same time that he exposes contradictions that the old did not recognize. His work testifies that during a paradigm shift, change arrives not by a single sweeping transformation but by complex compromises negotiated at specific sites" (*Chaos Bound: Orderly Disorder in Contemporary Literature and Science* [Ithaca and London: Cornell University Press, 1990], 140).

49. "When the light pulses from above / it awakens the oracles of sleep / and walks along me, and before the countryside / it gives me shape. Thus another new / morning. Thus again and before anyone, / even the least decisive breeze, / feeling myself live, alone, in the clean light."

50. This pattern will repeat in vv. 37–38 at the end of the poem.

51. "But I make some gesture, I have some / magic wand because, look, suddenly / beings dawn, they point me out. / I am innocent. How everything unites / and in simple movements to the limit, / yes, for my punishment: the litheness / of the cottonwood tree for every gaze! Doors / with misty fleece for doorposts / open there, surpassing the peak."

52. Miguel de Unamuno uses this image in the first section of *El Cristo de Velázquez* in reference to the painter's brush. It can, of course, also refer to Unamuno's pen, giving his poem a self-referential dimension.

53. Aristotle, "On the Art of Poetry," in *Classical Literary Criticism,* trans. T. S. Dorsch (London: Penguin Books, 1965), 65; Eco, *Semiotics,* 89.

54. In English, the etymology of the verb "castigate" shows that "purify" is one of the primary connotations of this root, a pertinent issue in this poem. The use of archaic meanings is further evidence of Rodríguez's familiarity with early Spanish literature and philology.

55. See note 39 above.

56. "What simpler than that nodding / of the crops? What more persuasive / than the hay germinating? I touch nothing. / I do not wash in the dirt like a bird. / Yes, for my punishment, day is born / and one must separate the same relapse / from the others. . . ."

57. Rodríguez will continue to develop this trait over the years; see the last chapter of Mayhew's book *Claudio Rodríguez* and his article "*Casi una leyenda*: Repetición y renovación en el último libro de Claudio Rodríguez," *Insula* 541 (enero 1992): 11–12.

58. Here I employ a term used by Riffaterre: "The dual sign is an equivocal word situated at the point where two sequences of semantic or formal associations intersect. Nodal point might be a better image, since the word links together chains of association drawn along parallel paths by the sentence" (*Semiotics of Poetry*, 86). The nodal point may be roughly equivalent to a "strange attractor" in chaotics. "An attractor is simply any point within an orbit that seems to attract the system to it" (Hayles, *Chaos Bound*, 147).

59. "Warm respiration of recent breath / comes to me and thus the field raises forms / to a sublime aridity, and a moment / after, that which is lost amid the mystery / of one road and that of another narrower one, / we are the work of that which resuscitates. / I am distant, so distant. Still / bitter like the wild mulberry, does the rhythm / of things hurt me? Soul of the bird, / you will lie beneath the dome of a tree."

60. It may be necessary to clarify the distinction I see between "ahora" and "un momento." The latter is more specific, not a deictic, and it is modified with the indefinite article, which could be considered a number.

61. In "Literature, Complexity, Interdisciplinarity," William Paulson asserts,

> Literary texts inevitably contain elements that are not immediately decodable and that therefore
> function for their readers as what information theory would call noise. . . . [N]oise both within and
> outside the text can lead to the emergence of new levels of meaning neither predictable from lin-
> guistic and genre conventions nor subject to authorial mastery. . . . The artistic text begins as an
> attempt to go beyond the usual system of a language—in which the word is a conventional sign—
> to a specifically artistic system such as that of poetry, in which sounds, rhythms, positional relations
> between elements will signify in new ways. . . . New levels of constraint produce new kinds of
> variety and coding, new contexts in which aspects of language that in nonartistic communication
> would be extraneous to the message become elements that enter into secondary or tertiary signify-
> ing systems. (N. Katherine Hayles, ed., *Chaos and Order: Complex Dynamics in Literature and
> Science* [Chicago: University of Chicago Press, 1991], 43–44)

62. Cirlot, *A Dictionary of Symbols*, 228.

63. I will discuss the epigraphs at the end of this section.

64. "Ah, nothing is certain under the sky. / Nothing resists now. It happens when / my grief lifts me and makes me a pinnacle / that images begin to hide / and to give grain in each pore the act / of its light growth. Then / one must advance life as clear / as the air, the challenging air."

65. Jakobson concludes his discussion with the following affirmation: "The principle of similarity underlies poetry; the metrical parallelism of lines, or the phonic equivalence of rhyming words prompts the question of semantic similarity and contrast. . . . Prose, on the contrary, is forwarded essentially by contiguity. Thus, for poetry, metaphor and for prose, metonymy is the line of least resistance and, consequently, the study of poetical tropes is directed chiefly toward metaphor" ("Two Aspects of Language," 95–96).

66. We might compare this strategy to Roland Barthes's "writing degree zero," especially as it relates to noise and equivocation (double-voicing); see Hayles, *Chaos Bound*, 188.

67. Following Eric Charles White's discussion of Michel Serres's work in "Negentropy, Noise, and Emancipatory Thought," we might say that Rodríguez is seeking the *clinamen* of the sign. According to White (quoting Lucretius), the *clinamen* is "the smallest conceivable condition for the first formation of turbulence" (Hayles, ed., *Chaos and Order*, 265). However, "The onset of turbulence constitutes an increase in complexity" (264), and as we saw in "Libro primero," "literature creates meaning precisely by placing meaning in jeopardy" (269).

68. "The labyrinth is one of the metaphors that metafiction summons most frequently in the face of structure's absence. In its crossings and recrossings that rupture straight lines . . . it represents metafiction's disruption of linearity, and hence of fiction's previous hierarchical systems. . . . The activity of the labyrinth involves an infinite repetition or retracing that ob-structs memory, and hence origin, and in this way is metonymic of fiction's violated descent from reality that metafiction makes explicit. When extended to the dimensions of time, or voice, or causality, or symbolism, or closure, its relevance multiplies exponentially" (Peter Stoicheff, "The Chaos of Metafiction," in Hayles, ed., *Chaos and Order*, 88–89). If we substi-tute "metapoetry" for "metafiction" in this passage, we have an excellent description of "Canto del caminar."

69. David Porush defines a "bifurcation point" as "the origin of the dissipative struc-ture—a system-shattering moment when the previous, simpler organization can no longer sup-port the intensity or frequency of its own fluctuations, and either disintegrates or jumps to a new level of order and integration" ("Prigogine and Postmodernism's Roadshow," in Hayles, ed., *Chaos and Order*, 68). "The moment of greatest instability in an open system far from equilibrium is what statistical thermodynamicists call a 'bifurcation point'—from which the system generally leaps to one of two or more possible states of higher organization (72). Ac-cording to his discussion, "Canto del caminar" "leaps about with unexplained hiatuses and discontinuities in discrete packets of uneven length (fluctuates nonlinearly) following no ap-

parent order, except that time moves only forward" (71). "It takes for granted . . . the machinery or style of discontinuous narration, quick cuts to parallel strands of the story, lacunae, self-conscious manipulation of language and punctuation, layers of conflicting interpretations, and more importantly, a distrust of making sense out of the world through the application of system" (64).

70. In "Borges's Garden of Chaos Dynamics," in Hayles, ed., *Chaos and Order,* Thomas P. Weissert notes that "we can conceptualize the complex dynamics of culture as a fluid system in which each of the disciplines is a current of information. . . . These currents are not isolated but are constantly intermixing their ideas in a process which could only be described as stochastic. Each current carries a quantity of information for a while, processes it, changes it, and then returns it to the central flow. . . . With this model, all the interesting dynamic structures of fluids come into metaphorical play: eddies, flows, bifurcations, feedback loops, mixing, and, of course, the most interesting feature of all, turbulence. . . . In nonlinear dynamical systems, islands of order arise from the sea of chaos" (224). This passage is an apt description of "Canto del caminar" if we consider the "currents" as the interplay of metaphor and metonymy on the sign, whereas the "islands of stasis" are the bifurcation points at which the speaker addresses the other.

71. In a concise definition of Derrida's term, Jonathan Culler explains, "The supplement is an inessential extra, added to something complete in itself, but the supplement is added in order to complete, to compensate for a lack in what was supposed to be complete in itself" (*On Deconstruction: Theory and Criticism after Structuralism* [Ithaca: Cornell University Press, 1982], 103). Hayles adds, "To supplement something implies that the original is already full and self-sufficient, in contrast to the supplementary material, which comes after and is superfluous" (*Chaos Bound,* 181–82). The full import of supplementarity will become evident in the iteration of "Libro tercero," here prefigured by "Canto del caminar."

Discussing *The Education of Henry Adams,* Hayles equates the discovery of the "real self" with the gap. She remarks that "The 'real' self, manifesting itself within the text as absence, rupture, or gap, further complicates the linear flow of the narrative and punctuates the accretion of the inscripted self, rendering its evolution discontinuous or indeterminate" (*Chaos Bound,* 64–65). In the note at the bottom of p. 65, she clarifies that "In writing about a 'real' self, I mean to imply not a self that is essential in fact but one posited *within the text* as beyond the reach of textuality" (emphasis in original). Later in the same essay she says, "The pattern I want to highlight is a transition from a bipolar to a tripartite construction, with the third part being a rupture or gap" (70). The same can be said not only for the islands of stasis or bifurcation points in "Canto del caminar" but of "Libro segundo" in its entirety.

Hayles continues (and I substitute Rodríguez for Adams in her text):

[A] gap is never merely a void. Rather it is a fold that conceals or a tear that reveals. . . . The attraction [Rodríguez] feels toward the gap is intensely ambivalent. On the one hand, the encounter with chaos can be excruciatingly painful; on the other, it evokes in him an urgent need to make sense of the universe. If it were not for these ruptures, the text might circle endlessly. . . . The gaps provide the energy necessary to move the narrative forward in more than the superficial senses provided by elapsed time and a sequential turning of pages.

The gaps, partaking of a double nature in the fold/tear, have multiple significations. In some contexts they are associated with the "real" self. I remarked earlier on the complex dynamic of revelation and concealment that characterizes the "real" self, whose presence is constituted through the assertion of its absence. In other contexts, the gap is associated with a woman so desired by the "real" self that the two are inextricable. In still other passages, the gap is an entrance through which chaotic forces pour into the ordered world of the character's certainties. . . . Thus the void becomes the self, and the self becomes the void, each occupying the other's former position as if they were the inside and outside surfaces of a Möbius strip. (73–74, 80)

72. My understanding of chaos derives from three books by Hayles: *The Cosmic Web: Scientific Field Models & Literary Strategies in the Twentieth Century; Chaos Bound: Orderly*

Disorder in Contemporary Literature and Science; and *Chaos and Order: Complex Dynamics in Literature and Science.* Also see Deleuze and Guattari on how rhizomes function in literature, which is a similar and related concept.

Hayles questions the use of chaos theory as metaphor, asking, "Should terms appropriated from chaos theory be confined to their technical denotation, or is it valid to use them metaphorically or analogically? If they are used metaphorically, what do such arguments demonstrate?" (*Chaos and Order*, 15). Her discussion—and the purpose of the collection of essays in *Chaos and Order*—is to explore the interaction between science and aesthetics and to demonstrate the similarities and differences between chaos theory and postmodern literature and criticism.

73. "I had never known that my footstep / was different on red earth, / that it sounded more purely dry / the same as if it bore no man, / on foot, in his dimension. By that noise / perhaps some borders remember me. / Not for anything else. . . ."

74. Rodríguez has often spoken of the way he composed the poems of *Don de la ebriedad* while walking through the Castilian countryside. That is why he uses a hendecasyllable—the meter of walking and of orality—throughout these poems. For example, in "A manera de un comentario," the introduction to *Desde mis poemas*, Rodríguez wishes to clarify that "mis primeros poemas brotaron del contacto directo, vivido, recorrido, con la realidad de mi tierra, con la geografía y con el pulso de la gente castellana, zamorana. . . . Mal sabía, junto a mis pasos, que el paisaje y los hombres alentaban mis primeras andanzas o aventuras, y mi manera de escribir" (14) [my first poems sprang from direct contact, lived, traversed, with the reality of my land, with the geography and with the pulse of the Castilian, Zamoran people. . . . Little did I know, along with my steps, that the countryside and the people were stimulating my first wanderings or adventures, and my manner of writing]. In a statement recorded by Cañas, Rodríguez says, "Escribí casi todo el libro andando. Me sabía el libro de memoria y lo iba repitiendo, corrigiendo, modificando cuando andaba por el campo. Salir a campo abierto era una forma de desahogarme de mis frustraciones familiares. Pero en el campo también sentía a veces miedo; no miedo físico, sino miedo a las cosas desconocidas, asombro y placer y miedo frente a las cosas. En mis andanzas de sosiego y sin finalidad perdía la sensación del tiempo, o más bien alcanzaba a sentir el tiempo como algo estático" (*Claudio Rodríguez*, 23) [I wrote almost all of the book walking. I knew the whole book by memory and I would go along repeating, correcting, modifying it when I was walking through the fields. To go out into the open country was a form of unburdening myself of frustrations with my family. But in the country I also felt fear sometimes; not physical fear, but fear of the unknown, surprise and pleasure and fear before things. In my peace-filled wanderings without end I would lose track of time, or rather would attain a sense of time as something static].

75. See note 61 above.

76. Hayles, ed., *Chaos and Order*, 11. "The affinities of the science of chaos with other postmodern theories can now be detailed more precisely. It provides a new way to think about order, conceptualizing it not as a totalized condition but as the replication of symmetries that also allows for asymmetries and unpredictabilities. In this it is akin to post-structuralism, where the structuralist penchant for replicating symmetries is modified by the postmodern turn toward fragmentation, rupture, and discontinuity" (10–11).

77. ". . . The clouds change / form and advance to their change / dazzling in it, as the stream / within its flow; the fountains / contain outwardly their silence."

78. Hayles notes that "Systems of interest in chaos theory are dynamic. They change over time. . . . [N]onlinear systems are all around us, in every puff of wind and swirl of water" (*Chaos and Order*, 16, 17). Examples of turbulence cited by Hayles and others include clouds, wind-tossed trees, stains, strewn pebbles, flecks of sunlight, waterfalls, tree grains, mountain contours, leaves, snowflakes, and cigarette smoke.

79. See Merrell's description of the Klein bottle (*Semiotic Foundations*, 27–28).

80. According to the *Diccionario de la Real Academia Española* (hereafter *DRAE*), liter-

ally "contener" means "Llevar o encerrar dentro de sí una cosa a otra" (351) [To carry or enclose something else within a thing itself]. The expression "como en ello se contiene" signifies "con que se afirma que una cosa es puntualmente como se dice" [with which one affirms that something is exactly as one says]. Cf. Mayhew's article "'Cuartilla': Pedro Salinas and the Semiotics of Poetry," *Anales de la Literatura Española Contemporánea* 16 (1991): 119–27, where he talks about the contrast between whiteness and the words on the page (122).

81. See Rodríguez's discussions of the interaction of meditation and inspiration in his works. Also, Wheelwright notes that "wine, associated with the ancient idea of new life through mystical identification with the wine-god, carries also an overtone . . . of that which somehow transcends and escapes the doom of universal change" (*Metaphor and Reality*, 59).

82. In English, "static" as a noun also refers to noise as on a radio or other communication system. It interferes with the transmission and/or reception of the message. This verse has a similar effect because it creates static (noise) and causes stasis (a temporary halt in the turbulence).

This gradual realization on the part of the reader is similar to the emergence of a "strange attractor" in chaos theory. Adelaide Morris describes this experience thus: "They have a disorderly order that emerges slowly but surely, so slowly and so surely that the reader experiences something like the eerie inevitability one observer remembers feeling when he first watched a strange attractor form on the computer screen: the pattern 'appears,' he tells us, 'like a ghost out of the mist. New points scatter so randomly across the screen that it seems incredible that any structure is there, let alone a structure so intricate and fine' (Gleick 150)" ("The Case of H.D." in Hayles, ed., *Chaos and Order*, 214).

83. Hayles points out that "The word ['chaos'] derives from a Greek verb-stem, KHA, meaning 'to yawn, to gape'; from this comes the meaning given by the *Oxford English Dictionary*, 'a gaping void, yawning gulf, chasm, or abyss'" (*Chaos and Order*, 2).

84. "Even the sickle asks more than reaps. / Even the grackle curses more than shrieks. / A concert of wheat-spike against wheat-spike / comes with the rising of the sun. So much / space to die! So much vivid blue, / so much yellow field for the friction! / Nor will I know when I find it: they have transported / my vision, stone by stone, like a temple."

85. "That chaos has been negatively valued in the Western tradition may be partly due . . . to the predominance of binary logic in the West. . . . In chaos theory chaos may either lead to order, as it does with self-organizing systems, or in yin/yang fashion it may have deep structures of order encoded within it" (Hayles, ed., *Chaos and Order*, 3).

86. "Characteristic metaphors [of the field model] are a 'cosmic dance,' a 'network of events,' and an 'energy field.' A dance, a network, a field—the phrases imply a reality that has no detachable parts, indeed no enduring, unchanging parts at all. Composed not of particles but of 'events,' it is in constant motion, rendered dynamic by interactions that are simultaneously affecting each other. . . . [T]he field becomes concentrated at one point and disappearing as it thins out at another. Particles are not to be regarded as discrete entities, then, but rather . . . as 'energy knots' [in a web]" (Hayles, *Cosmic Web*, 15–16).

87. See vv. 59–60 and 80–81. In *Orality and Literacy: The Technologizing of the Word* (London and New York: Routledge, 1982), Walter Ong asserts, "One of the most startling paradoxes inherent in writing is its close association with death. . . . The paradox lies in the fact that the deadness of the text, its removal from the living human lifeworld, its rigid visual fixity, assures its endurance and its potential for being resurrected into limitless living contexts by a potentially infinite number of living readers" (81).

88. "To clear land of scrub and useless grasses before working them, either so that they sprout or for other reasons" (*DRAE*, 1160).

89. "A key concept . . . is self-organization. . . . It envisions a world that can renew itself rather than a universe that is constantly running down, as nineteenth-century thermodynamicists believed. Disorder in this view does not interfere with self-organizing processes. Instead disorder stimulates self-organization and, in a certain sense, enables it to take place" (Hayles, *Chaos and Order*, 12).

90. Hayles explains that "the hyper-real comes into existence when copies refer no longer to originals but to other copies; or more precisely, when it is impossible to distinguish any longer between a copy and an original. . . . [T]he hyper-real presupposes a radical erosion of context, for the sense that something is an original depends upon its association with a unique context. Consider: a London bridge is dismantled and transported stone by stone to the Arizona desert, where it is reassembled. The bridge is physically the same (within limits imposed by the plasticity of the material); but is it an original or a copy? The undecidability of the question illustrates how deeply the sense that something is a simulacrum is bound up with the loss of a stable context" (*Chaos Bound*, 276).

91. Mayhew (*Claudio Rodríguez*, 134–37) questions Martha Miller's discussion of referential mimesis.

92. Hayles, *Chaos Bound*, 263.

93. "What an hour: to launch the body towards the heights! / Active watering within and above / transparent quietude, in blocks, made / of the slenderness of distant music / very high in the soul and alone at the surface. / Now this flight of sight is your love."

94. Similar to Eric Charles White's description of speakers (or voices) in Thomas Pynchon's *The Crying of Lot 49*, we could assert that "the noisy babbling of one speaker would then provide an opportunity for the next noisy speaker to invent meaning stochastically, on the spur of the moment, without reiterating what has always already been said" ("Negentropy, Noise, and Emancipatory Thought," in Hayles, ed., *Chaos and Order*, 269). This repetition with renewal anticipates Rodríguez's discovery of new potentials of language in "Libro tercero" of *Don* (see below).

95. "You have always heard me when, free / with the growing day, I retire / to the dark swelling, to my work, / like the thistle before the rain to the harsh / viscous juice of its flower; and it is because / it has to be so: I am one furrow / more, not a road that embitters time. / He who plowed me wishes that it be so. —Profound / plow!— I am guilty. They shout it at me."

96. See *DRAE*, 437. The adjectival past participle "desabrido" is the form most commonly used in modern Spanish. One of the figurative meanings of this word is "Aspero y desapacible en el trato" [Harsh and unpleasant in relationships] (437), coinciding with the description of the thistle in vv. 36–37.

97. Another usage of "desabrido" has to do with the weather: "Tratándose del tiempo, destemplado, desigual" [Dealing with weather, off-beat, uneven]. Ibid., 437.

98. Rodríguez uses the Christ-figure and crucifixion often. See, for example, "El canto de linos" in *Conjuros*, "Elegía desde Simancas" in *El vuelo*, and "Balada de un treinta de enero" in *Casi una leyenda*.

99. The ambivalence within and between the expressions "Soy inocente" and "Soy culpable" resembles what chaos theorists call a "strange loop," "a loop of reasoning that cannot be resolved because to accept either statement as true is to begin a loop which circles around to say that the same statement must be false" (Hayles, *Cosmic Web*, 34), resulting in indeterminacy but also generating new meaning. Another instance of a strange loop on a different scale level can be found in the structural repetition of the same verses at the beginning and end of poem VII of "Libro tercero" and its counterpart in "Libro primero" (see below).

100. "Like a kneading of bread their voices pass / to the pulse, to the blood, to my insanity / for remembering, for augmenting fears, to this / insanity of bearing my song on my back, / another sheaf, a sheaf of what pile."

101. One thinks again of the image of a labyrinth, "its crossings and recrossings. . . . The activity of the labyrinth involves an infinite repetition or retracing that obstructs memory, and hence origin. . . ." See Stoicheff's discussion in "The Chaos of Metafiction," esp. 88–95.

102. "That they save you, no. Look: the washerwoman / at the river, who doesn't wash the morning / so as not to let it dry in her hands, because / she would dry it out like white clothing, / she saves herself in her own way. And the autumns / too. And each being. And the sea that holds sway / above the moor. Oh, not only the wind / from the North is like a sea, but the poplar

tree / trembles like the rigging of a ship. / Not even the fabulous sheepfold of the afternoons / invades me thus. . . ."

103.   Eric Charles White describes the ocean as a "traditional emblem of flux and dissolution" (Hayles, *Chaos and Order*, 265). The characteristics of the sea transfer metaphorically to the storm and hence to language.

104.   ". . . Your love, your love I fear, / central nave of my grief, and countryside. / But now I am far away, so far away / that no one would cry if I were to die. / I begin to confirm that our reign / is not of this world either."

105.   "I go on. The days pass, luminous / on the surface of the earth, and blind on the hills / for the intolerable height, and beautiful / just like the death rattle of a new lark. / I go on. To go on is my only hope. / To go on hearing the noise of my footstep / with the fruition of a blind man's poor guide. / But now you exist and you are in everything."

106.   We should not overlook the death/resurrection imagery in the name "Lázaro": The poet sees himself dying to an old self and aspiring to a lasting identity through his poetry. This metaphoric comparison sets up a metonymic chain (a *mise-en-abîme* of recursive symmetry) because Lazarus's resurrection is a prefiguration of Christ's.

107.   "But now you exist and you are in everything. / If I were to die, you would make of me a furrow, / an inalterable furrow: neither hail, / nor that mourning of the angels, snow, nor that / north wind with so many clandestine fires / would change their line, which interprets / the season clearly. . . ."

108.   ". . . And what places / more sober than these to go on waiting? / It is Castile, suffer it! In other times, / when they would call me her child, / I couldn't think that hers / would be the only voice that would remain to me, / the only intimacy so tranquil / that would leave in my eyes faith in the rootstock. / The mother rootstock. And you, heart, red / grape, the most inebriated, that least / harvested by men, how were you / to know that you were not on the vine, / that you were sustained by no stalk?"

109.   Hayles comments that "Anyone who has seriously studied how language works is aware . . . that it shapes even as it articulates thought. . . . [L]anguage is not a passive instrument but an active engagement with a vital medium that has its own currents, resistances, subversions, enablings, pathways, blockages. As soon as discovery is communicated through language, it is also constituted by language" (Hayles, ed., *Chaos and Order,* 5). These views are consonant with Rodríguez's understanding of poetry as "conocimiento." See "Unas notas sobre poesía," in Ribes, *Poesía última*, esp. 87–88.

110.   "—I have spoken thus, prematurely, and should I / protect myself from the sun of enthusiasm? / A light that in the air is barely air / comes from the sunset and separates / the intense shadow of the white maples / before separating two clarities: / that of total day and the clouded one / of the moon, confused an instant / within a last diffuse beam."

111.   "Who cares about March crowning almond trees. / And night, who cares if we are still / seeking a definitive radiance. / Oh, the night that launches its stars / from heavenly ramparts. There is no longer anything: / only sky and land. A sure target, / a sure target does my chest offer! / Oh, the star of the hidden dawn / piercing me at last, now nearer. / That when I fall I die or not, who cares. / Who cares if now I am on my way."

112.   The same effect is manifest in Nietzschean versus Platonic repetition as described by Hillis Miller in the introduction to *Fiction and Repetition: Seven English Novels* (Cambridge: Harvard University Press, 1982). See the next section of this book.

113.   Arthur Rimbaud, "Comédie de la Soif," in *Complete Works, Selected Letters*, trans. and ed. Wallace Fowlie (Chicago: University of Chicago Press, 1966), 134.

114.   See Roman Jakobson's "Shifters, Verbal Categories and the Russian Verb," where he defines shifters as words whose application always depends on a specific context.

115.   Both the image of unstable March and the length of poem I of "Libro tercero" are prefigured in "Canto del caminar."

116.   Benoit Mandelbrot invented fractal geometry. According to Hayles, "He coined the

word 'fractal' from the Latin adjective *fractus* (meaning 'broken') and fractional; it connotes both fractional dimensions and extreme complexity of form. . . . [I]n fractal geometry the emphasis on recursive symmetries makes [convoluted] orbits [of strange attractors] . . . created by iteration of the same form over and over" (*Chaos Bound*, 165). Elizabeth Sánchez defines a fractal as a

> new way of looking at complex systems and natural forms by attending to scale-dependent symmetries. . . . The new "ingredient" here is attention to scales of measurement and to the repetition of a particular pattern or irregularity at different levels of a complex form. . . . A fractal, then, is an infinitely complex form which is self-similar (not necessarily self-identical) at different scale levels. (255–56)

Sánchez's discussion, "*La Regenta* as Fractal," forms part of a critical dialogue on chaos theory published by the *Revista de Estudios Hispánicos* 26 (1992): 251–76.

As I have indicated in my discussion of the "Cantos" of "Libro segundo," Hayles has done an extensive amount of work applying chaos theory to literature. According to what I have read in her books, a fractal is a design (or image) predicated on "recursive symmetry," the repetition of the same or similar pattern(s) on different levels or "scales" of measurement. The pattern that recurs (repeats) throughout "Libro tercero" is repetition itself, which extends from the phonic scale (alliteration) to the repetition of words, phrases, metaphors, intertextualities, to patterns of organization of poems and even of the section itself and the pendulum-like swing of the entire collection. I have chosen to concentrate my critical attention on the theory of repetition to avoid a potentially tautological discussion of "the repetition of repetitions."

Steven Connor begins his study of Samuel Beckett with these observations: "[R]epetition is a central and necessary concept within all attempts to understand individual and social being and representation. While to a large extent repetition determines and fixes our sense of our experience and representations of that experience, it is also the place where certain radical instabilities in these operations can reveal themselves" (*Samuel Beckett: Repetition, Theory and Text* [New York and Oxford: Basil Blackwell, 1988], 1). Rodríguez explores this "place of radical instabilities" in "Libro tercero" at the same time that he identifies himself as a poet.

117.   Two other sources have been invaluable for my understanding of repetition. See Connor, *Samuel Beckett*, and Kartiganer, "Faulkner's Art of Repetition," in *Faulkner and the Craft of Fiction: Faulkner and Yoknapatawpha, 1987,* ed. Doreen Fowler and Ann J. Abadie (Jackson and London: University Press of Mississippi, 1989), 21–47. It is curious to note that these theories of repetition have been applied to fiction rather than poetry, strengthening my argument that Rodríguez structures his works sequentially and uses metonymic devices in the second half of *Don*. For a discussion of repetition in poetry that provides additional insights into these poems, see Herrnstein Smith's *Poetic Closure: A Study of How Poems End* (Chicago and London: University of Chicago Press, 1968).

118.   Hillis Miller, *Fiction and Repetition*, 6.

119.   Ibid., 6. Also see Connor's discussion (*Samuel Beckett*, 5–9). Connor mentions Bruce Kawin's distinction between "building time" and "continuing time," which is based on the same concept (12–14).

120.   Hillis Miller, *Fiction and Repetition*, 7.

121.   Ibid., 8.

122.   Ibid.

123.   Ibid., 9. "Each form of repetition calls up the other, by an inevitable compulsion. The second is not the negation or opposite of the first, but its 'counterpart,' in a strange relation whereby the second is the subversive ghost of the first, always already present within it as a possibility which hollows it out. If logical, daylight resemblances depend on a third thing, on a principle of identity which precedes them, the opaque similarities of dream are baseless, or, if based at all, then based on the difference between the two things. They create in the gap of that difference a third thing, what Benjamin calls the image [*das Bild*]. The image is the meaning

generated by the echoing of two dissimilar things in the second form of repetition. It is neither in the first nor in the second nor in some ground which preceded both, but in between, in the empty space which the opaque similarity crosses."

124. Jacques Derrida explores the relationship between original and copy in *Writing and Difference*. See Connor, *Samuel Beckett*, 3–5.

125. Connor notes the contrast between "the modernist imperative to 'make it new'" and the postmodern "desire to recirculate the old or the already known, if only in the attempt to subvert the grounds of familiar knowledge" (*Samuel Beckett*, 2). He goes on to say,

> It would surely be a mistake to see this as merely the emptying of life or urgency from cultural activity, however, since what underlies modernist and postmodernist experiments with the forms of repetition is not so much a movement between the fixed polarities of creative originality on the one hand and plagiarizing imposture on the other, as an attempt to shift and complicate the fixity of each of those positions, and to explore the problematic interrelationship that exists between originality and repetition. (2–3)

This problematization underlies Rodríguez's transition from modernity to postmodernity that I argue is a significant feature of *Don*.

126. Kartiganer posits a "middle ground repetition" that "both empties the ground of its original power to determine future versions or fulfillments of itself, *and* restores it, reempowering it, so to speak, but according to the desires of the present. Middle ground repetition effects a design that is neither locked within its center, restricted to the performance of variations on a given theme, nor completely uprooted, merely making and unmaking itself as a display of artful turns above the abyss. Repetition, in other words, becomes a mode of meaning in language and consciousness that invests the past with a new yet correspondent power that, in turn, constitutes the 'source' of a new design or narrative" ("Faulkner's Art of Repetition," 29).

127. "In explaining what he means by 'opaque similarity,' Benjamin has recourse to an emblem which is an example of what he is trying to define. The defined enters once more into the definition, disqualifying that definition, as in my own language here, according to a necessity of this second form of repetition. If the similarity is not logical or wakeful, but opaque, dreamlike, it cannot be defined logically but only exemplified. The example will then only present again the opacity" (Hillis Miller, *Fiction and Repetition*, 8–9).

With regard to exemplification, Kenneth J. Knoespel says, "Our use of language relies on examples. We learn language through examples and continually use examples to orient ourselves within discourse. If we wish, we may think of examples as providing surveying tools that help orient our discourse with others. Practically, examples comprise appeals that would establish a common terrain for listeners or readers. Seen in this way, communication functions through an elaborate network of exemplification. Examples help us make points and enforce stability, but they also open discourse by challenging an audience to revise the maps they have used to plot experience. Finally, examples remind us that all understanding is temporally mediated" (Hayles, *Chaos and Order*, 109). Knoespel formulates three functions of exemplification: to promote closure, to provoke openings, and to subvert the system (109–10).

128. "That which before was exact now doesn't find / its place. It doesn't find it and it's day, and it is blown away as from afar / the fountain, that sounds like lost light. / Blown away I also by dint of warm / hungers, of unheard-of mornings, / / I have seen in the incense on the peaks / and in my white writing a happiness / dispersed with vigor. And still all does not rise / to kiss? Don't the stars / lose their limits for something more beautiful / than a hidden fall? . . ."

129. Hillis Miller, *Fiction and Repetition*, 9.

130. Hayles notes, "Iteration produces chaos because it magnifies and brings into view these initial uncertainties. . . . The goal of iteration is thus to make visible the lack of ground for the alleged originary difference, thus rendering all subsequent distinctions indeterminate" (*Chaos Bound*, 183, 182).

131. These images are in accord with what Kartiganer discerns as a dialectic

between nostalgia and gaiety: those texts that still yearn, however secretly, for a lost origin they can never regain, and those texts that celebrate the loss, exposing the fictiveness of their repetitions—if not with joy, then at least with candor. This division is seldom if ever pure; it is the interaction of the two possibilities that is the field of deconstructionist practice. The adequate reading of a text demonstrates the nostalgia with which the text asserts its gaiety or the gaiety with which it exposes its nostalgia. The upshot is undecidability. Texts know not what they are or want, but at their best they force that very fact to the front of their language. ("Faulkner's Art of Repetition," 27)

132. We have already mentioned that clouds and mountain peaks are instances of turbulence and recursive symmetry in chaotics.

133. Drucilla L. Cornell notes that "Throughout his work, Lacan uses the term *significance* to refer to that 'movement in language against, or away from, the positions of coherence which language simultaneously constructs' (Jacques Lacan, 'Introduction—II,' in *Feminine Sexuality*, pp. 51–52). As Jacqueline Rose goes on to explain, '[t]he concept of *jouissance* (what escapes in sexuality) and the concept of *significance* (what shifts in language) are inseparable' (*Ibid.*, p. 52)." See Cornell, "Gender, Sex, and Equivalent Rights," in *Feminists Theorize the Political*, ed. Judith Butler and Joan W. Scott (New York: Routledge, 1992), 295 n. 2ʋ.
    Stoicheff notes, "The random patterning within a simple phenomenal system is creative, because it generates 'richly organized patterns, sometimes stable and sometimes unstable' (Gleick 43). The system of the metafictional text is creative as well, producing what Barthes terms the 'jouissance' of an inexhaustible possibility of interpretations" ("The Chaos of Metafiction," 87).

134. In fractal geometry, this is the concept of recursive symmetries on different scale levels.

135. ". . . If life / were to call on me in the middle of my body / like the clearing amid pines on the cold / breathing of the moon, because now / I can, and now it is there. . . . But no: breezes / of mountain silence, lightened / birds that stop and again / their flight in equilibrium anticipate."

136. I first became aware of the image of the pine-grove as a universal one upon reading Faulkner's *The Unvanquished*, where the family has hidden its cemetery amid evergreens. I have also found it in Conrad Richter's *The Trees*, where the protagonist's sister defiles the sacred space by making love to a profane and unethical man, and in the children's book *Bridge to Terabithia* by Katherine Paterson, where two children (one of whom dies) recognize the magical and sacred properties of this space. The "ciprés," an evergreen traditionally found in Spanish cemeteries, adds to the ambivalence of this image of death and eternal life. Although sacred groves are a mainstay of Western mythology and symbology, to date I have not been able to pin down a source such as Cirlot, *A Dictionary of Symbols;* Jean Chevalier and Alain Gheerbrandt, *Diccionario de los símbolos;* or J. A. Pérez-Rioja, *Diccionario de símbolos y mitos* to verify my interpretation of the pine grove in particular. However, the pine tree and cone are treated in a number of sources. Another possibility to be explored might be the conic (triangular) shape of conifers. Also see María Zambrano's *Claros del bosque* and García Jambrina's discussion of the philosophical affinity between Rodríguez and Zambrano. Rodríguez uses this image again in the final poem of *Conjuros*, "Pinar amanecido." See chap. 2, below.

137. *Pequeño Larousse Ilustrado 1992* (Madrid: Ed. Larousse, 1991), s.v. "montaraz."

138. Kartiganer, "Faulkner's Art of Repetition," 27.

139. "That which before was exact, that which before / was simple: a grain that germinates, / suddenly. How does the lone month advance / on us from outside. It smells of you, it imitates / your beauty, the night your words / —you on the frieze of dawn. / And that I can't see my virgin city / or my grinding stone without oblique / swallows awakening the wall / to know that nothing, no one migrates!"

140. "This abiding nostalgia is countered by the Nietzschean refusal of all ground—moreover, the refusal to consider this loss of ground *as* loss. Refusal takes the form of what Derrida terms '*affirmation*—the joyous affirmation of the free play of the world and without truth,

without origin, offered to an active interpretation.' The groundlessness of repetition, in other words, becomes in its Nietzschean extremity, a reason for joy rather than regret" (Kartiganer, "Faulkner's Art of Repetition," 26–27).

141.   Connor points out that the deconstruction of these two theories of repetition is integrally related to Derrida's discussion of the dichotomy between speech and writing.

> Repetition is at one and the same time that which stabilizes and guarantees the Platonic model of original and copy and that which threatens to undermine it. Repetition must always repeat originality, must always depend on some thing or idea which is by definition preexisting, autonomous and self-identical. Repetition is therefore subordinated to the idea of the original, as something secondary and inessential. For this reason, repetition is conventionally condemned in Western culture as parasitic, threatening and negative. But if repetition is dependent upon a preexisting originality, it is also possible to turn this round and argue that originality is also dependent upon repetition. If repetition requires something that is already fixed and finished, already constituted as an essence, then it is equally true that originality or essence can never be apprehended as such unless the possibility exists for it to be copied or reiterated. (*Samuel Beckett*, 3)

142.   Hillis Miller, *Fiction and Repetition*, 11.

143.   See my discussion of poem VIII of "Libro primero" where a similar phenomenon obtains in the image of the rain.

144.   We could describe this gap or middle-ground repetition as a "vacuum that produces something out of nothing. The fecund vacuum would not be the powerful image it is in contemporary thought if reflexivity had not prepared the way by intimating that a lack of ground can be productive and exhilarating rather than threatening. Even if there are no foundations, there may nevertheless be creation, evolution, and renewal" (Hayles, *Chaos Bound*, 223).

145.   This duality is reminiscent of Kierkegaard's distinction between "recollection" and "repetition." As Kartiganer describes it,

> Kierkegaard makes an important distinction [in *Repetition*, published in 1843] between what he calls "recollection" and "repetition": "Repetition and recollection are the same movement, except in opposite directions, for what is recollected has been, is repeated backward, whereas genuine repetition is recollected forward. Repetition, therefore, if it is possible, makes a person happy, whereas recollection makes him unhappy." What Kierkegaard calls "recollection" is the notion of remembering or actively duplicating, without change, the pattern of a completed past. This is what Miller means by a Platonic, grounded repetition, as the mind secures itself within the parameters of its apparent origins, never going beyond the imitation of what have been its generating assumptions. Kierkegaard's second type of repetition, a modern existentialist view, yet different from Miller's, emphasizes the potential for reexperiencing the past in a new key—revising its initial meanings *so as to signal an individual growth within repetition*. This is what Kierkegaard calls a "repetition forward," in that the past is rewritten, becoming part of a new narrative expanding into the future. Recollection, as one commentator [Louis Mackey] has put it, "is the immediate recoil of the then upon the now"; repetition "is the reflective reinterpretation of that immediacy."
>
> This second form of repetition has been linked by some critics with Heidegger's notion of repetition. . . . Kierkegaard's "repetition forward" is a synthesis of grounded and ungrounded repetitions—a synthesis that recovers new possibilities in repetition and yet avoids the alternative of the utter abandonment of meaning or some clarity of value. This new repetition is at once grounded and ungrounded. It loosens the control of the archetype . . . and yet it resists the condition of utterly free fictions, broken from all origin and unable to reconnect in a formation of meaning. As a "repetition forward," a mind, a character, a text can release itself from its enabling origins into the adventure of time; and yet it can also claim a continuity within an expanding intention, a possibility of adequate, demonstrable meaning that is not merely what Miller calls the "memory of a world that never was." Repetition becomes the fulfillment of possibilities only latent in the past, the completion of what only the present can awaken. ("Faulkner's Art of Repetition," 29; my emphasis)

Throughout "Libro tercero," Rodríguez explores the interplay between these two forces. This tension never attains resolution; on the contrary, the exacerbation of tension is prolonged through the final poem and endows the work with its unique dynamics. The ambivalence to "the agonizing, energizing void for which the gap is the textual signifier" (Hayles, *Chaos Bound*, 74) is typical of chaos.

146. "It is the gaze, / it is the water that awaits drinking. / The water. It grows sad upon contemplating itself / nude and with March already pregnant."

Baudelaire's poem reads as follows:

> We have, for certain, many corrupt nations,
> Whose unknown beauties were their tribulations:
> Visages graven by all the diseases of the heart
> Whose beauty languishes for lack of art:
> But these inventions of our modern Muses
> Could never hinder in sick races the abuses
> Which gave to youth the aspect of a stranger,
> —Nor from Saintly graces, nor from the wind's danger,
> Youth whose clear eyes were simple as water flowing
> *that flows forever over all things*, knowing
> The way the wind blows and the planet's visions,
> The heats, the perfumes and the sun's derisions!

("I Love the Memory," in *Baudelaire, Rimbaud, Verlaine: Selected Verse and Prose Poems*, ed. Joseph M. Bernstein [New York: Citadel Press, 1947], 13–14; my emphasis)

147. The frequent use of alliteration reinforces this concept on yet another level of the text. Is alliteration nothing but empty babbling, or does it too illuminate new realms of meaning?

148. While discussing Stanislaw Lem's writing, Hayles points out that "In Lem's view, literature—indeed, language itself—is engaged in a feedback loop in which articulating an idea changes the context, and changing the context affects the way the idea is understood, which in its turn leads to another idea, so that text and context evolve together in a constantly modulating interaction" (*Chaos Bound*, 128). In Rodríguez's poem, we see these "feedback loops" operating on a number of different scale levels simultaneously, producing the fractal design. The ambivalent relation between text and context is endemic to the principle of repetition.

149. "The affinities of the science of chaos with other postmodern theories . . . provides a new way to think about order, conceptualizing it not as a totalized condition but as the replication of symmetries that also allows for asymmetries and unpredictabilities. In this it is akin to poststructuralism, where the structuralist penchant for replicating symmetries is modified by the postmodern turn toward fragmentation, rupture, and discontinuity. . . . Another convergence is the emphasis on iterative techniques and recursive looping. In deconstruction, as in the science of chaos, iteration and recursion are seen as ways to destabilize systems and make them yield unexpected conclusions" (Hayles, ed., *Chaos and Order*, 10–11).

150. As Kartiganer states, "In its most ancient forms repetition is preeminently the way of knowing, the way of experiencing reality and significance" ("Faulkner's Art of Repetition," 23).

151. Kartiganer remarks that "Free of confirmation in mythic archetype, a completed history, the forms of knowledge, repetition assumes new and ghostlier guises, establishes coherences whose conviction and validity are of a different and far more problematic nature. Partly out of will, the knowing defiance of all anteriority, partly out of loss, the sense that the past may be our invention after all, the modern mind plots and destroys its repetitions in dazzling and at times dizzying ways" ("Faulkner's Art of Repetition," 25–26).

152. "Everything is new perhaps for us. / The clear-shining sun, the setting sun, / dies; that which rises is more brilliant and higher / each time, it is distinct, it is another new / form of life, of creation felt. / Thus each morning is the first. / So that we live it you and I alone, / nothing is the same or repeats. That / curve, of flowering almond trees, soft, / was it flowering yesterday? That bird there, / is it perhaps flying in wider circles? / After having snowed the sky finds / brilliances that before were clouds. / Everything is new perhaps. . . ."

153. Claudio met Clara in 1953; they wed in 1959. See Cañas, *Claudio Rodríguez*, for more details.

154. Kartiganer notes a connection between Mircea Eliade's discussion of the archaic mind's linking of the sacred and the profane and the Judeo-Christian perception of

> the shift from a theory of eternal return, in which events are important through their reproduction of prior events, to a theory of history, the replacement of cyclical time with what Eliade calls "one-way time": a linear, progressive development, with a beginning, middle, and end. . . .
> What links the archaic and the Judeo-Christian perceptions, however, is the continuing sense of repetition as a solidly grounded vehicle of knowing and identity. Although each moment in the life of the individual and in time is now a new moment, never to come again, it is yet a moment that resonates with a meaning rooted in the context of the whole—the whole history to be completed in the future, but whose intelligible pattern has been predicated in the past. Each new moment, then, takes its place within a pattern . . . and receives its highest meaning only as a fulfillment, a repetition in real, actual time of that which has been foretold. ("Faulkner's Art of Repetition," 24)

As we will see in poem VIII of "Libro tercero" (the last poem of *Don*), there is an "eternal return" to the beginning of *Don* and an historical progression into the future as *Don* comes to an end.

155. The deconstruction of the inside/outside opposition is characteristic of both deconstruction and chaos theory (cf. the Möbius strip).

156. This is another instance of a "strange loop," now on the sentence level.

157. It is also a structural repetition similar to poem I of this section but without the stanzaic break, and vaguely similar to the periods after "Sigo" in "Canto del caminar."

158. "Everything is new perhaps. If it weren't, / if in the midst of this hour images / were to adopt life in others, and with them / the memories of a day now past / were to return hiding that of today, were to return / clarifying it, yes, but hiding / its nascent clarity, what surprise / would it give to my being, what delirium, / what new light or what new labors?"

159. One could say (as Connor does, citing Foucault's commentary on Deleuze) that "repetition is simultaneously a point of weakness and of deconstructive strength" (*Samuel Beckett*, 7). Hayles explains that "Maximum information is conveyed when there is a mixture of order and surprise, when the message is partly anticipated and partly surprising"; "Once randomness was understood as maximum information, it was possible to envision chaos . . . as the source of all that is new in the world" (*Chaos Bound*, 53, 51). The month of March is emblematic of these statements and representative of Rodríguez's conception of language at this stage in his investigation.

160. "River water, sea water; star / fixed or wandering, star in nocturnal / repose. What truth, what clear scene / that of love, that never sees in things / the sad reality of their appearance."

161. This temporal distinction recalls the phrase "remembering forward" and Kierkegaard's distinction between recollection and repetition. See Kartiganer, "Faulkner's Art of Repetition"; and Hillis Miller, *Fiction and Repetition*.

162. "And am I to make it true? Could I / point out when there is sap and when must, / when the threshers change the landscape / anew and in the hour of return?"

163. "The contagion of you, of me, of all / that which one can see upon leaving / a bridge, between the space of its eyes"

164. "On the ascent. Relentlessly / close, even with the fear of pursuit, / you arrive going beyond the point of arrival, / opening yourself upon arriving like the autumn"

165. "the great danger of the lights / on the plain is leveled on the scarlet / background"

166. "Because it's one thing to think I'm alone / and another to make noise so as to walk firmly; / one thing the night, another the nearness / of that night that lives on in this one / and loses control of it. —Hush, cottonwood tree, sober / torch burned by the wait! . . ."

167. ". . . And it hushes, / and moves the boundaries of its voice in a chorus / of intimacy the same as if it were moving / voices of the air while I hear you / —I am hearing you even though I may hear nothing—, / shadow of a song now almost corporeal."

168. "From the earliest recorded times the circle has been widely recognized as the most perfect of figures, both because of its simple formal perfection and for the reason stated in Heraclitus' aphorism, 'In the circle the beginning and the end are the same.' . . . Like many another archetypal symbol the Wheel [circle] is potentially ambivalent" (Wheelwright, *Metaphor and Reality*, 125–26). This symbol is consistent with the ambivalence of repetition.

169. ". . . Without me the fence, / the river, actor of the oldest music. / Still and although they fathom stealthy footprints, / widest straight or curved, / the valley, the offering valley, perhaps / a valley with outstanding creatures. / So much of us goes in a risk!"

170. Cf. Heraclitus. Also see Cirlot, *A Dictionary of Symbols*, 274.

171. The gain/loss motif is a staple of Rodríguez's participation in the poetic act.

172. "The morning, / in the midst of the dark green trunk / and in the treetop of a strong leafy gray, / senses a thousand wing beats that illuminate it"

173. "She exacts many / lives and lives so many that she makes eternal / that of her lover, she makes it of a loam / of love, unbearably certain."

174. "Simply to love only one time. / Conduit of the months, old and new / ignorance of the metamorphosis / that goes from June to June. See: it waits for / nothing or no one from me. What do you need? / Nothing nor no one for my existence."

175. Kartiganer, "Faulkner's Art of Repetition," 30. See note 145 above.

176. "It's not that it's left me: it's never been here. / But to seek and not to recognize it, / and not to set it afire in a vivid future... / How will I leave only this moment? / No one sees here and the flames palpitate / and it is necessary that one extract from it / the form, so that again it may take form / like the wind in the battle with its gyre. / Like in the battle with its gyre. . . ."

177. "One generation passeth away, and another generation cometh; / And the earth abideth for ever. / The sun also ariseth, and the sun goeth down, / and hasteth to his place where he ariseth. / The wind goeth toward the south, / And turneth about unto the north; / It turneth about continually in its circuit, / and the wind returneth again to its circuits. / All the rivers run into the sea, / Yet the sea is not full; / Unto the place whither the rivers go, / Thither they go again. / All things toil to weariness; / Man cannot utter it, / The eye is not satisfied with seeing, / Nor the ear filled with hearing. / That which hath been is that which shall be, / And that which hath been done is that which shall be done; / And there is nothing new under the sun." (Eccles. 1:4–9)

178. Kartiganer, "Faulkner's Art of Repetition," 30.

179. "Yesterday the field was pulsing on its own. / Today it lacks the vineshoot of another mystery, / of the foot that is unaware of the grape though it has stepped / heavily on the rootstock. Today."

180. "Oh, farther than the air and the night / (The blue glazier, the glazier / of the morning!), amid death itself / that reveals to us a serene path to walk / whether the path goes backward or forward, / whether the road goes to the sea or inland."

181. Here I have paraphrased Kartiganer ("Faulkner's Art of Repetition," 30). This concept is deeply rooted in Heidegger's exposition of temporality and history in *Being and Time* (see esp. sections 54–83). Michael Gelven explains that

> the mode of the authentic understanding in the past ekstasis [is] *repetition*. Historicality is the authentic repetition of possibilities, not as a mere enslavement of what has gone before, but as a sharing in the decisiveness and guilt that made the situations of the past significant. To speak, then, of 'living in the past' is not to deny the future; rather, it is to take hold of the future in such a way that the future is indeed one's *own*. (*A Commentary on Heidegger's Being and Time*, rev. ed. [De Kalb: Northern Illinois University Press, 1989], 208)

182. Kartiganer, "Faulkner's Art of Repetition," 30.

183. See also Baudelaire's prose poem "The Evil Glazier" ("Mauvais vitrier"). I quote

from parts of that poem that seem applicable to Rodríguez's image and the concept of the poet's inspiration:

> There are natures which are purely contemplative and wholly unfit for action, which nevertheless, under a mysterious and unknown impulse, act sometimes with a rapidity of which they would never have considered themselves capable. . . . Such men sometimes feel themselves brusquely propelled into action by an irresistible force, like an arrow shot from a bow. The moralist and the doctor, who pretend to universal knowledge, cannot explain from whence so mad an energy suddenly springs in these idle and voluptuous souls, nor how, incapable of accomplishing the simplest and most necessary things, they find at a given moment a glorious courage for the execution of the most absurd and often the most dangerous actions.

The poem recounts the act of calling a glazier from "the foul and heavy atmosphere" of the streets of Paris to a sixth floor to examine his glass. When the speaker discovers, after careful examination, that the glazier has no rose- or blue-colored glass "through which one may see some beauty in life," he peremptorily throws the glazier back down the staircase to the street. The poem concludes with the statement, "But what matters an eternity of damnation to one who has found in a second an infinite joy?" (I have used the translation in Bernstein, *Baudelaire, Rimbaud, Verlaine*, 102–4.)

In "Mauvais vitrier," the color blue as an ideal that is both sought and found, the contrast between mundane reality and the "heavenly" (Edenic) sixth floor and other contrasts, the figure of the glazier and the (equivocal) search for beauty supply a provocative intertextual underpinning for Rodríguez's poem.

184. See Kartiganer's discussion of Mircea Eliade's sacred and profane, where he states that "the past verifies the present, provides the doubling context that rescues it from that singleness which, knowing only itself, knows nothing. . . . There is a structure here of interaction and exchange, a dependency whose result is neither meaninglessness nor old meaning but new meaning, meaning renewed, created now, for the millionth time and the first" ("Faulkner's Art of Repetition," 23, 31–32).

185. "What a difference of emotion exists / between the right furrow and the left one, / between that low branch and that high one! / Beauty anterior to all form / is making us in its own image."

186. "Repetition has a double nature in the work of Derrida. Repetition is at one and the same time that which stabilizes and guarantees the Platonic model of original and copy and that which threatens to undermine it. Repetition must always repeat originality, must always depend on some thing or idea which is by definition preexisting, autonomous and self-identical. Repetition is therefore subordinated to the idea of the original, as something secondary and inessential. . . . But if repetition is dependent upon a preexisting originality, it is also possible to turn this round and argue that originality is also dependent upon repetition. If repetition requires something that is already fixed and finished, already constituted as an essence, then it is equally true that originality or essence can never be apprehended as such unless the possibility exists for it to be copied or reiterated. The question 'How can you have a repetition without an original?' brings with it the less obvious question 'How can you have an original which it would be impossible to represent or duplicate?'" (Connor, *Samuel Beckett*, 3).

187. Martha Miller, "Elementos metapoéticos," 128.

188. "How (do) I see the trees now. / Not with falling leaves, not with branches / subject to the voice of growth. / And even the breeze that burns them in gusts / I feel it not as something of the land / or of the sky either, but lacking / in that pain of life with destiny."

189. See Freud's discussion of the repetition compulsion and its relation to death in *Beyond the Pleasure Principle*. As Kartiganer explains,

> For Freud, it is not enough for the death-drive simply to oppose the life-instincts. Rather, its function is to bind and control excitations in order that the individual can pass through life, taking 'ever

more complicated *détours'* on the way to death, experiencing difference in order to bend it back towards death. . . .

As Deleuze observes, the binding force of habit and repetition is not secondary to the pleasure principle; rather, pleasure must be seen as the product of repetition. Pleasure and unpleasure are therefore bound together, depending upon and successively producing each other, and providing another instance of the complex junction of difference and repetition discussed by Deleuze. . . . [R]epetition and the death-instinct do not stand against the pleasure principle in simple opposition, but enfold the pleasure principle within them, affirming life at the very moment of death, openness within the jaws of closure. . . . [F]inality is held back momentarily to allow the imminence of the ending to be relished. The text ends by repeating the fact of death in advance, ends by not ending. . . . ("Faulkner's Art of Repetition," 9–10)

This description recalls the relationship between metaphor and metonymy in "Libro segundo."

190. See note 3 above.

191. "The morning is not such, it is an ample / plain without combat, almost eternal, / almost unknown because in each / place where before time was a shadow, / now the light waits to be created. / Not only the air leaves more its breath: / it possesses neither canticle nor anything; / they are given to it, and it begins to move around it / with fleeting splendor of the rhythm of the wing / and tries to make a sufficient hollow / so as not to continue outside. No, not only / to continue outside perhaps, but at a distance. / Good and well: the air of today has its canticle. / If you could hear it! . . ."

192. My understanding of this process is that the poet—whether he remembers the precursor's exact words or not—retains his own personal emotional response to those words. That idiosyncratic response, dependent upon the poet-reader's individual life experiences, forms the nucleus of the new aesthetic expression, again whether the poet includes the precursor's words verbatim, elliptically, or indirectly. This metonymic displacement coincides completely with Rodríguez's approach to language in "Libro tercero." This phenomenon may be what Harold Bloom defines as a "strong reading" (see *Agon*, for example).

193. See Hillis Miller, *Fiction and Repetition*, 9–11. If we substitute the air for the sock and the bird for the gift inside the empty sack in the following passage, we get a glimpse of how Rodríguez conceives of language at the end of *Don*. The "ground" then would be "Cómo veo los árboles ahora," already another figure.

It is like a sock which is also an empty sack, but also at the same time a gift inside the sock, filling it, but also a sock again. The emblem turns on the oppositions, or rather counterparts, of inside/ outside; full/empty; waking/dream; remembering/forgetting; identity/similarity; container/thing contained. These pairs . . . function not as polar opposites but as differences which remain differences but can turn into one another. . . . The oddness [of the ratios established here] lies partly in the fact that the figure of the sock is an example of what it is supposed to clarify. It lies also partly in the difficulty of following out exactly what stands for what when the emblem is applied. . . . Each is clearly another form of the same object. The stocking is both the empty bag, sign of absence, and at the same time the precious contents of that bag, a present. As a present it is an object of value which is passed from one person to another and establishes the reciprocal interchange of gift-giving and gift-receiving between them. Such an interchange is a fundamental property of signs. . . . The obscurity of the similarity between the bag and the present lies in the fact that one cannot see through the similarity to its ground. This is true because the ground, namely the sock, is, literally, the possibility of being two apparently opposite things, both the container and what is contained, both the empty bag and the present. . . . From oneness to twoness, from figure to literal ground, the relation is continuously reversible. Each state of the object is both literal ground of the other and the figure of it.

194. ". . . And the sun, fire, water, / how they give possession to these eyes of mine. / Is it that I am going to live? Does the drunkenness end / so soon? Ay, and how I see now / the trees, how few day remain . . ."

195. See Herrnstein Smith, *Poetic Closure*.

CHAPTER 2. TRADITION AND THE IRONIC TALENT IN *CONJUROS* (1958)

1. In the introduction to Rodríguez's *Poesía 1953–1966*, "La poesía de Claudio Rodríguez," Carlos Bousoño erroneously affirms that a major change occurs in Rodríguez's poetic process between *Conjuros* and *Alianza y condena*. I have shown, however, that the major radical inversion of the poetic process occurs between *Don de la ebriedad* and *Conjuros*. In a recapitulative gesture, Rodríguez then returns to the process used in *Don* to begin *Alianza*. In "La trayectoria poética de Claudio Rodríguez (1953–1976): Análisis del ritmo," *Studia Zamorensia. Philologica* 8 (1987): 97–118, Luis García Jambrina has discussed the evolution of the use of metrics in Rodríguez's poetry.

2. Although commentators have called attention to Rodríguez's portrayal of typically Castilian scenes, they have also recognized that in *Conjuros* "el poema se convierte en una tensión que arranca siempre de algo muy concreto y en seguida asciende a otro plano trascendente" (Luis Jiménez Martos, "*Conjuros*" *Estafeta Literaria*, no. 164 [1959]: 19) [the poem becomes a tension that always starts off from something very concrete and suddenly ascends to another, transcendent plane]. Bousoño's definition of "realismo metafórico" underscores this tension:

> Acaso se me diga: el segundo libro de Claudio Rodríguez, *Conjuros*, está lleno de elementos rurales, de alusiones muy concretas a la vida de los pueblos y del campo castellanos; y eso, sin duda, se relaciona con el realismo de toda la poesía de la posguerra. A primera vista, no se puede negar que ello sea así. En *Conjuros* hallamos, al parecer, cosas tan cotidianas y costumbristas, y hasta domésticas y usaderas, como la ropa tendida, el fuego del hogar, una viga de mesón, una pared de adobe, la contrata de mozos, la labranza o el baile de las "águedas." Pero en cuanto apuramos nuestro análisis, nos percatamos de que ese realismo es sólo aparente y por de fuera: se aposenta exclusivamente en la primera capa del estilo, la más superficial, pues no es sino un medio para hablarnos de otra cosa que está detrás, metida, ella sí, en el entresijo y sustancia de tal estilo, lugar en que todo ese realismo y costumbrismo quedan como trascendidos, transfigurándose en su puesto: una consideración universal, sobrepasadora de cualquier concreción. . . .
>
> Nos hallamos, pues, ante lo que podríamos designar con una unión de contrarios: *realismo metafórico.* ("La poesía de Claudio Rodríguez," in Rodríguez, *Poesía, 1953–1966* [Barcelona: Plaza y Janés, 1971], 11–12, 13)

> [Perhaps someone will say to me: the second book of Claudio Rodríguez, *Conjuros*, is full of rural elements, of very concrete allusions to the life of the Castilian people and countryside; and that, without a doubt, is related to the realism of all the poetry of the postwar period. At first glance, one cannot deny that it is so. In *Conjuros* we find, apparently, things so quotidian and customary, and even domestic and useful, as clothes spread out to dry, fire in the hearth, the roofbeam of an inn, a wall of adobe, the contract of youths, field work, or the dance of Agathas. But if we persist in our analysis, we discover that that realism is only apparent and outward: it resides only in the first layer of style, the most superficial, but it is nothing but a way of speaking to us of something else that is behind, located, surely, in the interstices and substance of that style, where all that realism and custom become as if transcended, transfigured in its place: a universal consideration, going far beyond any concreteness. . . .
>
> We find ourselves, then, before what we could designate with a union of contraries: *metaphoric realism.*]

3. Cf. Heidegger's concept of the "thrownness" of *Dasein*, the unavoidable immersion in one's physical, cultural, and social context (*Dasein*'s "Being-in-the-world" and "Being-with-others").

4. For example, see my doctoral dissertation, "The Poetry of Claudio Rodríguez: Technique and Structure" (doctoral diss., University of Kansas, 1975); and Bousoño, "La poesía de Claudio Rodríguez."

5. Rodríguez has distributed the twenty-seven poems of *Conjuros* among four "Libros."

The first, second, and final sections consist of nine, eight, and eight poems, respectively; "Libro tercero" contains only two poems and represents a turning point in the process delineated in this work. This arrangement suggests a similarity with but expansion of the structure of *Don de la ebriedad*.

6. "Stop breathing, and let the earth breathe / you, let it burn you in its marvelous / lungs! Look / whoever may look, will he not see in the seasons / a trace as of air that is encouraged? / Death would be natural here. / One wouldn't even realize it / like light, like space, Death / by only breathing! . . ."

7. "Then Jesus said to his disciples, 'Whoever wishes to come after me must deny himself, take up his cross, and follow me. For whoever wishes to save his life will lose it, but whoever loses his life for my sake will find it. What profit would there be for one to gain the whole world and forfeit his life? Or what can one give in exchange for his life?'"

The motif of profit/loss is one that will occupy an ever greater place not only in *Conjuros* but in Rodríguez's later works as well.

8. D. C. Muecke, *The Compass of Irony* (London: Methuen & Co., 1969), 4.

9. Wayne Booth, *A Rhetoric of Irony* (Chicago and London: University of Chicago Press, 1974).

10. See Booth, *A Rhetoric of Irony*, 22–27, 176–78, for a discussion of this issue in the determination of the presence of irony.

11. And so following the advice of his mentor, Vicente Aleixandre (to whom the book is dedicated), to immerse himself in life. See "En la plaza" from *Historia del corazón* (1954).

> Cuando, en la tarde caldeada, solo en tu gabinete
> con los ojos extraños y la interrogación en la boca,
> quisieras algo preguntar a tu imagen,
>
>   no te busques en el espejo,
> en un extinto diálogo en que no te oyes.
> Baja, baja despacio y búscate entre los otros.
> Allí están todos, y tú entre ellos.
> Oh, desnúdate y fúndete, y reconócete.
>
>   (*Historia del corazón*, 2a ed. [Madrid: Espasa-Calpe, 1985], 64)

[When, in the heated afternoon, alone in your study / with eyes estranged and a question on your lips, / you would like to ask your image something, // don't look for yourself in the mirror, / in an extinct dialogue in which you don't hear yourself. / Go down, go down slowly and seek yourself in others. / Everyone is there, and you among them. / Oh, strip yourself and fuse yourself, and know yourself.]

That is precisely what most critics have concluded, that *Conjuros* is a book of "social" poetry and solidarity, so that they fail to perceive the irony and even sarcasm in the final poems of the work.

12. This is the most problematic step, given that we are questioning the author's identity in the very process of reading.

13. ". . . Would that it were day / now and I would remain without sensations / in these fields, and I would breathe / deeply like these trees, without noise. / That's why morning is still a flight / growing high over / the mountains, and an impulse skimming along the ground / that before it fuses and adopts / form it is already a furrow for new grain. / Oh, my chamber. . . ."

14. Also see the scientific concept of "noise," which I defined in the last half of *Don* in chapter 1 of this study.

15. Booth maintains that it is often difficult to pinpoint exactly why we perceive irony or if we should trust our perception that irony is present. We need more clues, to see a pattern of ironic clues that will confirm our intuitions (see Booth, "Is It Ironic?," chap. 3 of *A Rhetoric of Irony*, 47–86). I confess that I may be overreading the phrase "sin ruido."

16. ". . . What watering of the soul / this with which I give my life and gain / so many beautiful lives. Be calm / you who breath me, men and things. / I am yours. You are also mine. / How (do) the roses augment / their youth upon surrendering themselves. Open yourselves / to everything! The hay bursts in spring, / the pine tree gives health with its strong odor. / What a host, that of breath, what a way / of creating, what a clear workshop of death!"

17. "I don't know how I have lived / until now or in what body I have felt / but something lifts me to the day pure, / it communicates an immense heart to me, / like that of the plateau, and my magic spell / is that of the air, tense / because of the swollen breathing of the country / very near my soul in the moment / when I place life / on the voracious pace of any breath whatsoever."

18. "I have gone out so many times into the sun without realizing it. / Not one more day! Soon, as the market opens / or the workshop in the plaza, what task, what income / does today open to me. Go at my side / without any other gear than pure life, without anything but humility for equipment. / I won't wait any longer! Oh, be clothes spread out to dry. / Let the sun strike us and the old fruit / fall and serve as fertilizer / for the new season, and sustain it! / Replace your tools, heart, tenant farmer / of this terrain of mine. Let today be the winnowing, / let today be the raking of the flax / and let it soften us and may the grain be clean!"

19. See T. S. Eliot's essay "*Hamlet*" in *Selected Prose of T. S. Eliot*, ed. Frank Kermode (New York: Farrar, Straus and Giroux, 1975), 48.

20. See Antonio Núñez, "Encuentro con Claudio Rodríguez," *Insula*, no. 234 (1966): 4; and Dionisio Cañas, *Claudio Rodríguez*, 23.

21. Bonifacio Gil, comp., *Cancionero del campo (Antología)* (Madrid: Taurus, 1966).

22. Gil includes these topics: a preoccupation with time and weather; elements of nature (air, wind, water, clouds, mists, freezes, snow); the "Ciclo del trigo" [Wheat cycle]; different flowers, plants, and trees; the cultivation of grapes and the different types of wine; and varieties of birds.

23. Thomas Capuano has studied that aspect of Berceo's poetry in several articles and offers some intriguing insights into it that are applicable to Rodríguez's poetry. See my article "Medieval Models: Claudio Rodríguez and Early Spanish Literature," in *Estudios alfonsinos y otros escritos*, ed. Nicolás Toscano (New York: National Endowment for the Humanities, National Hispanic Foundation for the Humanities, 1991), 172–82, for a more complete discussion of this issue.

24. ". . . I'm going along my road / to the eternal yard, where in vain / I bathed in the sun with you so many times / without realizing. How many, many times / I waited for it to tan us beneath the surface of the skin. / It never went beyond that. I leave you, / you stay there. I'd like... / But not one more day! I advise you / that since you are fine like that, just be / with openness and faith. Why has this morning / come to give me such war, this sun to burn up what I have lost? / Cover your seed. Make a mound of earth. / Perhaps you will mature and you will have done your job."

25. I disagree with Bruflat's interpretation of "solana" as a "greenhouse."

26. Riffaterre, *Semiotics of Poetry*, 100.

27. The word "title" comes from the Latin "titulus" meaning "inscription, label, title, sign." See Jack Myers and Michael Simms, *The Longman Dictionary of Poetic Terms* (New York and London: Longman, 1989), s.v. "title."

28. Charles Mills Gayley, *The Classic Myths in English Literature and in Art*, rev. and enl. ed. (Boston: Ginn, 1939), 351.

29. See Robert Graves, *The Greek Myths* (Baltimore: Penguin Books, 1955), 2:212–15; and Edith Hamilton, *Mythology* (New York: Mentor Books, 1942), 294.

30. Hamilton, *Mythology*, 294.

31. Graves, *The Greek Myths*, 2:213.

32. Gayley, *The Classic Myths*, 103; H. J. Rose, *A Handbook of Greek Mythology: Including Its Extension to Rome*, 5th ed. (London: Methuen, 1953), 200.

33. Graves, *The Greek Myths*, 2:213–14. Another version of this myth has very little to do with Rodríguez's poem. In that version, Linus is the music teacher of Hercules, who, frustrated by his own lack of musical ability, kills Linus by striking him in the head with a lyre. This version may refer to a lack of skill which the poet laments. This tangential version of the myth mirrors the duality in the title, especially the aspect of the title as label estranged from the body of the poem.

34. "No matter how sunny it may be you will not be pure / and there is no longer any time. The air / is barely moving and with the light of day, / still far away in the hills, the country opens up / and man rises to his labor. / And see: The best hour. And what has happened / so that today in full season we / only remember that sowing, / that threshing, those tillings? / The harvest is nothing but the beginning!"

35. See Cirlot, *A Dictionary of Symbols*, 105–6.

36. Ibid., 271–72.

37. Retrospectively, the myth of Linus suggests similarities with Christ, but these similarities are apparent only after reading the poem and recognizing the biblical allusions. Myers and Simms, *The Longman Dictionary of Poetic Terms,* might call this a "layered title," although it does not fit their definition exactly.

38. Rodríguez dedicated *Conjuros* to Aleixandre who, as an established poet, gave generous help to younger poets such as Rodríguez.

39. See Wheelwright, *Metaphor and Reality*, 112.

40. "Away with the sickle, yes, away with / the short embrace of the tools even when / all the earth is hope! Always, / like the good worker who each year / sees his wheat grow tall and believes / that only his work put the grain there, / we always go out to await day / with our task on our backs, and we place / our life, our chest in the air and for a moment / we are pure to the air. But only / for a moment. . . ."

41. "Amen, amen, I say to you, unless a grain of wheat falls to the ground and dies, it remains just a grain of wheat; but if it dies, it produces much fruit."

42. "He said, 'This is how it is with the kingdom of God; it is as if a man were to scatter seed on the land and would sleep and rise night and day and the seed would sprout and grow, he knows not how. Of its own accord the land yields fruit, first the blade, then the ear, then the full grain in the ear. And when the grain is ripe, he wields the sickle at once, for the harvest has come.'"

43. "Everything is sacred now and it even seems / simple to prosper on this earth, / to load the carts with the same hay / of youth, to carry it / over that same bridge. But, where, / in which immense haystack will the fodder / of man fit, those heaps / that may even still be fresh? / Where, where? . . . / . . . / Where the thrush that would leave / from there with the open humility of its flight / as if it could still return always? / It will not return. I know well what I have lost."

44. See Russell P. Sebold, ed., *Gustavo Adolfo Bécquer* (Madrid: Taurus, 1982), 11–13.

45. "You first, / you, the elect of the seasons, / he of the great farming, come with me. / Teach me to sow in the direction / of the wind. . . . / . . . / But you, dance, triumph, you who can. / Let's not say it. No, let no one know / what has happened this morning. We go along / together. Don't say more than that your harvest, / though it be in your farmyard, at the foot of your house, / will never be yours."

46. These words foreshadow the last two poems in *Conjuros*, "El baile de águedas" and "Pinar amanecido," and prefigure the stance to which the poet and speaker will arrive.

47. Cf. the reference to the sun in the first verse of "El canto de linos." There exists a constant play on the image of the sun in these verses.

48. See Charles Caldwell Ryrie, *The Ryrie Study Bible: King James Version* (Chicago: Moody Press, 1978), 944.

49. Chevalier and Gheerbrant affirm that "la labranza es un acto sagrado. . . . Pues sobre todo es la toma de posesión y la fecundación de la tierra virgen por parte del hombre trascendente, intermediario entre cielo y tierra" (*Diccionario de los símbolos* [Barcelona: Herder, 1991],

622) [field work is a sacred act. . . . For above all it is a taking of possession and a fecundation of the virgin earth by transcendent man, intermediary between sky and earth].

50. "And as I saw / that I was so popular amid the streets, / I crossed the bridge and, farewell, I left all behind. / But even here it comes to me, take it away, I am always / hearing that noise and I ascend and ascend, / I walk from town to town, I place my ear / on the flight of the linnet, on the sun, on the air, / whatever, on the sky, on the breast of young women / and always the same sound, the same change. / What siege this without respite? What lofty combats enter to sack my soul at all hours, / overcome the tower of the white flag, / open that breach, the silent one, / the one never false? And it is / you, music of the river, my deep breath, / simplicity and voice and pulse of my men."

51. "How much better it would be / to wait. Today I can't, today I am hard / of hearing after the years that I have spent / with those of the evil earth. But I have returned. / Field of truth, what betrayal was there? / Hear how we have had day after day / so much purity at our side, at home, / and we have continued deaf! / Not even this afternoon now! Welcome, / morning. I'm early: Be my witnesses / you who still hear! Oh, river / founder of cities, / resounding in all except in your bed, / make your noise be our song, our workshop in life. And if some day / solitude, seeing man for sale, / wine, bad love, or discouragement / assault that which you have well made yours, / put yourself like today in a warlike stance, guard / all my doors and windows as / you have always done, / you, to whom I am listening just as back then, / you, river of my land, you, Lasting River."

52. See Riffaterre, *Semiotics of Poetry*, esp. chap. 4, "Interpretants" (81–114), for a definition of the dual sign.

53. Cirlot, *A Dictionary of Symbols*, 274.

54. Debicki, *Poetry of Discovery: The Spanish Generation of 1956–71* (Lexington: University Press of Kentucky, 1982), 42–47.

55. As a child, I remember my mother putting lemon juice on stains on white clothes and spreading them on the grass in our back yard. Need I comment again on the implications of the sun as metapoetic symbol in this passage?

56. Note the similarity between my discussion of dialogic tension and Debicki's description.

57. Debicki, *Poetry of Discovery*, 44–46.

58. Riffaterre, *Semiotics of Poetry*, 2.

59. "Don't spread it out in the patio: there, on the peak, / clothing trod by the sun and the rooster, / by the king always!"

60. Debicki, *Poetry of Discovery*, 44.

61. Riffaterre, *Semiotics of Poetry*, 136.

62. Cirlot, *A Dictionary of Symbols*, 51–52. Wheelwright notes that the cock has a "long recognized symbolic plurisignation. . . . He has four characteristics that have set him off by their symbolic suggestiveness: his faithful crowing at the end of each night to usher in the dawn, his red comb which is an ancient icon of the sun supplemented by a later reference to Christ's redeeming blood, his noisy sexuality (hence, by free symbolic logic, his potency) which he expresses by crowing in triumph after coition with a hen, and finally the Gospel story of the cock's crow in relation to Peter's denial of Christ" (*Metaphor and Reality*, 108). These symbolic properties have metapoetic dimensions in Rodríguez's poem as well as encompassing the tension between two levels of meaning (the concrete and the abstract, the sexual as both carnal and spiritual act).

63. Miguel de Cervantes Saavedra, *Don Quijote de la Mancha*, texto y notas de Martín de Riquer (Barcelona: Juventud, 1966), 685 n. 19.

64. Riffaterre, *Semiotics of Poetry*, 82.

65. See Matthew Bailey's article on "Lexical Ambiguity in Four Poems of Juan del Encina," *Romance Quarterly* 36 (1989): 431–43; and my article "Medieval Models."

66. The use of the colloquial phrase "¡No tendedla!" is intentional. See García Jambrina, "La poesía viva: El elemento oral y popular en la obra poética de Claudio Rodríguez," *Anuario*

del Instituto de Estudios Zamoranos "Florián de Ocampo" (1988): 491–99, for discussion of idiomatic language in Rodríguez's poetry.

67. "I have said this at mid-dawn / because again I find it, / again in the open air hale and hardy. / It was in the river, surely, in that river / where everything is washed, below the bridge. / It smells like the very water, like my body. / And now without a stain! If there is some brave one, / let him put it on! I know that it would drown him."

68. "I know well that in the depth of my heart it is not white / but who cares: One day . . . / What, one day, today, tomorrow which is a holiday! / Tomorrow with everyone in town in the streets / and they will recognize it and they will say, 'This / is his shirt, that one, the one that was / only a patch and already was useless. / What is this love? Who is his washerwoman?'"

69. Cf. Ramón J. Sender: "La boda fue como todos esperaban. Gran comida, música y baile. Antes de la ceremonia muchas camisas blancas estaban ya manchadas de vino al obstinarse los campesinos en beber en bota" (*Réquiem por un campesino español*, 13th ed. [Madrid: Destinolibro, 1986], 53) [The wedding was as everyone expected. A great feast, music and dance. Before the ceremony many white shirts were already stained with wine because of the farmhands' inveterate custom of drinking from a wineskin].

70. Chevalier and Gheerbrandt, *Diccionario de los símbolos*, 630. [The washerwoman is . . . a woman of the lower class. The tantrism has made of the washerwoman an important symbol, on one hand by associating the pertinence to an inferior class of the sexual deprivation judged necessary—symbolically or not—for the execution of certain rites. . . . The union of the wise man and the washerwoman, exalted by the texts, figures thus as a "coincidence of opposites," an alliance of extremes, a true alchemical operation. The paradox is therefore more than apparent, if the washerwoman is associated with wisdom and if her dance symbolizes the ascension of the wise man.] Cirlot adds that "Their nature is contradictory: they fulfil humble tasks, yet possess extraordinary powers. . . . Their powers, however, are not simply magical, but are rather the sudden revelation of latent possibilities . . ." (*A Dictionary of Symbols*, 101).

71. It was not until I read "Lluvia y gracia" carefully and investigated the word "Palencia" that I discovered another aspect of the "lavandera" who uses a wooden instrument to beat the dirt and excess water out of the clothing she washes. Metonymically, her action symbolizes a punishment meted out to the speaker, in accord with the verb "refregar" in v. 1 of "A mi ropa tendida." See the discussion of "Lluvia y gracia" in chapter 3.

72. Booth, *A Rhetoric of Irony*, 210.

73. "I see the stars, this roofbeam / lets the light pass through and doesn't hold up / even the house! Roofbeam / wide open to the brilliance that comes / and to the harsh task / of man, who has placed so many dreams under it, so much good / hope. Thus, thus. Not to have felt / the smoke of the city or the worker's hand! / Always thus. . . ."

74. "Why do you notice the splinter in your brother's eye, but do not perceive the wooden beam in your own eye? How can you say to your brother, 'Let me remove that splinter from your eye,' while the wooden beam is in your eye? You hypocrite, remove the wooden beam from your eye first; then you will see clearly to remove the splinter from your brother's eye." The Spanish version of this passage includes the word "viga": "¿Por qué miras la brizna de paja que está en el ojo de tu hermano, y dejas de ver la viga que está en tu propio ojo?"

75. "Oh, buttress / of the sky, immense eave, roofbeam that was / only a moment ago a lifeless trunk, / you, be, be the roof / for all men some day!"

76. "It is beginning to grow light. As if at a peak / I am looking at it. Listen: It would fall / on top of me, it would fall on me until I were / worthy of being beneath it and I wouldn't leave / here! . . ."

77. ". . . But, can anyone, does anyone hope / to be worthy, to raise his love on his work, / his shelter on his ground, / his roof on the decay of here below / in which there trembles now a nest of the sky?"

78. "'No one can serve two masters. He will either hate one and love the other or be devoted to one and despise the other. You cannot serve God and mammon.

"'Therefore I tell you, do not worry about your life, what you eat [or drink], or about your body, what you will wear. Is not life more than food and the body more than clothing? Look at the birds in the sky; they do not sow or reap, they gather nothing into barns, yet your heavenly Father feeds them. Are not you more important than they? Can any of you by worrying add a single moment to your life-span?"

79. "And you brush my forehead, / and enter through the lots as well as through the sky / and you make your nests here noisily, / among men? What thirst flight must have / of earth. Higher, higher. Don't let this body / feel you, don't let these noises hear / anything pure! When will you notice / the sun, that that wall / seeks your warmth. Perforate it / now, put your chest deeply into it / like mud in the nest; otherwise / abandon it! Oh, higher, higher. . . ."

80. ". . . Where, where shall I hide? / Here, in full shriek, in the full afternoon / of June, in my city? And how many times / toting this sky that burns so much / I saw you enter humble things, how many times I wanted to distance myself from you. Now / it is very different. Go away! Why today is there nothing that flees? / What are you still seeking if man ignores / that you live next to him and to his work / you give your blue chore / benefiting his labor, his grain / and his crops? . . ."

81. ". . . But let it be / always thus and though there is no light and in vain / you try to sustain it in open fire, / go ahead, / come down without discouragement. It was already / necessary to alight. How I awaken / hearing you. Come lower! . . ."

82. ". . . If I could / detain you, pose you here, make you / pure targets of the air. . . . If I could / say what afternoons, what mornings of mine / have been won. . . . Thanks, I give you thanks with my gaze / because you have brought me those days, / you, who can come and go without losing anything."

83. ". . . but he said to me, 'My grace is sufficient for you, for power is made perfect in weakness.' I will rather boast most gladly of my weaknesses, in order that the power of Christ may dwell with me. Therefore, I am content with weaknesses, insults, hardships, persecutions, and constraints for the sake of Christ; for when I am weak, then I am strong."

84. "Enough, wandering feet, / you aren't stepping on grapes, get going, march. / What are you doing in this street, / here, in the street of my mischief? / It might be better for you to walk through other neighborhoods. / Always so badly guided, / how weren't you going to fall. It's a trap, / a trap. What snare is this? / Who set it so well that it's not missing / a piece and today in the afternoon / this sidewalk as well as that balcony hunt me? / The season opened forever, and always, / after three flights, the partridge to ground."

85. "Main street of my hope, may there sound / in you the steps of my life, open / your dovecote and let them loose, / let them loose in the open air, / let everyone play with them in chorus, / let them sing without rhyme or reason, let them sing and dance / letting it all out! See, see how / that doorway is the bottomless wine cask / where my childhood ferments, and the other, / always full of little girls, my granary / of youth, and the other, the other, the other..."

86. Rodríguez wrote his dissertation on the children's "corro"; see his article "Viendo jugar al corro," which I discuss in chapter 4 below. Also cf. jump rope songs and games like "Red Rover" in American society.

87. *DRAE*, 1292. "A familiar and figurative adverbial locution, according to a supernatural order, counting on the will of God."

88. "Mr. Mayor, listen, Mr. Mayor, / don't ever let them pave it, don't let anyone / step on it except those of the land / of well-made bread and dark wine! / Pardon me, but whoever wants can go down the street / and I shouldn't talk like that. What fine / would they impose on me now, me first, / if they were to see how lame, / how vagrantly I have walked since then. / I halt, I halt my steps."

89. Chevalier and Gheerbrant, *Diccionario de los símbolos*, 315–16. "To limp is a sign of debility. It is equivalent also to finishing, in order to begin again: it is the absence of repose, the inconclusive, disequilibrium. In myths, legends, and stories, the lame hero finishes a cycle that could be expressed by the end of a journey and the announcement of another new one. The

lame one evokes the declining sun, or also the sun of the end and the beginning of the year. . . . To limp, from a symbolic point of view, signifies a spiritual defect. Such a defect is not necessarily of a moral order; it can designate an wound of the spiritual order."

90. Ibid., 316. In "A las estrellas," the second poem of "Libro primero," the speaker exclaims, "Y así, marcadme estrellas, como a una res. ¡Que el fuego / me purifique!" (72) [And thus, mark me, stars, like cattle. May the fire purify me!]. Cf. Miguel Hernández, *El rayo que no cesa*: "Como el toro he nacido para el luto / y el dolor, como el toro estoy marcado / por un hierro infernal en el costado / y por varón en la ingle con un fruto" (poem 23) [Like the bull I have been born for mourning / and grief, like the bull I am marked by the infernal iron on my flank / and as a male on the thigh with a fruit]. Rodríguez is very familiar with Hernández's poetry, which evinces many similar images as Rodríguez's. See his address of induction into the Real Academia de la Lengua, *Poesía como participación: hacia Miguel Hernández* (Madrid: Real Academia Española, 1992).

91. "Then those years / what a badly sown trousseau for the house, / what shineless earrings for the great wedding. / Let each stone be like a hot coal for me. / You who are there, in the sun, throw me out, throw me out. / Then I will return when / my heart gets in rhythm with these / steps that I invoke, / that I am hearing today in the afternoon / resound on this sidewalk, / in this alleyway that leads to life."

92. "Can a man take fire to his bosom, / and his garments not be burned? / Or can a man walk on live coals, / and his feet not be scorched?" (Prov. 6:27–28).

93. Could this perhaps be a reference to Rodríguez's father who died when the poet was only twelve years old?

94. "'Enter through the narrow gate; for the gate is wide and the road broad that leads to destruction, and those who enter through it are many. How narrow the gate and constricted the road that leads to life. And those who find it are few.'"

95. Walter Brueggemann, *Toward Praying the Psalms: Letting Experience Touch the Psalter* (Winona, Minn.: St. Mary's College Press, 1979).

96. Cf. Psalms 1, 32, 41, 112, 119, and 128, among many other Biblical passages.

97. "Happy the man who one fine day goes out humbly / and walks down the street, like so many / other days of his life, and doesn't expect it / and, suddenly, what's this?, looks up / and sees, places his ear to the world and hears, / walks, and feels the love of the earth rise / amid his steps, and continues, and opens / his true workplace, and in his hands / his trade clearly shines, and he hands it to us / from his heart because he loves, and he goes to work / trembling as a child taking communion / but without fitting into his skin, and when / he has realized at last how simple / everything has been, now with his wages earned, / he returns home happily and feels that someone / grasps his doorknocker, and it is not in vain."

98. See Angel Prieto de Paula, "Claudio Rodríguez entre la iluminación y la muerte," *Insula*, nos. 444–45 (1983): 7–8.

99. "Therefore, my beloved brethren, be ye stedfast, unmoveable, always abounding in the work of the Lord, forasmuch as ye know that your labour is not in vain in the Lord."

100. ". . . To have felt / the purity of the world to now contribute to this season, to the noise / of these feet! Why does the hour of watering / always arrive?"

101. ". . . Although it may be summer / and here, it arrives so strongly / that it doesn't calm, it doesn't cloud the sun, it gives the plain / another even deeper drought. What death / because of excess, passing / cloud that was going to save that which it now razes."

102. "Pierce, pierce us more. Let what was / dust rise in the water that is amassed / with earth, that is earth now and pure / punishment from on high! And what matter if it impede the threshing or burn the wheat / if it made us believe that it was life."

103. At the time I was writing this chapter, Rodríguez had not yet published *Casi una leyenda* (1991), where the poem "Manuscrito de una respiración" employs a similar ventriloquism as "El «Cerro de Montamarta» dice." See chapter 5 below.

104. I have punctuated the title of this poem as it appears in the Plaza y Janés edition of Rodríguez's works as it helps us see the disjunction between the speaker and the poet.

105. See Victor Shklovsky's discussion of defamiliarization in "Art as Technique" in *Russian Formalist Criticism*, Lee T. Lemon and Marion J. Reis, trans. and eds. (Lincoln: University of Nebraska Press, 1965), 3–24.

106. "A day will come when I reach the cloud. / Lift me, mornings, or burn me up! What setting / of the sun will bring the light that still doesn't raise me / or drive me? What night will lift in this / blind plain of mine the land to the skies? / All the air loves me / and opens around me, and does not rest."

107. ". . . So many / suns I opened to their eyes, so many months, in pure / rotation I brought near to their bodies, so many / days I was their horizon. Still there remains in their souls / my labor, like their clear deaths in mine."

108. "And now the afternoon loses light and there is nocturnal / calm. Let everything all around / awaken for the last time / come to me, and understand the deep / strength of love in my arid profile, / of the anxiety that someone put in my slope! / See that there are hills with snow, / with streams, with pines, with flowers in the spring. / See that I am naked, being only an immense / volcano toward the air. And my height is so little. / A plow, a plow so intense / that it can make my rock fructiferous, / that it may stir up my grain for me / and I may give it to you, and you may understand my life!"

109. See Chevalier and Gheerbrandt, *Diccionario de los símbolos*, 115, who say that the symbol of the plow as pen was used by many medieval writers.

110. "For I will be here only for a moment. In vain / am I all the mountains of the world. In vain, with night / gone the dawn will return again / and the color gray and red. Then when / just as a wave I advance / toward the sea of the skies, toward you, man, who now / contemplates me, you won't know it. There will be no one to see me, / who could walk all over me with his soaring feet, / who would purify in me love and work / as I purify the aroma of the crops."

111. "If I could reach the passing cloud / with the tension of my eyes, how would / its brilliance leave me on the earth? / How would it leave me obscured / if its labor is clear, and its material / is almost light, is at least on high? / Take away that limpid bonework / leaving exposed an airy heart, / strong with its stormy pulse! / What fulminating life and death. Let it be / like that also in my body! In pure assault / take it from me, make of it your task!"

112. "If it were to approach me, if it would inundate / my life with its life so intense. / I wouldn't resist it. But, could / anyone be worthy of it? Doesn't the cloud / strive to die in so much space / in order to incendiate it all at once? Surrender, / pure word of the skies, hymn: / Sound like the voice of man, sound / and pass, pass thus, tell us your vivid / truth in this clear earthly hour, / in this dark life that flees and passes / and never in that will be able to see the immense, / lone happiness of here below, cloud, / soul perhaps in which a body grows calm."

113. "And where are the clouds of other days, / in which immortal spring sky? / The blank space in which they were, does it still / feel its company and go with it / creating a new brilliance, just / as in the middle of the night on the plains there remains / all the impulse of dawn? / Far from where man has sold out, / that granary, for which harvest?"

114. "Oh, cloud that flees and changes with each instant / as if the highest town of bees / were there working in clean fire. / Cloud that is born without pain, so near. / And to live in the most beautiful place / for this, to fall to earth / or disappear! It doesn't matter how / but now, that cloud there, that one / that is ours and is there, if not to inhabit it, / now, who might at least retain it."

115. See Cirlot, *A Dictionary of Symbols;* and Chevalier and Gheerbrandt, *Diccionario de los símbolos*.

116. As noted above, the passage from Matthew reads: "Then Jesus said to his disciples, 'Whoever wishes to come after me must deny himself, take up his cross, and follow me. For whoever wishes to save his life will lose it, but whoever loses his life for my sake will find it.

What profit would there be for one to gain the whole world and forfeit his life? Or what can one give in exchange for his life?'"

117. *Pequeño Larousse Ilustrado 1992*, s.v. "retener."

118. Booth defines unstable ironies as "ironies in which the truth asserted or implied is that no stable reconstruction can be made out of the ruins revealed through the irony. The author—insofar as we can discover him, and he is often very remote indeed—refuses to declare himself, however subtly, *for* any stable proposition, even the opposite of whatever proposition his irony vigorously denies. . . . What we do with a work, or what it does with us, will depend on our decision, conscious or unconscious, about whether we are asked by it to push through its confusions to some final point of clarity or to see through it to a possibly infinite series of further confusions. No other step in the never completed process of mastering the arts of interpretation is more important than discovering how and when to cross and recross this borderline with agility and confidence" (*A Rhetoric of Irony*, 240–42).

119. "But that's my sister and she is sewing in the inner room / so peacefully and, suddenly, / poof!, the sun strikes her and a simple ray / threads her, and in it she remains well-stitched, / a white point in the light of the world! / and, close the windows!, that ray, / eternal yeast, falls right on top / of us, and ferments us, and in it congeals / our doughy heart and, like / the insurrection of a people, / it expands, advances, covers / all the earth now, it weaves and unweaves / the hostile tow of man and there, as one, / in the inn of time, always expensive, / there, at the door, in the beautiful loom, / we are weaving, warping / the shirt of God, the clean gown / of life and death. . . ."

120. Cirlot points out that spinning, sewing, and other domestic tasks of this sort pertain to fairies, who have special powers. See n. 70 above.

121. Rodríguez has commented upon this similarity (personal communication).

122. A passage from Saul Bellow's novel, *Humboldt's Gift* (New York: Viking Press, 1973), supports this view: "Must the imagination be asked to give up its own full and free connection with the universe—the universe as Goethe spoke of it? As the living garment of God?" (344). The reference to Goethe can be found in Part I Scene I of *Faust*:

SPIRIT.
In the tides of Life, in Action's storm,
A fluctuant wave,
A shuttle free,
Birth and the Grave,
An eternal sea,
A weaving, flowing
Life, all-glowing,
Thus at Time's humming loom 't is my hand prepares
The garment of Life which the Deity wears!

(Johann Wolfgang von Goethe, *Faust: A Tragedy* [New York: The Modern Library, 1950], 20)

123. ". . . But, now, / what happens?: When I was / seeing hung from the sky / the immortal banner, as in the days / of festival in my city there hangs the red and yellow / banner, hear me, when / I saw that immense canvas in which each / light thread is an entire life / occupy space, / here is a breath, a tenuous breeze, / afterward a clear voice / arises, and with such spirit, / with such metal that voice sounds now / that thread by thread singing it unravels / one life, another, another, / of that great gown, and one hears something like a hymn, / listen, and suddenly . . ."

124. Recall the initial reaction to impressionist painting or Picasso's desire to shock his viewers. Also consider Robert Mapplethorp's photographs, Madonna's videos, Two Live Crew and "rap" music in general, the American flag on the floor of the Chicago Art Institute, a comic strip such as "Doonesbury," or a film like *Boyz N the Hood*.

125. Rodríguez may also be responding to Bousoño's definition of a "visión." See "La visión," in *Teoría de la expresión poética*, 2a ed. (Madrid: Gredos, 1952), 95–100. Throughout this study I refer to the second edition of Bousoño's constantly expanding *Teoría* because it would have been the edition with which Rodríguez was most familiar as he was beginning his poetic career.

126. Cirlot, *A Dictionary of Symbols*, 71–72.

127. Chevalier and Gheerbrandt, *Diccionario de los símbolos*, 391. "Demiurge and civilizing hero, clairvoyant and prophet, solar and at the same time shadowy bird, it announces misfortune and death and at times protects."

128. "Because now we're playing for keeps, because my life goes / in it! If other days / you heard my shrill around this temple, / forget it. Because now / you will not see this grackle / peck the egg or sack the nest! / Now never snacking, / never seeking the provisions, / the pack-saddles of man, / because there was nothing there but ruinous sauce. / Hear me, thicket, air, / mallow, little thistle, salvia, millet, oregano, / you, my jealous mate, / all, hear me: that was never / my life. Bad leisure."

129. ". . . Leave me / where I am now, on the beautiful transept / of youth. And I see / the crenellations in light of hope / above, always above. / I pass the sheafed arch, festival sash, / and the flowered capital. Let the dance / go on, go on! More, maids, spring, / soul of man! And you, go on a spree, / wind of so many years. / Let this day fall like a fruit / of freedom. Remember / our golden wanderings, / you, remember, remember / the fleeting happiness / of men, their festival / so poor in days and so rich in time."

130. Ironically, the word "crucero" is more popularly used to mean a "cruise," playing "the beautiful cruise of youth" (illusion) and "the beautiful transept of youth" (crucifixion), death and resurrection, against one another.

131. ". . . Let the suffocation / begin now, for I carry / my crop badly filled as in time / of change, for barely / does my down stir! Who has placed / in the shaft of each of my feathers the harsh / gray marrow of discouragement? . . ."

132. "What a swell, what an immense squall / pounds my keel, breaks my steering / plumage. This grackle, / this ship takes on water. I want to return, / I want to return, to fly again with my mate. / Yes, festive assembly of the afternoons, / ah, companions, where, / where are you that I don't hear you? / It doesn't matter. I will arrive. From the dome / I will see better. And now, / up one lane and down the other, in which air, / by which road do I go? Because now I don't / even see, because I founder and crash / against the rock, against / the walls of this temple, of this homeland!"

133. "Children, come, tie me up, / I prefer that you tie my feet with your / blue line of purity! Quiet, / I would like to be at peace for a moment. / I will arrive. I will arrive. There is my life, / there is the altar, there shines my people. / A little more. Now almost . . . / You, good breath, go on / a little more, upsy-daisy, heart, only a little . . . / Thus, thus . . . Now, now . . . What bad luck! / Just for so little! A grackle here, now on the ground."

134. See Cirlot, *A Dictionary of Symbols*.

135. "Let's close now! Let's go quickly to another / fair where there is a good market, where / people bargain, and cheat, and grasp / our grape with their hands, and give it a feel / to see if it's overripe! For what other reason / have we come here but to sell ourselves? / And today there is credit, come, for today we aren't charging anything."

136. "We have come thus to this plaza always, / with the hope of one who offers his work, / his youth to the air. And only the air is going to be our client? Without a parish / will he continue, he who is for hire, he who comes to pay his income? Prosperous / was our merchandise in another time, / when the land bought everything from us. / Then, far from this plaza, then, / in the market of light. See now / in what good that resulted. Contract, / servile exchange, theater of dishonor."

137. "See here the young people. Let's see, who will buy / this one of few years, of the land

/ of bread, of good kidneys, of sober hand / for reaping; this other, from the land / of wine, somewhat of a balladeer, of such short / height and so strong an arm, he who produces most / in the commotion of transport? Dirt / cheap!"

138. "And no one is coming, and soon / the June sun will have set. Prosperous / was our merchandise in another time. / But wait, don't remember now. / Our fair is here! If not today, tomorrow; / if not tomorrow, one day. What matters / is that they will come, they will come from everywhere, / from a thousand towns around the world, from remote / homelands the great buyers will come, / those of the clean warehouse. . . . / . . . / and thus one morning and another have passed / but our grape does not soften, always, / it is always in its prime, it's never overripe. / Be calm, I hear them. There, there they come."

139. "He will always be my friend not the one who in spring / goes out into the country and loses himself amid the blue festivity / of the men who love, and doesn't see the old leather / beneath the new growth of fur, but you, true // friendship, celestial pedestrian, you, who in winter / at the break of dawn leave your house and begin / to walk, and in our cold weather find eternal shelter / and in our deep drought, the voice of harvests."

140. "You have heard that it was said, 'You shall love your neighbor and hate your enemy.' But I say to you, love your enemies, and pray for those who persecute you, that you may be children of your heavenly Father, for he makes his sun rise on the bad and the good, and causes rain to fall on the just and the unjust. For if you love those who love you, what recompense will you have? Do not the tax collectors do the same? And if you greet your brothers only, what is unusual about that? Do not the pagans do the same? So be perfect, just as your heavenly Father is perfect."

141. Grimal remarks that Quirinus was "A very early Roman god, one of the three archaic divinities whose worship made up the Indo-European background of Roman religion. In hierarchical order, he was the last of the three, behind Jupiter and Mars." Although some sources assert that Quirinus was a god of war, "The modern scholar G. Dumézil has put forward the hypothesis that Quirinus, far from being originally a god of war, was essentially the protector of farmers" (Pierre Grimal, *The Concise Dictionary of Classical Mythology*, ed. Stephen Kershaw, trans. A. R. Maxwell-Hyslop [Oxford: Basil Blackwell, 1986], 384). "Some of the functions of the priest of Quirinus were directed towards the worship of rural divinities, notably Consus, a god whose rites were celebrated by placing garlands of flowers around the necks of draught animals, horses, asses and mules, which were spared from work on the day of his feast" (105).

In the epithalamic song of the second act of *Bodas de sangre*, Federico García Lorca, who also evoked many popular beliefs and customs in his writings, exploits a similar image. The epithalamic purpose of this passage emphasizes the loss of virginity (a type of death), and fertility and production (the creation of life), the same contrast seen in Rodríguez's ironic reversals and interaction between the concrete and the symbolic throughout *Conjuros*, but particularly in "Libro cuarto."

142. "Let no one speak of death in this town! / Out of the neighborhood of the cypress this very day / on which the children are going to toss the branch, / to toss death into the river! / Come out of your houses: Let's go see it! / See that it goes there, look at it, see that it is child's / play! So much fear / for this. Throw, throw rocks at it / that goes there, that goes there. Yes, what matters / is that it be far away. . . ."

143. See Mikhail Bakhtin, *Rabelais and His World*, trans. Hélène Iswolsky (Bloomington: Indiana University Press, 1984); and Julio Caro Baroja, *El carnaval: Análisis histórico-cultural*, 2a ed. (Madrid: Taurus, 1979).

144. "Do you remember now / how the eternal fleet / of stars upon the water / sails every night, high invincible / armada?"

145. ". . . That branch / on the surface of the water also, on the surface of life! / Let no one stay at home today! To the river, / for there goes the branch, there goes death / more flower-laden than ever!"

146. See the final section of *Casi una leyenda* where Rodríguez revives this image in the almond trees and the figure of Marialba.

147. *Pequeño Larousse Ilustrado 1992*, s.v. "florido."

148. ". . . Now you can't see it. God knows / if it will return, but this year / will be springlike in our town."

149. See Riffaterre, *Semiotics of Poetry*, 99–105.

150. Cirlot, *A Dictionary of Symbols*, 76.

151. Gustavo Correa, ed., *Poesía Española del Siglo Veinte, Antología* (New York: Appleton-Century-Crofts, 1972), 511 n. 3. "A dance to celebrate the feast of St. Agatha . . . that takes place the fifth of February. . . . In the province of Zamora in Spain, there exist associations of women called 'águedas' who organize the festival. In the dance on the appointed day, the women invite the men to dance." See also Caro Baroja, *El carnaval*, 372–76.

152. Debicki, *Poetry of Discovery*, 47–48.

153. "They are already there, they are already coming / down the lane with the sun of hope, / men from everywhere. / I am in the middle / of the festival and almost already / the early night of February congeals."

154. *Webster's New World Dictionary,* 3d college ed., s.v. "February."

155. How many cloaks, how many white stockings, / how many soft woolen sashes, how many / short trousers. Very lively, like / that young woman places her kerchief, / put your soul like that, very lively!"

156. Debicki, *Poetry of Discovery*, 48.

157. "I miss now / those times when to his festivals / man joined himself like whey to cheese. / Then, yes, they gave / their life to the sun, their breath to the air, then, / yes, they were incarnate in the earth."

158. "Listen to me, you, who now / pass by my side and one moment, / without noticing, you look on high / and there descends to your heart / the eternal dance of the Agathas of the world, / listen to me, you, who know / that the festival is coming to an end and you can't / keep it at home like a clean tool kit, / and it slips away, and now never . . . / you, who tread the earth / and squeeze your partner, and dance, dance."

159. See Bruflat, "Ambivalence and Reader Response," 46; Debicki, *Poetry of Discovery*, 7.

160. "Traveler, you never / will forget if you tread these lands / of the pine. / How much health, how much clean / air it gives us. Don't you feel / the cure next to the pine grove, / the clear breathing of the new lung, / the fresh watering of life? That / is what matters. . . ."

161. *Pequeño Larousse Ilustrado 1992*, s.v. "salud."

162. This image may be an allusion to the type of poet who produces an overabundance of poetry or to the type of society that values overproduction for the sake of production.

163. ". . . All together, / wall to wall, all arm in arm / through the streets / awaiting the wedding / in earnest!"

164. *Pequeño Larousse Ilustrado 1992*, s.v. "solidaridad."

165. ". . . Ah, you, mother / dove: put your good beak, / put the good beautiful grain / down into the crop of your nestlings."

166. "And now, traveler, / when the cock crows a second time, / go to the pine grove and wait for me there."

167. "Let's never tell the truth in this / sacred hour of the day. / The poor guy who looks / and sees clearly, sees / enter sacking the pine grove the immense / justice of the light, who is in the siege / that the daring horde of the stars / has given to the city, the implacable host / of space. / Poor guy who sees / that what unites is defense, fear."

168. "What a subtle lure, ruinous dirty work, / well-trimmed bait / of appearance. / Where love, where valor, yes, where / companionship? Traveler, / go on singing the praises of fortunate friendship / in the dawning pine grove. Never / believe this that I have said: / sing and sing. You, never / say in these lands / that there is little love and much fear always."

CHAPTER 3. THE GAZE, THE OTHER, AND THE (RE)CONSTITUTION OF THE
SELF: THE POET'S COMING OF AGE IN *ALIANZA Y CONDENA* (1965)

1. I have already alluded to Bousoño's misreading of the change that occurs between *Conjuros* and *Alianza y condena*. See note 1 of chap. 2 above. I envision the reversal between "Libro primero" and "Libro segundo" of *Alianza* following Jacques Lacan's diagrams in "The Line and Light" (*The Four Fundamental Concepts of Psycho-Analysis*, ed. Jacques-Alain Miller, trans. Alan Sheridan [New York: W. W. Norton, 1981], 91). These two forms combine in "Libro tercero."

2. In the Imaginary order, "The child forms a syncretic unity with the mother, and cannot distinguish between itself and its environment. It has no awareness of its own corporeal boundaries. It is *ubiquitous*, with no separation between itself and 'objects', for it forms a 'primal unity' with its objects" (Elizabeth Grosz, *Jacques Lacan: A Feminist Introduction* [London and New York: Routledge, 1990], 34).

3. Lacan refers to imagoes as "veiled faces it is our privilege to see in outline in our daily experience and in the penumbra of symbolic efficacity" (Jacques Lacan, "The Mirror Stage as Formative of the Function of the I as Revealed in Psychoanalytic Experience," in *Ecrits: A Selection*, trans. Alan Sheridan [New York: W. W. Norton, 1977], 3). Grosz explains that "The ego can thus be seen as an intrasubjective relation founded on inter-subjectivity. It is the coagulation and residue of internalized images of others. . . .

"Relations between self and other thus govern the *imaginary order*. This is the domain in which the self is dominated by images of the other and seeks its identity in a reflected relation with alterity. Imaginary relations are thus two-person relations, where the self sees itself reflected in the other" (*Jacques Lacan*, 46).

4. Grosz explains the mirror stage in this way: "The child's recognition of absence is the pivotal moment around which the mirror stage revolves. The child is propelled into its identificatory relations by this first acknowledgement of lack or loss. Only at this moment does it become capable of distinguishing itself from the 'outside' world, and thus of locating itself *in* the world. Only when the child recognizes or understands the concept of absence does it see that it is not 'one', complete in itself, merged with the world as a whole and the (m)other. . . . This marks the primitive 'origins' of the child's separation of inside and outside, subject and object, self and other, and a number of other conceptual oppositions which henceforth structure its adult life.

"The child can only give up this hermetically sealed circuit of need and satisfaction by accepting that the (m)other is not within its control, being a separate object. The 'fullness', the completeness it needs is interrupted by lack. The child is no longer in that happy state of satisfaction, protected by and merged with the (m)other. From this time on, lack, gap, splitting will be its mode of being. It will attempt to fill its (impossible, unfillable) lack. Its recognition of lack signals an ontological rift with nature or the Real. This gap will propel it into seeking an identificatory image of its own stability and permanence (the imaginary), and eventually language (the symbolic) by which it hopes to fill the lack . . ." (ibid., 34–35). In short, the mirror stage "marks a first stage in the child's acquisition of an identity independent of the mother, the genesis of a sense of self or personal unity, the origin of the child's sexual drives and the first process of social acculturation" (32).

Ellie Ragland-Sullivan points out the connection between Lacan and Heidegger at the mirror stage, confirming the link between "Libro segundo" of *Alianza* and the poems of *Conjuros*. "[T]his early identification also constitutes the first alienation for an infant, a split between outer form (big and symmetrical) and an inner sense of incoherence and dissymmetry. Lacan places this split at the heart of human knowledge (Sheridan, *Ecrits*, 5). Human beings will forever after anticipate their own images in the images of others, a phenomenon Lacan refers to as a sense of 'thrownness' (akin to Heidegger's theory of the human subject)" (*Jacques Lacan and the Philosophy of Psychoanalysis* [Urbana and Chicago: University of Illinois Press, 1986], 25).

5. "The dual imaginary relation needs to be symbolically regulated or mediated. This occurs with the help of a term outside this dual structure, a third position beyond the mother-child dyad. This 'third term' is the Father; not the real, or rather, the imaginary father, who is a person, an other, to whom the child may relate. The imaginary father usually takes on the symbolic function of law, but in any case these laws and prohibitions must be culturally represented or embodied for the child by some authority figure. It is generally the father who takes on the role of (symbolic) castrator and the Name-of-the-Father" (Grosz, *Jacques Lacan*, 47). "This process of social construction is predicated on the *necessary* renunciation and sacrifice of the child's access to the maternal body and the child's submission to the Law of the Father. The paternal figure serves to separate the child from an all-encompassing, engulfing, and potentially lethal relation with the mother. The father intervenes into this imaginary dyad and represents the Law. The Father embodies the power of the phallus and the threat of castration. Accepting his authority and phallic status is the precondition of the child's having a place within the socio-symbolic order, a name, and a speaking position" (142).

In the poems of "Libro tercero" of *Alianza,* Rodríguez inscribes his speaking position as a "strong poet" within the poetic tradition—metapoetically, the "culture" or "society" in Lacanian terms.

6. Ragland-Sullivan states that in "Group Psychology and the Analysis of the Ego" Freud "referred to the narcissistic investment in self as an 'ideal ego,' and the objects toward whom ego libido flows as 'ego ideals'" (*Jacques Lacan and the Philosophy of Psychoanalysis*, 31). "Like the physical universe Lacan's mirror-stage psychic universe is the scene of constant movement and reverberations controlled by the action of the Imaginary order. . . . Introjection is on the Symbolic slope, then, and projection on the Imaginary one" (146). Rodríguez "projects" his ideal ego at the beginning of "Libro primero" (e.g., in the images of the witches and the wolves) and moves toward an "introjection" of his ego ideals (Eugenio de Luelmo), which he actualizes more fully in "Libro segundo."

7. "In Martin Thom's essay '*Verneinung, Verwerfung, Ausstossung*: A Problem in the Interpretation of Freud,' the author points out that in 'Instincts and Their Vicissitudes' (1915) and in 'Denial' (1925) Freud spoke of a pleasure ego which is built up by attribution, incorporating good qualities and expelling bad ones. Expulsion (*Ausstossung*) of 'bad' objects or effects leads to denial (*Verneinung, dénégation*) just as affirmation (*Bejahung*) leads to assimilation of 'good' objects. *Ausstossung* and *Bejahung* therefore constitute the first acts of judgment exercised to create a 'self.' Melanie Klein took over these Freudian ideas to make introjection and expulsion a simple matter of reality and literal imagination. Lacan's contribution showed that there is not a 'literal' introjecting of good objects and expelling of bad ones. At the most primitive level the *Ur-Ich* or *Lust-Ich* establishes itself even prior to categories of inside/outside, and certainly before objects are attributed in relation to any idea of container or contained. In other words, the question of 'self' boundaries . . . parallels the question of the material that makes up the 'self.' Primary introjection is linked, furthermore, to what Lacan called *l'écriture* (scripting) or the effect of language. What is introjected here is not objects in a literal sense, but objects as perceived in relation to an effect of language: the Other's *parole* (*Séminaire* I, p. 97)" (Ragland-Sullivan, *Jacques Lacan and the Philosophy of Psychoanalysis*, 144).

8. "In certain contexts the subject unravels, revealing a disintegration of its apparent unity: in dreams, jokes, slips of the tongue and pen, neurosis, psychosis, unexpected affects, obsessively repeated identity themes, love, anxiety, and so on" (Ragland-Sullivan, *Jacques Lacan and the Philosophy of Psychoanalysis*, 4). "[Lacan] shows 'truth' peeking out in language through syncopations, contradictions, repetitions, implied questions or doubt, and other such verbal or textual *aporia*" (ibid., 98). We might compare these slips with Riffaterre's concept of "ungrammaticalities" laying bare the semiosis of a text.

9. Persin (*Recent Spanish Poetry*, 77–78) has discussed the verbs "saber" and "conocer" as contributing to Rodríguez's syntax of assertion and his calling into question the ability to "know." Alan Sheridan, the translator of *Four Fundamental Concepts* (hereafter *FFC*), explains that "Most European languages make a distinction [between *savoir* and *connaissance*] (e.g. Hegel's *Wissen* and *Kenntnis*) that is lost in English. In modern French thinking, different writers use the distinction in different ways. In Lacan, *connaissance* (with its inevitable concomitant, '*méconnaissance*') belongs to the imaginary register, while *savoir* belongs to the symbolic register" (281).

The speaker's awareness ("recognition") of the imagoes he has absorbed (the witches) allows him to "know" himself better and in that way to move toward ("hacia") greater acclaim ("recognition") by condemning them and introjecting new ego ideals that he encounters ("knows") during the subsequent mirror stage. Obviously, the words "conocimiento" and "conocer" have multifarious meanings, all of which come into play in the subtitle. This process of knowing (epistemology) constantly interacts with the wisdom attained (ontology) in an unending give-and-take.

"By this criterion Lacanian *savoir* is the sum of prejudices which composes a person's knowledge. But 'knowledge' here refers to the Other's discourse—the Real *subject* of knowing—or *le savoir supposé sujet*—which forms the foundation of any conscious knowledge. Everything emanates from the Other(A) in the sense that this discourse feeds into *je* language as a kind of eternally active subterranean emitting station, which sends out to others, in inverted form, the messages about individuality that it wishes to receive. The reflection of one's own *moi* from others is a virtual reflection and, in this sense, the human subject is a circular body that remains always equal to itself (*Séminaire* II, p. 282)" (Ragland-Sullivan, *Jacques Lacan and the Philosophy of Psychoanalysis*, 49).

10. Persin, *Recent Spanish Poetry*, 70–71, 84.

11. Culler, *Pursuit of Signs*, 115.

12. Bloom, *Agon*, 60. In his essay "Negation," Freud states, "The subject-matter of a repressed image or thought can make its way into consciousness on condition that it is *denied*. Negation is a way of taking account of what is repressed; indeed, it is actually a removal of the repression, though not, of course, an acceptance of what is repressed" (*A General Selection*, 65).

13. "Neither old wives' tales / nor eyeless needles nor headless / pins. It doesn't flash, / like salt in a flame, this simple / sortilege, this old / maleficence. Neither hyssop / for sprinkling nor a candle / of virgin wax does it need. . . ."

14. ". . . Each / form of life has / a boiling point, a meteor / of bubbles. There, where the lottery / of the senses seeks / propriety, there, where / being gels, in that / live stamen, the witchcraft / lodges. . . ."

15. ". . . It is not only the body, / with its legendary clumsiness, that which / deceives us: in the very / constitution of matter, in such / clarity that is hoax, / winks, potions, tremulous / rouge, they would drive us mad. And it smells / of an oily, black headscarf, of pure / witch, this September noon; / and in the folds of the air, / on the altars of space, vices are / buried, places / where one can buy the heart, sinister / recipes for love. And in the tense / maturation of the day, not lips / but arid gums / suck from our blood / prayer and blasphemy, / memory, forgetfulness, / all that was relief or fever."

16. Feminist theorists have revealed the biased masculinist perspectives on witches and prostitutes, the images that Rodríguez has chosen to represent those parts of himself that he dislikes and wishes to alter. I would argue that at least to some extent Rodríguez recognizes his sexist attitudes and performs his own "re-vision" of them in the course of *Alianza*, specifically because of his love for his wife Clara.

17. Ragland-Sullivan reports that "In 1948 Lacan listed specific images as the archaic *imago* of the fragmented body, which constitute what used to be termed the 'instincts.' These are images—i.e., mental representations—of castration, mutilation, dismemberment, disloca-

tion, evisceration, devouring, bursting open of the body, and so forth and have a formative function in composing the human subject of identity and perception" (*Jacques Lacan and the Philosophy of Psychoanalysis*, 19; see *Ecrits*, 11). This characterization is captured in the image of the witches in "Brujas."

18. The same spelling appears in "Girasol," the moment of troping that epitomizes the mirror stage.

19. "Like one who reads in a scratched-out line / the repentance of a lifetime, / with tenacity, with pity, with faith, even with hate, / now, at noon, when it is / hot and taste is / deadened, we contemplate / the deep destruction and the tenacious progress / of things, their eternal / delirium, while swallows / shriek in their flight."

20. As a graduate student with a limited vocabulary in Spanish, I was amazed when I first looked up the word "estrago" in *Cassell's Spanish Dictionary*. The definitions I found there continue to influence my reading of this poem because of their scope and their appropriateness for Rodríguez's theme. According to *Cassell's* (New York: Funk & Wagnalls, 1959), "estrago" means: "ravage, ruin, waste, havoc; destruction, carnage, damage; wickedness, corruption of morals, depravity," all of which the witches symbolize.

21. "The mountain flower, aged lard, / a child's navel, the fair / on the morning of St. John's Day, the doll / missing its right hand, resin, / good for women's hips, / saffron, thistle under the Talaveran / pot with pepper and wine, / all that belongs to witches, natural / things, today are nothing beside this coven / of images that, now, / when beings cast little shadow, / gives a reflection: life."

22. "Life is not a reflection, / but what is its image? / One body on top of another, does it feel resurrection or death? How / to poison, cleanse / this air that is not our lungs? / Why is it that he who loves never / seeks truth, but seeks happiness? / How without truth / can happiness exist? Here is everything."

23. These three "orders" or "registers" constitute one of Lacan's fundamental contributions to psychoanalytic theory. Ragland-Sullivan succinctly summarizes them: "In a narrow and technical sense the Imaginary order is the domain of the *imago* and relationship interaction. The Symbolic is the sphere of culture and language; and the Real is that which is concrete and already 'full'—the world of objects and experiences" (*Jacques Lacan and the Philosophy of Psychoanalysis*, 130–31). I have already adumbrated definitions of the Imaginary and the Symbolic in notes 2, 3, 4, and 5 above. With regard to the "Real," Sheridan explains that "The 'real' emerges as a third term, linked to the symbolic and the imaginary: it stands for what is neither symbolic nor imaginary, and remains foreclosed from the analytic experience, which is an experience of speech. What is prior to the assumption of the symbolic, the real in its 'raw' state (in the case of the subject, for instance, the organism and its biological needs), may only be supposed, it is an algebraic *x*. This Lacanian concept of the 'real' is not to be confused with reality, which is perfectly knowable: the subject of desire knows no more than that, since for it reality is entirely phantasmatic" (*FFC*, 280).

The concept of a representation of a representation was stated by Charles Sanders Peirce; see Kaja Silverman, *The Subject of Semiotics* (New York and Oxford: Oxford University Press, 1983), 15. "Indeed, although at times in *The Interpretation of Dreams*, Freud seems to suggest that representations have their origin in some prior presence, upon closer scrutiny such presence reveals itself to be a representation that in turn refers to other representations" (Samuel Weber, *Return to Freud: Jacques Lacan's Dislocation of Psychoanalysis*, Michael Levine, trans. [Cambridge: Cambridge University Press, 1991], 3).

24. "Summing up his argument, Lacan writes: 'What this structure of the signifying chain discloses,' is the subject's possibility 'to signify something entirely different from what it says.' Insofar as this movement of signification is constitutionally anchored in language itself, and does not depend upon the conscious intention of the subject, the function of discourse is no longer that of disguising—or, one might add: of expressing—thought. Rather, it is to 'indicate the place of this subject in the search for truth'" (Weber, *Return to Freud*, 55).

As Ragland-Sullivan states, "Lacan first designed the project later taken up by Piaget: to study knowledge as a process instead of as a state or as essences. . . . [He] has blurred the kind of distinction that separates man from reality. He paints man as a biological creature of contingency, who is subjectivized and representationalized in his genesis by the imposition of culture (symbols and language) on his corporal nature. Knowledge is, indeed, a process, but one which divides itself into unconscious, repressed knowledge as 'truth,' and conscious knowledge which flees from 'truth' in the name of rationality, wisdom, and convention" (*Jacques Lacan and the Philosophy of Psychoanalysis*, 89–90).

25. Curiously enough, Lacan uses a similar expression when defining the field of the ego and of the Other and talking about *"the subjective positions of being."* See *FFC*, 246–47.

26. "But we never / touch the suture, / that stitching (at times a darning, / at times embroidery) / between our senses and things, / that fine little sand / that no longer smells sweet but salty, / where the river and the sea empty into one another, / an echo in another echo, the debris / of a dream in the quick lime / of that dream for which I gave a world / and will continue giving it. . . ."

27. This slippage or *"glissement"* is entwined with the Lacanian understanding of desire. "For Lacan, as for Saussure, if any particular signifier refers to any given signified, it does so only through the mediation of the whole chain of signifiers. It is only the *totality* of signifiers that corresponds with the *totality* of signifieds; no single signifier is definitively attached to a single signified. Their only direct relation is one described as a relation of *glissement* or sliding. The chain of signifiers incessantly slides over the chain of signifieds. . . .

"There is a continuous evacuation of meaning as soon as the signifier moves out of its concrete relations, its syntagmatic bonds in a given speech act, back into the signifying chain. This signals a *constitutive lack* at the core of language, a lack which marks the absence of a fixed anchoring point, the absence of a solid core of meaning for any term—its necessarily open, ambiguous potential. The sliding of the signifier over the signified is only momentarily arrested in specific contexts. This lack of a founding sign—a signifier tied firmly to a given signified—means that if each term is founded on *pure difference* and thus already requires another term to be understood, all terms can only be understood relative to language as a whole . . ." (Grosz, *Jacques Lacan*, 95).

"Metaphor, the substitution of one term for another, is identified by Lacan with the Freudian process of condensation. He equates metonymy with the process of displacement, that 'veering off of signification' which primary processes utilize to evade the censor. The metaphoric process, the submersion of one term underneath another, provides the general model for the unconscious symptom: the term having 'fallen below the bar', becomes repressed, and the signifier which replaces it or becomes its symptom. In metonymy, connections are not so much modelled to the relation between latent and manifest as based on the connection between a term and what substitutes for it. In this movement from one term to its substitute, Lacan will recognize the movement of *desire*. Desire too is based on a chain of substitution whereby the first (lost) object of desire generates a potentially infinite chain of (only partially satisfactory) substitutes" (100).

"Displacement or metonymy replaces the original (lost) object of a drive with a substitute. This is the same movement as the *glissement* of the signifier over the signified. The loss of the primal object creates a lack which the child will attempt to fill using language to signify its demands. The language at its disposal replaces an ontological lack (lack of nature, lack of identity, lack of fixed objects) with a lack at the level constitutive of language (the lack of anchorage between the signifier and the signified: the lack constitutive of each sign). This lack is the most basic feature of desire and is both assumed and covered over by signification. The child is propelled into its (imaginary and symbolic) capture in/by signification" (102).

28. I do not wish to imply that the subject is in control of language. "In place of a Cartesian *res cogitans*, a thinking being, Lacan posits the speaking subject, a subject defined by and in language. This subject is not simply a speaking being, a being who happens by chance to

speak, but a being constituted as such by being spoken *through* by language itself. It cannot be conceived as the source or master of discourse, but is the locus or site of the articulation *(énonciation)* of representations, inscriptions, meanings, and significances" (ibid., 148).

As Ragland-Sullivan puts it, "In the Lacanian context language is not a static or passive tool waiting to be manipulated by knowledge or thought. It finds its principal *raison d'être* in serving as a tool for exploring and elaborating unconscious experience within the conscious realm" *(Jacques Lacan and the Philosophy of Psychoanalysis*, 91). "For Lacan . . . the effect of the image becomes . . . constitutive of the ego itself" (Weber, *Return to Freud*, 16). "This aspect could be called 'the linguistic condition of the ego.' For it is nothing but language, or more exactly, a particular function of language, that permits the ego to constitute itself . . ." (86).

Grosz clarifies that "the subject no longer constitutes language or functions as its master, but conversely, is constituted as a subject by language. . . . The subject cannot be considered the agent of speech; it is (through) the Other (i.e. the unconscious) that language speaks the subject. The subject is the effect of discourse, no longer its cause" *(Jacques Lacan*, 97–98).

This concept is also Heideggerian; see the introduction to this book for further discussion of this topic.

29. "What is realized in my history [i.e. in that of the individual subject] is not the past definite of what was, since it is no more, or even the present perfect of what has been in what I am, but the future anterior of what I shall have been for what I am in the process of becoming" (Lacan, *Ecrits* 86, quoted in Weber, *Return to Freud*, 7). Weber elucidates "future anteriority": "In the psychoanalytic perspective, then, memory becomes something very different from what it was for metaphysics—not because of a future that the subject will never be able to catch up with fully, but because every attempt by the subject of the unconscious to grasp its history inevitably divides that history into a past that, far from having taken place once and for all, is always yet to come. Consequently, the living present *[lebendige Gegenwart]* (Husserl) of the subject emerges as a focal point whose actuality can reside in an anticipated belatedness" (Weber, *Return to Freud,* 9). "For Lacan, the concept is construed not as the presentation of a representation in thought through the determinate negation of its properties, but rather as a vehicle of a *search*" (10).

30. ". . . Amid the ruins / of the sun trembles / a nest with nocturnal warmth. Amid / the ignominy of our laws arises / the altarpiece with old / gold and old doctrine / of the new justice. In which markets of high pilfering is water / wine, the wine blood, thirst the blood? / Through which customs offices does / contraband flour pass / like flesh, the flesh / like dust and the dust / like future flesh?"

31. "While acknowledging the sign's fundamentally layered structure, Lacan reverses Saussure's formula, signified/signifier, giving primacy to the material element (the signifier) in the genesis of the concept (the signified). His own formula for the sign is thus 'S/s', 'which is read as "the signifier over the signified," "over" corresponding to the bar separating the two stages'. The signifier is granted priority because, in Lacan's understanding, the signified is in fact simply another signifier occupying a different position, a position 'below the bar' within signification . . ." (Grosz, *Jacques Lacan*, 94).

Weber adds that "The signification of the phallus is constituted through castration, even and especially if 'nothing' is castrated. In this sense the phallus is the signifier of signification in general, the signifier of difference. To put it more precisely, the phallus marks the *bar* and the *barrier*, which itself is meaningless, but which renders signification possible" *(Return to Freud,* 147). Cf. the "y" in the title *Alianza y condena*.

32. "This is foolishness. A common / offense, this walking amid the pinches / of witches. Because they / do not study but dance / and pee, they are friends / of wine-cellars. And now, / at noon, / if they kiss us from so many things, / where will their night be, / where their lips, where our mouths / to accept so many lies and so much / love?"

Rodríguez has changed the expression from "hacen pis" in the Plaza y Janés edition (1972) to "mean" in the Cátedra edition (1983) of his works. My reading of this change is that the verb "mear" ("to pee") is more banal, ordinary, and vulgar (both vernacular and crude) than "hacer pis," demystifying the witches even more.

33. At the time when Rodríguez dedicated *Alianza* to Clara, she was his recent bride: They married in 1959, and Rodríguez wrote *Alianza* during the next five years. Clara embodies otherness and the female figures that predominate throughout the work, and her love motivates the ethical and aesthetic changes sought by the speaker of the poems. This love is also metaphoric of the poet's search for readers who will understand and appreciate his work.

34. ". . . When my hand acts, / so thoughtlessly and ungoverned, / but with errabund resonance, / and probes, seeking / warmth and company in this space / where so many others / have vibrated, what does it / mean? How many, many gestures like / a morning dream / have slipped away."

35. "We, so gestural but so unhappy, / race that only knew how / to weave flags, race of parades, / of fantasies and of dynasties, / let us make other signs. / . . . / No, these are not times / for looking nostalgically / at that infinite wake of the passing of men. There is much to forget / and even more to expect. . . ."

36. The poet's wife has a collection of different figurines and other representations of owls, which seem to be her "totem animal." One might even say that Claudio vaguely resembles an owl, especially as he has aged. See also "La mañana del búho" in *Casi una leyenda*, discussed in chap. 5 below. Note the word "claro," which appears in the next verses, a play on Clara's name frequent in *Alianza* and other works.

37. ". . . As silent / as the flight of the owl, a clear gesture, / of simple baptism, / will speak, in a new air, / my new meaning, its new / use. I only ask, if it is possible, / that when the evil hour arrives for me, / the hour of missing so many beloved gestures, / I may have strength to find them / like he who finds a fossil / (perhaps a jawbone still with the kiss tremulous) / of an extinct race."

38. "Authentic analytic consciousness . . . resides in seeing oneself being seen *(se voir se voir)* in the Other(A). . . . The *regard* is not simply a glance cast from the eye, nor a glance from reflective consciousness, because the *regard* has the power to activate within consciousness an awareness of unconscious motivation and intentionality.

"The meaning Lacan gives to the phenomenon of 'seeing oneself seen' is linked to his theory that the gaze is one of the first structuring mechanisms of the human subject. It [is] introjected as a part-object in the pre-mirror stage before the eye acquire[s] its function of seeing and representing the subject and, consequently, before there [is] any sense of alterity. In the mirror stage the gaze is the dialectical bridge to self-recognition; perceptually speaking, the prespecular objects of Desire become permanently enmeshed in a network of inner vision. In consciousness the intersubjective element involved in 'seeing oneself seen' has to do with knowing that the other knows that one is being looked at (*Séminaire* I, p. 244)" (Ragland-Sullivan, *Jacques Lacan and the Philosophy of Psychoanalysis*, 94–95).

"The gaze must be located outside the subject's conscious control. If it is outside, for Lacan . . . this means that the gaze comes always from the field of the Other. . . . But it is not the gaze of an other; it is the Other's gaze. It is the result of being located in the field of the Other" (Grosz, *Jacques Lacan*, 79–80).

See *Four Fundamental Concepts* (67–119) for Lacan's discussion "Of the Gaze as *Objet Petit a*." Also see Anthony Pagden for a discussion of the act of seeing as an act of possession in Discovery accounts. Gergen, quoting Boswell on his visit to the Hebrides, also reports that "Seeing became a confirmation of the self rather than a process by which the outer world of nature was understood." Because of his studies in philology, Rodríguez may have been (consciously or unconsciously) aware of this latent meaning of the word "mirar."

39. In general, Lacan and other psychoanalytic theorists make a distinction between a more abstract concept of the Other—the "Autre" or "Other(A)"—and the more concrete manifestations of this concept in the other, which Lacan designates as "l'objet petit a," "autre" with a lowercase "a." Lacan has stated, "The Other is the locus in which is situated the chain of the

signifier that governs whatever may be made present of the subject—it is the field of that living being in which the subject has to appear" (*FFC*, 203). At times, these two concepts seem to overlap, making a clear-cut distinction moot, but I try to be consistent in following the standard distinction between the "Other" and the "other."

". . . [T]he child's wish to *be* the cause of the Other's Desire . . . remains at the heart of adult sexual relations. In 1960 Lacan talked about *le désir de l'Autre*, purposely playing on the preposition *de* to make the phrase mean variously: desire is the Desire of/for/by the Other(A)" (Ragland-Sullivan, *Jacques Lacan and the Philosophy of Psychoanalysis*, 76).

Weber elaborates on this seeming contradiction: "Yet insofar as desire is directed towards something else which 'itself' can never simply be a self-identical object, it is not only desirous *of another*, but is 'itself' another's desire. It is 'the desire for the other's desire,' the desire *of* a signifier, defined as the signifier of another desire.

". . . So long as the desired end entails the consumption of natural objects, the subject is defined as a natural being caught up in the struggle for self-preservation. Only a desire seeking not a natural object, but rather acknowledgment through another desire raises the subject above its natural and material existence to the level of pure self-consciousness. What ensues from this account is the struggle for mastery. In this interpretation, desire seeks recognition from another desire. Recognition, however, is a moment in the autonomous constitution of self-consciousness. . . .

"As Lacan remarks, we are not dealing with a process of identification here—for . . . the metonymic movement of desire excludes any kind of identification—but with 'the condition that obliges the subject to find the constitutive structure of its desire in the very rift [*béance*] opened by the effect of the signifiers in those who come to represent the Other for it, insofar as its demand is subjected to them" (*Return to Freud*, 128–29).

In her explanation of the difference between demand and desire, Grosz elaborates the effects of this situation: "If need is a function of the Real and demand is a product of imaginary identifications, the third term in Lacan's libidinal trilogy is *desire*, the symbolic 'equivalent' or counterpart of need and demand. Rather than rely simply on Freud's two basic views of erotic desire, libido, and the structure of the wish . . . , Lacan derives his conception of desire from Hegel, particularly from *The Phenomenology of Spirit*, where Hegel posits desire as a lack and absence. Desire is a fundamental lack, a hole in being that can be satisfied only by one 'thing'— another('s) desire. Each self-conscious subject desires the desire of the other as its object. Its desire is to be desired by the other, its counterpart. Following Hegel, Lacan assumes a concept of desire as the *difference* or gap separating need from demand . . ." (*Jacques Lacan*, 64).

"Like demand, desire is in principle insatiable. It is always an effect of the Other, an 'other' with whom it cannot engage, in so far as the Other is not a person but a place, the locus of law, language, and the symbolic. The child must find his or her place within this order to become a speaking being. Indeed, as far as Lacan is concerned, the relation between desire and language constitute the twin axes of psychoanalytic interpretation. Together they serve to locate the subject as *split* and divided, a being who fades in the unfolding of discourse . . ." (67).

Grosz also explains that "The gaze must be located outside the subject's conscious control. If it is outside, for Lacan, unlike Sartre, this means that the gaze comes always from the field of the Other. It is only the gaze which can, as Sartre astutely observed, reduce me to shame at my very existence. But it is not the gaze of an other; it is the Other's gaze. It is the result of being located in the field of the Other. . . . Desire always refers to a triangle—the subject, the other and the Other. The other is the object through whom desire is returned to the subject; the Other is the locus of signification which regulates the movement by which this return is made possible. The subject's desire is always the desire of the Other" (80).

40. Emilio Alarcos Llorach explains that "Cuando se hace hincapié en la importancia de la causa, puede anteponerse la oración degradada" [When one emphasizes the importance of the cause, one can place the secondary clause beforehand] (*Gramática de la lengua española* [Madrid: Espasa-Calpe, 1994], 366). However, he also begins his discussion by saying that

these clauses can express two different causalities: "uno, cuando la oración transpuesta se refiere a la causa real de la experiencia evocada por el llamado verbo principal; otro, cuando la oración transpuesta explica meramente el motivo por el cual se expresa el núcleo del enunciado" [one, when the secondary clause explains the real cause of the experience evoked by the so-called main verb; another, when the secondary clause merely explains the motive for which one expresses the nucleus of the statement] (ibid., 365). Alarcos Llorach exemplifies each type with the following sentences: First, "Está enfermo porque ha llevado mala vida" [He is sick because he has led a bad life]; second, "Está enfermo porque tiene mal aspecto" [He is sick because he looks bad]. Magnified by the reversal of the clauses, ambivalence exists as to which type of sentence Rodríguez is uttering.

41. ". . . The combustion of the eye at this / hour of day, when the light, cruel / because it is so truthful, hurts / the gaze, no longer brings me that / simplicity. I no longer know what it is that dies, / what that resuscitates. But I look, / I seize fervor, and the gaze becomes / a kiss, I no longer know whether loving or betraying."

42. This effect reminds us of the word "deslumbrar" from *Don* and the ironic play of light and darkness in that work.

43. Lacan has described this phenomenon as the "inside-out structure of the gaze" (*FFC*, 82). He also alludes to the circularity of movement between self and other in the psychoanalytic setting: "Here the processes are to be articulated, of course, as circularity between the subject and the Other—from the subject called to the Other, to the subject of that which he has himself seen appear in the field of the Other, from the Other coming back. This process is circular, but, of its nature, without reciprocity. Because it is circular, it is disymmetrical" (207). Although the love relationship is the metaphoric situation Rodríguez foregrounds in *Alianza*, the psychoanalytic approach reveals that the poet is attempting to "seduce" the reader, "desiring" to find a reader who will constitute him through the act of reading. Rodríguez is thus defining the type of reader he seeks. Though he speaks of painting, Lacan's comments are pertinent. He calls this phenomenon the artist's "mapping" of himself onto the text in an appeal to the spectator/reader to "lay down the gaze." See his comments in *FFC*, 100–101.

44. "It wants to emboss things, / to detain their gloomy hurry / to take leave, to dress, to cover / their fierce nudity of farewell / with whatever: with that delicate / membrane of air, / though it were only / with the subtle tenderness / of the veil that separates the tiny cells / of the pomegranate. It wants to smear its grease, / dense with youth and with fatigue, / on so many luminous hinges that reality / opens, to enter / leaving there, in such fecund bedrooms, / its dregs and its scraps, / its nest and its storm, / without being able to inhabit them. What a dark / gaze seeing things / so clear. . . ."

45. ". . . Look, look: / There smoke rises, men / begin to leave that factory, / their eyes lowered, their heads lowered. / There is the Tormes with its high sky, / children on its banks, amid the debris / where chickens scratch. Look, look: / See how already, even with grooves and pegs, / with scowls and asperities, / things go flowing by. . . ."

46. Cirlot, *A Dictionary of Symbols*, 300.

47. The Tormes River makes us think of Salamanca and the *pícaro* Lazarillo. Does the speaker see himself as a disillusioned, rootless *pícaro?*

48. ". . . Spring forth, fount / of rich vein, my gaze, my only / salvation, seal, carve, as lovers on a tree, / the harmonious insanity of life / in your speedily passing waters."

49. "Es la mirada, / es el agua que espera ser bebida. / El agua." See Baudelaire's "I Love the Memory" and note 146 of chap. 1 above.

50. Here we might adduce Lacan's comments on tattooing and scarification: "One of the most ancient forms in which this unreal organ [the libido] is incarnated in the body, is tattooing, scarification. The tattoo certainly has the function of being for the Other, of situating the subject in its marking his place in the field of the group's relations, between each individual and all the others. And, at the same time, it obviously has an erotic function. . . . [I]n the profound relation of the drive, what is essential is that the movement by which the arrow that sets out

towards the target fulfills its function only by really reemerging from it, and returning on to the subject" (*FFC*, 205–6). This image appears occasionally in Rodríguez's poetry; recall the branding with a hot iron in "A las estrellas" in *Conjuros*. It seems, however, that the limp has replaced scarification as the more prominent identificatory mark of the poet.

51. Grosz says that "Of all the senses, vision remains the one which most readily confirms the separation of subject from object. Vision performs the distancing function, leaving the looker unimplicated or uncontaminated by its object" (*Jacques Lacan*, 38). Consonant with the paradoxical reciprocity of "alliance" and "condemnation," we discover a sense of "complementary transitivism" operating at this crucial moment in the speaker's progress through "Libro primero." As Grosz explains, "The roles of master and slave, actor and audience, doctor and patient are complementary, a relation of active to passive" (41). However, Freud has postulated "an intermediate stage in between the active and passive forms of the (scopic or aggressive) drive . . . the self-reflexive position represented by Freud's dazzling metaphor of the mouth kissing itself. . . . [T]his is no mere auto-erotic pleasure. It implies that the subject is already a being at the mercy of language, a subject positioned as such through language. What designates . . . active and . . . passive forms of sexual drives is not the amount or kind of energy invested in the process (passivity involves as much activity as activity!); but the fact that they are governed by a grammatical function, which is itself mediated by the self-reflexive position: 'I look', 'I am looked at', mediated by 'I look at myself'" (77). In the three intermediate poems of "Libro primero," Rodríguez begins the process of examining himself and his attitudes in his search for individuation. Note below the personification of youth knocking on the speaker's eyelids and the acknowledgment of the evil eye as one's own.

52. "The mysteriously constant youth / of that which exists, its marvellous / eternity, today knock / with their little scraped knuckles on this / imprisoned pupil. A while back / (how well I know the reason now) it was the same for me / to see a flower that wounds, a snare that caresses; / but this afternoon has brought into the open my solitude and I look / with a different gaze. . . ."

53. This image may be a variation of a line in T. S. Eliot's *The Waste Land*: "pressing lidless eyes and waiting for a knock upon the door." Rodríguez wrote most of *Alianza* while a lecturer in Spanish at the Universities of Nottingham and Cambridge in England, where he read English poetry assiduously.

54. ". . . Companions, / false and taciturn, / fattened on watchwords, while so rich / in propaganda, so poor in song; / I myself, who erred, so many cities / with that coat-of-arms of the arid mud / of greed, so many rapacious people, / whom in spite of myself I love, / I went along, surreptitiously, / giving myself the evil eye, and I continued / amid the dirty winks, awaiting / a moment. This one today. . . ."

55. In his essay "Dracula's Women, and Why Men Love to Hate Them," George Stade explains "the evil eye—which means that his gaze is a projection of your guilt; you see him seeing in you what you have tried to hide from yourself" (Gerald I. Fogel et al., eds., *The Psychology of Men: Psychoanalytic Perspectives* [New Haven and London: Yale University Press, 1996], 30). The same relationship obtains for the speaker of Rodríguez's poem.

When speaking of the gesture in "What Is a Picture?" Lacan remarks, "This terminal time of the gaze, which completes the gesture, I place strictly in relation to . . . the evil eye. The gaze in itself not only terminates the movement, it freezes it. Take those dances I mentioned—they are always punctuated by a series of times of arrest in which the actors pause in frozen attitude. What is that thrust, that time of arrest of the movement? It is simply the fascinatory effect, in that it is a question of dispossessing the evil eye of the gaze, in order to ward it off. The evil eye is the *fascinum*, it is that which has the effect of arresting movement and, literally, of killing life. At the moment the subject stops, suspending his gesture, he is mortified. The anti-life, anti-movement function of this terminal point is the *fascinum*, and it is precisely one of the dimensions in which the power of the gaze is exercised directly. The moment of seeing can intervene here only as a suture, a conjunction of the imaginary and the symbolic, and it is taken up again in a dialectic, that sort of temporal progress that is called haste, thrust, forward movement, which is concluded in the *fascinum*" (*FFC*, 117–18).

56. ". . . The last light / trembles in the air. It is the hour / when our gaze / becomes graceful and ladylike. / The hour when, at last, with all / the shame on my face, I look and exchange / my whole life for a gaze, / that one which now is distant, / the only one that serves my purpose, for the only / thing for which I want these two eyes: / that gaze which has no master."

57. Philip Silver has chosen this line as the basis for his commentary on Rodríguez in *La casa de Anteo* (see the bibliography). Though his argument takes a different direction from mine, his opening comments concerning originality are highly apropos to this discussion.

58. This attitude corresponds to the Lacanian concept of demand. "Demand is able to borrow the forms of instinctual need because of its fundamental ambiguity; demand always has two objects, one spoken, the other unspoken: the object or thing demanded (this or that object), and the other to whom the demand is ostensibly addressed. The thing demanded—food, attention, a 'cure' from the analyst, the undying love of another—are all relatively insignificant, or rather, they function as excuses for access to the second object, the (m)other. The thing demanded is a rationalization for maintaining a certain relation to the other. Where need aims at an object which satisfied it, demand appeals to an other in such a way that even if the demanded object is given, there can be no satisfaction. This is because the demand is really for something else, for the next thing the other can give, for the thing that will 'prove' the other's love. Demand requires the affirmation of an ego by the other to such a degree that only an imaginary union or identification with them, an identity they share, could bring satisfaction—and only then with the annihilation of the self, for it is now invaded by and exists as the other" (Grosz, *Jacques Lacan*, 61).

59. "The names of things, which are lies," "the suit / that covers the beloved body," "the four drinks that make us tipsy," "the caution of the envelope," and "the immense scar that hides the deep wound."

60. "that dark bandage / of custom, that covers our eye / so that we don't go blind, / the vain piece of candy of one day and another day / soothing our mouths"; "they are a venomous / and merciful deceit."

61. "where / the opportunity of love, / of free contemplation or, at the least, / of deep sadness, of true pain?"; "the husk and the mask / . . . / must they give life to so much / macerated youth, so much corrupted faith?"

62. "But you, burn, burn / all the letters, all the portraits, / the haylofts of time, the oats of infancy."

63. "Kneeling upon / so many lost days, / I contemplate today my work like that / distant city, in the open / country" / * * * / "Standing upon / so many happy days, / I continue my march. I will not be able to inhabit you, / nearby city. I will always be a guest, / never a neighbor."

64. "And you blame me for it, / heart, harsh master. / That I remember and forget, / that I lighten up and that I sing / to pass the time, / to lose my fear; / that so many years go to waste / in case something comes to us / that will protect men. / As always, is that what you want?"

65. "In a herd, not astute / but distrustful, / sometimes haughty / at others needy, because of inertia / and ignorance, in the arms / of rancor, with the honor / of their crude garlic and their pure wine, / remember, remember / how much in their company / we gained and we lost. / How will you now bring into balance obligation / with happiness, good fortune / with money? But go on."

66. "death," "envy," "cowards," "poverty," "arrogance," "anxiety," "social / notes, lineage, public favor," "adulation," "greed," "enemies," "those men . . . so avid only of munitions and rations."

67. "Those / mornings with their strong / light of the plateau, so consoling"; "Those girls who were going to school."

68. "At other times I was not worried / about the high night, / remember that. I know it

was lamentable, / that treatment, the hollow / repertoire of ramshackle / gestures, / above bodies of varied / assortment and with so little / grace for acting. . . ."

69. "men / with diminutive triangular eyes / like those of the bee, / officially legitimating / the fraud, the perfidy, / and making life negotiable."

70. "As in the old story, I heard those / words in the middle of the night, tipsy, / either like suede / or leathery, horny, never human. / I saw the decrepitude, the black wicker. / I saw that the bells were painful / in the clear light of dawn."

71. Chevalier and Gheerbrandt affirm that "El mimbre posee carácter sagrado de protección; acompaña los nacimientos milagrosos. . . . El papel principal del Logos (el Verbo, la Palabra) aparece simbolizado, en Oriente y Occidente, de modo análogo, por el mimbre y el sauce. La cesta de mimbre asegura la protección" (*Diccionario de los símbolos*, 713). [Wicker possesses a sacred character of protection; it accompanies miraculous births. . . . The principal role of the Logos (the Word) appears symbolized, in East and West, in analogous ways, by wicker and willow. The wicker basket assures protection.]

72. "At times, however, in those lands / friendship flourished. And often / even love. I give thanks." / * * * / "The hour is very late / but I want to enter the city. And I go on. / It is going to dawn. Where will I find lodging?"

73. "When someone dawns with grace, so simple / as things are at his side that they almost / seem new, we almost / feel the punishment, the dark fear / of possessing. . . ."

74. ". . . the effectiveness of this man, / unrehearsed, the business / of the sea that were his gestures, wave by wave, / flower and fruit at the same time, and death, and birth / at the same time, and that great danger / of his tenderness, of his way of going / through the streets, gave us / the sole justice: happiness."

75. "Like one who smokes at the foot / of a powder magazine without realizing it, we would go with him / and, since he was so easy / to invite, we didn't see / that he kissed when he drank and that when we cheated / at tute, even more at mus, he played / honestly, with his cards / unmarked. . . ." (Note: "tute" and "mus" are Spanish card games.)

76. ". . . He, whose occupation without schedule / was companionship, how was he / to know that his Duero / is a bad neighbor?"

77. In Spanish, "genio" means "disposition, nature, character, special nature, peculiarities" as well as "genius." The name "Eugenio" may be an ironic pun, consistent with the psychoanalytic stance we have adopted in *Alianza*.

78. "how shall we now / celebrate what was pure happening, / news without history, work that is achievement?"

79. "Blind to the mystery / and, therefore, one-eyed / for the real."

80. "I do not bow my head, / Eugenio, though I know well that now / they wouldn't recognize me even at home."

81. "Death is not a river, like the Duero, / nor is it a sea. Like love, the sea / always ends between four / walls. And you, Eugenio, through a thousand channels / without flooding or drought, / without bridges, without women / washing clothes, in what waters / have you placed yourself? / But you do not reflect, like water; / like earth, you possess."

82. I understand the riverbed as a variation on the symbol of the "camino" (the road of life). The water imagery associated with the riverbed augments the richness and inspiration that Eugenio provided for those around him.

83. "And the stitching of these streets / of your quarter next to the river, / and the shabby cards, / and shaking hands without giving now summer / or reality, nor life / without risk and the tongue / now silly from saying 'hi,' 'bye,' / and the thieving, fleeing sun, / and these towers of damp / gunpowder, of a lost / calibre, and I, with this air of the first of June / that makes noises in my chest, / and my friends . . . Much, / in so little time much has ended."

84. "Now uphill or downhill, / toward the plaza or toward the workshop, / everything looks at us now / aslant, catches us / out of place. / It gives us shame almost / to live, it gives us shame / to breath, to see how beautifully / the afternoon falls. But / into the keyhole of all the

locks of the world / your key passes, and opens / familiarly, luminously, / and thus we enter our home / like he who returns from an engagement kept."

85. We could therefore assert that Eugenio represents the "third term" in the oedipal structure. But complete identification with that male figure is still pending for the speaker. He has yet to solidify his position "beyond the structure of dual imaginary relations within the framework of culture" (Grosz, *Jacques Lacan*, 47). He still does not have a name, a speaking position as a poet, within the sociosymbolic order, that is, within the poetic tradition.

86. "Never tentatively, thus, like now, enter / this neighborhood. Thus, thus, without alms, / without truce, enter, round up, / place your crude forge / in these houses. Once for all come down, open / and scar this deep / misery. Come down now that there is no one here, / my night, don't go away, don't take away / your infinite, avid pulse. Finish / now hovering above, pursue / once for all this prey which no one / wants to value. . . .' "

87. ". . . May I only hear, / my night, after so many years, / the voracious sound of your luminous horde / sacking to the depths / so much orphanhood, the bitter, coarse poverty / of this block in silence that is almost / in the country and lodges / a vivid, vibrant sowing. May your light / dismantle our injustice and put it / in the air for us, and corrode it, / and shake it, and make it sticky / like this earth, and may we realize / that it is here, two steps away. Never / protective, yes, audacious. / Accuse. And may the race, / the manhood of fine lime, the dreams, the work, / the naked framework of life / be set on edge."

88. This is another instance of the "future anterior"; see note 28 above.

89. "And you are alone, / you, night, maddened with justice, / stunned with compassion, / above this tremulous neighborhood to which no one / will come because it is the history / of everyone, but to which you always, sooner / or later, / take, and bring, and wound, and seduce / without anyone knowing it, / without anyone hearing the noise / of your immense pulses, that overflow."

90. As we have already seen in *Conjuros* and as we shall see in "Libro segundo" of *Alianza*, this relationship is analogous to Bousoño's term "realismo metafórico." To "frame the Other," then, is to perceive its manifestation in concrete, everyday scenes and objects (the *objets a*) which the speaker encounters as reflections of sameness and difference with himself.

Grosz clarifies this concept: "The child sees itself as a unified totality, a *gestalt* in the mirror: it experiences itself in a schism, as a site of fragmentation. The child's identification with its specular image impels it nostalgically to seek out a past symbiotic completeness, even if such a state never existed and is retrospectively imposed on the pre-mirror phase; and to seek an anticipatory or desired (ideal or future) identity in the coherence of the totalized specular image. Lacan claims that the child is now enmeshed in a system of confused recognition/ misrecognition: it sees an image of itself that is both accurate (since it is an inverted reflection, the presence of light rays emanating from the child: the image as icon): as well as delusory (since the image prefigures a unity and mastery that the child still lacks). It is the dual ambivalent relation to its own image that is central to Lacan's account of subjectivity. If the child simply *recognizes* the image, we would have another version of Freud's realist view of the ego—an ego essentially in contact with reality. But if, on the other hand, the child merely misrecognizes its image, it is the subject of error and falsehood, unable to produce knowledge, a subject of ideology. Instead, Lacan posits a divided, vacillating attitude that is incapable of a final resolution. This 'divided' notion of self and the problem of self-recognition are crucial in so far as they may explain processes of social inculcation and positioning. Neither ignorant nor aware of its own socialization, the child must be both induced to accept social norms and values as natural, and yet to function as an agent within a social world, an agent who has the capacity for rebellion against and rejection of its predesignated social place. [Cf. the poet versus the tradition.]

"In identifying with its mirror-image, the child introjects it into the subject's ego; yet the subject's relation to the image is also alienated. The image both is *and* is not an image of itself" (*Jacques Lacan*, 39–40).

91. The connection of "Libro segundo" with *Conjuros*, where the speaker-poet must accept his cultural inheritance but also separate himself from it, both actions necessary to the constitution of his identity, is again evident in this mirror-image relationship of self and other, similarity and difference. This intertextual aspect was suggested to me by Philip Silver's outstanding paper presented at the 1991 Convention of the Modern Language Association, "The Spectacle of Poetics: From the Ridiculous to the Sublime," where he maps the intertextual relationship between "Espuma" and Leopardi's "Idilio" along with a definition of the tripartite division of the poem corresponding to the three stages of the Kantian sublime.

92. In Lacanian terms, then, Rodríguez subscribes to the notion of the "split subject," and that splitting is a part of the process necessary to constitute subjectivity. Lacan has asserted that "The relation of the subject to the Other is entirely produced in a process of gap" (*FFC*, 203). In another place, Lacan reminds his audience that "one should not then forget the interval that separates [perception and consciousness], in which the place of the Other is situated, in which the subject is constituted" (45). He goes on to remark, "By separation, the subject finds, one might say, the weak point of the primal dyad of the signifying articulation, in so far as it is alienating in essence. It is in the interval between these two signifiers that resides the desire offered to the mapping of the subject in the experience of the discourse of the Other, of the first Other he has to deal with, let us say, by way of illustration, the mother. It is in so far as his desire is beyond or falls short of what she says, of what she hints at, of what she brings out as meaning, it is in so far as his desire is unknown, it is in this point of lack, that the desire of the subject is constituted. The subject—by a process that is not without deception, which is not without presenting that fundamental twist by which what the subject rediscovers is not that which animates his movement of rediscovery—comes back, then, to the initial point, which is that of his lack as such, of the lack of his *aphanisis* [the disappearance or fading of the subject behind the signifier]" (218–19).

Weber notes that "The 'fissures' mentioned by Lacan are, as it were, the materialization of difference in 'actual discourse.' Difference materializes as a gap, a fissure, a hole or shadow that interferes with the semantic progress of discourse, puncturing and punctuating it. Such interruptions, as Freud emphasized in his discussion of dreams, constitute the favored markers of the unconscious. Despite its name, then, an 'expletive' like *ne* does not so much fill up a hole as mark its borders" (*Return to Freud*, 113). This gap or lack is equivalent to the threat of castration as defined in the oedipal configuration.

93. As Paul Ricoeur has pointed out in *Oneself as Another* (trans. Kathleen Blamey [Chicago: University of Chicago Press, 1992], 1–3), the word "identity" is problematic because it can connote both similarity (*idem*) and difference (*ipse*). When we say, for example, that twins are "identical," we mean that they look so much alike that it is difficult to distinguish one from the other. In this regard, "identity" refers to "sameness" (*idem*). But twins would be the first to insist that each of them—like each of us—has a unique personality constituted by the cluster of traits that (like fingerprints) makes each of us a distinct individual. In this sense, "identity" means "difference" (*ipse*).

94. "This structure [the entire structure of language] is determined through the distinctive properties of the signifier, which is constituted on the one hand through opposition, on the other, through a capacity to combine with other signifiers to form a chain, 'in accordance with the laws of a closed order.' This order consists of two radically heterogeneous but interdependent dimensions: that of the signifier and that of the signified, which are separated from each other by a bar—derived from the Saussurean division of the sign, but above all, from its graphic representation. But this bar is not merely a mark of separation: it is also a limit that must necessarily be transgressed, for the signifier is also precipitated into the realm of the signified, leaving its mark upon the latter, and allowing it to be designated as an 'effect.' Lacan therefore emphasizes a certain 'primacy of the signifier over the signified'" (Weber, *Return to Freud*, 59).

95. This uniqueness depends upon the *aphanisis* or "fading" of the subject: "The differential nature of the signifier thereby affects the metonymic movement itself: it does not merely

carry the subject somewhere else, but rather locates the subject in a place where it can never arrive. The signifying structure of the subject assumes value only through its position relative to others, within the chain, but also without. The place of the subject thereby becomes impossible to demarcate fully, since it is always 'there where I am not, because I cannot situate myself there,' as Lacan puts it. One can even go so far as to say that the subject, in the Lacanian perspective, *determines itself* in and as this impossibility. The latter, translated into an image, is called: *fader*. The subject only appears, insofar as it *fades*. The emergence of the subject is its *fading*" (ibid., 90).

96. In speaking of the *moi* (ego), Ragland-Sullivan provides insight into the process taking place in "Libro segundo": "As the nonverbal agent of specularity and identifications, the *moi* leads the game of human interaction. But it is essentially in an unstable posture. Subjects reconstitute themselves for each other, Lacan says, by exchanging ego (*moi*) through language (*je*) as symbols. . . . [T]he *moi* can only experience itself in relation to external images and to the gaze of others. . . . It began as a dialectical structure and, throughout life, each metamorphosis and successive identification with others again challenge its delimitations (*Ecrits* 19–20). It is possible therefore to say—another paradox—that the subject's identity is both fixed and continually *en jeu*. Put another way, the two major aspects of the *moi* are (1) the formal stagnation or fixation of feelings and images, which constitute the subject and its objects (others) with attributes of permanence, identity, and substantiality; and (2) the inherent gaps, ambiguities, and scars in the *moi*, which surface in the speaking subject and throw its apparent, although illusory and contradictory unity into question (*Ecrits* 17)" (*Jacques Lacan and the Philosophy of Psychoanalysis*, 43).

97. See, for example, the analyses of Gonzalo Sobejano, "'Espuma' de Claudio Rodríguez," *Consenso-Revista de Literatura* 2 (1978): 37–50; and Alicia Vargas-Churchill, "La coherencia de 'Espuma' de Claudio Rodríguez," *Explicación de Textos Literarios* 14 (1985–86): 25–34. Before his untimely death Aníbal Núñez wrote a marvelous commentary on the first two verses of "Espuma." See "¿Dónde la ebriedad? (Retórica en dos versos de Claudio Rodríguez)," *La Ciudad* (Valladolid) (abril 1988): 16–17.

98. "I look at the foam, its delicacy / that is so distinct from that of ashes. / Like one who looks at a smile, that one / for which he gives his life and that is for him fatigue / and shelter, I look now at the modest / foam. . . ."

99. "Lacan renews this Freudian tradition through which psychoanalytic writing gestures towards a stage whose borders are not only provisionally determined by what is called the 'reader' (or 'auditor' . . .). This 'reader' or 'audience,' as the provisional 'representative of the other' . . . serves to delimit the borders of a stage that will always have been at a remove from the place we occupy as self-conscious subjects" (Weber, *Return to Freud*, 10).

"It is only by means of identifying with another, even if that other is its 'own' mirror-image, that the ego is constituted. Yet to seek to appropriate that other is tantamount to denying the difference that makes it a suitable object of identification in the first place. The imaginary thus becomes a 'trap,' or a double-bind: the ego can only emerge by binding itself to the other; but for it to fulfill its image of wholeness, as a Gestalt, it is bound to deny the bond that constitutes it" (107).

"While the mirror-stage identification with the mother provided a sense of triumph over an original experience of fragmentation, secondary identification with the father divides this already tenuous sense of unity. For Lacan, this split forms the ontological foundation of human knowledge and identity in terms of a cultural self-alienation and allusive Desire, which are both born of Law. Underlying all 'meaning,' then, is a drama of fusion and separation, which has created the unconscious as a system whose knowledge is elementally structural and transformational.

". . . The two major experiences of identificatory fusion and subsequent separation mark the subject for life. An implicit intentionality thereby sets individuals off on a paradoxical quest for Imaginary sameness and Symbolic difference" (Ragland-Sullivan, *Jacques Lacan and the Philosophy of Psychoanalysis*, 282).

"The mirror stage both affirms and denies the subject's separateness from the other" (Grosz, *Jacques Lacan*, 42).

100. Cirlot, *A Dictionary of Symbols*, 241.

101. "The mirror stage relies on and in turn provides a condition for the body-image or imaginary anatomy, which in turn helps distinguish the subject from its world. By partitioning, dividing, representing, inscribing the body in culturally determinant ways, it is constituted as a social, symbolic, and regulatable body. It becomes the organizing site of perspective, and, at the same time, an object available to others from their perspectives—in other words both a subject and an object.

"The child sees an image of itself as an organized and integrated totality. The image is positioned in a physical environment. It comes to have a fixed but partial, limited perspective on itself through the externalization provided by the mirror; and it is or can become the object of another's perspective. . . . [T]he child's recognition of its own image means that it has adopted the perspective of exteriority on itself" (Grosz, *Jacques Lacan*, 37–38).

102. An intriguing play of rhyme and rhythm in these opening verses replicates the movement of the waves and may be connected with the union of antitheses that the sea represents (see Cirlot, *A Dictionary of Symbols*, 241). It may also be an instance of what Weber calls *"vehicles of repetition and recurrence" (Return to Freud*, 95) in his discussion "The Subject as Stylus." Given the erotic overtones of "Espuma" (evident in the stylus or pen as phallus, the act of writing) and the process of (re)constituting the subject, the parallelism between Rodríguez's poetry and psychoanalytic theory is manifest. Also, repetition, as we have seen in *Don*, is symptomatic of separation anxiety and the acquisition of language (see Freud's description of the *fort-da* game in *Beyond the Pleasure Principle*).

103. ". . . It is the harsh and beautiful moment / of usage, the friction, the act of surrender / creating it. The incarcerated pain / of the sea saves itself in such a lithe fiber; / beneath the keel, in front of the dike, where / plowed love exists, as on land / the flower, the foam is born. . . ."

104. Cirlot, *A Dictionary of Symbols*, 241–42.

105. ". . . And it is in it / where death breaks, in its skein / where the sea adopts being, as in the height / of his passion man is man, outside / of other business: in his essence."

106. Weber, *Return to Freud*, 137, 143.

107. "Lacan has referred to such unconscious signifying effects in language as crossroad words or 'knots' of meaning—not unlike the *Knotenpunkte* Freud attributed to dreams—or symbolic 'anchoring points' *(points de capiton) (Ecrits*, 1966, p. 503)" (Ragland-Sullivan, *Jacques Lacan and the Philosophy of Psychoanalysis*, 109).

108. "To this railing, the curb of matter / that is a fountain, not an exit, / I now come forth, when the tide / rises, and there I shipwreck, there I drown / very silently, with full / acceptance, unharmed, renewed / in the imperishable foams."

109. See note 30 above. Consistent with Rodríguez's poetics of discovery, then, he focuses on the site of the making of signification, the bar or gap.

110. Weber, *Return to Freud*, 143.

111. While defining Lacan's concept of the Real, Ragland-Sullivan notes, "The Real itself is unmoveable and complete. But man's interpretations of the Real are moveable. The latter combine language with 'self'-experience. The resulting interpretations compose 'reality,' but not the real. The 'real' Real is both beyond and behind Imaginary perception and Symbolic description" (*Jacques Lacan and the Philosophy of Psychoanalysis*, 188). Also see note 22 above.

112. "The child identifies with an image that is manifestly different from itself, though it also clearly resembles it in some respects. It takes as its own an image which is other, an image which remains out of the ego's control. The subject, in other words, recognizes itself at the moment it loses itself in/as the other. This other is the foundation and support of its identity, as well as what destabilizes or annihilates it. The subject's 'identity' is based on a (false) recognition of an other as the same" (Grosz, *Jacques Lacan*, 41).

113. "The phallus is . . . situated, decisively and incisively, on the border that separates the imaginary from the symbolic. It emerges out of the gaps of a perception that apprehends only presence or absence. . . . What it represents is not the absence of a presence, but a difference impossible to apprehend in terms of presence or absence. What it represents, but only by effacing it, is the differential relation of the sexes" (Weber, *Return to Freud*, 145).

114. This paradox is fundamental to Lacan's understanding of "the dislocation of the subject," of the "decentered subject," or of the subject as "fader." Weber explains, "Insofar as language is defined as a system of articulation governed by the play of signifiers, a subject constituted through this play can never be reduced to a reflexive identity and transparency generally associated with the ego. Instead, it must go the way of the 'I' construed as a shifter, or, we could add, as a drifter" (*Return to Freud*, 89). See note 97 above for Weber's definition of the subject as fader.

115. The word "sublime" is entangled in the Lacanian relationship of signifier to signified since it consists of the two elements "sub-" and "-lime." Literally, meaning "below the lintel, threshold, or bar," "sublime" describes the dominance of the signifier over the signified in Lacanian thought. But the sublime is that which carries us beyond ordinary, concrete reality to that which is "elevated or lofty in thought, language, etc., impressing the mind with a sense of grandeur or power, inspiring awe, veneration, etc." (*Random House Webster's College Dictionary*, 1995 ed., s.v. "sublime"). As Henry Hart affirms, "the word [sublime] derives from Latin roots meaning both 'uplifted' (*sublimis*) and 'under the threshold' (*sublimen*)" (*Robert Lowell and the Sublime* [Syracuse, N.Y.: Syracuse University Press, 1995], xxiii). This contradiction in the word "sublime" is congruent with Lacan's understanding of the relationship between signifier and signified and the dissymmetrical exchange between self and other, as well as with Rodríguez's use of "realismo metafórico."

116. Weber, *Return to Freud*, 109; original emphasis. "The Imaginary in adult life valorizes the Other(A) in its links to the mirror-stage quest for sameness and the Oedipal injunction to difference. . . . Imaginary logic stands behind the human tendency of moralizing (good or bad) and ethical judgments, therefore, as well as behind all binary and oppositional thinking. . . .

". . . [W]ithout the Imaginary there would be no sense of identity, no basis for Desire, no representational reference point for reality perception, no mechanism by which to anchor language to any coherent sense of being a 'self.' But without the Symbolic to stabilize, give form to, and 'translate' the Imaginary, man would remain at the same perceptual level as common animals that lack speech. The Imaginary must be sought, then, not just as a separate category, but at the join between Real events and Symbolic naming.

"This join leads to the origin of knowledge as well as to the source of affect" (Ragland-Sullivan, *Jacques Lacan and the Philosophy of Psychoanalysis*, 154, 156).

117. "The word 'I' thus entails a double reference: on the one hand, it refers to the speaker designating himself as part of the content of a particular statement [*énoncé*]; on the other hand, and at the same time, it refers to the speaker designating himself as the subject of a more general process of enunciation that is irreducible to any determinate statement" (Weber, *Return to Freud*, 83).

"With the entry of the subject into the language of the signifier—into verbal language in this case—it enters into a structure of articulation in which direct identification no longer functions; the subject can never again hope to find itself in the signifier, because the latter only receives its identity by virtue of its place in the signifying chain. Signifiers 'are,' only by virtue of their difference. The subject is thereby split between the 'said' and the 'saying,' between the enunciated and the enunciation; it is inscribed in a structure of representation that cannot be traced back to an original presence, but is instead constituted by an irreducible movement of repetition" (134–35).

118. Ibid., 107.

119. "If it places the subject's tumultuous, unlocatable experiences within its corporeal

boundaries and organs, the mirror-stage also engenders social relations with others with whom the subject identifies. These two effects are not clearly separable, particularly if the metaphor of the mirror represents the child's relation to the mother. It is by identifying with and incorporating the image of the mother that it gains an identity as an ego. The image is always the image of another. Yet the otherness of the other is not entirely alien. The subject, to be a subject at all, internalizes otherness as its condition of possibility. It is thus radically *split*, unconscious of the processes of its own production, divided by lack and rupture. The ego illusorily sees itself as autonomous and self-determined, independent of otherness. It feels itself to be its own origin, unified and developed *in/by nature*. There is thus a form of fixity built upon misrecognized dependencies. It is an attempt to arrest rigidly the tensions of the opposition between the fragmented perceived body and the unified, specular body" (Grosz, *Jacques Lacan*, 43).

"The ego is split, internally divided between self and other. It can represent the person as a whole (as in the realist view) only in so far as it denies this internal rupture and conceives of itself as the source of its own origin and unity. It maintains an active, aggressive, and libidinal relation to the other on whom it depends. It comes to distinguish itself as subject from its own body, over which it establishes a hierarchical distance and control. It gains from, as well as loses itself in, the other" (47).

120. The intertextuality underlying all the poems of "Libro segundo" remits us to the question of originality (individuality) and the anxiety of influence that especially pervades *Conjuros*, again demonstrating the link between "Libro segundo" and the earlier book. I use the word "parody" here in the specific sense defined by Linda Hutcheon: "What I mean by 'parody' . . . is *not* the ridiculing imitation of the standard theories and definitions that are rooted in eighteenth-century theories of wit. The collective weight of parodic *practice* suggests a redefinition of parody as repetition with critical distance that allows ironic signalling of difference at the very heart of similarity" (*A Poetics of Postmodernism: History, Theory, Fiction* [New York and London: Routledge, 1988], 26).

121. "Not even the body resists / so much resurrection, and it seeks shelter / in the face of this wind that now softens and brings / smells, and new intimacy. Now all that / was hunger has become sustenance. And life / grows lighter, and a generous gleam / vibrates through our streets. But our retina / continues cloudy, and our saliva / dry, and our feet wander about, as always. . . ."

122. "this wind that now tempers and brings / aroma, and new intimacy"; "a generous gleam [that] vibrates through the streets"

Cf. "Canto del caminar" *(Don)* and "Dando una vuelta" *(Conjuros)*. The duality of wind and light recalls C. Christopher Soufas's title *Conflict of Wind and Light*, suggesting that in his rewriting of Guillén's poem Rodríguez perhaps is considering issues similar to those posed by Soufas's reading of the Generation of 1927.

123. ". . . And then, / this spirited pressure that brings us / the still fragile body of spring, / circles around the winter / of our hearts, seeking a spot / through which to enter them. And here, on turning / the corner, lying in wait, / in fierce meandering, / it ripples our clothes, / aerates our work, / sweeps the house, greases our doors / hard from the dark locks, and opens them / to who knows what beautiful hospitality / and overflows us and, although / we never realize / so much youth, it completely / demolishes us. . . ."

124. ". . . Yes, a little / after sunrise, a now pleasant wind, / serene with seed, blew around / our drought, the injustice / of our years, it inspired something / more beautiful than so much / distrust and so much despair, / more valiant than our / fear of its deep rebellion, of its high / resurrection. . . ."

125. Weber, *Return to Freud*, 14.

126. ". . . And now / I, who lost my freedom for everything, / I want to hear how the poor / noise of our pulse goes dragging itself along / after the warm sound of this alliance / and both make devastating / music, without rhythm, deafly, / for which I know that a day will arrive, / perhaps in mid-January, in which all of us / will know the reason for the name: 'spring / wind.'"

127. Weber, *Return to Freud*, 3.

128. Rodríguez used this same technique and grappled with this transition in "Al ruido del Duero" in *Conjuros*, further evidence of the connection between this section and that book.

129. Guillén does a similar reversal in the final verse of "Impaciente vivir," a possible intertextual echo.

130. Cf. Freud's account of the "realistic ego": "In *The Ego and The Id*, Freud describes the ego as an agency which intervenes in the conflict between anti-social, endogenous, sexual impulses or wishes, which originate in the id, and the demands of reality, which impinge on the organism from the outside. The ego acts like a filter in both directions, from the id to reality and from reality to the id" (Grosz, *Jacques Lacan*, 25).

131. "At this point it is important to bear in mind that any interpretation of a discourse whose temporal medium is the future anterior must itself be caught up in processes of repetition difficult to master or to situate temporally. In short, such interpretations will themselves have been inscribed precisely in the temporal *non-identity of the text read*. They are inscribed literally as *inter-pretations*—as attempts to ascertain the price *(pretium)* of textual gaps—of the *inter*. At the same time, interpretation itself strives to reach the future anterior, when it will have done its work, repeating and displacing the gaps, replacing them with other, supplementary gaps that will in turn elicit yet other retrospective anticipations" (Weber, *Return to Freud*, 12).

132. "What does he seek in our dark / life? What love does he find / in our hard bread?"

133. "Now when Jesus saw great multitudes about him, he gave commandment to depart unto the other side. And a certain scribe came, and said unto him, Master, I will follow thee whithersoever thou goest. And Jesus saith unto him, The foxes have holes, and the birds of the air have nests; but the Son of man hath not where to lay his head. And another of his disciples said unto him, Lord, suffer me first to go and bury my father. But Jesus said unto him, Follow me; and let the dead bury their dead" (Matt. 8:18–22). I am grateful to Rodríguez for clarifying this allusion for me.

134. "If left to itself, the mother-child relation would entail a vicious cycle of imaginary projections, identifications, internalizations, fantasies, and demands that leave no room for development or growth. Lacan claims that if the child and mother form an enclosed, mutually defined relation, relations with a third, independent term become impossible. . . . The unmediated two-person structure of imaginary identifications leaves only two possibilities for the child, between which it vacillates but cannot definitively choose; being overwhelmed by the other, crowded out, taken over (the fantasy of the devouring mother/voracious child); and the wretched isolation and abandonment of all self-worth by the other's absence or neglect (the fantasy of the bad or selfish mother/child)" (Grosz, *Jacques Lacan*, 50–51).

135. Weber, *Return to Freud*, 137; original emphasis.

136. Debicki, *Poetry of Discovery*, 52.

137. "From the bus, full / of laborers, of priests and of roosters, / upon arriving in Palencia, / I see that man."

138. Debicki, *Poetry of Discovery*, 52.

139. Debicki, *Spanish Poetry of the Twentieth Century: Modernity and Beyond*, 111. I do not mean that Rodríguez uses traditional allegory, however. Bousoño attempted to define the phenomenon I am treating here as "alegoría disémica" [bisemic allegory], though he does not distinguish clearly between this concept and "realismo metafórico."

La técnica de *Conjuros* que penetra (aunque característicamente de otro modo . . .) en *Alianza y condena*, consiste . . . en tomar un elemento concreto de la vida real, generalmente un elemento rural o costumbrista (aunque no siempre posea aquél tan atenido carácter: véase el poema «A las estrellas»), e «interpretarlo» en dirección ascendente y trascendentalizadora. ¿Cuál es la extraña consecuencia de este método poético? La aparición de un tipo metafórico de aspecto insólito; algo que podríamos clasificar como «alegoría disémica», especie nueva de recurso retórico. ("La poesía de Claudio Rodríguez," 14)

[The technique of *Conjuros* that penetrates (although characteristically in a different way . . .) *Alianza y condena* consists . . . in taking a concrete element of real life, generally a rural element or custom (although it does not always possess such a foregone character: see the poem "A las estrellas" {To the stars}), and "interpret" it in an ascendent and transcendentalizing direction. What is the unusual consequence of this poetic method? The appearance of an unheard of metaphoric type; something that we could classify as "bisemic allegory," a new type of rhetorical recourse.]

If "alegoría disémica" points in two directions simultaneously, suggesting a distension between the two different levels, it also suggests a tension between them as they are imbricated in the same language of the poem. See notes 270 and 298 below for what I believe to be superb examples of "alegoría disémica."

140.   This situation is similar to the Lacanian notion of the gap opened by the Other which the subject feels obliged to "paper over." As Ragland-Sullivan explains, "Mirror-stage identifications entail the *discovery* of difference, and the concomitant experience of awareness or delimiting alienation. . . . Mirror-stage identification with an external image of the human form both symbolizes the acquisition of a mental permanence and also marks the subject's destined alienation away from the naturalness of spontaneous fusion and toward a cultural dependency. Society and language further widen a gap for which means must then be devised to paper it over" (*Jacques Lacan and the Philosophy of Psychoanalysis*, 25).

141.   Debicki, *Poetry of Discovery*, 52.

142.   "It begins to rain hard, it almost pours / and he won't have enough time / to seek refuge in the city. And he runs / like an assassin. And he doesn't understand / the punishment of the water, his simple / servitude; only to be safe / is what he wants. For that reason he doesn't know / that like a fertile renewal there grows / in his accelerated breathing, / which is live bait, love now irremediable, / rich quarry. . . ."

143.   "Servidumbre" refers to humbling oneself in order to exalt oneself; cf. several parables and scenes in the New Testament. In an interview with Juan Carlos Suñén following the publication of *Casi una leyenda* in 1991, Rodríguez has confirmed, "Servidumbre no es ser servil, es aceptar, y aceptar es aceptar y condenar: alianza y condena son casi sinónimos. La vida está asentada sobre esa urdimbre. Condenamos, rechazamos, pero al mismo tiempo hay que seguir, moverse hacia adelante, como todos los adjetivos del destino humano. Es una servidumbre festiva" [Servitude is not being servile, it is acceptance, and to accept is to accept and to condemn: alliance and condemnation are almost synonymous. Life is based upon that warp. We condemn, we reject, but at the same time one must go on, move forward, like all the adjectives of human destiny. It is a festive servitude] ("Claudio Rodríguez: 'El hombre no puede ser libre,'" *El Urogallo* 62–63 [julio–agosto 1991]: 11).

144.   Sheridan notes that "The French word [*leurre*] translates variously 'lure' (for hawks, fish), 'decoy' (for birds), 'bait' (for fish) and the notion of 'allurement' and 'enticement'. In Lacan, the notion is related to '*méconnaissance*'" (*FFC*, 281). Lacan says that "from the outset, we see, in the dialectic of the eye and the gaze, that there is no coincidence, but, on the contrary, a lure. When, in love, I solicit a look, what is profoundly unsatisfying and always missing is that—*You never look at me from the place from which I see you*.

"Conversely, *what I look at is never what I wish to see*. And the relation that I mentioned earlier, between the painter and the spectator, is a play, a play of *trompe-l'oeil*" (*FFC*, 102–3).

The "lure" or "bait" in "Lluvia y gracia" hinges upon the reflection of sameness and difference between self and other. We shall see that the speaker is in the end result "hooked" by his own observation of the other.

145.   ". . . And, faced with the surprise / of such fecundity, he stumbles and fears; / he feels, very deep in his heart, that he is clean / forever, but he can't stand it; / and he looks, and seeks, and flees, / and, upon arriving at safety, / he enters soaked and free, and takes shelter, / and breathes tranquilly in his ignorance / upon seeing how his clothes / little by little dry out."

146.   Cirlot, *A Dictionary of Symbols*, 51–52. Cf. "A mi ropa tendida."

147.   This image also explains the last line of "A mi ropa tendida (El alma)" from *Conjuros*:

"¿Quién es su lavandera?" The earlier poem also entails the image of water and purification as a "castigo."

148. Cirlot, *A Dictionary of Symbols*, 271–72. See poem VIII in "Libro primero" of *Don*.

149. Cf. "espuma/ceniza/fatiga/amparo" above.

150. Cf. Blake's sunflower poem and Miguel Hernández's in *El rayo que no cesa*.

151. Debicki, *Poetry of Discovery*, 50–52.

152. Chevalier and Gheerbrandt, *Diccionario de los símbolos*, 556.

153. Ibid. [The common name of the heliotrope sufficiently indicates its solar character, which results, on the other hand, not only from a well-known tropism, but also from the radiated form of the flower].

154. The Greek roots of the word "trope" encompass not only a literal turning ("*trópos* turn, turn or figure of speech, akin to *trépein* to turn") (*Random House Webster's College Dictionary*, 1995 ed., s.v. "trope"). A "tropism" is "the orientation of an organism *toward or away from* a stimulus, as light" (my emphasis), and the prefix "tropo-" defines a reaction, response, change, suggesting a metamorphosis, the sort of transformation the speaker undergoes in reacting to his shortcomings, turning away from them in order to turn toward other attitudes.

In keeping with the troping that occurs in "Girasol" in "Libro segundo" of *Alianza*, Weber states, "The *stade du miroir* is thereby defined . . . as a *phase* and as a turning-point or trope, destined to be repeated incessantly, in accordance with a schema whose moments are inadequacy, anticipation, and defensive armoring, and whose result is an identity that is not so much *alienated* as *alienating*" (*Return to Freud*, 14).

155. Saussurean linguistic theory posits that meaning is determined differentially. "The smallest unit of analysis in semiotics, the sign, is composed of two components, which Saussure called the signifier and the signified. The signifier is the material (phonic, graphic) component and the signified is the conceptual (meaningful) component, and together, they are the bases of all languages and representational systems. For Saussure, the sign is not the attachment of a label or name to a pregiven concept. Rather, the sign is active in constituting its ingredients. Neither the signifier nor the signified pre-exist their relations in the sign. The sign is in fact the coupling of a difference in/as the signifier with a difference in/as the signified. Saussure claims, in other words, that the elements composing the sign, as well as the sign itself, can only have identity by virtue of their *pure difference*. Neither the signifier nor the signified have any positive identity. Each can only be defined in terms of what it is *not*" (Grosz, *Jacques Lacan*, 93).

"Lacan problematized psychoanalysis by taking the differences between 'I' and 'me' seriously. By opposing the subject of opacification to the psychological subject, and by showing the subject of certainty as divided, he showed that there are no clear-cut polarities between subject and object, inside and outside, self and other, conscious and unconscious" (Ragland-Sullivan, *Jacques Lacan and the Philosophy of Psychoanalysis*, 65).

156. I wonder if this is an allusion to Guillén's "Perfección."

157. See the discussion of "Brujas" in the first section of this chapter.

158. ". . . of good / fortune because now you, valiant / sunflower, with your gaze / so blind, you were lacking for me / with your posture of pardon, after that / sunny campaign / of haughtiness, toward earth / your head, overcome / by so much grain, such a crazy enterprise."

159. Cf. *Conjuros* and the mirror stage as turning point or trope (note 133 above).

160. Cf. the myth of Clitia: "En la leyenda griega, Clitia es amada y luego abandonada por el Sol, por el amor de otra joven. Inconsolable, Clitia se consume de tristeza y se transforma en heliotropo, la flor que siempre gira hacia el Sol, como alrededor del amante perdido. Simboliza la incapacidad de sobreponerse a su pasión y la receptividad al influjo del ser amado" (Chevalier and Gheerbrandt, *Diccionario de los símbolos*, 556). [In the Greek legend, Clitia is loved and then abandoned by the Sun for the love of another young woman. Inconsolable, Clitia is consumed with sadness and is transformed into a heliotrope, the flower that always turns toward

the Sun, as around the lost lover. She symbolizes the incapacity of overcoming her passion and receptivity to the influence of the beloved being.]

161. See note 97 above concerning the subject as "fader."

162. Grosz summarizes Freud's discussion of the contradictory feelings provoked by the resolution of the oedipal complex, which may underlie the tension the speaker feels in these poems: "In the 'Contributions to the Psychology of Love' (1911), Freud outlines some of the effects of the boy's resolution of the oedipus complex on his later love relations. The requirements of symbolic functioning are contradictory: on the one hand, the boy's sexuality is virile, active, predatory; yet, on the other hand, it must be controlled, repressed, sublimated, and redirected. This split attitude may effect the man's choice of love-object. For example, Freud suggests that men may feel split between feelings of tenderness, respect, affection, and sexual 'purity'; and feelings of a highly sexual yet debasing kind. Affection and sexual desire seem to inhabit different spheres, often being resolved only by splitting his relations between two kinds of women—one noble, honourable, and pure (the virgin figure), the other a sexual profligate (the prostitute figure). He treats the first with asexual admiration, while he is sexually attracted to, yet morally or socially contemptuous of, the second" (*Jacques Lacan*, 128–29).

163. "The light enthused with conquest / loses confidence now, / tremulous with impotence, and doesn't know / if it is on earth or in the sky. It divests itself / of its intimate tenderness / and retires slowly. . . ."

164. Weber provides a brief commentary on the metaphysical theory of language which provides a basis for Lacan's use of linguistics to explain psychoanalytic concepts ("The Unconscious Chess Player," in *Return to Freud*, 20–37). This discussion includes comments on the truth, which Rodríguez has earlier questioned in "Brujas a mediodía, II." In light of the Aristotelian tradition he notes that "truth itself becomes increasingly difficult to distinguish from non-truth" because "language is inherently neither true nor false, but rather a process of signification" (ibid., 21).

165. ". . . What alms / without delight? What dry repose / does evening bring us? What mercy / does this sun of faded red leave? / Who spoke to us from the deep / pity of the sky? . . ."

166. ". . . There still remain / remnants of the audacious forge / of the light, but few / new ones come to us from life: a noise, / some odor badly kneaded, this gloomy / serenity of sunset, when / far away are the fields and even farther / the fire of the hearth, and this defeat / of ours, because of cowardice or arrogance, / because of inertia or because of glory / like that of this light, now without justice / or rebellion, or dawn."

167. Lacan's explanation of the concept of "negative quantity" is pertinent to this moment in the speaker's evolution: "[M]en survive only by being at each moment so forgetful of all their conquests, I am speaking of their subjective conquests. Of course, from the moment they forget them, they are nevertheless conquered, but it is rather they who are conquered by the effects of these conquests. And the fact of being conquered by something that one does not know sometimes has formidable consequences, the first of which is confusion.

"Negative quantity, then, is the term that we shall find to designate one of the supports of what is called the castration complex, namely, the negative effect in which the phallus object enters into it" (*FFC*, 252–53).

168. Cf. Quevedo, "Poderoso caballero es don Dinero" [A powerful lord is Mr. Money].

169. "Shall I sell my words, today when I lack / usefulness, income, today when no one trusts me? / I need money for love, poverty / in order to love. And the price of a memory, the auction / of a vice, the inventory of a desire, / give value, not virtue, to my needs, / ample vocabulary to my clumsiness, / license to my limestone / solitude. . . ."

170. For commentary distinguishing need, demand, and desire see Grosz, *Jacques Lacan*, 59–67; and Ragland-Sullivan, *Jacques Lacan and the Philosophy of Psychoanalysis*, 69–89.

171. ". . . Because money, at times, is dream / itself, it is life / itself. And its triumph, its monopoly, gives fervor, / change, imagination, takes off age and smooths / brows, and multi-

plies friends, / and raises skirts, and is honey crystalizing light, warmth. Not a plague, leprosy / like today; happiness, / not frivolity; law, not impunity. . . ."

172. "Rich from so much loss, / without dealings, without a stock market, even without temptation / and even without gilt ruin, to what purpose the lair / of these words that if they give breath, / they don't give money? Do they promise bread or arms? / Or rather, like a badly contrived balance, / do they attempt to give order to a time of lack, / to give meaning to a life propriety or eviction?"

173. Rodríguez will return to this imagery in "Oda a la hospitalidad."

174. Cf. "Espuma" and "Lluvia y gracia." In these poems that call attention to the frame the scene is depicted as a staging of reality in which the speaker is both actor and audience, part of the scene observed and an observer. Also see note 92 above.

175. This reading differs with Bousoño's in "La poesía de Claudio Rodríguez," 22–24.

176. The awareness of this dark spot resembles Lacan's discussion of the "scotoma." Ragland-Sullivan explains: "A person may feel scrutinized by someone whose eyes and physical being are invisible. A mere suspicion of the presence of others can trigger an inner resonance: a window, darkness, a feeling—suddenly the window itself becomes a *regard*. . . . In moments like these the limitations of consciousness may be witnessed in what Lacan has de scribed as a *scotoma* (Greek, obscuration of part of the field of vision). . . . The *regard* is no simply a glance cast from the eye, nor a glance from reflective consciousness, because the *regard* has the power to activate within consciousness an awareness of unconscious motivation and intentionality" (*Jacques Lacan and the Philosophy of Psychoanalysis*, 94).

177. Several aspects of Lacan's thinking expressed in "Tuché and Automaton" (*FFC*, esp 55–60) are applicable here. Lacan remarks that in this encounter, which seems as if it were a dream, "the idea of another locality, another space, another scene, *the between perception and consciousness*" (56) opens up. "Thus the encounter, forever missed, has occurred between dream and awakening, between the person who is still asleep and whose dream we will no know and the person who has dreamt merely in order not to wake up" (59).

178. Continuing with Lacan's comments on the scotoma, "At the perceptual level, this is the phenomenon of a relation that is to be taken in a more essential function, namely, that in its relation to desire, reality appears only as marginal" (ibid., 107–8). In essence, then, the central (the scene of the snowfall) becomes marginal so that the speaker can focus on his blind spot.

179. "And you say: «Wake up, / for it is dawning». (And it is night / at its darkest.) You say «Close, / for the sun enters». And I do not want / to lose yet again before this / snowfall. No, I do not want / to lie to you again. I have / to lift the mask / from this enemy face / that feigns for me at my door / the innocence that returns / and the foot that leaves its mark."

180. "Transparent quietude. In front of the reddish / land, desiccated to the marrow, / with aridity that is now rigidity, / the Mediterranean opens. There are low pines, / sabinas, century plants, and there grows thyme / and the faithful rosemary, so austerely / yet they barely smell i not of saltpeter. / The north wind burns. Evening falls."

181. "Truth of submission, of surrender, of / dethronings, collapsings / in front of the pure blue sea that on the shore / becomes emerald green. Old and new / erosion. Plates, laminas cornises, / cliffs and breakwaters, agile / bevel edge, groove, lucidity of rock / of millenary permanence. Here / the truth of the stone, never mute / but in internal reverberation, / in a shivering of perennial / harvest, giving its sure office, / its secret sober tenderness next / to the sea, that is too much creature, / too much beauty for man."

182. "Ancient Latin sea that today does not sing, / barely speaks, whispers, prisoner / of its implacable power, with / the pulsing of suffocation, without waves, / almost in the silence o clairvoyance / while the sky grows dark and there arrives, / massive and dry, the last occasion / for loving. . . ."

183. ". . . Amid stones and amid foams, / what is surrender, what supremacy? / What calm us, what torments us: The terse sea or the desolate land?"

184. I am grateful to Luis García Jambrina for pointing this fact out to me. Edited by

Antonio Molina, the anthology *Poesía cotidiana* [Quotidian poetry] was published in February of 1966, subsequent to the first edition of *Alianza y condena* (1965). It is curious that Rodríguez's poems included in this anthology are mostly from *Conjuros* and *Alianza*, but they are chronologically (and aesthetically, according to Rodríguez's ordering in his works) shuffled. The anthology also has three different titles: at the head of the title page appears "*Poesía española contemporánea: Antología (1939–1964),*" which is followed by three asterisks and the title "*Poesía cotidiana.*" On the final page, which contains the publishing history, one reads the following: "Esta primera edición de la *Antología de la Poesía Cotidiana*, con prólogo y notas de Antonio Molina, quedó lista el día 2 de marzo de 1966." However, on the back of the title page the date reads "Primera edición: 20 de febrero de 1966." The publishing history of "Llegada" and "Ciudad" bears an uncanny resemblance to Jane Gallup's account of Lacan's "The Mirror Stage"; see her chapter "Where to Begin?" in *Reading Lacan* (Ithaca and London: Cornell University Press, 1985), 74–92. "Llegada" can be found in *Poesía española contemporánea: antología 1939–1964; Poesía cotidiana*, comp. Antonio Molina (Madrid: Alfaguara, 1966), 515–18.

185. "Arrival at the Station in Avila" "Avila, such healthful air / as yours doesn't exist elsewhere, / but I come not / to be cured of anything, though a cure / would be good for my lung, after these / years on the bad earth."

186. "Like that around here / such healthful air doesn't exist, but I don't come / to get cured of anything. I come to know what deed / vibrates in the light, what dark rebellion / razes our life today."

187. "Here no longer are there banners, / or walls, or towers, as if now / everything could resist the impetus / of the land, the looting / of the sky. And our view / is swept away, our bodies are / a candid market, our voices dwellings / and love and years / doors for one and for a thousand who would enter. / Yes, so groundless always, / when today we walk through the old streets / our heels are stained / with a new grape, and we hear / I know well what waters / spill over the murmurous channels of our ears."

188. "And knowing what distance / there is from man to man, from one life to another, / what planetary dimension separates / two pulses, what immense distance / there is between two gazes / or from a mouth to a kiss. / . . . / Never houses: barracks, / never streets: trenches, / never work: duty. / For what have such strong plazas, / deep moats, solid battlements, walled enclosures / served? / Fear, defense, / self-interest and vengeance, hate, / solitude: Here is what made us / live in proximity, not in company. / Such is the cruel scene / that they left us as an inheritance. Then, / how to fortify life here / if it is only alliance?"

189. "Old ambition that now / only the tourist or the archeologist admires / or he who likes stamps or coats of arms. / This is no national / monument, but light of the upper plains, / fresh air that waters the arid lung / and expands it, and makes of / total, renewed surrender, homeland / in the open country. Here there are no coasts, seas, / north or south: here all is material for harvest. . . ."

190. "Avila, like your healthful air / such air doesn't exist, and this little wine / seeps into us with it in deep breaths. / Recently arrived and a moment together, / out of here anyone who would remind us now / of that voracious fall of night / above the high fields / of our land!"

191. ". . . Because everything / surrenders all around and there are no borders, or distance, or history. / Only voracious space and the October dew / above these high fields / of our land."

192. Chevalier and Gheerbrandt, *Diccionario de los símbolos*, 887–88.

193. "A metaphoric relation between father and son is instituted, for the boy must be like his father (i.e., acquire the characteristics of masculinity the father represents) while also *not* being like him (by not desiring the woman the father desires). This may explain why, instead of resting the power of the complex on the personage of the father, Lacan speaks of the 'paternal metaphor' or 'the name-of-the-father'" (Grosz, *Jacques Lacan*, 68).

194. In addition to his thorough familiarity with Greek and Roman mythology, Rodríguez surely knew of Nietzsche's distinction between Dionysian and Apollonian traits expounded in *The Birth of Tragedy* because of his extensive reading in philosophy.

195. See Chevalier and Gheerbrandt, *Diccionario de los símbolos*, 420–22. Again, see Mayhew (*Claudio Rodríguez*, 26) on "ebriedad" and the discussion of *Don* in chap. 1 above.

196. The tale of Daphne and Apollo is perhaps the most well known. See Chevalier and Gheerbrandt, who note that Apollo "realiza el equilibrio y la armonía de los deseos, no por suprimir las pulsiones humanas, sino por orientarlas hacia una espiritualización progresiva, gracias al desarrollo de la conciencia" (*Diccionario de los símbolos*, 111) [achieves equilibrium and harmony of his desires, not by suppressing his human impulses, but by orienting them toward a progressive spiritualization, thanks to the development of conscience].

197. In note 1 above, I refer to the pair of diagrams in "The Line and the Light" (Lacan, *FFC*, 91). Lacan subsequently imbricates these two complementary diagrams in "What Is a Picture?" (*FFC*, 105). These diagrams visually depict the concepts I am describing in "Libro tercero." Lacan follows his diagram with the following comments: "What is at issue here is not the philosophical problem of representation. From that point of view, when I am presented with a representation, I assure myself that I know quite a lot about it, I assure myself as a consciousness that knows that it is only representation, and that there is, beyond, the thing, the thing itself. Behind the phenomenon, there is the noumenon, for example. I may not be able to do anything about it, because my *transcendental categories*, as Kant would say, do just as they please and force me to take the thing in their way. . . .

"In my opinion, it is not in this dialectic between the surface and that which is beyond that things are suspended. For my part, I set out from the fact that there is something that establishes a fracture, a bi-partition, a splitting of the being to which the being accommodates itself, even in the natural world" (106).

198. "It is through castration that the phallus is constituted as a signifier. Castration is thus nothing other than an effect upon the subject caused by the falling out or *striking down* of the signifier. This function of the phallus thus derives from the structure of language conceived as a movement of signifiers, a movement to which the subject is sub-jected. This subjection not only splits the subject, but also supports and suspends it in the incessant reiteration of an irremediable division: not between subject and object, but between enunciated and enunciation, signified and signifier. It is in this sense that the individual subject is dependent upon the symbolic, or as Freud writes in a letter to Fliess, upon that 'prehistoric, unforgettable other, who is never equaled by anyone later.' This Other, however, is not a person or even a subject, but instead that 'somewhere else,' that localized difference which emerges from and moves towards the signifying chain. This negative place, this 'dislocation' comes to be occupied by various instances: first by the mother as that utterly Other in the sense of the demand for love; then by the father as the forbidding, castrating instance which also introduces the law; and finally by the phallus 'itself,' as the selfless, self-effacing mark that bars the place and splits the subject. While the phallus thus marks the *decisive* moment of bifurcation in the trajectory of the subject, it at the same time remarks the structural condition of the latter's subjection—to language as medium of articulation and of difference" (Weber, *Return to Freud*, 148).

199. As indicated in note 5 above, the Law of the Name-of-the-Father defines an individual's acceptance of the threat of castration (loss), permitting entry into the symbolic and language, "giving the child access to a (sexual [poetic]) identity and speaking position within culture [the poetic tradition]" (Grosz, *Jacques Lacan*, 122).

200. "Through the 'name-of-the-father', the child is positioned beyond the structure of dual imaginary relations within the broader framework of culture, where genuine exchange may become possible (exchange requires the third term, the object exchanged between the subject and the other). However, the resolution of the oedipus complex or the assumption of the name-of-the-father, is rarely if ever entirely successful. The imaginary returns, being only partially repressed, resurfacing in both pathological and 'normal' forms in adult life as symptoms, dreams, and amorous relations, in those relations where the self strives to see itself in the other" (ibid., 47).

Weber says of the orders, "If the arresting images of the imaginary order are effectively inscribed in the force-field of the signifier, the latter would have neither field nor force without the dissimulation by the imaginary. Left to its own devices, the symbolic, like the primary process, would tend to dissolve and to displace the very determinations upon which it 'itself' depends. In short: without the imaginary, the symbolic would self-destruct. It is therefore no less dependent on the imaginary than the imaginary on it. . . . [T]he imaginary and the symbolic constitute neither an ethical opposition nor an ontological hierarchy, but a differential relationship that disorders each of these 'orders,' . . .; each order sets itself apart *from* the other, but in so doing reveals its dependency upon the other and thereby sets *itself apart*" (*Return to Freud*, 108–9; original emphasis). Also see note 114 above.

201. "In adult life," notes Ragland-Sullivan, "subjects constantly reconstitute their identities within a synchronic, cultural signifying context—a Symbolic order—to secure themselves a fixed value in terms of their Imaginary 'self'-fables. A subject represents him- or herself to an-other person as signifying something cultural (a title, a profession) within a given Symbolic order, or something more basic and personal in terms of his or her own narcissism, and tries to confirm the merit of the Symbolic and Imaginary aspects of identity in light of Real events. When a subject's Imaginary ideal is confirmed by Symbolic labels and approved by Real events, the accompanying feeling is one of wholeness or *jouissance*. But the ever-jostling, power-bent signifying chain of society continually threatens the constancy and fixity of any subject's Imaginary, Symbolic, and Real constellation of joy" (*Jacques Lacan and the Philosophy of Psychoanalysis*, 223).

202. In effect, this inversion is precisely how Lacan understands the movement of signification in the sign and the path of the drive. See his well-known diagram in "The Partial Drive and Its Circuit" (*FFC*, 178). Weber elucidates this movement: "In the word, so understood, the movement of signification proceeds from the signified, as its beginning, traverses the signifier, as its middle—and manifestation—and comes full circle, ending again in the signified" (*Return to Freud*, 88).

203. These verses are from Villon's "Le Testament" where the poet "half-seriously, half-comically" looks back on his life. He acknowledges that he has lost his youth, squandered opportunities to improve himself, and led a dissipated life. Yet at the same time that he confesses these faults, he says that he does not regret these experiences because of what he has learned from them. See *The Penguin Book of French Verse*, vol. 1: *To the Fifteenth Century*, ed. Brian Woledge (Baltimore: Penguin Books, 1966), xvii, 308.

204. "Perhaps, being worth what a day is worth, / it may be better that today end soon. / The novelty of this event, of this / girl, almost a child but with already experienced / eyes and flesh on the verge / of honey, with her short steps, with her light chestnut-colored / bun, her ankle dimpled / so harmoniously, with her graceful / breast that dazzles more than anything / my tongue . . ."

205. I am grateful to Laura Demaría for these insights.

206. The image of the "moño" ("bun" or "twist": hair formed into a "knot" on the top of a woman's head) recurs in other poems by Rodríguez, most memorably in "Hilando" (*El vuelo*). This image seems to represent an ideal image of Woman for Rodríguez, but may also be an image of the text ("knotted," "plaited," or "woven" language). Wearing one's hair in this fashion highlights the shape of the face and the head, and accentuates the features (according to several women whom I have consulted). It also suggests vulnerability by exposing the nape, and reserve as opposed to "letting one's hair down." It may therefore be a symbol of availability.

As yet, I have not been able to find any sources that would confirm (or negate) these hypotheses, although two dictionaries of symbols provide some insight under the entry "hair." Chevalier and Gheerbrandt ambivalently note, "Por ser la cabellera una de las principales armas de la mujer, el hecho de mostrarla o esconderla, anudarla o desatarla es frecuentemente signo de la disponibilidad, de don o de reserva de una mujer. María Magdalena, en la iconografía cristiana, se representa siempre con los cabellos largos y sueltos, signo de abandono a Dios, más aún que recuerdo de su antigua condición de pecadora" (*Diccionario de los símbolos*, 220)

[By being one of the principal weapons of woman, the fact of showing it or hiding it, knotting it or untying it is frequently a sign of the availability, of the gift or of the reserve of a woman. Mary Magdalene, in Christian iconography, is always represented with long, loose hair, a sign of abandonment to God, still more than a reminder of her former condition of sinner].

"A hairstyle," Nadia Julien remarks, "expresses the persona; it reflects the individual's attitude to instinctive drives. Whether women wear their hair long or short, up or down, reveals availability or reserve, whether they show or hide it, a desire to please, or get themselves noticed, or avoid being noticed or lusted after (such as the puritan with hair scragged back)" (*The Mammoth Dictionary of Symbols: Understanding the Hidden Language of Symbols* [New York: Carroll and Graf, 1996], 188).

207. This chance meeting corresponds with Lacan's discussion of the *tuché*, which can take the form of either a fortuitous or an unfortunate encounter ("the *eutuchia* or the *dustuchia*, the happy encounter and the unhappy encounter" [*FFC*, 80]). "For what we have in the discovery of psycho-analysis is an encounter, an essential encounter—an appointment to which we are always called with a real that eludes us, . . . the *tuché*, which we have borrowed . . . from Aristotle, who uses it in his search for cause. We have translated it as *the encounter with the real*. The real is beyond the *automaton*, the return, the coming-back, the insistence of the signs, by which we see ourselves governed by the pleasure principle. The real is that which always lies beyond the automaton" (53–54).

Speaking of the gaze in another lecture, Lacan seems to define "esa mirada que no tiene dueño" which causes shame and suspends the subject in vacillation. "But what is the gaze?" he asks, answering, "it is a question of recentring the subject as speaking in the very lacunae of that in which, at first sight, it presents itself as speaking. . . .

"It is here that I propose that the interest the subject takes in his own split is bound up with that which determines it—namely, a privileged object, which has emerged from some primal separation, from some self-mutilation induced by the very approach of the real, whose name, in our algebra, is the *objet a*.

"In the scopic relation, the object on which depends the phantasy from which the subject is suspended in an essential vacillation is the gaze. . . . From the moment that this gaze appears, the subject tries to adapt himself to it, he becomes that punctiform object, that point of vanishing being with which the subject confuses his own failure. Furthermore, of all the objects in which the subject may recognize his dependence in the register of desire, the gaze is specified as unapprehensible. That is why . . . the subject manages, fortunately, to symbolize his own vanishing and punctiform bar *(trait)* in the illusion of the consciousness of *seeing oneself see oneself*, in which the gaze is elided.

"If, then, the gaze is that underside of consciousness, how shall we try to imagine it?

"The expression is not inapt, for we can give body to the gaze . . . in the dimension of the existence of others. Others would remain suspended in the same, partially de-realizing, conditions that are, in Sartre's definition, those of objectivity, were it not for the gaze. The gaze, as conceived by Sartre, is the gaze by which I am surprised—surprised in so far as it changes all the perspectives, the lines of force, of my world, orders it, from the point of nothingness where I am, in a sort of radiated reticulation of the organisms. As the locus of the relation between me, the annihilating subject, and that which surrounds me, the gaze seems to possess such a privilege that it goes so far as to have me scotomized, I who look, the eye of him who sees me as object. In so far as I am under the gaze, Sartre writes, I no longer see the eye that looks at me and, if I see the eye, the gaze disappears. . . .

"The gaze sees itself—to be precise, the gaze of which Sartre speaks, the gaze that surprises me and reduces me to shame, since this is the feeling he regards as the most dominant. The gaze I encounter . . . is, not a seen gaze, but a gaze imagined by me in the field of the Other" (82–85).

The gaze of the young woman in "Un suceso" reduces the speaker to shame, precisely because he sees himself seeing himself; he recognizes her gaze as the projection of his desire.

"The intrasubjective element appears mysteriously to consciousness when a person experiences 'self' as an object of an-other's gaze—whether present or absent—and the gaze catalyzes a phenomenology of judgment in the form of shame, modesty, blushing, fear, prestige, rage, or so on. . . . The Other's gaze triumphs over the eye, subjectivizing the relationship between gaze and eye, or seeing and knowing. . . . This state of affairs derives partly from the incongruous and asymmetrical relationship among gaze, eye, and knowledge: a relationship that is really one of specular lure, opacity, illusion, and trap.

". . . If 'seeing' basically involves projecting one's own inner reality outward to be refracted through an-other's eyes, then 'knowing' is complicated at the primordial level of 'self'-image and representation, long before 'knowing' culminates in conscious thought" (Ragland-Sullivan, *Jacques Lacan and the Philosophy of Psychoanalysis*, 95).

208. See note 149 above concerning the contradictory outcomes of the resolution of the oedipal complex and a man's ambivalent sexual reaction to woman.

209. ". . . And there is no remedy, and I speak to her hoarsely / like a gull, at the surface of the lips / (of my wasted mouth), and I get excited / dissimulating knowledge and innocence / like one who doesn't distinguish a glass bead / from a diamond, and I speak to her of details / of my life, and I lose my voice, and I hear myself / and I pursue myself, very distrustful / of my studied assurance, and I am careful of my breath, of my gaze / and of my hands, and I almost forgive myself / for feeling such precious liberty / near me. . . ."

210. ". . . I know very well that this is not only / temptation. How (do) I renounce my desire / now. I feel sorry for myself and I blush / beside this girl whom today I love, / whom today I lose, whom very soon / I will kiss very chastely without / her knowing that in that kiss goes a sob."

211. "Everything emerges from the structure of the signifier," asserts Lacan. ". . . Psychoanalysis . . . reminds us that the facts of human psychology cannot be conceived in the absence of the function of the subject defined as the effect of the signifier.

"Here the processes are to be articulated, of course, as circular between the subject and the Other—from the subject called to the Other, to the subject of that which he has himself seen appear in the field of the Other, from the Other coming back. This process is circular, but, of its nature, without reciprocity. Because it is circular, it is disymmetrical. . . .

"The whole ambiguity of the sign derives from the fact that it represents something for someone. This someone may be many things, it may be the entire universe, in as much as we have known for some time that information circulates in it, as a negative of entropy. Any node in which signs are concentrated, in so far as they represent something, may be taken for a someone. What must be stressed at the outset is that a signifier is that which represents a subject for another signifier.

"The signifier, producing itself in the field of the Other, makes manifest the subject of its signification. But it functions as a signifier only to reduce the subject in question to being no more than a signifier, to petrify the subject in the same movement in which it calls the subject to function, to speak, as subject" (*FFC*, 206–7).

212. "The drive gains satisfaction even in the deflection of its aim, as is the case in the vicissitude of sublimation. The drive is motivated by but always falls short of satisfaction. There is an ambiguity in its aim *(zeil):* the aim of the drive is always both the attainment of its object, *and* ultimately, a gain in satisfaction. In spite of renouncing its object, as in the process of sublimation, the drive is still able to gain satisfaction. . . .

"Lacan suggests . . . that even when the subject has renounced a certain satisfaction through the attainment of its aim, there is still a satisfaction. There can be satisfaction, in other words, at giving up satisfaction" (Grosz, *Jacques Lacan*, 74–75).

213. Rodríguez has taken the title of his poem from Shakespeare's *The Winter's Tale*, where in act 2, scene 1, the young prince Mamillius tells his mother Hermione a story of "sprites and goblins," for "A sad tale's best for winter." When Mamillius climbs into her lap, Hermione asks him to "Come on, then, / And give't me in mine ear." Although the play is a comedy, the

oedipal conflict lies at the heart of this drama because of King Leontes' jealousy and his harsh and unjust treatment of his wife. The king also causes the death of his son, but Mamillius is later reinstated in the figure of Florizel, who marries Leontes' daughter Perdita.

214. "With me don't you have / any remorse, mother. I give you the only thing / that I can give you now: if not love, / then reconciliation. Now I know the failure, / the victory that fits / in a body. The falling, the ruining of oneself / for so many years against the flint / of grief, the fleeing / with impunity with laws / that were on my side, a cruel massage / to distance me from you; stories / of money and of cots, / of rents without taxes, / when my life consisted of being ready to pounce / on your fall, on your / wound, on which I placed if not my teeth, not / my tongue either, / give me today the measure / of my sin."

215. "One of Lacan's most convincing arguments for a functioning of the signifier beyond language and system lies in his theory that the *tu* constitutes a signifier. . . .

"The human tendency is to want to objectify the other to make sense of the prototypical *tu* within one's own 'self'-myth system and thereby to stabilize the ambiguities and miscommunications which characterize human interaction. But the independent other or *tu* exists as a reminder of the difficulty of such endeavor. Lacan shows that 'communication' systems work best on paper. *Tu*, said Lacan, is the fishhook (*hameçon*) of the other in the wave of meaning. *Tu* has no univocal value as a signifier, then, and keeps people from making a Real thing out of their abstract objectivizations of others. *Tu*—an undetermined signifier—serves as a point of psychic punctuation by which we try to fix the other in a point of meaning. . . . In the interior of our own intrasubjective discourse, the *tu* supports something comparable to our own *moi* ideal ego while not being it. Instead, the *tu* signifies our myth of the other (*Séminaire* III, pp. 337–38). Since the relationship of *moi* and *toi* is one of Imaginary exclusion or confusion (that is, we cannot readily know who the other really is or how the other truly receives us), any address to the *tu* is an invocation of our own Other(A); an effort to learn what one does not know about oneself (*Seminaire* III, pp. 342–43). The difficulty of the *moi/toi* relation (with its implicit narcissistic and aggressive fusions) forces upon Symbolic order dealings what Lacan has called the 'general notion of the other'—a notion marked by 'normal distance.' Lacan therefore concluded that the basic reason people 'communicate' is not really to secure feedback or for the effect of a message's content, but for the action itself, the goal being love and recognition" (Ragland-Sullivan, *Jacques Lacan and the Philosophy of Psychoanalysis*, 218–19).

216. "I have grown only in skeleton: look at me. / Come over as before / to the window. You, don't ever think / about that crude rod that raised me / sixteen years ago. Come, come, / see how clear the night is now, / see that I love you, that it's true, / see how, where there were / parcels of land, there are plains, / see your son who returns / pathless and cloakless, as then, / to your lap with remorse."

217. This request for confirmation is underscored in the later poem "Adiós." The speaker is looking for confirmation from an outside source, but he looks for the mother's gaze, as indicated by the presence of the window.

"It is th[e] imperfection of the child's jubilant recognition—its contamination by something *else*, something unsettling, that impels the child to *turn around*, for such verification can only come from somewhere else, from another place. It does not take place in the ostensibly perceptual relationship of the child to the mirror, of subject to object, or even, despite appearances, of subject to subject. It takes place in the encounter of look and look. The look is no longer determined by the object it seems to perceive: the mirror image, but rather by its encounter with another look. . . . What is now added to the mirror image is the *glance of the other* and the *gesture* of turning around that *returns* the child to the signifier" (Weber, *Return to Freud*, 117).

"The mirror stage is not negated or invalidated, far from it; it is given a new twist by a *gesture* that turns away from the image in a silent *appeal* to the *look* as such. The place of the subject is thus no longer framed by the mirror, but relegated to the enabling margins of the visible. On this margin, the manifestation of a certain 'prematuration' is replaced by another, a 'much more critical one, the concealment of which is the secret of the subject's jubilation.' The new twist, the look that is lacking, sets the stage for a very different kind of drama: that of desire conceived as the desire of the other" (119).

218. "In his continuing effort to show the connections between 'self'-misrecognition and the proximity of the Imaginary to the Symbolic and the Real," Ragland-Sullivan writes, "Lacan used the example of the Real of the human body whose form first appears to the infant Imaginarily, that is, as a 'mirror' reflection. People can see themselves reflected in a window, for example, at the same time that they see Real objects outside the window. Although the 'self'-reflection also seems real, it is only 'virtual' or Imaginary" (*Jacques Lacan and the Philosophy of Psychoanalysis*, 151).

219. Also see Matthew Arnold's "Dover Beach" where the speaker says, "Come to the window, sweet is the night-air!"

220. "A subject does not represent an idea by means of a signifier for another subject (a version of the commonly held communicational model of language, whereby the sender transmits a message to a receiver); rather, a signifier represents a subject for another signifier" (Grosz, *Jacques Lacan*, 97). "Yet insofar as desire is directed towards something else which 'itself' can never simply be a self-identical object, it is not only desirous *of another*, but is 'itself' another's desire. It is 'the desire for the other's desire,' the desire *of* a signifier, defined as the signifier of another desire" (Weber, *Return to Freud*, 128).

"By introducing an awareness of otherness into the structure of the subject, the Phallus subverts not only the illusory symmetry of the Imaginary infant/mother dyad but also the possibility of the independent unity of any one term. Identity only 'means' henceforth in relation to responses to and from others" (Ragland-Sullivan, *Jacques Lacan and the Philosophy of Psychoanalysis*, 176).

221. See Luke 15:11–32.

222. Weber, *Return to Freud*, 81, 90.

223. "Mirror-stage identification with an external image of the human form both symbolizes the acquisition of a mental permanence and also marks the subject's destined alienation away from the naturalness of spontaneous fusion and toward a cultural dependency. Society and language further widen a gap" (Ragland-Sullivan, *Jacques Lacan and the Philosophy of Psychoanalysis*, 25). "The space between the *moi* and the Other(A) is . . . Desire, a space that widens throughout life" (76–77).

224. Grosz succinctly defines the *objet a* in this way: "The 'object' providing satisfaction is not the object *of* the drive. It is always a divergence, a metonymy, a lack of the real, displaced onto a substitute. The object of satisfaction is represented by Lacan's formulaic expression, the *objet a*. The *objet a* is not the drive's *objekt*, but the *cause of desire*" (*Jacques Lacan*, 75). "The drive thus strives for an (impossible) object to satisfy its bivalent aims by filling the lack or gap. It is because of its essential lack of an essence, its capacity to substitute one object for another to gain satisfaction, the drive is the field in which desire is manifested" (ibid., 76).

"The first meeting between an infant and the Real," says Ragland-Sullivan, "is symbolized by Lacan as the *objet a*, which refers both to the primordial gap between body experience and perception and to the images which quickly fill in this gap (*Séminaire* XI, pp. 76, 78). From the start, *objet a* carries the dual meaning of 'lack' and that which compensates for lack" (*Jacques Lacan and the Philosophy of Psychoanalysis*, 190–91).

Sheridan describes the "*objet petit a*" by saying that "The '*a*' in question stands for '*autre*' (other), the concept having been developed out of the Freudian 'object' and Lacan's own exploitation of 'otherness'. The '*petit a* (small '*a*') differentiates the object from (while relating it to) the '*Autre*' or '*grand Autre*' (the capitalized 'Other')" (*FFC*, 282).

225. "The elemental dramas of separation, alienation, and Desire link knowledge, language, and love" (Ragland-Sullivan, *Jacques Lacan and the Philosophy of Psychoanalysis*, 131).

226. "In Seminar Twenty Lacan said that demand emanates from the *je* and resides in the

substitution of finite and concrete objects for the denied and obscure, infinite object of Desire (p. 114); these substitutions are just so many metonymous ways to compensate for the split between being and wanting that marked the end of the mirror stage. Thus, demand begins with the ideal ego's formation and answers finally to the superego, or the limits intrinsic to a specific *moi*. Substitute objects include language itself in the sense that it serves the same mastery function as objects (Lacan's interpretation of the *Fort! Da!* for example): Lacan has said that speaking is in and of itself a *jouissance*" (ibid., 86).

227. See Lacan's and Weber's discussion of future anteriority in note 28 above.

228. "I know very well how the flower / shines throughout Sanabria, / near Portugal, in lands poor in production and in consumption, / but of great quality of wheat and trills."

229. "It isn't your memory. Today it's only / the enterprise, the adventure, / not the memory that which I seek. It is that / tension of distance, / the faithful kilometerage. No, I don't want / duration, the guarantee of an / image, today expansive and already tomorrow / shrivelled. I want to see that terrain, / to tread the unforgettable route, to hear / the song of that light there, to see / how love, the early / rains today have made / this mud, to live / that naturalness of the breeze / that blows there. . . ."

230. Walter Starkie (*The Road to Santiago: Pilgrims of St. James* [Berkeley: University of California Press, 1965], 302) mentions a pilgrimage route from the south of Spain that passes through La Sanabria before joining the main route of the "Camino de Santiago" [the Way of St. James] at Lestedo in the province of Lugo. In Spanish, the "Camino de Santiago" is synonymous with the "Vía láctea" [the Milky Way].

231. ". . . No, today I do not / struggle still with your body / but with the way that takes me to it. / I want my senses, / without you, / to continue being advantageous to me. / Between one stop / and another, to greet those men / to see what I am capable of giving / and capable of accepting, to see what I refuse, / what is still useful to me; to enter cities, to breathe / with native breath in them, be they / those they may be. . . ."

232. ". . . I do not seek / to chew that dry / slice of memory, / to buy that hardware, to contrive such a poor / botched job. I seek the place, the distance, / the concrete tense, vibrating, the lone / remarkable company, that which unites so much dispersed life. . . ."

233. ". . . Not only / your flesh, that now already burns like tow / and of which I am the flame, / but pure calibre, the very area / of your separation and of the land. / Of that land where the sun ripens / that which does not last."

234. "The aim, then, is always a return, a reintegration into the circuit of a perfectly self-enclosed auto-eroticism which has succeeded in replacing the lost object with its own processes and parts. The drive describes the residue or remainder left over of the primal object that ensures no substitute (even the Real itself) will ever plug the rim, fill it to completion" (Grosz, *Jacques Lacan*, 77). "Desire too is based on a chain of substitution whereby the first (lost) object of desire generates a potentially infinite chain of (only partially satisfactory) substitutes" (100).

In "The Most Prevalent Form of Degradation in Erotic Life" Freud says that "something in the nature of the sexual drive itself is unfavorable to the achievement of absolute gratification. . . . [T]he ultimate object of the sexual drive is never again the original one, but only a surrogate for it. . . . [W]hen the original object of a wishful excitation becomes lost in consequence of repression, it is often replaced by an endless series of substitute objects, none of which ever give full satisfaction" (quoted in Weber, *Return to Freud*, 125).

". . . [T]he *moi* continually (re-)constitutes itself in anticipation of an ideal image being refracted, in anticipation of narcissism (re-)verified and pre-Castration *jouissance* restored. Not unlike the mirror-stage infant joyfully anticipating its own unity through body mastery, the adult anticipates psychic mastery (wholeness, constancy, glory, certainty, and joy), deploring its evanescence" (Ragland-Sullivan, *Jacques Lacan and the Philosophy of Psychoanalysis*, 149).

235. "Every operation of the signifier consists of both substitution and concatenation, each

depending upon the other, since the signifier is determined only through its relationship to its surroundings, and more precisely, through exchanges that define linguistic 'value' as a function of substitution" (Weber, *Return to Freud*, 61). "Metonymy thus could be said to *actualize* the differential articulation of the signifier" (65).

"Lacan's concept of metonymy lies on the diachronic slope of unstable meanings, of evocative *paroles* and the gaps implied by Desire. Metaphor creates synchronic words of the Symbolic order. But metaphor is anchored, paradoxically, in the metonymic chain of being and could itself be called the metonymy of being: the link between language, symbol, self, and process" (Ragland-Sullivan, *Jacques Lacan and the Philosophy of Psychoanalysis*, 252). "Unconscious language is not only materially unstable, i.e., not anchored by normal conventions and rules of grammar, but the laws of condensation and displacement also create enigmatic associational groupings. All this underlines Lacan's second difference with Jakobson: that metaphor only takes on the fuller sense of its meanings in relation to metonymy" (249).

236. "for, what must one do, if his lips are still / too dirty to kiss, if his arms / are still cold?" The intertextual echo is to the final line of the seventh stanza of the "Cántico espiritual" [Spiritual Canticle], which reads as follows:

> Y todos cuantos vagan,
> de ti me van mil gracias refiriendo.
> Y todos más me llagan,
> y déjame muriendo
> un no sé qué que quedan balbuciendo.

[And all those who wander / of you to me a thousand graces keep referring. / And all wound me more, / and I am left dying / by I know not what they keep on stammering.] See Elías Rivers, ed., *Renaissance and Baroque Poetry of Spain* (New York: Dell, 1966), 131–32.

237. In her discussion of "Repetition, Repression, and Regression," Ragland-Sullivan states that Lacan "echoes Kierkegaard's idea that the principle of identity is precisely that of repetition" (*Jacques Lacan and the Philosophy of Psychoanalysis*, 111).

"To explain the metaphorical/metonymical character of the mirror-stage assumption of identity, Lacan used Frege's system where numbers are primary unities, each of which implies another number in an ongoing chain. But Lacan adds what Frege failed to see: that the human subject is produced and unified by language. The combined impact of a logicomathematical—i.e., structural—drama with the materiality of language means that every individual's history has both a universal structure (Desire and Law) and a unique story. . . . Individuals realize themselves in the measure that their subjective structures are integrated into a social myth with an extended human value (*Séminaire* I, p. 215)" (182).

238. "One must remove the trace / . . . / . . . even though it be in the end / for a moment, this one now, and nobody / may ever be its master / while, light in the light, it slips away from us."

239. "The paradox and tragedy of being human stems from the fact that, by accepting language as a substitute for an impossible union, language itself as a symbol builds absence—Castration—into the structure of the subject and ensures that the human condition will be marked by eternal wanting. . . . Lacan can claim, therefore, that the structure of self or ontology comes from Real gaps (wants) in being, which Desire causes (in the form of various *objets a*) and for which Desire compensates by expressing itself in language (*Séminaire* XX, p. 100). In connecting language to Desire, Lacan makes sense of the observation that both language and Desire are marked by a sense of seeking" (Ragland-Sullivan, *Jacques Lacan and the Philosophy of Psychoanalysis*, 172). For a discussion of the Compton effect see Hayles, ed., *Chaos and Order*.

240. "in that city of gloomy / census, of misery and of honor. / Amid the old custom of rapacity and of flattery . . ."

241. "I am ashamed of my mouth / not because of those words / but because of that mouth / that it kissed."

242. "A taste of bitter almonds / remains, a taste of rot; / a taste of betrayal, of a body / sold, of an overripe caress."

243. "Lacan . . . taught that an individual will not reach any unconscious truth along the path of reminiscence (delving into the past), but along the path of repetition in the here and now (*Séminaire* II, p. 110, *Séminaire* XI, p. 131). Lacan distinguishes, therefore, between *reminiscence*, which partakes of memory (and thus of consciousness), and *remémoration*, which belongs to the *moi* and drives human beings to relive unconsciously each instant of their history in the present (*Séminaire* II, p. 218). . . . Repetition is a behavior begun in the past, but reproduced in the present" (Ragland-Sullivan, *Jacques Lacan and the Philosophy of Psychoanalysis*, 111–12). "Psychic maturation occurs . . . by a liberation of one's 'self'-image from the Other's Desire which, although established in the past, is always active in the present" (118).

244. "Would that time were only / that which one loves. One hates / and it is time also. And it is song."

245. "I hated you then and today it is important for me / to remember you, to see you before me / without anyone helping us / and to love you again, and to hate you / anew. I kiss you now / and I betray you now upon / your body. . . .' "

246. ". . . Who doesn't negotiate / with the little he possesses? / If yesterday it was sell, today it's buy; / tomorrow, regret. / Dawn is not the only hour."

247. Lacan uses the same expression with regard to alienation and the relation between the *Lust* and the *Ich*. "The *Lust-Ich* stands out and, by the same token, *Unlust*, the foundation of the non-ego, falls back. . . . You simply see being produced at a primitive level that breaking-off, that splitting-off, which I indicated in the dialectic of the subject with the Other, but here in the opposite direction.

"This is expressed in the expression, *No good without evil, no good without pain*, which preserves in this good and in this evil a character of alternation, of a possible calibration, in which the articulation that I gave earlier of a dyad of signifiers will be reduced, and incorrectly. For, to return things at the level of good and evil, everyone knows that hedonism is unable to explain the mechanism of desire. This is because in passing over to the other register, to the alienating articulation, it is expressed quite differently. I almost blush to repeat here such catchphrases as *beyond good and evil*, which idiots have been playing around with for so long without knowing exactly what they were doing. Nevertheless, we must articulate what occurs at the level of the alienating articulation thus—no evil without there resulting some good from it, and when the good is there, there is no good that holds with evil" (*FFC*, 241–42).

248. See note 205 above. Orpheus's looking back might be explained in terms of the mirror stage, where the child looks to the (m)other for confirmation after looking in the mirror. However, does this action represent an incipient awareness of otherness, or does it fall back into dependency on the (m)other? Does Orpheus lose his autonomy (his life, by being dismembered) because of his refusal to accept Pluto's "law"? Or does his song become even more poignant and plaintive because he cannot return to the "womb" (the Underworld) a second time? Note that the speaker is both similar to and different from the mythical figure. See Hamilton (*Mythology*, 105), who says that "Farewell" was the last word Eurydice spoke.

249. "Any little thing might be worth my life / this afternoon. Any small little thing / if there is anything. For me it is / martyrdom to hear the serene noise, scrupulous, without return, / of your low shoe. What victories / does he who loves seek? Why are these streets / so straight? . . ."

250. ". . . I neither look back nor can I / lose sight of you now. This is the land / of punishment: even friends / give bad information. My mouth kisses / that which dies, and accepts it. And the skin / of the lip itself is that of the wind. Farewell. It is useful, / normal, this event, they say. Keep / for yourself our things, you who can, / for I will go where the night wills."

251. I have appropriated this term from Lacan's formula for metaphor given in the "Agency of the Letter in the Unconscious." As Ragland-Sullivan explains, "The S(+)s denotes a crossing of the 'bar' between consciousness and unconsciousness in the creation of meaning (Sheridan, *Ecrits*, p. 158). The new formation of S is a condensed image or signifier plus a signified

(personal meaning)" (*Jacques Lacan and the Philosophy of Psychoanalysis*, 246–47). "Crossing the Bar" is also the title of one of Tennyson's last poems, which deals with death but more importantly (poetic) immortality. For Rodríguez, symbolically crossing the bar in the center of "Libro tercero" figuratively represents the death of his old self, even though the process will continue indefinitely.

252. Joseph Campbell, *The Hero with a Thousand Faces* (New York: Pantheon, 1949), 82.

253. "Actaeon discovered the goddess Diana bathing nude; she then turned her attendant nymphs into hunting dogs that tore Actaeon to pieces for his 'privileged knowledge.' But in Lacan's version the discovery of unconscious truth leads not to death, but to life. For only by pushing further and grasping the Other's Desire and extracting oneself from its superimposed meanings, does one find a measure of freedom" (Ragland-Sullivan, *Jacques Lacan and the Philosophy of Psychoanalysis*, 300). Compare Orpheus's death with Actaeon's and the price the poet must pay for his "privileged knowledge."

254. "Welcome is the night for whoever goes surely / and with clear eyes looks serenely at the countryside / and with a clean life looks peacefully at the sky, / his city and his house, his family and his work. // But for whoever walks tentatively and sees shadow, sees the hard / brow of the sky and lives the condemnation of his land / and the malevolence of his beloved beings, / an enemy is the night and its compassion, pursuit."

255. "And still more so on this barren plain of the upper Rioja / where [night] opens itself with such clarity that it dazzles, / it palpitates so near that it catches unawares, and very / deeply into the soul it enters and stirs it to its depth."

256. "Because night always, like fire, reveals, / refines, polishes time, prayer, and sobbing, / it gives gloss to sin, limpidity to memory, / punishing and redeeming an entire life."

257. Chevalier and Gheerbrandt, *Diccionario de los símbolos*, 69; my emphasis. [Hence proceeds the double color of its leaves, and on this difference is founded the symbolism of the cottonwood tree. *It signifies the duality of every being.* . . . This tree also appears connected with hells, with *grief*, and with *sacrifice*, as well as with tears.]

258. In *Mythic Masks* (Chapel Hill and London: University of North Carolina Press, 1986), Dorothy Z. Baker discusses these comparisons and contrasts and concludes, "The mythology, then, might be said to bear witness to the increasingly complex conception of the unique role of the poet as one who reconciles the Apollonian and Dionysian forces in man, the rational and the manic, the divine and the human, the individual and the universal" (22–23).

259. "True grief makes no noise: / It leaves a whisper like that of the leaves / of the cottonwood tree rocked by the wind, / an intimate rumor, of such deep vibration, so sensitive to the least brush, / that it can become solitude, discord, / injustice, or wrath. . . ."

260. ". . . I am hearing / its murmuring sound, that does not agitate / but gives harmony, so sharp / and subtle, so resonant with spacious / serenity, in the midst of this afternoon, / that it is almost now painful wisdom, / pure resignation. A betrayal that came / from the ruinous advice of the dry mouth / of envy. It's the same thing. . . ."

261. In his discussion of the gaze and the evil eye, Lacan discusses envy ("envidia"), which is linked here to the witches of "Brujas" and the speaker's former way of life. Noting that "*Invidia* comes from *videre* [to see]," Lacan says, "The powers that are attributed to [the evil eye], of drying up the milk of an animal on which it falls—a belief as widespread in our time as in any other, and in the most civilized countries—of bringing with it disease or misfortune— where can we better picture this power than in *invidia*? . . .

"In order to understand what *invidia* is in its function as gaze it must not be confused with jealousy. . . . Everyone knows that envy is usually aroused by the possession of goods which would be of no use to the person who is envious of them, and about the true nature of which he does not have the least idea.

"Such is true envy—the envy that makes the subject pale before the image of a completeness closed upon itself, before the idea that the *petit a*, the separated *a* from which he is hanging may be for another the possession that gives satisfaction . . ." (*FFC*, 115–16).

262. "... I am hearing / that which obliges me and enriches me, at the cost / of wounds that still ooze. Pain that I hear / very withdrawn, as of a frond / rocked, without seeking signs, words, or meaning. Only music, / without enigmas, sound alone that pierces / my heart, pain that is my victory."

263. Walter Strauss, *Descent and Return: The Orphic Theme in Modern Literature* (Cambridge: Harvard University Press, 1971), 6, 7.

264. See Cirlot, *A Dictionary of Symbols*, 347.

265. See Bousoño, *Teoría de la expresión poética*, 106–50, for a definition of "símbolo bisémico."

266. "What clear countersign / has opened the hidden to me? What air comes / and with cautious delicacy / leaves on my body its deep burden and touches / with vehement skill that secret / threshold of the senses where there trembles / the new action, the new / alliance? ..."

267. "What form of matter has come together / in the light gust that now / brings what was lost and brings / what is gained, and brings time / and brings memory, and brings / freedom and condemnation?"

268. "The imaginary represents the child's earliest entry into social life. Through an intense, mutually defining relation with the mother, the child gradually understands that it is distinct from her, and has an identity of its own, an identity which is fundamentally alienated. The child is constituted as a libidinal subject and confined to the limits of its body through the establishment of the ego. Its identity is thus always incomplete, dependent on the other. The other is thus not simply an external, independent other, but the internal condition of the identity, the core of the self" (Grosz, *Jacques Lacan*, 50).

269. "I give thanks to this gust / that smells of a beloved body and of an afternoon / and of a city, to this air / intimate with erosion, that penetrates to the depth / and works on me silently / giving me aroma and stench. / To this smell that is my life."

270. See "Lluvia de verano" in *Conjuros* and "Lluvia y gracia."

271. "In the dream a person is no longer subjected to the *regard* of the conscious world, which can offer comfort, judgment, seduction, and so on. Instead, the gaze of the Other(A) both sees and shows, ensuring that the subject does not grasp itself as it does in conscious thought. Awake, one is such-and-such for others; asleep, one is such-and-such for no one. Lacan interprets this to mean that the primitiveness of the *regard* is marked in the dream, where the roots of identity and essence are linked to seeing as gaze rather than seeing as eye, and therefore show themselves as prior to intersubjective (mirror-stage) imperatives (*Séminaire* XI, p. 72). . . . Viewed in this way, dreams are the home of the primordial source of being in terms of anteriority and narcissism (*Séminaire* XI, pp. 72–73). But dreams are not the unconscious; they are distortions of a Real unconscious (Other) part of being as it regresses to the level of perception" (Ragland-Sullivan, *Jacques Lacan and the Philosophy of Psychoanalysis*, 45).

272. "Already the roosters crow / my love. Go now: / see that it is dawning."

The "cantiga de amigo" is a traditional Spanish verse form, that has its roots in Galician-Portuguese lyrics, forming part of the oral tradition. In these poems, the speaker is normally a woman who, according to José Manuel Blecua's "Introducción," protests "la llegada del alba, que obliga a dejar amorosos brazos" [the arrival of dawn, which obliges one to leave the lover's arms] (Dámaso Alonso and José Manuel Blecua, *Antología de la poesía española: Lírica de tipo tradicional*, 2a ed. corr. [Madrid: Gredos, 1964], lxix). This pattern of female speaker and male addressee is reversed in Rodríguez's poem, creating a chiasmus consonant with his differential idiom.

Francisco Rico explains that "La tradición gallego-portuguesa convirtió la *cansó* trovadoresca en la austera y abstracta *cantiga d'amigo* . . . , versión literaria de la canción de la muchacha enamorada. . . . Las cantigas de amigo . . . eran sin duda la parte más estimada del repertorio de los cantores, palaciegos o vagabundos, y en su ejecución tenían especial oportunidad de lucirse las juglaresas que los acompañaban, convirtiendo el poema en una pequeña representación dramática" (*Mil años de poesía española: Antología comentada* [Barcelona: Planeta, 1996], 54). [The Galician-Portuguese tradition converted the troubadoresque "song" into the austere and abstract *cantiga d'amigo* . . . , the literary version of the song of the young woman in love. . . . The "cantigas de amigo" . . . were without a doubt the most valued part of the repertory of the singers, those of the palace or those wandering about, and in their execution the female singers who accompanied them had a special opportunity to display their abilities, converting the poem into a small dramatic presentation.]

See Alonso and Blecua, *Antología de la poesía española*, 40–41, for the complete text of the poem.

273. ". . . Is the body / the question or the answer to so much / uncertain luck? A small, dry cough, / a pulse that becomes fresher now and extinguishes / the old ceremony of the flesh / while there remain neither gestures nor words / to go back to interpret the scene / like novices. I love you. . . ."

274. Staging is a key concept in Lacanian thinking. "In Lacan's innovative linking of Freudian thought to structural linguistics, this [Freud's] 'other scene' or stage in a theater *(ein anderer Schauplatz)* becomes the radical Otherness of the unconscious: the inscribing of an alien discourse in an individual" (Ragland-Sullivan, *Jacques Lacan and the Philosophy of Psychoanalysis*, 15). Here the bed as stage and the lovers as actors vaguely suggests a scene from Romeo and Juliet, an ideal but evanescent love comparable to the *objet a*.

275. ". . . Like a war without / heroes, like a peace without alliances, / night has passed. And I love you. / I look for spoils, I look for a broken / medal, a living trophy of this time / that they want to rob from us. You are tired / and I love you. It's time. Will our flesh / be the recompense, the shrapnel / that would justify so much pure struggle / without victors or vanquished? Hush, / for I love you. It's time. There enters now a tremulous / dawn. Never was the light so early."

276. "Clouds / of ashy brown, turquoise blue, / for a moment bring quietude, raise / life and enlarge its small light."

277. "how / can I doubt, not bless the dawn / if still in my body there is youth and there is / love on my lips?"

278. "Let me speak to you, at this hour / of grief, with happy / words. One already knows / that the scorpion, the leech, the flea, / cure at times. . . ."

279. ". . . But listen, let me / tell you that, in spite / of such a deplorable life, yes, / in spite and even now / that we are in defeat, never in command, / grief is the cloud, / happiness the space; / grief is the guest, / happiness the house. / That grief is honey, / symbol of death, and happiness / is acrid, dry, new, / the only thing that has / true meaning."

280. Chevalier and Gheerbrandt, *Diccionario de los símbolos*, 710.

281. Ibid., 567.

282. "Let me, with old / wisdom, say: / in spite, in spite / of all the regrets / and though it may be painful, and though / it may at times be indecent, always, always, / the deepest truth is happiness. / That which of a turbulent river / makes clear waters, / that which causes me to say / these words, now so unworthy, / that which comes to us as / night arrives and morning arrives, / as the wave arrives / to the shore / irremediably."

283. "evokes strength from weakness . . . / . . . from vicious breath / it makes a prayer, tenderness from lasciviousness, / and it raises flame from the ashes, and gives alliance to salt"; "in chores of love and quietude."

284. Chevalier and Gheerbrandt, *Diccionario de los símbolos*, 312. [It represents fundamentally the element of water, vital principle of all things; but also . . . the word, also fecundating; sperm that wraps itself around the female matrix.]

285. "the trembling of a leaf, the hand clasped / with faith, the yeast of these eyes / which you make see things clearly."

286. ". . . I don't want your fleeting / footstep, your beautiful visit to me / to go away ever again, like other times / that I turned my back on you, in a red / autumn, like today's, and let you / die in your luminous diapers."

287. Because of the process of identification with mythical figures that takes place in "Libro tercero," it obtains that "every individual's history has both a universal structure (Desire and Law) and a unique story. Normal language unifies that history within the transference of interhuman relations (*Séminaire* I, pp. 221–22). Individuals realize themselves in the measure that their subjective structures are integrated into a social myth with an extended human value (*Séminaire* I, p. 215)" (Ragland-Sullivan, *Jacques Lacan and the Philosophy of Psychoanalysis*, 182). In the odes, Rodríguez realizes the connection between the two levels, but he reverses the relationship between the personal and the universal of "Libro tercero," making the odes of "Libro cuarto" consummate examples of Bousoño's "alegoría disémica."

288. Speaking about the ego that appears in dreams, Weber describes the ambivalent process of "filling in the ego": "'I may fill in my ego,' [*Ich darf mein Ich ergänzen*] Freud remarks. The German phrase is notably ambiguous: 'to fill in my ego' means both to complete my ego, and to complete the scene by adding my ego to it, in the place of the non-ego that appears. But it would be more accurate to say, 'I may conceal and distort my ego.' . . . And yet, precisely that is what 'filling in one's ego' amounts to: creating the illusion of fullness, of completeness, of the ego as a self-identical subjective instance" (*Return to Freud*, 81).

289. "And this is your welcome, / March, in order to leave home happily: / with the humid and cold wind of the plateau?"

Recall that "Libro primero" of *Alianza* recuperates the poetic process of *Don*.

290. "Always now, at the door, / and still to our regret, there returns, returns / this childhood destiny that explodes / everywhere: in the street, in this / voracious breathing of the day, in the / simplicity of the first tasty smoke, / in the gaze, in each labor / of man. / Always thus, vanquished, / only for fear of such punishment, of such / combat, now we make / a confused shouting through cities, / through factories, through areas / of neighborhoods. . . ."

291. Cf. the beginning of "Canto del caminar."

292. ". . . But beneath our clothing a trembling / of bells rings us, and upon leaving through so many streets / without compassion and without commotion / clear scenes of dawn / break, and so many / dirty bricks without health are baked / with the intimacy of bed and stew. Then, / there is nothing that can part us / from our deep profession of innocence; / then, already at our task, / we cross this plaza with a new foot / and, even amid the snowstorm, as if it were June, / our tremulous lung of dawn opens / and, as at midday, / rich are our eyes / with dark dignity."

293. "Many men have passed by our side, but / they were not of our community. / They leave cornered lives throughout these neighborhoods, / they, who were the neighborhood without walls. / They looked, but they did not see; neither truth nor lie / but an empty bagatelle / did they desire, did they live. All have been / to blame that they heard only the blind pulse / of injustice, the bloody march / of the cold helmet of rancor. The setting / of the sun was only a setting / of the heart. . . ."

294. "What are the palm fronds doing there / on those balconies without the white bow / of our deep orphanhood? What this market / through which I am passing now; / the quarters, the factories, the clouds, / life, air, everything, / without the tempest of our childhood / that raises waves forever?"

295. "Always upon leaving we think / of the distance, never / of the company. And any place is a good place / to make friendships. / Although today is dangerous. Much dust / lies amid the folds / of propaganda. The sooner / we get to work, the better. An evil / welcome yours, March. And our streets, / clear as if they led to the fields, / where are they leading now? Why is everything infancy?"

296. "But now the light gathers, / little by little it grows redder; the wind softens / and in its harvests vibrates / a grain of alliance, a waving / of the immense pastures of the future."

297. "A truth has been uttered without a wound, / without the dirty business / of tears, / with the same tenderness with which snow bestows itself. / See that all is infancy."

298. "The fidelity of the earth, / the presence of the intolerable sky / that seeps into us here,

even into the morning / shot of white lightning / the days / that dawn with trills and close with gargling, the noise / of the bus that finally arrives. . . ."

299. *DRAE*, 1984.

300. "Years of buying and selling / . . . / have brought us to the fear of the great adventure / of our race, to childhood."

301. ". . . Ah, quiet, / quiet beneath that iron / that marks us, and cures us, and gives us a master. / A master who is servitude, reins that make us brothers."

302. "And they will take everything away from us / except these / seven-league boots. / Here, here, well shod / on our insipid feet of short steps. / Here, here, these everyday / shoes, those in the windows / on the sixth of January. / And they will take everything away from us / except the dirty suit / of Communion, this one, the one we always wear, the one we have on."

303. At the beginning of his essay "Nuestra América," José Martí uses a variation of this idiom sarcastically to refer to the high aspirations and great ideas of some thinkers. I am indebted to Juan José Daneri for pointing out this instance to me.

304. María Ramos has enlightened my understanding of these customs, for which I am grateful.

305. "That then was a dream. It was a phase. This now / is neither present nor past, / nor even future: it is the origin. / This is the only wealth / of man. . . ."

306. ". . . And when we are / arriving and already the rain / founders on rapid clouds and sinks / throughout these neighborhoods / tremulous with luminous death rattles. . . ."

307. Cf. "Entonces, / nada hay que nos aleje / de nuestro hondo oficio de inocencia" from part I with the following verses from the end of part IV: "Y nadie, / nada hay que nos aleje / de nuestro oficio de felicidad / sin distancia ni tiempo."

308. "Now is the moment / in which, who would have said it, high, blind, there is reborn / the springtime sun of innocence, / now without sunset over our land."

309. We might more appropriately call this *plus-de-jouir*, following Lacan's terminology. "The phallic signifier does not denote any sexual gender of superiority. Nor does it place sameness above difference in any order of preference. . . . The Phallus is, instead, the signifier or creator of the lack that establishes substitutive Desire as a permanent ontological state and makes adult 'wanting' a shadow pantomime of the primordial drama of Desire between mother and infant.

"Lacanian Desire is beyond physical need, therefore, and refers to the implicit 'appeal' *(demande)* for knowledge of the absent Other(A) through the dynamics of identification and a person's relationship to the social order (*Séminaire* XI, p. 172). Its libidinal source is a lack in the Other (Sheridan, *Ecrits*, p. 287). The 'want-in-being' of alienation is a 'subversion' of the subject, which makes him or her aim not at renunciation or repression, but at the realization of Desire, the re-finding of the presocial self. . . . The goal sought is a repetition, the replacement of the pleasure *(jouissance)* in the illusion of wholeness which was characteristic of the prephallic period. *Jouissance* means sexual pleasure, but at an abstract level it could be described as the temporary pleasure afforded by substitute objects or by others' recognition (substitutes for the original other). At this juncture *jouissance* and Desire meet in the concept of the *plus-de-jouir*" (Ragland-Sullivan, *Jacques Lacan and the Philosophy of Psychoanalysis*, 271).

310. "In whatever time and in whatever terrain / there is always a man who / walks as vagrantly as smoke, / doer of good, doer of evil, / baptized with the acrid / milk of our laws. And he finds / his salvation in / hospitality."

311. "In a series of essays called *On the Way to Language*, Heidegger continues his revolutionary reappraisal of this peculiar philosophical phenomenon [the nature of language]. The most revealing, if not the most readily accessible of these essays is 'A Dialogue on Language,' which Heidegger holds with a Japanese visitor. In the course of the dialogue, language is characterized as 'the House of Being.' . . . By calling language the house of Being we are at least made aware of the enormous range of language as well as of its elusive character. A house is what gives location and significance to all the other items essential for dwelling (the furniture),

but it also shelters and establishes a foundation of human meaning. If language is the house of Being, then all the different ways of Being, all the multifarious ways of existence, are made intelligible and even recognizable only under the curious roof of language. . . . The image of the 'house of Being' suggests . . . that language as the very protective enclosure that gives a place for existence and Being to occur cannot be isolated as merely another event or as an entity alongside other entities" (Michael Gelven, *A Commentary on Heidegger's Being and Time*, rev. ed. [De Kalb: Northern Illinois University Press, 1989], 226). See also Martin Heidegger, "The Way to Language," in *On the Way to Language*, trans. Peter D. Hertz (New York: Harper & Row, 1971), 135.

312. "As clothing attracts the moth, / as love all / its relatives of lust and grace, / of fear and of luck, / so a house seduces him. And not / for being a honeycomb or an anchor, but for that dark / divorce between the sequestration of his years, / the deep captivity of time past / there, between its walls, / and his damaged liberty of the present."

313. See entries for both "almendra" and "almendro" in Chevalier and Gheerbrandt, *Diccionario de los símbolos*, 82–83. This image will reappear in the first section of *El vuelo de la celebración*.

314. ". . . This is the struggle, this / is the time, the terrain / where he must conquer if it is the case that he seeks / not merely memories / and hopes. / If it is the case that he seeks / founding, servitude."

315. Heidegger refers to language as "the foundation of human meaning." See Gelven, *A Commentary*, 226, quoted in note 293 above.

316. This seems to me a perfect example of Bousoño's "alegoría disémica." See note 131 above.

317. "And today, like the rain / washes the leaf, this clear morning, / so prematurely Aprilish / cleans so much time of dust and / of tinsel, and germinates, and creates / almost a miracle of deeds and events, / and finishes and adjusts / so much ambulant life, so much luck and fraud / throughout the days, / purifying faces and cities, / enriching a needful / youth, preparing, / situating life. . . ."

318. ". . . But can anyone / make of the past / the simple material of the surface: / wax, lacquer, varnish, that which very soon / fades, very soon / like the lip's flower? / Or rather must he wait to be with those / true friends, those who will give meaning / to his life, to his land, and to his home?"

319. "It is hospitality. It is the origin / of festivity and of song. / Because song is not just / a hospitable word: that which redeems / though it leave a wound. And love is merely / a hospitable wound, though it has no cure; / and freedom fits / in a humble, hospitable hand, / perhaps sore and tremulous / but founding and faithful, extended in servitude / and in confidence, not in / submission or domination."

320. "In spite of the fact that we make / of conviviality techniques / of oppression and measures for security, and / of hospitality hospices, always / there is a simple man and a clear morning, / with the high transparency of this land, / and a house, and an hour / of prosperity. And this man / sees around his table / his beloved beings. He asks not, / but invites, he does not display cups of unpleasantness or silver flatware. / He barely speaks, and still less of his exile. / That for which he hoped, he has found / and he celebrates it, far away from / incense and powder, that money, that resentment."

321. "Now his native land is this generous / occasion and, serenely, / somewhat fearfully in the face of such goodness, he welcomes / and names, one by one, / his nonaristocratic friends, since birth. Now never / a stranger, he gives thanks very intimately, like a beggar. And he knows, / he understands at last. . . ."

322. "And he looks happily, with that intimacy of frankness that is the only efficacy, / at the faces and the objects, / the truth of his life / recently gained here, between the walls / of a free youth and a hearth without borders."

CHAPTER 4. PRESENCE AND ABSENCE, WOUND AND SUTURE, ELEGY AND QUEST: THE CRISIS OF IDENTITY IN *EL VUELO DE LA CELEBRACIÓN* (1976)

1. The original edition of *El vuelo*, published by Editorial Visor in 1976, delineates what I consider the definitive structure of the work, in spite of the erratum in the table of contents where the fifth and final Roman numeral is missing. In that text, each of the five sections is introduced by a page with a Roman numeral on it. "Elegía desde Simancas" is unequivocally the fifth section. A recent edition of *El vuelo*, published by Ediciones La Palma in 1992, seems to be an exact reproduction of the Visor edition. A major deviation exists in the Cátedra collection *Desde mis poemas*, where the first and second sections are elided, changing the numeration of the ensuing sections but separating "Elegía" as a distinct section. In a personal conversation, Luis García Jambrina has agreed with me that the work should be divided into five sections, with "Herida en cuatro tiempos" and "Elegía desde Simancas" forming the peripheral framing sections.

2. I have relied principally upon the excellent and extensive works of Peter M. Sacks, *The English Elegy: Studies in the Genre from Spenser to Yeats* (Baltimore: Johns Hopkins University Press, 1985); and Jahan Ramazani, *Poetry of Mourning: The Modern Elegy from Hardy to Heaney* (Chicago: University of Chicago Press, 1994), for this discussion of elegy. See also W. David Shaw, *Elegy and Paradox: Testing the Conventions* (Baltimore and London: Johns Hopkins University Press, 1994).

3. "Despite the common misconception that twentieth-century poets forsake mourning and genre, many of them perpetuate and intensify the ancient literary dialogue with the dead.

"Yet modern poets reanimate the elegy not by slavishly adopting its conventions; instead, they violate its norms and transgress its limits. They conjoin the elegiac with the anti-elegiac, at once appropriating and resisting the traditional psychology, structure, and imagery of the genre" (Ramazani, *Poetry of Mourning*, 1).

Sacks also remarks on "the relation between mourning and the quest for poetic inheritance" (*The English Elegy*, 41), especially in his discussion of Spencer's *The Shepheardes Calender*. Commenting on Milton's "Lycidas," he remarks, "Now what could agitate that desire for immortality more urgently than death itself . . .? And what could appease that same desire for immortality more fully than a work that was itself not merely a promise of approaching fame but a poem designed precisely to create a figure for what surpasses death?" (91).

4. In a letter, Freud stresses, "Although we know that after such a loss the acute state of mourning will subside, we also know we shall remain inconsolable and will never find a substitute. No matter what may fill the gap, even if it be filled completely, it nevertheless remains something else. And actually, this is how it should be, it is the only way of perpetuating that love which we do not want to relinquish" (*The Letters of Sigmund Freud*, ed. Ernst L. Freud, trans. Tania and James Stern [New York: Basic Books, 1960], 386; quoted in Ramazani, *Poetry of Mourning*, 375–76 n. 84). For Rodríguez, the elegy becomes a way of perpetuating the love of his lost family members and his commitment to poetry.

5. Augustine's definition of time is representative of this tradition: "[Y]et purchance it might be properly said, 'There be three times; a present of things past, a present of things present, and present of things future.' For these three do exist in some sort . . . present of things past, memory; present of things present, sight; present of things future, expectation" (*The Confessions of St. Augustine*, trans. E. B. Pusey [New York: E. P. Dutton, 1907], 266–67). Hans Meyerhoff gives the following version of this definition in *Time in Literature* (Berkeley and Los Angeles: University of California Press, 1955): "What happens, happens *now*; that is, it is always an experience, idea, or thing which is 'present.' Nevertheless, we cannot construct a meaningful temporal series accounting for past and future in terms of memory and expectation.

By 'past' we then mean the present memory or experience of a thing past; by 'future,' the present expectation or anticipation of a future thing" (10). Also, see Heidegger's discussion of the three ectases of time mentioned in the introduction to this study and in *Being and Time*, sec. 65.

6. Sacks insists that "almost any elegy requires a progression of voice, a sequence by which the mourner supersedes his grieving self" (*The English Elegy*, 125). Thus, the elegy is an apt genre for Rodríguez to pursue, given the sequencing characteristic of all of his works.

7. Freud asserts that "The complex of melancholia behaves like an open wound, drawing to itself cathectic energy from all sides . . . and draining the ego until it is utterly depleted; it proves easily able to withstand the ego's wish to sleep" ("Mourning and Melancholia," *A General Selection from the Works of Sigmund Freud*, John Rickman, ed. [New York: Doubleday, 1957], 134). The images of the wound and sleeplessness are pertinent to Rodríguez's poem, although the poet moves away from melancholia through the healthy work of mourning.

8. "How familiar are the cotton and the thread of this pillow / wounded by my dreams, / mourned and deserted, / where I grew during fifteen years. / Of this pillow from which my eyes / saw the sky / and the purity of dawn / and the nocturnal splendor / when my sweat, an orphaned thief, and the transparent fruit / of my innocence, and the germination of my body / were already almost a blessing."

9. See Martha Miller, "Linguistic Skepticism in *El vuelo de la celebración*," *Anales de la Literatura Española Contemporánea* 6 (1981): 105–21.

10. We could also read this number as being composed of five and ten, both important symbols of metapoetic and existential layers of meaning. According to Chevalier and Gheerbrandt, the number five "[e]s signo de unión, número *nupcial* dicen los Pitagóricos; número también del centro, de la armonía y el equilibrio. . . . Símbolo igualmente del universo, dos ejes, uno vertical y otro horizontal, pasando por un mismo centro; símbolo del orden y la perfección; finalmente, símbolo de la voluntad divina que no puede desear más que el orden y la perfección" (*Diccionario de los símbolos*, 291) [is a sign of union, a nuptial number say the Pythagoreans; a number also of the center, of harmony and balance. . . . Symbol equally of the universe, two axes, one vertical and the other horizontal, passing through the same center; symbol of order and perfection; finally, symbol of a divine will that desires nothing more than order and perfection]. "[Diez] es el número de la *Tetraktys* pitagórica: la suma de los cuatro primeros números (1 + 2 + 3 + 4). Tiene el sentido de la totalidad, del acabamiento, del retorno a la unidad tras el desarrollo del ciclo de los nueve primeros números. . . . No sorprenderá en estas condiciones que el diez pueda expresar tanto la muerte como la vida, su alternancia, o más bien su co-existencia, que está ligada a este dualismo. . . . Diez es también el número de los mandamientos de Dios: el decálogo simboliza el conjunto de la Ley; en sus múltiples aspectos, no es más que una; con sus múltiples negaciones, no deja de ser positiva" (418–19) [{Ten} is the number of the Pythagorean *Tetraktys:* the sum of the first four numbers (1 + 2 + 3 + 4). It has the sense of totality, of completion, of a return to unity after the development of a cycle of the first nine numbers. . . . It will not be surprising under these conditions that ten can express death as well as life, their alternance, or rather their coexistence, and it is tied to this dualism. . . . Ten is also the number of the commandments of God: the Decalogue symbolizes the unity of the Law; in its multiple aspects, it is only one; with its multiple negations, it never ceases to be positive].

11. "A similar reading [to an investigation into the significance of flowers] is often required for a deeper appreciation of images of *light* so crucial to elegies. As with the images of flowers, there are several levels of meaning, and similar currents run beneath the obvious significance of this figure for an elegy that conquers darkness and outlasts human mortality. . . .

"Like that of the fertility god, the figure of the sun and the associated figures of light and of fire have undergone a history of resignification throughout the development of the elegy. . . . [W]hether the sun or the light signifies Achilles' angrily renewed martial strength . . . , or Milton's resurrective vision, or Hardy's memory, beneath this figure there plays a heritage of powerful contradictions associated with the original positing of any imagery of light on the far side of darkness, or of presence in the space of an absence" (Sacks, *The English Elegy*, 33–34).

12. This issue comes to the fore in the fourth section of *El vuelo*, in which eroticism is a key element. Sacks asserts that

> one of the most profound issues to beset any mourner and elegist is his surviving yet painfully altered sexuality. Although it is crucial for the mourner to assert a continued sexual impulse, that assertion must be qualified, even repressively transformed or rendered metaphorical, by the awareness of loss and mortality. Indeed, our consoling images are most often figures for an immortal but metaphorized sexual force. (Ibid., 7)

The emphasis on personal, perhaps even biographical information is typical of the modern elegy, according to Ramazani: "From the mid-nineteenth century to the present, the elegy's representations of the dead and mourners have tended to move away from the categorical and universal to the intimate and particular" (*Poetry of Mourning*, 18).

13. The gain/loss motif appears repeatedly in elegiac poetry. For example, Tennyson has written "But who shall so forecast the years / And find in loss a gain to match?" ("In memoriam"; see Sacks, *The English Elegy*, 172). The prominence of this motif in Rodríguez's work attests yet again to the appropriate choice of the elegiac genre to advance his poetic status.

14. "It is becoming clear that there is a significant similarity between the process of mourning and the oedipal resolution. . . . [T]he work of mourning appears to recapitulate elements of the earlier resolution. . . . Each procedure or resolution is essentially defensive, requiring a detachment of affection from a prior object followed by a reattachment of the affection elsewhere. At the core of each procedure is the renunciatory experience of loss and the acceptance, not just of a substitute, but of the very means and practice of substitution. In each case such an acceptance is the price of survival, and in each case a successful resolution is not merely deprivatory, but offers a form of compensatory reward. . . .

". . . According to Lacan, it is the figure of the father, representing the symbolic order, that formally intervenes between the child and the child's first object of attachment. The child's imaginary dyadic relationship with its prior 'love-object' is thus interrupted and mediated by a signifying system, which acts as a third term. . . . In the elegy, the poet's preceding relationship with the deceased (often associated with the mother, or Nature, or a naively regarded Muse) is conventionally disrupted and forced into a triadic structure including the third term, death (frequently associated with the father, or Time, or the more harshly perceived necessity of linguistic mediation itself). The dead, like the forbidden object of a primary desire, must be separated from the poet, partly by a veil of words" (Sacks, *The English Elegy*, 8–9).

15. According to Sacks, "Eyes are the emblems of virility and of a father's gaze" (ibid., 106).

16. "The trembling bed / where the nightmare became flesh, / where my breath was fertile, / bold as the rain, / with its luminous weave and without an ash. / And my bed was a nest / and now it is vermin; / now its wood without varnish, dark, / without comfort."

17. "[Healthy mourners] accept their loss and can retain their identities by what we may call a healthy work of mourning, a work that, as Freud points out, requires a withdrawal of affection from the lost object and a subsequent reattachment of affection to some substitute for that object. . . . Of course only the object *as lost*, and not the object itself, enters into the substitutive sign, and the latter is accepted only by a turning away from the actual identity of what was lost. Consolation thus depends on a trope that remains at an essential remove from what it replaces" (Sacks, *The English Elegy*, 6).

"One of the dangers besetting a mourner is the imprisonment of his affective energies, the locking up within himself of impulses previously directed toward or attached to the deceased. . . . One obvious function of elegiac questioning is to set free the energy locked in grief or rage and to organize its movement in the form of a question that is not merely an expression of ignorance but a voicing of protest.

"More significantly, when the question is addressed to someone else, the mourner succeeds in shifting his focus from the lost object or from himself and turns outward to the world. If tinged with anger, as they often are, such questions actually carry that anger away from its possible attachment to the self . . . . He may thereby also deflect the closely related element of mourning—guilt—which if unalleviated would drag him toward melancholy" (22).

18. Another source that readers may wish to consult is Sheldon Brivic's *The Veil of Signs: Joyce, Lacan, and Perception* (Urbana and Chicago: University of Illinois Press, 1991).

19. "I will not sleep again in this hurt, in this / ruin, / wrapped in debris, sheetless, / without love or family, / in the very dregs themselves. / And at the same time I want to warm myself / in it, see / how it dawns, how / the light hits me in the face, here, in my bed."

20. "Elegiac questioning, like the *fort-da* game and like the ritual origins of the genre, is marked by a significant use of repetition. . . .

"Repetition creates a sense of continuity, of an unbroken pattern such as one may oppose to the extreme discontinuity of death. Time itself is thereby structured to appear as a familiar, filled-in medium rather than as an open-ended source of possible catastrophe. Repetition is, moreover, one of the psychological responses to trauma. The psyche repeats the shocking event, much as the elegy recounts and reiterates the fact of death. . . . By such repetitions, the mind seeks retroactively to create the kind of protective barrier that, had it been present at the actual event, might have prevented or softened the disruptive shock that initially caused the trauma.

"At the same time, the repetition of words and refrains and the creation of a certain rhythm of lament have the effect of controlling the expression of grief while also keeping that expression in motion. It is as if the grief might be gradually conjured forth and exorcised. This returns us to the idea of ceremony, and to the idea that repetition may itself be used to create the sense of ceremony. Certainly, by confessing its repetitive nature at large, the elegy takes comfort from its self-insertion into a longstanding convention of grief. And by repeating the form of the vegetation rites, for example, an individual elegy may borrow the ritual *context* of consolation" (Sacks, *The English Elegy*, 23).

21. Speaking of the mirror stage, Sacks notes that "this phase foreshadows the elegist's consoling construction of a fictional identity not only for the dead but for himself as well" (ibid., 10).

22. See Sacks (ibid., 15–17) on the renunciation of desire in oedipal and Freudian terms.

23. "Yours, my father, my mother, / my brothers and sisters, / where my salvation was your death."

24. In his interview with Mauro Armiño, Rodríguez states: "Y es que fue así: su muerte fue mi salvación. Fíjate si es doloroso, dolorosísimo decirlo. . . . Muertos mis padres y mi hermana, sólo me queda un hermano, que vive en Ginebra, y otra hermana, en Holanda" ("Claudio Rodríguez: oficio de palabras," *Cambio 16*, no. 840 [4 enero 1988]: 90). [And that's just how it happened: their death was my salvation. Imagine how painful it is, how very painful it is to say it. . . . Dead my parents and my sister, I only have left a brother, who lives in Geneva, and another sister, in Holland.]

Sacks talks of "warning signals, miniature reversals that prepare us for the catastrophic reversal to come. The characteristic form of these reversals is the turning of a word or line against itself. . . . This creates a cushion of expectation, but it also instills a vertiginous instability, as though within language, as in life, there were this sudden tendency for reversal or cancellation, the sudden opening of a chasm" (*The English Elegy*, 55).

25. "Each substitution seems to repeat a prior change, just as each loss recapitulates a prior loss and each turn to consolation repeats an earlier deflection of desire. Our experiences of loss fold upon themselves in gathers, creating the highly stratified 'occasion' that each elegy 'begin[s] again' or enters 'yet once more'" (ibid., 18).

Ramazani analyzes Hardy's guilt for what he calls "the economic problem of poetic mourning—the production of poems from . . . loss" (*Poetry of Mourning*, 53). Whereas Hardy's guilt may stem from the failure of his marriage, Rodríguez's may derive from his inability to protect his sister from death or from being in a situation where she would be susceptible to violence (see Cañas, *Claudio Rodríguez*).

Sacks also remarks the elegist's guilt and self-effacement: "We are familiar with the mourner's impulse to self-abasement. . . . [T]his is partly the mourner's penitence for having survived, for choosing to live on, for having been unable to protect the dead, or simply for being unable to mourn him more effectively" (*The English Elegy*, 171).

26. "Such reality testing is by nature repetitive, for it must not only drive home the resisted fact of the death but also constantly undo the repeated illusions that the dead are still present" (ibid., 239; see also 24–25).

Freud states, "The testing of reality, having shown that the loved object no longer exists, requires forthwith that all the libido shall be withdrawn from its attachments to this object. Against this demand a struggle of course arises. . . . This struggle can be so intense that a turning away from reality ensues. . . . The normal outcome is that deference for reality gains the day. Nevertheless its behest cannot be at once obeyed. The task is now carried through bit by bit, under great expense of time and cathectic energy, while all the time the existence of the lost object is continued in the mind. Each single one of the memories and hopes which bound the libido to the object is brought up and hyper-cathected, and the detachment of the libido from it accomplished" ("Mourning and Melancholia," in *A General Selection*, 126).

27. See Sacks (*The English Elegy*, 10–11) on the *fort-da* game, which Freud describes in *Beyond the Pleasure Principle*. Sacks explains,

> Whenever the child's mother left the room, he controlled his anger and grief by repeatedly casting away and then retrieving a wooden reel, to the accompaniment of the syllables *fort* and *da*. Freud saw the reel as a surrogate for the mother and he interpreted the syllables to mean approximately "gone" (away) and "there" or "here" (in the sense of regained presence). Freud regarded this game of "disappearance and return" as "related to the child's great cultural achievement—the instinctual renunciation (that is, the renunciation of instinctual satisfaction) which he had made in allowing his mother to go away without protesting. He compensated himself for this, as it were, by himself staging the disappearance and return of the objects within his reach." By a primitive form of mourning, the child not only comes to terms with the otherness and absence of his first love-object, he also learns to *represent absence*, and to make the absent present, by means of a substitutive figure accompanied by an elementary language. (Ibid., 11)

28. Sacks discusses the antiphonal voice at ibid., 34–36. Of the three partial interpretations of this "conventional fracturing" he provides, the third—"the confrontational structure required for the very recognition of loss"—seems the most applicable to Rodríguez's poems, especially in relation to "reality testing."

> [T]hrough a kind of repetitive dialogue the bereaved is forced to accept a reality that he might otherwise refuse. Allied to this is the general function of controlling or criticizing the mourner. . . .
> A separation of voices thus reflects and carries forward the necessarily dialectical movement of the work of mourning, not merely in the process of recognition but for the entire project of withdrawal and reattachment of affections. If the mourner must break off and replace his attachments, the self that survives in this way has, in a sense, begun again, putting its former position behind it. (35–36)

29. "Time is in your hands: / touch it, touch it. Now night falls and there is / pus in the odor of the body, there is high tide / in the sea of sleep, and the open furrow / amid the sheets, / the cross of the eyelashes / about to fall, the lips toward the sky of the ceiling, / toward the melody of the wheat stalk, / toward this lamp of a now pale blue, / in this room that rises up on me / with the pitiless window, / damned and olorous, pierced by stars."

30. "And in my eyes the star, here, making me ache, / enclosing me, inhabiting me astutely / in the breathing of the night, in the clear autumn / of the eyelid's poppy, / in the needles of the pine-grove of sleep."

31. My colleague Randolph Pope has noted (in a personal communication) that the poppy is associated with opium (cf. Coleridge). The poppy as a source of opium dulls the senses and simultaneously relieves pain. Ramazani identifies the poppy as belonging to the elegiac tradition and emphasizes its ambivalent symbolism: "like the anemones, violets, and poppies of elegiac tradition, the figure of the flower signifies not only beauty and transcendence but also mortality" (*Poetry of Mourning*, 331). Pérez-Rioja's entry says the following: "En general, se la considera símbolo de fertilidad, sueño, ignorancia, pasión o extravagancia. A veces, alude a la Pasión de Cristo por su color rojo-sangre, que evoca la idea de la muerte. Vida efímera. Separada de la planta se marchita rápidamente" (*Diccionario de símbolos y mitos*, 4a ed. [Madrid: Tecnos, 1992], 59). [In general, it is considered a symbol of fertiligy, dream, ignorance, passion or extravagance. At times, it alludes to the Passion of Christ because of its blood-red color, which evokes the idea of death. Ephemeral life. Separated from the plant, it quickly wilts.] According to Nadia Julien, "The poppy was an attribute of Demeter, goddess of fertility and harvests, who found her daughter, Persephone, again in the underworld. It symbolizes Nature's eternal cycle of death and rebirth" (*The Mammoth Dictionary of Symbols*, 339). See also "Sombra de la amapola," the second poem of part II of *El vuelo*, where the red of the poppy is contrasted with and superseded by its shadow (again the light/dark, passion/death contrast).

32. "The streets, the almond trees, / some with mauve leaves, / others in late bloom before / the solitude of the bridge / where the light is woven in eyes / too young to hate. And the water of the Duero / passes, never too late to love, / emotional and slow, / burning infancy."

33. "[M]an creates a fiction whereby nature and its changes, the occasions of his grief, appear to depend on him. The withering vegetation is now no more the *cause* of human grief but rather the mourner or even the effect of a human-divine loss. . . . Thus the so-called pathetic fallacy of nature's lament, one of the prominent elegiac conventions so frequently criticized for artifice and contrivance, actually has a naturalistic basis in the notation of seasonal change. . . .

"From this point of view, the elegy's elaborate observations of nature's decline are not the fallacious products of man's self-pity but rather the expression of his attempted mastery of and vengeance against nature, or more precisely change" (Sacks, *The English Elegy*, 20–21).

34. Sacks explicates the importance of the vegetation deity in elegy at ibid., 19–21. He goes on to say, "The immortality suggested by nature's self-regenerative power rests on a principle of recurrent fertility" (27).

35. Of weaving Sacks notes, "Since we have been stressing the ways in which the mourner or elegist must submit to the mediating fabric of language, a tissue of substitutions that may cover a preceding lack, few readers would need to be reminded how the word *text* refers back to a woven fabric rather than to an intrinsically more solid substance. Nor would they need to recall Freud's rather fanciful version of the invention of writing as an instance of hair-braiding. But it *is* worth noting the significant frequency with which the elegy has employed crucial images of weaving, of creating a fabric in the place of a void. . . .

"To speak of weaving a consolation recalls the actual weaving of burial clothes and shroud, and this emphasizes how mourning is an action, a process of work" (ibid., 18–19).

The aspect of weaving, hair-braiding, Penelope as the weaver of a shroud, and the act of writing will appear prominently again in "Hilando." See my article "Ekphrasis, Intertextuality and the Reader's Role in Poems by Francisco Brines and Claudio Rodríguez," *Studies in Twentieth Century Literature* 14 (1990): 279–300, for a fuller discussion of these issues.

36. "The stream is a figure . . . for the mourner's sexuality, and for its necessary willingness to accept not only a detour but a sacrificial change" (Sacks, *The English Elegy*, 112). This image appears again in the mention of the Pisuerga River in "Elegía desde Simancas."

37. "What shall I do with my sweat, with these years / without money and without watering, / without perfidy even now in my bed? / And shall I dream this nightmare / again? You, be still, be still. / Put your head high and put your hands / on the back of your neck. And above all see / that it is dawning, even here, / in the corner of the use of your dreams, / next to the crime of the darkness, / next to the almond tree. How well I know its shadow."

38. See Sacks (*The English Elegy*, 21–23) on the purpose of questioning and its relation to repetition.

39. Ibid., 231.

40. Margaret Persin *(Recent Spanish Poetry)* has discussed this contrast in her discussion of "Brujas a mediodía."

41. "And is the wound now without its deep petal, / without warmth, / but fecund with its own pollen, / sewn by hand, almost like a sigh, / with the venom of its melody, / with the harvest of its fruit, / consoling, enshrouding / my life?"

42. "It embraces me. And it is enough. / But nothing happens. / It's not the same old thing, it's not my love on sale, / the nudity of my desire, nor / the innocent pain, without advantage, / nor the sacrifice of that on which we put a price, / nor the abandonment of the light, nor even / the hollow, knotted / stem, like that of wheat, of / injustice. No, / it's not the cinnamon color / of malicious laziness, / nor the flowering, whispering / skeleton of hate. Nor even the old / mouth of the rite / of violence."

43. Sacks analyzes the stories of Apollo and Daphne as well as Pan and Syrinx from Ovid's *Metamorphoses*. See *The English Elegy*, 3–8.

44. "There is still no sweat, only volubility; / there is still no love, only the poor beads / of empty deceit. / With neither crevices nor bandages / you come to me, my wound, with so much full night, / worn out, / without my being able to embrace you. And you embrace me."

45. "How my gaze aches / upon entering so blindly into the day. / How the odor of the sky, / the light of the city / today crude, bitter, cure / my oozing wound with its breath / and with its rottenness, / surprised and slim, / and now without lips, / talking to itself with its scars / so surely, without echo, / toward its destiny, arising so early, / until it reaches gangrene."

46. Sacks, *The English Elegy*, 10.

47. Ibid. Sacks mentions the importance of echo as a form of repetition and reality testing (23–25). His commentary omits the myth of Echo and Narcissus, although narcissism is a vital part of the elegiac process of mourning as opposed to melancholia. "One of the major tasks of the work of mourning and of the elegy is to repair the mourner's damaged narcissism—but without allowing that repair to have permanent recourse either to the melancholy form of secondary narcissism or to the fantasies of the primitive narcissism associated with the mirror stage" (10). See also Freud, "Mourning and Melancholia."

48. "But / the renewed apparition of the wind, / mute in its clarity, / wafts the broom of this wound that never / closes blindly. / Embrace me, my wound. And rest."

49. Chevalier and Gheerbrandt state that "La flor de genista (retama) o de aliaga (Aulaga) podría haber originado, según se dice, la flor de lis heráldica, o la rama de oro (muérdago). . . . Las ramas floridas de retama se utilizaban en los funerales; se cubría con ellas el cuerpo de los difuntos.

"La flor está por su color y su fragancia, asociada a la llegada del nuevo primaveral y al amor" (*Diccionario de los símbolos*, 530).

[The genista flower (broom) or furze (gorse) could have originated, according to what they say, the heraldic *fleur de lis*, or the golden bough (mistletoe). . . . Flowering branches of broom were used in funerals; they covered the body of the dead with them.

The flower is, by its color and its fragrance, associated with the arrival of the springtime new and with love.]

Sacks discusses several variations on the descent into the Underworld, beginning with the vegetation deity and passing through Dionysus, Orpheus, Demeter and Persephone, the Eleusinian mysteries, and the Christian commemoration of Christ's resurrection in the Eucharist. See *The English Elegy*, 29–32.

50. "How is grief, so clean and so moderate, / innocent grief, which is the greatest mystery, / slipping away from me? / It has happened little by little, / with the suture of solitude / and the space without snares, without routine / of your death and mine. / But your soul rings, and the nest is / here, in the coffin, / with a soft light."

51. To quote Sacks, "[I]t is important to see how the energy of the poem is braced . . . by being directed to some kind of addressee. The poem is thus tautened by a sinew of address, a compelling tone of engagement, . . . for the . . . passage may be read as an intensifying exercise in making up or evoking a presence where there is none—a fundamentally elegiac enterprise. So, too the . . . vocative mood not only palliates the solitude of the bereaved but grips the reader as though he, too, were being continually addressed" (*The English Elegy*, 96).

52. "You've gone. Don't go. You've given me your hand. / You won't go. You, forgive, my life, / my sister, / that the air is ringing for you, that there are no roofs / nor are there windows with love to the wind, / that the bribe of the traitorous sky / does not enter into your youth, into your death, / so white and vile. / And that your murder awaits my vengence, and that it saves us, / because you are the almond / in the coffin. Always ripe."

53. This apology forms part of the mourner's self-effacement and abasement (Sacks, *The English Elegy*, 171). See note 25 above.

54. Conversion of the loved one into a seed is reminiscent of the metamorphoses of the myths and the displacement of the mourner's loss with some object, as well as of the vegetation deity and flowers.

55. This process reflects the child's learning to substitute the spool for the absent mother in the *fort-da* game.

56. We recall the escape and loss of the female figures in Ovid's *Metamorphoses*; but flight also represents the power to save (Sacks, *The English Elegy*, 33). "Continuing the work of mourning, the [poet] pursues the traditional strategy by which an elegist summons female figures only to repeat his required detachment from them" (319).

57. "The sand, so naked and so helpless, / so pursued, / never deceitful, agile, / with its submissive liberty without mourning, / is now washing me. // Behold: the dark vainglory of rock / here, between the tips of / my fingers, / with the whispering of its farewell / and with its odor of early wing."

58. Chevalier and Gheerbrandt, *Diccionario de los símbolos*, 137, 138.

59. Ibid., 137.

60. "Fly, fly away, / my little sand, / sing in my body, in every pore, enter / into my life, please, now when I need / your cadence, already very pulsating in light, / with the mystery of the melody / of your serenity, / of your profound tenderness."

61. Sacks remarks upon "the active and redemptive power of song" (*The English Elegy*, 89). "The self-consciously dramatized performance in which the poet translates the bird's song represents the elegist's familiar recapitulation of his entry into language—in this case a scenario even more than usually fraught with questions of echo in tension with originality. And the form of the song, with its 'limitless,' inclusive, almost undifferentiated flow, is a carefully wrought aesthetic displacement and figuring of the actually undifferentiated flux of reunion . . . that the poet both desires and renounces. In fact, we might see the bird as an unusual reminder of the vegetation deity, one whose power and whose transgressive, even incestuous, yearning for a surpassal of differentiation the elegist comes to imitate only within the mediating fabric of his language" (317–18). Cf. Whitman's thrush in "Out of the Cradle Endlessly Rocking," an elegy for his brother.

62. Ramazani defines "two primary consolations of the pastoral elegy: the association of the dead person with a vegetation god that dies and revives ('a three-days personage' such as Orpheus, Adonis, or Christ) and the alignment of the human with a sympathetic and cyclical nature. Traditionally, nature reflects the changes in the dead person (autumn or winter, then spring) and in the mourner's grief (Milton's mournful vines, then fresh woods). Both the theological and the seasonal tropes are anthropomorphic, projecting the human onto the natural" (*Poetry of Mourning*, 99). But Ramazani also notes that this "elegiac topos contrasts nature's relentless cyclicality with human finitude" (100). Certainly, the ebb and flow of the tide represents a cyclical aspect of nature.

63. "The presence of these gathering fabrics of shadow, veil, and curtain testifies to an

elegist's acceptance not only of Death's castrative power but also of the elegist's recapitulated entry into, and submission to, those very mediations of language that interpose between him and his object of loss or desire" (Sacks, *The English Elegy*, 150).

64. "How it is plaited and how it welcomes us, / the nerve, the encircling of this rope, / so intimate with salt, / and with this firmness trembling with adventure, / well woven, in the port. The esparto fiber / has become very hard and very tempered, / somewhat rusty. It is low tide. / Fair weather. And the iodine in each thread, / where sweaty hands, / amid the odor of fish scales, narrows the course, and the silence / of the saltpeter, / in each knot."

65. Further echoes of the first section of *El vuelo* are evident in the words "aventura" and "hilada," among others.

66. These adjectives also recall the opening verses of "Un rezo": "¿Cómo el dolor, tan limpio y tan templado, / el dolor inocente . . . ?"

67. If we rearrange this sentence, we read: "Y el yodo en cada hebra, donde [hay también] el sudor de manos, entre el olor de las escamas y el silencio del salitre, ciñe el rumbo en cada nudo."

68. The following poems contain a stanzaic gap: "Arena," "Sombra de la amapola," "Ciruelo silvestre," "Ballet del papel," "Lágrima." Significantly, the last two poems of the section are those that do not contain a break, indicating that suturing and healing are taking place.

69. "The rigging trembles without agitation on / the railing of the dock, / when my life is tied without breach, / now without return at last and having touched bottom. / But what does it matter now. And the esparto fiber / has become very hard and very sure, / without the palpitation of tides, / of the dirty waves, of the spume / of destiny. / But what does it matter now. And the rope / has become tense and wounded. / And where, oh where is the prayer of the sea / and its blasphemy?"

70. See his discussion of the "economic problem" of elegy—"the exchange of the work for the life (his own and others'), the gain of poetic benefit from human loss"—with regard to both Yeats and Heaney (*Poetry of Mourning*, 343).

71. "Probably the greatest influence on the form of the elegy has been the rituals associated with the death and rebirth of vegetation gods. . . . An obvious influence of such rites is the residually ceremonial structure of the elegy. The form has a measured pace and direction and develops the effect not only of an event but of a performance. The performance is in fact foregrounded by the genre's staging devices, a convention that draws attention to the mourner or cast of mourners" (Sacks, *The English Elegy*, 19).

72. Ibid., 35. Sacks posits three partial suggestions for interpreting the fracturing or separation of voices. The first two apply to "Ballet."

> The first relates to the "splitting" and self-suppression that accompanied the self's first experiences of loss and substitution, its discovery of signs both for lost objects and for the self. The second is associated with the dramatizing strategy by which mourners not only lend ceremony to their rites but also intensify and indicate their own "work" as survivors. Thus the lament would have to include the semblance of another voice as stage director, introducing and spotlighting apparently other voices or choruses. (35)

73. According to Fernando Lázaro Carreter ("Imitación compuesta y diseño retórico en la oda de Juan de Grial," *Anuario de Estudios Filológicos* 2 [1979]: 89–119), in classical literature bees are a metaphor for "compound imitation"; they represent the appropriate means for achieving originality because they draw from different sources to create their own individual honey. I am grateful to David Thompson for this insight.

74. "It is growing dark. The wind smells of rain / and its rhythm alters. And I live the harmony, / now fugitive, / of the pulse of the paper beneath the clouds / . . . / . . . very near / my lost childhood and now recently gained / so delicately, thanks to this dew / of these papers, that tiptoe away, / light and barefoot, / with a smile and with a stain. / Farewell, and good luck. Good luck."

75. Sacks calls this a "form of interpositional texture or cloud" (*The English Elegy*, 150). See Mayhew's discussion of this poem in *Claudio Rodríguez*, as well as Carole Bradford's "Francisco Brines and Claudio Rodríguez: Two Recent Approaches to Poetic Creation" and Pedro Ojeda Escudero's article.

76. According to Sacks, "a mourner should wish to associate himself with . . . a purified or distilled force that involves individual death but also has the power to survive extinction. In this case, dew may connote spiritual purity, but it retains its earlier relation to the immortal seminal potency on which . . . images for the spirit . . . have been based" (*The English Elegy*, 84).

77. This phrase originates (in poetry, at least) with Catullus's elegy for his brother:

> By strangers' coasts and waters, many days at sea,
>   I came here for the rites of your unworlding,
> Bringing for you, the dead, these last gifts of the living,
>   and my words—vain sounds for the man of dust.
>   Alas, my brother,
> You have been taken from me. You have been taken from me,
>   By cold Chance turned a shadow, and my pain.
>
> Here are the foods of the old ceremony, appointed
>   Long ago for the starvelings under earth:
> Take them; your brother's tears have made them wet; and take
>   Into eternity my hail and my farewell.

(L. R. Lind, ed., *Latin Poetry in Verse Translation: From the Beginnings to the Renaissance* [Boston: Houghton Mifflin, 1957], 52.)

Tennyson also uses the last line as the title of his elegy "Ave atque vale," written shortly after the death of his brother.

78. See Debicki, *Poetry of Discovery*.

79. See Matthew Arnold's "Geist's Grave" (written for the poet's dachshund) as a possible precedent for this type of elegiac statement. W. David Shaw says of this poem, "In its pathos, waggish affection, and blend of both high seriousness and humor, 'Geist's Grave' is one of Arnold's most charming, yet deeply felt, elegies" (*Elegy and Paradox*, 38).

80. See Cañas *(Claudio Rodríguez)* for a discussion of Aleixandre's role in Rodríguez's life.

81. "The oedipal resolution also governs the creation of a superego, and here, too, we find an important relation to the work of mourning and the elegy. At the most obvious level, we recall Freud's suggestion that the superego is made up of the 'illustrious dead,' a sort of cultural reservoir, or rather cemetery, in which one may also inter one's renounced love-objects and in which the ruling monument is the internalized figure of the father. Since the father . . . intervenes and governs precisely as a *figure*, a totemic metaphor or name—the *Nom du Père*— any actual father thus has himself been displaced by a substitutive image with which the child seeks to identify. This displacement of the actual father by an idealized totemic figure involves an act very much like the child's castrative creation or adoption of the phallus" (Sacks, *The English Elegy*, 15).

"[M]any elegies pivot around the issue of poetic inheritance. In this case, the heir apparent must demonstrate a greater strength or proximity to the dead than any rival may claim, but he must also wrest his inheritance *from* the dead. More than a mere ingestion, some act of alteration of surpassal must be made, some device whereby the legacy may be seen to have entered a new successor. . . . [T]he elegy clarifies and dramatizes this emergence of the true heir." (37)

82. See Cañas, *Claudio Rodríguez*. Rodríguez is extremely reluctant to discuss biographical issues since he believes that his poetry stands on its own. The critic, however, must take these issues into account to augment and deepen the reading of this poetry. Moreover, a complete

separation of the poet as human being and as implied author and speaker of the poems is a concept put in question by Rodríguez's poetry on many levels.

83. A picture of Aleixandre and Sirio appears in the Austral edition of *Historia del corazón*, 2a ed. (Madrid: Espasa-Calpe, 1985), 114.

84. "To you, who caressed / the infinite glint of the human suit when / within it the poem boils up. / To you, of wandering baptism, / who with blue saliva and a flattering tongue / licked fresh pulses tremulous with high reins, / some creative hands, with salty affection always, / now that I recall / years of clear friendship, / to you I whistle. Do you know me?"

85. "It was six years ago, when / my chain was made of air, like that which your master / put on you in the garden. You looked at one another, treading, / you on his immense region without walls, / he on your trackless realm. / Who was the servant? Who the master? / No one will ever know / but seeing your gazes was joyous."

86. This may be another manifestation of the umbilical cord that we saw in "Amarras."

87. "One fine day, stoked by all the swallows of the / world / until it glowed red, / you became silent to howl an eternal howl. / You did not bark at children or at the poor / but at bad poets, whose odor / you detected at a distance, fine tracker. / Perhaps they were their children / who, at that hour of ruinous jargon, hung / from your tail, from your deep, easily frightened heart / the noisy pewter, cruel and stamped / by their sold fathers. It was the same thing. / You became silent. . . ."

88. ". . . But now / I play with you again from this dirty mist / with which the clear air of our Guadarrama Mountains / would make a July sun, along with your friends, / seeing on your back the loyal hand, tanned, / and I whistle to you, and I speak to you, and I caress / your pure breed, your offered life / now forever, «Sirius», good friend of the man, / companion of the poet, star that up there shines / with inflamed jaws / in which today I place at last, fearlessly, entirely, / this hand bitten by your beautiful memory."

89. This section "correspond[s] to the intermediate phase of mourning . . . in which there is a detachment of affections and interest from the lost love-object and a temporary return of these upon the self. From this stage the mourner works outward once more, trying to find or invent a new object of attachment" (Sacks, *The English Elegy*, 58).

90. "It is time, it is fear / that most reveal to us / our misery and our treasure. / Fear on top of a body, / fear of losing it, / fear mouth to mouth. / Fear at seeing this soil, / old and red, as so many times, / placing in it the rhythm of my life, / going back over my steps, / from Logroño to Burgos. . . ."

91. "So that I cannot flee, / so that I cannot rest and do not dare / to declare my palpable love, so / that now the shiver, / which is almost innocence, cannot smell / of the smoke of those bonfires of this autumn, / you come, my fear, my friend, / with your mouth closed, / with your hands so caressing, / with your way of walking emotionally, / enamoringly, as if you were getting closer / instead of going away."

92. "I want to see your face / with your lascivious nose, / and your serene brow, without wrinkles, / cold, rebellious water, / and your narrow eyes very black and round, / like those of the people of these lands. // Small in stature, like all saints, / somewhat stoop-shouldered and weak / in voice, with short, infantile arms, / left-handed, / in a striped suit, always your Sunday best, / with miraculous gestures and hands / of voracious size."

93. Sacks notes, "Instead of withdrawing from the dead, . . . the common psychological response of identification . . . may involve a lethal deformation of the self" (*The English Elegy*, 57). He later remarks, "Even more intriguing is the expressly elegiac element of the daemon. . . . By means of an artistic figure, the self finds or creates an image of its opposite, which it may then strive to imitate in an act of contemplative self-transformation or self-completion" (281, 280–81).

94. "What does your figure matter / if you are with me now breathing, trembling / with the wind from the East. / And in it we would find the innocent sigh, / the impact of the senses, / the harvest of happiness next to that / of despair."

95. "It is fear, it is fear. / The blind leading the blind, / fear that is the source of mistrust, / of evil, loss of faith, / ridicule and castle wall. Yes, the worst wedge: / that of the very wood. But also it is clay / improving the soil."

96. In this passage from Matthew, the Pharisees and scribes ask Jesus why his disciples do not wash their hands when they eat a meal. When the disciples ask Jesus if he is aware that the Pharisees took offense at his response, he replies: "Every plant that my heavenly Father has not planted will be uprooted. Let them alone; they are blind guides [of the blind]. If a blind person leads a blind person, both will fall into a pit" (Matt. 15:13–14). When asked to explain this parable, he adds, "Do you not realize that everything that enters the mouth passes into the stomach and is expelled into the latrine? But the things that come out of the mouth come from the heart, and they defile. For from the heart come evil thoughts, murder, adultery, unchastity, theft, false witness, blasphemy. These are what defile a person, but to eat with unwashed hands does not defile" (Matt. 15:17–20).

97. See my comments on "Libro segundo" of *Don*.

98. "Take up this glass of water"; "Touch this female body"; "Open that door, close it"; "Walk through those streets."

99. "Will the sun never dry / that which we put out / in the air: our fear, / our small love?"

100. "As powerful as hope / or memory is fear, / I know not if dark or luminous, but / leveling, straightening, rebuilding / our life."

101. "Let's go, my friend, my fear. / Untruthful as sinners, / have courage, have courage. / Try to seduce me / with money, with gestures, / with your piercing grace on the street corners, / seeking that somber and fervid / kiss, / that pleasureless embrace, / the bed that separates, like flax, / the stalk from the fiber."

102. See chap. 2 for a more detailed discussion of this poem.

103. "I want to see your tears, / though they be of cider or of vinegar, / never of domestic honey. / I want to see your tears / and I want to see my own, / these right now when I despise you / and I sing to you, / when I see you with such clarity / that I feel your pulse that wounds me, / pursues me, whispers to me, and almost dominates me, / and cures me of you, of you, of you."

104. "Forgive me, for you are / my friend, my companion. / You, damned old accomplice. / The least traitorous?"

105. "Viendo jugar al corro," *ABC* (18 January 1987): 3.

106. Rodríguez says that these "corros" are less frequent in contemporary society but still fulfill an important societal function. For other definitions, see *DRAE* and *Enciclopedia Universal Sopena*. Both mention only little girls, but Rodríguez uses the plural "niños."

107. Sacks, *The English Elegy*, 4. In his article, Rodríguez emphasizes the magical, incantatory quality of participation in the "corro." The "corro" has a creative function to personify reality and/or dreams, allowing for the modification of reality. This creative, incantatory power can be seen in the abundance of "fórmulas imperativas" [imperative formulae], "conjuros en una palabra" [conjurations in a word], and "expresiones propiciatorias o impetratorias" [propitiatory or impetrative expressions].

108. Sacks, *The English Elegy*, 5.

109. "These children who sing and raise / life / in the choruses of the world / that are not a wall but an open door / where if once one truly enters / one never leaves, / because one never leaves a miracle. . . ."

110. "These children who call the sky the sky / because it's very high, / and who have seen the dream, / sky blue, with white polka dots, / dance with a mouse amid the generous / and horrible furniture of infancy, / and mysterious . . ."

111. Another important factor in this function of the "corro" is gesture, "la pantomima como creación." As Rodríguez explains,

[E]n el niño, el «plano motriz», según la terminología de Piaget . . . , es mucho más profundo y valedero que el verbal y tiene un mayor acento comunicativo. . . . Lo importante . . . es que el puente entre la etapa emocional y la intelectual está cimentado por un repertorio de gestos estereotipados que casi siempre adquieren un valor mágico-supersticioso. Esta valencia reside en la magia de la interdependencia entre gestos y objetos. ("Viendo jugar la corro," 3)

[{I}n a child, the «motoric plane», according to the terminology of Piaget . . . , is much more profound and invested with meaning than the verbal and has a greater communicative accent. . . . The important thing . . . is that the bridge between the emotional stage and the intellectual is cemented by a repertory of stereotyped gestures that almost always acquire a magical-superstitious value. This valence resides in the magic of the interdependence between gestures and objects.]

Rodríguez further states that these gestures are the source of theater and masks that help objectify reality and emotions, the point of contiguity between gestures and objects.

112. "As was true for Apollo, Pan's pursued object changes to a form in the natural world, a form that, like the laurel tree, must be further altered to yield a consoling sign or instrument. Once again, that subsequent alteration, moving from nature to artifice, requires both a cutting off and a refashioning of the cut fragment. Both episodes portray a turning away from erotic pursuits and attachments to substitutive, artificial figures of consolation. Unlike many other grievers in the *Metamorphoses* . . . Apollo and Pan are successful mourners. . . . For unlike the others, they accept their loss and can retain their identities by what we may call a healthy work of mourning, a work that, as Freud points out, requires a withdrawal of affection from the lost object and a subsequent reattachment of affection to some substitute for that object. Ovid presents a condensed version of this process, a metamorphosis in which the lost object seems to enter or become inscribed in the substitute, in this case the found sign or art" (Sacks, *The English Elegy*, 6).

113. "I now contemplate the smallest child: / she who places her infancy / beneath the firewood. / We must save her. She sings and dances clumsily / and we must save her. / That delicacy that there is in her clumsiness / is what we must save."

114. Sacks, *The English Elegy*, 7.

115. Another fundamental characteristic of the "corro" related to its incantatory power is "la invención fonética" [phonetic invention]. In the "corro," words cease to have meaning per se; instead, one finds "la preponderancia del elemento sonoro sobre el lógico" [a preponderance of the sonorous element over the logical one]. Rodríguez affirms that "Es en el corro donde el niño halla el escenario más apto y luminoso para desarrollar su capacidad creadora a base de lo fonético y lo paródico" [It is in the "corro" where a child finds the most apt and luminous scenario for developing his/her creative capacity based on the phonetic and the parodic]. Frequently, "estribillos" [refrains] function "como formas rítmicas de invocación" [as rhythmic forms of invocation]. The "estribillo," according to Rodríguez, often displaces, weakens, and even unravels the logic of the song. "¿Y qué es lo que ha sucedido? El estribillo ha asumido la significación cobrando la categoría de conjuro, intentando modificar la realidad de la canción y la ley del juego por medio de una participación teúrgica" [And what has happened? The refrain has assumed a signification worthy of the category of a magic spell, attempting to modify the reality of the song and the law of the game by means of a theurgical participation].

116. "Come here, I don't know, I don't know, / but I want to tell you / something that perhaps no one has told you, / a story that now for me is a lament. / Come, come, and feel / the pure rain, like you, fall, / hear its sound, and how / it gives us a song in exchange / for grief, for injustice. You, come, come, / blessed pollen, give me / your clarity, your liberty, and put / your lemon yellow bow / at more of an angle. I want, I want / you to move your hair more, to raise / the adventure of your waist more, / and for your body to be sonorous and redemptive."

117. "And how many times, without being worthy, / I am next to this chorus, next to this / cupola, / next to the children who have no shadow. / And I hear it sing, solid and alive, / and it elates me, and it accuses me, / so full of tenderness and secrecy, / offered and useless until now . . ."

118. Sacks, *The English Elegy*, 5.

119. "And I follow the chorus, / and I live in it, in the full interior sea, / with these children, / never captive but with fierce / seeds in my soul, as the rain falls."

120. "I only ask that I may, / when the years pass, / again enter with the pulse of now / in this body, lasting and pure, / enter this chorus, / in this house open forever."

121. See my article "Ekphrasis, Intertextuality and the Reader's Role," 286–92.

122. I am thinking particularly here of Europa, the victim of a crime of passion, as Rodríguez has described his sister's death in an interview with Armiño: "Esa pesadilla la escribí hace unos trece años; a una de mis hermanas, la persona que yo más quise, la asesinaron por la calle, en Madrid, de una puñalada en el corazón, un crimen de pasión" ("Claudio Rodríguez," 90) [I wrote that nightmare some thirteen years ago; one of my sisters, the person I loved most in the world, was murdered in the street, in Madrid, stabbed in the heart, a crime of passion]. But even Arachne entails loss while her metamorphosis into a spider and her continued weaving is resurrective and compensatory. For more recent, feminist discussions of the myth of Arachne, see Marcia Welles, *Arachne's Tapestry: The Transformation of Myth in Seventeenth-Century Spain* (San Antonio, Tex.: Trinity University Press, 1985); and Nancy Miller, "Arachnologies: The Woman, the Text, and the Critic," in *Subject to Change: Reading Feminist Writing* (New York: Columbia University Press, 1988).

123. Debicki has pointed out the allusion to "A mi ropa tendida," which, if we recall "Lluvia y gracia," involves both chastening and exultation.

124. Ramazani provides additional insight into the acacia tree as traditionally associated with mourning (*Poetry of Mourning*, 383 n. 36), perhaps because of their contradictory color (blue/green, dark/light).

125. See Debicki's discussion of the life/art dichotomy in "Hilando" in the introduction to *Poesía del conocimiento* (Madrid: Júcar, 1986), 43–48. Ramazani also suggests that the poet "tries to make sense of death by superimposing the thinkable opposition, life/art, on the unthinkable opposition, life/death" (*Poetry of Mourning*, 130).

126. "With the velocity of the sky gone, / with the workshop, with / the rhythm of the tides of the streets, / she is here, without lies, / with her love so mute and returning, / with her celebration and with her servitude."

127. See my discussion in "Ekphrasis" of Penelope and the unraveling of the text.

128. Cf. Milton's "November Eclogue," for example.

129. Chevalier and Gheerbrandt, *Diccionario de los símbolos*, 762.

130. See Gonzalo Sobejano's seminal article on the epiphanic structure in Rodríguez's poems, "Impulso lírico y epifanía en la obra de Claudio Rodríguez," in *De los romances-villancico a la poesía de Claudio Rodríguez: 22 ensayos sobre las literaturas española e hispano-americana en homenaje a Gustav Siebenmann*, ed. José Manuel López de Abiada and Augusta López (Madrid: José Esteban, 1984), 409–27.

131. "Again November is coming, which is the month I love most, / because I know its secret, because it gives me more life. / The quality of its air, which is song, / almost revelation, / and its mornings that are so restorative, / its greedy tenderness, / its intimate loneliness. / And to find a street in a mouth, / a house in a body while, so fleeting, / with their melody of ambition lost, / the chestnuts and the spider webs fall."

132. Also see Heidegger on the poet's (*Dasein's*) act of uncovering. As Michael Gelven explains, "Heidegger's claim is that the essence or nature of truth is disclosure *(Erschlossenheit)*. He points out the etymology of the Greek word for 'truth,' *aletheia* (ἀλήθεια): 'unhiddenness'" (*A Commentary*, 129).

133. "These chestnuts, of yellowish ocher, / sure, half-opened, giving me liberty / along with the tremor in the shadow of their shells. / The spider webs, with their geometry / so cautious and sticky, and / also with their silence, / with their dark palpitation / like that of coral or the tenderest / sponge, or that of the opened / pineapple, / or the heart when it beats without tyranny when / it resuscitates and cleanses itself."

134. "After such a long time without love, this morning, / how redeeming. What / an intimate light. It enters me and gives me music / without pause / at the very moment when I love you, / when I surrender myself to you with joy, / tremulously and impatiently, / without looking at that door where the goodbye calls." (Note that I have used the Visor edition, where the final word of v. 31 is "adiós" instead of "dios" in the Cátedra edition.)

135. Cf. the myth of Orpheus and Eurydice.

136. "Again November has come. Far away are the days / of petty dreams, of faded kisses. / You are the month that I love. May your greedy, forgetful, violet light / never leave me in darkness / as winter nears."

137. In *Mirar un cuadro en el Museo del Prado* (Barcelona and Madrid: Lunwerg, 1991), 174.

138. "When St. John of the Cross attempts to clarify the verses and afterwards says: 'See that the pain of love is not cured except with the presence and the figure,' he brings us near to contemplation, vivid contemplation. It has to do with a transfiguration, so to speak. But the interpretation is not only an existing version of the contemplated object, but the entire life of the painter, of the creator, of art in this case, in contact with the object, that is to say, one begins to wonder in order to question again if existence isn't an image, a figure. In effect, I think, the creator attempts to lose his personality to a certain degree. Hence the respect that Velázquez has for his scenes, his objects, his figures, his portraits. This respect of this transformation consists, naturally, of reaching to the very heart. Reaching in that manner to the very heart of an object, of the figure in which the very creator loses his personality or, rather than losing it, nourishes himself, recognizes himself, renews himself in the figure, in the contemplation, he comes to possess vivid contemplation.

"The relationship between the multiple traces of things and their secret tends towards a vigilant moment in which one is bound to establish, that is to say, is bound to acquire eternity without fleetingness. This is essential" (Rodríguez, "El Bufón," 174).

139. "These sure eyes, / eyes never traitorous, / this beneficial gaze that makes / life pure, here in February, / with mysterious nearness. This woman / passes, and she looks me straight in the eye, and I possess the secret, / not the pleasure, of her life, / by means of the most / risky and whole / adventure: vivid contemplation."

140. "And I see her gaze / which transfigures, and I do not know, she does not know, / and ignorance is our appetite. / Well do I see that she is brunette, / short, a little flabby, / but this moment does not give time / to notice the color, the dimension, / or even the age of her look, / but, yes, the intensity of this moment."

141. "And the fertility of that which flees, / and of that which destroys me: / This passing, this gazing / on this street in Avila with its noon light / between gray and copper, / causes my liberty, my rebellion, my gratitude / to grow."

142. "There are those who touch the tablecloth, but not the table; / the glass, but not the water. / Those who tread many lands, / never their own."

143. "But before this gaze that has passed / and has wounded me well with its limpid quietude, / with such moving simplicity / that it leaves me and gives me / happiness and shock, / and, above all, reality, / I am left vanquished. And I see, I see, and I know / that which one expects, which is that which one dreams."

144. "The pathos of knowledge in these eyes, / so fleeting, instead of in the lips. / Because the lips rob / and the eyes implore. // She's gone. // When all has gone, when I have gone, / this gaze that asked and gave without time / will remain."

145. I am grateful to Philip Silver for this insight (personal communication).

146. ". . . / with the sober and haughty desiccation / of his very dirty hands, / with his clouded teeth, / in darkness, in the pollen of his mouth."

147. We could give a Lacanian reading of this image in the mirror, especially concerning the child's perception of wholeness (the recognition of identity) in contrast with his perception of fragmentation and dependence. See Jacques Lacan, "The Mirror Stage."

148. "And he said: 'There's a sound / in the glass' . . . / What color?, I said. You're lying. / He took out a small plate and sketched in the depth / of the porcelain, / with his mature fingernails, / with his breath and the smoke of a cigarette, / a house, / a path of trembling stone, / just like a child. / —You see? / Don't you hear the wind in the stone now? / He blew on the drawing / and there was nothing. 'Farewell. / I am the King of Smoke.'"

149. Carmen Ruiz Barrionuevo, "La poesía de Claudio Rodríguez a la vista de *El vuelo de la celebración*," *Alamo* 57 (setiembre–octubre 1976): [30–33].

150. "Although I don't know you, a child barely / but with the dark skin of a woman, / I have the silent / feverish key with which I am entering, / without clarity and without a goal, / and perhaps at an inappropriate moment, / into your half-open mouth / just for a moment, like the love of the air / or the surprise of solitude."

151. "And the column of breath, / so fugitive and imperishable, / the hidden movement of your fleshy lips, / so very poised and deceitful, / make me live in them: / in your gums, in your teeth, not / in your eyes."

152. "Farewell, farewell. I will remember, in the shadow / of other lips clearer than yours / this silent adventure. / It has been nothing: only a smile."

153. "Forgive my frivolous / betrayal of two months ago, but I love you, come, / you, you, come, / and hear with me how the fruit grows, / because without you I don't know, / because without you I don't love. . . ."

154. "The hushed sound. I hear the streets, / generous and unjust, of my hometown / as in my infancy, / in this party of your lips, of / your flesh that is a whisper and is a cadence / from the tips of your toes, sounding like the tides, / to your somewhat gray hair, like the murmur of quiet / water or that of the poplar trees at dusk."

155. "What more? What more? Shall we hear only, / after so much love and so much failure, / the music of the shadow and the sound of the dream?"

156. "I have heard and I have believed in many voices / though not in the words. / I have believed in the lips / but not in the kiss."

157. "Let them tell lies, those words of yours. / I want their sound: There, in it, I have / the truth of your life, like the wind, / now serene, of March. Hear it. It speaks."

158. "I have known you by the light of this moment, / so silent and clean, / upon entering your body, its secret, / the cavern that is altar and clay, / and erosion. / The redeeming mist, the blind smoke shape me / there, where nothing grows dark."

159. ". . . / there, in the dry pulse, in the cell of sleep, / in the tremulous leaf / illuminated and pierced to the depth / by the purity of the dawn. / Where one kisses in the dark, / blindly, as children kiss, / beneath the deep tenderness of this dome, / of this cavern open to the brilliance / where I give you my life. / Right there: in the dark / innocence."

160. According to *Webster's New World Dictionary* (3d College Edition, s.v. "innocence"), the word "innocence" derives from the Old French based on the Latin *innocentia*. This word can be divided into the negative prefix *in-*, not + *nocere*, to do wrong to. The latter is related to *nex*, death, and *necare*, to kill, evoking the loved one's death but also negating it by the negative prefix. The elegy has a similar function of recalling the loved one's death but also perpetuating his/her life through poetry.

161. ". . . / dangerous the trace, the promise / between the offering of things / and that of life. // Miserable the moment if it is not song."

162. This inference is consonant with the elegist's need to celebrate the passage of time. Rodríguez is "a poet who [is] struggling to reconcile the instantaneous with the passage of time and who need[s] to preserve an assurance of identity despite temporal change," who finds "a preservation and fulfillment of any discrete moment or identity by a revelation of its higher, timeless character" (Sacks, *The English Elegy*, 193–94). Consistent with the statements made in chap. 2 regarding "realismo metafórico," however, let us recognize that the transient and the lasting coexist in the same experience.

163. "How different love is next to the sea / than in my native, my captive land, to which I

will always / sing, / on the shore of the temper of its rivers / with their innocence and their clairvoyance, / with that company that shudders, / seeing the true tear fall / from the sky / when the night is long / and the dawn is clear."

164. "I never know why I feel / my body is a companion, that it is omen and refuge. / And now, before the sea, / what warping that of the wheat, / that of the waves, / what spinning, what full harvest / encase, fuse, curve / my love."

165. "The curved movement of the waves, / in the morning, so distinct from the night / so similar to that of the fields, / is entering / the mysterious murmur of your body, / today when there is high tide / and love is pearl gray, almost matte, / like the color of the poplar in October."

166. "Dreaming is simple, but not contemplation. / And now, at dawn, when it is time / to know and to do, / how this naked coast sounds like you. / When love and the sea / are one tide, without the northeast wind / being able to break through this retreat, / this astonishing seed, / this land, this water / here, in port, / where there are no longer any farewells, only pure anchor."

167. *Enciclopedia Universal Sopena*, 8:8037.

168. Ibid.

169. Simancas is a very small, unimpressive town outside of Valladolid, and a visit to it is a disappointing experience. Access to the fortress/archives is limited to one display room and the viewing of a videotape unless one has obtained special permission to do research in the archives.

170. In addition to the image of the river as "a figure . . . for the mourner's sexuality, and for its necessary willingness to accept not only a detour but a sacrificial change" noted in relation to the Duero above and applicable to the Pisuerga here, Sacks's comments on the image of the tower in Yeats's "In Memory of Major Robert Gregory" are pertinent here:

> [T]he tower's elegiac properties are particularly impressive. On the simplest level, it is an image of defensive fortitude. . . . Not only has the tower withstood time but it has remained as though at the center of time, a kind of temporal as well as spatial omphalos measuring the movements of the sun and moon. . . .
>
> Associated with the ancient centers of philosophy and astronomy, Yeats's tower is thus also closely bound up with a specifically Irish history [as is Rodríguez's fortress with Spanish history]. The concern for national heritage, thus embedded in the very stones of [this castle], will be important to the elegy. . . . But in addition, the tower suggests the isolated but lofty retreats [of other poets]. . . . (*The English Elegy*, 272)

Sacks further remarks that "submission to ritual, or to the imitation of perfect images discovered in art or scholarship, demands renunciation, an ascetic chastity that we have seen to be closely related to the work of mourning, with its unavoidable deflections of desire" (277), "a plunge into the abyss of solitary contemplation, an abyss associated with the subjective pursuit of art and literature" (280).

171. In this regard, we must deconstruct our temporal progression according to the tripartite definition of time and recognize that past, present, and future coexist in each section, as the tripartite definition suggests, because the present underlies all three temporal planes.

172. "Now with April well over half-completed when the light never / ends, / and even less at night, / night so dawn-like that it resuscitates us, / and walks us / from this well-polished stone, / we breathe history, here, in Simancas."

173. Because "caminar" means "recorrer caminando" [to traverse by walking] and walking is Rodríguez's idiom for writing, the act of writing exacts a thorough, painstaking examination of oneself, whereas writing an elegy means making repairs in the form of suturing the wound.

174. "Originally, as we have seen in the vegetation rites and in their spiritualized successors, the act of mourning quite simply *included* the act of inheritance, for the participant ingested the god or its symbol. . . . The connection between mourning and inheritance has remained a close one throughout history. Most interesting for any reader of the elegy is the fact

that in Greece the right to mourn was from earliest times legally connected to the right to inherit. There were, predictably enough, contests, even at the gravesite, over who should most legitimately mourn. . . . Few elegies can be fully read without an appreciation of their frequently combative struggles for inheritance.

"Furthermore, the ancient law prevented anyone from inheriting *unless* he mourned. . . . [M]any elegies pivot around the issue of poetic inheritance. In this case, the heir apparent must demonstrate a greater strength or proximity to the dead than any rival may claim, but he must also wrest his inheritance *from* the dead. More than a mere ingestion, some act of alteration or surpassal must be made, some device whereby the legacy may be seen to have entered a new successor. . . . In its earliest conflictual structures, as also in successive adaptations of the eclogue form, the elegy clarifies and dramatizes this emergence of the true heir" (Sacks, *The English Elegy*, 37).

175. "And it goes along illuminating / the curve of the furniture, / the fibers of paper burning on the main crag, / the apse of the parchments, / the dome of the letters. And the names singing / with grief, with lies, with perjury, / with their nuance of greed and of / pestilence and love . . . ."

176. "The lines emphasize the slow labor of craft and texture, the turning aside from passion to artifice" and "the elegiac stress on artifice and its materials (metal, wood, plaster, stone)" (Sacks, *The English Elegy*, 291).

177. "Like the rocks, the circle is a figure for the past and perhaps for the elegies themselves—a harsh version of wreath or garland" (ibid., 259).

178. ". . . And it goes along lifting / the crystal, where a new bubbling / cleans its pores and molds to the depth / its transparency, beside the holm-oaks / in praise with their open shadows."

179. "The unifying effect is reinforced by a subtle mesh of imagery . . . almost all of which represent the poet's mind, that delicate yet uncertain source of light that depends on the surrounding gloom for its definition and that, as we now recognize, is a light invariably associated with some veil or texture" (Sacks, *The English Elegy*, 191).

180. The Eucharist suggested here in the image of bread is "reminiscent of primitive mourners' ingestion of the dead god" (ibid., 221), nourishing the poet's soul through his inheritance from the past, the tradition. "[A]n elegist's consolation depends on his celebration of and subsequent association with the power of the father" (222). "To take the wafer and wine is still an act of repeated inheritance" (37).

181. "The crust of bread, that now is in morning's / hands, / and the dough that sounds / like a bell / cleanses, calms us, / still hiding the ocher gaze / of envy, / the shoulder of haughtiness, the dry lips of injustice, / the caustic lime, the dust of desire, / with a silence that shivers and lasts / amid the vertebrae of history, in the leaf / decrepit and pierced in each vein / by the light that accompanies / and blinds, and purifies time / above these fields, with its intimate science, / beneath this sky that is wisdom."

182. Cf. Quevedo, "Polvo será, mas polvo enamorado."

183. Again quoting Sacks, "The metaphor only drives home the substitution of the literary for the natural" (*The English Elegy*, 191).

184. As noted above, Persin has discussed the difference between these two concepts in her discussion of "saber" and "conocer" in "Brujas al mediodía" (*Recent Spanish Poetry*).

185. "Never in retreat, and still less at night, / with head held high, / so simple, amassed / on the cornice of the half light, / amid the bars of knowledge, / in the palpitation of the soul / dawn arrives. / And the splendor opens / giving flight to shadow."

186. "Like a lynx hunting on the slope, / lying in wait, looking almost with its snout, / like the royal kite or the sooty / rook, in the time / of hibernation, thus come now / the rapacity, the kiss, / the image of the centuries, / that of my own life."

187. Cf. Ramazani's "economic problem" for the elegist profitting from the loss of a loved one.

188. ". . . There are nests / of doves, and falcons / there, on the towers, while the rooster

crows / on the altar, and pecks / the offered, humble shirt blowing in the wind / on the right bank of the Pisuerga."

189.   The two primary definitions of the verb "suceder" found in the *DRAE* have express bearing on the elegiac text. The first maintains that "suceder" means "Entrar una persona o cosa en lugar de otra o seguirse a ella" [For a person or a thing to enter in place of another or to follow that other], indicative of the veil of language of the text and the suturing process of closing the wound of loss and grief. The second definition is "Entrar como heredero o legatario en la posesión de los bienes de un difunto" [To enter as an inheritor or legatee in possession of the goods of a deceased person], describing the poet's inheritance from the tradition.

190.   "Air that marks us / and that never allows us / to wither because you enfold / in a thousand ways, / so sure and bold, from the choirs / of the lungs, / to the corners of the mouth, / come. You are all."

191.   See Shakespeare's sonnet 73:

> That time of year thou mayst in me behold
> When yellow leaves, or none, or few, do hang
> Upon those boughs which shake against the cold,
> Bare ruined choirs, where late the sweet birds sang.
> In me thou see'st the twilight of such day
> As after sunset fadeth in the west;
> Which by and by black night doth take away,
> Death's second self, that seals up all in rest.
> In me thou see'st the glowing of such fire,
> That on the ashes of his youth doth lie,
> As the deathbed whereon it must expire,·
> Consumed with that which it was nourished by.
> This thou perceiv'st, which makes thy love more strong,
> To love that well which thou must leave ere long.

192.   In keeping with the eternal present that has emerged in "Elegía" through the temporal progression of the work of mourning in *El vuelo*, we see "a reconciliation of the timebound with the timeless in a music that smoothly encompasses the occasions of grief" (Sacks, *The English Elegy*, 192).

193.   "History is not even / a sigh, / or a tear, pure or rotten / or deceitful: perhaps a derisive laugh."

194.   See "Lágrima" in the second section of *El vuelo* and note 75 above.

195.   "But here is the sweat, / and the grief, here, protected / by the wool and the worked leather, / in the silk, the esparto grass, / in the humility of the oil, / in the harmony of the flour, / in the saliva in flower, licked and expectorated / and pleading for / the pulp of a date or a cowardly love / in the cities awaiting the traffic."

196.   "I am amid the living / streets of the words: many can be seen written, / fine as coral, / a dark reddish color, / in manuscripts: others / flapping their wings on so many walls, / said straightforwardly, / while you are before me, my sky, / and you give me no rest. . . ."

197.   Sacks asserts that "elegies often end with an indication of further movement" (*The English Elegy*, 210).

198.   ". . . Hush, hush. / Here no longer is history or even legend; / only time made song / and the light that opens its arms, recently crucified / beneath this sky always at noon."

199.   As Sacks notes of Jonson's "On My First Son," "[T]here is something characteristically Neoclassical in the way Jonson's elegy ends in a voice that is and is not quite his own. We have seen how almost any elegy requires a progression of voice, a sequence by which the mourner supersedes his grieving self. But in the Neoclassical era, with its high incidence of personae, it is interesting to note how often the elegist actually concludes as though with someone else's voice" (*The English Elegy*, 126).

For Heidegger, speaking is first listening: "Only when we give thought to our human saying . . . , only then do we arrive at an adequate definition of what is essentially present in all speaking. Speaking is known as the articulated vocalization of thought by means of the organs of speech. But speaking is at the same time also listening. It is the custom to put speaking and listening in opposition: one man speaks, the other listens. But listening accompanies and surrounds not only speaking such as takes place in conversation. The simultaneousness of speaking and listening has a larger meaning. Speaking is of itself a listening. Speaking is listening to the language which we speak. Thus, it is a listening not *while* but *before* we are speaking" (Martin Heidegger, "The Way to Language," in *On the Way to Language*, trans. Peter D. Hertz [New York: Harper & Row, 1971], 123).

200. Sacks, *The English Elegy*, 289.

CHAPTER 5. PROMETHEUS DOUBLE-BOUND: THE ROLE OF THE POET IN CONTEMPORARY LIFE IN *CASI UNA LEYENDA* (1991)

1. I have used Claudio Rodríguez, *Casi una leyenda* (Barcelona: Tusquets, 1991) for all quotes from this text. Page numbers will appear in parentheses after each quote.

Recent studies of *Casi* include an excellent discussion by Angel Rupérez in the otherwise off-target introduction to Claudio Rodríguez, *Poesías escogidas* (Madrid: Mondadori, 1992), 29–38. Also see Philip Silver's "Poesía última de Claudio Rodríguez: 'Casi una leyenda,'" *Revista Hispánica Moderna* 46 (1993): 340–42; and Fernando Yubero's "La noche clara de Claudio Rodríguez: Hacia *Casi una leyenda*," *Compás de Letras* 6 (1995): 131–46.

2. See Mayhew, "*Casi una leyenda*: Repetición y renovación en el último libro de Claudio Rodríguez," *Insula* 541 (enero 1992): 11–12.

3. The concept of the sublime is a knotty theoretical issue with a long history in both philosophy and literary theory, beginning with Longinus's treatise. As Suzanne Guerlac avers in *The Impersonal Sublime: Hugo, Baudelaire, Lautréamont* (Stanford, Calif.: Stanford University Press, 1990), "In each treatise the sublime emerges in a problematic relationship to the expository framework that presents it, eluding theoretical mastery" (1). In his discussion of *The Kantian Sublime: From Morality to Art* (Oxford: Clarendon Press, 1989), Paul Crowther adds that "sublimity of expression has no intrinsic link with any specific signifying device" (161), giving the poet latitude to develop a personal mode of expression to attain sublimity. Jean-Luc Nancy affirms: "The sublime properly constitutes our *tradition* (in aesthetics at the very least, but then this restriction already entangles us in some of the questions which are today tied to the sublime). The tradition passes on [*La tradition* transmet]. What it passes on to us in the name of the sublime is not *an* aesthetics. It is above all not an aesthetics of the grandiose, the monumental, or the ecstatic, with which the sublime is often confused—admittedly not without certain historical reasons, which must be handled with discretion, even as this all-too-heavy word *sublime* must perhaps gradually be effaced. The tradition passes on the aesthetic as question" ("Preface to the French Edition," in *Of the Sublime: Presence in Question*, ed. Jeffrey S. Librett [Albany: State University of New York, 1993], 1).

In consonance with Rodríguez's aesthetic project, Crowther proffers the following: "the sublime is an item or set of items which, through the possession or suggestion of perceptually, imaginatively, or emotionally overwhelming properties, succeeds in rendering the scope of some human capacity vivid to the senses" (*The Kantian Sublime*, 162). "In the context of the sublime . . . a rather different experience of what it is to be a finite rational being emerges. What is important here is not simply the fact that the sublime vivifies the extraordinary scope of rational comprehension (in a way that pierces through our normal desensitization); but also the fact that it is experienced as profoundly and inseparably connected with—indeed, as *called forth and projected from*—finite being's struggle to launch itself into and articulate the world.

In this experience, in other words, both rationality and finitude are experienced as a kind of positive and integrated continuity. They are felt to embody a fundamental thrust where the primal drama of the very origin and essence of the human condition itself is re-enacted and exemplified" (167). "Given this, one might say that to experience the sublime in these terms is to have a full and complete primordial experience of spatio-temporality. . . .

"I am arguing, then, that our various experiences of the sublime can have a broader *metaphysical* significance in terms of what might be called 'primordial disclosure'. By this, I mean that the sublime is an affective experience which *qua* aesthetic is logically distinguishable from those connected with the immediate vicissitudes of everyday life, but which, if understood correctly, reveals a foundation in ultimate structures which are immanent to, but customarily concealed within, that life" (171–72).

Throughout this chapter, I will elaborate on this definition, following the model provided by Guerlac *(The Impersonal Sublime)* by reading primarily Longinus and Kant through the lens of Heidegger and finally linking it with Heidegger's belief that *Dasein*'s confrontation with death (as "the scope of some human capacity") provides most insight into and awareness of what it means to be. Jean-François Lyotard addresses many of these issues in his essay "The Interest of the Sublime," in Librett, ed., *Of the Sublime*, 109–32; also see Éliane Escoubas, "Kant or the Simplicity of the Sublime" and Jeffrey S. Librett's afterword, "Positing the Sublime: Reading Heidegger Reading Kant," in the same volume (55–70 and 193–219, respectively).

In addition to Crowther and Guerlac, the sources I have consulted include Longinus, "On the Sublime" in *Classical Literary Criticism*, T. S. Dorsch, trans. (London: Penguin Books, 1965); Immanuel Kant, *Observations on the Feeling of the Beautiful and Sublime*, John T. Goldthwait, trans. (Berkeley, Los Angeles, and Oxford: University of California Press, 1960); Henry Hart, *Robert Lowell and the Sublime* (Syracuse, N.Y.: Syracuse University Press, 1995); Neil Hertz, *The End of the Line: Essays on Psychoanalysis and the Sublime* (New York: Columbia University Press, 1985); Librett, ed., *Of the Sublime;* and Thomas Weiskel, *The Romantic Sublime: Studies in the Structure and Psychology of Transcendence* (Baltimore and London: Johns Hopkins University Press, 1976).

4. Philip Silver, a longtime and valued friend of the poet, has written "Diré que la personalidad pública de Claudio despista y confunde. Claudio rehuye ser considerado poeta. . . . Conclusión provisional: es imposible desmitificar al verdadero poeta. Cuanto más se insiste en su «llaneza», más misterioso se nos hace" ("«El rey del humo», un poeta misterioso"). [I will say that the public personality of Claudio misleads and confuses. Claudio shies from being considered a poet. . . . Provisional conclusion: it is impossible to demythify the true poet. However much one insists on his "openness," the more mysterious he becomes for us.]

In support of this statement, following the publication of *Casi*, Rodríguez was feted in the media with a number of interviews and articles and was the recipient of two major literary awards: the "Reina Sofía" and the "Príncipe de Asturias."

5. The paradoxical consequences of the issues treated in *Casi* reflect Rodríguez's commitment to the moral aspect of writing. As Crowther says, "The pursuit of happiness, and even selfishness, [Kant] admits, is always active in us, and is merely temporarily checked by the moral law. However, 'self-conceit'—stipulatively defined as the view that features contingent upon the human condition (such as happiness, or other-regarding emotions such as sympathy) constitute the supreme principle of morality—is something which determination by the moral law 'strikes down' and 'humiliates' altogether. It is by the thwarting of sensible impulses and the principles unwarrantably derived from such impulses that a feeling akin to pain is produced. But this negative effect has two rewarding consequences. First, by checking and humiliating our impulses and 'self-conceit' it clears away obstacles to authentic moral decision, that is, makes it easier for our will to be determined by the moral law on future occasions. Second, it reinforces our awareness that that which has destroyed our 'self-conceit' is an 'intellectual causality' (i.e. a manifestation of our wholly rational supersensible self). The feeling akin to

pain thus serves to elevate us with a sense of our ultimate rational vocation" (*The Kantian Sublime*, 23).

6. With regard to *Casi*, Silver asserts, "Su temario: la misma revelación que acabamos de explicar, lo sublime y su engranaje cotidiano, y la manera en que la experiencia de lo sublime configura su comprensión del amor y la muerte.

"Pretende recuperar la presencia e inocencia que la noche y los años le han restado, y poder partir así de nuevo hacia la aventura . . ." ("Todo misterio"). [Its thematics: the very revelation that we have just explained, the sublime and its daily meshing of gears, and the way in which the experience of the sublime configures his comprehension of love and death. He pretends to recuperate the presence and innocence that night and the years have taken from him, and thus to be able to depart anew toward adventure.]

When asked in an interview with Dionisio Cañas to clarify the title of this work, Rodríguez has stated: "Significa, simplemente, la vida como leyenda, no como historia. Lo que pasa es que parece confusa, incierta esa vida, como si la experiencia no hubiera sucedido o hubiera sucedido de otra manera. Es algo fabuloso, legendario, y ahí está el origen del título. Siempre me acuerdo, lo he dicho ya, de un verso de Dante que dice «así como la vista parece y no parece verdadera», yo lo cambio a «así como la vida parece y no parece verdadera». Esto viene a ser lo mismo que la idea de Calderón de que la vida es sueño, ilusión." [It means, simply, life as legend, not as history. What happens is that it seems confused, uncertain, that life, as if experience hadn't happened or had happened in a different way. It is something fabulous, legendary, and there is the origin of the title. I always remember, I've already mentioned it, a verse by Dante that says "just as sight seems and does not seem real," I change it to "just as life seems and does not seem real." This is the same as Calderón's idea that life is dream, illusion.] He repeats this definition with some slight modifications in other interviews.

7. Guerlac makes a similar point when discussing Baudelaire's prose poems. "In the shift from the poetry to the prose poems, Baudelaire's 'passionate taste for the obstacle' is no longer engaged in terms of a challenge to beautiful representation. Whereas in the poetry the infinite is thematized through the finite instrument of beautiful presentation, in the prose poems a relation of obstruction between the infinite and the finite (or of interference between beauty and its obstructions) is thematized through a language that advertises no literary self-justification, no privilege over its representations. As a result, it offers no firm ground for interpretation. The language of the prose poems tends either to follow thematic shifts, in which case beauty of presentation becomes another element of the text that requires interpretation, or toward self-effacement, an effect of 'art without art' often misconstrued as 'realism.'

"The dualism that operates both thematically and structurally in the prose poems is often characterized in terms of the 'ideal' and the 'real,' or of idealization and its demystification" (*The Impersonal Sublime*, 97).

8. *Casi* is the first work in which Rodríguez has provided such specific titles for his sections although he anticipates this procedure in the opening and closing sections of *El vuelo*. These three sections vaguely resemble the tripartite intermediate sections of that work. I believe, however, that Rodríguez has altered the "temporal" sequence in *Casi* to present, past, and future. The process of renewal and variation is a constant in Rodríguez's aesthetic trajectory. It is of particular importance in *Casi* not only because of the need to revitalize his own work, but his obligation to transmit the poetic tradition and to redirect the moral values of contemporary society as well.

In an article published in the Spanish newspaper *Diario 16* ("Todo misterioso"), Silver suggests that the themes of the three sections are "amor, tiempo, muerte" [love, time, death], and he notes that Rodríguez has taken these titles from the "romancero." Note that all three are octasyllabic.

9. The anonymous author of an article in *El Urogallo* has defined the structure of this work as divided into five sections, preceded by a "poema-prólogo." According to this critic, "el autor se pregunta continuamente si podrá captar esa visión intuida, si podrá atrapar la verdad

absoluta que se desprende de esa visión que las palabras producen y elevarla a eternidad" ("Claudio Rodríguez," *El Urogallo,* September–October 1991, n.p.) [the author continuously wonders if he will be able to capture that intuited vision, if he will be able to capture the absolute truth that is connected with that vision words produce and to elevate it to eternity].

10. Weiskel delineates a contrast between the positive and negative sublime which we can posit as an imbrication of fixed and fluid, grotesque and symmetrical, in Rodríguez's structuring of the work and the definition of his identity in *Casi:* "Unlike the positive sublime, whose ultimate form is repetitive and circular, the negative sublime theoretically aims toward a unique disillusionment—the unmasking of the 'subreption' by which an object seems sublime" (*The Romantic Sublime,* 77). In his afterword, Librett arrives at a similar conclusion: "Accordingly, Kant determines the 'moment' or the 'nonce' of this nonce-sense once as a *sequence* of two feelings, the one negative, the other positive, so to speak, and once as a quasi simultaneous *alternation* between negative and positive feelings. . . . From the description of a linear sequence, then, we move to the description of a circularity or simultaneous repetition of opposed tendencies. Between the two descriptions and within each, the moment, the nonce, is broken or multiplied to several nonces at (n)once. The nonce-sense of the sublime is a nonnonce, always the anon of the nonce" ("Positing the Sublime," 217). Summarizing simply Librett's play on words, we can say that the structure of *Casi* is both circular and spiral, as the poet's identity is both (re)defined and called into question, demystified and aggrandized. Again, we might invoke the image of the Moebius strip to envision these paradoxical configurations.

11. In a personal communication, Rodríguez himself mentioned that the book seems "cojo" [lame]. We shall see the added significance of that statement later in this chapter.

12. Cf. the "good thief" who was crucified with Christ on Golgotha.

13. Guerlac, *The Impersonal Sublime,* 7.

14. "'Art without art' is the grounding principle of the 'five genuine sources of the sublime' Longinus proposes to us. . . . 'Metaphors make for sublimity, we read, yet we are also told that 'a figure is always most effective when it conceals the very fact of its being a figure.' How is this fact concealed? Precisely through the effect of sublimity itself: 'The sublimity and the effect on the emotions are a wonderfully helpful antidote against the suspicion that accompanies the use of figures.' Art achieves its force of sublimity through a dissimulation of its artifice, that is, by appearing as nature: 'For art is only perfect when it looks like nature'" (Guerlac, *Impersonal Sublime,* 2). Also see Hertz (*End of the Line,* 15–20) for a discussion of the deceptive aspect of the sublime and the relationship between concealment and truth, revelation and falsity, and Michel Deguy's discussion of Longinus:"The Discourse of Exaltation (Μεγαληγορειν): Contribution to a Rereading of Pseudo-Longinus," in Librett, ed., *Of the Sublime,* 22–23.

On the basis of Kant's discussion in the *Critique of Judgment,* Crowther postulates four varieties of the sublime: cognitive, artefactual, personalized, and expressive. "I have, then, reconstructed Kant's theory of the sublime in terms of four varieties. The first of these (which I shall call the *cognitive* variety) divides into the mathematical and dynamical modes; it arises when some vast or powerful object (whether real or occurring as the subject-matter in art) makes vivid the scope of rational cognition as such. The second variety—which I shall call the *artefactual* sublime—arises when some vast or mighty man-made product (or a representation of one) makes vivid the scope of human artifice. The third variety—which I shall call the *personalized* sublime—involves some overwhelming personal significance that an artwork holds for us making vivid the scope of artistic creation. The final variety—which I shall term the *expressive* sublime—arises when an artist's originality is able to evoke a sense of his subject-matter's universal significance and, in so doing, makes vivid the extraordinary scope of artistic expression" (*The Kantian Sublime,* 162).

Although all four varieties are manifest in *Casi* to some extent or another, I would submit that the cognitive and the expressive varieties predominate and interact throughout the collection, positing a friction between what Crowther designates the descriptive (the cognitive and the artefactual) and the evaluative (the personalized and the expressive) aspects of the sublime

(*The Kantian Sublime*, 162). (I have used the terms "descriptive" and "prescriptive," "constative" and "performative" to define this effect.)

15. Victor Hugo stressed the effect of the grotesque. See his "Preface" to *Cromwell*. We will encounter the grotesque in *Casi* but only after we have stepped over the threshold into the sublime. Also, Burke has stressed that the sublime consists of both pain and pleasure, commensurate with Rodríguez's poetics. See his *A Philosophical Enquiry into the Origin of our Ideas of the Sublime and the Beautiful*. As Weiskel explains, "So Burke argues that obscurity has a greater affective appeal than clarity, which 'is in some sort an enemy to all enthusiasms whatever.' In nature, 'dark, confused, uncertain images have a greater power on the fancy to form the grander passions than those have which are more clear and determinate'" (*The Romantic Sublime*, 16–17).

Crowther suggests that there is some precedence for this attitude on the poet's part when he remarks Heidegger's commentary on a painting by Van Gogh. "The fact that sublimity of expression does not presuppose intrinsically sublime subject-matter can be shown by the example (amongst others) of Van Gogh's famous painting of a pair of peasant boots. This is about as unsublime a subject-matter as one could hope for. However, as Heidegger has sensitively shown, Van Gogh's sheer style of expression can open out a sense of the immense possibilities of toil and the passage of the seasons across the earth which inform the boots' truth as 'a piece of equipment.' . . . I would suggest, though that sublimity of expression has no intrinsic link with any specific signifying device. . . . Indeed, the tendency to use overt symbolism, metaphor, and the like can meet with the same fate as the conventionalized 'sublime' content of the Gothic novel and late eighteenth-century landscape painting (i.e. degenerate into clichéd theatricality). . . .

"I have, by developing themes in Kant's theory of art, shown that, despite his reservations, the sublime can arise in a threefold distinctively artistic sense. Either through the overwhelming perceptual scale of a work making vivid the scope of human artifice, or through a work's overwhelming personal significance making vivid the scope of artistic creation, or, finally, through the imaginatively overwhelming character of some general truth embodied in a work, making vivid the scope of artistic expression" (*The Kantian Sublime*, 160–61).

For Heidegger's discussion of Van Gogh's painting, see "The Origin of the Work of Art," in *Poetry Language Thought*, trans. Albert Hofstadter (New York: Harper & Row, 1971), 17–87; or "El origen de la obra de arte," in *Arte y poesía*, trad. Samuel Ramos (México: Fondo de Cultura Económica, 1958), 37–123.

16. Again speaking of Baudelaire, Guerlac addresses the supplementarity of the reader's role: "The imagination, Baudelaire writes in the 'Salon de 1859,' includes a 'permission to supplement' that it owes to its 'divine origin.' The imagination is also said to include a critical spirit that supplements its artistic operations. This is the basis for the critical moment when the artist wants to *raissoner son art*, which Baudelaire invoked in connection with Wagner. In the act of aesthetic reception, furthermore, the imagination of the beholder is said to supplement the production of the work of art through the act of reception—'In music, as in painting and even in written speech, there is always a gap filled in by the imagination of the listener.'

"It is here that we find a link between Longinian hypsos—the crossing of positions of enunciation and the appropriation by the listener of the act of speaking—and the Kantian sublime of genius" (*The Impersonal Sublime*, 104–5).

17. According to Weiskel, "the discourse of identity is, on the one hand, a discourse of origins and, on the other, a discourse of fictions. In both phases the structure of identity is circular and the transcendence it accomplishes is spiral. Because memory has no origin and desire no finality, identity can never be completely accomplished" (*The Romantic Sublime*, 157).

18. Rodríguez comments on the lack of inspiration in the city during an interview with Cañas published in *Cambio 16,* 10 June 1991, 104–5. The title of that piece summarizes his attitude: "'La ciudad no me inspira, aunque casi todo lo escribo callejeando'" ["The city doesn't inspire me, though I write almost everything wandering through the streets"].

19. Denis Donoghue, *Thieves of Fire* (London: Faber & Faber, 1973), 113.

20. In her discussion of Trakl's poetry in relation to Heidegger's philosophy, Véronique M. Fóti comments "on the figure of the wandering stranger and the locality or 'landscape,' as Heidegger calls it, of his exile or wandering" (*Heidegger and the Poets: Poiēsis / Sophia / Technē* [Atlantic Highlands, N.J.: Humanities Press], 15). She notes that "The figure of the wandering poet who is 'of another sense' and who has become a stranger to the contemporary cast *(Geschlecht)* of man (which itself is deeply estranged from man's disclosive *essence*) is not a figure capable of what Heidegger earlier called 'spiritual legislation,' but one who can trace out, in the depth of night, the uncertain itinerary of a possible transition" (14). The speaker of *Casi una leyenda* wanders in the same kind of landscape and fulfills a similar role with regard to himself and others.

21. "And is there no danger, salvation, punishment, / maleficence of October / after the deep promise of the night, / next to the pursuit of the rain that before / was a very fecund secret and now is washing / my memory, echoing without loyalty, / serene enemy in this street? / And the dark palpitation of destiny, / still not mature today?"

22. In the article in *El Urogallo* mentioned above, the author states that "La lluvia . . . simboliza, como en César Vallejo y Blas de Otero, el recuerdo, la memoria, y, así, la memoria recuperada aparece como una ciudad recién llovida. La puerta cerrada como símbolo del poema que avanza hacia el conocimiento oculto aparece en los siguientes versos de «Calle». . . . Y sólo dentro de esta configuración simbólica en sentido la «llave» como elemento que facilita el conocimiento de la realidad a través del poema" [The rain . . . symbolizes, as in Cesar Vallejo and Blas de Otero, remembering, memory, and, thus, recuperated memory appears as a city recently rained upon. The closed door as symbol of the poem that advances toward hidden knowledge appears in the following verses of "Calle." . . . And only within this symbolic configuration of meaning the "key" as an element that facilitates knowledge of reality by means of the poem].

23. See Rodríguez's comments about the title *Casi una leyenda* in note 6 above.

24. "I hear the nocturnal clarity and the astuteness of the wind / as thirsty and fugitive always. / But where is it, where / that secret nest of dawned wings / of swallows?"

25. "Someone calls to me from / these windows awaiting the dawn, / from these transparent houses, alone, / with gleams and ashes / and with the inheritance of their scars while / this closed door becomes music / awaiting a hand that will open it / without fear and without dust. And where the neighbors?"

26. "Whereas beauty is aroused by specific, tangible properties of objects such as smallness or smoothness—properties easily imitated or represented in art or painting—the sublime in nature is associated with what Burke calls 'privations.' These include 'Vacuity, Darkness, Solitude, Silence' and above all infinity—something that (if it can be considered a thing at all) cannot be represented, because it has no limits, something that is, as Burke puts it, 'presentable but by language'" (Guerlac, *The Impersonal Sublime*, 6). The cityscape substitutes for "nature" in this definition, for it emblematizes the "privations" Burke enumerates.

In his discussion of a passage in Heidegger, Lacoue-Labarthe also observes that "Defamiliarity, alienation and derangement, shock, simplicity, transport, retreat, and reservation: all of this . . . is the vocabulary of the sublime . . . or at least its transcription in the Heideggerian idiom" ("Sublime Truth," in Librett, ed., *Of the Sublime*, 94–95).

27. Following upon the previous quote, Lacoue-Labarthe says, "But what happens in this experience or trial [*épreuve*]? On the borders of a being that 'estranges' the entirety of what is, and in accordance with the proper glow or radiance of this being, it *happens* to become present (or to appear): that there is (such a thing as) the being and not nothing. The work is that absolutely paradoxical being . . . which nihilates [*né-antise*] the being in order to make Being itself appear and come to light, glow, and scintillate. The work opens the clearing, the luminous opening in which, as a being, it holds itself, and on the (empty) ground—the groundless ground— of which the being comes to manifest itself. The work presents Λ-λήθεια, the no-thing, lumi-

nous with an 'obscure illumination,' which 'is' the Being of what is. And this is sublimity" (ibid., 95). The play between light and darkness will become even more pronounced and significant when we reread this poem at the end of *Casi*.

28. The question "¿Y dónde los vecinos?" echoes a verse from Hölderlin's "Andenken" that speaks of friendship. As Fóti explains,

> Friendship is here conceived as essentially a form of truth. Its aletheic character neglects Spinoza's insight that man is God to man, as well as the Graeco-Roman and political model of friendship (based on reciprocity), in favor of what Derrida describes as the "heterology, asymmetry, and infinity" of non-reciprocity and non-requital. For Heidegger, such asymmetry has positive import, for he sees mortals as first of all oriented toward "the holy" and bound into the configuration of the Fourfold, rather than as being in the situation of human encounter. He therefore hears Hölderlin's question, "Wo aber sind die Freunde?" ("Where, however, are the friends?") which opens the fourth strophe of "Andenken," as a question concerning "the essence of friendship yet to come," a friendship which exceeds human communion. The poet's bereaved singularization is, for him the mark attesting to "the respect of the one first sacrificed before the sacrifice." This sacrifice sets the poet apart from those who . . . dedicate themselves to a dialectical exploration of what is alien, and remain unable to accomplish "the transition into the homelike." These, . . . Heidegger concludes, are incapable of understanding either the alien or the homelike, for they lack the courage to accept "the essential-original poverty" [of thought] and to turn toward what is "simple and originary." (*Heidegger and the Poets*, 65)

(The parentheses are Fóti's. The Derridean text to which she refers is "The Politics of Friendship," *Journal of Philosophy* 82, no. 11 (November 1988): 632–49. The quotes from Heidegger are from *Gesamtausgabe (Collected Works)*, 52:169, 52:176.)

Major themes of Rodríguez's *Casi una leyenda* are the poet's sacrifice, the search for truth and for readers who will share in the truth and sacrifice necessary to attain it, the asymmetry and infinity of the work's structure, and the title "Andenken" ("memory" and "commemoration"). Fóti explains that Heidegger identifies commemorating with greeting, the poetic word per se.

> Every poetic word, for Heidegger, is "a greeting word," and this characterization carries a double sense. First, in the *essential* sense, greeting bespeaks mindfulness of the differential origin of manifestation; it holds in memory *(Andenken)* the enigma of the Differing as that which already-was *(das Gewesene)*. . . . At the same time, however, greeting opens up the historical place-scape of *essential* poetic practice. In coming-into-its-own . . . , such poetizing keeps in memory the "alien" which it has sought out but surpassed, the Greek "fire from heaven." . . . Heidegger insists . . . that what is greeted in such poetic commemoration "swings across" the straits of the present and encounters a people from out of the future, as what is still "to come." In greeting it, the poet and thinker prepare for its advent. (Fóti, *Heidegger and the Poets*, 51–52; original emphasis)

29. "It is getting lighter. / And when the seeds of the rain / fecundate the silence and the mystery, / the spume of the trace / echoing in disquietude, with a shiver, / as if it were the first time / amid the air and the light and a caress, / they are no longer important as before, / the vivid song forging / the shape of the iron on the balconies / the sunstruck rooftiles / neither the dark, dull blue / of the cement and of the sky. . . ."

30. Fóti again makes an illuminating comment concerning Trakl's poetry and Heidegger's commentary: "The other cast of standpoint is that of enlightened vision . . ., which allows the *Fortriss* driven by pain (the unrecognized pull of the Differing at the heart of manifestation) to be checked and stilled by the countermovement of a backward pull or *Rückriss* that brings the dynamic intensities into equipoise and transforms singeing wildness into a 'flaming regard.' . . . Through the double pull of *Fortriss* and *Rückriss*, the 'great soul' is brought to a standpoint where it responds receptively to the double, if not duplicitous, movement of the holy, the movement of the trace which is Being's self-withdrawing bestowal. Heidegger, appropriating Trakl's imagery and diction, calls the movement of the holy 'the brightness sheltered into the dark,' or

speaks of it as the somber luminosity of the color blue. Through being irradiated with blueness, the radiance of the holy, the wildness of human existence is calmed and its pain 'stilled' without being assuaged" (*Heidegger and the Poets*, 19–20).

31. ". . . And who treads it? / Must one let his step, like water, / strip down and wash / sometimes dry, agile or poorly tempered; / other times, like now / so little friendly, without surrender or audacity, / walking without a path and with distrust / amid a deceived, corrupted people, / with life without season, / with liberty without song? // This sidewalk is talking to me like a wing, / this wall in shadow that fixes me and shapes me / with limestone without thyme and without flight without luck / a lost youth. One must go on. Farther . . ."

32. With reference to Longinus, Deguy says, "Mimesis is a representation of what has come before by means of a special effort of retrospective preparation, *as* 'at the beginning.' . . . Figures favor a general rapprochement of the before and after, of natural and artificial. In short, the reorganization and reunification of all that is separate. . . . Thus, the illumination their light favors covers figures over again with the very shadow of their 'brightness' (κατακαλύψει)" ("The Discourse of Exaltation," 21).

33. "If it is taken alone—on its own, asynthetically (not asyndetically for asyndeton augments the fusional temperature of the sublime mixture), bereft of all alliance or grounding in the reunification the ingredients of which Pseudo-Longinus treats exhaustively as the catalysts of the whole—rhythm—this corybantic rhythm that 'constrain[s] the listener to move rhythmically'—runs away with itself, lets fall its sense, communicates only the trepidations of trance, traceless of sense. As opposed to those votaries of the frenetic, the 'crazy' rockers of today, Pseudo-Longinus takes the risk of risk itself" (ibid., 18).

34. The alternation between the interrogative and affirmative use of the motif "Y" is implicated in the ambivalence of the sublime (see Guerlac's introductory remarks on theories of the sublime in *The Impersonal Sublime*, 1–12). What appears to be a very simple and insignificant rhetorical device signifies by means of the "context" of the verbal mode. Rodríguez subtly calls attention to this device by beginning the poem and the entire collection with it.

35. "And I go from door to door / up and down the street / and before I leave / I want to see that face there at mid-window, / transparent and hushed / next to the surprise of its intimacy / with the cadence of the glass without a nest / very well transfigured by the light, / by the harsh reflection of the plateau, / with useless modesty, / looking out in silence and adventure. / I want to see that face. And to see myself in it."

36. Deguy concludes his essay by noting that "words are forever ruses, and it is only in and through words that what one desires will appear, the (in)credible salvation, which is other than words, the other of words, and which one calls *silence*. Discourses are for making silence, and Pseudo-Longinus himself does not escape from the topos where words abolish themselves. "It is thus in words insofar as they *render themselves forgotten*, insofar as they appear as wordless! . . . Is *denegation* inscribed in the very heart of speech? As a kind of 'performative' constitutive of eloquence? This negativity of a *work against oneself*: a sort of self-destruction at work in the heart of 'words' and of the poem? Poetry annuls the poem which annuls itself in poetry (consumes itself there in favor of what surpasses it and which is itself?)" ("The Discourse of Exaltation," 24).

37. "It has dawned. And each corner sings, / trembles recently rained on. The cement and the sky / are very high. / The air is calling me routinely, / newly. / The new violet of the clouds / vacillates, grows cowardly. And very open / the swallows fly and the city without thresholds, / the flowering bronze of the bells. Where, / where my steps?"

38. "The Longinian sublime introduces a dynamic of limitation, actively marking the limit between positions of enunciation, between rule and infraction (or tradition and innovation), between repetition and difference, art and nature, and sincerity and deceit. In the very different terms of transcendental philosophy, Kant's theory of the sublime introduces the problem of the limits of representation. What is sublime is unrepresentable, and the Kantian sublime involves the presentation of this nondemonstrability. . . .

"The limits of what might loosely be called a problematic of the sublime could thus be said to include an overwhelming force of enunciation on the one hand and the presentation of the nondemonstrable on the other. Each implies a certain excess and ambivalence" (Guerlac, *The Impersonal Sublime*, 11).

39. *Diccionario de los símbolos*, 1074. "Color of moderation, made of an equal proportion of red and of blue, of lucidity and of reflex action, of equilibrium between earth and sky, the senses and the mind, passion and intelligence, love and wisdom."

40. This "other voice" reminds us of the final verses of "Elegía desde Simancas," the point from which *Casi* departs.

41. "You, don't walk anymore. Say good-bye. / You, let this street / continue talking for you, though you never return."

42. "Pseudo-Longinus treats not the relation between rhetoric and persuasion but the relation between the 'stupefying' (θαυμάσιον) and 'ecstasy' (ἐκστασις).There is a power of discursive abduction that overcomes all obstacles, all ἐφ᾽ἡμῖν, all that 'which depends on us.' The question is whether there is an art of teaching this access to the dimension of βάθος and of ὕψος (of the profound and the elevated), a τέχνη, a μέθοδος. Thus, Pseudo-Longinus interweaves two main threads: (1) he reminds his reader that the sublime exists, that there is this *high* in things to the level of which the λόγος of a Being who is 'by nature *logical*' ought to elevate itself, and (2) he teaches his reader how this *can* be done" (Deguy, "The Discourse of Exaltation," 13).

43. "Pseudo-Longinus is . . . one who looks at the past in order to reestablish through his own discourse some hope of a truly exalted discourse, precisely *for* the generation that follows him. . . .

"In a certain sense, his interest is the 'phenomenological' interest in a return to the things themselves, in this case, insofar as they are those things that had a meaning for one's ancestors, a return which inclines toward what has been and a return which is carried out for the sake of a tradition or a culture by means of a reading of past utterances" (ibid., 7).

44. Referring to Emerson and Marcel Mauss, Donoghue states that "a stolen gift is surrounded by an entirely different set of connotations from those which surround the innocent gift. A gift of any kind starts a cycle of obligation. . . . Obligations are incurred and returned. But a gift which has been stolen is a much more complex matter because it cannot release itself from its origin in violence, risk, and guilt; the receiver is incriminated in the donor's crime. What kind of obligation is incurred by a man who accepts a stolen gift? In an innocent gift, two people are joined in a relation, but in a stolen gift there are three, the third being the original owner, who is related to the receiver through the thief. . . . The interest of the myth [of Prometheus] consists in the ambiguity with which it surrounds the lucidity of knowledge, the moral darkness from which its brightness came" (*Thieves of Fire*, 17–18).

45. Guerlac (*The Impersonal Sublime*, 2–4) comments on this effect of the sublime, calling it a "cocreating" of the text through reception of an original utterance, and linking this with Heidegger's concepts of the "preserving" and "solitariness" of the work of art in which both poet and reader participate. We will observe this effect quite explicitly in the final poem of this section, "Manuscrito de una respiración."

46. Lacoue-Labarthe addresses this issue in his discussion of an inscription on the temple of Isis ("I am all that is, that was, and that will be, and no mortal has lifted my veil"): "What does it mean, in effect, 'to tell the truth'? By an immemorial constraint . . . which does not arise out of any metaphorical decision, telling the truth is unveiling the truth. Truth-telling, in this sense, as we know since Aristotle, and as paragraph 7B of *Being and Time* reminds us, is *apophantic*: it lets us see (or lets appear: φαίνεσθαι) on the basis of (ἀπό) that of which it speaks. It renders manifest or patent, it unveils. Truth-telling is the λόγος ἀληθής. But what is produced in Isis's sentence . . . is that telling the truth about itself, telling the truth of the truth and unveiling itself as the truth, truth (unveiling) unveils itself as the impossibility of unveiling or the necessity, for finite (mortal) Being, of its veiling. Speaking of itself, unveiling itself,

truth says that the essence of truth is nontruth—or that the essence of unveiling is veiling. The truth (the unveiling) unveils itself as veiling itself" ("Sublime Truth," 91). This statement corresponds with his previous observation that paradox is "a key word since Longinus, and perhaps the major concept of the theory of the sublime" (88), which epitomizes Rodríguez's poetry.

47. "Without old age and without death the high shadow, / which is not consolation and even less affliction, / is illuminated and hovers / surrounded now by the light of sunset / and the infancy of the sky. . . ."

48. Longinus describes the sublime moment as when "'the rational aspect of the mind is *violently* overcome . . . and "dazzled"' by the event of sublimity" (Guerlac, *The Impersonal Sublime*, 1).

49. ". . . / and life that shows / its darkness and its fatigue, / it mysterious truth, pore by pore, / with its hope and its moth round / about the small light, about the shadow without sleep."

50. Rodríguez notes that this image comes to him via St. Theresa: "La imagen de la polilla es una imagen clásica de Santa Teresa. . . . Lo que yo sé es que esa *claridad* no es una claridad física, exterior, sino interior. . . . No es sólo la luz, es también algo espiritual (una fulguración interior, un resplandor)" (Juan Carlos Suñén, "Entrevista a Claudio Rodríguez," *El Urogallo* 62–63 [July–August 1991]: 8–10) [The image of the moth is a classic image of St. Theresa. . . . What I know is that that *clarity* is not a physical, exterior clarity, but an interior one. . . . It is not only light, it is also something spiritual (an interior flash, a brilliance)].

51. Weiskel comments upon the concept of the "negative sublime" in Kant's "Analytic of the Sublime": "On the principle of homeostasis, any excess of stimuli will be felt as pain, even if the stimuli themselves are pleasurable. . . . There is simultaneously a wish to be inundated or engulfed by pleasurable stimuli and a fear of being incorporated, overwhelmed, annihilated. . . . Fascination and dread coincide" (*The Romantic Sublime*, 104).

52. "And where the caress of your repentance, / fresh in the fig tree and in the white acacia, / very tenuous in the hawthorn at noon, / deep in the holm-oak, in steel, shaped almost without / a curve, / in nickel and quartz, so near in the threads of honey, / a blue tempered in ash in the streets, / with pity and with flight in the gaze, / with anxiety of surrender?"

53. "If I could give you belief, / the clean, enlightened power / of this serene afternoon . . . / Why does the light curse and the shadow pardon? / The wind is losing its mature shadow / and you are going away / and you are accusing me, / you are illuminating me. Hush, hush. / And don't follow me and don't pursue me. / Now it is never late. But what have I done to you / if I owe you everything I have?"

54. "Go away with your shivering innocence / flying blindly, certainly, / younger than the light. Light in my light."

55. Hertz's commentary on Longinus includes a discussion of the poet's commitment to a fall: "But the point is not simply that to force one's talent past its natural limit, as Euripides is said to have done, is a transgression equivalent to Phaeton's. Rather, I think, the authenticity of the father's language—and it is appropriate here that the father is Helios—can be attained only by means of a sacrificial act. . . . But what is the status of such an oath? It could be said to occupy an equivocal middle ground, somewhere between the transgressions of the son and either the admonitions or the creative word of the father. It can be seen as the mortal's attempt to capture for his language some of the prestige and stability of the divine by placing limits on his actions or binding himself (the Greek word for oath, *horkos*, derives from *herkos*, the word for an enclosure or wall); hence the oath's connection with sacrifice and invariably a figure for self-sacrifice, a gesture in the direction of one's own death. . . .

"Yet because oaths (and their analogues in literary language) are never more than merely attempts at divine stability, there is always the risk that they will turn into—or turn out to be—merely a fancier form of transgression" (*The End of the Line*, 9–10).

We can posit a clear connection here between "Revelación" (the poem under consideration, the first following the overture) and the later and pivotal "Brindis por un seis de enero," where Rodríguez makes his oath and transgresses (steps over) the threshold into the sublime experience.

56. See Cañas, *Claudio Rodríguez,* 195–97, for an earlier version of this poem, there titled "La mañana de la lechuza." A comparison of the two versions reveals how significantly Rodríguez has "muted" the version eventually included in *Casi.*

57. Discussing Kant's concept of the "mathematical sublime" in the *Critique of Judgment,* Crowther notes a complication in Kant's thinking in two passages on the same page. "In the first passage, Kant talks as though the experience of the sublime involves two distinct stages—one negative, the other positive. In the second passage, however, he talks as though the experience is much more complex—involving *alternations* of attraction and repulsion towards the object" (*The Kantian Sublime,* 81).

58. In an interview published in *El sol* (18 mayo 1991), "Nadie sabe hoy quién es el lector ni dónde se le encuentra" [No one knows today who the reader is or where s/he is found], Antonio Puente asks Rodríguez about the title "La mañana del búho":

—Habla en su libro de "La mañana del búho". ¿Qué significado tiene ese ave recurrente, y, sobre todo, ese contrasentido?

—Sí, es una paradoja profunda; sobre todo cuando el búho es, tan erróneamente, símbolo de la sabiduría. *La mañana del búho* representa la impotencia del conocimiento. Los ojos están abiertos como platos, pero no funcionan en plena luz; nada ven, o tal vez lo están viendo todo, pero entonces ya no lo conocen. Es uno de los *leit-motiv* de mi poesía.

Yo suscribo a Plotino cuando dice que la "llamada naturaleza es un alma, producto de un alma anterior que poseía una vida más potente". De manera que la impotencia, el destierro, abarca también a la propia naturaleza. ¿No ves esta luz? (dice del rayo de sol que se filtra por la ventana). . . . Aspira, como todo, a quedarse y a extinguirse, al mismo tiempo. Esa intermitencia de todas las cosas, entre su autoafirmación y su autodestrucción, es lo que me obsesiona" (42).

[—You speak in your book about "The Morning of the Owl." What meaning does that recurrent bird have, and, above all, that countersense?

—Yes, it is a profound paradox; above all when the owl is, so erroneously, symbol of wisdom. *The morning of the owl* represents the impotence of knowledge. Its eyes are as big as saucers, but they don't function in the full light; they see nothing, or perhaps they see everything, but then they don't even know it. It is one of the *leitmotifs* of my poetry.

I subscribe to Plotinus when he says that "so-called nature is a soul, the product of a former soul that possessed a more potent life." So that impotence, exile, also includes nature itself. Do you see that light? (he says of a beam of sunlight that filters through the window). . . . It aspires, like everything, to remain and to extinguish itself, both at the same time. That intermittence of everything, between its self-affirmation and its self-destruction, is what obsesses me.]

59. "The naked seed, here, in the center / of the pupil in full / rotation / toward so much sudden whiteness / of this wave without windows / near the wall of sleep between high seas / and low tide, / toward what does it carry me? / If that which I see is invisible, it is pure / illumination, / it is the origin of premonition."

60. See *Webster's New World Dictionary,* 3d College Edition, s.v. "Prometheus," and Hamilton, *Mythology,* 68. The contrast between Prometheus and his twin Epimetheus (whose name means "afterthought") will reappear in the "Segundo interludio de enero," where Janus looks both to the past and to the future.

61. Mayhew defines self-consciousness in twentieth-century Spanish poetry as "awareness of the theoretical problems surrounding poetic language" (*The Poetics of Self-Consciousness,* 11), and he has thoroughly explored Rodríguez's self-conscious meditation on the sign in his book *Claudio Rodríguez.* As he has demonstrated, this characteristic is a constant of Rodríguez's poetry. Later, I will use the term "Self-consciousness" more narrowly, following the lead of Bettina L. Knapp in her discussion of "the Prometheus syndrome," and distinguish it for the purposes of this study with an uppercase "S" (see note 99 below).

62. "It is this autumn of wood and of echoes / of olive and birch trees / with the rapacity of the slow wing / tilting and gyring, / with the old miserly flight of night, / with the equilibrium of a nightmare, / with a beak without wax, without milk and without oil, / and plumage without smoke, the spume that softens / the saliva, the salt, the excrement / of the nest . . ."

63. Rodríguez's hair is still very dark in spite of his 64 years of age.

64. Chevalier and Gheerbrandt explain that, "Considerados como receptáculo de fuerza, los excrementos simbolizan un poder biológico sagrado que reside en el hombre y que, evacuado, puede en cierto modo ser recuperado. Así, lo que aparentemente estaría más desprovisto de valor, sería lo más cargado: las significaciones del oro y de las heces se juntan en muchas tradiciones" (*Diccionario de los símbolos*, 553). [Considered receptacles of strength, excrement symbolizes a sacred biological power that resides in man and that, evacuated, can in a certain sense be recuperated. Thus, that which would apparently be the most worthless would be the most valuable: The significance of gold and lees are united in many traditions.]

Cirlot adds, "All this symbolism is contained within Nietzsche's phrase: 'Out of the lowest the highest reaches its peak'" (*A Dictionary of Symbols*, 99). This concept is therein related to the Longinian sublime, as Deguy states: "The sublime measures our failure. If it is a *sacred* relation to the *divine* that constitutes the sublime, then our failure will be equivalent to our distance from the sacred, or to our unbelief, our incapacity to navigate through the straits of the difference (κρίσις) between immortal and mortal" ("The Discourse of Exaltation," 7). He later adds, "The high does not raise itself without the support of the low, of what is underneath; height can only hold by rising in a pile from the low, which renders itself forgotten in the service that is 'naturally' its own, specifically, to support like a slave that in which it consists and into which it disappears: the high" (19).

65. ". . . There is a sound / of height, molded / in figures, in a vapor / of eucalyptus. I do not see, I do not possess. / And that lark, that grape-leaf / both so innocent on the vine now, / and the swift of firewood and of cramp, / and the capture of the hare, the nacre / of dawn and the transparency / in orange high tide of contemplation?"

66. "And everything is invisible? But this moment / pierced with dawn is clear! / This moment that I will never see. / This morning that no one will see / because it is not created, / this morning that takes me closer to the capital and to the nest. / And this beating of wings without fear or wind, / the epidemic, the mastiff and the cocoon / with the light of the plateau? / How May was singing in the January night."

67. According to Guerlac, "readers throughout history have found the text [Longinus's *On the Sublime*] to be confused, an impression reinforced by the fragmented state in which the manuscript has come down to us. Consequently there has been a tendency to trivialize the Longinian sublime as merely rhetorical, with rhetoric construed in modern terms as the packaging of an *énoncé* ready for expression, rather than in terms of a logic of enunciation. Instead, the Longinian sublime occurs as a force of enunciation determined neither by subjective intention nor by mimetic effect. It implies a premetaphysical articulation between nature and man, or physis and logos. . . . The Longinian sublime involves a reciprocity between art and nature that neutralizes opposition between the two terms and therefore renders problematic the application of a mimetic framework of analysis in the conventional sense" (*The Impersonal Sublime*, 1–2).

68. "Next to the relief and the chisel, the rasp / and the burin, there is a city, / hand of work and secret in each crevice / of the prayer and of the redemption, / and the temperature of the stone / oriented toward the east / with a science of polished erosion, / of quietude of suspended wave, of adventure / that enters and leaves at the same time. There the scenes / of history, theology, fauna, myths / and the law of granite, pore by pore, / its scar in each ochre streak, the rite of the tear / in cold and crystalline risk in rain / and with the sunflower that now washes / between the owl and the virgin. There is neither space nor time: the sacrament / of matter."

69. "Now all art, as a mode of artifice, necessarily involves the following of rules pertaining to means and ends. Yet whereas in 'mechanical' and 'agreeable' art [cf. the lark and the

swift] the artist's creativity is reducible to the following of established rules, in fine art it is not. Indeed, the very appearance of the fine art work has the unforced spontaneity of a natural object—thus belying its rule-governed origin in human artifice. . . .

"Hence originality is the 'primary property' of genius. It should not, however, be thought that this is a sufficient condition. For, as Kant himself suggests, there can be 'original nonsense'. What is required in addition is that the artist must have mastered the academic rules and conventions governing his medium. This not only allows him systematically to develop his gift of originality, but also enables the observer to judge that such originality is not just a passing fluke. . . . All that is required to distinguish fine art as a broad category from mechanical and agreeable art is that the former has an original element of handling which, while rule-governed, cannot be reduced to the following of rules" (Crowther, *The Kantian Sublime*, 155–56).

70. Some commentators have identified this as the theme of *Casi*, but we are still in the first section of the work.

71. "So much presence that it is rebirth, / and it is renunciation, and it is anchor / of the pious shipwreck / of my illusion of liberty, my flight . . . / A guess, almost a thought / next to the deep dew / of the dust of the light, the mystery that illuminates / this sure air, / this health of the new wood / and arrives germinating / to the nectar without haste, well shaped / in the burned rockrose."

72. "It is grace, it is grace, vision, / the color of the oracle of sleep, / the veining of the laurel leaf, / the madness of contemplation / and how many times curse, childhood, / ringing in each wing with surprise. / The early fountain and the star / of morning!"

73. Speaking of the concept of "art without art" in Longinus's treatise, Guerlac notes this ambivalence: "Whereas earlier in the text sincerity was associated with genius as natural gift, and sublimity was defined in terms of force of conviction, here in the discussion of figurativity it is posed as a contrived effect. Art as seduction (which replaces a notion of art as system or method given earlier in the text) implies the successful production of an impression or effect of sincerity through a strategic concealment of figures as devices of rhetorical manipulation. Thus, considered as a function of nature, the sublime implies nobility and sincerity. Considered as a function of art, it implies the reverse. Since the specificity of the sublime is the reciprocity of nature and art—art without art—it carries a force both of sincerity and duplicity, of truth and falsity; it implies a force that undermines precisely this opposition" (*The Impersonal Sublime*, 2).

74. "And the pleasure, the lust, the ruinous support / of disillusionment, the brush / of my heavy wings, so caressing, / almost half-opened when / there is no longer flight nor still knowledge / before there now arrives / the interminable blush . . . Day / that never will be mine and that is entering / my ascent toward the darkness!"

75. In conjunction with the earlier "la lujuria, el ruin amparo / de la desilusión," this image reminds us of the witches as prostitutes in "Brujas a mediodía"; even the title is similar to "La mañana del búho" in its ambivalence.

76. "Will I live the movement, the images / never in repose / of this morning without autumn always?"

77. In formulating "a genealogical tree of the 'faculties of the soul'" and analyzing Kant's *Critique of Judgment*, Lyotard avers, "In the sublime, the imagination must be subjected to violence, because it is by way of its suffering, the mediation of its violation, that the joy of seeing—or almost seeing—the law can be obtained. The sublime 'renders so to speak intuitable the superiority of the rational destiny of our faculty of knowledge over the greatest power of sensibility' (*CJ*, §27, 96; 96). And this 'joy . . . is only possible by the mediation of pain' (*CJ*, §27, 98; 99). . . . The sublime . . . requires suffering. It is supposed to hurt" ("The Interest of the Sublime," 124, 125).

78. Deguy says that "The elevation to the sublime is a strange operation. It is a matter of reattaining the ground, of raising up and carrying away—what? Culture (τέχνη: διδάκτικός) leads back to nature (φισικός: γενναῖος) on condition that nature—for example, the gift of innate eloquence (a person is by nature a being of logos)—is conceived as a movement of *self-*

surmounting" ("The Discourse of Exaltation," 16; my emphasis). Lyotard adds, "When it is a matter of morality, the chains that must be shed are the chains by which inclinations restrain the exercise of good will. . . . The purely reasonable practical motive cannot assert itself except in the company of a 'pain' (*Critique of Pure Reason*, 86; 75), a mourning for attractive objects, a withdrawal of previous investments and fixations. This mourning thus has to affect the 'object' *par excellence* which poses an obstacle to respect and the good motive: the *ego* (*CPrR*, 89–90; 79). . . . This dark aspect of respect is the 'humiliation' of the 'presumption' and 'arrogance' of the empirical ego, of its 'overestimation' of itself (*CPrR*, 86–87; 76). Narcissism must be thrown down [*jeté à bas*], vanquished" ("The Interest of the Sublime," 122–23).

79.   "And there is no way to save life. / And there is no way of going where there is no one. / I am walking in thirst of a meeting, in the absence / of light. / I am walking off the road. / Why the error, why the love and where / the footprint without pity?"

80.   "It's becoming night. And what does it matter. / It is the same old thing but everything is new."

81.   "And the stars of cold whiteness / in the curved space / of gravitation, and the temperature, / the legends of the constellations, / the deep pulse of the constellations, / the deep pulse of the whole sky / and its sidereal harmony and science, / are entering alone / with a silent and beautiful dominance, vivid in melody / in this house."

82.   "It is the distrust in the material. / It is the material far from men / that doesn't make itself and is making itself. / It is the very material that lies / like the crazy oats of memory, / like the delirium of the nocturnal glass, / the windows of the sky, / presentiment of solitude."

83.   "This house, this night / that penetrate each other and are wounding each other / with I know not what fecundity . . ."

84.   "the honey without death of the pilgrim, the blond / rooster of fine feather, / the rainbow of the skin of the trout, / the amber of the eyes and the howl of the wolf of Sanabria."

85.   "the kitchen and the eel / of Christmas, the whipped cream / and the fine flour"; "the empty sepulchre and the folded winding sheet, / the linen sheet, / the reverberation of the resin, / of the myrrh and the aloe." Note again the allusion to Linus.

86.   In conjunction with the notion of "cocreating" discussed in note 45 above, Guerlac remarks this problematic situation: "At the moment of the sublime utterance, it is as if the words were wrung from the speakers. It is as if the speakers merged with the message, while the listeners were overwhelmed or subjugated by the force of the sublime enunciation that 'scatters everything before it like a thunderbolt'—including the subjectivity, or self-presence, of the listeners. In a second moment, the interlocutors come to feel as if they had produced the sublime utterance themselves. This is the moment of 'proud flight,' the moment of elevation and transport associated with *hypsos*. The listener is displaced to the position of speaker, raised to the status of master, and the force of enunciation continues to operate inscribed in memory. This paradoxical moment is presented by the text as being both the effect and the origin of the sublime, which engenders itself through 'impregnating' the soul of the listener [cf. the verses 'Esta casa, esta noche / que se penetran y se están hiriendo / con no sé qué fecundidad . . .']. There results a problematic relationship between imitation of the discourse of another as a way of achieving sublimity and the value of originality—a mysterious gap between citation and citability, or worthiness of repetition" (*The Impersonal Sublime*, 2–3).

87.   Knapp has appropriated these terms from Keréneyi's *Prometheus* (xviii). She explains, "In *The Prometheus Syndrome* the 'myth' is to be understood as the narration of a primordial experience, not necessarily personal but rather, transcendental; not something invented for the sake of entertainment, though it may be also that, but rather, a living and burning reality that exists in the psyche and culture of a people. A myth is ectypal (it deals with the existential world) and archetypal (it deals with eternal experiences). Existence on these two levels contains past, present, and future within its structure.

"A myth, then, lives outside of temporal time. Not bound within the limits of eschatological, linear, or historical time, it flows in a cyclical, sacred, or eternal dimension. . . . The events narrated in the Prometheus myth are perpetual. . . . In that the myth is ectypal, it reveals and relives 'the structure of reality.' It may then become the model or the prototype of the period or periods that brought it into being; and it reflects in its many transformations and recountings throughout the centuries, the needs, obsessions, and longings of the individual cultures" (Bettina L. Knapp, *The Prometheus Syndrome* [Troy, N.Y.: Whitston, 1979], 2–3).

88. "May the doors and windows sing at last / and the forgotten stars, sing / the light of the soul that I might have loved, / the fleeting which is the approaching / like the song of the lark on this night / of the morning of St. John and sound / the new flute of the curved rooftiles / on the lost house; / . . ."

89. Weiskel addresses the issue of the inexorability of the sublime poet's quest: "Poets, however, are up to such risks, which in any case they have no choice about. It is not in the assumption of spiritual risks that the egotistical romantic pays for the hybris of his sublimation. Nothing is got for nothing. The cost is there, and it is paid in the text, not in extrinsic circumstance" (*The Romantic Sublime*, 58).

90. "After so many aimless and homeless / and even painless days and the lone bells / and the dark wind like that of memory / this day arrives. // When yesterday breath was a mystery / and the dry gaze, without resin, / was seeking a definitive brilliance, / there arrives, so delicately and so simply, / so serene with new leaven / this morning . . ."

91. "It is the surprise of clarity, / the innocence of contemplation, / the secret that opens with shape and astonishment / the first snowfall and the first rain / washing the hazel tree and the olive tree / already very near the sea."

92. "Invisible quietude. Breeze wafting / the melody that I no longer expected. / It is the illumination of happiness / with the silence that has no time. / A grave pleasure that of solitude."

93. Cf. the slippage from "pain" to "delight" as characteristic of the sublime.

94. "And don't look to the sea because it knows everything / when the hour arrives / where thought never arrives / but yes the sea of the soul, / but yes this moment of air in my hands, / of this peace that awaits me / when the hour arrives / —two hours before midnight— / of the third wave, which is mine."

95. In the interview with Puente cited above, Rodríguez has addressed the issue of process: "No me interesa la terminal del viaje sino sólo el proceso mismo de escritura, su temperatura; trajinar, y tejer y destejer, y como la vida misma, bifurcarme" ("Nadie sabe hoy quién es el lector," 42). [I'm not interested in the end of the trip but only in the process itself of writing, its temperature; tinkering, and weaving and unweaving, and like life itself, bifurcating myself.]

96. See note 21 above.

97. Neil Hertz makes a similar comment when discussing the "doubling of consciousness" resulting from Wordsworth's use of the third person in "A Night-Piece": "Yet Wordsworth was insisting that there was a gap between poet and traveller of the same sort that exists between poet and reader, and that that gap may be bridged but is not thereby removed" (*The End of the Line*, 26). See his discussion of "A Night-Piece" on pp. 22–27.

98. "Within the sublime, in the Kantian sense, there is no ambiguity: the sublime does not risk quietism by naturalizing the domain of art. Instead of the achieved stasis, the *discordia concors* of ideal and real, there is oscillation, movement over the widening gap between two terms, culminating in the withdrawal of consciousness from the sensible world. In the sublime moment, dualism is legitimated and intensified. The beautiful intimates reconciliation, however precariously and ambiguously; the sublime splits consciousness into alienated halves" (Weiskel, *The Romantic Sublime*, 48).

99. Knapp has defined these terms: "Prometheus represents the ego. Once the ego acquires the strength and courage necessary to steal Zeus' fire—or symbolically speaking, transforms amorphous visions into the *creative act*—the existing psychological and social structures are displaced. To accomplish such a feat, the ego has to do battle in a solitary struggle. . . .

"For the purpose of simplification the Promethean struggle, lived in two psychological stages, may be labeled *ego-consciousness* and *Self-consciousness*. In the initial stage the individual experiences the creative impulse and attempts to concretize his vision. . . . In the ego-conscious stage the creative individual wrestles heroically against the prevailing archaic and perhaps decadent forces within his own being and in society. It is the ego in this stage that usually finds change or new ideations unacceptable. The ego-conscious phase is marked by a preoccupation with mundane personal needs: the creative act per se; the new concepts and visions coming into being in the terrestrial and subjective sense; and the energy needed to endure the excoriatingly painful period of sacrifice and solitude that birth of a new way engenders. Chaos and turmoil mark these arduous times. Intransigence in attitude is the rule.

"The second stage of the Promethean development, *Self-consciousness*, brings about a state of differentiation and objectivity by the individual. The struggle implicit in the concretization of the new vision (such as the creation of a work of art or scientific discovery) leads to the involvement of the whole psyche, the total personality. It also taps the collective forces of society in which this action takes place. . . . Despite its harshness, the struggle Prometheus experiences, brings him to a state of expanded consciousness. No longer limited to his isolated domain, the ordeal to achieve his vision puts him in touch with transpersonal forces. Thus his frame of reference is enriched by new values; new sets of priorities and insights are brought into focus. What previously had been disparate and unrelated facets within the personality have become integrated (individuated) and fall into place. The vision has taken on form and substance. The Promethean now views his creative act in terms of the whole psyche—or the Self— with regard not only to his own being but in terms of the collective domain: man and the gods; man and the cosmos" (*The Prometheus Syndrome*, 4–6).

Rodríguez's progression from ego-consciousness to Self-consciousness takes place not only "diachronically" from *Don* to *Casi* but also "synchronically" within *Casi*, similar to the distinctions between intra- and intertextuality, metaphor and metonymy, that concerned us in his first book of poems.

100. Cf. the intertextual allusion to the Book of Ecclesiastes in "El canto de linos" *(Conjuros)*. It seems that Rodríguez has become increasingly and particularly conscious of the reader's role in the actualization of the text, perhaps because he feels that the reader, too, must make a moral commitment in the act of reading. The reader as recipient of the Promethean gift is complicit in the theft. In the lengthy but superb interview coaxed out of him by Juan Carlos Suñén for *El Urogallo*, Rodríguez reveals that Carlos Bousoño had suggested a parenthetical subtitle to "La mañana del búho." In response, Rodríguez remonstrates, "Me lo sugirió con el mismo argumento que Aleixandre: facilitar el camino al lector. Pero ¿por qué un poeta tiene que abdicar ante el lector? El lector debe hacer un esfuerzo. ¿Para qué poner notas? La obra debe contener sus propias claves y, además, entre tú y yo, como decía Larra, ¿dónde está el público? ¿quién es el lector? ¿cómo se llama? ¿dónde ha estudiado? ¿cuáles son sus gestos? ¿qué lecturas tiene? ¿qué sensibilidad? O es parte del libro, o está también dentro del libro, o no es nada" ("Entrevista a Claudio Rodríguez," 13). [He suggested it to me with the same argument as Aleixandre: to facilitate the way for the reader. But why should a poet have to abdicate to the reader? The reader ought to make an effort. Why put notes? The work ought to contain its own keys and, besides, between you and me, as Larra would say, Where is the public? Who is the reader? What's his/her name? Where has s/he studied? Which are his/her gestures? What reading has s/he done? What sensitivity does s/he have? Either s/he is part of the book, or s/he is also within the book, or s/he is nothing.] Note also that the question "¿Dónde está el público?" echoes the verse from "Calle sin nombre," "¿Y dónde los vecinos?"

101. "The bed stirs me and purifies me / with an odor very March-like, / with a gaze of rain amid the folds / of the sheet and a / caress of virgin wool. / The darkness of the thorax, the lime of grape of the lip, / the shadow of the bone and the shadow / of saliva, / the spinal marrow badly sustained / by its wings that ache / when it begins to grow clear and there arrives / a trembling of innocence."

102. Cf. the story of Pyramus and Thisbe.

103. "And who calls to me through it, who / has chosen me, who / is asking something of me and does not surrender? / And you are going away from me, / you go and come and go and are as if lost, / as if fled anew. . . ."

104. "you are feeling now / this air of the plateau, that which knows more, / that of your salvation that one doesn't hear / because you are its music"

105. "And you heal me, / and I give you thanks for coming / so delicately that I can almost see you."

106. See Itziar Elizondo, "Claudio Rodríguez: «Sigo creyendo en la poesía como un don y un entusiasmo» [I continue believing in poetry as a gift and an enthusiasm], *El Independiente* (Madrid), 23 May 1991, *Libros* 31.

> —¿Quién es el ladrón del poema «El robo»?
> —Me baso en una leyenda de la catedral de Zamora. Una persona había entrado a robar y en el momento de huir la ventana se estrechó y se quedó aprisionado. Para mí, esto simboliza el oficio del poeta, es Prometeo, la incapacidad del hombre para conocer la verdad. Es un ladrón que quiere robar pero queda condenado. Los poetas estamos condenados a escribir porque no podemos poseer la verdad.

> [—Who is the thief in the poem "The Theft"? —I am basing myself on a legend of the Cathedral of Zamora. A person had entered to rob and in the moment of fleeing, the window shrank and he became imprisoned. For me, this symbolizes the profession of the poet, he is Prometheus, the incapacity of man to know the truth. He is a thief who wants to rob but remains condemned. We poets are condemned to write because we cannot possess the truth.]

See also the interview with José Esteban, "¡Queremos tanto a Claudio . . . !" [We Love Claudio So Much!], *La Esfera*, 16 June 1991, 1–2.

> [S]e me ocurrió por una leyenda zamorana, y esto no lo he contado hasta ahora. Esta leyenda se llama «El robo» que da título a uno de los poemas más extensos del libro. Verás. En el ábside de la catedral hay un rostro humano, ya corroído por los siglos y borroso, y según cuentan es el ladrón que entró a robar en la catedral y cuando con el botín intentó escapar por la ventana ésta comenzó a estrecharse y quedó aprisionado con el rostro fuera y el cuerpo dentro. Porque ese es el origen de la poesía, buscar la verdad, pero la verdad no se consigue, es lo secreto, lo sagrado. Y esta leyenda y el rostro contraído me han acompañando siempre. De ahí casi una leyenda. (2)

> [{I}t occurred to me because of a Zamoran legend, and I have not told anyone this before. This legend is called "The Theft" which gives title to one of the most extensive poems in the book. Look. In the apse of the Cathedral there is a human face, now corroded by the centuries and blurry, and according to what they say, it is the thief who entered to rob the Cathedral and when with the booty in hand he tried to escape through the window, it began to narrow and he remained imprisoned with his face on the outside and his body on the inside. Because that is the source of poetry, to seek the truth, but the truth can't be gotten, it's secret, sacred. And this legend and the contracted face have accompanied me always. Therefore, almost a legend.]

In his chronology of Rodríguez's life in *Hacia el canto*, García Jambrina also reports that Rodríguez himself once stole a chalice from a church in Zamora (see p. 24). An early version of "El robo" accompanies an interview with Jesús Fernández Palacios in *Fin de Siglo* 8 (1984): 30–34.

107. Knapp offers some insights into what she calls the Prometheus syndrome: "The prototype of the rebel, Prometheus sought to conquer a past that no longer answered his needs and to dominate a present that might otherwise have engulfed him. . . . As a fine psychologist, Prometheus knew that hope was an important factor in helping man experience a positive life process. He therefore endowed him with a sense of illusion, thus relieving him from feelings of perpetual discouragement that might accrue from recognizing the absurdity of his condition.

He also instilled in man the meaning and value of energy, action, ambition, liberty—all of which give purpose to his life struggle" (*The Prometheus Syndrome*, 1).

108. Crowther's comments are pertinent here: "The sublime is thus, at heart, both a paradoxical and intense experience. It is the sensible world in its excess which limits perceptual cognition, yet it is a particular instance of this excess which gives the scope of rational cognition such a dramatic impact. We feel ourselves to be both imprisoned and liberated by the very same force. This, I would suggest, is why the felt compatibility between world and cognition in the experience of sublimity takes the form of awe and astonishment, or even ecstatic bewilderment" (*The Kantian Sublime*, 150).

Rodríguez has stated that "El robo" "Es una imagen del poeta que desea encontrar lo secreto, lo sagrado. Está basado en una leyenda de Zamora. Para mí era como un correlato de la experiencia del poeta, de la poesía. El ladrón entra en la catedral y cuando alcanza la verdad, su robo, descubre que no puede escapar con él, porque es simbólico, es interior, le aprisiona y le condena. Su propio robo le roba" (Juan Carlos Suñén, "Entrevista a Claudio Rodríguez," 11). [It is an image of the poet who desires to find the secret, the sacred. It is based on a Zamoran legend. For me it was like a correlate of the experience of the poet, of poetry. The thief enters the cathedral and when he attains the truth, his theft, he discovers that he cannot escape with it, because it is symbolic, it is interior, it imprisons and condemns him. His own theft robs him.]

109. "Not that these fruits are in their natures tart / and unformed, but that you still lack the vision / of such high things. The defect is on your part." I have used John Ciardi's translation of Dante Alighieri, *The Divine Comedy* (Franklin Center, Pa.: The Franklin Library, 1983), 534. Dante's *Divina Commedia* in general is a superb example of the sublime as the speaker transits from the Inferno to the Paradiso.

110. Crowther notes that "we can, against our natural inclinations, transcend fear and face destruction courageously—thus acting on principles of moral conduct which testify to our true vocation as rational supersensible beings. . . . Our pleasure in the destructive object is explicable through its leading us to imagine a situation where, through our courageous moral bearing, we refute its (and thereby nature's) claim to dominion over us" (*The Kantian Sublime*, 111).

111. "Now is the moment of pursuit, / of the silent siege, / of the corner of the hand with its curve / and its roof of greed. Now / is the moment of this so tenuous light, / high in the intimacy of the dry cold, / of this so lonely March. / And one has to pay the price, the sale and the fraud, / because you have promised and you have not come, / and you have not known what is presaged: / the adventure in secrecy, the dexterity / of so much doubt."

112. Guerlac makes a similar observation of Lautréamont's *Les Chants de Maldoror*: "[H]e dramatizes writing itself as one spectacle among other representations of transgression. . . . Transgression is presented as spectacle, as 'theatrical scenes'" (*The Impersonal Sublime*, 152).

113. In his summary of Kant's threefold structure of the sublime, Weiskel speaks of the relationship between poet, reader, and the sublime experience. "The three-phase model has limitations, but it serves to emphasize two features of the sublime moment without which an analytic is in danger of collapsing into merely another thematic exercise. In the first place, the model renders the sublime moment as an *economic* event, a series of changes in the distribution of energy within a constant field. . . . [N]othing is got for nothing" (*The Romantic Sublime*, 25). Weiskel posits this duality with reference to the metaphorical and the metonymical. "We may call the mode of the sublime in which the absence of determinate meaning becomes significant the *metaphorical* sublime, since it resolves the breakdown of discourse by substitution. This is, properly, the natural or Kantian sublime, and we might think of it as the hermeneutic or 'reader's' sublime. . . . The other mode of the sublime may be called *metonymical*. Overwhelmed by meaning, the mind recovers by displacing its excess of signified into a dimension of contiguity which may be spatial or temporal. . . . The metonymical mode suggest[s] the *poet's* as opposed to the *reader's* sublime" (28–29, 30). Cf. my usage of the constative versus the performative.

114. "It is the memory, ruinous and luminous, / and the half-open hand, malicious and

rapacious, / and the astute fingers now mature / with the trembling of their wisdom. / It is when touch shines with astonishment and with vice, / the gaze backlit, / the crossroads in the shadow of money. / It is the orphanage of the body that does not know / how to continue being a poor thief, without benefit."

115. "The oil is very intimate and rebellious, / as suspicious as the pulse. Leave it, / let it slip and hide, / let it console and animate us, / let it accuse me / of the crime. / Remember how before an aroma of chestnut, / of raspberry, of cherry, of sugar cane, / of the harmony of wash in the open air / enlightened you, gave you shelter, direction, divination / and even today liberty / amid perfidy and bonanza. / Now is the moment of the key, / of the deep lock. Hit or miss."

116. "Thus, lying in ambush, amid the thieves, / the uncertainty of solitude, / such delirium in the humid / hands of gold, / with the prudence of the evergreen-oak hearing / the signal of the rabbit, / the fence rail, the wire / next to the course of the river today very temperate, / I give you the white stones of destiny. / Engrave them with your breath / so that you may know that that which you have gained / you have lost."

117. Again in reference to *Les Chants de Maldoror,* Guerlac asserts, "According to [Henri] Birault . . . , the problematic of finitude, in which finitude is determined through freedom, is identified with the emergence of the problematic of the subject. Freedom achieved through, or experienced as, transgression (associated with the desire to be God—the desire for nonlimitation or for absolute autonomy) as an individuating principle for the subject. Through transgression, the subject replaces the infinite term through the incorporation (as infinite will) of the infinity, or absolute autonomy, of the transcendent term. Promethean man—the man of infinite will— replaces God, and yet, as Promethean man, the subject remains a kind of mirror of the conception of the infinite powers of the Omnipotent. . . .

"In recent decades transgression has become a critical or philosophical theme—a philosopheme—as well as a literary one. Writing, or textual productivity, has itself become identified with a critical or ideological thematics of transgression. . . . As Birault suggests, transgression belongs to the thinking of finitude, to the developments in the history of philosophy from Descartes through Kant, to an 'essential "insurrection"' through which, from Descartes to Nietzsche and in the death of God, a new figure of Being constitutes itself, that of subjectivity'" (*The Impersonal Sublime*, 149–50, 151–52).

Guerlac refers to Birault's article "Heidegger et la pensée de la finitude" (*Revue Internationale de Philosophie* 52 [1960]: 135–62) and his book *Heidegger et l'expérience de la pensée* (Paris: Gallimard, 1978).

118. "You haven't lost it. Wait. / Anybody knows and much less now when / you have forgotten to surrender your soul / to the air, / and the more you breathe, the more it escapes you / and calls you, and then never . . . / But your body and the muscatel grape / that is a burn in light, / the fever and the surprise, / still discover you, in high inclemency / while the fingers crack, they become agile / and even familiar with the dome of smoke."

119. See note 97 above.

120. "And what are you waiting for? What do you fear now? / The clarity again, the risk, the clumsiness / or the serene audacity of your rebellion / next to the treachery of the night / and the strategy of the shadowy mist / of those lilacs that were your aid / with the aroma of lilies / where you took refuge and little by little / fled from your death, from that crime, / while you are going . . . ? / You know very well where and you have always known."

121. At first the inclusion of the lilacs seems ridiculous, but it may be relevant. If we remember that lilacs are a symbol of death and resurrection (cf. Whitman's use of them in the elegiac mode) and that their violet color connotes a delicate balance, the speaker may be attempting to surmount his achievement in *El vuelo* by mocking and humiliating himself. On another level, he may also be referring to the difficult course he is pursuing in *Casi* by deflating his own image, effacing the surface of his language, and thereby taking a tremendous risk, walking a tightrope, tiptoeing toward his theft of the sublime. The image is certainly enigmatic and equivocal.

122. "But there arrives the mastery of the profession, / that of the solemn iron and the perverse steel, / the decorated hinges, the madness of the nail, / the chiselled rhythm / without noticing the trace of the cruel solder, / and the head of the screw opening / the swing and the lace / of the hinge; / the lyre of the key, the pierced and well-polished haft, / illuminated amid the clean folds / marked by the light, by the sulphur, / by the smoke of salt and coal."

123. "No one has conquered but they have not given you / freedom but deep / slavery. / That which is disgrace is discovery / and birth. / It is not pain but the sacrilege / amid the metal and the soul / while the new lark sings in the wounds, / dry and lonely, of the lock. / And that which you seek is that which you love? / Be quiet and don't remember. And throw the keys into the sea!"

124. Crowther remarks that "psychologically speaking, the feeling of sublimity is characteristically one of awe, or astonishment, or exhilaration, etc., rather than the restful contemplation we enjoy in relation to beauty. . . . The sublime is thus, at heart, both a paradoxical and intense experience. . . . We feel ourselves to be both imprisoned and liberated by the very same force" (*The Kantian Sublime*, 150).

125. See again Silver's use of the word "engranaje" to describe the relation between the everyday and the sublime (note 6 above).

126. "Don't wash your hands and don't pick up sand / because the sand is asking for night, / the nakedness of sleep, / grain of myrtle. / You sought a house where there was no one, / near the river, / but destiny had already made a hard / brilliance on the wings of infancy. / You go down the road, which is that of suffering, / of illusion, of ambition, torture, / confused by the distance. / You are a thief. Wait."

127. "Look at the iris of the valley, the pine-groves / entering the city when today barely / is there any traffic, police / sirens. / Each step that you may take is dangerous / amid the rubbish and ruins where the mallow grows / as impatiently as / the delicate half moon in mother-of-pearl / on the touched fingernail, / of the play of the tips of the fingers. / Go on calmly and reach the altar, / reach furtively in a dance / the vivid silver, the gold of the chalice, / the sapphire and the emerald; / reach your saliva that curses, / smooth and dry, your body."

128. I have already mentioned Deguy's comments regarding the past and the future for the sake of continuing the tradition and culture (see note 43 above). Lyotard adds that "The sacred requires *potlatch*, the destruction or consumption of the given, the present 'wealth' (presence, gift) . . . or natural form, in order to obtain in return the countergift of the nonpresented (of *manna*?). . . . All sacrifice entails this sacrilege. Pardon can be obtained only by the abandonment, the banishment, of a prior gift, which must itself be infinitely precious. Sacrificed nature is sacred. The sublime interest evokes such a sacrilege. One is tempted to say: an ontological sacrilege" ("The Interest of the Sublime," 130).

129. "And the river flows illusioned . . . / you are arriving at such clarity / that now you do not even see that it is spring / sober in the poplars there before you. But / what have you done to yourself? / Why, you have had the truth / in your hands! / You have not been able to get out of the dizziness / of this miraculous and sure window / that drowns you and hangs you."

130. "The erosion of the rock, / that is you, / alone and ocher in the apse. / But it's you yourself, you, with the bitter / plasticity of the prow on your face / century after century, day after day, / in transfiguration! / You, with your entire life / awakening and calling to the city / while the morning that robs the morning / is singing through the streets, / so much time that robs even love / and even myself, without knowing who you are, / old thief without fleeing."

131. I asked Rodríguez if this poem simply had no title or if its title was the same as that of the section, "De amor ha sido la falta," to which he responded "yes."

132. "Here now is the miracle, / here, at mid-road / amid blessing, amid silence, / and fecundation and lust / and light without fatigue."

133. "And the seed of prophecy, / the yeast of pleasure that amasses / sex and song?"

134. Cf. the concept of the sublime turning on pain.

135. "This July night, in quietude and in pity, / serene the wind from the west and very /

beloved it raises me / up to your clear body, / up to the accursed sky that is entering / next to your love and mine."

136. These aspects link the sublime with Rodríguez's aesthetic project, as defined most recently in *El vuelo*. In Deguy's words, "A 'life' that does not revolt against its mortality, seeking instead the figure and flourishing of the nonmortal, is not 'worthy of being lived.' . . . The mortal condition and the moment of perishing are always at stake when the *sublime* appears. The sublime is the concentration, the start of the startling that weighs in speech against death. . . . The sublime is the ephemeral immortality of the point gained, adverse speech snatched from death where the totality of becoming-and-passing-away concentrates itself. . . . Perhaps the only *present* is at this moment, 'snatched from the order of time,' as Proust will say, the present of salvation. . . . The poet is the witness who passes on the legacy of their eternal final word" ("The Discourse of Exaltation," 9–10).

137. Hertz (*The End of the Line*, 16) notes that pairs of antithetical terms perform the sublime reversal. Guerlac also stipulates that "The Longinian sublime introduces a dynamic of limitation, actively marking the limit between positions of enunciation, between rule and infraction (or tradition and innovation), between repetition and difference, art and nature, and sincerity and deceit" (*The Impersonal Sublime*, 11). It is in this section of *Casi* that Rodríguez begins to experiment, to take greater risks with language.

138. The text of Shelley's "The Nest of Love" can be found in *The Romantics*, an anthology by Geoffrey Grigson (London: Routledge, 1942), 206.

> . . When hearts have once mingled
> Love first leaves the well-built nest;
> The weak one is singled
> To endure what it once possessed.
> O Love! who bewailest
> The frailty of all things here,
> Why choose you the frailest
> For your cradle, your home, and your bier?
>
> Its passions will rock thee
> As the storms rock the ravens on high;
> Bright reason will mock thee,
> Like the sun from a wintry sky.
> From thy nest every rafter
> Will rot, and thine eagle home
> Leave thee naked to laughter,
> When leaves fall and cold winds come.

139. Alfriston is in Sussex, located near Eastbourne (to the northwest of Sussex Downs). According to Rodríguez (personal communication), in the past members of Parliament kept their mistresses at Alfriston because it is located near London, making a rendezvous easily accessible, but far enough away to maintain the privacy and discretion necessary for such arrangements. They referred to Alfriston among themselves as "the nest of lovers."

140. This deployment of past and present is defined as the "egotistical sublime," a characteristic for which Wordsworth is well known. According to Hertz: "We most frequently find Wordsworth, in his major poems, writing in the first person and engaged in the imaginative retrieval of events in the more or less distant past. He is, we know, the poet of the egotistical sublime" (*The End of the Line*, 22). Weiskel also links this process with the theme of identity and the following passages, gleaned across several pages, are most appropriate to Rodríguez's poetic project and its continuation in *Casi*: "Wordsworth's sublimation was so massive and thorough that he was able to embrace identity as a redemptive program. . . . Identity is the terminus of one vacancy but, as it turns out, the opening of another. . . . The myth of memory

and the myth of loss are mutually implied in the dialectic of presence and absence. Identity is similarly equivocal with respect to the plot of desire, and indeed desire and memory are so intimately related that the one may be virtually transposed into the other. . . . Our line of thought has yielded the result that the discourse of identity is, on the one hand, a discourse of origins and, on the other, a discourse of fictions. In both phases the structure of identity is circular and the transcendence it accomplishes is spiral. Because memory has no origin and desire no finality, identity can never be completely accomplished" (*The Romantic Sublime*, 152–57).

See Cañas (*Claudio Rodríguez*, 57–72) concerning Rodríguez's years in England.

141. The vastness and grandeur of this natural scene, prototypical of the Romantic period in England, evokes what Kant calls the "mathematical sublime," "that mode which is embodied in our encounter with *vast* objects" (Crowther, *The Kantian Sublime*, 146). However, as Rodríguez breaks off his utterance with ellipsis, in this poem he also includes a visit to the interior of a pub whose owner ("el viejo Terry") and a child or young woman ("la niña Carol") are named. This interiority, as opposed to the exteriority, as well as the specificity (one could even say triviality) of the names and the presence of a girl demonstrate that, as Jacob Rogozinski states, "Magnitude is the Being-great of all quantity or greatness, that which gives it its size, the gesture of a tracing, of a first measure which no finite quantity could measure. If the finite is the quantitative, the measured, the commensurable, magnitude is infinite by its un-measure. It can present itself as an immense quantity, 'in comparison with which all the rest is small.' But quantitative immensity is not un-measure: magnitude is a 'greatness which is equal only to itself,' great 'beyond all comparison,' *infinitely other* than all finite quantity. In this sense, it is neither large nor small, and the colossal is as little sublime as the most extreme smallness. It even happens that, in a time dominated by emphasis on grandeur, the sublime finds refuge in the tiny or the laughable, the grain of a voice, the brilliance of an instant" ("The Gift of the World," in Librett, ed., *Of the Sublime*, 151).

142. Weiskel's discussion of Wordsworth's "Tintern Abbey" sounds very similar to what is happening in "'The Nest of Lovers.'" "The central event, the reviving of the 'picture of the mind,' is curiously opaque and inaccessible; presumably the genitive is possessive—picture from the mind—but picture of what? Probably of the first visit. . . . The subtle redundance 'revives again' suggests that the picture is *re*curring without having quite *oc*curred except in an origin retrospectively posited by a mind whose every cognition is brought to consciousness as recognition. . . . It is a picture without content—actually, the possibility of picturing and the necessity of it: the formal, empty envelope of signification. Of course, it is filled by a version of the past that comes into being as a differential function of the present in the process Freud called *Nachträglichkeit* ('deferred action'). . . . Both 'myself-as-I-am-now' and the 'some-other-Being' of the . . . past are objective states of the self, identities that can be recognized and compared. The vacancy stretches between two known points and thus becomes an extensive attribute of the implicit identity that subsumes both states and whose medium is time. . . . The myth (or plot) of memory is not a problem but an answer. The vacancy, the absolute insufficiency of the *now*, is objectified as the distance between identities which can be signified. A known version of crystallization of the self—an ideal image of the ego—answers and as it were fills up the absence created by pure subjectivity. Identity seems to imply a discourse, and a succession of identities deployed in time constitutes a 'perpetual logic' of knowable terms. Without the myth of memory, . . . self-consciousness can not be formalized and remains outside the discourse . . . converting the present into the past, into 'life and food / For future years'" (*The Romantic Sublime*, 141–42, 143).

143. "Raise your face more because it is not an image / and there is neither memory nor remorse / . . . / of the lover, / the silence that lasts, is lasting."

144. "And I see it because I love you. / It is love that makes no sense. / Lift your face now to mid-wind / with transparency and without destiny round / about the promise of spring, / the apple trees with joy in your body / that is harmony and is felicity, / with the terseness of timidity

/ when it becomes night and the sky grows / and the sea goes away and does not return / when now I live the new happiness, / very far from the memory, the only grief, / the truth of love that is yours and mine."

145. As noted, this conflict underlies the theory of the sublime as well as the Prometheus syndrome.

146. "Now the lone words leave me / and I am waiting for you / next to the wind envious of the light, / very near the plaza. And I am seeing / the ankles recently arisen / ringing like an oven. It is the first curve / beloved, vein by vein, / before entering the mystery. How / the day is opening for me. And it is for your / deep hips never for your thighs, / that odor of underarm that matures / with the sweat that I love and smells of salty / wheat, of pitch, of the fever of wood, / of the illusion of infancy / easy to awaken like smiling / but astute men, / the color of the wing of that dove / that flies through the plaza / rising again in a gyre of lust."

147. "In this plaza of golden space / where the stone dances with its shadow / there arrives the pleasure of all the senses, / and the visitation of benavides, / and the happiness of the flesh, the pure / festive body when the rooster sings / to the dark, / the agile trill of the brown nipple. . . .'"

148. "From this plaza to the uncovered sky / . . . / I am losing more and more of my soul / although I may gain in sense."

149. "I am singing what is never *mine. / . . . / . . .* It is enough only / the morning without end that enters and desires / in *your* body which is *mine. . . . / . . . /* And I let myself get carried away, you are carrying me / toward the dry appointment, without domicile, / toward the wait without good-bye, very far / from true love, which is *yours*."

150. ". . . a «Mari» se le llama también «la dama» . . ., la «señora», la «bruja» y la «maligna». Sus moradas son las sierras . . . y cuevas o espeluncas de diversas localidades . . . ; así se le designa también con el nombre de Mari de la cueva. Aparece en formas diversas. Corrientemente, es la mujer de extraordinaria belleza. Va de un lado a otro, por el aire, rodeada de fuego, y se producen grandes estampidos cuando se oculta en uno de sus antros. Pero no faltan viejos caseros que aseguran que la han visto en figura de árbol, rodeado también de llamas, y de cuervo, de hoz o globo de fuego, de nube, de caballo o montada en un carro tirado por cuatro caballos. También aparece como un buitre, rodeada de sus compañeras, que están en la misma forma, o peinando hilos de oro, haciendo madejas en los cuernos de un carnero.

"Mari atrae a los pastores, verificando algunos robos, hasta sus habitaciones, llenas de oro y piedras preciosas. Pero si les da algo de aquello, al salir se transforma en materia deleznable. No faltan casos, sin embargo, en que un trozo de carbón regalado por la misma se cambia en oro puro" (Caro Baroja, *Los Vascos*, 194).

[. . . "Mari" is also called "the lady" . . ., the "missus," the "witch" and the "evil one." Her haunts are the mountains . . . and caves or grottos of diverse localities . . . ; hence she is also called Mari of the cave. She appears in diverse forms. Most usually, in that of a woman of extraordinary beauty. She moves from one place to another, through the air, surrounded by fire, and immense explosions are produced when she hides in one of her caves. But there is no lack of old inhabitants who affirm having seen her in the figure of a tree, surrounded also by flames, and of a raven, of a sickle, or as a sphere of fire, of cloud, on horseback or mounted in a cart pulled by four horses. She also appears as a vulture, surrounded by her companions, who are in the same form, or combing threads of gold, winding skeins on the horns of a ram.

"Mari attracts shepherds, verifying some thefts, to her rooms, full of gold and precious gems. But if she gives them something of all that, upon leaving, it is transformed into worthless matter. There is no lack of cases, however, in which a piece of coal given as a gift by Mari changed into pure gold. . . .]

151. "Originally, Mari was a mortal youth. Her mother cursed her because of her disobedience or offered her to the devil with great imprudence, and in accord with this deed the enemy of humankind took her to his subterranean mansions, from which she presides over droughts and rains. . . . 'Mari' is, thus, at times, a type of Basque 'Koré' or 'Proserpina.' . . ."

152. "It is almost better that this scene arrive thus / because you are not figure but breath. /

The spring returns but love does not / return, Mari. And much less that now / all appears and disappears. / And much less that I am going so early in the morning / that the body does not surrender, it is lost."

153. "Is it that which was, that which is, that which still awaits / remorse, reconciliation / or disdain or compassion? And there is no longer jealousy / that gives sap to love, nor ingenuity / that gives more freedom to beauty. / Who would have said so? And who knew, / after the aged delicacy, / when now without pain there is no illusion, / when the wounded light goes away blindly / in this never fugitive plaza, / that purity was purity, / that the truth was not our truth?"

154. "Who sought duration? Who farewell? / There is no longer any love and there is no distrust, / deceitful salvation. It is the serene, / happy misery, when it is still cold / as the upper plains, Mari, and day shines / with the ash in rain, with a gleam / of shame on your face and on mine, / with the shadow that curses misfortune. / How early, how late, how long do they last, / this scene, this wind, this morning!"

155. Miguel Manzano's collection *Canciones zamoranas* (Madrid: Editorial Alpuerto, 1986) includes "El tío Babú," in the second and third verses of which "Los Cinco Pilares" is mentioned (13). As yet, I have not been able to identify these geographic locations in any other sources. See note 172 below.

156. "It is love that returns. And what shall we do now / if the lark of dawn is singing in the resin / of the five pine-groves of your death and mine?"

157. "It is love without a master, it is our creation: / the mystery that saves and the life that lives!"

158. We might see in these images the "sublime turn" or "sublime reversal," "the turning away from near-annihilation, from being 'under death' to being out from under death" (Hertz, *The End of the Line*, 6). This turn receives its full due in the rereading and recontextualization of the overture as epilogue.

159. *The New Princeton Encyclopedia of Poetry and Poetics*, ed. Alex Preminger and T. V. F. Brogan (Princeton: Princeton University Press, 1993), mentions incremental repetition as one of the elements of traditional ballads (117). "In incremental repetition a line or stanza is repeated successively with some small but material substitution at the same crucial spot" (581).

160. "Here I am under the sky, / under that which I have to earn money. / The clarity that is illusion comes, / serene fear along with joy / newborn / from the innocence of this night that enters / through all the windows without glass, / from morning to morning / and is divination and is the vision, / that which always is expected and now arrives, / is arriving as I lift my glass / and my hand trembles, life to life, / with miracle and with sky / where nothing darkens. And I toast and I toast."

161. "I continue toasting until day may open / for this night which is true night."

162. Rogozinski's remarks in "The Gift of the World" are apropos here: "The sublime is the formless-limitless, which exceeds all presentation and all finite duration. The infinity of the past is sublime, and even more the faceless infinity of the future.

"What the sublime revelation discovers, at the limit of the formless and at the risk of chaos, is the event of origination. Even more than Being-unto-death, Being-in-origination is the possibility of the impossible. The feeling of the sublime overtakes us the instant the chain of phenomena breaks apart, when time gives itself another chance, delivering all at once the horizon of possibilities. It is thus that passion of Law and of Ideas can suddenly seize a nation; that the work of the genius invents itself without a model; that the call of the Law liberates us from a bad repetition, in a change of direction, a *Bekehrung* which is, Kant says, 'like a new origination.' The sublime schematizes the freedom of the world, the power to commence afresh. It thus makes it possible to think an aesthetics of innovation, an ethics of conversion, a politics of revolution" ("The Gift of the World," 146).

163. Weiskel makes some incisive comments about the poet's sacrifice and the role of the poet in society: "Culture is very largely constituted by this crucial supererogation, and hence it is the measure by which the merely personal history of poet or man is exceeded by his sense of

destiny—what he *must* do. The inevitable symbol for the initiatory identification which founds and empowers the culture-ego is the profoundly ambivalent symbolic image of the sacrifice. . . . It is enough to note that the sacrifice, posited, no doubt mythically, as the founding moment of culture, is also the first symbolic act and thereby the origin of the symbolic order, of language in the wider sense" (*The Romantic Sublime*, 190).

The irony of this poem is heightened by the well-known fact that Rodríguez unremittingly imbibes red wine.

164. "Someone is knocking at the door and it isn't time yet. / Something is nearby, something is half-opening. / And how is belief becoming / mysterious innocence, / a vivid moment when still the years, / in rebellion, display / solitude or pleasure? From these stones / that shudder upon joining like / a cross or a four-pointed / nail, / can one hear the signal? / Can one hear how the water / is speaking to itself forever?"

165. "And I hear the beard of the wheat, / the chorus of dreams and the pitiless light, / captive of so much distance toward / the west wind and the dusk of a crystal, / the poverty in ashes, / so much happiness toward the clarity, / such a deep winter season. / And the body on edge / in the deep night that now / one sees and one will not see / and will not even have breath."

166. "And children playing from snow to snow in the plaza of air, / with transparent redemption. / Time, the betrayal of the blue oval, / of greed and envy, / and this shadowy wall. / This sure signal, this knocking, / this mature, calm call."

167. "And what was I going to know if I was there / knocking from door to door, in the streets, / very shamefaced, / with the brilliance of my hands / today so empty and vivid, / covered with plasterwork! I haven't had time. / It is the day, it is the day. / And the airy wood, with hail, / and the frozen wounds of the windows, / the pulse of January and the luminous cold."

168. "Someone is knocking at the door. It is painful / to believe. But the palms of my hands / open wide; / the worn knuckles / plead, sing / on the threshold that is mine on this 30th of January, / and the lintel without malice / with the fragility of repentant dream / amid the low branches of the cherry tree."

169. "Already everything has arisen. And I am seeing / a crucifixion from behind. I smell now / of this resin, of this sawdust without dust. // Now is the moment. And what more can it give. / Whoever it may be, go out and open the door. / For the messenger of your birth?"

170. "According to Heidegger, the most important aspect of the death phenomenon is that one's awareness of death *can* focus one's attention on the self *as it belongs to* the individual Dasein—i.e., the authentic self. . . . Hence one major function that the interpretation of the phenomenon of death has for Heidegger is to reveal authentic Dasein" (Gelven, *A Commentary*, 142).

171. I am grateful to Rodríguez for introducing me to this music.

172. "How it rains in Bardales, Uncle Babú . . . / also in Valdespino. / The white-grape vines of Marialba, Uncle Babú . . . / the river has carried them away." See Manzano, *Canciones zamoranas*, 13.

173. *Random House Webster's College Dictionary*, 1995 ed., s.v. "bogeyman."

174. Rodríguez's sister was named Maricarmen.

175. "Twenty-four maids were going to a wedding / there were twenty-five because the bride was going too; / because the bride was going because the godfather was going, / twenty-four maids were going down the road."

176. "The frozen afternoons / between a February little by little more intimate / and a March still very timorous, / the branch noble after the neat pruning, / the network of the tender leaf like / memory without thresholds or wingbeats, / the mild weather, the tillage / with the white oil of winter, / is all this resurrection?"

177. According to Fóti (*Heidegger and the Poets*, 69), Hölderlin uses a similar image that conjoins snow and flowers amid the new green of the alpine meadows in his poem "Mnemosyne" (the muse of memory, perhaps related to the poetic tradition in Rodríguez's poem).

178. "The rise in the river has not carried them off, / without a backwater possible, like then, / these almond trees of Maridawn. Now / it is the prodigy before us, on the red / hillside. One must look at them / with the gaze high, without curves, / awaiting this wind so early, / this night faded and accompanying, / this clear odor before / entering the prime season of the rain, / in the very fine stalk of death."

179. *Pequeño Larousse Ilustrado 1992*, s.v. "prodigio."

180. See Graves, *The Greek Myths*, 1:144; and Donoghue, *Thieves of Fire*, 36. The Spanish word for fennel, an herb that has a "sabor dulce y olor aromático y es condimenticia y medicinal" (*Enciclopedia Sopena*, 4332) [a sweet taste and an aromatic smell and is a condiment and medicinal], is "hinojo," suggesting the humility of placing oneself on one's knees ("ponerse de hinojos") in an act of prayer or obeisance.

According to Chevalier and Gheerbrandt, fennel is "Símbolo de rejuvenecimiento espiritual. . . . «El hinojo, al decir de Plinio, tiene la propiedad de aclarar la vista y, además, gustando de él las serpientes adquieren precisamente el poder maravilloso de rejuvenecerse periódicamente»" (*Diccionario de los símbolos*, 571). [Symbol of spiritual rejuvenation. . . . «Fennel, according to Pliny, has the property of clarifying sight and, also, by enjoying it snakes acquire precisely the marvelous power of rejuvenating themselves periodically.»]

181. "How many times have I been next to this cold cradle, / with the enemy light, / with stamens very sweet to the tongue, / next to these pitiless branches. And today / how I breathe this brilliance, / this health of the new growth / that arrives germinating / with the sap of death without hurry. / Without hurry, modeled / with the benign river / between the autumn of knowledge / and the casket of tenuous shadow, next to / these almond trees awaiting always / the future crops, / is all this resurrection?"

182. "Never in repose, almond trees / of Maridawn / because the earth is springy and clean, / because the almond is barely lasting / high and trembling / with its fidelity, its confidence, / very much to the size of the hands that now / dry themselves and open / to the fingertip and to the fruit, / to fecundity, to fatigue, / to the emotion of the ground / next to the light without nests. / Is all this resurrection?"

183. "According to Henri Birault, in its specifically modern version finitude is considered a privation imposed by the infinite term, the Divine or Perfect Being. The infinite term is the agent of negativity as cause of the limitations of the finite term. In the modern version of the problem of finitude, the subject attempts to fight back, to overcome the limitations of its finite character, through the infinite reach of his or her will or desire. The desire to be God is the expression of an unlimited freedom of the will, which links the idea of finitude with freedom and transgression. Freedom as transgression depends upon the Christian thinking of the fall and of sin. Interpreting the idea of finitude as a 'speculative transposition of the theme of sin,' Birault suggests, enables us to see 'the very essence of modern subjectivity as the freedom of negativity.' According to Birault, therefore, the problematic of finitude, in which finitude is determined through freedom, is identified with the emergence of the problematic of the subject. Freedom achieved through, or experienced as, transgression (associated with the desire to be God—the desire for nonlimitation or for absolute autonomy) is an individuating principle for the subject. Through transgression, the subject replaces the infinite term through the incorporation (as infinite will) of the infinity, or absolute autonomy, of the transcendent term. Promethean man—the man of infinite will—replaced God, and yet, as Promethean man, the subject remains a kind of mirror of the conception of the infinite powers of the Omnipotent. . . .

"In recent decades transgression has become a critical or philosophical theme—a philosopheme—as well as a literary one. Writing, or textual productivity, has itself become identified with a critical or ideological thematics of transgression" (Guerlac, *The Impersonal Sublime*, 149–50).

Also, "reflection upon the possibility of not-being (to-be-able-not-to-be) reveals the possibility of being (to-be-able-to-be) in a way in which 'possibility' is no longer seen merely as an abstract logical function of not-yet-actual, but is seen rather as an essential manner in which a human being exists; and that essential manner is given the name *'freedom.' Heidegger's analysis of death, then, is not the basis for morbidity and despair; it is rather the source of freedom and authentic existence"* (Gelven, *A Commentary*, 155; emphasis added).

184.   "There is a sigh where there is no air, / only the secret of the melody / becoming purer and more painful / of these almond trees that grew before / innocence and suffering were / the sure flower, / purified with its solitude / that does not fade in vain."

185.   Cf. the biblical passage "Unless a seed of grain shall fall upon the ground and die, it remains just a single grain; but if it falls and dies, it produces abundant life."

186.   "And it is the entire year and it is the spring / of these almond trees that are in your soul / and are singing in it and I hear them, / I hear the sap of the light with nests / in this body where there is no longer anyone / and the river / carries it off, is carrying it off / far away, far away, / there in the open water, / there, with the mauve leaf, / the river."

187.   I am indebted to Juan Bruce-Novoa of the University of California, Irvine, for this insight.

188.   Cf. Eco and my discussion of language in *Don* in chap. 1 above.

189.   "'The blue glazier, the glazier / of morning!' And you go limping along, / whistling. Enter the dance / without funeral, with the sound of birth / speaking with the passersby / when the road arrives at the summit / and the invisible is transparency in flame / like the odor of the bonfire in November. / In a little while, / who will even hear / the sunflower that no one will ever see? / Everything is dark but you are clear. / Everything corrupt but you are pure."

190.   "Enter with limpid audacity, / buried in your wings, / enter the dance, enter each letter of this name, each / headstone that is secret and sacrifice, / and fruit and salvation. / . . ."

191.   ". . . / Enter the dance, / dance with a lively body, / with haughty and beautiful grace, / give me your hand and cast / your scarf to the wind. / Dance upon this headstone. / «The blue glazier, the glazier / of morning!»"

192.   "Before the unfinished melody / is heard you remain there, / there, very alone, alone, / alone in the dance."

193.   "Day of wrath, Day of mourning, / Lo, the world in ashes burning— / Seer and Sibyl gave the warning." See *A Manual of Prayers for the Use of the Catholic Laity*, prep. and enj. by order of the Third Plenary Council of Baltimore (New York: P. J. Kennedy & Sons, 1930), 610.

194.   Christophe Nyrop says, *"Solvet seclum*—'The world is falling asunder, the world is perishing': so it runs in the old psalm about the Day of Judgment. *Solvet seclum in favilla*— 'The world is perishing in a sea of flames.' These words of the Middle Ages, with their prophetic menace and exhortation, again arouse fear and gloomy forebodings in the minds of men all over the earth. Is it not the *dies irae*, the day of wrath, of which the Psalm sings, that is now approaching? Is it for the end of the world we are steering for? . . .

"*Solvet seclum*—'The old world is perishing'; but, as Leconte de Lisle says in his powerful paraphrase of these words about the Day of Judgment, its impure dross shall fertilize the furrows, where the new world is already germinating" (*Is War Civilization?*, trans. H. G. Wright [London: William Heinemann, 1917], 244, 256).

195.   My first intuition was that "favilla" is a diminutive. According to John T. White, *The White Latin Dictionary* (Chicago: Follett, 1948), "favilla" is derived from "facula," the diminutive of "fax." "Favilla" is "A small torch, i.e., a small shining or glowing thing . . . . Hot cinders or ashes, embers; The ashes of the dead still glowing; Fig., A glimmering spark, i.e., beginning, origin." "Facula" is "A little torch," and "Fax," literally the shining or brilliant thing, is "A torch, flambeau, link; . . . The light of the heavenly bodies; A fiery meteor, fire-ball, shooting-star; Fig., Flame in good or bad sense; anything that inflames or incites; incitement, stimulus, cause of ruin, destruction."

Both Graves (*The Greek Myths*, 1:144) and Hamilton (*Mythology*, 69) mention a torch Prometheus used to obtain fire for mankind, another link between the poet and the Promethean myth.

196. This verse echoes a similar statement in "A la respiración en la llanura," where the
?et writes, "No sé cómo he vivido / hasta ahora" (*Desde mis poemas*, 70).

197. The translations of vv. 7 and 16 are self-evident. Verses 21–24 read: "corrosion in full
divination / and annihilation in full creation, / amid delirium and science."

198. "The plains of the countryside, with soft slopes, / valiant in vineshoots . . . / How the
?n enters the grape / and trembles, becomes light in it, / and they mature and they abandon, /
?ey give beauty and they open / to their future death. . . ."

199. "The skeleton amid the lime and the sand / and the ash of cowardice, / the servitude of
?e flesh in voice, / on the wing, / of the bone that is about to be a flute, / and the brain to be a
?oneycomb or a wicker basket / next to the violins of the worm, / the melody in the flower of
?e woodrot, / the gnawed and crystalline petal, / the golden tooth in the vivid ossuary, / and the
?aves and the wind / with the incense of the high waves / and the saltiness of the high tide, / the
?turgical abyss of the body in the hour / of the supremacy of a flash of light, / of the dome in
?ames without space / with the putrefaction that is pure love, / where death no longer has a
?ame. . . ."

200. "And can you hear the nightingale? / Where the new vineshoot, / where the tremulous
?ermentation / of meditation, / far from the vain thought, from the life / that one never has to
wait / but be ripe / to receive, from sons / to sons, in the aurora / of the pollen?"

201. See Barbara Herrnstein Smith, *Poetic Closure: A Study of How Poems End* (Chicago
?nd London: University of Chicago Press, 1968).

202. "You didn't know that death is beautiful / and that it became in your body. You didn't
?now / that the family, generous streets, / were lies. // But not that rain of childhood, / and not
?he taste of disillusionment, / the sheet without shadow and the caress / unknown."

203. "For the light never forgets or pardons, / more dangerous with your clarity / so inno-
?ent that it says it all: / revelation. // And now I cannot even live your life, / and now I cannot
?ven live my life / with the open hands of this afternoon / accursed and clear."

204. "Now that which has been lost is saved / with the sacrifice of love, the incest / of the
?ky, and with pain, remorse, / serene grace. // And if the spring is true? / I no longer know what
?o say. I go away happy. / You didn't know that death is beautiful, / sad maid."

205. "they were a lie / unknown // revelation / damned and clear // serene grace / sad maid"

206. Guerlac remarks, "For the circle is the figure of totalization and closure. Transgression is what keeps the 'circulatory apparatus' of the text turning. The opposition between sublime and grotesque is the principal mechanism of transgressive reversal" (*The Impersonal Sublime*, 153).

207. Guerlac notes Boileau's emphasis on the accoutrements of the speech act in his translation of Longinus. "If the French translation veils a number of the paradoxical or ambivalent
features of the Longinian sublime, Boileau nevertheless retains the Longinian emphasis on the
act of enunciation. He develops this aspect of the sublime in the direction of a pragmatics of
discourse that attends to the contextual situation of an act of speech—who is speaking, upon
what occasion, and at which moment" (*The Impersonal Sublime*, 4–5).

208. See note 19 above.

Conclusion and Prologue: The Poet/Artist as *Dasein*

1. Although these poems have mostly been published for some time, they have only
now become accessible to the greater audience thanks to the inclusion of an early love sonnet
in Cañas's anthology and the more recent appendage of several poems in the selection edited
by Luis García Jambrina, *Hacia el canto* (Salamanca: Ediciones Universidad de Salamanca,
1993). I have used this edition for the text of the first two poems I will discuss.

2. In this regard, I take an approach in contradistinction to García Jambrina, who catego-

rizes them as homages. Of the poems in García Jambrina's collection, I have opted not to re: either "Inscripción en una frente" [Inscription on a forehead] because of a similar homage Vicente Aleixandre in "Perro de poeta" [Dog of the poet] of *El vuelo* (both were published the same year, 1959), or "Despertar de Antonio Machado en Soria" [Awakening of Antoni Machado in Soria]. It is clear, however, that these poems fall into the same category not only homages but also of depictions of the poet/artist. The third poem I have chosen is not include in García Jambrina's anthology.

3. See the introduction of this book for additional discussion of the underpinning Heidegger's philosophy in Rodríguez's poetry and a fuller definition of the concept of *Dasei*

4. "Blas de Otero" can be found in García Jambrina, *Hacia el canto*, 283–84. "To se how the Duero flows / and how the plaster and the cement, / how the bread, the tool / singin and accusing in the hands / of Ramon and of Julio, and of Marcelo, / of Thomas and of Antonic / above all of Eugenio, / you were there."

5. "Yes, amid/between the mud / and the soul, / when the light becomes melody / an fount and the sky / 'very luminously red,' as you say, / then, two steps away, / the bridge wa opening itself and was embracing the water, / to intimate and fecund, / and was weaving it ami its limpid eyes, / and was kneading it freely, / with the mold sweated and breathed / along wit the friends."

6. Blas de Otero, *Con la inmensa mayoría* (Buenos Aires: Losada, 1960), 24. "The Duero The water mills of Zamora. / the sky luminously red. / Companions. I write from memory what I had before my eyes."

7. "There, in that workshop of yours you are shaping / (I copy your style) / not only tru words / but also salvation, the search / and the protest. The water / passes by, there, two step away, / the water of the Duero."

8. "And the workshop, and the beat / of the rhythm of the work and of the hand, / are there, with you, / beside the thighs of the washerwomen / without the river dying in our arms because the water of the Duero is now quicklime."

9. "Cal hirviente" is another image from Blas's poetry. See the sonnet "Pido vivir" in *Ancia*. See *Cuatro poetas de hoy*, sel. de María de Gracia Ifach, 2a ed. (Madrid: Taurus, 1965), 154.

10. This poem also can be found in *Hacia el canto*, 285. "It is this symphony / of the cape that sounds / like what? Here is the mystery. / All, the cloth, the air / of distance, all the charge, / aggressive and solemn, / and when the spirit arrives, it is already song. / Here is the bullfighter who, although he may have a name, / gives even more of himself, and he desires, and he saves. / That way of walking through the bullring, / the internal movement, that of the reckoning, / grows palpable, / and becomes touch and air at the same time / when the onslaught arrives."

11. I am condensing and paraphrasing Véronique M. Fóti, who explains, "*Poiēsis*, Heidegger insists, is essentially linked to technicity insofar as it is the differential, un-principled mode of articulation characteristic of *technē* in its ancient sense. With respect to language (which enables un-concealment), *poiēsis* is poetic articulation, which contrasts with the challenging-forth and the unconditional command characteristic of technicity. Since *poiēsis* remains mindful of the 'mystery' or the lack of any inherent, positable reality in the happening of manifestation, it is able to awaken awareness of the destinal-historical ambiguity between totalizing and differential modalities of un-concealment in the *essence* of *Ge-stell*. By showing forth this ambiguity, *poiēsis* situates *Ge-stell* within an epochal destiny of manifestation granting *(ge/währt)*. As soon, however, as *Ge-stell* can be thus situated, we have gained what Heidegger calls a 'free relationship' to it, so that its 'entrapment' *(nachstellen)* of man's disclosive *essence* is foiled; and the extremity of 'danger' becomes transmuted into 'that which saves' by enabling an epochal turning" (*Heidegger and the Poets*, 13).

12. "Apparition without time. / Frontal or circular? Is it movement / or is it repose? / The distance, the proximity, / here they are. He knows well / the religiosity of smoke and of blood: / the most vivid. And there reaches him / an obscure revelation, from the left / or rather from the

ght, and the body is / offered, totally, here in his chest, in dominion and marble, between the agic and the wisdom."

13. Heidegger quotes this verse in his essay "What Are Poets For?," in *Poetry, Language, hought*, 118. The translation there reads "But where there is danger, there grows also what aves." I have used the translation in Steiner, *Martin Heidegger*, 141. The original German is Wo aber Gefahr ist, wächst / Das Rettende auch" (141).

14. I am grateful to Beatriz Celaya for information concerning the bullfighter Antoñete. she recalls that this bullfighter retired from the ring for several years, but eventually made a reappearance, similar to Rodríguez's long hiatus from publication following *El vuelo*. As a bullfighter, Antoñete was extremely immobile and dignified, displaying his imperturbability, serenity, courage, and dignity in the face of death.

15. *Vía Crucis del arte zamorano: 14 poetas 14 pintores* (Zamora: Diputación de Zamora, 1991), 16–17.

16. "This is my liberty and my condemnation. / It is my condemnation and your salvation. / And the injustice will be life to life, / rebellion and love and sacrifice. / That is how I want it. Like that. See me offered. / And my cross will be a canticle. And my death / your resurrection."

17. As noted in chap. 5, Gelven asserts that "reflection upon the possibility of not-being (to-be-able-not-to-be) reveals the possibility of being (to-be-able-to-be) in a way in which 'possibility' is no longer seen merely as an abstract logical function of not-yet-actual, but is seen rather as an essential manner in which a human being exists; and that essential manner is given the name 'freedom.' Heidegger's analysis of death, then, is not the basis for morbidity and despair; it is rather the source of freedom and authentic existence" (*A Commentary*, 155).

18. These quotes are adapted from Steiner, *Martin Heidegger*, 112–13.

19. "But the gift is not like the transgression. For if by that one person's transgression the many died, how much more did the grace of God and the gracious gift of the one person Jesus Christ overflow for the many. And the gift is not like the result of the one person's sinning. For after one sin there was the judgment that brought condemnation; but the gift, after many transgressions, brought acquittal. For it, by the transgression of one person, death came to reign through that one, how much more will those who receive the abundance of grace and of the gift of justification come to reign in life through the one person Jesus Christ. In conclusion, just as through one transgression condemnation came upon all, so through one righteous act acquittal and life came to all. For just as through the disobedience of one person the many were made sinners, so through the obedience of one the many will be made righteous. The law entered in so that transgression might increase but, where sin increased, grace overflowed all the more, so that as sin reigned in death, grace also might reign through justification for eternal life through Jesus Christ our Lord" (Rom. 5:15–21). With regard to the two modes of "Being-toward," see also the frequent use of the ambivalent verb "esperar" throughout Rodríguez's poetry.

20. I have used the definition of sacrifice in *Webster's New World Dictionary*, 3d College Edition, to formulate this statement.

21. Cf. the Canticle of Mary, also called "the Magnificat" (Luke 1:46–56), and Jorge Guillén's *Cántico*. Also see Heidegger's definition of song, poetry, art, discussed in the introduction of this book.

22. Note that the "pie quebrado" suggests a "limp," emblematic of Rodríguez's walking as writing.

Bibliography

Works by Claudio Rodríguez

Editions of Poetry Consulted

Poesía, 1953–1966. Barcelona: Plaza & Janés, 1971.
El vuelo de la celebración. Madrid: Visor, 1976.
Desde mis poemas. Madrid: Cátedra, 1983.
Casi una leyenda. Barcelona: Tusquets, 1991.
Hacia el canto. Edited by Luis García Jambrina. Salamanca: Ediciones Universidad de Salamanca, 1993.

Articles and Introductions

"Algunos comentarios sobre el tema de la fauna en la poesía de Vicente Aleixandre." *Insula,* nos. 374–75 (1978): 17.
"El bufón «Calabacillas», llamado erróneamente «el bobo de Coria» Diego Velázquez de Silva (1599–1660)." In *Mirar un cuadro en el Museo del Prado,* 174. Barcelona and Madrid: Lunwerg, 1991.
"Cautiva del aire." In *El Libro de Tamar,* Almudena Guzmán, 7–9. Melilla: Rusadir, 1989.
"Leopardi." *ABC,* 13 junio 1987, 3.
"Prólogo." In *Poemario (1967–1981),* by Alfonso Gil, 7–9. Zaragoza, 1983.
"Prólogo." In *Obra poética (1943–1981),* by Rafael Morales, 13–20. Madrid: Espasa-Calpe, 1982.
Reflexiones sobre mi poesía. Madrid: Universidad Autónoma, 1985.
"Unas notas sobre la poesía de Jorge Guillén." *Insula,* nos. 435–36 (1983): 7, 8.
"Unas notas sobre poesía." *Olvidos de Granada* 13 (1987): 131, 133.
"Unas palabras sin título." In *El suplicante y otras escenas parabólicas,* by Alfredo Castellón, 11–12. Madrid: Endymion, 1988.
"Viendo jugar al corro." *ABC,* 18 January 1987, 3.

Studies of Rodríguez's Poetry

Aguada, J. A. "Una nueva poética para la muerte." *Diario de Terrassa* (11 October 1991).

Aguirre, Francisca. "La dolorida alegría de leer a Claudio Rodríguez." *República de las Letras* 9 (1984): 38–39.

Albornoz, Aurora de. "Claudio Rodríguez: palabras superpuestas." *Olvidos de Granada* 14 (1986): 26–27.

Alejo, Justo. "Los poemas humanos de Claudio Rodríguez." *Triunfo* 4, núm. 721 (20 November 1976): 61.

Aller, César. "El conocimiento en la poesía de Claudio Rodríguez." *Arbor,* núm. 309–10 [n.d.]: 131–34.

———. "La poesía de Claudio Rodríguez." *La Estafeta Literaria,* no. 335 (1966): 14.

———. "*El vuelo de la celebración.*" *Arbor,* núm. 372 (1976): 124–26.

Alonso, Santos. "*Casi una leyenda*: La sorpresa de la ciudad." *Reseña,* núm. 279 (July–August 1991): 17.

Armiño, Mauro. "Claudio Rodríguez: oficio de palabras." *Cambio 16,* no. 840 (4 January 1988): 88–90.

Ayuso, César Augusto. "«Casi una leyenda», de Claudio Rodríguez." *El Norte de Castilla. Letras* (8 June 1991): vii.

Barrón, Amalia. "Nuestros cuatro mejores poetas revelan el nombre de sus musas." *El Diario Vasco* (1965): 8.

Benito de Lucas, Joaquín. "Claudio Rodríguez [1934]." In *Literatura de la postguerra: La poesía,* 77–80. Madrid: Cincel, 1981.

———. "*Conjuros.*" *Poesía Española,* no. 87 (1960): 8–10.

Berasátegui, Blanca. "Claudio Rodríguez: El alma es una colmena vibrante." *ABC,* 20 March 1977, 36.

———. "1980: Nueva frontera de la literatura española." *Los domingos de ABC,* 16 December 1979, 17–19, 21–22.

Bourne, Louis. "*Desde mis poemas.*" *Libros,* no. 26 (1984): 3–4.

———. "Plotino y las hermosas agresiones de Claudio Rodríguez." *Libros* 25 (1984): 3–4.

Bousoño, Carlos. "La ebriedad de un poeta puro." *El País,* 21 May 1989, Libros 17.

———. "La poesía de Claudio Rodríguez." *ABC,* 8 March 1986, v.

———. "La poesía de Claudio Rodríguez." In *Poesía, 1953–1966,* Claudio Rodríguez, 9–35. Barcelona: Plaza y Janés, 1971.

Bradford, Carole A. "Francisco Brines and Claudio Rodríguez: Two Recent Approaches to Poetic Creation." *Crítica Hispánica* 2 (1980): 29–40.

———. "From Vicente Aleixandre to Claudio Rodríguez: Love as a Return to the Cosmos." *Hispanic Journal* 4 (1982): 97–104.

———. "Transcendent Reality in the Poetry of Claudio Rodríguez." *Journal of Spanish Studies—Twentieth Century* 7 (1979): 133–46.

Bruflat, Alan Scott. "Ambivalence and Reader Response in the Poetry of Claudio Rodríguez." Doctoral diss., University of Kansas, 1986.

———. "Claudio Rodríguez's 'Brujas a mediodía': Meaning and Intelligibility." *Romance Notes* 29 (1988): 39–44.

———. "Doubt and Affirmation in Claudio Rodríguez's *Conjuros.*" *Hispanófila* 96 (1989): 55–64.

————. "Process as Metaphor in the Poetry of Claudio Rodríguez." *Confluencia* 6 (1990): 45–53.

Buenaventura, Ramón. "Leyenda crecedera." *Cinco Días,* 12 August 1991.

Campbell, Federico. *Infame turba.* Barcelona: Lumen, 1971.

Cañas, Dionisio. "Carta a Claudio Rodríguez." *El Mundo,* 22 May 1991.

————. "'La ciudad no me inspira, aunque casi todo lo escribo callejeando." *Cambio 16,* 10 June 1991, 104–5.

————. *Claudio Rodríguez.* Madrid: Júcar, 1988.

————. *Poesía y percepción (Francisco Brines, Claudio Rodríguez y José Angel Valente).* Madrid: Hiperión, 1984.

————. "La vida, a pesar de todo, es real." *El Mundo. La Esfera,* 16 June 1991, 3.

Cano, José Luis. "La poesía de Claudio Rodríguez." *Insula,* no. 230 (1966): 8–9.

————. "La poesía de Claudio Rodríguez y su nuevo libro *Conjuros.*" *Insula,* no. 147 (1959): 6–7.

————. *Poesía española contemporánea: Las generaciones de posguerra.* Madrid: Guadarrama, 1974.

————. "Un nuevo libro de Claudio Rodríguez: *El vuelo de la celebración.*" *Insula,* no. 359 (1976): 8–9, 11.

————. "Un poeta de la novísima generación: Claudio Rodríguez." In *Poesía española del siglo XX: De Unamuno a Blas de Otero,* 527–31. Madrid: Ediciones Guadarrama, 1960.

Cantavella, Juan. "Ultimo poemario de Claudio Rodríguez." *Heraldo de Aragón,* 29 May 1991.

Celis, Mary Carmen de. "El paraíso abierto de Claudio Rodríguez." *El Adelanto,* 3 March 1973, 5.

Chacón, Juan. "Evolución en la poesía de Claudio Rodríguez." *La Hora XXV,* 1966, 157–58, 160–61.

Cid, Alicia. "Un nuevo libro de Claudio Rodríguez." *Blanco y Negro,* 14 February 1976, 65.

Ciria Matilla, Soledad. Review of *Desde mis poemas,* by Claudio Rodríguez. *Cuadernos de Investigación de Literatura Hispánica* 8 (1987): 269.

Ciriza, María. "Una aventura lúcida y controlada." *Informaciones de las Artes y las Letras,* 2 marzo 1972, 5.

Compás de Letras: Monografías de literatura española. Vol. 6. June 1995.

Conte, Rafael. "La voz de Claudio Rodríguez." *El Sol,* 17 May 1991, 3.

Cuadernos de la lechuza (May 1987). Núm. monográfico dedicado a Claudio Rodríguez.

Cuenca, Luis Alberto de. "Claudio y yo." *ABC,* 8 marzo 1986, x.

Debicki, Andrew P. "Claudio Rodríguez: Language Codes and Their Effects." In *Poetry of Discovery: The Spanish Generation of 1956–71.* Lexington: University Press of Kentucky, 1982.

————. "Los códigos y la experiencia en poemas de Claudio Rodríguez." *Journal of Spanish Studies: Twentieth Century* 5 (1977): 97–110.

————. *Poesía del conocimiento: La generación española de 1956–1971.* Translated by Alberto Cardín. Madrid: Júcar, 1986.

Demel, Marjorie Jean. "Nature and the Patterns for Giving in the Poetry of Claudio Rodríguez." Master's thesis, Texas A&M University, 1979.

Díaz-Plaja, Guillermo. "Poesía de Claudio Rodríguez." In *Al pie de la poesía: Páginas críticas, 1971–1973,* 188–92. Madrid: Editora Nacional, 1974.

Domínguez Rey, Antonio. "A la búsqueda de una justificación." *El País,* 27 June 1976, Libros 21.

————. "Hacia una interpretación de la poesía: *Don de la ebriedad*, de Claudio Rodríguez." *Antípodas* 2 (1989): 187–206.

————. "Transfiguración de la materia." *El Independiente. Libros,* 6 June 1991, 34.

Echeverría, Rosa María. "Claudio Rodríguez: «Los poetas tenemos fecha de caducidad, como los yogures»." *Blanco y Negro,* 29 March 1992, 78–83.

Elizondo, Itziar. "Claudio Rodríguez: «Sigo creyendo en la poesía como un don y un entusiasmo»." *El Independiente,* 23 May 1991, 31.

Encuentros con el 50: La voz poética de una generación. Oviedo: Fundación Municipal de Cultura, 1990.

"Encuentros con el 50: La voz poética de una generación." *Insula,* no. 494 (1988): 21–24.

Esteban, José. "¡Queremos tanto a Claudio . . . !" *El Mundo. La Esfera,* 16 June 1991, 3.

Ezquerra, Iñaki. "Poesía vivencial." *El Correo Español,* 4 September 1991.

Fernández Almagro, Melchor. "*Alianza y condena.*" *ABC,* 13 January 1966, n.p.

Fernández-Braso, Miguel. "Claudio Rodríguez." *Pueblo,* 23 June 1971, 32.

Fernández Palacios, Jesús. "Claudio Rodríguez. A su manera." *Fin de Siglo* 8 (1984): 29–32.

Gallego, Vicente. "Claudio Rodríguez: *Conjuros,* veintiocho años después." *Insula,* no. 483 (1987): 9.

García, Angeles. "Claudio Rodríguez: 'Los galardones no influyen en el ejercicio del poeta.'" *El País,* 1 December 1983, 26.

García Hortelano, Juan. "Claudio o el acierto." *El País,* 1 December 1983, 26.

García Jambrina, Luis Miguel. "Comentario de un poema de Claudio Rodríguez: «Hacia la luz»." In *La poesía de postguerra,* edited by Ricardo de la Fuente, 176–79. Vol. 47 of *Historia de la literatura española.* Madrid: Ediciones Júcar, in press.

————. "De *Don de la ebriedad* a «¿dónde la ebriedad?»" *El Correo de Zamora,* 29 March 1992, Dominical VIII–IX.

————. "De *Don de la ebriedad* a «¿dónde la ebriedad?»" (y II)." *El Correo de Zamora,* 5 April 1992, Dominical XII–XIV.

————. "De *Don de la ebriedad* a «¿dónde la ebriedad?»": *Casi una leyenda* en la trayectoria poética de Claudio Rodríguez." Texto presentado en los Primeros Encuentros de Poética: Congreso sobre Jaime Gil de Biedma y su generación poética. Universidad de Zaragoza, 1991.

————. "Lección y lectura de un clásico actual." *Insula,* no. 545 (May 1992): 5–6.

————. "Pensamiento y poesía según María Zambrano: Una aplicación a la lectura de Claudio Rodríguez." *Philosophica Malacitana* 4 (1991): 131–42.

————. "Poesía como participación: hacia Claudio Rodríguez." *Diálogo de la Lengua,* núm. 1 (1992): 107–14.

————. "La poesía viva: El elemento oral y popular en la obra poética de Claudio Rodríguez." *Anuario del Instituto de Estudios Zamoranos "Florián de Ocampo,"* 1988, 491–99.

————. "La trayectoria poética de Claudio Rodríguez (1953–1976): Análisis del ritmo." *Studia Zamorensia. Philologica* 8 (1987): 97–118.

————. "El vuelo de la palabra de Claudio Rodríguez." In *La poesía de postguerra,* edited by Ricardo de la Fuente, 72–79. Vol. 47 of *Historia de la literatura española.* Madrid: Ediciones Júcar, in press.

García Jambrina, Luis M., and Luis Ramos de la Torre. *Claudio Rodríguez para niños.* Madrid: Ediciones de la Torre, 1988.

————. *Guía de lectura de Claudio Rodríguez.* Madrid: Ediciones de la Torre, 1988.

García Lorenzo, Luciano. "*Alianza y condena.*" *Revista de Literatura,* nos. 55–56 (1965): 308–9.

———. "*Conjuros:* En busca del paraíso perdido." In *Conjuros,* by Claudio Rodríguez, 11–20. Zamora: Diputación de Zamora, 1988.

García Martín, José Luis. Review of *Casi una leyenda,* Claudio Rodríguez. *La Nueva España,* 28 June 1991, 53.

———. *La segunda generación poética de posguerra.* Badajoz: Diputación de Badajoz, 1986.

García Ortega, Adolfo. "Algunas consideraciones sobre la poesía de Claudio Rodríguez." *Olvidos de Granada* 13 (1986): 94–98.

———. "Todo lo que el hombre hace es moral." *El País,* 11 December 1986, 4.

García Posada, Miguel. "*Casi una leyenda.*" *ABC,* 18 May 1991, 3.

———. "Pureza." *El País,* 29 May 1993, 35.

Garciasol, Ramón de. "*Don de la ebriedad.*" *Insula,* no. 99 (1954): 7.

Gimferrer, Pere. "*Alianza y condena.*" *El Ciervo* 15, núm. 146 (1966): 14.

———. "La poesía de Claudio Rodríguez." *Triunfo* 26 (1971): 54–55.

———. "Poesía de hoy y de siempre." *ABC,* 30 May 1991, 3.

———. "Claudio Rodríguez: *Alianza y condena.*" *La Trinchera,* 2ª ép., 2 (July 1966): 39–40, 42.

González, Angel. "Una obra valiosa y valerosa." *El Mundo,* 29 May 1993, 51.

González, Angel, et al. "Coloquio sobre poesía." *Olvidos de Granada* 13 (1984): 129–30, 134, 138, 142, 145.

González Martín, J. P. "Claudio Rodríguez." In *Poesía hispánica 1939–1969 (Estudio y antología).* Barcelona: El Bardo, 1970.

González Muela, Joaquín. *La nueva poesía española.* Madrid: Alcalá, 1973.

González Roncero, María-Isabel. "Claudio Rodríguez diserta sobre su propia poesía." *El Correo de Zamora,* 31 January 1975.

Guinda, Angel. "La leyenda es Claudio Rodríguez." *El Periódico,* 30 May 1991, 3.

Hernández, Antonio. "Claudio Rodríguez." *La Estafeta Literaria,* 15 September 1971, 15–17.

Hernández R., Jesús. "Claudio Rodríguez y la salvación de la materia." *El Correo de Zamora,* 23 April 1972, 12.

———. "La ebriedad amanecida del canto." *Diario Regional,* 5 November 1976, Artes y Letras 1, 4–5.

Hierro, José. "Alianza y condena." *Atlántida,* January–February 1967, 101–3.

Hilario Tundidor, Jesús. *6 poetas de Zamora.* Zamora: Caja de Ahorros Provincial de Zamora, 1976.

Hodgson, Irene Belle. "The Poetic Works of Claudio Rodríguez." Doctoral diss., Purdue University, 1986.

Iglesias, Amalia. "Claudio Rodríguez." *Diario 16,* 26 April 1991, 27.

Infante, José. "Obra poética (1953–1966) de Claudio Rodríguez." *Sol de España,* 12 August 1971, 13.

Janés, Clara. "El momento de la amapola." *ABC,* 8 March 1986, x.

Jiménez, José Olivio. "Claudio Rodríguez entre la luz y el canto: Sobre *El vuelo de la celebración.*" *Papeles de Son Armadans* 87 (1977): 103–24.

———. *Diez años de poesía española (1960–1970).* Madrid: Insula, 1972.

———. "Para una antología esencial de Claudio Rodríguez." *Cuadernos Hispanoamericanos,* no. 414 (1984): 92–110.

————. "La poesía última de Claudio Rodríguez (Sobre *Alianza y condena*)." *Revista de Estudios Hispánicos* 1 (1967): 209–41.

Jiménez Martos, Luis. "*Alianza y condena*." *La Estafeta Literaria*, no. 336 (1966): 19.

————. "*Conjuros*." *La Estafeta Literaria*, no. 164 (1959): 19.

Jové Lamenca, Jordi. "La poesía de Claudio Rodríguez: Un momento de infancia a través de la mirada." *Antípodas* 2 (1989): 179–85.

Juárez, R. "Desde sus poemas: Claudio Rodríguez." *Las Nuevas Letras* 1 (1984): 85–87.

Logroño, Miguel. "La poesía en su estado puro." *El Mundo*, 29 May 1993, 52.

López, Julio. "Claudio Rodríguez: La celebración de un gran poeta." *La Patria*, 2 September 1979, Revista Dominical 3.

López Castro, Armando. "La mirada natural de Claudio Rodríguez." *Hora de Poesía* 45 (1986): 5–32.

López Gorgé, Jacinto. "Cinco poetas de distantas promociones tratan de poner en claro el confusionismo reinante." *La Estafeta Literaria* 482 (1971): 12–14.

López-Sueiras, Manuel. "Después de quince años, Claudio Rodríguez publica un nuevo libro." *El Correo de Zamora*, 29 April 1991.

Lucio, Francisco. "Dos poetas en sus libros: Francisco Brines-Claudio Rodríguez." *Insula*, no. 304 (1972): 4–5.

Luna Borje, José. "Casi una fantasía." *Sur,* 19 October 1991, Cultural 3. Also in *Diario de Jerez,* 5 October 1991.

Mainer, José-Carlos. "El don de la poesía." *El Sol*, 10 May 1991.

Malpartida, Juan. "La mirada fundacional (Sobre Claudio Rodríguez)." *Cuadernos Hispanoamericanos,* núm. 497 (1991): 101–9.

Mandlove, Nancy. "Carnal Knowledge: Claudio Rodríguez and *El vuelo de la celebración*." *The American Hispanist* 4 (1979): 20–23.

————. "Revelation and Communion: Contrasting Reader-Speaker Relationships in the Poetry of Jorge Guillén and Claudio Rodríguez." In *LA CHISPA '81: Selected Proceedings* (26–28 February 1981), edited by Gilbert Paolini, 191–98. New Orleans, La.: Tulane University, 1981.

Marco, Joaquín. "Evolución de la poesía de Claudio Rodríguez." In *Ejercicios literarios.* Barcelona: Táber, 1969.

Martínez, José Enrique. "*Casi una leyenda*." *El Diario de León,* 18 August 1991.

————. "Claudio Rodríguez: La poesía como un don." In *Anuario de Castilla y León: 1994,* 477–84. N.p.: Ambito, 199?

Martínez Ruiz, Florencio. "*El vuelo de la celebración*." *Blanco y Negro* 341 (15 mayo 1976): 66–67.

Masoliver, Juan Ramón. "Ignacio, de la novela; la poesía, de Claudio." *La Vanguardia Española,* 21 April 1966, 59.

Mayhew, Jonathan. "*Casi una leyenda*: Repetición y renovación en el último libro de Claudio Rodríguez." *Insula,* no. 541 (1992): 11–12.

————. *Claudio Rodríguez and the Language of Poetic Vision.* Lewisburg, Pa.: Bucknell University Press, 1990.

————. "The Dialectic of the Sign in Claudio Rodríguez's *Alianza y condena*." *Hispania* 72 (1989): 516–25.

————. "The Motive for Metaphor: Claudio Rodríguez's *Conjuros* and the Rhetoric of Social Solidarity." *Symposium* 43 (1989): 37–55.

————. "Reading as Self-Sacrifice in Claudio Rodríguez's *Don de la ebriedad.*" *Modern Language Studies* 19 (1989): 12–24.

Méndez, José. "Claudio Rodríguez: El vuelo de la paloma tiene tres tiempos." *ABC,* 8 March 1986, vi–vii.

Miller, Elizabeth Gamble. "Unraveling and Reweaving the Enigmatic Fabric of Claudio Rodríguez's Poetry." *Translation Review* 38–39 (1992): 55–63.

Miller, Martha LaFollette. "Elementos metapoéticos en un poema de Claudio Rodríguez." *Explicación de Textos Literarios* 8 (1979–80): 127–36.

————. "Linguistic Skepticism in *El vuelo de la celebración.*" *Anales de la Literatura Española Contemporánea* 6 (1981): 105–21.

————. "Order and Anarchy: Cosmic Song in Jorge Guillén and Claudio Rodríguez." *Anales de la Literatura Española Contemporánea* 12 (1987): 259–72.

Millner, Curtis. "Entrevista con Claudio Rodríguez." *Anales de la Literatura Española Contemporánea* 9 (1984): 285–94.

Miró, Emilio. "*Alianza y condena,* Claudio Rodríguez." *Cuadernos Hispanoamericanos,* no. 201 (1966): 809–12.

Molero, Juan Carlos. "*Poesía 1953–1966,* de Claudio Rodríguez." *Madrid,* 16 July 1971.

————. "La poesía de Claudio Rodríguez." *Levante,* 15 May 1966, 17; 22 May 1966, 19; 5 June 1966, 25; 19 June 1966, 17; 10 July 1966, 17; 31 July 1966, 17.

Molitoris, Joan I. "Diferencias críticas: El continuo crítico-lírico en Angel González, Claudio Rodríguez y Jaime Gil de Biedma." *Romance Languages Annual* 1 (1989): 553–58.

Monmany, Mercedes. "Claudio Rodríguez: «La vida parece y no parece verdadera, es casi como una leyenda»." *El Europeo* 32 (May 1991): 75–77.

Mostaza, B. "Palabra y realidad unificadas." *Ya,* 16 April 1966.

Mudrovic, William Michael. "Claudio Rodríguez's *Alianza y condena*: Technique, Development and Unity." *Symposium* 33 (1979): 248–62.

————. "Dialogic Perspective, Linguistic Skepticism and the Cultural Code in Claudio Rodríguez's *Conjuros.*" *Letras Peninsulares* 1 (1988): 151–67.

————. "Dreams, Frames, Impromptu Stages: Spectacle in Poems by Claudio Rodríguez." *Revista Hispánica Moderna* 46 (1993): 313–21.

————. "Edenic Language in Claudio Rodríguez's *Don de la ebriedad.*" *Anales de la Literatura Española Contemporánea* 18 (1993): 137–56.

————. "Ekphrasis, Intertextuality and the Reader's Role in Poems by Francisco Brines and Claudio Rodríguez." *Studies in Twentieth Century Literature* 14 (1990): 279–300.

————. "Medieval Models: Claudio Rodríguez and Early Spanish Poetry." In *Estudios alfonsinos y otros escritos,* edited by Nicolás Toscano, 172–82. New York: National Endowment for the Humanities, National Hispanic Foundation for the Humanities, 1991.

————. "The Poetry of Claudio Rodríguez: Technique and Structure." Doctoral diss., University of Kansas, 1976.

————. "The Progression of Distance in Claudio Rodríguez's *Conjuros.*" *Hispania* 63 (1980): 328–34.

————. Review of *Casi una leyenda,* by Claudio Rodríguez. *Letras Peninsulares* 5 (1993): 486–87.

————. "Time and Reality in Claudio Rodríguez's *El vuelo de la celebración.*" *Anales de la Literatura Española Contemporánea* 6 (1981): 123–40.

————. "The Title as Pun in Claudio Rodríguez's 'El canto de linos'." *Hispanófila* 106 (1992): 31–40.

Murciano, Carlos. Review of *Casi una leyenda*, by Claudio Rodríguez. *Valor de la Palabra*, núm. 26 (1991): 69.

Núñez, Aníbal. "¿Dónde la ebriedad? (Retórica en dos versos de Claudio Rodríguez)." *La Ciudad* 5 (April 1988): 16–17.

Núñez, Antonio. "Encuentro con Claudio Rodríguez." *Insula*, no. 234 (1966): 4.

Ojeda Escudero, Pedro. "El 'Poderío de las sensaciones' en la poesía de Claudio Rodríguez (a través del poema 'Lágrima')." In *Literatura contempóranea en Castilla y León*, edited by Víctor García de la Concha et al., 244–49. Valladolid: Junta de Castilla y León, Consejería de Educación y Cultura, 1986.

Olson, Paul R. "Dos metafísicas del texto poético: Jiménez, Rodríguez, Celaya." In *Actas del Sexto Congreso Internacional de Hispanistas*, edited by Alan M. Gordon and Evelyn Rugg, 539–41. Toronto: Dept. of Spanish and Portuguese, University of Toronto, 1980.

Pablos, Luis. "José Luis Cano habló sobre la poesía de Claudio Rodríguez." *El Correo de Zamora*, 4 March 1978, 6.

Panero, Leopoldo. "Crecimiento en la noche: *Conjuros* de Claudio Rodríguez." *Blanco y Negro*, June 1959. Reprinted in Leopoldo Panero, *Obras completas*, vol. 2 (Madrid: Editora Nacional, 1973), 211–14.

Persin, Margaret H. "La ambigüedad versus la indeterminancia en la poesía española del siglo XX." In *Actas del IX Congreso de la Asociación Internacional de Hispanistas*, edited by Sebastian Neumeister, 337–44. Frankfurt: Vervuert, 1989.

———. "The Syntax of Assertion in the Poetry of Claudio Rodríguez." In *Recent Spanish Poetry and the Role of the Reader*. Lewisburg, Pa.: Bucknell University Press, 1987.

Pons, Agustín. "Claudio Rodríguez. La poesía se escribe con palabras, no con ideas." *El Noticiero Universal* (Barcelona), 8 June 1971, 23.

Prado, Benjamín. "Los trucos de Claudio Rodríguez." *Olvidos de Granada*, summer 1985, 13–14.

Preciado, Nativel. "«Alianza y condena» Premio de la Crítica 1965." *Arriba*, 20 April 1965.

Prieto de Paula, Angel L. "Claudio Rodríguez entre la iluminación y la muerte." *Insula*, nos. 444–45 (1983): 7–8.

———. "De la dualidad a la unión en la poesía de Claudio Rodríguez." In *Literatura contemporánea en Castilla y León*, edited by Víctor García de la Concha et al, 238–43. Valladolid: Junta de Castilla y León, Consejería de Educación y Cultura, 1986.

———. *La llama y la ceniza*. Salamanca: Universidad de Salamanca y Colegio Universitario de Zamora, 1989.

———. "La noche solar de Claudio Rodríguez." In *La lira de Arión: De poesía y poetas españoles del siglo XX*, 159–88. Alicante: Secretariado de Publicaciones de la Universidad; Caja de Ahorros Provincial, 1991.

———. "La voz de Claudio Rodríguez." *El País*, 5 June 1983, Libros 4.

Provencio, Pedro. *Poéticas españolas contemporáneas: La generación del 50*. Madrid: Hiperión, 1988.

Puente, Antonio. "Nadie sabe hoy quién es el lector ni dónde se le encuentra." *El Sol*, 18 May 1991, 42.

Puente, J. L. "Una oración desde el amor." *La Crónica*, 20 September 1991.

Pulido, Natividad. "Claudio Rodríguez: «El amor es el que lo mueve todo en la poesía»." *ABC*, 6 July 1996, Cultura 64.

Revista Hispánica Moderna, vol. 46, no. 2 (1993).

«Rimart». "Claudio Rodríguez: Premio Nacional de Poesía." *República de las Letras* 9 (1984): 38.

Rodríguez, Emma. "«El don de la ebriedad sigue latiendo en mí»: Claudio Rodríguez se alza con el Príncipe de Asturias de las Letras." *El Mundo,* 29 May 1993, 51–52.

Rubio, Andrés, and Javier Cuartas. "Claudio Rodríguez gana el Príncipe de Asturias de las Letras por la iluminación de su poesía." *El País,* 29 May 1993, 35.

Ruiz Barrionuevo, Carmen. "La poesía de Claudio Rodríguez a la vista de *El vuelo de la celebración.*" *Alamo* 57 (September–October 1976): [30–33].

Ruiz Peña, Juan. "Claudio Rodríguez." *Diario de Burgos,* 6 September 1961.

Rupérez, Angel. "Poemas de la privación: La belleza de la muerte, tema del nuevo libro de Claudio Rodríguez." *El País,* 16 June 1991, Libros 3.

———. "La vida para siempre (Sobre la poesía de Claudio Rodríguez)." In *Poesías escogidas,* by Claudio Rodríguez, 7–40. Madrid: Mondadori, 1992.

Sala, José María. "Algunas notas sobre la poesía de Claudio Rodríguez." *Cuadernos Hispanoamericanos,* no. 334 (1978): 125–41.

———. "De la exaltación a la meditación: Claudio Rodríguez." *La Vanguardia Española,* 16 September 1971, 49.

Sánchez Pascual, Angel. "El vuelo de la celebración, de Claudio Rodríguez." *Hoy,* 12 August 1976.

Sánchez Santiago, Tomás. "Claudio Rodríguez, según Sánchez Santiago." *Lateral,* July–August 1996, 10.

———. "La presencia de Zamora en la obra de Claudio Rodríguez." *El Periódico de Guadalete. Azul,* 4 March 1989, 28–29.

Sánchez Valles, Joaquín. "La función del poeta." *Turia,* no. 18 (1991): 198–200.

Santiago, Tomás S. "Inocencia y responsabilidad: La obra poética de Claudio Rodríguez." *Anuario del Instituto de Estudios Zamoranos "Florián de Ocampo,"* 1984, 261–77.

Sanz Echevarría, Alfonso. "*El vuelo de la celebración* de Claudio Rodríguez." *Jugar con Fuego. Poesía y crítica* 2 (1976): 47–51.

Scarano, Laura R. "*El vuelo de la celebración* de Claudio Rodríguez: entre la desmitificación y la ilusión simbólica." *España Contemporánea. Revista de Literatura y Cultura* 2 (1989): 7–24.

Segovia, Tomás. "Retórica y sociedad: Cuatro poetas españoles." In *Contracorrientes,* 275–98. México: Universidad Nacional Autónoma de México, 1973.

Siebenmann, Gustav. "La contemplación viva." In *Los estilos poéticos en España desde 1900,* 419–22, 463–66. Madrid: Gredos, 1973.

Siles, Jaime. "Dos versos de Claudio Rodríguez y una prosa de Pedro Salinas: Ensayo de reconstrucción." *Insula,* nos. 444–45 (1983): 6–7.

———. "La palabra fundadora." *Quimera,* no. 10 (1981): 75–77.

Silver, Philip W. "Claudio Rodríguez o la mirada sin dueño." In *Antología poética,* by Claudio Rodríguez, 7–22. Madrid: Alianza, 1981. Also in *Essays on Hispanic Literature in Honor of Edmund L. King,* edited by Sylvia Molloy and Luis Fernández Cifuentes (London: Tamesis, 1983). Also in *La casa de Anteo: Ensayos de poética hispana (de Antonio Machado a Claudio Rodríguez)* (Madrid: Taurus, 1985), 220–39.

———. "Poesía última de Claudio Rodríguez." *Revista Hispánica Moderna* 45 (1992): 128–30.

———. "«El rey del humo», un poeta misterioso." *Diario 16,* 26 April 1991, 27.

———. "Todo misterio." *Diario 16,* 30 May 1991, Libros ix.

Sobejano, Gonzalo. "'Espuma' de Claudio Rodríguez." *Consenso-Revista de Literatura* 2 (1978): 37–50.

———. "Impulso lírico y epifanía en la obra de Claudio Rodríguez." In *De los romances-villancico a la poesía de Claudio Rodríguez: 22 ensayos sobre las literaturas española e hispanoamericana en homenaje a Gustav Siebenmann*, edited by José Manuel López de Abiada and Augusta López Bernasocchi, 409–27. Madrid: José Esteban, 1984.

Suárez, Marian. "Don de la celebración." *La Voz de Aviles*, 11 July 1991.

Suñén, Juan Carlos. "Claudio Rodríguez: La emoción del suelo." *El crítico* 1 (1991): 1–2.

———. "Claudio Rodríguez: 'El hombre no puede ser libre.'" *El Urogallo* 62–63 (July–August 1991): 8–13.

Suñén, Luis. "Claudio Rodríguez, la comunión con el mundo." *El Observador,* 13 July 1991, Libros iv.

———. "Un libro decisivo en la poesía española: *El vuelo de la celebración*, Claudio Rodríguez." *Reseña* 13, núm. 99 (1976): 11–12.

Tarín Martínez, Juan José. *Palabra y deseo (La poesía de Claudio Rodríguez).* Valencia: Universidad de Valencia, Colegio Universitario de Castellón, 1990.

Tovar, Antonio. "Ni un día sin línea." *Gaceta Ilustrada,* 15 October 1967.

Ullán, José-Miguel. "Escribo mientras camino." *El País,* 20 September 1981, Libros 4.

———. "Una lectura superrealista de Claudio Rodríguez." *El País,* 20 September 1981, Libros 4.

———. "Poesía histórica." *El Adelanto,* 26 December 1965.

Valente, José Angel. "Claudio Rodríguez." *Indice de Artes y Letras* 10, núm. 84 (1955): 18.

Vaquero, Isabel. "En la biblioteca de Claudio Rodríguez." *Leer* 8 (April–June 1987): 40–41.

Vara Fínez, José. "Claudio Rodríguez, el poeta más completo de la literatura española contemporánea." *El Correo de Zamora,* 1971.

Vargas-Churchill, Alicia. "La coherencia de 'Espuma' de Claudio Rodríguez." *Explicación de Textos Literarios* 14 (1985–86): 25–34.

Vilumara, Martín. "Alianza, que no condena." *Alamo*, September–December 1966.

Villán, Javier. "Claudio Rodríguez: leyenda y celebración." *El Mundo,* 29 December 1991, La Esfera 3.

Villar, Arturo del. "Claudio Rodríguez, viajero de la luz." *El Correo de Zamora,* 1 August 1976, 3.

———. "El don de la claridad de Claudio Rodríguez." *La Estafeta Literaria,* nos. 592–93 (1976): 20–23.

BIBLIOGRAPHY OF WORKS CITED

Alarcos Llorach, Emilio. *Gramática de la lengua española.* Real Academia Española, Colección Nebrija y Bello. Madrid: Espasa Calpe, 1994.

Aleixandre, Vicente. *Algunos caracteres de la nueva poesía española.* Madrid: Imprenta Góngora, 1975.

———. *Historia del corazón.* Prol. José Luis Cano. 2a ed. Madrid: Espasa-Calpe, 1985.

Alonso, Dámaso, and José Manuel Blecua. *Antología de la poesía española: Lírica de tipo tradicional.* 2a ed. corregida. Madrid: Gredos, 1964.

Bahktin, Mikhail M. *The Dialogic Imagination: Four Essays.* Edited by Michael Holquist.

Translated by Caryl Emerson and Michael Holquist. Austin: University of Texas Press, 1981.

———. *Rabelais and His World.* Translated by Hélène Iswolsky. Bloomington: Indiana University Press, 1984.

Bailey, Matthew. "Lexical Ambiguity in Four Poems of Juan del Encina." *Romance Quarterly* 36 (1989): 431-43.

Baker, Dorothy Zayatz. *Mythic Masks in Self-Reflexive Poetry: A Study of Pan and Orpheus.* Chapel Hill and London: University of North Carolina Press, 1986.

Barthes, Roland. "The Death of the Author." In *Image—Music—Text.* Translated by Stephen Heath. New York: Noonday Press, 1988.

Bellow, Saul. *Humboldt's Gift.* New York: Viking Press, 1973.

Bernasconi, Robert. *Heidegger in Question: The Art of Existing.* Atlantic Highlands, N.J.: Humanities Press, 1993.

Bernstein, Joseph M., ed. *Baudelaire, Rimbaud, Verlaine: Selected Verse and Prose Poems.* New York: Citadel Press, 1947.

Bloom, Harold. *Agon: Towards a Theory of Revisionism.* Oxford and New York: Oxford University Press, 1982.

———. *The Anxiety of Influence: A Theory of Poetry.* New York: Oxford University Press, 1973.

Booth, Wayne. *A Rhetoric of Irony.* Chicago and London: University of Chicago Press, 1974.

Bousoño, Carlos. *Teoría de la expresión poética.* 2d ed. Madrid: Gredos, 1952.

Brivic, Sheldon. *The Veil of Signs: Joyce, Lacan, and Perception.* Urbana and Chicago: University of Illinois Press, 1991.

Bruggeman, Walter. *Toward Praying the Psalms: Letting Experience Touch the Psalter.* Winona, Minn.: St. Mary's College Press, 1979.

Bruns, Gerald. *Modern Poetry and the Idea of Language.* New Haven and London: Yale University Press, 1974.

Burke, Kenneth. "Four Master Tropes." In *A Grammar of Motives,* 503-17. Berkeley: University of California Press, 1969.

Burke, Sean. *The Death & Return of the Author: Criticism and Subjectivity in Barthes, Foucault, and Derrida.* Edinburgh: Edinburgh University Press, 1992.

Butler, Judith, and Joan W. Scott, eds. *Feminists Theorize the Political.* New York: Routledge, 1992.

Campbell, Joseph. *The Hero with a Thousand Faces.* The Bollingen Series 17. New York: Pantheon Books, 1949.

Caro Baroja, Julio. *El carnaval: Análisis histórico-cultural.* 2a ed. Madrid: Taurus, 1979.

———. *Los Vascos.* Madrid: Istmo, 1971.

Carreter, Fernando Lázaro. "Imitación compuesta y diseño retórico en la oda de Juan de Grial." *Anuario de Estudios Filológicos* 2 (1979): 89-119.

Cervantes Saavedra, Miguel de. *Don Quijote de la Mancha.* Texto y notas de Martín de Riquer. Barcelona: Editorial Juventud, 1966.

Chevalier, Jean, and Alain Gheerbrant. *Diccionario de los símbolos.* Barcelona: Herder, 1991.

Cirlot, Juan Eduardo. *Diccionario de símbolos.* Undécima ed. Barcelona: Labor, 1995.

———. *A Dictionary of Symbols.* Translated by Jack Sage. 2d ed. New York: Appleton-Century-Crofts, 1972.

Connor, Steven. *Samuel Beckett: Repetition, Theory, and Text.* New York and Oxford: Basil Blackwell, 1988.

Crowther, Paul. *The Kantian Sublime: From Morality to Art.* Oxford: Clarendon Press, 1989.

Culler, Jonathan. *On Deconstruction: Theory and Criticism after Structuralism.* Ithaca: Cornell University Press, 1982.

Debicki, Andrew P. *Spanish Poetry of the Twentieth Century: Modernity and Beyond.* Lexington: University Press of Kentucky, 1994.

Deleuze, Gilles, and Felix Guattari. *Rizoma (Introducción).* Valencia: Pre-Textos, 1977.

Derrida, Jacques. *Writing and Difference.* Translated by Alan Bass. Chicago: University of Chicago Press, 1978.

de Saussure, Ferdinand. *Course in General Linguistics.* Edited by Charles Bally and Albert Sechehaye, with Albert Riedlinger. Translated and introduced by Wade Baskin. New York: McGraw-Hill, 1959.

Diccionario de la Real Academia Española. 19a ed. Madrid: Real Academia Española, 1970.

Donoghue, Denis. *Thieves of Fire.* London: Faber & Faber, 1973.

Eco, Umberto. *The Role of the Reader: Explorations in the Semiotics of Texts.* Bloomington: Indiana University Press, 1979.

———. *Semiotics and the Philosophy of Language.* Bloomington: Indiana University Press, 1984.

Eliot, Thomas Stearns. "*Hamlet.*" In *Selected Prose of T. S. Eliot,* edited by Frank Kermode, 45–49. New York: Farrar, Straus and Giroux, 1975.

Enciclopedia Universal Sopena: Diccionario Ilustrado de la Lengua Española. 9 vols. Barcelona: Editorial Ramón Sopena, 1963.

Fogel, Gerald I., Frederick M. Lane, and Robert S. Liebert, eds. *The Psychology of Men: Psychoanalytic Perspectives.* New Haven and London: Yale University Press, 1996.

Fóti, Véronique M. *Heidegger and the Poets: Poiēsis / Sophia / Technē.* Atlantic Highlands, N.J.: Humanities Press, 1992.

Foucault, Michel. "What Is an Author?" In *The Foucault Reader,* edited by Paul Rabinow, 101–20. New York: Pantheon Books, 1984.

Freud, Sigmund. *Beyond the Pleasure Principle.* In *The Standard Edition,* translated and edited by James Strachey. New York and London: W. W. Norton, 1961.

———. *A General Selection from the Works of Sigmund Freud.* Edited by John Rickman. New York: Doubleday, 1957.

Gallup, Jane. *Reading Lacan.* Ithaca and London: Cornell University Press, 1985.

Gayley, Charles Mills. *The Classic Myths in English Literature and in Art.* Rev. and enl. ed. Boston: Ginn, 1939.

Gelven, Michael. *A Commentary on Heidegger's Being and Time.* Rev. ed. De Kalb: Northern Illinois University Press, 1989.

Gergen, Kenneth J. *The Saturated Self: Dilemmas of Identity in Contemporary Life.* New York: Basic Books, 1991.

Gil, Bonifacio, comp. *Cancionero del campo (Antología).* Madrid: Taurus, 1966.

Goethe, Johann Wolfgang von. *Faust: A Tragedy.* New York: The Modern Library, 1950.

Graves, Robert. *The Greek Myths.* Rev. ed. Vols. 1-2. London: Penguin Books, 1960.

Grigson, Geoffrey. *The Romantics.* London: George Routledge & Sons, 1942.

Grimal, Pierre. *The Concise Dictionary of Classical Mythology.* Edited by Stephen Kershaw. Translated by A. R. Maxwell-Hyslop. Oxford: Basil Blackwell, 1986.

Grosz, Elizabeth. *Jacques Lacan: A Feminist Introduction.* London and New York: Routledge, 1990.

Guerlac, Suzanne. *The Impersonal Sublime: Hugo, Baudelaire, Lautréamont.* Stanford, Calif.: Stanford University Press, 1990.

Guignon, Charles B. *Heidegger and the Problem of Knowledge.* Indianapolis: Hackett, 1983.

Hamilton, Edith. *Mythology.* Boston: Little, Brown, 1942.

Hart, Henry. *Robert Lowell and the Sublime.* Syracuse, N.Y.: Syracuse University Press, 1995.

Hayles, N. Catherine. *Chaos Bound: Orderly Disorder in Contemporary Literature and Science.* Ithaca and London: Cornell University Press, 1990.

———. *The Cosmic Web: Scientific Field Models and Literary Strategies in the Twentieth Century.* Ithaca and London: Cornell University Press, 1984.

———, ed. *Chaos and Order: Complex Dynamics in Literature and Science.* Chicago: University of Chicago Press, 1991.

Heidegger, Martin. *Arte y poesía.* Translated by Samuel Ramos. México: Fondo de Cultura Económica, 1958.

———. *Being and Time.* Translated by John Macquarrie and Edward Robinson. San Francisco: Harper & Row, 1962.

———. *On the Way to Language.* Translated by Peter D. Hertz. San Francisco: Harper & Row, 1971.

———. *Poetry, Language, Thought.* Translated by Albert Hofstadter. New York: Harper & Row, 1971.

Hertz, Neil. *The End of the Line: Essays on Psychoanalysis and the Sublime.* New York: Cornell University Press, 1985.

Hugo, Víctor. "Prefacio." In *Cromwell,* 11–51. 4a ed. Madrid: Espasa-Calpe, 1979.

Hutcheon, Linda. *A Poetics of Postmodernism: History, Theory, Fiction.* New York and London: Routledge, 1988.

Jakobson, Roman. "Two Aspects of Language and Two Types of Aphasic Disturbances." In *Fundamentals of Language,* by Roman Jakobson and Morris Halle, 67-96. 2d, rev. ed. The Hague and Paris: Mouton, 1975.

Julien, Nadia. *The Mammoth Dictionary of Symbols: Understanding the Hidden Language of Symbols.* New York: Carroll and Graf, 1996.

Kant, Immanuel. *Observations on the Feeling of the Beautiful and Sublime.* Translated by John T. Goldthwait. Berkeley, Los Angeles, and Oxford: University of California Press, 1960.

Kartiganer, Donald M. "Faulkner's Art of Repetition." In *Faulkner and the Craft of Fiction: Faulkner and Yoknapatawpha, 1987,* edited by Doreen Fowler and Ann J. Abadie, 21-47. Jackson and London: University Press of Mississippi, 1989.

Knapp, Bettina L. *The Prometheus Syndrome.* Troy, N.Y.: Whitston, 1979.

Kruger-Robbins, Jill. *Frames of Referents: The Postmodern Poetry of Guillermo Carnero.* Lewisburg, Pa.: Bucknell University Press, 1997.

Lacan, Jacques. *The Four Fundamental Concepts of Psycho-Analysis.* Edited by Jacques-Alain Miller. Translated by Alan Sheridan. New York: W. W. Norton, 1981.

———. "The Mirror Stage as Formative of the Function of the I as Revealed in Psychoanalytic Experience." In *Ecrits: A Selection,* translated by Alan Sheridan, 1–7. New York: W. W. Norton, 1977.

LeGuern, Michel. *La metáfora y la metonimia.* 4a ed. Madrid: Cátedra, 1985.

Librett, Jeffrey S., ed. and trans. *Of the Sublime: Presence in Question.* Albany: State University of New York Press, 1993.

Lind, L. R., ed. *Latin Poetry in Verse Translation: From the Beginnings to the Renaissance.* Boston: Houghton Mifflin, 1957.

Lodge, David. *The Modes of Modern Writing: Metaphor, Metonymy, and the Typology of Modern Literature.* Ithaca: Cornell University Press, 1977.

Longinus. "On the Sublime." In *Classical Literary Criticism. Aristotle: On the Art of Poetry; Horace: On the Art of Poetry; Longinus: On the Sublime,* translated by T. S. Dorsch. London: Penguin Books, 1965.

Luna Borge, José. *La generación poética del 70: Cuestión de perspectiva.* Sevilla: Qüásyeditorial, 1991.

A Manual of Prayers for the Use of the Catholic Laity. Prep. and enj. by order of the Third Plenary Council of Baltimore. New York: P. J. Kennedy & Sons, 1930.

Manzano, Miguel, comp. *Canciones zamoranas.* Madrid: Editorial Alpuerto, 1986.

Martín Gaite, Carmen. *Usos amorosos de la posguerra española.* 10a ed. Barcelona: Anagrama, 1992.

Mayhew, Jonathan. "'Cuartilla': Pedro Salinas and the Semiotics of Poetry." *Anales de la Literatura Española Contemporánea* 16 (1991): 119-27.

———. *The Poetics of Self-Consciousness: Twentieth-Century Spanish Poetry.* Lewisburg, Pa.: Bucknell University Press, 1994.

Merrell, Floyd. *Semiotic Foundations: Steps toward an Epistemology of Written Texts.* Bloomington: Indiana University Press, 1982.

Metzidakis, Stamos. *Repetition and Semiotics.* Birmingham, Ala.: Summa Publications, 1986.

Miller, J. Hillis. "Ariachne's Broken Woof." *Georgia Review* 31 (1977): 44-60.

———. *Fiction and Repetition: Seven English Novels.* Cambridge: Harvard University Press, 1982.

Miller, Nancy K. *Subject to Change: Reading Feminist Writing.* New York: Columbia University Press, 1988.

Muecke, D. C. *The Compass of Irony.* London: Methuen, 1969.

Mulhall, Stephen. *Heidegger and "Being and Time."* New York: Routledge, 1996.

Myers, Jack and Michael Simms. *The Longman Dictionary of Poetic Terms.* New York and London: Longman, 1989.

Nyrop, Christophe. *Is War Civilization?* Translated by H. G. Wright. London: William Heinemann, 1917.

Ong, Walter J. *Orality and Literacy: The Technologizing of the Word.* London and New York: Routledge, 1982.

Pequeño Larousse Ilustrado 1992. Edited by Ramón García-Pelayo y Gross. París: Editorial Larousse, 1991.

Pérez-Rioja, J. A. *Diccionario de símbolos y mitos.* 4a ed. Madrid: Tecnos, 1992.

Preminger, Alex, and T. V. F. Brogan, eds. *The New Princeton Encyclopedia of Poetry and Poetics.* Princeton: Princeton University Press, 1993.

Ragland-Sullivan, Ellie. *Jacques Lacan and the Philosophy of Psychoanalysis.* Urbana and Chicago: University of Illinois Press, 1986.

Ramazani, Jahan. *Poetry of Mourning: The Modern Elegy from Hardy to Heaney.* Chicago: University of Chicago Press, 1994.

Rico, Francisco. *Mil años de poesía española: Antología comentada.* Barcelona: Planeta, 1996.

Ricoeur, Paul. *Oneself as Another.* Translated by Kathleen Blamey. Chicago: University of Chicago Press, 1992.

Riffaterre, Michael. *Semiotics of Poetry.* Bloomington: Indiana University Press, 1978.

Rivers, Elias L., ed. *Renaissance and Baroque Poetry of Spain.* New York: Dell, 1966.

Rose, H. J. *A Handbook of Greek Mythology: Including Its Extension to Rome.* 5th ed. London: Methuen, 1953.

Ryrie, Charles Caldwell. *The Ryrie Study Bible: King James Version.* Chicago: Moody Press, 1978.

Sacks, Peter M. *The English Elegy: Studies in the Genre from Spenser to Yeats.* Baltimore: Johns Hopkins University Press, 1985.

Sánchez, Elizabeth. "*La Regenta* as Fractal." *Revista de Estudios Hispánicos* 26 (1992): 251-76.

Sebold, Russell P., ed. *Gustavo Adolfo Bécquer.* Madrid: Taurus, 1982.

Sender, Ramón J. *Réquiem por un campesino español.* 13a ed. Madrid: Destinolibro, 1986.

Shaw, W. David. *Elegy and Paradox: Testing the Conventions.* Baltimore and London: Johns Hopkins University Press, 1994.

Shklovsky, Victor. "Art as Technique." In *Russian Formalist Criticism*, translated and edited by Lee T. Lemon and Marion J. Reis, 3–24. Lincoln: University of Nebraska Press, 1965.

Smith, Barbara Herrnstein. *Poetic Closure: A Study of How Poems End.* Chicago and London: University of Chicago Press, 1968.

Soufas, C. Christopher. *Conflict of Light and Wind: The Spanish Generation of 1927 and the Ideology of Poetic Form.* Middletown, Conn.: Wesleyan University Press, 1989.

Steiner, George. *Martin Heidegger.* Chicago: University of Chicago Press, 1987.

Strauss, Walter. *Descent and Return: The Orphic Theme in Modern Literature.* Cambridge: Harvard University Press, 1971.

Todorov, Tzetvan. "The Origin of Genres." *New Literary History* 8 (1976): 159-70.

Vattimo, Gianni. *Más allá del sujeto: Nietzsche, Heidegger, y la hermenéutica.* 2a ed. Barcelona: Paidós, 1992.

Weber, Samuel. *Return to Freud: Jacques Lacan's Dislocation of Psychoanalysis.* Translated by Michael Levine. Cambridge: Cambridge University Press, 1991.

Weiskel, Thomas. *The Romantic Sublime: Studies in the Structure and Psychology of Transcendence.* Baltimore and London: Johns Hopkins University Press, 1976.

Welles, Marcia. *Arachne's Tapestry: The Transformation of Myth in Seventeenth-Century Spain.* San Antonio, Tex.: Trinity University Press, 1985.

Wheelwright, Philip. *Metaphor and Reality.* Bloomington: Indiana University Press, 1962.

White, John T. *The White Latin Dictionary.* New ed. Chicago: Follett, 1948.

Index

573